Psychological Testing

ANNE ANASTASI

Department of Psychology, Fordham University

Psychological Testing

FIFTH EDITION

MACMILLAN PUBLISHING CO., INC.
New York

Collier Macmillan Publishers
London

MACMILLAN PUBLISHING CO., INC.
866 Third Avenue, New York, New York 10022

COLLIER MACMILLAN CANADA, INC.

Library of Congress Cataloging in Publication Data

Anastasi, Anne, (date)
  Psychological testing.

  Bibliography: p.
  Includes indexes.
  1. Psychological tests. I. Title.
BF176.A5 1982   150'.76   81–6018
ISBN 0–02–302960–9 (Hardbound)   AACR2
ISBN 0–02–977510–8 (International Edition)

Printing: 8 9   Year: 6 7 8 9

ISBN   0-02-302960-9

PREFACE

WHILE preparing this fifth edition, I was frequently reminded that psychological testing today does not stand still long enough to have its picture taken. During the time required to review and update the content of twenty chapters, so much was happening in this area that I felt I was constantly running at top speed in order to snap a photograph of my galloping subject. More than a third of the tests discussed in this edition are either new or have been substantially revised since their inclusion in the 1976 edition. Of the approximately 250 tests listed in Appendix E, 11% have been revised since they were last reviewed in the *Mental Measurements Yearbooks*. Conspicuous examples include the WAIS-R, Otis-Lennon School Ability Test, Cognitive Abilities Test, Peabody Picture Vocabulary Test, SCAT-III, STEP-III, Iowa Tests of Basic Skills, and Metropolitan Achievement Tests. An additional 13% have not been included at all in the MMY series. Although a few of the latter may fall outside the scope of tests covered in these yearbooks, the large majority appeared too late for inclusion in the eighth MMY, published in 1978.

Of more general interest are the substantive developments that have occurred in the field as a whole and that are reflected in the present edition. Major theoretical and methodological advances include applications of item response theory (IRT) in test construction, especially in the development of individually tailored, adaptive testing; continuing research on test bias and the clarification of decision models for fair use of tests; Bayesian approaches to validity generalization; further applications of decision theory in personnel selection, including research on the relation of test validity to productivity; growing emphasis on construct validation in both ability and personality testing; contributions of cognitive psychology to an understanding of the constructs measured by intelligence tests; theoretical and methodological progress in the analysis of trait, state, and situational variables in the personality domain; and increasing recognition of the need for psychometrically sound assessment techniques in behavior modification programs.

Several developments concern chiefly test use and the interpretation of test results. Major topics in this area include the causes and treatment of test anxiety; the effects of coaching and other training programs; population changes in test performance, such as the widely publicized score decline on the College Board's SAT; and the testing implications of the 1978 *Uniform Guidelines on Employee Selection Procedures* and related court cases, of Public Law 94-142 on the education of all handicapped children, and of legislation pertaining to the disclosure of test content.

Another noteworthy trend is the application of psychometric procedures in new areas. Among the varied instruments developed for these purposes are tests of minimum competency in basic skills, standardized neuropsychological batteries, health-related inventories, career exploration programs and indices of career maturity, tests for assessing sex roles and androgyny, and measures of environmental or ecological attitudes.

In the present edition, every effort was made to incorporate new material into the framework of the previous edition. Accordingly, the chapter organization remains largely unchanged, and earlier chapter titles have been retained, with a single necessary exception (Ch. 18). The decision to follow this organization was based on two considerations. First, current users of the text find it inconvenient to adapt their courses to frequent changes in topical organization. Second, the chapter structure of the previous edition seems to fit the new material as well as any other I could devise. The changes begin to emerge in the organization and headings of the major sections within chapters and become more evident in the subsections.

At a more basic level, the objectives and general approach of the book are the same as those in all earlier editions. The primary goal of the text is to contribute toward the proper evaluation of psychological tests and the correct interpretation and use of test results. This goal calls for several kinds of information: (1) an understanding of the major principles of test construction, (2) psychological knowledge about the behavior being assessed, (3) sensitivity to the social and ethical implications of test use, and (4) broad familiarity with the types of available instruments and the sources of current information about tests. As heretofore, particular tests discussed in the text have been chosen either because they are outstanding examples of a major category of testing instruments or because they illustrate some special point of test construction or interpretation. The classified list in Appendix E contains not only all tests cited in the text but also others added to provide a more representative sample.

As the field of psychological testing expands at an increasing rate, it becomes necessary to rely more and more on direct contact with colleagues for current information. I am indebted to the many researchers, authors, and test publishers who provided reprints, unpublished manuscripts, specimen sets of tests, and answers to my innumerable inquiries by mail, telephone, or personal conferences. For contributions beyond the normal expectations, I owe special thanks to Lorraine D. Eyde, Frank L. Schmidt, and Vern W. Urry, U.S. Office of Personnel Management; Robert C. Droege, Employment and Training Administration, U.S. Department of Labor; Edith M. Huddleston, National Center for Educational Statistics; Gerry Ann Bogatz, Harold Gulliksen, and Barbara Lerner, Educational Testing Service; Michael D. Beck and David O. Herman, The Psychological Corporation; Esther E. Diamond, Science Research Associates; Leo A. Munday, Riverside Publishing Company; Gary J. Robertson, American Guidance Service; John D.

Black, Consulting Psychologists Press; Franklin Evans, Law School Admissions Services; Shanna Richman, Professional Examination Service; John W. Atkinson, University of Michigan; Marilyn Bergner, Department of Health Services, University of Washington; Charles J. Golden, University of Nebraska Medical Center; Robert M. Kaplan, Department of Community Medicine, University of California at San Diego; Douglas N. Jackson, University of Western Ontario; Paul McReynolds, University of Nevada; Theodore Millon, University of Miami; Melvin R. Novick, University of Iowa; Jerome M. Sattler, San Diego State University; Charles D. Spielberger, University of South Florida; Donald E. Super, Teachers College, Columbia University; and David J. Weiss, University of Minnesota.

To my colleagues in the Fordham University Department of Psychology, I am grateful for their continued interest, ready cooperation, and helpful suggestions. I am pleased to acknowledge the special bibliographic services rendered by members of the Fordham University libraries, particularly Mary F. Riley, Chief Reference Librarian, Lucy Valentino of the Circulation Staff, and Victoria Overton of the Periodicals Staff. Special thanks are due my husband, John Porter Foley, Jr., who participated in the solution of countless problems of both content and form throughout the preparation of the book.

A. A.

CONTENTS

PART TWO
TECHNICAL AND METHODOLOGICAL PRINCIPLES

PART THREE
TESTS OF GENERAL INTELLECTUAL LEVEL

PART FOUR
TESTS OF SEPARATE ABILITIES

PART ONE

Context of Psychological Testing

CHAPTER 1

Functions and Origins of Psychological Testing

A NYONE reading this book today could undoubtedly illustrate what is meant by a psychological test. It would be easy enough to recall a test the reader has taken in school, in college, in the armed services, in a counseling center, or in a personnel office. Or perhaps the reader has served as a participant in an experiment that used standardized tests. This would certainly not have been the case before the 1920s. Psychological testing is a relatively young branch of one of the youngest of the sciences.

USES OF PSYCHOLOGICAL TESTS

Traditionally, the function of psychological tests has been to measure differences between individuals or between the reactions of the same individual on different occasions. One of the first problems that stimulated the development of psychological tests was the identification of the mentally retarded. To this day, the detection of intellectual deficiencies remains an important application of certain types of psychological tests. Related clinical uses of tests include the examination of the emotionally disturbed, the delinquent, and other types of behavioral deviants. A strong impetus to the early development of tests was likewise provided by problems arising in education. At present, schools are among the largest test users. The classification of children with reference to their ability to profit from different types of school instruction, the identification of the intellectually retarded on the one hand and the gifted on the other, the diagnosis of academic failures, the educational and vocational counseling of high school and college students, and the selection of applicants for professional and other special schools are among the many educational uses of tests.

The selection and classification of industrial personnel represent another major application of psychological testing. From the assembly-line operator or filing clerk to top management, there is scarcely a type of job for which some kind of psychological test has not proved helpful in such matters as

3

hiring, job assignment, transfer, promotion, or termination. To be sure, the effective employment of tests in many of these situations, especially in connection with high-level jobs, usually requires that the tests be used as an adjunct to skillful interviewing, so that test scores may be properly interpreted in the light of other background information about the individual. Nevertheless, testing constitutes an important part of the total personnel program. A closely related application of psychological testing is to be found in the selection and classification of military personnel. From simple beginnings in World War I, the scope and variety of psychological tests employed in military situations underwent a phenomenal increase during World War II. Subsequently, research on test development has been continuing on a large scale in all branches of the armed services.

The use of tests in counseling has gradually broadened from a narrowly defined guidance regarding educational and vocational plans to an involvement with all aspects of the person's life. Emotional well-being and effective interpersonal relations have become increasingly prominent objectives of counseling. There is growing emphasis, too, on the use of tests to enhance self-understanding and personal development. Within this framework, test scores are part of the information given to the individual as aids to his or her own decision-making processes.

It is clearly evident that psychological tests are currently being employed in the solution of a wide range of practical problems. One should not, however, lose sight of the fact that such tests are also serving important functions in basic research. Nearly all problems in differential psychology, for example, require testing procedures as a means of gathering data. As illustrations, reference may be made to studies on the nature and extent of individual differences, the organization of psychological traits, the measurement of group differences, and the identification of biological and cultural factors associated with behavioral differences. For all such areas of research—and for many others—the precise measurement of individual differences made possible by well-constructed tests is an essential prerequisite. Similarly, psychological tests provide standardized tools for investigating such varied problems as life-span developmental changes within the individual, the relative effectiveness of different educational procedures, the outcomes of psychotherapy, the impact of community programs, and the influence of environmental variables on human performance.

From the many different uses of psychological tests, it follows that some knowledge of such tests is needed for an adequate understanding of most fields of contemporary psychology. It is primarily with this end in view that the present book has been prepared. The book is not designed to make the individual either a skilled examiner and test administrator or an expert on test construction. It is directed, not to the test specialist, but to the general student of psychology. Some acquaintance with the leading current tests is necessary in order to understand references to the use of such tests in the psychological literature. And a proper evaluation and interpretation of test results must ultimately rest on a knowledge of how the tests were constructed, what they can be expected to accomplish, and what are their peculiar limitations. Today a familiarity with tests is required, not only by those who give or construct tests, but by the general psychologist as well.

A brief overview of the historical antecedents and origins of psychological testing will provide perspective and should aid in the understanding of present-day tests.[1] The direction in which contemporary psychological testing has been progressing can be clarified when considered in the light of the precursors of such tests. The special limitations as well as the advantages that characterize current tests likewise become more intelligible when viewed against the background in which they originated.

The roots of testing are lost in antiquity. DuBois (1966) gives a provocative and entertaining account of the system of civil service examinations prevailing in the Chinese empire for some three thousand years. Among the ancient Greeks, testing was an established adjunct to the educational process. Tests were used to assess the mastery of physical as well as intellectual skills. The Socratic method of teaching, with its interweaving of testing and teaching, has much in common with today's programmed learning. From their beginnings in the Middle Ages, European universities relied on formal examinations in awarding degrees and honors. To identify the major developments that shaped contemporary testing, however, we need go no farther than the nineteenth century. It is to these developments that we now turn.

EARLY INTEREST IN CLASSIFICATION AND TRAINING OF THE MENTALLY RETARDED

The nineteenth century witnessed a strong awakening of interest in the humane treatment of the mentally retarded and the insane. Prior to that time, neglect, ridicule, and even torture had been the common lot of these unfortunates. With the growing concern for the proper care of mental deviates came a realization that some uniform criteria for identifying and classifying these cases were required. The establishment of many special institutions for the care of the mentally retarded in both Europe and America made the need for setting up admission standards and an objective system of classification especially urgent. First it was necessary to differentiate between the insane and the mentally retarded. The former manifested emotional disorders that might or might not be accompanied by intellectual deterioration from an initially normal level; the latter were characterized essentially by intellectual defect that had been present from birth or early

[1] A more detailed account of the early origins of psychological tests can be found in Goodenough (1949) and J. Peterson (1926). See also Boring (1950) and Murphy and Kovach (1972) for more general background, DuBois (1970) for a brief but comprehensive history of psychological testing, and Anastasi (1965) for historical antecedents of the study of individual differences.

infancy. What is probably the first explicit statement of this distinction is to be found in a two-volume work published in 1838 by the French physician Esquirol (1838), in which over one hundred pages are devoted to mental retardation. Esquirol also pointed out that there are many degrees of mental retardation, varying along a continuum from normality to low-grade idiocy. In the effort to develop some system for classifying the different degrees and varieties of retardation, Esquirol tried several procedures but concluded that the individual's use of language provides the most dependable criterion of his or her intellectual level. It is interesting to note that current criteria of mental retardation are also largely linguistic and that present-day intelligence tests are heavily loaded with verbal content. The important part verbal ability plays in our concept of intelligence will be repeatedly demonstrated in subsequent chapters.

Of special significance are the contributions of another French physician. Seguin, who pioneered in the training of the mentally retarded. Having rejected the prevalent notion of the incurability of mental retardation, Seguin (1866) experimented for many years with what he termed the physiological method of training; and in 1837 he established the first school devoted to the education of mentally retarded children. In 1848 he emigrated to America, where his ideas gained wide recognition. Many of the sense-training and muscle-training techniques currently in use in institutions for the mentally retarded were originated by Seguin. By these methods, severely retarded children are given intensive exercise in sensory discrimination and in the development of motor control. Some of the procedures developed by Seguin for this purpose were eventually incorporated into performance or nonverbal tests of intelligence. An example is the Seguin Form Board, in which the individual is required to insert variously shaped blocks into the corresponding recesses as quickly as possible.

More than half a century after the work of Esquirol and Seguin, the French psychologist Alfred Binet urged that children who failed to respond to normal schooling be examined before dismissal and, if considered educable, be assigned to special classes (T. H. Wolf, 1973). With his fellow members of the Society for the Psychological Study of the Child, Binet stimulated the Ministry of Public Instruction to take steps to improve the condition of retarded children. A specific outcome was the establishment of a ministerial commission for the study of retarded children, to which Binet was appointed. This appointment was a momentous event in the history of psychological testing, of which more will be said later.

THE FIRST EXPERIMENTAL PSYCHOLOGISTS

The early experimental psychologists of the nineteenth century were not, in general, concerned with the measurement of individual differences. The principal aim of psychologists of that period was the formulation of generalized descriptions of human behavior. It was the uniformities rather than the differences in behavior that were the focus of attention. Individual differences were either ignored or accepted as a necessary evil that limited the applicability of the generalizations. Thus, the fact that one individual reacted differently from another when observed under identical conditions was regarded as a form of error. The presence of such error, or individual variability, rendered the generalizations approximate rather than exact. This was the attitude toward individual differences that prevailed in such laboratories as that founded by Wundt at Leipzig in 1879, where many of the early experimental psychologists received their training.

In their choice of topics, as in many other phases of their work, the founders of experimental psychology reflected the influence of their backgrounds in physiology and physics. The problems studied in their laboratories were concerned largely with sensitivity to visual, auditory, and other sensory stimuli and with simple reaction time. This emphasis on sensory phenomena was in turn reflected in the nature of the first psychological tests, as will be apparent in subsequent sections.

Still another way in which nineteenth-century experimental psychology influenced the course of the testing movement may be noted. The early psychological experiments brought out the need for rigorous control of the conditions under which observations were made. For example, the wording of directions given to the subject in a reaction-time experiment might appreciably increase or decrease the speed of the subject's response. Or again, the brightness or color of the surrounding field could markedly alter the appearance of a visual stimulus. The importance of making observations on all subjects under standardized conditions was thus vividly demonstrated. Such standardization of procedure eventually became one of the special earmarks of psychological tests.

CONTRIBUTIONS OF FRANCIS GALTON

It was the English biologist Sir Francis Galton who was primarily responsible for launching the testing movement. A unifying factor in Galton's numerous and varied research activities was his interest in human heredity. In the course of his investigations on heredity, Galton realized the need for measuring the characteristics of related and unrelated persons. Only in this way could he discover, for example, the exact degree of resemblance between parents and offspring, brothers and sisters, cousins, or twins. With this end in view, Galton was instrumental in inducing a number of educational institutions to keep systematic anthropometric records on their students. He also set up an anthropometric laboratory at the International Exposition of 1884 where, by paying threepence, visitors could be measured in certain physical traits and could take tests of keenness of vision and hearing, muscular strength, reaction time, and other simple sensorimotor functions. When the exposition closed, the laboratory was transferred to South Kensington Museum, London, where it operated for six years. By such methods, the first large, systematic body of data on individual differences in simple psychological processes was gradually accumulated.

Galton himself devised most of the simple tests administered at his anthropometric laboratory, many of which are still familiar either in their original or in modified forms. Examples include the Galton bar for visual discrimination of length, the Galton whistle for determining the highest audible pitch, and graduated series of weights for measuring kinesthetic discrimination. It was Galton's belief that tests of sensory discrimination could serve as a means of gauging a person's intellect. In this respect, he was partly influenced by the theories of Locke. Thus, Galton wrote: "The only information that reaches us concerning outward events appears to pass through the avenue of our senses; and the more perceptive the senses are of difference, the larger is the field upon which our judgment and intelligence can act" (Galton, 1883, p. 27). Galton had also noted that idiots tend to be defective in the ability to discriminate heat, cold, and pain—an observation that further strengthened his conviction that sensory discriminative capacity "would on the whole be highest among the intellectually ablest" (Galton, 1883, p. 29).

Galton also pioneered in the application of rating-scale and questionnaire methods, as well as in the use of the free association technique subsequently employed for a wide variety of purposes. A further contribution of Galton is to be found in his development of statistical methods for the analysis of data on individual differences. Galton selected and adapted a number of techniques previously derived by mathematicians. These techniques he put in such form as to permit their use by the mathematically untrained investigator who might wish to treat test results quantitatively. He thereby extended enormously the application of statistical procedures to the analysis of test data. This phase of Galton's work has been carried forward by many of his students, the most eminent of whom was Karl Pearson.

CATTELL AND THE EARLY "MENTAL TESTS"

An especially prominent position in the development of psychological testing is occupied by the American psychologist James McKeen Cattell. The newly established science of experimental psychology and the still newer testing movement merged in Cattell's work. For his doctorate at Leipzig, he completed a dissertation on individual differences in reaction time, despite Wundt's resistance to this type of investigation. While lecturing at Cambridge in 1888, Cattell's own interest in the measurement of individual differences was reinforced by contact with Galton. On his return to America, Cattell was active both in the establishment of laboratories for experimental psychology and in the spread of the testing movement.

In an article written by Cattell in 1890, the term "mental test" was used for the first time in the psychological literature. This article described a series of tests that were being administered annually to college students in the effort to determine their intellectual level. The tests, which had to be administered individually, included measures of muscular strength, speed of movement, sensitivity to pain, keenness of vision and of hearing, weight discrimination, reaction time, memory, and the like. In his choice of tests, Cattell shared Galton's view that a measure of intellectual functions could be obtained through tests of sensory discrimination and reaction time. Cattell's preference for such tests was also bolstered by the fact that simple functions could be measured with precision and accuracy, whereas the development of objective measures for the more complex functions seemed at that time a well-nigh hopeless task.

Cattell's tests were typical of those to be found in a number of test series developed during the last decade of the nineteenth century. Such test series were administered to schoolchildren, college students, and miscellaneous adults. At the Columbian Exposition held in Chicago in 1893, Jastrow set up an exhibit at which visitors were invited to take tests of sensory, motor, and simple perceptual processes and to compare their skill with the norms (J. Peterson, 1926; Philippe, 1894). A few attempts to evaluate such early tests yielded very discouraging results. The individual's performance showed little correspondence from one test to another (Sharp, 1898–1899; Wissler, 1901), and it exhibited little or no relation to independent estimates of intellectual level based on teachers' ratings (Bolton, 1891–1892; J. A. Gilbert, 1894) or academic grades (Wissler, 1901).

A number of test series assembled by European psychologists of the period tended to cover somewhat more complex functions. Kraepelin (1895), who was interested primarily in the clinical examination of psychiatric patients, prepared a long series of tests to measure what he regarded as basic factors in the characterization of an individual. The tests, employing chiefly simple arithmetic operations, were designed to measure practice effects, memory, and susceptibility to fatigue and to distraction. A few years earlier, Oehrn (1889), a pupil of Kraepelin, had employed tests of perception, memory, association, and motor functions in an investigation on the interrelations of psychological functions. Another German psychologist, Ebbinghaus (1897), administered tests of arithmetic computation, memory span, and sentence completion to schoolchildren. The most complex of the three tests, sentence completion, was the only one that showed a clear correspondence with the children's scholastic achievement.

Like Kraepelin, the Italian psychologist Ferrari and his students were interested primarily in the use of tests with pathological cases (Guicciardi & Ferrari, 1896). The test series they devised ranged from physiological measures and motor tests to apprehension span and the interpretation of pictures. In an article published in France in 1895, Binet and Henri criticized most of the available test series as being too largely sensory and as concentrating unduly on simple, specialized abilities. They argued further that, in the measurement of the more complex functions, great precision is not necessary, since individual differences are larger in these functions. An extensive and varied list of tests was proposed, covering such functions as memory, imagination, attention, comprehension, suggestibility, aesthetic appreciation, and many others. In these tests, we can recognize the trends that were eventually to lead to the development of the famous Binet intelligence scales.

BINET AND THE RISE OF INTELLIGENCE TESTS

Binet and his co-workers devoted many years to active and ingenious research on ways of measuring intelligence. Many approaches were tried, including even the measurement of cranial, facial, and hand form and the analysis of handwriting. The results, however, led to a growing conviction that the direct, even though crude, measurement of complex intellectual functions offered the greatest promise. Then a specific situation arose that brought Binet's efforts to immediate practical fruition. In 1904, the Minister of Public Instruction appointed Binet to the previously cited commission to study procedures for the education of retarded children. It was in connection with the objectives of this commission that Binet, in collaboration with Simon, prepared the first Binet-Simon Scale (Binet & Simon, 1905).

This scale, known as the 1905 scale, consisted of 30 problems or tests arranged in ascending order of difficulty. The difficulty level was determined empirically by administering the tests to 50 normal children aged 3 to 11 years, and to some mentally retarded children and adults. The tests were designed to cover a wide variety of functions, with special emphasis on judgment, comprehension, and reasoning, which Binet regarded as essential components of intelligence. Although sensory and perceptual tests were included, a much greater proportion of verbal content was found in this scale than in most test series of the time. The 1905 scale was presented as a preliminary and tentative instrument, and no precise objective method for arriving at a total score was formulated.

In the second, or 1908, scale, the number of tests was increased, some unsatisfactory tests from the earlier scale were eliminated, and all tests were grouped into age levels on the basis of the performance of about 300 normal children between the ages of 3 and 13 years. Thus, in the 3-year level were placed all tests passed by 80–90% of normal 3-year-olds; in the 4-year level, all tests similarly passed by normal 4-year-olds; and so on to age 13. The child's score on the entire test could then be expressed as a *mental level* corresponding to the age of normal children whose performance he or she equaled. In the various translations and adaptations of the Binet scales, the term "mental age" was commonly substituted for "mental level." Since mental age is such a simple concept to grasp, the introduction of this term undoubtedly did much to popularize intelligence testing.[2] Binet himself, however, avoided the term "mental age" because of its unverified developmental implications and preferred the more neutral term "mental level" (T. H. Wolf, 1973).

A third revision of the Binet-Simon Scale appeared in 1911, the year of Binet's untimely death. In this scale, no fundamental changes were introduced. Minor revisions and relocations of specific tests were instituted. More tests were added at several year levels, and the scale was extended to the adult level.

Even prior to the 1908 revision, the Binet-Simon tests attracted wide attention among psychologists throughout the world. Translations and adaptations appeared in many languages. In America, a number of different revisions were prepared, the most famous of which is the one developed under the direction of L. M. Terman at Stanford University and known as the Stanford-Binet (Terman, 1916). It was in this test that the intelligence quotient (IQ), or ratio between mental age and chronological age, was first used. The latest revision of this test is widely employed today and will be more fully considered in Chapter 9. Of special interest, too, is the first Kuhlmann-Binet revision, which extended the scale downward to the age level of 3 months (Kuhlmann, 1912). This scale represents one of the earliest efforts to develop preschool and infant tests of intelligence.

GROUP TESTING

The Binet tests, as well as all their revisions, are *individual scales* in the sense that they can be administered to only one person at a time. Many of the tests in these scales require oral responses from the examinee or necessitate the manipulation of materials. Some call for individual timing of responses. For these and other reasons, such tests are not adapted to group administration. Another characteristic of the Binet type of test is that it requires a highly trained examiner. Such tests are essentially clinical instruments, suited to the intensive study of individual cases.

Group testing, like the first Binet scale, was developed to meet a pressing practical need. When the United States entered World War I in 1917, a committee was appointed by the American Psychological Association to consider ways in which psychology might assist in the conduct of the war.

[2] Goodenough (1949, pp. 50–51) noted that in 1887, 21 years before the appearance of the 1908 Binet-Simon Scale, S. E. Chaille published in the *New Orleans Medical and Surgical Journal* a series of tests for infants arranged according to the age at which the tests are commonly passed. Partly because of the limited circulation of the journal and partly, perhaps, because the scientific community was not ready for it, the significance of this age-scale concept passed unnoticed at the time. Binet's own scale was influenced by the work of some of his contemporaries, notably Blin and Damaye, who prepared a set of oral questions from which they derived a single global score for each child (T. H. Wolf, 1973).

This committee, under the direction of Robert M. Yerkes, recognized the need for the rapid classification of the million and a half recruits with respect to general intellectual level. Such information was relevant to many administrative decisions, including rejection or discharge from military service, assignment to different types of service, or admission to officer-training camps. It was in this setting that the first group intelligence test was developed. In this task, the army psychologists drew on all available test materials, and especially on an unpublished group intelligence test prepared by Arthur S. Otis, which he turned over to the army. A major contribution of Otis's test, which he designed while a student in one of Terman's graduate courses, was the introduction of multiple-choice and other "objective" item types.

The tests finally developed by the army psychologists came to be known as the Army Alpha and the Army Beta. The former was designed for general routine testing; the latter was a nonlanguage scale employed with illiterates and with foreign-born recruits who were unable to take a test in English. Both tests were suitable for administration to large groups.

Shortly after the termination of World War I, the army tests were released for civilian use. Not only did the Army Alpha and Army Beta themselves pass through many revisions, but they also served as models for most group intelligence tests. The testing movement underwent a tremendous spurt of growth. Soon group intelligence tests were being devised for all ages and types of persons, from preschool children to graduate students. Large-scale testing programs, previously impossible, were now being launched with zestful optimism. Because group tests were designed as mass testing instruments, they not only permitted the simultaneous examination of large groups but also simplified the instructions and administration procedures so as to demand a minimum of training on the part of the examiner. Schoolteachers began to give intelligence tests to their classes. College students were routinely examined prior to admission. Extensive studies of special adult groups, such as prisoners, were undertaken. And soon the general public became IQ-conscious.

The application of such group intelligence tests far outran their technical improvement. That the tests were still technically crude was often forgotten in the rush of gathering scores and drawing practical conclusions from the results. When the tests failed to meet unwarranted expectations, skepticism and hostility toward all testing often resulted. Thus, the testing boom of the 1920s, based on the indiscriminate use of tests, may have done as much to retard as to advance the progress of psychological testing.

APTITUDE TESTING

Although intelligence tests were originally designed to sample a wide variety of functions in order to estimate the individual's general intellectual level, it soon became apparent that such tests were quite limited in their coverage. Not all important functions were represented. In fact, most intelligence tests were primarily measures of verbal ability and, to a lesser extent, of the ability to handle numerical and other abstract and symbolic relations. Gradually, psychologists came to recognize that the term "intelligence test" was a misnomer, since only certain aspects of intelligence were measured by such tests.

To be sure, the tests covered abilities that are of prime importance in our culture. But it was realized that more precise designations, in terms of the type of information these tests were able to yield, would be preferable. For example, a number of tests that would probably have been called intelligence tests during the 1920s later came to be known as scholastic aptitude tests. This shift in terminology was made in recognition of the fact that many so-called intelligence tests measure that combination of abilities demanded by academic work.

Even prior to World War I, psychologists had begun to recognize the need for tests of special aptitudes to supplement the global intelligence tests. These *special aptitude tests* were developed particularly for use in vocational counseling and in the selection and classification of industrial and military personnel. Among the most widely used are tests of mechanical, clerical, musical, and artistic aptitudes.

The critical evaluation of intelligence tests that followed their widespread and indiscriminate use during the 1920s also revealed another noteworthy fact: an individual's performance on different parts of such a test often showed marked variation. This was especially apparent on group tests, in which the items are commonly segregated into subtests of relatively homogeneous content. For example, a person might score relatively high on a verbal subtest and low on a numerical subtest, or vice versa. To some extent, such internal variability is also discernible on a test like the Stanford-Binet, in which, for example, all items involving words might prove difficult for a particular individual, whereas items employing pictures or geometric diagrams may place her or him at an advantage.

Test users, and especially clinicians, frequently utilized such intercomparisons in order to obtain more insight into the individual's psychological makeup. Thus, not only the IQ or other global score but also scores on subtests would be examined in the evaluation of the individual case. Such a practice is not to be generally recommended, however, because intelligence tests were not designed for the purpose of differential aptitude analysis. Often the subtests being compared contain too few items to yield a stable or reliable estimate of a specific ability. As a result, the obtained difference between subtest scores might be reversed if the individual were retested on a different day or with another form of the same test. If such intraindividual comparisons are to be made, tests are needed that are specially designed to reveal differences in performance in various functions.

While the practical application of tests demonstrated the need for multiple aptitude tests, a parallel development in the study of trait organization was gradually providing the means for constructing such tests. Statistical studies on the nature of intelligence had been exploring the interrelations among scores obtained by many persons on a wide variety of different tests. Such investigations were begun by the English psychologist Charles Spearman (1904, 1927) during the first decade of the present century. Subsequent methodological developments, based on the work of such American psychologists as T. L. Kelley (1928) and L. L. Thurstone (1938, 1947b), as well as on that of other American and English investigators, have come to be known as "factor analysis."

The contributions that the methods of factor analysis have made to test construction will be more fully examined and illustrated in Chapter 13. For the present, it will suffice to note that the data gathered by such procedures have indicated the presence of a number of relatively independent factors, or traits. Some of these traits were represented, in varying proportions, in the traditional intelligence tests. Verbal comprehension and numerical reasoning are examples of this type of trait. Others, such as spatial, perceptual, and mechanical aptitudes, were found more often in special aptitude tests than in intelligence tests.

One of the chief practical outcomes of factor analysis was the development of *multiple aptitude batteries*. These batteries are designed to provide a measure of the individual's standing in each of a number of traits. In place of a total score or IQ, a separate score is obtained for such traits as verbal comprehension, numerical aptitude, spatial visualization, arithmetic reasoning, and perceptual speed. Such batteries thus provide a suitable instrument for making the kind of intraindividual analysis, or differential diagnosis, that clinicians had been trying for many years to obtain, with crude and often erroneous results, from intelligence tests. These batteries also incorporate into a comprehensive and systematic testing program much of the information formerly obtained from special aptitude tests, since the multiple aptitude batteries cover some of the traits not ordinarily included in intelligence tests.

Multiple aptitude batteries represent a relatively late development in the testing field. Nearly all have appeared since 1945. In this connection, the work of the military psychologists during World War II should also be noted. Much of the test research conducted in the armed services was based on factor analysis and was directed toward the construction of multiple aptitude batteries. In the Air Force, for example, special batteries were constructed for pilots, bombardiers, radio operators, range finders, and scores of other military specialists. A report of the batteries prepared in the Air Force alone occupies at least 9 of the 19 volumes devoted to the aviation psychology program during World War II (Army Air Forces, 1947–1948). Research along these lines is still in progress under the sponsorship of various branches of the armed services. A number of multiple aptitude batteries have likewise been developed for civilian use and are being widely applied in educational and vocational counseling and in personnel selection and classification. Examples of such batteries will be discussed in Chapter 13.

To avoid confusion, a point of terminology should be clarified. The term "aptitude test" has been traditionally employed to refer to tests measuring relatively homogeneous and clearly defined segments of ability; the term "intelligence test" customarily refers to more heterogeneous tests yielding a single global score such as an IQ. Special aptitude tests typically measure a single aptitude. Multiple aptitude batteries measure a number of aptitudes but provide a profile of scores, one for each aptitude.

STANDARDIZED ACHIEVEMENT TESTS

While psychologists were busy developing intelligence and aptitude tests, traditional school examinations were undergoing a number of technical improvements (Caldwell & Courtis, 1923; Ebel & Damrin, 1960). An important step in this direction was taken by the Boston public schools in 1845, when written examinations were substituted for the oral interrogation of students by visiting examiners. Commenting on this innovation, Horace Mann cited arguments remarkably similar to those used much later to justify the replacement of essay questions by objective multiple-choice items. The written examinations, Mann noted, put all students in a uniform situation, permitted a wider coverage of content, reduced the chance element in question choice, and eliminated the possibility of favoritism on the examiner's part.

After the turn of the century, the first standardized tests for measuring the outcomes of school instruction began to appear. Spearheaded by the work of E. L. Thorndike, these tests utilized measurement principles developed in the psychological laboratory. Examples include scales for rating the quality of handwriting and written compositions, as well as tests in spelling, arithmetic computation, and arithmetic reasoning. Still later came the achievement batteries, initiated by the publication of the first edition of the Stanford Achievement Test in 1923. Its authors were three early leaders in test development: Truman L. Kelley, Giles M. Ruch, and Lewis M. Terman. Foreshadowing many characteristics of modern testing, this battery provided comparable measures of performance in different school subjects, evaluated in terms of a single normative group.

At the same time, evidence was accumulating regarding the lack of agreement among teachers in grading essay tests. By 1930, it was widely recognized that essay tests were not only more time-consuming for examiners and examinees but also yielded less reliable results than the "new type" of objective items.[3] As the latter came into increasing use in standardized achievement tests, there was a growing emphasis on the design of items to

---

[3] Research bearing on the relative effectiveness of essay and objective item types will be cited in connection with the educational use of tests in Chapter 14.

test the understanding and application of knowledge and other broad educational objectives. The decade of the 1930s also witnessed the introduction of test-scoring machines, for which the new objective tests could be readily adapted.

The establishment of statewide, regional, and national testing programs was another noteworthy parallel development. Probably the best known of these programs is that of the College Entrance Examination Board (CEEB). Established at the turn of the century to reduce duplication in the examining of entering college freshmen, this program has undergone profound changes in its testing procedures and in the number and nature of participating colleges—changes that reflect intervening developments in both testing and education. In 1947, the testing functions of the CEEB were merged with those of the Carnegie Corporation and the American Council on Education to form Educational Testing Service (ETS). In subsequent years, ETS has assumed responsibility for a growing number of testing programs on behalf of universities, professional schools, government agencies, and other institutions. Mention should also be made of the American College Testing Program established in 1959 to screen applicants to colleges not included in the CEEB program, and of several national testing programs for the selection of highly talented students for scholarship awards.

Achievement tests are used not only for educational purposes but also in the selection of applicants for industrial and government jobs. Mention has already been made of the systematic use of civil service examinations in the Chinese empire, dating from 1115 B.C. In modern times, selection of government employees by examination was introduced in European countries in the late eighteenth and early nineteenth centuries. The United States Civil Service Commission installed competitive examinations as a regular procedure in 1883 (Kavruck, 1956). Test construction techniques developed during and prior to World War I were introduced into the examination program of the United States Civil Service with the appointment of L. J. O'Rourke as director of the newly established research division in 1922. Today this work is conducted by a large and technically sophisticated research staff within the unit designated as the United States Office of Personnel Management.

As more and more psychologists trained in psychometrics participated in the construction of standardized achievement tests, the technical aspects of achievement tests increasingly came to resemble those of intelligence and aptitude tests. Procedures for constructing and evaluating all these tests have much in common. The increasing efforts to prepare achievement tests that would measure the attainment of broad educational goals, as contrasted to the recall of factual minutiae, also made the content of achievement tests resemble more closely that of intelligence tests. Today the difference between these two types of tests is chiefly one of degree of specificity of content and extent to which the test presupposes a designated course of prior instruction.

ASSESSMENT OF PERSONALITY

Another area of psychological testing is concerned with the affective or nonintellectual aspects of behavior. Tests designed for this purpose are commonly known as personality tests, although some psychologists prefer to use the term "personality" in a broader sense, to refer to the entire individual. Intellectual as well as nonintellectual traits would thus be included under this heading. In the terminology of psychological testing, however, the designation "personality test" most often refers to measures of such characteristics as emotional states, interpersonal relations, motivation, interests, and attitudes.

An early precursor of personality testing may be recognized in Kraepelin's use of the free association test with abnormal patients. In this test, the examinee is given specially selected stimulus words and is required to respond to each with the first word that comes to mind. Kraepelin (1892) also employed this technique to study the psychological effects of fatigue, hunger, and drugs and concluded that all these agents increase the relative frequency of superficial associations. Sommer (1894), also writing during the last decade of the nineteenth century, suggested that the free association test might be used to differentiate between the various forms of mental disorder. The free association technique has subsequently been utilized for a variety of testing purposes and is still currently employed. Mention should also be made of the work of Galton, Pearson, and Cattell in the development of standardized questionnaire and rating-scale techniques. Although originally devised for other purposes, these procedures were eventually employed by others in constructing some of the most common types of current personality tests.

The prototype of the personality questionnaire, or *self-report inventory*, is the Personal Data Sheet developed by Woodworth during World War I (DuBois, 1970; Symonds, 1931, Ch. 5; Goldberg, 1971). This test was designed as a rough screening device for identifying seriously neurotic men who would be unfit for military service. The inventory consisted of a number of questions dealing with common neurotic symptoms, which respondents answered about themselves. A total score was obtained by counting the number of symptoms reported. The Personal Data Sheet was not completed early enough to permit its operational use before the war ended. Immediately after the war, however, civilian forms were prepared, including a special form for use with children. The Woodworth Personal Data Sheet, moreover, served as a model for most subsequent emotional adjustment inventories. In some of these questionnaires, an attempt was made to subdivide emotional adjustment into more specific forms, such as home adjustment, school adjustment, and vocational adjustment. Other tests concentrated more intensively on a narrower area of behavior or were concerned with more distinctly social responses, such as dominance–submission in interpersonal contacts. A later development was the construction of tests for quantifying the expression of interests and attitudes. These tests, too, were based essentially on questionnaire techniques.

Another approach to the measurement of personality is through the application of *performance* or *situational tests*. In such tests, the examinee has a task to perform whose purpose is often disguised. Most of these tests simulate everyday-life situations quite closely. The first extensive application of such techniques is to be found in the tests developed in the late 1920s and early 1930s by Hartshorne, May, and their associates (1928, 1929, 1930). This series, standardized on schoolchildren, was concerned with such behavior as cheating, lying, stealing, cooperativeness, and persistence. Objective, quantitative scores could be obtained on each of a large number of specific tests. Another illustration, for the adult level, is provided by the series of situational tests developed during World War II in the Assessment Program of the Office of Strategic Services (OSS, 1948). These tests were concerned with relatively complex and subtle social and emotional behavior and required rather elaborate facilities and trained personnel for their administration. The interpretation of the individual's responses, moreover, was relatively subjective.

Projective techniques represent a third approach to the study of personality and one that has shown phenomenal growth, especially among clinicians. In such tests, the subject is given a relatively unstructured task that permits wide latitude in its solution. The assumption underlying such methods is that the individual will project her or his characteristic modes of response into such a task. Like the performance and situational tests, projective techniques are more or less disguised in their purpose, thereby reducing the chances that the respondent can deliberately create a desired impression. The previously cited free association test represents one of the earliest types of projective techniques. Sentence-completion tests have also been used in this manner. Other tasks commonly employed in projective techniques include drawing, arranging toys to create a scene, extemporaneous dramatic play, and interpreting pictures or inkblots.

All available types of personality tests present serious difficulties, both practical and theoretical. Each approach has its own special advantages and disadvantages. On the whole, personality testing has lagged far behind aptitude testing in its positive accomplishments. But such lack of progress is not to be attributed to insufficient effort. Research on the measurement of personality has attained impressive proportions since 1950, and many ingenious devices and technical improvements are under investigation. It is rather the special difficulties encountered in the measurement of personality that account for the slow advances in this area.

SOURCES OF INFORMATION ABOUT TESTS

Psychological testing is in a state of rapid change. There are shifting orientations, a constant stream of new tests, revised forms of old tests, and additional data that may refine or alter the interpretation of scores on existing tests. The accelerating rate of change, together with the vast number of available tests, makes it impracticable to survey specific tests in any single text. More intensive coverage of testing instruments and problems in special areas can be found in books dealing with the use of tests in such fields as counseling, clinical practice, personnel selection, and education. References to such publications are given in the appropriate chapters of this book. In order to keep abreast of current developments, however, anyone working with tests needs to be familiar with more direct sources of information about tests.

One of the most important sources is the series of *Mental Measurements Yearbooks* (MMY) edited by Buros (1978). These yearbooks cover nearly all commercially available psychological, educational, and vocational tests published in English. The coverage is especially complete for paper-and-pencil tests. Each yearbook includes tests published during a specified period, thus supplementing rather than supplanting the earlier yearbooks. The *Eighth Mental Measurements Yearbook,* for example, is concerned principally with tests appearing between 1971 and 1977. Tests of continuing interest, however, may be reviewed repeatedly in successive yearbooks, as new data accumulate from pertinent research. The earliest publications in this series were merely bibliographies of tests. Beginning in 1938, however, the yearbook assumed its current form, which includes critical reviews of most of the tests by one or more test experts, as well as a complete list of published references pertaining to each test. Routine information regarding publisher, price, forms, and age of persons for whom the test is suitable is also regularly given.

A comprehensive bibliography covering all types of published tests available in English-speaking countries is provided by *Tests in Print II* (Buros, 1974). Other reference sources in the series include *Personality Tests and Reviews* (Buros, 1970, 1975b), *Intelligence Tests and Reviews* (Buros, 1975a), and *Vocational Tests and Reviews* (Buros, 1975c), as well as similar volumes covering particular educational subjects, such as reading and mathematics. These area monographs contain the relevant sections of the MMY, together with some additional tests not found in the MMY.

Since 1970, several sourcebooks have appeared that provide information about unpublished or little-known instruments, largely supplementing the material listed in the MMY. A comprehensive survey of such instruments can be found in *A Sourcebook for Mental Health Measures* (Comrey, Backer, & Glaser, 1973). Containing approximately 1,100 abstracts, this sourcebook includes tests, questionnaires, rating scales, and other devices for assessing both aptitude and personality variables in adults and children. Another similar reference is entitled *Measures for Psychological Assessment* (Chun, Cobb, & French, 1976). For each of 3,000 measures, this volume gives the original source as well as an annotated bibliography of the studies in which the measure was subsequently used. The entries were located through a search of 26 measurement-related journals for the years 1960 to 1970. Still another general source is the two-volume *Directory of Unpublished Experimental Mental Measures* (Goldman & Busch, 1978; Goldman & Saunders, 1974).

Information about assessment devices suitable for children from birth to 18 years is summarized in *Tests and Measurements in Child Development* (*Handbook I*, Johnson & Bommarito, 1971; *Handbook II*, O. G. Johnson, 1976). Covering tests not listed in the MMY, these handbooks describe non-commercial instruments located through an extensive search of journals and other research reports. Selection criteria include availability of the test to professionals, adequate instructions for administration and scoring, sufficient length, and convenience of use (i.e., not requiring expensive or elaborate equipment). A more highly specialized and timely compendium brings together information on over 200 tests and measures relevant to research on women and women's issues (Beere, 1979). Among the many types of instruments described are measures of sex-role behaviors and attitudes, sex stereotyping, and gender-related personality variables.

Finally, it should be noted that the most direct source of information regarding specific current tests is provided by the catalogs of test publishers and by the manual that accompanies each test. A comprehensive list of test publishers, with addresses, can be found in the latest *Mental Measurements Yearbook*. For ready reference, the names and addresses of some of the larger American publishers and distributors of psychological tests are given in Appendix D. Catalogs of current tests can be obtained from each of these publishers on request. Manuals and specimen sets of tests can be purchased by qualified users.

The test manual should provide the essential information required for administering, scoring, and evaluating a particular test. In it should be found full and detailed instructions, scoring key, norms, and data on reliability and validity. Moreover, the manual should report the number and nature of persons on whom norms, reliability, and validity were established and the methods employed in computing indices of reliability and validity. In the event that the necessary information is too lengthy to fit conveniently into the manual, references to the printed sources in which such information can be readily located should be given. The manual should, in other words, enable test users to evaluate the test before choosing it for their specific purposes. It might be added that many test manuals still fall short of this goal. But some of the larger and more professionally oriented test publishers are giving increasing attention to the preparation of manuals that meet adequate scientific standards. An enlightened public of test users provides the firmest assurance that such standards will be maintained and improved in the future.

A succinct but comprehensive guide for the evaluation of psychological tests is to be found in *Standards for Educational and Psychological Tests* (1974), published by the American Psychological Association. These standards represent a summary of recommended practices in test construction, based on the current state of knowledge in the field. They are concerned with the information about validity, reliability, norms, and other test characteristics that ought to be reported in the manual. In their current edition, the *Standards* also provide a guide for the proper use of tests and for the correct interpretation and application of test results. Relevant portions of these *Standards* will be cited in the following chapters, in connection with the appropriate topics. A further revision of the *Standards* is in preparation and will probably be published in 1983. It will incorporate technical advances in testing and give increased attention to the social impact of test use.

Chapter 2

Nature and Use of Psychological Tests

THE HISTORICAL introduction in Chapter 1 has already suggested some of the many uses of psychological tests, as well as the wide diversity of available tests. Although the general public may still associate psychological tests most closely with "IQ tests" and with tests designed to detect emotional disorders, these tests represent only a small proportion of the available types of instruments. The major categories of psychological tests will be discussed and illustrated in Parts Three, Four, and Five, which cover tests of general intellectual level, traditionally called intelligence tests; tests of separate abilities, including multiple aptitude batteries, tests of special aptitudes, and achievement tests; and personality tests, concerned with measures of emotional and motivational traits, interpersonal behavior, interests, attitudes, and other noncognitive characteristics.

In the face of such diversity in nature and purpose, what are the common differentiating characteristics of psychological tests? How do psychological tests differ from other methods of gathering information about individuals? The answer is to be found in certain fundamental features of both the construction and the use of tests. It is with these features that the present chapter is concerned.

WHAT IS A PSYCHOLOGICAL TEST?

BEHAVIOR SAMPLE. A psychological test is essentially an objective and standardized measure of a sample of behavior. Psychological tests are like tests in any other science, insofar as observations are made on a small but carefully chosen *sample* of an individual's behavior. In this respect, the psychologist proceeds in much the same way as the biochemist who tests a patient's blood or a community's water supply by analyzing one or more samples of it. If the psychologist wishes to test the extent of a child's vocabulary, a clerk's ability to perform arithmetic computations, or a pilot's eye–hand coordination, he or she examines their performance with a representative set of words, arithmetic problems, or motor tests. Whether or not the test adequately covers the behavior under consideration obviously depends on the number and the nature of items in the sample. For example, an arithmetic test consisting of only five problems, or one including only multiplication items, would be a poor measure of the individual's computational skill. A vocabulary test composed entirely of baseball terms would hardly provide a dependable estimate of a child's total range of vocabulary.

The *diagnostic* or *predictive value* of a psychological test depends on the degree to which it serves as an indicator of a relatively broad and significant area of behavior. Measurement of the behavior sample directly covered by the test is rarely, if ever, the goal of psychological testing. The child's knowledge of a particular list of 50 words is not, in itself, of great interest. Nor is the job applicant's performance on a specific set of 20 arithmetic problems of much importance. If, however, it can be demonstrated that there is a close correspondence between the child's knowledge of the word list and his total mastery of vocabulary, or between the applicant's score on the arithmetic problems and her computational performance on the job, then the tests are serving their purpose.

It should be noted in this connection that the test items need not resemble closely the behavior the test is to predict. It is only necessary that an empirical correspondence be demonstrated between the two. The degree of similarity between the test sample and the predicted behavior may vary widely. At one extreme, the test may coincide completely with a part of the behavior to be predicted. An example might be a foreign vocabulary test in which the students are examined on 20 of the 50 new words they have studied; another example is provided by the road test taken prior to obtaining a driver's license. A lesser degree of similarity is illustrated by many vocational aptitude tests administered prior to job training, in which there is only a moderate resemblance between the tasks performed on the job and those incorporated in the test. At the other extreme one finds projective personality tests such as the Rorschach inkblot test, in which an attempt is made to predict from the respondent's associations to inkblots how he or she will react to other people, to emotionally toned stimuli, and to other complex, everyday-life situations. Despite their superficial differences, all these tests consist of samples of the individual's behavior. And each must prove its worth by an empirically demonstrated correspondence between the examinee's performance on the test and in other situations.

Whether the term "diagnosis" or the term "prediction" is employed in this connection also represents a minor distinction. Prediction commonly connotes a temporal estimate, individuals' future performance on a job, for example, being forecast from their present test performance. In a broader sense, however, even the diagnosis of present condition, such as mental retardation or emotional disorder, implies a prediction of what the individual will do in situations other than the present test. It is logically simpler to regard all tests as behavior samples from which predictions regarding other behavior can be made. Different types of tests can then be characterized as variants of this basic pattern.

Another point that should be considered at the outset pertains to the concept of *capacity*. It is entirely possible, for example, to devise a test for predicting how well an individual can learn French before he or she has even begun the study of French. Such a test would involve a sample of the types of behavior required to learn the new language, but would in itself presuppose no knowledge of French. It could then be said that this test measures the individual's "capacity" or "potentiality" for learning French. Such terms should, however, be used with caution in reference to psychological tests. Only in the sense that a present behavior sample can be used as an indicator of other, future behavior can we speak of a test measuring "capacity." No psychological test can do more than measure behavior. Whether such behavior can serve as an effective index of other behavior can be established only by empirical tryout.

STANDARDIZATION. It will be recalled that in the initial definition a psychological test was described as a standardized measure. Standardization implies *uniformity of procedure* in administering and scoring the test. If the scores obtained by different persons are to be comparable, testing conditions must obviously be the same for all. Such a requirement is only a special application of the need for controlled conditions in all scientific observations. In a test situation, the single independent variable is usually the individual being tested.

In order to secure uniformity of testing conditions, the test constructor provides detailed directions for administering each newly developed test. The formulation of directions is a major part of the standardization of a new test. Such standardization extends to the exact materials employed, time limits, oral instructions, preliminary demonstrations, ways of handling queries from examinees, and every other detail of the testing situation. Many other, more subtle factors may influence performance on certain tests. Thus, in giving instructions or presenting problems orally, consideration must be given to the rate of speaking, tone of voice, inflection, pauses, and facial expression. In a test involving the detection of absurdities, for example, the correct answer may be given away by smiling or pausing when the crucial word is read. Standardized testing procedure, from the examiner's point of view, will be discussed further in a later section of this chapter dealing with problems of test administration.

Another important step in the standardization of a test is the establishment of *norms*. Psychological tests have no predetermined standards of passing or failing; performance on each test is evaluated on the basis of empirical data. For most purposes, an individual's test score is interpreted by comparing it with the scores obtained by others on the same test. As its name implies, a norm is the normal or average performance. Thus, if normal 8-year-old children complete 12 out of 50 problems correctly on a particular arithmetic reasoning test, then the 8-year-old norm on this test corresponds to a score of 12. The latter is known as the raw score on the test. It may be expressed as number of correct items, time required to complete a task, number of errors, or some other objective measure appropriate to the content of the test. Such a raw score is meaningless until evaluated in terms of suitable interpretive data.

In the process of standardizing a test, it is administered to a large, representative sample of the type of persons for whom it is designed. This group, known as the standardization sample, serves to establish the norms. Such norms indicate not only the average performance but also the relative frequency of varying degrees of deviation above and below the average. It is thus possible to evaluate different degrees of superiority and inferiority. The specific ways in which such norms may be expressed will be considered in Chapter 4. All permit the designation of the individual's position with reference to the normative or standardization sample.

It might also be noted that norms are established for personality tests in essentially the same way as for aptitude tests. The norm on a personality test is not necessarily the most desirable or "ideal" performance, any more than a perfect or errorless score is the norm on an aptitude test. On both types of tests, the norm corresponds to the performance of typical or average persons. On dominance–submission tests, for example, the norm falls at an intermediate point representing the degree of dominance or submission manifested by the average person. Similarly, in an emotional adjustment inventory, the norm does not ordinarily correspond to a complete absence of unfavorable or maladaptive responses, since a few such responses occur in the majority of "normal" individuals in the standardization sample.

OBJECTIVE MEASUREMENT OF DIFFICULTY. Reference to the definition of a psychological test with which this discussion opened will show that such a test was characterized as an objective as well as a standardized measure. In what specific ways are such tests objective? Some aspects of the objectivity of psychological tests have already been touched on in the discussion of standardization. Thus, the administration, scoring, and interpretation of scores are objective insofar as they are independent of the subjective judgment of the particular examiner. Any one individual should theoretically obtain the identical score on a test regardless of who happens to be the examiner. This is not entirely so, of course, since perfect standardization and objectivity have not been attained in practice. But at least such objectivity is the goal of test construction and has been achieved to a reasonably high degree in most tests.

There are other major ways in which psychological tests can be properly described as objective. The determination of the difficulty level of an item or of a whole test is based on objective, empirical procedures. When Binet and Simon prepared their original, 1905 scale for the measurement of intelligence, they arranged the 30 items of the scale in order of increasing difficulty. Such difficulty, it will be recalled, was determined by trying out the items on 50 normal and a few mentally retarded children. The items correctly solved by the largest number of children were, *ipso facto*, taken to be the easiest; those passed by relatively few children were regarded as more difficult items. By this procedure, an empirical order of difficulty was established. This early example typifies the objective measurement of difficulty level, which is now common practice in psychological test construction.

Not only the arrangement but also the selection of items for inclusion in a test can be guided by the proportion of examinees in the trial samples who pass each item. Thus, if there is a bunching of items at the easy or difficult end of the scale, some items can be discarded. Similarly, if items are sparse in certain portions of the difficulty range, new items can be added to fill the gaps. More technical aspects of item analysis will be considered in Chapter 8.

RELIABILITY. How good is this test? Does it really work? These questions could—and occasionally do—result in long hours of futile discussion. Subjective opinions, hunches, and personal biases may lead, on the one hand, to extravagant claims regarding what a particular test can accomplish and, on the other hand, to stubborn rejection. The only way questions such as these can be conclusively answered is by empirical trial. The *objective evaluation* of psychological tests involves primarily the determination of the reliability and the validity of the test in specified situations.

As used in psychometrics, the term reliability always means consistency. Test reliability is the consistency of scores obtained by the same persons when retested with the identical test or with an equivalent form of the test. If a child receives an IQ of 110 on Monday and an IQ of 80 when retested on Friday, it is obvious that little or no confidence can be put in either score. Similarly, if in one set of 50 words an examinee identifies 40 correctly, whereas in another, supposedly equivalent set she gets a score of only 20 right, then neither score can be taken as a dependable index of her verbal comprehension. To be sure, in both illustrations it is possible that only one of the two scores is in error, but this could be demonstrated only by further retests. From the given data, we can conclude only that both scores cannot be right. Whether one or neither is an adequate estimate of the individual's ability in vocabulary cannot be established without additional information.

Before a psychological test is released for general use, a thorough, objective check of its reliability should be carried out. The different types of test reliability, as well as methods of measuring each, will be considered in Chapter 5. Reliability can be checked with reference to temporal fluctuations, the particular selection of items or behavior sample constituting the test, the role of different examiners or scorers, and other aspects of the testing situation. It is essential to specify the type of reliability and the method employed to determine it, because the same test may vary in these different aspects. The number and nature of persons on whom reliability was checked should likewise be reported. With such information, test users can predict whether the test will be about equally reliable for the group with which they expect to use it, or whether it is likely to be more reliable or less reliable.

VALIDITY. Undoubtedly the most important question to be asked about any psychological test concerns its validity, that is, the degree to which the test actually measures what it purports to measure. Validity provides a direct check on how well the test fulfills its function. The determination of validity usually requires independent, external *criteria* of whatever the test is designed to measure. For example, if a medical aptitude test is to be used in selecting promising applicants for medical school, ultimate success in medical school would be a criterion. In the process of validating such a test, it would be administered to a large group of students at the time of their admission to medical school. Some measure of performance in medical school would eventually be obtained for each student on the basis of grades, ratings by instructors, success or failure in completing training, and the like. Such a composite measure constitutes the criterion with which each student's initial test score is to be correlated. A high correlation, or *validity coefficient*, would signify that those individuals who scored high on the test had been relatively successful in medical school, whereas those scoring low on the test had done poorly in medical school. A low correlation would indicate little correspondence between test score and criterion measure and hence poor validity for the test. The validity coefficient enables us to determine how closely the criterion performance could have been predicted from the test scores.

In a similar manner, tests designed for other purposes can be validated against appropriate criteria. A vocational aptitude test, for example, can be validated against on-the-job success of a trial group of new employees. A pilot aptitude battery can be validated against achievement in flight training. Tests designed for broader and more varied uses are validated against a number of independently obtained behavioral indices; and their validity can be established only by the gradual accumulation of data from many different kinds of investigations.

The reader may have noticed an apparent paradox in the concept of test validity. If it is necessary to follow up the examinees or in other ways to obtain independent measures of what the test is trying to predict, why not dispense with the test? The answer to this riddle is to be found in the distinction between the validation group on the one hand and the groups on which the test will eventually be employed for operational purposes on the other. Before the test is ready for use, its validity must be established on a representative sample of persons. The scores of these persons are not them-selves employed for operational purposes but serve only in the process of testing the test. If the test proves valid by this method, it can then be used on other samples in the absence of criterion measures.

It might still be argued that we would need only to wait for the criterion measure to mature, to become available, on *any* group in order to obtain the information that the test is trying to predict. But such a procedure would be so wasteful of time and energy as to be prohibitive in most in-stances. Thus, we could determine which applicants will succeed on a job or which students will satisfactorily complete college by admitting all who apply (or a random sample of them) and waiting for subsequent develop-ments! It is the very wastefulness of this procedure—and its deleterious emotional impact on individuals—that tests are designed to minimize. By means of tests, the person's present level of prerequisite skills, knowledge, and other relevant characteristics can be assessed with a determinable mar-gin of error. The more valid and reliable the test, the smaller will be this margin of error.

The special problems encountered in determining the validity of dif-ferent types of tests, as well as the specific criteria and statistical procedures employed, will be discussed in Chapters 6 and 7. One further point, how-ever, should be considered at this time. Validity tells us more than the de-gree to which the test is fulfilling its function. It actually tells us *what* the test is measuring. By studying the validation data, we can objectively de-termine what the test is measuring. It would thus be more accurate to define validity as the extent to which we know what the test measures. The inter-pretation of test scores would undoubtedly be clearer and less ambiguous if tests were regularly named in terms of the empirically established rela-tionships through which they had been validated. A tendency in this direc-tion can be recognized in such test labels as "scholastic aptitude test" and "personnel classification test" in place of the vague title "intelligence test."

REASONS FOR CONTROLLING THE USE OF PSYCHOLOGICAL TESTS

"May I have a Stanford-Binet blank? My nephew has to take it next week for admission to School X and I'd like to give him some practice so he can pass."

"To improve the reading program in our school, we need a culture-free IQ test that measures each child's innate potential."

"Last night I answered the questions in an intelligence test published in a maga-zine and I got an IQ of 80—I think psychological tests are silly."

"My roommate is studying psych. She gave me a personality test and I came out neurotic. I've been too upset to go to class ever since."

"Last year you gave a new personality test to our employees for research purposes. We would now like to have the scores for their personnel folders."

The above remarks are not imaginary. Each is based on a real incident, and the list could easily be extended by any psychologist. Such remarks illustrate potential misuses or misinterpretations of psychological tests in such ways as to render the tests worthless or to hurt the individual. Like any scientific instrument or precision tool, psychological tests must be properly used to be effective. In the hands of either the unscrupulous or the well-meaning but uninformed user, such tests can cause serious damage. There are two principal reasons for controlling the use of psychological tests: (a) to ensure that the test is used by a qualified examiner; and (b) to prevent general familiarity with the test content, which would invalidate the test.

QUALIFIED EXAMINER. The need for a qualified examiner is evident in each of the three major aspects of the testing situation: selection of the test, administration and scoring, and interpretation of scores. Tests cannot be chosen like lawn mowers, from a mail-order catalog. They cannot be evaluated by name, author, or other easy marks of identification. To be sure, it requires no psychological training to consider such factors as cost, bulkiness and ease of transporting test materials, testing time required, and ease and rapidity of scoring. Information on these practical points can usually be obtained from a test catalog and should be taken into account in planning a testing program. For the test to serve its function, however, an evaluation of its technical merits in terms of such characteristics as validity, reliability, difficulty level, and norms is essential. Only in such a way can test users determine the appropriateness of any test for their particular purpose and its suitability for the type of persons with whom they plan to use it.

The introductory discussion of test standardization earlier in this chapter has already suggested the importance of a trained examiner. An adequate realization of the need to follow instructions precisely, as well as a thorough familiarity with the standard instructions, is required if the test scores obtained by different examiners are to be comparable or if any one individual's score is to be evaluated in terms of the published norms. Careful control of testing conditions is also essential. Similarly, incorrect or inaccurate scoring may render the test score worthless. In the absence of proper checking procedures, scoring errors are far more likely to occur than is generally realized.

The proper interpretation of test scores requires a thorough understanding of the test, the examinee, and the testing conditions. What is being measured can be objectively determined only by reference to the specific procedures through which the particular test was validated. Other information, pertaining to reliability, nature of the group on which norms were established, and the like, is likewise relevant. Some background data regarding the individual being tested are essential in interpreting any test score. The same score may be obtained by different persons for very different reasons. The conclusions to be drawn from such scores would therefore be quite dissimilar. Finally, some consideration must also be given to special factors that may have influenced a particular score, such as unusual testing conditions, the temporary emotional or physical state of the examinee, and the extent of the examinee's previous experience with tests.

PROTECTION OF TEST CONTENT. Obviously, if one were to memorize the correct responses on a test of color blindness, such a test would no longer be a measure of color vision for that person. Under these conditions, the test would be completely invalidated. Test content clearly has to be restricted in order to forestall deliberate efforts to fake scores. In other cases, however, the effect of familiarity may be less obvious, or the test may be invalidated in good faith by misinformed persons. A schoolteacher, for example, may give a class special practice in problems closely resembling those on an intelligence test, "so that the children will be well prepared to take the test." Such an attitude is simply a carry-over from the usual procedure of preparing for a school examination. When applied to an intelligence test, however, it is likely that such specific training or coaching will raise the scores on the test without appreciably affecting the broader area of behavior the test tries to sample. Under such conditions, the validity of the test as a predictive or diagnostic instrument is reduced.

Ensuring the security of specific test content need not—and should not—interfere with the effective communication of testing information to examinees, concerned professionals, and the general public. Such communication serves several purposes. First, it tends to dispel any mystery that may have become associated with testing and thereby helps to correct prevalent misconceptions about what tests are designed to do and what their scores mean. A number of clearly written publications distributed by some of the larger test publishers were prepared for this purpose. A second type of communication is designed to report fully the technical procedures whereby particular tests were constructed and evaluated, and to present the relevant data about reliability, validity, and other psychometric properties of the tests. This type of information is typically included in the technical manual prepared for each test and is available to any interested person.

A third purpose of test communication is to familiarize examinees with testing procedures, dispel anxiety, and ensure that each will perform to the best of her or his ability. Several explanatory booklets have been prepared for this purpose, some of a general nature and others for specific tests such as the College Board's Scholastic Aptitude Test. These materials will be discussed further in a later section of this chapter. A fourth and highly significant type of communication is the feedback provided to examinees regarding their own performance on any test they have taken. Psychologists have given considerable attention to the most useful and meaningful ways of conveying such information in different contexts. Appropriate procedures will be examined in Chapter 3.

The dissemination of information about testing is of fundamental importance. There are helpful as well as harmful ways of carrying it out. An example of the latter is provided by some overhasty legislative attempts to introduce government controls at both state and federal levels (Lerner, 1980b). State laws regulating the disclosure of testing information were actually enacted in the late 1970s in California and New York. The New York law, which was the more extreme of the two, required the unlimited disclosure of test questions and answers in all large-scale testing programs for admission to institutions of higher learning. Because this condition necessitates the preparation of a new form of each test for each administration, it can have any of several adverse effects. These include, among others, fewer available testing dates during the year, increase in applicant fees, and decline in the quality-control procedures that can be followed in test construction. The desirable goals that motivated the proposal of such laws can be attained more effectively and without deleterious side effects by strengthening available procedures for communicating information about tests.[1]

TEST ADMINISTRATION

The basic rationale of testing involves generalization from the behavior sample observed in the testing situation to behavior manifested in other, nontest situations. A test score should help us to predict how the client will feel and act outside the clinic, how the student will achieve in college courses, and how the applicant will perform on the job. Any influences that are specific to the test situation constitute error variance and reduce test validity. It is therefore important to identify any test-related influences that may limit or impair the generalizability of test results.

A whole volume could easily be devoted to a discussion of desirable procedures of test administration. But such a survey falls outside the scope of the present book. Moreover, it is more practicable to acquire such techniques within specific settings, because no one person would normally be concerned with all forms of testing, from the examination of infants to the clinical testing of psychotic patients or the administration of a mass testing program for military personnel. The present discussion will therefore deal principally with the common rationale of test administration rather than with specific questions of implementation. For detailed suggestions regard-

---

[1] Much testimony was presented, at both state and federal levels, detailing the potential harm that could result from the proposed legislation. Statements were submitted by individuals from many sectors of the public and by professional associations. Excerpts of views on the test-disclosure legislation expressed by various educational leaders are reproduced in a special testing supplement of *The College Board Review* (1980, pp. A12–A13).

ing testing procedure, see Palmer (1970), Sattler (1982), and Terman and Merrill (1960) for individual testing, and Clemans (1971) for group testing.

ADVANCE PREPARATION OF EXAMINERS. The most important requirement for good testing procedure is advance preparation. In testing there can be no emergencies. Special efforts must therefore be made to foresee and forestall emergencies. Only in this way can uniformity of procedure be assured.

Advance preparation for the testing session takes many forms. Memorizing the exact verbal instructions is essential in most individual testing. Even in a group test in which the instructions are read to the examinees, some previous familiarity with the statements to be read prevents misreading and hesitation and permits a more natural, informal manner during test administration. The preparation of test materials is another important preliminary step. In individual testing and especially in the administration of performance tests, such preparation involves the actual layout of the necessary materials to facilitate subsequent use with a minimum of search or fumbling. Materials should generally be placed on a table near the testing table so that they are within easy reach of the examiner but do not distract the examinee. When apparatus is employed, frequent periodic checking and calibration may be necessary. In group testing, all test blanks, answer sheets, special pencils, or other materials needed should be carefully counted, checked, and arranged in advance of the testing day.

Thorough familiarity with the specific testing procedure is another important prerequisite in both individual and group testing. For individual testing, supervised training in the administration of the particular test is usually essential. Depending upon the nature of the test and the type of persons to be examined, such training may require from a few demonstration and practice sessions to over a year of instruction. For group testing, and especially in large-scale projects, the preparation may include advance briefing of examiners and proctors, so that each is fully informed about the functions he or she is to perform. In general, the examiner reads the instructions, takes care of timing, and is in charge of the group in any one testing room. The proctors hand out and collect test materials, make certain that instructions are followed, answer the individual questions of examinees within the limitations specified in the manual, and prevent cheating.

TESTING CONDITIONS. Standardized procedure applies not only to verbal instructions, timing, materials, and other aspects of the tests themselves but also to the testing environment. Some attention should be given to the selection of a suitable testing room. This room should be free from undue noise and distraction and should provide adequate lighting, ventilation, seating facilities, and working space for examinees. Special steps should also be taken to prevent interruptions during the test. Posting a sign on the door to indicate that testing is in progress is effective, provided all personnel have learned that such a sign means no admittance under any circumstances. In the testing of large groups, locking the doors or posting an assistant outside each door may be necessary to prevent the entrance of late-comers.

It is important to realize the extent to which testing conditions may influence scores. Even apparently minor aspects of the testing situation may appreciably alter performance. Such a condition as the use of desks or of chairs with desk arms, for example, proved to be significant in a group testing project with high school students, the groups using desks tending to obtain higher scores (Kelley, 1943; Traxler & Hilkert, 1942). There is also evidence to show that the type of answer sheet employed may affect test scores (Bell, Hoff, & Hoyt, 1964). Because of the establishment of independent test-scoring and data-processing agencies that provide their own machine-scorable answer sheets, examiners sometimes administer group tests with answer sheets other than those used in the standardization sample. In the absence of empirical verification, the equivalence of these answer sheets cannot be assumed. The Differential Aptitude Tests, for example, may be administered with any of five different answer sheets. On the Clerical Speed and Accuracy Test of this battery, separate norms are provided for three of the five answer sheets, because they were found to yield substantially different scores than those obtained with the answer sheets used by the standardization sample.

In testing children below the fifth grade, the use of *any* separate answer sheet may significantly lower test scores (Cashen & Ramseyer, 1969; Harcourt Brace Jovanovich, 1973; Ramseyer & Cashen, 1971). At these grade levels, having the child mark the answers in the test booklet itself is generally preferable.

Many other, more subtle testing conditions have been shown to affect performance on ability as well as personality tests. Whether the examiner is a stranger or someone familiar to the examinees may make a significant difference in test scores (Sacks, 1952; Tsudzuki, Hata, & Kuze, 1957). In another study, the general manner and behavior of the examiner, as illustrated by smiling, nodding, and making such comments as "good" or "fine," were shown to have a decided effect on test results (Wickes, 1956). In a projective test requiring the respondent to write stories to fit given pictures, the presence of the examiner in the room tended to inhibit the inclusion of strongly emotional content in the stories (Bernstein, 1956). In the administration of a typing test, job applicants typed at a significantly faster rate when tested alone than when tested in groups of two or more (Kirchner, 1966).

Examples could readily be multiplied. The implications are threefold. First, follow standardized procedures to the minutest detail. It is the responsibility of the test author and publisher to describe such procedures fully and clearly in the test manual. Second, record any unusual testing conditions, however minor. Third, take testing conditions into account when interpreting test results. In the intensive assessment of a person through individual testing, an experienced examiner may occasionally depart from the standardized test procedure in order to elicit additional information for special reasons. In such a case, he or she can no longer interpret the responses in terms of the test norms. Under these circumstances, the test stimuli are used only for qualitative exploration; and the responses should be treated in the same way as any other informal behavioral observations or interview data.

RAPPORT

In psychometrics, the term "rapport" refers to the examiner's efforts to arouse the examinee's interest in the test, elicit cooperation, and ensure that he or she follows the standard test instructions. In ability tests, the instructions call for careful concentration on the given tasks and for putting forth one's best efforts to perform well; in personality inventories, they call for frank and honest responses to questions about one's usual behavior; in certain projective tests, they call for full reporting of associations evoked by the stimuli, without any censoring or editing of content. Still other kinds of tests may require other approaches. But in all instances, the examiner endeavors to motivate the examinee to follow the instructions as fully and conscientiously as he or she can.

The training of examiners covers techniques for the establishment of rapport as well as those more directly related to test administration. In establishing rapport, as in other testing procedures, uniformity of conditions is essential for comparability of results. If a child is given a coveted prize whenever she solves a test problem correctly, her performance cannot be directly compared with the norms or with that of other children who are motivated only with the standard verbal encouragement or praise. Any deviation from standard motivating conditions for a particular test should be noted and taken into account in interpreting performance.

Although rapport can be more fully established in individual testing, steps can also be taken in group testing to motivate examinees and relieve their anxiety. Specific techniques for establishing rapport vary with the nature of the test and with the age and other characteristics of the persons tested. In testing preschool children, special factors to be considered include shyness with strangers, distractibility, and negativism. A friendly, cheerful, and relaxed manner on the part of the examiner helps to reassure the child. The shy, timid child needs more preliminary time to become familiar with the surroundings. For this reason, it is better for the examiner not to be too demonstrative at the outset, but rather to wait until the child is ready to make the first contact. Test periods should be brief, and the tasks should be varied and intrinsically interesting to the child. The testing should be presented to the child as a game and his curiosity aroused before each new task is introduced. A certain flexibility of procedure is necessary at this age level because of possible refusals, loss of interest, and other manifestations of negativism.

Children in the first two or three grades of elementary school present many of the same testing problems as the preschool child. The game approach is still the most effective way of arousing their interest in the test. The older schoolchild can usually be motivated through an appeal to the competitive spirit and the desire to do well on tests. When testing children from educationally disadvantaged backgrounds or from different cultures, however, the examiner cannot assume they will be motivated to excel on academic tasks to the same extent as children in the standardization sample. This problem and others pertaining to the testing of persons with dissimilar experiential backgrounds will be considered further in Chapters 3, 7, and 12.

Special motivational problems may be encountered in testing emotionally disturbed persons, prisoners, or juvenile delinquents. Especially when examined in an institutional setting, such persons are likely to manifest a number of unfavorable attitudes, such as suspicion, insecurity, fear, or cynical indifference. Special conditions in their past experiences are also likely to influence their test performance adversely. As a result of early failures and frustrations in school, for example, they may have developed feelings of hostility and inferiority toward academic tasks, which the tests resemble. The experienced examiner makes special efforts to establish rapport under these conditions. In any event, he or she must be sensitive to these special difficulties and take them into account in interpreting and explaining test performance.

In testing any school-age child or adult, one should bear in mind that every test presents an implied threat to the individual's prestige. Some reassurance should therefore be given at the outset. It is helpful to explain, for example, that no one is expected to finish or to get all the items correct. The examinee might otherwise experience a mounting sense of failure as she or he advances to the more difficult items or is unable to finish any subtest within the time allowed.

It is also desirable to eliminate the element of surprise from the test situation as far as possible, because the unexpected and unknown are likely to produce anxiety. Many group tests include a preliminary explanatory statement that is read to the group by the examiner. An even better procedure is to provide each examinee in advance with materials that explain the purpose and nature of the tests, offer general suggestions on how to take tests, and contain a few sample items. Such explanatory booklets are regularly available to participants in many large-scale testing programs, such as those conducted by the College Board (1981a, 1981b).

Adult testing presents some additional problems. Unlike the schoolchild, the adult is not so likely to work hard at a task merely because it is assigned. It therefore becomes more important to "sell" the purpose of the tests to the adult, although high school and college students also respond to such an appeal. Cooperation of examinees can usually be secured by convincing them that it is in their own interests to obtain a valid score, i.e., a score correctly indicating what they can do rather than overestimating or underestimating their abilities. Most persons will understand that an incorrect decision, which might result from invalid test scores, would mean subsequent failure, loss of time, and frustration for them. This approach can serve not only to motivate examinees to try their best on ability tests but also to reduce faking and encourage frank reporting on personality inventories, because examinees realize that they themselves would otherwise be the losers. It is certainly not in the best interests of individuals to be admitted to a course of study for which they are not qualified or assigned to a job they cannot perform or would find uncongenial.

TEST ANXIETY

Many of the practices designed to enhance rapport serve also to reduce test anxiety. Procedures tending to dispel surprise and strangeness from the testing situation and to reassure and encourage the examinee should certainly help to lower anxiety. The examiner's own manner and a well-organized, smoothly running testing operation will contribute toward the same goal.

Individual differences in test anxiety have been studied with both school-children and college students (Gaudry & Spielberger, 1974; I. G. Sarason, 1980; Spielberger, 1972). Much of this research was initiated by S. B. Sarason and his associates at Yale (Sarason, Davidson, Lighthall, Waite, & Ruebush, 1960). The first step was to construct a questionnaire to assess the individual's test-taking attitudes. The children's form, for example, contained items such as the following:

Do you worry a lot before taking a test?

When the teacher says she is going to find out how much you have learned, does your heart begin to beat faster?

While you are taking a test, do you usually think you are not doing well?

Of primary interest is the finding that both school achievement and intelligence test scores yielded significant negative correlations with test anxiety. Similar correlations have been found among college students (I. G. Sarason, 1961). Longitudinal studies likewise revealed an inverse relation between changes in anxiety level and changes in intelligence or achievement test performance (Hill & Sarason, 1966; Sarason, Hill, & Zimbardo, 1964).

Such findings, of course, do not indicate the direction of causal relationships. It is possible that students develop test anxiety because they perform poorly on tests and have thus experienced failure and frustration in previous test situations. In support of this interpretation is the finding that within subgroups of high scorers on intelligence tests, the negative correlation between anxiety level and test performance disappeared (Denny, 1966; Feldhusen & Klausmeier, 1962). On the other hand, there is evidence suggesting that at least some of the relationship results from the deleterious effects of anxiety on test performance. In one study (Waite, Sarason, Lighthall, & Davidson, 1958), high-anxious and low-anxious children equated in intelligence test scores were given repeated trials in a learning task. Although initially equal in the learning test, the low-anxious group improved significantly more than the high-anxious.

Several investigators have compared test performance under conditions designed to evoke "anxious" and "relaxed" states. Mandler and Sarason (1952), for example, found that ego-involving instructions, such as telling examinees that everyone is expected to finish in the time allotted, had a beneficial effect on the performance of low-anxious persons, but a deleterious effect on that of high-anxious persons. Other studies have likewise found an interaction between testing conditions and such individual characteristics as anxiety level and achievement motivation (Lawrence, 1962; Paul & Eriksen, 1964). It thus appears likely that the relation between anxiety and test performance is nonlinear, a slight amount of anxiety being beneficial while a large amount is detrimental. Individuals who are customarily low-anxious benefit from test conditions that arouse some anxiety, while those who are customarily high-anxious perform better under more relaxed conditions.

It is undoubtedly true that a chronically high anxiety level exerts a detrimental effect on school learning and intellectual development. Such an effect, however, should be distinguished from the test-limited effects with which this discussion is concerned. To what extent does test anxiety make the individual's test performance unrepresentative of his or her customary performance level in nontest situations? Because of the competitive pressure experienced by college-bound high school seniors in America today, it has been argued that performance on college admission tests may be unduly affected by test anxiety. In a thorough and well-controlled investigation of this question, French (1962) compared the performance of high school students on a test given as part of the regular administration of the Scholastic Aptitude Test with performance on a parallel form of the test administered at a different time under "relaxed" conditions. The instructions on the latter occasion specified that the test was given for research purposes only and scores would not be sent to any college. The results showed that performance was no poorer during the standard administration than during the relaxed administration. Moreover, the concurrent validity of the test scores against high school course grades did not differ significantly under the two conditions. Several recent investigations have also called into question the common stereotype of the test-anxious student who knows the subject matter but "freezes up" when taking a test (see Culler & Holahan, 1980). This research found that students who score high on a test anxiety scale obtain lower grade-point averages and tend to have poorer study habits than do those who score low in test anxiety.

Research on the nature, measurement, and treatment of test anxiety is continuing at an ever-increasing pace (I. G. Sarason, 1980; Spielberger, Anton, & Bedell, 1976; Spielberger, Gonzalez, & Fletcher, 1979; Spielberger, Gonzalez, Taylor, Algaze, & Anton, 1978; G. S. Tryon, 1980). With regard to the nature of test anxiety, two important components have been identified, namely, emotionality and worry. The emotionality component comprises feelings and physiological reactions, such as tension and increasing heartbeat. The worry or cognitive component includes negative self-oriented thoughts, such as expectation of doing poorly and concern about the consequences of failure. These thoughts draw attention away from the task-oriented behavior required by the test and thereby disrupt performance. Both components are measured by several test anxiety· inventories. Although widely used in research, such inventories have until recently been available only through reports in the research literature. The Test Anxiety Inventory developed by Spielberger and his co-workers is now available in published form; it is described in Chapter 17 and listed in Appendix E.

Considerable effort has been devoted to the development and evaluation of methods for treating test anxiety. These include several behavior therapy procedures (Ch. 16) for reducing the emotional component of test anxiety. The results have generally been positive, but it is difficult to attribute the improvement to any particular technique because of methodological flaws in the evaluation studies (G. S. Tryon, 1980). In fact, the emotionality component of test anxiety tends to decrease from test to retest even in control groups with no therapeutic intervention, as well as in special control groups given a credible pseudotherapy. Moreover, reduction in the emotionality component has little or no effect on performance level.

Performance in both tests and course work is more likely to improve when treatment is directed to the self-oriented cognitive reactions. Available research thus far suggests that the best results are obtained from combined treatment programs, which include the elimination of emotionality and worry, as well as the improvement of study skills. Test anxiety is a complex phenomenon with multiple causes, and the relative contribution of different causes varies with the individual. To be effective, treatment programs should be adapted to individual needs. It must also be recognized that test anxiety is only one manifestation of a more general set of conditions that reduce the individual's effectiveness as a learner.

EXAMINER AND SITUATIONAL VARIABLES

Comprehensive surveys of the effects of examiner and situational variables on test scores have been published periodically (Masling, 1960; Moriarty, 1961, 1966; Palmer, 1970; S. B. Sarason, 1954; Sattler, 1970, 1982; Sattler &

Theye, 1967). Although some effects have been demonstrated with objective group tests, most of the data have been obtained with either projective techniques or individual intelligence tests. These extraneous factors are more likely to operate with unstructured and ambiguous stimuli, as well as with difficult and novel tasks, than with clearly defined and well-learned functions. In general, children are more susceptible to examiner and situational influences than are adults; in the examination of preschool children, the role of the examiner is especially crucial. Emotionally disturbed and insecure persons of any age are also more likely to be affected by such conditions than are well-adjusted persons.

There is considerable evidence that test results may vary systematically as a function of the examiner (E. Cohen, 1965; Masling, 1960). These differences may be related to personal characteristics of the examiner, such as her or his age, sex, race, professional or socioeconomic status, training and experience, personality characteristics, and appearance. Several studies of these examiner variables, however, have yielded misleading or inconclusive results because the experimental designs failed to control or isolate the influence of different examiner or examinee characteristics. Hence, the effects of two or more variables may be confounded.

The examiner's behavior before and during test administration has also been shown to affect test results. For example, controlled investigations have yielded significant differences in intelligence test performance as a result of a "warm" versus a "cold" interpersonal relation between examiner and examinees, or a rigid and aloof versus a natural manner on the part of the examiner (Exner, 1966; Masling, 1959). Moreover, there may be significant interactions between examiner and examinee characteristics, in the sense that the same examiner characteristics or testing manner may have a different effect on different examinees as a function of the examinee's own personality characteristics. Similar interactions may occur with task variables, such as the nature of the test, the purpose of the testing, and the instructions given to examinees. Dyer (1973) adds even more variables to this list, calling attention to the possible influence of the test givers' and the test takers' diverse perceptions of the functions and goals of testing.

Still another way in which an examiner may inadvertently affect the examinee's responses is through his or her own expectations. This is simply a special instance of the self-fulfilling prophecy (Rosenthal, 1966; Rosenthal & Rosnow, 1969). An experiment conducted with the Rorschach will illustrate this effect (Masling, 1965). The examiners were 14 graduate student volunteers, 7 of whom were told, among other things, that experienced examiners elicit more human than animal responses, while the other 7 were told that experienced examiners elicit more animal than human responses. Under these conditions, the two groups of examiners obtained significantly different ratios of animal to human responses from their examinees. These differences occurred despite the fact that neither examiners nor examinees reported awareness of any influence attempt. Moreover, tape recordings of all testing sessions revealed no evidence of verbal influence on the part of any examiner. The examiners' expectations apparently operated through subtle postural and facial cues to which the examinees responded.

Apart from the examiner, other aspects of the testing situation may significantly affect test performance. Military recruits, for example, are often examined shortly after induction, during a period of intense readjustment to an unfamiliar and stressful situation. In one investigation designed to test the effect of acclimatization to such a situation on test performance, 2,724 recruits were given the Navy Classification Battery during their ninth day at the Naval Training Center (Gordon & Alf, 1960). When their scores were compared with those obtained by 2,180 recruits tested at the conventional time, during their third day, the 9-day group scored significantly higher on all subtests of the battery.

The examinees' activities immediately preceding the test may also affect their performance, especially when such activities produce emotional disturbance, fatigue, or other handicapping conditions. In an investigation with third- and fourth-grade schoolchildren, there was some evidence to suggest that IQ on the Draw-a-Man Test was influenced by the children's preceding classroom activity (McCarthy, 1944). On one occasion, the class had been engaged in writing a composition on "The Best Thing That Ever Happened to Me"; on the second occasion, they had again been writing, but this time on "The Worst Thing That Ever Happened to Me." The IQ's on the second test, following what may have been an emotionally depressing experience, averaged 4 or 5 points lower than on the first test. These findings were corroborated in a later investigation specifically designed to determine the effect of immediately preceding experience on the Draw-a-Man Test (Reichenberg-Hackett, 1953). In this study, children who had had a gratifying experience involving the successful solution of an interesting puzzle, followed by a reward of toys and candy, showed more improvement in their test scores than those who had undergone neutral or less gratifying experiences. Similar results were obtained by W. E. Davis (1969a, 1969b) with college students. Performance on an arithmetic reasoning test was significantly poorer when preceded by a failure experience on a verbal comprehension test than it was in a control group given no preceding test and in one that had taken a standard verbal comprehension test under ordinary conditions.

Several studies have been concerned with the effects of feedback regarding test scores on the individual's subsequent test performance. In a particularly well-designed investigation with seventh-grade students, Bridgeman (1974) found that "success" feedback was followed by significantly higher performance on a similar test than was "failure" feedback in students who had actually performed equally well to begin with. This type of motivational feedback may operate largely through the goals the participants set for themselves in subsequent performance and may thus represent another example of the self-fulfilling prophecy. Such general motivational feedback, however, should not be confused with corrective feedback, whereby the individual is informed about the specific items he or she missed and given remedial instruction; under these conditions, feedback is much more likely to improve the performance of initially low-scoring persons.

The examples cited in this section illustrate the wide diversity of test-related variables that may affect test scores. In the majority of well-administered testing programs, the influence of these variables is negligible for practical purposes. Nevertheless, the skilled examiner is constantly on guard to detect the possible operation of such variables and to minimize their influence. When circumstances do not permit the control of these conditions, the conclusions drawn from test performance should be qualified.

EFFECTS OF TRAINING ON TEST PERFORMANCE

In evaluating the effects of training or practice on test scores, a fundamental question is whether the improvement is limited to the specific items included in the test or whether it extends to the broader behavior domain that the test is designed to assess. The answer to this question represents the difference between coaching and education. Obviously, any educational experience the individual undergoes, either formal or informal, in or out of school, should be reflected in her or his performance on tests sampling the relevant aspects of behavior. Such broad influences will in no way invalidate the test, since the test score presents an accurate picture of the individual's standing in the abilities under consideration. The difference is, of course, one of degree. Influences cannot be classified as either narrow or broad but obviously vary widely in scope, from those affecting only a single administration of a single test, through those affecting performance on all items of a certain type, to those influencing the individual's performance in the large majority of activities. From the standpoint of effective testing, however, a workable distinction can be made. Thus, it can be stated that a test score is invalidated only when a particular experience raises the score without appreciably affecting the behavior domain that the test is designed to measure.

COACHING. The effects of coaching on test scores have been widely investigated. Several early studies were conducted by British psychologists, with special reference to the effects of practice and coaching on the tests formerly used in assigning 11-year-old children to different types of secondary schools (Yates et al., 1953–1954). As might be expected, the extent of improvement depends on the ability and earlier educational experiences of the examinees, the nature of the tests, and the amount and type of coaching provided. Individuals with deficient educational backgrounds are more likely to benefit from special coaching than are those who have had superior educational opportunities and are already prepared to do well on the tests. It is obvious, too, that the closer the resemblance between test content and coaching material, the greater will be the improvement in test scores. On the other hand, the more closely instruction is restricted to specific test content, the less likely is improvement to extend to criterion performance.

In America, the College Entrance Examination Board has been concerned about the spread of ill-advised commercial coaching courses for college applicants. To clarify the issues, the College Board conducted several well-controlled experiments to determine the effects of such coaching on its Scholastic Aptitude Test (SAT) and surveyed the results of similar studies by other, independent investigators (Angoff, 1971a; College Board, 1979a, 1979b; Messick, 1980a). These studies covered a variety of coaching methods and included students in both public and private high schools; one investigation was conducted with black students in 15 urban and rural high schools in Tennessee. The conclusion from all these studies is that intensive drill on items similar to those on the SAT is unlikely to produce appreciably greater gains than occur when students are retested with the SAT after a year of regular high school instruction.

It should also be noted that in its test construction procedures, the College Board investigates the susceptibility of new item types to coaching (Angoff, 1971a; Pike & Evans, 1972). Item types on which performance can be appreciably raised by short-term drill or instruction of a narrowly limited nature are not included in the operational forms of the tests. An obvious example would be the type of problem that requires a simple insightful solution which, once attained, can be applied directly to solving all similar problems. When encountered in the future, such problems would thus test recall rather than problem-solving skills.

TEST SOPHISTICATION. The effects of test sophistication, or sheer test-taking practice, should also be considered in this connection. In studies with alternate forms of the same test, there is a tendency for the second score to be higher. Significant mean gains have been reported when alternate forms were administered in immediate succession or after intervals ranging from one day to three years (Angoff, 1971a; Droege, 1966; Peel, 1951, 1952). Similar results have been obtained with normal and intellectually gifted schoolchildren, high school and college students, and employee samples. Data on the distribution of gains to be expected on a retest with a parallel form should be provided in test manuals, and allowance for such gains should be made when interpreting test scores.

Nor are score gains limited to alternate forms. The individual who has had extensive prior experience in taking standardized tests enjoys a certain advantage in test performance over one who is taking his or her first test (Millman, Bishop, & Ebel, 1965; Rodger, 1936). Part of this advantage stems from having overcome an initial feeling of strangeness, as well as from having developed more self-confidence and better test-taking attitudes. Part is the result of a certain amount of overlap in the type of content and functions covered by many tests. Specific familiarity with common item types and practice in the use of objective answer sheets may also improve performance slightly. It is particularly important to take test sophistication into account when comparing the scores obtained by persons whose test-taking experience may have varied widely.

Short orientation and practice sessions can be quite effective in equalizing test sophistication (Wahlstrom & Boersman, 1968). Such familiarization training reduces the effects of prior differences in test-taking experience as such. Since these individual differences are specific to the test situation, their diminution should permit a more valid assessment of the broad behavior domain the test is designed to measure. This approach is illustrated by the College Board publication entitled *Taking the SAT* (College Board, 1981b), a booklet distributed to all college applicants who register for this test. The booklet offers suggestions for effective test-taking behavior, illustrates and explains the different types of items included in the test, and reproduces a complete form of the test, which students are advised to take under standard timing conditions and to score with the given key.

More general test orientation procedures have also been developed. An example is the *Test Orientation Procedure* (TOP), designed chiefly for job applicants with little prior testing experience (Bennett & Doppelt, 1967). It comprises a booklet and a tape recording on how to take tests, with easy test-like exercises; and a second, 20-page booklet of sample tests, which the prospective applicant can take home for practice. The United States Employment Service has likewise prepared a booklet on how to take tests, as well as a more extensive pretesting orientation technique, for use with educationally disadvantaged applicants tested at state employment services (U.S. Department of Labor, 1968, 1970b, 1971).

INSTRUCTION IN BROAD INTELLECTUAL SKILLS. Some researchers have been exploring the opposite approach to the improvement of test performance. Their goal is the development of widely applicable intellectual skills, work habits, and problem-solving strategies. The effects of such interventions should be manifested in *both* test scores and criterion performance, such as college courses. In accordance with the distinction introduced at the opening of this section, this type of program is designed to provide education rather than coaching. Some of these investigators have been working with educable mentally retarded children and adolescents (Babad & Budoff, 1974; Belmont & Butterfield, 1977; A. L. Brown, 1974; Budoff & Corman, 1974; Campione & Brown, 1979; Feuerstein, 1979, 1980). Others have concentrated on college and professional school students from educationally disadvantaged backgrounds (Whimbey, 1975, 1977, 1980).

Many of the training procedures employed in these programs are designed to develop effective problem-solving behavior, such as careful analysis of problems or questions; consideration of all alternatives, relevant details, and implications in arriving at a solution; deliberate rather than impulsive formulation or choice of a solution; and the application of high standards in evaluating one's own performance. These are obviously strategies that should improve one's intellectual functioning not only on tests but also in academic work and in many other everyday-life activities that depend on school learning. A crucial question, however, pertains to the degree of transfer and generalizability of effects beyond the types of contents and settings employed in the training. Results thus far reported are promising. But the programs are still in an exploratory stage and more research is needed to establish the breadth and durability of the improvement attained.

OVERVIEW. We have considered three types of pretest training that are quite dissimilar in their objectives. How do these types of training affect the validity of a test and its practical usefulness as an assessment instrument? The first was coaching, in the sense of intensive, massed drill on items similar to those on the test. It was noted that well-constructed tests choose item types so as to minimize their susceptibility to such drill; and they also protect the security of specific test items. Insofar as such coaching might improve test performance, it would do so without a corresponding improvement in criterion behavior. Hence, it would thereby reduce test validity. The test would become a poorer measure of the broad abilities it was designed to assess and a less accurate means of ascertaining whether the individual has acquired the skills and knowledge prerequisite for success in the criterion situation.

Test orientation procedures, on the other hand, are designed to rule out or equalize differences in prior test-taking experience. Like the effects of coaching, these differences represent conditions that affect test scores as such, without necessarily being reflected in the broader behavior domain to be assessed. Hence, the test orientation procedures should make the test a more valid instrument by reducing the influence of test-specific factors.

Finally, training in broadly applicable intellectual skills, if effective, should improve the trainee's ability to cope with subsequent intellectual tasks. This improvement will and should be reflected in test performance. Insofar as both test scores and criterion performance are improved, such training leaves test validity unchanged; but it enhances the individual's chances of attaining desired goals.

CHAPTER 3

Social and Ethical
Implications of Testing

I N BOTH their research and the practical applications of their procedures, psychologists have long been concerned with questions of professional ethics. A concrete example of this concern is the systematic
empirical program followed in the early 1950s to develop the first formal
code of ethics for the profession. This extensive undertaking resulted in the
preparation of a set of standards which were officially adopted by the American Psychological Association and first published in 1953. These standards
undergo continual review and refinement, leading to the periodic publication of revised editions. The current version, *Ethical Principles of Psychologists,* is reproduced in Appendix A. Beginning in 1979, illustrative cases on
ethical problems have been published annually in the *American Psychologist*
(Sanders, 1979). These reports are disguised summaries of actual ethics
cases adjudicated by the APA Committee on Scientific and Professional
Ethics and Conduct.

The distribution and use of psychological tests constitutes a major area
of the *Ethical Principles.* Principle 8 (Assessment Techniques) is specifically directed to testing, being concerned with the development, publication, and utilization of psychological assessment techniques. Principle 5
(Confidentiality), although broader in scope, is also highly relevant to testing, as are portions of most of the other principles. Some of the matters discussed in the *Ethical Principles* are closely related to points covered in the
Standards for Educational and Psychological Tests (1974) cited in Chapter 1. In fact, much of the content of the test *Standards* themselves helps to
define the professionally responsible use of tests. A survey of sources reporting ethical standards in the use of tests for personnel decisions can be found
in London and Bray (1980).

At a broader level, the 1970s evidenced a heightened concern with the
question of values in all fields of both theoretical and applied psychology.
An enlightening discussion of the ethical dilemmas and value conflicts that
may arise in research with human participants can be found in a book by
Diener and Crandall (1978). Within the testing area, a thoughtful and provocative analysis of the role of values is provided by Messick (1975, 1980b).

45

Ethical and social responsibility regarding the use of tests can be approached from several angles and at different levels. Major current approaches are illustrated in this chapter.

USER QUALIFICATIONS

The requirement that tests be used only by appropriately qualified examiners is one step toward protecting the individual against the improper use of tests. Of course, the necessary qualifications vary with the type of test. Thus, a relatively long period of intensive training and supervised experience is required for the proper use of individual intelligence tests and most personality tests, whereas a minimum of specialized psychological training is needed in the case of educational achievement or vocational proficiency tests. It should also be noted that students who take tests in class for instructional purposes are not usually equipped to administer the tests to others or to interpret the scores properly.

Well-trained examiners choose tests that are appropriate for both the particular purpose for which they are testing and the persons to be examined. They are also cognizant of the available research literature on the chosen test and able to evaluate its technical merits with regard to such characteristics as norms, reliability, and validity. In administering the test, they are sensitive to the many conditions that may affect test performance, such as those illustrated in Chapter 2. They draw conclusions or make recommendations only after considering the test score (or scores) in the light of other pertinent information about the individual. Above all, they should be sufficiently knowledgeable about the science of human behavior to guard against unwarranted inferences in their interpretations of test scores. When tests are administered by psychological technicians or assistants, or by persons in other professions, it is essential that an adequately qualified psychologist be available, at least as a consultant, to provide the needed perspective for a proper interpretation of test performance.

Misconceptions about the nature and purpose of tests and misinterpretations of test results underlie many of the popular criticisms of psychological tests. In part, these difficulties arise from inadequate communication between psychometricians and their various publics—educators, parents, legislators, job applicants, and so forth. Probably the most common examples center on unfounded inferences from IQs. Not all misconceptions about tests, however, can be attributed to inadequate communication between psychologists and the public. Psychological testing itself has tended to become dissociated from the mainstream of behavioral science (Anastasi, 1967). The growing complexity of the science of psychology has inevitably been accompanied by increasing specialization among psychologists. In this process, psychometricians have concentrated more and more on the technical refinements of test construction and have tended to lose contact with developments in other relevant specialties, such as learning, child development, individual differences, and behavior genetics. Thus, the technical aspects of test construction have tended to outstrip the psychological sophistication with which test results are interpreted. Test scores can be properly interpreted only in the light of all available knowledge regarding the behavior that the tests are designed to measure.

Who is a qualified psychologist? Obviously, with the diversification of the field and the consequent specialization of training, no psychologist is equally qualified in all areas. In recognition of this fact, the *Ethical Principles* specify: "Psychologists recognize the boundaries of their competence and the limitations of their techniques. They only provide services and only use techniques for which they are qualified by training and experience" (Principle 2, Competence). A useful distinction is that between a psychologist working in an institutional setting, such as a school system, university, clinic, or government agency, and one engaged in independent practice. Because the independent practitioner is less subject to judgment and evaluation by knowledgeable colleagues than is the institutional psychologist, he or she needs to meet higher standards of professional qualifications. The same would be true of a psychologist responsible for the supervision of other institutional psychologists or one who serves as an expert consultant to institutional personnel.

A significant step, both in upgrading professional standards and in helping the public to identify qualified psychologists, was the enactment of state licensing and certification laws for psychologists. Nearly all states have such laws. Although the terms "licensing" and "certification" are often used interchangeably, in psychology certification typically refers to legal protection of the title "psychologist," whereas licensing controls the practice of psychology. Licensing laws thus need to include a definition of the practice of psychology. In either type of law, the requirements are generally a PhD in psychology, a specified amount of supervised experience, and satisfactory performance on a qualifying examination. Violations of the APA ethics code constitute grounds for revoking a certificate or license. Although most states began with the simpler certification laws, there has been continuing movement toward licensing.

At a more advanced level, specialty certification within psychology is provided by the American Board of Professional Psychology (ABPP). Requiring a high level of training and experience within designated specialties, ABPP grants diplomas in such areas as clinical, counseling, industrial and organizational, and school psychology. The Biographical Directory of the APA contains a list of current diplomates in each specialty, which can also be obtained directly from ABPP. The principal function of ABPP is to provide information regarding qualified psychologists. As a privately constituted board within the profession, ABPP does not have the enforcement authority available to the agencies administering the state licensing and certification laws.

TESTING INSTRUMENTS AND PROCEDURES

The purchase of tests is generally restricted to persons who meet certain minimal qualifications. The catalogs of major test publishers specify requirements that must be met by purchasers. Usually, individuals with a master's degree in psychology or its equivalent qualify. Some publishers classify their tests into levels with reference to user qualifications, ranging from educational achievement and vocational proficiency tests, through group intelligence tests and interest inventories, to such clinical instruments as individual intelligence tests and most personality tests. Distinctions are also made between individual purchasers and authorized institutional purchasers of appropriate tests. Graduate students who may need a particular test for a class assignment or for research must have the purchase order countersigned by their psychology instructor, who assumes responsibility for the proper use of the test.

Efforts to restrict the distribution of tests have a dual objective: security of test materials and prevention of misuse. It should be noted, however, that while test distributors may make sincere efforts to implement these objectives, the control they are able to exert is necessarily limited. In some cases, they may fail to investigate and verify the alleged qualifications of test purchasers (see, e.g., Oles & Davis, 1977). Moreover, the formal qualifications provide only a rough screening device. It is evident, for example, that an MA degree in psychology—or even a PhD, a state license, and an ABPP diploma—do not necessarily signify that the individual is qualified to use a particular test or that his or her training is relevant to the proper interpretation of the results obtained with that test. The major responsibility for the proper use of tests ultimately resides in the individual user or institution concerned.

Another professional responsibility pertains to the marketing of psychological tests by authors and publishers. Tests should not be released prematurely for general use. Nor should any claims be made regarding the merits of a test in the absence of sufficient objective evidence. When a test is distributed early for research purposes only, this condition should be clearly specified and the distribution of the test restricted accordingly. The test manual should provide adequate data to permit an evaluation of the test itself as well as full information regarding administration, scoring, and norms. The manual should be a factual exposition of what is known about the test rather than a selling device designed to put the test in a favorable light. It is the responsibility of the test author and publisher to revise tests and norms often enough to prevent obsolescence. The rapidity with which a test becomes outdated, of course, varies widely with the nature of the test.

Tests or major parts of tests should not be published in a newspaper, magazine, or popular book, either for descriptive purposes or for self-evaluation. Under these conditions, self-evaluation would not only be subject to such drastic errors as to be well-nigh worthless, but it might also be psychologically injurious to the individual. Moreover, any publicity given to specific test items will tend to invalidate the future use of the test with other persons. It might also be added that presentation of test materials in this fashion tends to create an erroneous and distorted picture of psychological testing in general. Such publicity may foster either naive credulity or indiscriminate resistance on the part of the public toward all psychological testing.

Another unprofessional practice is testing by mail. An individual's performance on either aptitude or personality tests cannot be properly assessed by mailing test forms to her or him and having them returned by mail for scoring and interpretation. Not only does this procedure provide no control of testing conditions, but usually it also involves the interpretation of test scores in the absence of other pertinent information about the individual. Under these conditions, test results may be worse than useless.

PROTECTION OF PRIVACY

A question arising particularly in connection with personality tests is that of invasion of privacy. Insofar as some tests of emotional, motivational, or attitudinal traits are necessarily disguised, the examinee may reveal characteristics in the course of such a test without realizing that he or she is so doing. Although there are few available tests whose approach is subtle enough to fall into this category, the possibility of developing such indirect testing procedures imposes a grave responsibility on the psychologist who uses them. For purposes of testing effectiveness, it may be necessary to keep the examinee in ignorance of the specific ways in which the responses on any one test are to be interpreted. Nevertheless, a person should not be subjected to any testing program under false pretenses. Of primary importance in this connection is the obligation to have a clear understanding with the examinee regarding the use that will be made of the test results.

Although concerns about the invasion of privacy have been expressed most commonly about personality tests, they logically apply to any type of test. Certainly any intelligence, aptitude, or achievement test may reveal limitations in skills and knowledge that an individual would rather not disclose. Moreover, any observation of an individual's behavior—as in an interview, a casual conversation, or other personal encounter—may yield information that the individual would prefer to conceal and that he or she may reveal unwittingly. The fact that psychological tests have often been singled out in discussions of the invasion of privacy probably reflects prevalent misconceptions about tests. If all tests were recognized as measures of behavior samples, with no mysterious powers to penetrate beyond behavior, popular fears and suspicion would be lessened.

It should also be noted that all behavior research, whether employing tests or other observational procedures, presents the possibility of invasion of privacy. Yet, as scientists, psychologists are committed to the goal of advancing knowledge about human behavior. Conflicts of values may thus arise, which must be resolved in individual cases. Many examples of such conflict resolutions can be found in *Ethical Principles in the Conduct of Research with Human Participants* (APA, 1973), which describes actual incidents under each principle.

The problem is obviously not simple; and it has been the subject of extensive deliberation by psychologists and other professionals. In a report entitled *Privacy and Behavioral Research* (1967), prepared for the Office of Science and Technology, the right to privacy is defined as "the right of the individual to decide for himself how much he will share with others his thoughts, his feelings, and the facts of his personal life" (p. 2). It is further characterized as "a right that is essential to insure dignity and freedom of self-determination" (p. 2). To safeguard personal privacy, no universal rules can be formulated; only general guidelines can be provided. In the application of these guidelines to specific cases, there is no substitute for the ethical awareness and professional responsibility of the individual psychologist. Solutions must be worked out in terms of the particular circumstances.

One relevant factor is the purpose for which the testing is conducted—whether for individual counseling, institutional decisions regarding selection and classification, or research. In clinical or counseling situations, clients are usually willing to reveal themselves in order to obtain help with their problems. The clinician or examiner does not invade privacy where he or she is freely admitted. Even under these conditions, however, clients should be warned that in the course of the testing or interviewing they may reveal information about themselves without realizing that they are so doing; or they may disclose feelings of which they themselves are unaware.

When testing is conducted for institutional purposes, the examinee should be fully informed as to the use that will be made of his or her test scores. It is also desirable, however, to explain to examinees that correct assessment will benefit them, since it is not to their advantage to be placed in a position where they will fail or which they will find uncongenial. The results of tests administered in a clinical or counseling situation, of course, should not be made available for institutional purposes, unless the examinee gives her or his consent.

When tests are given for research purposes, anonymity should be preserved as fully as possible and the procedures for ensuring such anonymity should be explained in advance to the participants. Anonymity does not, however, solve the problem of protecting privacy in all research contexts. Some individuals may resent the disclosure of facts they consider personal, even when complete confidentiality of responses is assured. In most cases, however, cooperation may be elicited if participants are convinced that the information is needed for the research in question and if they have sufficient confidence in the integrity and competence of the investigator. All research on human behavior, whether or not it utilizes tests, may present conflicts of values. Freedom of inquiry, which is essential to the progress of science, must be balanced against the protection of the individual. The investigator must be alert to the values involved and must carefully weigh alternative solutions (APA, 1973, 1981; *Privacy and Behavioral Research*, 1967; Ruebhausen & Brim, 1966).

Whatever the purposes of testing, the protection of privacy involves two key concepts: relevance and informed consent. The information that the individual is asked to reveal must be *relevant* to the stated purposes of the testing. An important implication of this principle is that all practicable efforts should be made to ascertain the validity of tests for the particular diagnostic or predictive purpose for which they are used. An instrument that is demonstrably valid for a given purpose is one that provides relevant information. It also behooves the examiner to make sure that test scores are correctly interpreted. An individual is less likely to feel that her or his privacy is being invaded by a test assessing readiness for a particular educational program than by a test allegedly measuring "innate intelligence."

The concept of *informed consent* also requires clarification; and its application in individual cases may call for the exercise of considerable judgment (APA, 1973; Ruebhausen & Brim, 1966). The examinee should certainly be informed about the purpose of testing, the kinds of data sought, and the use that will be made of the scores. It is not implied, however, that he or she be shown the test items in advance or told how specific responses will be scored. Nor should the test items be shown to a parent, in the case of a minor. Such information would usually invalidate the test. Not only would the giving of this information seriously impair the usefulness of an ability test, but it would also tend to distort responses on many personality tests. For example, if an individual is told in advance that a self-report inventory will be scored with a dominance scale, his or her responses are likely to be influenced by stereotyped (and often erroneous) ideas he or she may have about this trait, or by a false or distorted self-concept.

In the testing of children, special questions arise with regard to parental consent. Following an interdisciplinary conference, the Russell Sage Foundation (1970) published a set of *Guidelines for the Collection, Maintenance, and Dissemination of Pupil Records*. In reference to informed consent, the *Guidelines* differentiate between individual consent, given by the child, the parents, or both, and representational consent, given by the parents' legally elected or appointed representatives, such as a school board. While avoiding rigid prescriptions, the *Guidelines* suggest aptitude and achievement tests as examples of the type of instruments for which representational consent should be sufficient; at the other extreme, personality assessment is cited as requiring individual consent. A helpful feature of these *Guidelines* is the inclusion of sample letters and forms for obtaining written consent. There is also a selected bibliography on the ethical and legal aspects of school rec-ord-keeping.

Testing procedures and experimental designs that protect the individual's right to decline to participate and that adequately safeguard privacy, while yielding scientifically meaningful data, present a challenge to the psychologist's ingenuity. With proper rapport and the establishment of attitudes of mutual respect, however, the number of refusals to participate may be reduced to a negligible quantity. The technical difficulties of biased sampling and volunteer error may thus be avoided. Evidence from both national and statewide surveys suggests that this goal *can* be achieved, both in testing educational outcomes and in the more sensitive area of personality research (Holtzman, 1971; Womer, 1970). There is also some evidence that the number of respondents who feel that a personality inventory represents an invasion of privacy or who consider some of the items offensive is significantly reduced when the test is preceded by a simple and forthright explanation of how items were selected and how scores will be interpreted (Fink & Butcher, 1972). From the standpoint of test validity, it should be added that, in the cited study, such an explanation did not affect the mean profile of scores on personality inventories.

CONFIDENTIALITY

Like the protection of privacy, to which it is related, the problem of confidentiality of test data is multifaceted. The fundamental question is: Who shall have access to test results? Several considerations influence the answer in particular situations. Among them are the security of test content, the hazards of misunderstanding test scores, and the need of various persons to know the results.

There has been a growing awareness of the right of individuals to have access to the findings in their own test reports. The examinee should also have the opportunity to comment on the contents of the report and if necessary to clarify or correct factual information. Counselors are now trying more and more to involve clients as active participants in their own assessment. For these purposes, test results should be presented in a form that is readily understandable, free from technical jargon or labels, and oriented toward the immediate objective of the testing. Proper safeguards must be observed against misuse and misinterpretation of test findings.

In the case of minors, one must also consider the parents' right of access to the child's test record. This presents a possible conflict with the child's own right to privacy, especially in the case of older children. In a searching analysis of the problem, Ruebhausen and Brim (1966, pp. 431–432) wrote: "Should not a child, even before the age of full legal responsibility, be accorded the dignity of a private personality? Considerations of healthy personal growth, buttressed with reasons of ethics, seem to command that this be done." The previously mentioned *Guidelines* (Russell Sage Foundation, 1970, p. 27) recommend that "when a student reaches the age of eighteen and no longer is attending high school, or is married (whether age eighteen or not)," he or she should have the right to deny parental access to his or her records. However, this recommendation is followed by the caution that school authorities check local state laws for possible legal difficulties in implementing such a policy.

Apart from these possible exceptions, the question is not *whether* to communicate test results to parents of a minor but *how* to do so. Parents normally have a legal right to information about their child; and it is usually desirable for them to have such information. In some cases, moreover, a child's academic or emotional difficulties may arise in part from parent–child relations. Under these conditions, the counselor's contact with the parents is of prime importance, both to fill in background data and to elicit parental cooperation.

Discussions of the confidentiality of test records have usually dealt with accessibility to a *third* person, other than the individual tested (or parent of a minor) and the examiner. The underlying principle is that such records should *not* be released without the knowledge and consent of the individual.

When tests are administered in an institutional context, as in a school system, court, or employment setting, the individual should be informed at the time of testing regarding the purpose of the test, how the results will be used, and their availability to institutional personnel who have a legitimate need for them. Under these conditions, no further permission is required at the time results are made available within the institution. A different situation exists when test results are requested by outsiders, as when a prospective employer or a college requests test results from a school system. In these instances, individual consent for release of the data is required. The same requirement applies to tests administered in clinical and counseling contexts, or for research purposes. The previously cited *Guidelines* (Russell Sage Foundation, 1970, p. 42) contain a sample release form for the use of school systems in clearing the transmission of such data.

Another problem pertains to the retention of records in institutions. On the one hand, longitudinal records on individuals can be very valuable, not only for research purposes but also for understanding and counseling the person. As is so often the case, these advantages presuppose proper use and interpretation of test results. On the other hand, the availability of old records opens the way for such misuses as incorrect inferences from obsolete data and unauthorized access for other than the original testing purpose. It would be manifestly absurd, for example, to cite an IQ or a reading achievement score obtained by a child in the third grade when evaluating him for admission to college. Too much may have happened to him in the intervening years to make such early and isolated test scores meaningful.

Similarly, when records are retained for many years, there is danger that they may be used for purposes that the individual (or his parents) never suspected and would not have approved.

To prevent such misuses, when records are retained either for legitimate longitudinal use in the interest of the individual or for acceptable research purposes, access to them should be subject to unusually stringent controls. In the *Guidelines* (Russell Sage Foundation, 1970, pp. 20–22), school records are classified into three categories with regard to their retention. A major determining factor in this classification is the degree of objectivity and verifiability of the data; another is relevance to the educational objectives of the school. It would be wise for any type of institution to formulate similar explicit policies regarding the destruction, retention, and accessibility of personal records.

The problems of maintenance, security, and accessibility of test results—and of all other personal data—have been magnified by the development of computerized data banks. In his preface to the *Guidelines* (Russell Sage Foundation, 1970, pp. 5–6), Ruebhausen wrote:

Modern science has introduced a new dimension into the issues of privacy. There was a time when among the strongest allies of privacy were the inefficiency of man, the fallibility of his memory, and the healing compassion that accompanied both the passing of time and the warmth of human recollection. These allies are now being put to rout. Modern science has given us the capacity to record faithfully, to maintain permanently, to retrieve promptly, and to communicate both widely and instantly.

The unprecedented advances in storing, processing, and retrieving data made possible by computers can be of inestimable service both in research and in the more immediate handling of social problems. The potential dangers of invasion of privacy and violation of confidentiality need to be faced squarely, constructively, and imaginatively. Rather than fearing the centralization and efficiency of complex computer systems, we should explore the possibility that these very characteristics may permit more effective procedures for protecting the security of individual records.

Several ingenious solutions have been devised which illustrate what can be accomplished in this regard with the facilities of a large-scale computerized data bank (see, e.g., Boruch & Cecil, 1979; Laska & Bank, 1975, Part 4; Renninger, 1974). Among the procedures utilized are numerical coding of individuals and a dual– or even triple–file system. Through such techniques, it is possible to ensure that no one person will have access to the information needed to link individuals with all the data about them, even when names and addresses are required for follow-up contact (Astin & Boruch, 1970). Considerable attention has been given to the design of computer systems that provide mechanisms for isolating data with regard to specific user needs. Legislative action at federal and state levels represents another approach to the protection of privacy of personal records.

COMMUNICATING TEST RESULTS

Psychologists have given much thought to the communication of test results in a form that will be meaningful and useful. It is clear that the information should not be transmitted routinely, but should be accompanied by interpretive explanations by a professionally trained person. When communicating scores to parents, for example, a recommended procedure is to arrange a group meeting at which a counselor or school psychologist explains the purpose and nature of the tests, the sort of conclusions that may reasonably be drawn from the results, and the limitations of the data. Written reports about their own children may then be distributed to the parents, and arrangements made for personal interviews with any parents wishing to discuss the reports further. Regardless of how they are transmitted, however, an important condition is that test results should be presented in terms of descriptive performance levels rather than isolated numerical scores. This is especially true of intelligence tests, which are more likely to be misinterpreted than are achievement tests.

In communicating results to teachers, school administrators, employers, and other appropriate persons, similar safeguards should be provided. Broad levels of performance and qualitative descriptions in simple terms are to be preferred over specific numerical scores, except when communicating with adequately trained professionals. Even well-educated laypersons have been known to confuse percentiles with percentage scores, percentiles with IQs, norms with standards, and interest ratings with aptitude scores. But a more serious misinterpretation pertains to the conclusions drawn from test scores, even when their technical meaning is correctly understood. A familiar example is the popular assumption that an IQ indicates a fixed characteristic of the individual which predetermines his or her lifetime level of intellectual achievement.

In all test communication, it is desirable to take into account the characteristics of the person who is to receive the information. This applies not only to that person's general education and his or her knowledge about psychology and testing, but also to his or her anticipated emotional response to the information. In the case of a parent or teacher, for example, personal emotional involvement with the child may interfere with a calm and rational acceptance of factual information.

Last but by no means least is the problem of communicating test results to the examinees themselves, whether children or adults. The same general safeguards against misinterpretation apply here as in communicating with a third party. The emotional reaction to the information is especially important, of course, when persons are learning about their own assets and shortcomings. When an individual is given his or her own test results, not only should the data be interpreted by a properly qualified person, but facilities should also be available for counseling anyone who may become emotionally disturbed by such information. For example, a college student might become seriously discouraged when she learns of her poor performance on a scholastic aptitude test. A gifted schoolchild might develop habits of laziness and shiftlessness, or he might become uncooperative and unmanageable, if he discovers that he is much brighter than any of his associates. A severe personality disorder may be precipitated when a maladjusted individual is given her score on a personality test. Such detrimental effects may, of course, occur regardless of the correctness or incorrectness of the score itself. Even when a test has been accurately administered and scored and properly interpreted, a knowledge of such a score without the opportunity to discuss it further may be harmful to the individual.

Counseling psychologists have been especially concerned with the development of effective ways of transmitting test information to their clients (see, e.g., Goldman, 1971, Ch. 14–16). Although the details of this process are beyond the scope of our present discussion, two major guidelines are of particular interest. First, test reporting is to be viewed as an integral part of the counseling process and incorporated into the total counselor–client relationship. Second, insofar as possible, test results should be reported as answers to specific questions raised by the counselee. An important consideration in counseling relates to the counselee's acceptance of the information presented to her or him. The counseling situation is such that if the individual rejects any information, for whatever reasons, then that information is likely to be totally wasted.

TESTING AND THE CIVIL RIGHTS OF MINORITIES

THE SETTING. The decades since 1950 have witnessed an increasing public concern with the rights of minorities,[1] a concern that is reflected in the enactment of civil rights legislation at both federal and state levels. In connection with mechanisms for improving educational and vocational opportunities of such groups, psychological testing has been a major focus of attention. The psychological literature of the 1960s and 1970s contains many discussions of the topic, whose impact ranges from clarification to obfuscation. Among the more clarifying contributions are several position papers by professional associations (see, e.g., APA, 1969; Cleary, Humphreys, Kendrick, & Wesman, 1975; Deutsch, Fishman, Kogan, North, & Whiteman, 1964; *The Responsible Use of Tests*, 1972). A brief but cogent paper by Flaugher (1974) also helps to clear away some prevalent sources of confusion. A summary of objections to standardized testing expressed by special-interest groups is provided by Samuda (1975, Ch. 1).

[1] Although women represent a statistical majority in the national population, legally, occupationally, and in other ways they have shared many of the problems of minorities. Hence when the term "minority" is used in this section, it will be understood to include women.

Much of the concern centers on the lowering of test scores by cultural conditions that may have affected the development of aptitudes, interests, motivation, attitudes, and other psychological characteristics of minority group members. Some of the proposed solutions for the problem reflect misunderstandings about the nature and function of psychological tests. Differences in the experiential backgrounds of groups or individuals are inevitably manifested in test performance. Every psychological test measures a behavior sample. Insofar as culture affects behavior, its influence will and should be detected by tests. If we rule out all cultural differentials from a test, we may thereby lower its validity as a measure of the behavior domain it was designed to assess. In that case, the test would fail to provide the kind of information needed to correct the very conditions that impaired performance.

Because the testing of minorities represents a special case within the broader problem of cross-cultural testing, the underlying theoretical rationale and testing procedures are discussed more fully in Chapter 12. A technical analysis of the concept of "test bias" is given in Chapter 7, in connection with test validity. In the present chapter, our interest is primarily in the basic issues and social implications of minority group testing.

TEST-RELATED FACTORS. In testing culturally diverse persons, it is important to differentiate between cultural factors that affect both test and criterion behavior and those whose influence is restricted to the test. It is the latter, test-related factors that reduce validity. Examples of such factors include previous experience in taking tests, motivation to perform well on tests, rapport with the examiner, and any other variables affecting performance on the particular test but irrelevant to the broad behavior domain under consideration. Special efforts should be made to reduce the operation of these test-related factors when testing persons with dissimilar cultural backgrounds. A desirable procedure is to provide adequate test-taking orientation and preliminary practice, as illustrated by the booklets and tape recordings cited in Chapter 2. Retesting with a parallel form is also recommended with low-scoring examinees who have had little or no prior test-taking experience.

Specific test content may also influence test scores in ways that are unrelated to the ability the test is designed to assess. In a test of arithmetic reasoning, for example, the use of names or pictures of objects unfamiliar in a particular cultural milieu would represent a test-restricted handicap. Ability to carry out quantitative thinking does not depend upon familiarity with such objects. On the other hand, if the development of arithmetic ability itself is more strongly fostered in one culture than in another, scores on an arithmetic test should not eliminate or conceal such a difference.

Another, more subtle way in which specific test content may spuriously affect performance is through the examinee's emotional and attitudinal responses. Stories or pictures portraying typical suburban middle-class family scenes, for example, may alienate a child reared in a low-income inner-city home. Exclusive representation of the physical features of a single racial type in test illustrations may have a similar effect on members of an ethnic minority. In the same vein, women's organizations have objected to the perpetuation of sex stereotypes in test content, as in the portrayal of male doctors or executives and female nurses or secretaries. Certain words, too, may have acquired connotations that are offensive to minority groups. As one test publisher aptly expressed it, "Until fairly recently, most standardized tests were constructed by white middle-class people, who sometimes clumsily violate the feelings of the test-taker without even knowing it. In a way, one could say that we have been not so much culture biased as we have been 'culture blind'" (Fitzgibbon, 1972, pp. 2–3).

The major test publishers now make special efforts to weed out inappropriate test content. Their own test construction staffs have become sensitized to potentially offensive, culturally restricted, or stereotyped material. Members of different ethnic groups participate either as regular staff members or as consultants. And the reviewing of test content with reference to possible minority implications is a regular step in the process of test construction.

INTERPRETATION AND USE OF TEST SCORES. By far the most important considerations in the testing of culturally diverse groups—as in all testing—pertain to the interpretation of test scores. The most frequent misgivings regarding the use of tests with minority group members stem from misinterpretations of scores. If a minority examinee obtains a low score on an aptitude test or a deviant score on a personality test, it is essential to investigate why he or she did so. For example, an inferior score on an arithmetic test could result from low test-taking motivation, poor reading ability, or inadequate knowledge of arithmetic, among other reasons. Some thought should also be given to the type of norms to be employed in evaluating individual scores. Depending on the purpose of the testing, the appropriate norms may be general norms, subgroup norms based on persons with comparable experiential backgrounds, or the individual's own previous score.

In predicting outcome, such as performance on a job or in an educational program, we must also consider the effects of differential treatments. It is one of the contributions of decision theory to psychometrics that it provides ways of incorporating differential treatment into the prediction of outcomes from test scores (Ch. 7). For example, given certain test scores obtained by an individual with a specified cultural background, what will be his or her predicted college grades if we introduce remedial teaching programs, counseling designed to modify educational attitudes and motivation, or other appropriate treatments?

Tests are designed to show what an individual can do at a given point in time. They cannot tell us *why* he performs as he does. To answer that question, we need to investigate his background, motivations, and other pertinent circumstances. Nor can tests tell how able a culturally or educationally disadvantaged child might have been if she had been reared in a more favorable environment. Moreover, tests cannot compensate for cultural deprivation by eliminating its effect from their scores. On the contrary, tests should reveal such effects, so that appropriate remedial steps can be taken. To conceal the effects of cultural disadvantages by rejecting tests or by trying to devise tests that are insensitive to such effects can only retard progress toward a genuine solution of social problems. Such reactions toward tests are equivalent to breaking a thermometer because it registers a body temperature of 101°. Test scores should be used constructively: by the individual in enhancing self-understanding and personal development and in educational and vocational planning; by teachers in improving instruction and in adjusting instructional content to individual needs; and by employers in achieving a better match between persons and jobs, recognizing that persons can be trained and jobs can be redesigned.

The tendency to categorize and label, as a shortcut substitute for understanding, is all too prevalent. The diagnostic categories of classical psychiatry, whereby patients are assigned such labels as "paranoid schizophrenic" or "manic–depressive," are well known. Aware of the many deficiencies of this system of classification, clinical psychologists have turned increasingly to personality descriptions. Unlike the diagnostic labels, these descriptions focus on the origins and individual significance of deviant behavior and provide a more effective basis for therapy. But the traditional labels are not easily dislodged.

Another example of the categorizing tendency is provided by popular misinterpretations of the IQ. A common criticism of intelligence tests is that they encourage a rigid, inflexible, and permanent classification of individuals. A low IQ, it is argued, places an indelible stamp of inferiority on a child. In the case of culturally disadvantaged children, such an IQ would thus serve to perpetuate their handicap. It is largely because implications of permanent status have become attached to the IQ that in 1964 the use of group intelligence tests was discontinued in the New York City public schools (H. B. Gilbert, 1966; Loretan, 1966). Soon, other communities followed suit. That it proved necessary to discard the tests in order to eliminate the misconceptions about the fixity of the IQ is a revealing commentary on the tenacity of the misconceptions. It should also be noted that the ban did not usually extend to individual intelligence tests like the Stanford-Binet, which are administered and interpreted by trained examiners and school psychologists. It was the mass testing and routine use of IQs by relatively unsophisticated persons that was considered hazardous.

According to a popular misconception, the IQ is an index of innate intellectual potential and represents a fixed property of the organism. As will be seen in Chapter 12, this view is neither theoretically defensible nor supported by empirical data. When properly interpreted, intelligence test scores should not foster a rigid categorizing of persons. On the contrary, intelligence tests—and any other test—may be regarded as a map on which the individual's present position can be located. When combined with information about experiential background, test scores should facilitate effective planning for the optimal development of the individual.

OBJECTIVITY OF TESTS. When social stereotypes and prejudice may distort interpersonal evaluations, tests provide a safeguard against favoritism and arbitrary or capricious decisions. As the civil rights movement gained momentum, several observers called attention to the positive function that standardized testing can serve. Commenting on the use of tests in schools, Gardner (1961, pp. 48–49) wrote: "The tests couldn't see whether the youngster was in rags or in tweeds, and they couldn't hear the accents of the slum. The tests revealed intellectual gifts at every level of the population."

In the same vein, the *Guidelines for Testing Minority Group Children* (Deutsch et al., 1964, p. 139) contains the following observation:

Many bright, non-conforming pupils, with backgrounds different from those of their teachers, make favorable showings on achievement tests, in contrast to their low classroom marks. These are very often children whose cultural handicaps are most evident in their overt social and interpersonal behavior. Without the intervention of standardized tests, many such children would be stigmatized by the adverse subjective ratings of teachers who tend to reward conformist behavior of middle-class character.

With regard to personnel selection, the contribution of tests was aptly characterized in the following words by John W. Macy, Jr., then Chairman of the United States Civil Service Commission (*Testing and Public Policy*, 1965, p. 883):

The necessity to measure characteristics of people that are related to job performance is at the very root of the merit system, which is the basis for entry into the career services of the Federal Government. Thus, over the years, the public service has had a vital interest in the development and application of psychological testing methods. I have no doubt that the widespread public confidence in the objectivity of our hiring procedures has in large part been nurtured by the public's perception of the fairness, the practicality, and the integrity of the appraisal methods they must submit to.

The *Guidelines on Employee Selection Procedures*, first prepared by the Equal Employment Opportunity Commission (1970) as an aid in the implementation of the Civil Rights Act, began with the following statement of purpose:

The guidelines in this part are based on the belief that properly validated and standardized employee selection procedures can significantly contribute to the implementation of nondiscriminatory personnel policies, as required by Title VII. It is also recognized that professionally developed tests, when used in conjunction with other tools of personnel assessment and complemented by sound programs of job design, may significantly aid in the development and maintenance of an efficient work force and, indeed, aid in the utilization and conservation of human resources generally.

In summary, tests *can* be misused in testing culturally disadvantaged persons—as in testing anyone else. When properly used, however, they serve an important function in preventing irrelevant and unfair discrimination. When evaluating the social consequences of testing, we need to assess carefully the social consequences of *not* testing and thus having to rely upon alternative procedures for decision making (Ebel, 1964; Messick, 1975).

LEGAL REGULATIONS. Since 1960, there have been rapid developments pertaining to the employment testing of minorities. These developments include legislative actions at state and federal levels, executive orders, and court decisions. Increasingly, the courts have played an important part in interpreting and applying civil rights laws. The implications of several famous court cases have been widely discussed in the personnel and testing literature by persons trained in psychology, law, or both (see Albright et al., 1976; Fincher, 1973; Lerner, 1977, 1978a, 1978b, 1979, 1980a; Novick & Ellis, 1977; *Summaries*, 1978; U.S. Office of Personnel Management, 1979). The most pertinent federal legislation is provided by the Equal Employment Opportunity Act (Title VII of the Civil Rights Act of 1964 and its subsequent amendments). Responsibility for implementation and enforcement is vested in the Equal Employment Opportunity Commission (EEOC), which developed a set of guidelines for this purpose (EEOC, 1970). In 1978, in the interests of simplified procedure and improved coordination, the *Uniform Guidelines on Employee Selection Procedure* were jointly adopted by the EEOC, the Civil Service Commission (now the U.S. Office of Personnel Management), and the Departments of Justice and Labor. A copy of these *Guidelines* is reproduced in Appendix B.

Some major provisions of the *Uniform Guidelines* should be noted. The Equal Employment Opportunity Act prohibits discrimination on the grounds of race, color, religion, sex, or national origin in selection procedures leading to employment decisions. These regulations apply to employers (both private and governmental), labor organizations, employment agencies, and licensing and certification boards. When the use of a test or other selection procedure results in a significantly higher rejection rate for minority candidates than for nonminority candidates ("adverse impact"),[2] its utility must be justified by evidence of validity for the job in question (Sec. 3, 4). In defining acceptable procedures for establishing validity, the

---

[2] The inconsistencies in ways of assessing adverse impact in different court cases have been thoughtfully analyzed by Lerner (1980a).

Guidelines make explicit reference (Sec. 5C) to the *Standards for Educational and Psychological Tests* (1974) published by the American Psychological Association. A major portion of the *Guidelines* (Sec. 14) covers minimum requirements for acceptable validation. The reader may find it profitable to review these requirements after reading the more detailed technical discussion of validity in Chapters 6 and 7 of this book.

The same regulations specified for tests are also applied to all other formal and informal selection procedures, including educational and work-history requirements, application forms, and interviews (Sec. 2B, 16Q). A survey of judicial decisions suggests that thus far the courts have tended to apply somewhat less stringent requirements in establishing the validity of interviews than has been done with tests. When the content of interview questions appears to be job-related and the interviews are conducted in a uniform and systematic manner, they have been accepted as valid (Arvey, 1979). From another angle, Lerner (1980a) has argued convincingly that the job relevance or validity of tests should be evaluated no more stringently than that of interviewing procedures, particularly in situations where full-scale local validation is not technically feasible. In neither case can one *assume* either validity or lack of validity in the absence of evidence.

In the discussion of affirmative action, the *Guidelines* (Sec. 13, 17) point out that even when selection procedures have been satisfactorily validated, if disproportionate rejection rates result for minorities, steps should be taken to reduce this discrepancy as much as possible. Affirmative action implies that an organization does more than merely avoiding discriminatory practices. Psychologically, affirmative action programs may be regarded as efforts to compensate for the residual effects of past social inequities. Such effects may include deficiences in aptitudes, job skills, attitudes, motivation, and other job-related behavior. They may also be reflected in a person's reluctance to apply for a job not traditionally open to minority candidates, or in his or her inexperience in job-seeking procedures. Examples of affirmative actions in meeting these problems include recruiting through the media most likely to reach minorities; explicitly encouraging minority candidates to apply and following other recruiting practices designed to counteract past stereotypes; and, when practicable, providing special training programs for the acquisition of prerequisite skills and knowledge. It should be noted, however, that the goal of affirmative action does not imply the neglect of relevant qualifications in job selection. In reference to affirmative action plans, the *Guidelines* (Sec. 17–4) state:

Selection under such plans should be based upon the ability of the applicant(s) to do the work. Such plans should not require the selection of the unqualified, or the unneeded, nor should they require the selection of persons on the basis of race, color, sex, religion, or national origin.

PART TWO

Technical and Methodological Principles

Chapter 4

Norms and the
Interpretation of Test Scores

IN THE absence of additional interpretive data, a raw score on any psychological test is meaningless. To say that an individual has correctly solved 15 problems on an arithmetic reasoning test, or identified 34 words in a vocabulary test, or successfully assembled a mechanical object in 57 seconds conveys little or no information about his or her standing in any of these functions. Nor do the familiar percentage scores provide a satisfactory solution to the problem of interpreting test scores. A score of 65% correct on one vocabulary test, for example, might be equivalent to 30% correct on another, and to 80% correct on a third. The difficulty level of the items making up each test will, of course, determine the meaning of the score. Like all raw scores, percentage scores can be interpreted only in terms of a clearly defined and uniform frame of reference.

Scores on psychological tests are most commonly interpreted by reference to *norms* which represent the test performance of the standardization sample. The norms are thus empirically established by determining what the persons in a representative group actually do on the test. Any individual's raw score is then referred to the distribution of scores obtained by the standardization sample, to discover where he or she falls in that distribution. Does the score coincide with the average performance of the standardization group? Is it slightly below average? Or does it fall near the upper end of the distribution?

In order to determine more precisely the individual's exact position with reference to the standardization sample, the raw score is converted into some relative measure. These derived scores are designed to serve a dual purpose. First, they indicate the individual's relative standing in the normative sample and thus permit an evaluation of her or his performance in reference to other persons. Second, they provide comparable measures that permit a direct comparison of the individual's performance on different tests. For example, if a girl has a raw score of 40 on a vocabulary test and a raw score of 22 on an arithmetic reasoning test, we obviously know nothing about her relative performance on the two tests. Is she better in vocabulary or in arithmetic, or equally good in both? Since raw scores on different tests are usually expressed in different units, a direct comparison of such scores is impossible. The difficulty level of the particular test would also affect such a comparison between raw scores. Derived scores, on the other hand, can be expressed in the same units and referred to the same or to closely similar normative samples for different tests. The individual's relative performance in many different functions can thus be compared.

There are various ways in which raw scores may be converted to fulfill the two objectives stated above. Fundamentally, however, derived scores are expressed in one of two major ways: (1) developmental level attained; (2) relative position within a specified group. These types of scores, together with some of their common variants, will be considered in separate sections of this chapter. But first it will be necessary to examine a few elementary statistical concepts that underlie the development and utilization of norms. The following section is included simply to clarify the meaning of certain common statistical measures. Simplified computational examples are given only for this purpose and not to provide training in statistical methods. For computational details and specific procedures to be followed in the practical application of these techniques, the reader is referred to any recent textbook on psychological or educational statistics.

STATISTICAL CONCEPTS

A major object of statistical method is to organize and summarize quantitative data in order to facilitate their understanding. A list of 1,000 test scores can be an overwhelming sight. In that form, it conveys little meaning. A first step in bringing order into such a chaos of raw data is to tabulate the scores into a *frequency distribution,* as illustrated in Table 1. Such a distribution is prepared by grouping the scores into convenient class intervals and tallying each score in the appropriate interval. When all scores have been entered, the tallies are counted to find the frequency, or number of cases, in each class interval. The sums of these frequencies will equal N, the total number of cases in the group. Table 1 shows the scores of 1,000 college students in a code-learning test in which one set of artificial words, or nonsense syllables, was to be substituted for another. The raw scores, giving number of correct syllables substituted during a two-minute trial, ranged from 8 to 52. They have been grouped into class intervals of 4 points, from 52–55 at the top of the distribution down to 8–11. The frequency column reveals that two persons scored between 8 and 11, three between 12 and 15, eight between 16 and 19, and so on.

The information provided by a frequency distribution can also be presented graphically in the form of a distribution curve. Figure 1 shows the data of Table 1 in graphic form. On the baseline, or horizontal axis, are the scores grouped into class intervals; on the vertical axis are the frequencies, or number of cases falling within each class interval. The graph has been

TABLE 1
Frequency Distribution of Scores of 1,000 College Students
on a Code-Learning Test

(Data from Anastasi, 1934, p. 34)

Class Interval	Frequency
52–55	1
48–51	1
44–47	20
40–43	73
36–39	156
32–35	328
28–31	244
24–27	136
20–23	28
16–19	8
12–15	3
8–11	2
	$N = 1,000$

plotted in two ways, both forms being in common use. In the *histogram*, the height of the column erected over each class interval corresponds to the number of persons scoring in that interval. We can think of each individual standing on another's shoulders to form the column. In the *frequency polygon*, the number of persons in each interval is indicated by a point placed in the center of the class interval and across from the appropriate frequency. The successive points are then joined by straight lines.

Except for minor irregularities, the distribution portrayed in Figure 1 resembles the bell-shaped *normal curve*. A mathematically determined, perfect normal curve is reproduced in Figure 3. This type of curve has important mathematical properties and provides the basis for many kinds of statistical analyses. For the present purpose, however, only a few features will be noted. Essentially, the curve indicates that the largest number of cases cluster in the center of the range and that the number drops off gradually in both directions as the extremes are approached. The curve is bilaterally symmetrical, with a single peak in the center. Most distributions of human traits, from height and weight to aptitudes and personality characteristics, approximate the normal curve. In general, the larger the group, the more closely will the distribution resemble the theoretical normal curve.

A group of scores can also be described in terms of some measure of *central tendency*. Such a measure provides a single, most typical or representative score to characterize the performance of the entire group. The most familiar of these measures is the average, more technically known

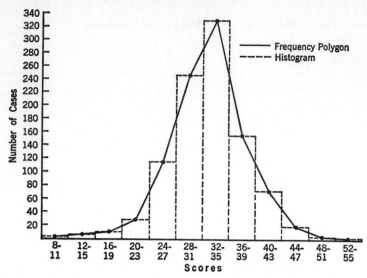

Fig. 1. Distribution Curves: Frequency Polygon and Histogram.
(Data from Table 1.)

as the *mean* (M). As is well known, this is found by adding all scores and dividing the sum by the number of cases(N). Another measure of central tendency is the *mode,* or most frequent score. In a frequency distribution, the mode is the midpoint of the class interval with the highest frequency. Thus, in Table 1, the mode falls midway between 32 and 35, being 33.5. It will be noted that this score corresponds to the highest point on the distribution curve in Figure 1. A third measure of central tendency is the *median,* or middlemost score when all scores have been arranged in order of size. The median is the point that bisects the distribution, half the cases falling above it and half below.

Further description of a set of test scores is given by measures of *variability,* or the extent of individual differences around the central tendency. The most obvious and familiar way of reporting variability is in terms of the *range* between the highest and lowest score. The range, however, is extremely crude and unstable, for it is determined by only two scores. A single unusually high or low score would thus markedly affect its size. A more precise method of measuring variability is based on the difference between each individual's score and the mean of the group.

At this point, it will be helpful to look at the example in Table 2, in which the various measures under consideration have been computed on 10 cases. Such a small group was chosen in order to simplify the demonstration, although in actual practice we would rarely perform these computations on so few cases. Table 2 serves also to introduce certain standard statistical symbols that should be noted for future reference. Original raw scores are

TABLE 2
Illustration of Central Tendency and Variability

	Score (X)	Deviation $(x = X - M)$	Dev. Squared (x^2)
	48	+8	64
50% of cases	47	+7	49
	43	+3 ⎤ +20	9
	41	+1	1
	41	+1 ⎦	1
Median = 40.5 →	40	0	0
	38	−2	4
50% of cases	36	−4 ⎤ −20	16
	34	−6	36
	32	−8 ⎦	64
	$\Sigma X = 400$		$\Sigma x^2 = 244$

$$M = \frac{\Sigma X}{N} = \frac{400}{10} = 40$$

$$\text{Variance} = \sigma^2 = \frac{\Sigma x^2}{N} = \frac{244}{10} = 24.40$$

$$SD \text{ or } \sigma = \sqrt{\frac{\Sigma x^2}{N}} = \sqrt{24.40} = 4.9$$

Note. The symbols Σ and σ given in this table are the capital and lower case of the same Greek letter, pronounced "sigma." In many statistical writings, SD (or simply S) refers to the standard deviation of the sample on which the data were actually obtained, while σ refers to the estimated value of the standard deviation in the population from which the sample was drawn. The latter value is useful in a number of further computations.

conventionally designated by a capital X, and a small x is used to refer to deviations of each score from the group mean. The symbol Σ means "sum of." It will be seen that the first column in Table 2 gives the data for the computation of mean and median. The mean is 40; the median is 40.5, falling midway between 40 and 41—five cases (50%) are above the median and five below. There is little point in finding a mode in such a small group, since the cases do not show clear-cut clustering on any one score. Technically, however, 41 would represent the mode, because two persons obtained this score, while all other scores occur only once.

The second column shows how far each score deviates above or below the mean of 40. The sum of these deviations will always equal zero, because the positive and negative deviations around the mean necessarily balance, or cancel each other out $(+20 - 20 = 0)$. If we ignored signs, of course, we could average the absolute deviations, thus obtaining a measure of the average amount by which each person deviates from the group mean. Although of some descriptive value, such an "average deviation" is not suitable for use in further mathematical analyses because of the arbitrary discarding of signs and is therefore not employed in practice.

A much more serviceable measure of variability is the *standard deviation* (symbolized by either *SD* or σ), in which the negative signs are legitimately eliminated by squaring each deviation. This procedure has been followed in the last column of Table 2. The sum of this column divided by the number of cases $\left(\dfrac{\Sigma x^2}{N}\right)$ is known as the *variance,* or *mean square deviation,* and is symbolized by σ^2. The variance has proved extremely useful in sorting out the contributions of different factors to individual differences in test performance. For the present purposes, however, our chief concern is with the *SD*, which is the square root of the variance, as shown in Table 2. This measure is commonly employed in comparing the variability of different groups. In Figure 2, for example, are two distributions having the same mean but differing in variability. The distribution with wider individual differences yields a larger *SD* than the one with narrower individual differences.

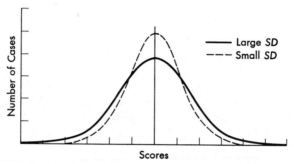

FIG. 2. Frequency Distributions with the Same Mean but Different Variability.

The *SD* also provides the basis for expressing an individual's scores on different tests in terms of norms, as will be shown in the section on standard scores. The interpretation of the *SD* is especially clear-cut when applied to a normal or approximately normal distribution curve. In such a distribution, there is an exact relationship between the *SD* and the proportion of cases, as shown in Figure 3. On the baseline of this normal curve have been marked distances representing one, two, and three standard deviations above and below the mean. For instance, in the example given in Table 2, the mean would correspond to a score of 40, $+1\sigma$ to 44.9 ($40 + 4.9$), $+2\sigma$ to 49.8 ($40 + 2 \times 4.9$), and so on. The percentage of cases that fall between the mean and $+1\sigma$ in a normal curve is 34.13. Because the curve is symmetrical,

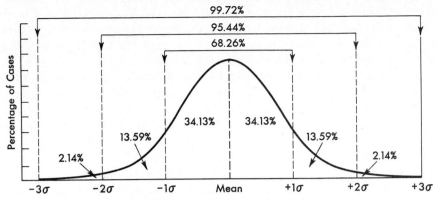

FIG. 3. Percentage Distribution of Cases in a Normal Curve.

34.13% of the cases are likewise found between the mean and -1σ, so that between $+1\sigma$ and -1σ on both sides of the mean there are 68.26% of the cases. Nearly all the cases (99.72%) fall within $\pm 3\sigma$ from the mean. These relationships are particularly relevant in the interpretation of standard scores and percentiles, to be discussed in later sections.

DEVELOPMENTAL NORMS

One way in which meaning can be attached to test scores is to indicate how far along the normal developmental path the individual has progressed. Thus an 8-year-old who performs as well as the average 10-year-old on an intelligence test may be described as having a mental age of 10; a mentally retarded adult who performs at the same level would likewise be assigned an MA of 10. In a different context, a fourth-grade child may be characterized as reaching the sixth-grade norm in a reading test and the third-grade norm in an arithmetic test. Other developmental systems utilize more highly qualitative descriptions of behavior in specific functions, ranging from sensorimotor activities to concept formation. However expressed, scores based on developmental norms tend to be psychometrically crude and do not lend themselves well to precise statistical treatment. Nevertheless, they have considerable appeal for descriptive purposes, especially in the intensive clinical study of individuals and for certain research purposes.

MENTAL AGE. In Chapter 1, it was noted that the term "mental age" was widely popularized through the various translations and adaptations of the Binet-Simon scales, although Binet himself had employed the more neutral term "mental level." In age scales such as the Binet and its revisions, items are grouped into year levels. For example, those items passed by the majority of 7-year-olds in the standardization sample are placed in the 7-year level, those passed by the majority of 8-year-olds are assigned to the 8-year level, and so forth. A child's score on the test will then correspond to the highest year level that he or she can successfully complete. In actual practice, the individual's performance shows a certain amount of *scatter*. In other words, the examinee fails some tests below his mental age level and passes some above it. For this reason, it is customary to compute the *basal age*, i.e., the highest age at and below which all tests are passed. Partial credits, in months, are then added to this basal age for all tests passed at higher year levels. The child's mental age on the test is the sum of the basal age and the additional months of credit earned at higher age levels.

Mental age norms have also been employed with tests that are not divided into year levels. In such a case, the child's raw score is first determined. Such a score may be the total number of correct items on the whole test; or it may be based on time, on number of errors, or on some combination of such measures. The mean raw scores obtained by the children in each year group within the standardization sample constitute the age norms for such a test. The mean raw score of the 8-year-old children, for example, would represent the 8-year norm. If an individual's raw score is equal to the mean 8-year-old raw score, then her or his mental age on the test is 8 years. All raw scores on such a test can be transformed in a similar manner by reference to the age norms.

It should be noted that the mental age unit does not remain constant with age but tends to shrink with advancing years. For example, a child who is one year retarded at age 4 will be approximately three years retarded at age 12. One year of mental growth from ages 3 to 4 is equivalent to three years of growth from ages 9 to 12. Since intellectual development progresses more rapidly at the earlier ages and gradually decreases as the individual approaches his or her mature limit, the mental age unit shrinks correspondingly with age. This relationship may be more readily visualized if we think of the individual's height as being expressed in terms of "height age." The difference, in inches, between a height age of 3 and 4 years would be greater than that between a height age of 10 and 11.Owing to the progressive shrinkage of the MA unit, one year of acceleration or retardation at, let us say, age 5 represents a larger deviation from the norm than does one year of acceleration or retardation at age 10.

GRADE EQUIVALENTS. Scores on educational achievement tests are often interpreted in terms of grade equivalents. This practice is understandable because the tests are employed within an academic setting. To describe a pupil's achievement as equivalent to seventh-grade performance in spelling, eighth-grade in reading, and fifth-grade in arithmetic has the same popular appeal as the use of mental age in the traditional intelligence tests.

Grade norms are found by computing the mean raw score obtained by children in each grade. Thus, if the average number of problems solved correctly on an arithmetic test by the fourth-graders in the standardization sample is 23, then a raw score of 23 corresponds to a grade equivalent of 4. Intermediate grade equivalents, representing fractions of a grade, are usually found by interpolation, although they can also be obtained directly by testing children at different times within the school year. Because the school year covers ten months, successive months can be expressed as decimals. For example, 4.0 refers to average performance at the beginning of the fourth grade (September testing), 4.5 refers to average performance at the middle of the grade (February testing), and so forth.

Despite their popularity, grade norms have several shortcomings. First, the content of instruction varies somewhat from grade to grade. Hence, grade norms are appropriate only for common subjects taught throughout the grade levels covered by the test. They are not generally applicable at the high school level, where many subjects may be studied for only one or two years. Even with subjects taught in each grade, however, the emphasis placed on different subjects may vary from grade to grade, and progress may therefore be more rapid in one subject than in another during a particular grade. In other words, grade units are obviously unequal and these inequalities occur irregularly in different subjects.

Grade norms are also subject to misinterpretation unless the test user keeps firmly in mind the manner in which they were derived. For example, if a fourth-grade child obtains a grade equivalent of 6.9 in arithmetic, it does *not* mean that she has mastered the arithmetic processes taught in the sixth grade. She undoubtedly obtained her score largely by superior performance in fourth-grade arithmetic. It certainly could not be assumed that she has the prerequisites for seventh-grade arithmetic. Finally, grade norms tend to be incorrectly regarded as performance standards. A sixth-grade teacher, for example, may assume that all pupils in her class should fall at or close to the sixth-grade norm in achievement tests. This misconception is certainly not surprising when grade norms are used. Yet individual differences within any one grade are such that the range of achievement test scores will inevitably extend over several grades.

ORDINAL SCALES. Another approach to developmental norms derives from research in child psychology. Empirical observation of behavior development in infants and young children led to the description of behavior typical of successive ages in such functions as locomotion, sensory discrimination, linguistic communication, and concept formation. An early example is provided by the work of Gesell and his associates at Yale (Ames, 1937; Gesell & Amatruda, 1947; Halverson, 1933; Knobloch & Pasamanick, 1974). The Gesell Developmental Schedules show the approximate developmental level in months that the child has attained in each of four major areas of behavior, namely, motor, adaptive, language, and personal–social. These levels are found by comparing the child's behavior with that typical of eight key ages, ranging from 4 weeks to 36 months.

Gesell and his co-workers emphasized the sequential patterning of early behavior development. They cited extensive evidence of uniformities of developmental sequences and an orderly progression of behavior changes. For example, the child's reactions toward a small object placed in front of her or him exhibit a characteristic chronological sequence in visual fixation and in hand and finger movements. Use of the entire hand in crude attempts at palmar prehension occurs at an earlier age than use of the thumb in opposition to the palm; this type of prehension is in turn followed by the use of the thumb and index finger in a more efficient pincerlike grasp of the object. Such sequential patterning was likewise observed in walking, stair climbing, and most of the sensorimotor development of the first few years. The scales developed within this framework are ordinal in the sense that developmental stages follow in a constant order, each stage presupposing mastery of prerequisite behavior characteristic of earlier stages.[1]

Since the 1960s, there has been a sharp upsurge of interest in the developmental theories of the Swiss child psychologist Jean Piaget (see Flavell, 1963; Ginsburg & Opper, 1969; Green, Ford, & Flamer, 1971). Piaget's research has focused on the development of cognitive processes from infancy to the midteens. He is concerned with specific concepts rather than broad abilities. An example of such a concept, or schema, is object permanence, whereby the child is aware of the identity and continuing existence of objects when they are seen from different angles or are out of sight. Another widely studied concept is conservation, or the recognition that an attribute remains constant over changes in perceptual appearance, as when the same quantity of liquid is poured into differently shaped containers, or when rods of the same length are placed in different spatial arrangements.

Piagetian tasks have been used widely in research by developmental psychologists and some have been organized into standardized scales, to be discussed in Chapters 10 and 14 (Goldschmid & Bentler, 1968b; Loretan, 1966; Pinard & Laurendeau, 1964; Užgiris & Hunt, 1975). In accordance with Piaget's approach, these instruments are ordinal scales, in which the attainment of one stage is contingent upon completion of the earlier stages in the development of the concept. The tasks are designed to reveal the dominant aspects of each developmental stage; only later are empirical data gathered regarding the ages at which each stage is typically reached. In this

[1] This usage of the term "ordinal scale" differs from that in statistics, in which an ordinal scale is simply one that permits a rank-ordering of individuals without knowledge about amount of difference between them; in the statistical sense, ordinal scales are contrasted to equal-unit interval scales. Ordinal scales of child development are actually designed on the model of a Guttman scale or simplex, in which successful performance at one level implies success at all lower levels (Guttman, 1944). An extension of Guttman's analysis to include nonlinear hierarchies is described by Bart and Airasian (1974), with special reference to Piagetian scales.

respect, the procedure differs from that followed in constructing age scales, in which items are selected in the first place on the basis of their differentiating between successive ages.

In summary, ordinal scales are designed to identify the stage reached by the child in the development of specific behavior functions. Although scores may be reported in terms of approximate age levels, such scores are secondary to a qualitative description of the child's characteristic behavior. The ordinality of such scales refers to the uniform progression of development through successive stages. Insofar as these scales typically provide information about what the child is actually able to do (e.g., climbs stairs without assistance; recognizes identity in quantity of liquid when poured into differently shaped containers), they share important features with the criterion-referenced tests to be discussed in a later section of this chapter.

WITHIN-GROUP NORMS

Nearly all standardized tests now provide some form of within-group norms. With such norms, the individual's performance is evaluated in terms of the performance of the most nearly comparable standardization group, as when comparing a child's raw score with that of children of the same chronological age or in the same school grade. Within-group scores have a uniform and clearly defined quantitative meaning and can be appropriately employed in most types of statistical analysis.

PERCENTILES. Percentile scores are expressed in terms of the percentage of persons in the standardization sample who fall below a given raw score. For example, if 28% of the persons obtain fewer than 15 problems correct on an arithmetic reasoning test, then a raw score of 15 corresponds to the 28th percentile (P_{28}). A percentile indicates the individual's relative position in the standardization sample. Percentiles can also be regarded as ranks in a group of 100, except that in ranking it is customary to start counting at the top, the best person in the group receiving a rank of one. With percentiles, on the other hand, we begin counting at the bottom, so that the lower the percentile, the poorer the individual's standing.

The 50th percentile (P_{50}) corresponds to the median, already discussed as a measure of central tendency. Percentiles above 50 represent above-average performance; those below 50 signify inferior performance. The 25th and 75th percentile are known as the first and third quartile points (Q_1 and Q_3), because they cut off the lowest and highest quarters of the distribution. Like the median, they provide convenient landmarks for describing a distribution of scores and comparing it with other distributions.

Percentiles should not be confused with the familiar percentage scores. The latter are raw scores, expressed in terms of the percentage of correct items; percentiles are derived scores, expressed in terms of percentage of persons. A raw score lower than any obtained in the standardization sample would have a percentile rank of zero (P_0); one higher than any score in the standardization sample would have a percentile rank of 100 (P_{100}). These percentiles, however, do not imply a zero raw score and a perfect raw score.

Percentile scores have several advantages. They are easy to compute and can be readily understood, even by technically untrained persons. Moreover, percentiles are universally applicable. They can be used equally well with adults and children and are suitable for any type of test, whether it measures aptitude or personality variables.

The chief drawback of percentile scores arises from the marked inequality of their units, especially at the extremes of the distribution. If the distribution of raw scores approximates the normal curve, as is true of most test scores, then raw score differences near the median or center of the distribution are exaggerated in the percentile transformation, whereas raw score differences near the ends of the distribution are greatly shrunk. This distortion of distances between scores can be seen in Figure 4. In a normal curve, it will be

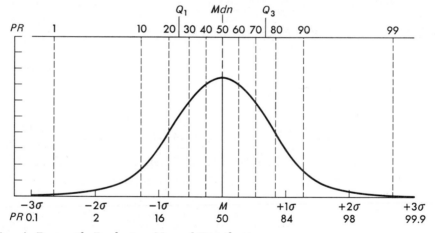

Fig. 4. Percentile Ranks in a Normal Distribution.

recalled, cases cluster closely at the center and scatter more widely as the extremes are approached. Consequently, any given percentage of cases near the center covers a shorter distance on the baseline than does the same percentage near the ends of the distribution. In Figure 4, this discrepancy in the gaps between percentile ranks (PR) can readily be seen if we compare the distance between a PR of 40 and a PR of 50 with that between a PR of 10 and a PR of 20. Even more striking is the discrepancy between these distances and that between a PR of 10 and PR of 1. (In a mathematically derived normal curve, zero percentile is not reached until infinity and hence cannot be shown on the graph.)

The same relationship can be seen from the opposite direction if we examine the percentile ranks corresponding to equal σ-distances from the mean of a normal curve. These percentile ranks are given under the graph in Figure 4. Thus, the percentile difference between the mean and $+1\sigma$ is 34 $(84 - 50)$. That between $+1\sigma$ and $+2\sigma$ is only 14 $(98 - 84)$.

It is apparent that percentiles show each individual's relative position in the normative sample but not the amount of difference between scores. If plotted on arithmetic probability paper, however, percentile scores can also provide a correct visual picture of the differences between scores. Arithmetic probability paper is a cross-section paper in which the vertical lines are spaced in the same way as the percentile points in a normal distribution (as in Figure 4), whereas the horizontal lines are uniformly spaced, or vice versa (as in Figure 5). Such *normal percentile charts* can be used to plot the scores of different persons on the same test or the scores of the same person on different tests. In either case, the actual interscore difference will be correctly represented. Many aptitude and achievement batteries now utilize this technique in their score profiles, which show the indi-

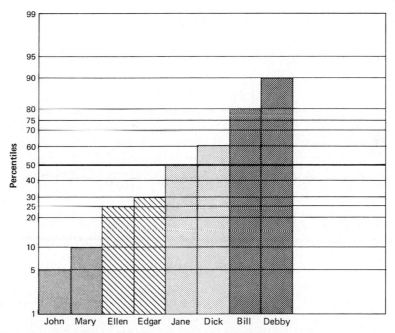

FIG. 5. A Normal Percentile Chart. Percentiles are spaced so as to correspond to equal distances in a normal distribution. Compare the score distance between John and Mary with that between Ellen and Edgar; within both pairs, the percentile difference is 5 points. Jane and Dick differ by 10 percentile points, as do Bill and Debby.

vidual's performance in each test. An example is the Individual Report Form of the Differential Aptitude Tests, reproduced in Figure 13 (Ch. 5).

STANDARD SCORES. Current tests are making increasing use of standard scores, which are the most satisfactory type of derived score from most points of view. Standard scores express the individual's distance from the mean in terms of the standard deviation of the distribution.

Standard scores may be obtained by either linear or nonlinear transformations of the original raw scores. When found by a *linear transformation,* they retain the exact numerical relations of the original raw scores, because they are computed by subtracting a constant from each raw score and then dividing the result by another constant. The relative magnitude of differences between standard scores derived by such a linear transformation corresponds exactly to that between the raw scores. All properties of the original distribution of raw scores are duplicated in the distribution of these standard scores. For this reason, any computations that can be carried out with the original raw scores can also be carried out with linear standard scores, without any distortion of results.

Linearly derived standard scores are often designated simply as "standard scores" or "z scores." To compute a z score, we find the difference between the individual's raw score and the mean of the normative group and then divide this difference by the SD of the normative group. Table 3 shows the computation of z scores for two individuals, one of whom falls 1 SD above the group mean, the other .40 SD below the mean. Any raw score that is exactly equal to the mean is equivalent to a z score of zero. It is apparent that such a procedure will yield derived scores that have a negative sign for all persons falling below the mean. Moreover, because the total range of most groups extends no farther than about 3 SDs above and below the mean, such standard scores will have to be reported to at least one decimal place in order to provide sufficient differentiation among individuals.

TABLE 3
Computation of Standard Scores

$$z = \frac{X - M}{SD} \qquad\qquad M = 60 \qquad\qquad SD = 5$$

JOHN'S SCORE	BILL'S SCORE
$X_1 = 65$	$X_2 = 58$
$z_1 = \dfrac{65 - 60}{5}$	$z_2 = \dfrac{58 - 60}{5}$
$= +1.00$	$= -0.40$

Both the above conditions, viz., the occurrence of negative values and of decimals, tend to produce awkward numbers that are confusing and difficult to use for both computational and reporting purposes. For this reason, some further linear transformation is usually applied, simply to put the scores into a more convenient form. For example, the scores on the Scholastic Aptitude Test (SAT) of the College Entrance Examination Board are standard scores adjusted to a mean of 500 and an *SD* of 100. Thus a standard score of -1 on this test would be expressed as 400 ($500 - 100 = 400$). Similarly, a standard score of $+1.5$ would correspond to 650 ($500 + 1.5 \times 100 = 650$). To convert an original standard score to the new scale, it is simply necessary to multiply the standard score by the desired *SD* (100) and add it to or subtract it from the desired mean (500). Any other convenient values can be arbitrarily chosen for the new mean and *SD*. Scores on the separate subtests of the Wechsler Intelligence Scales, for instance, are converted to a distribution with a mean of 10 and an *SD* of 3. All such measures are examples of linearly transformed standard scores.

It will be recalled that one of the reasons for transforming raw scores into any derived scale is to render scores on different tests comparable. The linearly derived standard scores discussed in the preceding section will be comparable only when found from distributions that have approximately the same form. Under such conditions, a score corresponding to 1 *SD* above the mean, for example, signifies that the individual occupies the same position in relation to both groups. His score exceeds approximately the same percentage of persons in both distributions, and this percentage can be determined if the form of the distribution is known. If, however, one distribution is markedly skewed and the other normal, a *z* score of $+1.00$ might exceed only 50% of the cases in one group but would exceed 84% in the other.

In order to achieve comparability of scores from dissimilarly shaped distributions, nonlinear transformations may be employed to fit the scores to any specified type of distribution curve. The mental age and percentile scores described in earlier sections represent nonlinear transformations, but they are subject to other limitations already discussed. Although under certain circumstances another type of distribution may be more appropriate, the normal curve is usually employed for this purpose. One of the chief reasons for this choice is that most raw score distributions approximate the normal curve more closely than they do any other type of curve. Moreover, physical measures such as height and weight, which use equal-unit scales derived through physical operations, generally yield normal distributions.[2]

---

[2] Partly for this reason and partly as a result of other theoretical considerations, it has frequently been argued that, by normalizing raw scores, an equal-unit scale could be developed for psychological measurement similar to the equal-unit scales of physical measurement. This, however, is a debatable point that involves certain questionable assumptions.

Another important advantage of the normal curve is that it has many useful mathematical properties, which facilitate further computations.

Normalized standard scores are standard scores expressed in terms of a distribution that has been transformed to fit a normal curve. Such scores can be computed by reference to tables giving the percentage of cases falling at different *SD* distances from the mean of a normal curve. First, the percentage of persons in the standardization sample falling at or above each raw score is found. This percentage is then located in the normal curve frequency table, and the corresponding normalized standard score is obtained. Normalized standard scores are expressed in the same form as linearly derived standard scores, viz., with a mean of zero and an *SD* of 1. Thus, a normalized score of zero indicates that the individual falls at the mean of a normal curve, excelling 50% of the group. A score of −1 means that he or she surpasses approximately 16% of the group; and a score of +1, that he or she surpasses 84%. These percentages correspond to a distance of 1 *SD* below and 1 *SD* above the mean of a normal curve, respectively, as can be seen by reference to the bottom line of Figure 4.

Like linearly derived standard scores, normalized standard scores can be put into any convenient form. If the normalized standard score is multiplied by 10 and added to or subtracted from 50, it is converted into a *T* score, a type of score first proposed by W. A. McCall (1922). On this scale, a score of 50 corresponds to the mean, a score of 60 to 1 *SD* above the mean, and so forth. Another well-known transformation is represented by the *stanine* scale, developed by the United States Air Force during World War II. This scale provides a single-digit system of scores with a mean of 5 and an *SD* of approximately 2.[3] The name "stanine" (a contraction of "*sta*ndard *nine*") is based on the fact that the scores run from 1 to 9. The restriction of scores to single-digit numbers has certain computational advantages, for each score requires only a single column on computer punched cards.

Raw scores can readily be converted to stanines by arranging the original scores in order of size and then assigning stanines in accordance with the normal curve percentages reproduced in Table 4. For example, if the group

TABLE 4
Normal Curve Percentages for Use in Stanine Conversion

Percentage	4	7	12	17	20	17	12	7	4
Stanine	1	2	3	4	5	6	7	8	9

[3] Kaiser (1958) proposed a modification of the stanine scale that involves slight changes in the percentages and yields an *SD* of exactly 2, thus being easier to handle quantitatively. Other variants are the *C* scale (Guilford & Fruchter, 1978, pp, 484–487), consisting of 11 units and also yielding an *SD* of 2, and the 10-unit *sten* scale, with 5 units above and 5 below the mean (Canfield, 1951).

consists of exactly 100 persons, the 4 lowest-scoring persons receive a stanine score of 1, the next 7 a score of 2, the next 12 a score of 3, and so on. When the group contains more or fewer than 100 cases, the number corresponding to each designated percentage is first computed, and these numbers of cases are then given the appropriate stanines. Thus, out of 200 cases, 8 would be assigned a stanine of 1 (4% of 200 = 8). With 150 cases, 6 would receive a stanine of 1 (4% of 150 = 6). For any group containing from 10 to 100 cases, Bartlett and Edgerton (1966) have prepared a table whereby ranks can be directly converted to stanines. Because of their practical as well as theoretical advantages, stanines are being used increasingly, especially with aptitude and achievement tests.

Although normalized standard scores are the most satisfactory type of score for the majority of purposes, there are nevertheless certain technical objections to normalizing all distributions routinely. Such a transformation should be carried out only when the sample is large and representative and when there is reason to believe that the deviation from normality results from defects in the test rather than from characteristics of the sample or from other factors affecting the behavior under consideration. It should also be noted that when the original distribution of raw scores approximates normality, the linearly derived standard scores and the normalized standard scores will be very similar. Although the methods of deriving these two types of scores are quite different, the resulting scores will be nearly identical under such conditions. Obviously, the process of normalizing a distribution that is already virtually normal will produce little or no change. Whenever feasible, it is generally more desirable to obtain a normal distribution of raw scores by proper adjustment of the difficulty level of test items rather than by subsequently normalizing a markedly nonnormal distribution. With an approximately normal distribution of raw scores, the linearly derived standard scores will serve the same purposes as normalized standard scores.

THE DEVIATION IQ. In an effort to convert MA scores into a uniform index of the individual's relative status, the ratio IQ (Intelligence Quotient) was introduced in early intelligence tests. Such an IQ was simply the ratio of mental age to chronological age, multiplied by 100 to eliminate decimals (IQ = 100 X MA/CA). Obviously if a child's MA equaled his CA, his IQ was exactly 100. An IQ of 100 thus represented normal or average performance IQs below 100 indicated retardation, those above 100, acceleration.

The apparent logical simplicity of the traditional ratio IQ, however, soon proved deceptive. A major technical difficulty is that, unless the *SD* of the IQ distribution remains approximately constant with age, IQs will not be comparable at different age levels. An IQ of 115 at age 10, for example, may indicate the same degree of superiority as an IQ of 125 at age 12, since both may fall at a distance of 1 *SD* from the means of their respective age distributions. In actual practice, it proved very difficult to construct tests that met the psychometric requirements for comparability of ratio IQs throughout their age range. Chiefly for this reason, the ratio IQ has been largely replaced by the so-called deviation IQ, which is actually another variant of the familiar standard score. The deviation IQ is a standard score with a mean of 100 and an SD that approximates the SD of the Stanford-Binet IQ distribution. Although the SD of the Stanford-Binet ratio IQ (last used in the 1937 edition) was not exactly constant at all ages, it fluctuated around a median value slightly greater than 16. Hence, if an SD close to 16 is chosen in reporting standard scores on a newly developed test, the resulting scores can be interpreted in the same way as Stanford-Binet ratio IQs. Since Stanford-Binet IQs have been in use for many years, testers and clinicians have become accustomed to interpreting and classifying test performance in terms of such IQ levels. They have learned what to expect from individuals with IQs of 40, 70, 90, 130, and so forth. There are therefore certain practical advantages in the use of a derived scale that corresponds to the familiar distribution of Stanford-Binet IQs. Such a correspondence of score units can be achieved by the selection of numerical values for the mean and SD that agree closely with those in the Stanford-Binet distribution.

It should be added that the use of the term "IQ" to designate such standard scores may be somewhat misleading. Such IQs are not derived by the same methods employed in finding traditional ratio IQs. They are not ratios of mental ages and chronological ages. The justification lies in the general familiarity of the term "IQ," and in the fact that such scores *can* be interpreted as IQs provided that their SD is approximately equal to that of previously known IQs. Among the first tests to express scores in terms of deviation IQs were the Wechsler Intelligence Scales. In these tests, the mean is 100 and the SD 15. Deviation IQs are also used in a number of current group tests of intelligence and in the latest revision of the Stanford-Binet itself.

With the increasing use of deviation IQs, it is important to remember that deviation IQs from different tests are comparable only when they employ the same or closely similar values for the SD. This value should always be reported in the manual and carefully noted by the test user. If a test maker chooses a different value for the SD in making up the deviation IQ scale, the meaning of any given IQ on that test will be quite different from its meaning on other tests. These discrepancies are illustrated in Table 5, which shows the percentage of cases in normal distributions with SDs from 12 to 18 who would obtain IQs at different levels. These SD values have actually been employed in the IQ scales of published tests. Table 5 shows, for example, that an IQ of 70 cuts off the lowest 3.1% when the SD is 16 (as in the Stanford-Binet); but it may cut off as few as 0.7% (SD = 12) or as many as 5.1% (SD = 18). An IQ of 70 has been used traditionally as a cutoff point for identifying mental retardation. The same discrepancies, of course, apply to IQs of 130 and above, which might be used in selecting children for special programs for the intellectually gifted. The IQ range

TABLE 5

Percentage of Cases at Each IQ Interval in Normal Distributions with Mean of 100 and Different Standard Deviations

(Courtesy of Test Department, Harcourt Brace Jovanovich, Inc.)

IQ Interval	Percentage Frequency			
	$SD = 12$	$SD = 14$	$SD = 16$	$SD = 18$
130 and above	0.7	1.6	3.1	5.1
120–129	4.3	6.3	7.5	8.5
110–119	15.2	16.0	15.8	15.4
100–109	29.8 ⎫ 59.6	26.1 ⎫ 52.2	23.6 ⎫ 47.2	21.0 ⎫ 42.0
90– 99	29.8 ⎭	26.1 ⎭	23.6 ⎭	21.0 ⎭
80– 89	15.2	16.0	15.8	15.4
70– 79	4.3	6.3	7.5	8.5
Below 70	0.7	1.6	3.1	5.1
Total	100.0	100.0	100.0	100.0

between 90 and 110, generally described as normal, may include as few as 42% or as many as 59.6% of the population, depending on the test chosen. To be sure, test publishers are making efforts to adopt the uniform *SD* of 16 in new tests and in new editions of earlier tests. There are still enough variations among currently available tests, however, to make the checking of the *SD* imperative.

INTERRELATIONSHIPS OF WITHIN-GROUP SCORES. At this stage in our discussion of derived scores, the reader may have become aware of a rapprochement among the various types of scores. Percentiles have gradually been taking on at least a graphic resemblance to normalized standard scores. Linear standard scores are indistinguishable from normalized standard scores if the original distribution of raw scores closely approximates the normal curve. Finally, standard scores have become IQs and vice versa. In connection with the last point, a reexamination of the meaning of a ratio IQ on such a test as the Stanford-Binet will show that these IQs can themselves be interpreted as standard scores. If we know that the distribution of Stanford-Binet ratio IQs had a mean of 100 and an *SD* of approximately 16, we can conclude that an IQ of 116 falls at a distance of 1 *SD* above the mean and represents a standard score of +1.00. Similarly, an IQ of 132 corresponds to a standard score of +2.00, an IQ of 76 to a standard score of −1.50, and so forth. Moreover, a Stanford-Binet ratio IQ of 116 corresponds to a percentile rank of approximately 84, because in a normal curve 84% of the cases fall below +1.00 *SD* (Figure 4).

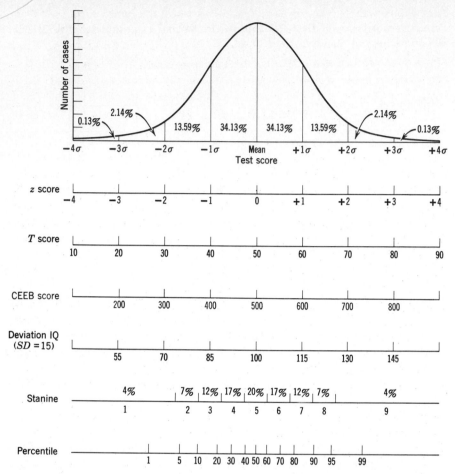

Fig. 6. Relationships among Different Types of Test Scores in a Normal Distribution.

Figure 6 summarizes the relationships that exist in a normal distribution among the types of scores so far discussed in this chapter. These include z scores, College Entrance Examination Board (CEEB) scores, Wechsler deviation IQs ($SD = 15$), T scores, stanines, and percentiles. Ratio IQs on any test will coincide with the given deviation IQ scale if they are normally distributed and have an SD of 15. Any other normally distributed IQ could be added to the chart, provided we know its SD. If the SD is 20, for instance, then an IQ of 120 corresponds to $+1$ SD, an IQ of 80 to -1 SD, and so on.

In conclusion, the exact form in which scores are reported is dictated largely by convenience, familiarity, and ease of developing norms. Standard scores in any form (including the deviation IQ) have generally replaced other types of scores because of certain advantages they offer with regard to test construction and statistical treatment of data. Most types of within-group derived scores, however, are fundamentally similar if carefully derived and properly interpreted. When certain statistical conditions are met, each of these scores can be readily translated into any of the others.

RELATIVITY OF NORMS

INTERTEST COMPARISONS. An IQ, or any other score, should always be accompanied by the name of the test on which it was obtained. Test scores cannot be properly interpreted in the abstract; they must be referred to particular tests. If the school records show that Bill Jones received an IQ of 94 and Terry Brown an IQ of 110, such IQs cannot be accepted at face value without further information. The positions of these two students might have been reversed by exchanging the particular tests that each was given in his or her respective school.

Similarly, an individual's relative standing in different functions may be grossly misrepresented through lack of comparability of test norms. Let us suppose that a student has been given a verbal comprehension test and a spatial aptitude test to determine her relative standing in the two fields. If the verbal ability test was standardized on a random sample of high school students, while the spatial test was standardized on a selected group of students attending elective shop courses, the examiner might erroneously conclude that the individual is much more able along verbal than along spatial lines, when the reverse may actually be the case.

Still another example involves longitudinal comparisons of a single individual's test performance over time. If a schoolchild's cumulative record shows IQs of 118, 115, and 101 at the fourth, fifth, and sixth grades, the first question to ask before interpreting these changes is, "What tests did he take on these three occasions?" The apparent decline may reflect no more than the differences among the tests. In that case, he would have obtained these scores even if the three tests had been administered within a week of each other.

There are three principal reasons to account for systematic variations among the scores obtained by the same individual on different tests. First, tests may differ in *content* despite their similar labels. So-called intelligence tests provide many illustrations of this confusion. Although commonly described by the same blanket term, one of these tests may include only verbal content, another may tap predominantly spatial aptitudes, and still another may cover verbal, numerical, and spatial content in about equal proportions. Second, the *scale units* may not be comparable. As explained earlier in this chapter, if IQs on one test have an *SD* of 12 and IQs on another have an *SD* of 18, then an individual who received an IQ of 112 on the first test is most likely to receive an IQ of 118 on the second. Third, the composition of the *standardization samples* used in establishing norms for different tests may vary. Obviously, the same individual will appear to have performed better when compared with a less able group than when compared with a more able group.

Lack of comparability of either test content or scale units can usually be detected by reference to the test itself or to the test manual. Differences in the respective normative samples, however, are more likely to be overlooked. Such differences probably account for many otherwise unexplained discrepancies in test results.

THE NORMATIVE SAMPLE. Any norm, however expressed, is restricted to the particular normative population from which it was derived. The test user should never lose sight of the way in which norms are established. Psychological test norms are in no sense absolute, universal, or permanent. They merely represent the test performance of the persons constituting the standardization sample. In choosing such a sample, an effort is usually made to obtain a representative cross-section of the population for which the test is designed.

In statistical terminology, a distinction is made between *sample* and *population*. The former refers to the group of persons actually tested. The latter designates the larger, but similarly constituted, group from which the sample is drawn. For example, if we wish to establish norms of test performance for the population of 10-year-old, urban, public school boys, we might test a carefully chosen sample of 500 10-year-old boys attending public schools in several American cities. The sample would be checked with reference to geographical distribution, socioeconomic level, ethnic composition, and other relevant characteristics to ensure that it was truly representative of the defined population.

In the development and application of test norms, considerable attention should be given to the standardization sample. It is apparent that the sample on which the norms are based should be large enough to provide stable values. Another, similarly chosen sample of the same population should not yield norms that diverge appreciably from those obtained. Norms with a large sampling error would obviously be of little value in the interpretation of test scores.

Equally important is the requirement that the sample be representative of the population under consideration. Subtle selective factors that might make the sample unrepresentative should be carefully investigated. A number of such selective factors are illustrated in institutional samples. Because such samples are usually large and readily available for testing purposes, they offer an alluring field for the accumulation of normative data. The special limitations of these samples, however, should be carefully analyzed. Testing persons in school, for example, will yield an increasingly superior selection of cases in the successive grades, owing to the progressive dropping out of the less able students. Nor does such elimination affect different subgroups equally. For example, the rate of selective elimination from school is greater for boys than for girls, and it is greater at lower than at higher socioeconomic levels.

Selective factors likewise operate in other institutional samples, such as prisoners, patients in mental hospitals, or institutionalized mental retardates. Because of many special factors that determine institutionalization itself, such groups are not representative of the entire population of criminals, psychotics, or mental retardates. For example, mental retardates with physical handicaps are more likely to be institutionalized than are the physically fit. Similarly, the relative proportion of severely retarded persons will be much greater in institutional samples than in the total population.

Closely related to the question of representativeness of sample is the need for defining the specific population to which the norms apply. Obviously, one way of ensuring that a sample is representative is to restrict the population to fit the specifications of the available sample. For example, if the population is defined to include only 14-year-old schoolchildren rather than all 14-year-old children, then a school sample would be representative. Ideally, of course, the desired population should be defined in advance in terms of the objectives of the test. Then a suitable sample should be assembled. Practical obstacles in obtaining participants, however, may make this goal unattainable. In such a case, it is far better to redefine the population more narrowly than to report norms on an ideal population which is not adequately represented by the standardization sample. In actual practice, very few tests are standardized on such broad populations as is popularly assumed. No test provides norms for the human species! And it is doubtful whether many tests give truly adequate norms for such broadly defined populations as "adult American men," "10-year-old American children," and the like. Consequently, the samples obtained by different test constructors may be unrepresentative of their alleged populations and biased in different ways. Hence, the resulting norms may not be comparable.

NATIONAL ANCHOR NORMS. One solution for the lack of comparability of norms is to use an anchor test to work out equivalency tables for scores on different tests. Such tables are designed to show what score in Test A is equivalent to each score in Test B. This can be done by the *equipercentile method*, in which scores are considered equivalent when they have equal percentiles in a given group. For example, if the 80th percentile in the same group corresponds to an IQ of 115 on Test A and to an IQ of 120 on Test B, then Test-A-IQ 115 is considered equivalent to Test-B-IQ 120. This approach has been followed to a limited extent by some test publishers, who have prepared equivalency tables for a few of their own tests (e.g., Lennon, 1966a).

More ambitious proposals have been made from time to time for calibrating each new test against a single anchor test, which has itself been administered to a highly representative, national normative sample (Lennon, 1966b). No single anchor test, of course, could be used in establishing norms for *all* tests, regardless of content. What is required is a battery of anchor tests, all administered to the same national sample. Each new test could then be checked against the most nearly similar anchor test in the battery.

The data gathered in Project TALENT (Flanagan et al., 1964) so far come closest to providing such an anchor battery for a high school population. Using a random sample of about 5% of the high schools in this country, the investigators administered a two-day battery of specially constructed aptitude, achievement, interest, and temperament tests to approximately 400,000 students in Grades 9 through 12. Even with the availability of anchor data such as these, however, it must be recognized that independently developed tests can never be regarded as completely interchangeable.[4] At best, the use of national anchor norms would appreciably *reduce* the lack of comparability among tests, but it would not eliminate it.

The Project TALENT battery was employed to calibrate several test batteries in use by the Navy and the Air Force (Dailey, Shaycoft, & Orr, 1962; Shaycoft, Neyman, & Dailey, 1962). The general procedure is to administer both the Project TALENT battery and the tests to be calibrated to the same sample. Through correlational analysis, a composite of Project TALENT tests is identified that is most nearly comparable to each test to be normed. By means of the equipercentile method, tables are then prepared giving the corresponding scores on the Project TALENT composite and on the particular test. For several other batteries, data have been gathered to identify the Project TALENT composite corresponding to each test in the battery (Cooley, 1965; Cooley & Miller, 1965). These batteries include the General Aptitude Test Battery of the United States Employment Service, the Differential Aptitude Tests, and the Flanagan Aptitude Classification Tests.

Of particular interest is the Anchor Test Study conducted by Educational Testing Service under the auspices of the U.S. Office of Education (Jaeger, 1973). This study represents a systematic effort to provide comparable and truly representative national norms for seven of the most widely used reading achievement tests for elementary schoolchildren. Through a well-controlled experimental design, over 300,000 fourth-, fifth-, and sixth-grade schoolchildren were examined in 50 states. The anchor test consisted of the reading comprehension and vocabulary subtests of the Metropolitan Achievement Test, for which new norms were established in one phase of the project. In the equating phase of the study, each child took the reading comprehension and vocabulary subtests from two of the seven batteries, each battery being paired in turn with every other battery. Some groups

---

[4] For an excellent analysis of some of the technical difficulties involved in efforts to achieve score comparability with different tests, see Angoff (1964, 1966, 1971b).

took parallel forms of the two subtests from the same battery. In still other groups, all the pairings were duplicated in reverse sequence, in order to control for order of administration. From statistical analyses of all these data, score equivalency tables for the seven tests were prepared by the equipercentile method. A manual for interpreting scores is provided for use by school systems and other interested persons (Loret, Seder, Bianchini, & Vale, 1974).

The data from the equating phase of the Anchor Test Study were subsequently used to develop a single score scale, designated as the National Reference Scale (Rentz & Bashaw, 1977). The conversion table thus developed permits the transformation of a score from any form of the seven tests at any of the grade levels into a three-place score on a uniform, continuous scale. This scale was constructed by using the item analysis and scaling methods of the Rasch model, one of the simplest of the latent trait models discussed in a later section of this chapter and described more fully in Chapter 8.

SPECIFIC NORMS. Another approach to the nonequivalence of existing norms—and probably a more realistic one for most tests—is to standardize tests on more narrowly defined populations, so chosen as to suit the specific purposes of each test. In such cases, the limits of the normative population should be clearly reported with the norms. Thus, the norms might be said to apply to "employed clerical workers in large business organizations" or to "first-year engineering students." For many testing purposes, highly specific norms are desirable. Even when representative norms are available for a broadly defined population, it is often helpful to have separately reported *subgroup norms.* This is true whenever recognizable subgroups yield appreciably different scores on a particular test. The subgroups may be formed with respect to age, grade, type of curriculum, sex, geographical region, urban or rural environment, socioeconomic level, and many other factors. The use to be made of the test determines the type of differentiation that is most relevant, as well as whether general or specific norms are more appropriate.

Mention should also be made of *local norms,* often developed by the test users themselves within a particular setting. The groups employed in deriving such norms are even more narrowly defined than the subgroups considered above. Thus, an employer may accumulate norms on applicants for a given type of job within a particular company. A college admissions office may develop norms on its own student population. Or a single elementary school may evaluate the performance of individual pupils in terms of its own score distribution. These local norms are more appropriate than broad national norms for many testing purposes, such as the prediction of subsequent job performance or college achievement, the comparison of a child's relative achievement in different subjects, or the measure.nent of an individual's progress over time.

FIXED REFERENCE GROUP. Although most derived scores are computed in such a way as to provide an immediate normative interpretation of test performance, there are some notable exceptions. One type of nonnormative scale utilizes a fixed reference group in order to ensure *comparability and continuity* of scores, without providing normative evaluation of performance. With such a scale, normative interpretation requires reference to independently collected norms from a suitable population. Local or other specific norms are often used for this purpose.

One of the clearest examples of scaling in terms of a fixed reference group is provided by the score scale of the College Board Scholastic Aptitude Test (Angoff, 1971a). Between 1926 (when this test was first administered) and 1941, SAT scores were expressed on a normative scale, in terms of the mean and SD of the candidates taking the test at each administration. As the number and variety of College Board member colleges increased and the composition of the candidate population changed, it was concluded that scale continuity should be maintained. Otherwise, an individual's score would depend on the characteristics of the group tested during a particular year. An even more urgent reason for scale continuity stemmed from the observation that students taking the SAT at certain times of the year performed more poorly than those taking it at other times, owing to the differential operation of selective factors. After 1941, therefore, all SAT scores were expressed in terms of the mean and SD of the approximately 11,000 candidates who took the test in 1941. These candidates constitute the fixed reference group employed in scaling all subsequent forms of the test. Thus, a score of 500 on any form of the SAT corresponds to the mean of the 1941 sample; a score of 600 falls 1 SD above that mean, and so forth.

To permit translation of raw scores on any form of the SAT into these fixed-reference-group scores, a short anchor test (or set of common items) is included in each form. Each new form is thereby linked to one or two earlier forms, which in turn are linked with other forms by a chain of items extending back to the 1941 form. These nonnormative SAT scores can then be interpreted by comparison with any appropriate distribution of scores, such as that of a particular college, a type of college, a region, and so on. These specific norms are more useful in making college admission decisions than would be annual norms based on the entire candidate population. Any changes in the candidate population over time, moreover, can be detected only with a fixed-score scale. It will be noted that the principal difference between the fixed-reference-group scales under consideration and the previously discussed scales based on national anchor norms is that the latter require the choice of a single group that is broadly representative and appropriate for normative purposes. Apart from the practical difficulties in obtaining such a group and the need to update the norms, it is likely that for many testing purposes such broad norms are not required.

Scales built from a fixed reference group are analogous in one respect to scales employed in physical measurement. In this connection, Angoff (1962, pp. 32–33) commented:

There is hardly a person here who knows the precise original definition of the length of the foot used in the measurement of height or distance, or which king it was whose foot was originally agreed upon as the standard; on the other hand, there is no one here who does not know how to evaluate lengths and distances in terms of this unit. Our ignorance of the precise original meaning or derivation of the foot does not lessen its usefulness to us in any way. Its usefulness derives from the fact that it remains the same over time and allows us to familiarize ourselves with it. Needless to say, precisely the same considerations apply to other units of measurement—the inch, the mile, the degree of Fahrenheit, and so on. In the field of psychological measurement it is similarly reasonable to say that the original definition of the scale is or should be of no consequence. What is of consequence is the maintenance of a constant scale—which, in the case of a multiple-form testing program, is achieved by rigorous form-to-form equating—and the provision of supplementary normative data to aid in interpretation and in the formation of specific decisions, data which would be revised from time to time as conditions warrant.

LATENT TRAIT MODELS.[5] The late 1970s witnessed a sharp upsurge of interest in a class of mathematically sophisticated procedures for scaling the difficulty of test items (Jaeger, 1977). Because of the extensive computations required, these procedures became practicable only with the increasing availability of high-speed computers. Although differing in complexity and in specific mathematical procedures, these approaches are based on what are generally characterized as "latent trait models." The concept of latent traits is employed in deriving an index of item difficulty, the basic measure being the probability that a person of specified ability succeeds on an item of specified difficulty. There is no implication, however, that such latent traits or underlying abilities "exist" in any physical or physiological sense, nor that they cause behavior. The latent traits are statistical constructs that arise from a particular analysis of empirically observed relations among test responses. A crude estimate of an examinee's latent trait is the total score he or she obtains on the test; but some of the models apply several refinements to this estimate.

Essentially, latent trait models are used to establish a uniform, "sample-free" scale of measurement, which is applicable to individuals and groups of widely varying ability levels and to test content of widely varying difficulty levels. Like the use of a fixed reference group described in the preceding section, latent trait models need anchor items as a bridge across examinee

[5] Also designated as "item response theory" (IRT) models.

samples and across tests or sets of items. However, rather than using the mean and *SD* of a specific reference group to define the origin and the unit size of the scale, latent trait models set origin and unit size in terms of data representing a wide range of ability and item difficulty, which may come from several samples. Usually the origin is set near the center of this range. Latent trait models also use a specially derived unit that has several advantages, both theoretically and practically. Further description of the latent trait approach will be given in Chapter 8, in connection with techniques of item analysis.

COMPUTER UTILIZATION IN THE INTERPRETATION OF TEST SCORES

Computers have already made a significant impact upon every phase of testing, from test construction to administration, scoring, reporting, and interpretation. The obvious uses of computers—and those developed earliest —represent simply an unprecedented increase in the speed with which traditional data analyses and scoring processes can be carried out. Far more important, however, are the adoption of new procedures and the exploration of new approaches to psychological testing which would have been impossible without the flexibility, speed, and data-processing capabilities of computers. As Baker (1971, p. 227) succinctly put it, computer capabilities should serve "to free one's thinking from the constraints of the past." A good example of the role of computers in the adoption of more sophisticated test-construction procedures is provided by the previously cited latent trait models for sample-free scaling.

Various other testing innovations resulting from computer utilization will be discussed under appropriate topics throughout the book. In the present connection, we shall examine some applications of computers in the evaluation of test performance. At the simplest level, most current tests, and especially those designed for group administration, are now adapted for *computer scoring* (Baker, 1971). Several test publishers, as well as independent test-scoring organizations, are equipped to provide such scoring services to test users. Although separate answer sheets are commonly used for this purpose, optical scanning equipment available at some scoring centers permits the reading of responses directly from test booklets. Many innovative possibilities, such as diagnostic scoring and path analysis (recording a student's progress at various stages of learning), have barely been explored.

At a somewhat more complex level, certain tests now provide facilities for *computer interpretation* of test scores. In such cases, the computer program associates prepared verbal statements with particular patterns of test responses. This approach has been pursued with both personality and aptitude tests. For example, with the Minnesota Multiphasic Personality Inventory (MMPI), to be discussed in Chapter 17, test users may obtain computer printouts of diagnostic and interpretive statements about the examinee's personality tendencies and emotional condition, together with the numerical scores. Similarly, the Differential Aptitude Tests (see Ch. 13) provide a Career Planning Report, which includes a profile of scores on the separate subtests as well as an interpretive computer printout. The latter contains verbal statements that combine the test data with information on interests and goals given by the student on a Career Planning Questionnaire. These statements are typical of what a counselor would say to the student in going over test results in an individual conference (Super, 1973).

Individualized interpretation of test scores at a still more complex level is illustrated by *interactive computer systems,* in which the individual is in direct contact with the computer by means of response stations and in effect engages in a dialogue with the computer (J. A. Harris, 1973; Holtzman, 1970; M. R. Katz, 1974; Super et al., 1970). This technique has been investigated with regard to educational and vocational planning and decision making. In such a situation, test scores are usually incorporated in the computer data base, together with other information provided by the student or client. Essentially, the computer combines all the available information about the individual with stored data about educational programs and occupations; and it utilizes all relevant facts and relations in answering the individual's questions and aiding her or him in reaching decisions. Examples of such interactive computer systems, in various stages of operational development, include IBM's Education and Career Exploration System (ECES) and ETS's System for Interactive Guidance Information (SIGI). Preliminary field trials show good acceptance of these systems by high school students and their parents (J. A. Harris, 1973).

Test results also represent an integral part of the data utilized in *computer-assisted instruction* (CAI). In order to present instructional material appropriate to each student's current level of attainment, the computer must repeatedly score and evaluate the student's responses to preceding material. On the basis of his response history, the student may be routed to more advanced material, or to further practice at the present level, or to a remedial branch whereby he receives instruction in more elementary prerequisite material. Diagnostic analysis of errors may lead to an instructional program designed to correct the specific learning difficulties identified in individual cases. An example of a widely used CAI system for teaching reading to first- second-, and third-grade children is described by R. C. Atkinson (1974).

A less costly and operationally more feasible variant of computer utilization in learning is *computer-managed instruction* (CMI—see Hambleton, 1974). In such systems, the learner does not interact directly with the computer. The role of the computer is to assist the teacher in carrying out a plan of individualized instruction, which may use self-instruction packages or more conventional types of instruction. A major contribution of the computer is to process the rather formidable mass of data accumulated daily regarding the performance of each student, in a classroom where each may be involved in a different activity, and to utilize these data in prescribing the next instructional step for each student. Several CMI systems, in varying stages of development and implementation, are described in Talmage (1975).

CRITERION-REFERENCED TESTING

NATURE AND USES. An approach to testing that has aroused a surge of activity, particularly in education, is generally designated as "criterion-referenced testing." First proposed by Glaser (1963), this term is still used somewhat loosely and its definition varies among different writers. Moreover, several alternative terms are in common use, such as content-, domain-, and objective-referenced. These terms are sometimes employed as synonyms for criterion-referenced and sometimes with slightly different connotations. "Criterion-referenced," however, seems to have gained ascendancy, although it is not the most appropriate term.

Typically, criterion-referenced testing uses as its interpretive frame of reference a specified *content* domain rather than a specified population of *persons*. In this respect, it has been contrasted with the usual norm-referenced testing, in which an individual's score is interpreted by comparing it with the scores obtained by others on the same test. In criterion-referenced testing, for example, an examinee's test performance may be reported in terms of the specific kinds of arithmetic operations he has mastered, the estimated size of his vocabulary, the difficulty level of reading matter he can comprehend (from comic books to literary classics), or the chances of his achieving a designated performance level on an external criterion (educational or vocational).

Thus far, criterion-referenced testing has found its major applications in several recent innovations in education. Prominent among these are computer-assisted, computer-managed, and other individualized, self-paced instructional systems. In all these systems, testing is closely integrated with instruction, being introduced before, during, and after completion of each instructional unit to check on prerequisite skills, diagnose possible learning difficulties, and prescribe subsequent instructional procedures.

From another angle, criterion-referenced tests are useful in broad surveys of educational accomplishment, such as the National Assessment of Educational Progress (Womer, 1970), and in meeting demands for educational accountability (Gronlund, 1974). From still another angle, testing for the attainment of minimum requirements, as in qualifying for a driver's license or a pilot's license, illustrates criterion-referenced testing. A related application is in testing for job proficiency where the mastery of a small number of clearly defined job skills is to be assessed, as in military occupational specialties (Maier & Hirshfeld, 1978; Swezey & Pearlstein, 1975).

Finally, familiarity with the concepts of criterion-referenced testing can contribute to the improvement of the traditional, informal tests prepared by teachers for classroom use. Gronlund (1973) provides a helpful guide for this purpose, as well as a simple and well-balanced introduction to criterion-referenced testing. A brief but excellent discussion of the chief limitations of criterion-referenced tests is given by Ebel (1972); and a readable account of common misconceptions about the construction and use of criterion-referenced tests in education can be found in Shaycoft (1979).

CONTENT MEANING. The major distinguishing feature of criterion-referenced testing (however defined and whether designated by this term or by one of its synonyms) is its interpretation of test performance in terms of content meaning. The focus is clearly on *what* the person can do and what he knows, not on how he compares with others. A fundamental requirement in constructing this type of test is a clearly defined domain of knowledge or skills to be assessed by the test. If scores on such a test are to have communicable meaning, the content domain to be sampled must be widely recognized as important. The selected domain must then be subdivided into small units defined in performance terms. In an educational context, these units correspond to behaviorally defined instructional objectives, such as "multiplies three-digit by two-digit numbers" or "identifies the misspelled word in which the final *e* is retained when adding *-ing*." In the programs prepared for individualized instruction, these objectives run to several hundred for a single school subject. After the instructional objectives have been formulated, items are prepared to sample each objective. This procedure is admittedly difficult and time-consuming. Without such careful specification and control of content, however, the results of criterion-referenced testing could degenerate into an idiosyncratic and uninterpretable jumble.

When strictly applied, criterion-referenced testing is best adapted for testing basic skills (as in reading and arithmetic) at elementary levels. In these areas, instructional objectives can also be arranged in an ordinal hierarchy, the acquisition of more elementary skills being prerequisite to the acquisition of higher-level skills.[6] It is impracticable and probably undesirable, however, to formulate highly specific objectives for advanced levels of knowledge in less highly structured subjects. At these levels, both the content and sequence of learning are likely to be much more flexible.

On the other hand, in its emphasis on content meaning in the interpretation of test scores, criterion-referenced testing may exert a salutary effect on testing in general. The interpretation of intelligence test scores, for example, would benefit from this approach. To describe a child's intelligence test performance in terms of the specific intellectual skills and knowledge it represents might help to counteract the confusions and misconceptions that

---

[6] Ideally such tests follow the simplex model of a Guttman scale (see Popham & Husek, 1969), as do the Piagetian ordinal scales discussed earlier in this chapter.

have become attached to the IQ. When stated in these general terms, however, the criterion-referenced approach is equivalent to interpreting test scores in the light of the demonstrated validity of the particular test, rather than in terms of vague underlying entities. Such an interpretation can certainly be combined with norm-referenced scores.

MASTERY TESTING. A second major feature commonly associated with criterion-referenced testing is the procedure of testing for mastery. Essentially, this procedure yields an all-or-none score, indicating that the individual has or has not attained the preestablished level of mastery. When basic skills are tested, nearly complete mastery is generally expected (e.g., 80–85% correct items). A three-way distinction may also be employed, including mastery, nonmastery, and an intermediate, doubtful, or "review" interval.

In connection with individualized instruction, some educators have argued that, given enough time and suitable instructional methods, nearly everyone can achieve complete mastery of the chosen instructional objectives. Individual differences would thus be manifested in learning time rather than in final achievement as in traditional educational testing (Bloom, 1968; J. B. Carroll, 1963, 1970; Cooley & Glaser, 1969; Gagné, 1965). It follows that in mastery testing, individual differences in performance are of little or no interest. Hence, as generally constructed, criterion-referenced tests minimize individual differences in performance after appropriate training. Mastery testing is regularly employed in the previously cited programs for individualized instruction. It is also characteristic of published criterion-referenced tests for basic skills, suitable for elementary school. Examples of such tests include the Prescriptive Reading Inventory and the Diagnostic Mathematics Inventory (CTB/McGraw-Hill), the Skills Monitoring System in Reading (Psychological Corporation), and Diagnosis: An Instructional Aid in Reading and in Mathematics (Science Research Associates).

In the construction of such tests, two important questions are: (1) How many items must be used for reliable assessment of each of the specific instructional objectives covered by the test? (2) What proportion of items must be correct for the reliable establishment of mastery? In much current testing, these two questions have been answered by judgmental decisions. Substantial progress has been made, however, in developing appropriate statistical techniques that may provide objective, empirical answers (Ferguson & Novick, 1973; Glaser & Nitko, 1971; Hambleton, 1980; Hambleton & Novick, 1973; Millman, 1974). A few examples will serve to illustrate the nature and scope of these efforts.

The two questions about number of items and cutoff score can be incorporated into a single hypothesis, amenable to testing within the framework of decision theory and sequential analysis (Glaser & Nitko, 1971; Lindgren & McElrath, 1969; Wald, 1947). Specifically, we wish to test the hypothesis that the examinee has achieved the required level of mastery in the content domain or instructional objective sampled by the test items. Sequential analysis consists in taking observations one at a time and deciding after each observation whether to (1) accept the hypothesis; (2) reject the hypothesis; or (3) make additional observations. Thus, the number of observations (in this case, number of items) needed to reach a reliable conclusion is itself determined during the process of testing. Rather than being presented with a fixed, predetermined number of items, the examinee continues taking the test until a mastery or nonmastery decision is reached. At that point, testing is discontinued and the student is either directed to the next instructional level or returned to the nonmastered level for further study. With the computer facilities described earlier in this chapter, such sequential decision procedures are feasible and can reduce total testing time while yielding reliable estimates of mastery (Glaser & Nitko, 1971).

Some investigators have been exploring the use of Bayesian estimation techniques, which lend themselves well to the kind of decisions required by mastery testing. Because of the large number of specific instructional objectives to be tested, criterion-referenced tests typically provide only a small number of items for each objective. To supplement this limited information, procedures have been developed for incorporating collateral data from the student's previous performance history, as well as from the test results of other students (Ferguson & Novick, 1973; Hambleton & Novick, 1973).

When individually tailored procedures are impracticable, cutoff scores can be established empirically by analyzing preinstruction and postinstruction scores of appropriate groups on the given test. A cutting score is then selected that best discriminates between those who have and those who have not received the relevant training (e.g., Panell & Laabs, 1979). Judgment is required in specific situations to assess the relative seriousness of "passing" a person who is not qualified versus "failing" one who is. The cutoff would be accordingly raised or lowered to adjust to the seriousness of the consequences of misclassification.

Still another approach is represented by defining, through consensus or other a priori means, a desired mastery level for the content domain sampled by the test, and then determining how many test items must be correctly completed to attain that level. Through the application of appropriate mathematical models, sets of tables have been constructed that show the required number of items and cutting scores for different domain mastery levels (Millman, 1972, 1973; Shaycoft, 1979, Appendix A).

RELATION TO NORM-REFERENCED TESTING. Beyond basic skills, mastery testing is inapplicable or insufficient. In more advanced and less structured subjects, achievement is open-ended. The individual may progress almost without limit in such functions as understanding, critical thinking, appreciation, and originality. Moreover, content coverage may proceed in many different directions, depending upon the individual's abilities, interests, and goals, as well as local instructional facilities. Under these conditions, complete mastery is unrealistic and unnecessary. Hence, norm-referenced evaluation is generally employed in such cases to assess degree of attainment. Some published tests are so constructed as to permit both norm-referenced and criterion-referenced applications. An example is provided by the Stanford diagnostic tests in reading and in mathematics. While providing appropriate norms at each level, these tests permit a qualitative analysis of the child's attainment of detailed instructional objectives.

It should be noted that criterion-referenced testing is neither as new nor as clearly divorced from norm-referenced testing as some of its proponents imply. Evaluating an individual's test performance in absolute terms, such as by letter grades or percentage of correct items, is certainly much older than normative interpretations. More precise attempts to describe test performance in terms of content meaning also antedate the introduction of the term "criterion-referenced testing" (Ebel, 1962; Flanagan, 1962—see also Anastasi, 1968, pp. 69–70). Other examples may be found in early product scales for assessing the quality of handwriting, compositions, or drawings by matching the individual's work sample against a set of standard specimens. Ebel (1972) observed, furthermore, that the concept of mastery in education—in the sense of all-or-none learning of specific units —achieved considerable popularity in the 1920s and 1930s and was later abandoned.

A normative framework is implicit in all testing, regardless of how scores are expressed (Angoff, 1974). The very choice of content or skills to be measured is influenced by the examiner's knowledge of what can be expected from human organisms at a particular developmental or instructional stage. Such a choice presupposes information about what other persons have done in similar situations. Moreover, by imposing uniform cutoff scores on an ability continuum, mastery testing does not thereby eliminate individual differences. To describe an individual's level of reading comprehension as "the ability to understand the content of the *New York Times*" still leaves room for a wide range of individual differences in degree of understanding. Applying a cutoff point to dichotomize performance simply ignores the remaining individual differences within the two categories and discards potentially useful information.

EXPECTANCY TABLES. Test scores may also be interpreted in terms of expected criterion performance, as in a training program or on a job. This usage of the term "criterion" follows standard psychometric practice, as when a test is said to be validated against a particular criterion (see Ch. 2). Strictly speaking, the term "criterion-referenced testing" should refer to this type of performance interpretation, while the other approaches discussed in this section can be more precisely described as content-referenced. This terminology, in fact, is used in the APA test *Standards* (1974).

An expectancy table gives the probability of different criterion outcomes for persons who obtain each test score. For example, if a student obtains a score of 530 on the CEEB Scholastic Aptitude Test, what are the chances that her or his freshman grade-point average in a specific college will fall in the A, B, C, D, or F category? This type of information can be obtained by examining the bivariate distribution of predictor scores (SAT) plotted against criterion status (freshman grade-point average). If the number of cases in each cell of such a bivariate distribution is changed to a percentage, the result is an expectancy table, such as the one illustrated in Table 6. The

TABLE 6

Expectancy Table Showing Relation Between DAT Verbal Reasoning Test and Course Grades in American History for 171 Boys in Grade 11

(Adapted from Fifth Edition Manual for the Differential Aptitude Tests, Forms S and T, p. 114. Reproduced by permission. Copyright © 1973, 1974 by The Psychological Corporation, New York, N.Y. All rights reserved.)

Test Score	Number of Cases	Percentage Receiving Each Criterion Grade			
		Below 70	70–79	80–89	90 & above
40 & above	46		15	22	63
30–39	36	6	39	39	17
20–29	43	12	63	21	5
Below 20	46	30	52	17	

data for this table were obtained from 171 high school boys enrolled in courses in American history. The predictor was the Verbal Reasoning test of the Differential Aptitude Tests, administered early in the course. The criterion was end-of-course grades. The correlation between test scores and criterion was .66.

The first column of Table 6 shows the test scores, divided into four class intervals; the number of students whose scores fall into each interval is given in the second column. The remaining entries in each row of the table indicate the percentage of cases within each test-score interval who received each grade at the end of the course. Thus, of the 46 students with scores of 40 or above on the Verbal Reasoning test, 15% received grades of 70–79, 22% grades of 80–89, and 63% grades of 90 or above. At the other extreme, of the 46 students scoring below 20 on the test, 30% received grades below 70, 52% between 70 and 79, and 17% between 80 and 89. Within the limitations of the available data, these percentages represent the best estimates of the probability that an individual will receive a given criterion grade. For example, if a new student receives a test score of 34 (i.e., in the 30–39 interval), we would conclude that the probability of his obtaining a grade of 90 or above is 17 out of 100; the probability of his obtaining a grade between 80 and 89 is 39 out of 100, and so on.

In many practical situations, criteria can be dichotomized into "success" and "failure" in a job, a course of study, or other undertaking. Under these conditions, an *expectancy chart* can be prepared, showing the probability of success or failure corresponding to each score interval. Figure 7 is an example of such an expectancy chart. Based on a pilot selection battery developed by the Air Force, this expectancy chart shows the percentage of pilot cadets scoring within each stanine on the battery who failed to complete primary flight training. It can be seen that 77% of the cadets receiving a stanine of 1 were eliminated in the course of training, while only 4% of those at stanine 9 failed to complete the training satisfactorily. Between these extremes, the percentage of failures decreases consistently over the successive stanines. On the basis of this expectancy chart, it could be predicted, for example, that approximately 40% of pilot cadets who obtain a stanine score of 4 will fail and approximately 60% will satisfactorily complete primary flight training. Similar statements regarding the probability of success and failure could be made about individuals who receive each stanine.

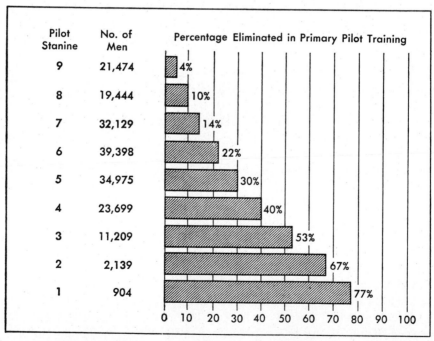

Fig. 7. Expectancy Chart Showing Relation between Performance on Pilot Selection Battery and Elimination from Primary Flight Training.
(From Flanagan, 1947, p. 58.)

Thus, an individual with a stanine of 4 has a 60:40 or 3:2 chance of completing primary flight training. Besides providing a criterion-referenced interpretation of test scores, it can be seen that both expectancy tables and expectancy charts give a general idea of the validity of a test in predicting a given criterion.

CHAPTER 5

Reliability

RELIABILITY refers to the consistency of scores obtained by the same persons when reexamined with the same test on different occasions, or with different sets of equivalent items, or under other variable examining conditions. This concept of reliability underlies the computation of the *error of measurement* of a single score, whereby we can predict the range of fluctuation likely to occur in a single individual's score as a result of irrelevant, chance factors.

The concept of test reliability has been used to cover several aspects of score consistency. In its broadest sense, test reliability indicates the extent to which individual differences in test scores are attributable to "true" differences in the characteristics under consideration and the extent to which they are attributable to chance errors. To put it in more technical terms, measures of test reliability make it possible to estimate what proportion of the total variance of test scores is *error variance*. The crux of the matter, however, lies in the definition of error variance. Factors that might be considered error variance for one purpose would be classified under true variance for another. For example, if we are interested in measuring fluctuations of mood, then the day-by-day changes in scores on a test of cheerfulness-depression would be relevant to the purpose of the test and would hence be part of the true variance of the scores. If, on the other hand, the test is designed to measure more permanent personality characteristics, the same daily fluctuations would fall under the heading of error variance.

Essentially, any condition that is irrelevant to the purpose of the test represents error variance. Thus, when examiners try to maintain uniform testing conditions by controlling the testing environment, instructions, time limits, rapport, and other similar factors, they are reducing error variance and making the test scores more reliable. Despite optimum testing conditions, however, no test is a perfectly reliable instrument. Hence, every test should be accompanied by a statement of its reliability. Such a measure of reliability characterizes the test when administered under standard conditions and given to persons similar to those constituting the normative sample. The characteristics of this sample should therefore be specified, together with the type of reliability that was measured.

There could, of course, be as many varieties of test reliability as there are conditions affecting test scores, since any such conditions might be irrelevant for a certain purpose and would thus be classified as error variance. The types of reliability computed in actual practice, however, are relatively few. In this chapter, the principal techniques for measuring the reliability of test scores will be examined, together with the sources of error variance identified by each. Since all types of reliability are concerned with the degree of consistency or agreement between two independently derived sets of scores, they can all be expressed in terms of a *correlation coefficient*. Accordingly, the next section will consider some of the basic characteristics of correlation coefficients, in order to clarify their use and interpretation. More technical discussion of correlation, as well as more detailed specifications of computing procedures, can be found in any elementary textbook of educational or psychological statistics, such as Guilford and Fruchter (1978).

THE CORRELATION COEFFICIENT

MEANING OF CORRELATION. Essentially, a correlation coefficient (r) expresses the degree of correspondence, or *relationship*, between two sets of scores. Thus, if the top-scoring individual in variable 1 also obtains the top score in variable 2, the second-best individual in variable 1 is second best in variable 2, and so on down to the poorest individual in the group, then there would be a perfect correlation between variables 1 and 2. Such a correlation would have a value of +1.00.

A hypothetical illustration of a perfect positive correlation is shown in Figure 8. This figure presents a scatter diagram, or bivariate distribution.

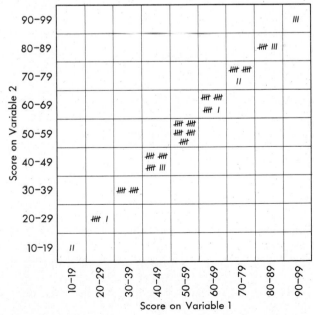

FIG. 8. Bivariate Distribution for a Hypothetical Correlation of +1.00.

Each tally mark in this diagram indicates the score of one person in both variable 1 (horizontal axis) and variable 2 (vertical axis). It will be noted that all of the 100 cases in the group are distributed along the diagonal running from the lower left- to the upper right-hand corner of the diagram. Such a distribution indicates a perfect positive correlation (+1.00), since it shows that each person occupies the same relative position in both variables. The closer the bivariate distribution of scores approaches this diagonal, the higher will be the positive correlation.

Figure 9 illustrates a perfect negative correlation (−1.00). In this case, there is a complete reversal of scores from one variable to the other. The best individual in variable 1 is the poorest in variable 2 and vice versa, this reversal being consistently maintained throughout the distribution. It will be noted that, in this scatter diagram, all persons fall on the diagonal extending from the upper left- to the lower right-hand corner. This diagonal runs in the reverse direction from that in Figure 8.

A zero correlation indicates complete absence of relationship, such as might occur by chance. If each person's name were pulled at random out of a hat to determine his or her position in variable 1, and if the process were repeated for variable 2, a zero or near-zero correlation would result. Under these conditions, it would be impossible to predict an individual's relative standing in variable 2 from a knowledge of her or his score in variable 1. The top-scoring person in variable 1 might score high, low, or average in variable 2. By chance, some persons might score above average in both

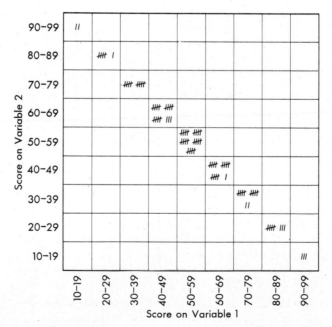

FIG. 9. Bivariate Distribution for a Hypothetical Correlation of −1.00.

variables, or below average in both; others might fall above average in one variable and below in the other; still others might be above the average in one and at the average in the second, and so forth. There would be no regularity in the relationship from one individual to another.

The coefficients found in actual practice generally fall between these extremes, having some value higher than zero but lower than 1.00. Correlations between measures of abilities are nearly always positive, although frequently low. When a negative correlation is obtained between two such variables, it usually results from the way in which the scores are expressed. For example, if time scores are correlated with amount scores, a negative correlation will probably result. Thus, if each person's score on an arithmetic computation test is recorded as the number of minutes required to complete all items, while the score on an arithmetic reasoning test represents the number of problems correctly solved, a negative correlation can be expected. In such a case, the poorest (i.e., slowest) individual will have the numerically highest score on the first test, while the best individual will have the highest score on the second.

Correlation coefficients may be computed in various ways, depending on the nature of the data. The most common is the *Pearson Product-Moment Correlation Coefficient*. This correlation coefficient takes into account not only the person's position in the group, but also the amount of his deviation above or below the group mean. It will be recalled that when each person's standing is expressed in terms of standard scores, persons falling above the average receive positive standard scores, while those below the average receive negative scores. Thus, an individual who is superior in both variables to be correlated would have two positive standard scores; one inferior in both would have two negative standard scores. If, now, we multiply each individual's standard score in variable 1 by his standard score in variable 2, all of these products will be positive, provided that each person falls on the same side of the mean on both variables. The Pearson correlation coefficient is simply the mean of these products. It will have a high positive value when corresponding standard scores are of equal sign and of approximately equal amount in the two variables. When persons above the average in one variable are below the average in the other, the corresponding cross-products will be negative. If the sum of the cross-products is negative, the correlation will be negative. When some products are positive and some negative, the correlation will be close to zero.

In actual practice, it is not necessary to convert each raw score to a standard score before finding the cross-products, since this conversion can be made once for all after the cross-products have been added. There are many shortcuts for computing the Pearson correlation coefficient. The method demonstrated in Table 7 is not the quickest, but it illustrates the meaning of the correlation coefficient more clearly than other methods that utilize computational shortcuts. Table 7 shows the computation of a Pearson *r* between the mathematics and reading scores of 10 children. Next to each

TABLE 7

Computation of Pearson Product-Moment Correlation Coefficient

Pupil	Mathematics X	Reading Y	x	y	x^2	y^2	xy
Bill	41	17	+1	−4	1	16	− 4
Carol	38	28	−2	+7	4	49	−14
Geoffrey	48	22	+8	+1	64	1	8
Ann	32	16	−8	−5	64	25	40
Bob	34	18	−6	−3	36	9	18
Jane	36	15	−4	−6	16	36	24
Ellen	41	24	+1	+3	1	9	3
Ruth	43	20	+3	−1	9	1	− 3
Dick	47	23	+7	+2	49	4	14
Mary	40	27	0	+6	0	36	0
Σ	400	210	0	0	244	186	86
M	40	21					

$$SD_x = \sqrt{\frac{244}{10}} = \sqrt{24.40} = 4.94 \qquad SD_y = \sqrt{\frac{186}{10}} = \sqrt{18.60} = 4.31$$

$$r_{xy} = \frac{\Sigma xy}{(N)\,(SD_x)\,(SD_y)} = \frac{86}{(10)\,(4.94)\,(4.31)} = \frac{86}{212.91} = .40$$

child's name are his or her scores in the mathematics test (X) and the reading test (Y). The sums and means of the 10 scores are given under the respective columns. The third column shows the deviation (x) of each mathematics score from the mathematics mean; and the fourth column, the deviation (y) of each reading score from the reading mean. These deviations are squared in the next two columns, and the sums of the squares are used in computing the standard deviations of the mathematics and reading scores by the method described in Chapter 4. Rather than dividing each x and y by its corresponding SD to find standard scores, we perform this division only once at the end, as shown in the correlation formula in Table 7. The cross-products in the last column (xy) have been found by multiplying the corresponding deviations in the x and y columns. To compute the correlation (r), the sum of these cross-products is divided by the number of cases (N) and by the product of the two standard deviations (SD_xSD_y).

STATISTICAL SIGNIFICANCE. The correlation of .40 found in Table 7 indicates a moderate degree of positive relationship between the mathematics and reading scores. There is some tendency for those children doing well in mathematics also to perform well on the reading test and vice versa, although the relation is not close. If we are concerned only with the performance of these 10 children, we can accept this correlation as an adequate description of the degree of relation existing between the two variables in this group. In psychological research, however, we are usually interested in generalizing beyond the particular *sample* of individuals tested to the larger *population* which they represent. For example, we might want to know whether mathematics and reading ability are correlated among American schoolchildren of the same age as those we tested. Obviously, the 10 cases actually examined would constitute a very inadequate sample of such a population. Another comparable sample of the same size might yield a much lower or a much higher correlation.

There are statistical procedures for estimating the probable fluctuation to be expected from sample to sample in the size of correlations, means, standard deviations, and any other group measures. The question usually asked about correlations, however, is simply whether the correlation is significantly greater than zero. In other words, if the correlation in the population is zero, could a correlation as high as that obtained in our sample have resulted from sampling error alone? When we say that a correlation is "significant at the 1% (.01) level," we mean the chances are no greater than one out of 100 that the population correlation is zero. Hence, we conclude that the two variables are truly correlated. Significance levels refer to the risk of error we are willing to take in drawing conclusions from our data. If a correlation is said to be significant at the .05 level, the probability of error is 5 out of 100. Most psychological research applies either the .01 or the .05 levels, although other significance levels may be employed for special reasons.

The correlation of .40 found in Table 7 fails to reach significance even at the .05 level. As might have been anticipated, with only 10 cases it is difficult to establish a general relationship conclusively. With this size of sample, the smallest correlation significant at the .05 level is .63. Any correlation below that value simply leaves unanswered the question of whether the two variables are correlated in the population from which the sample was drawn.

The minimum correlations significant at the .01 and .05 levels for groups of different sizes can be found by consulting tables of the significance of correlations in any statistics textbook. For interpretive purposes in this book, however, only an understanding of the general concept is required. Parenthetically, it might be added that significance levels can be interpreted in a similar way when applied to other statistical measures. For example, to say that the difference between two means is significant at the .01 level indicates that we can conclude, with only one chance out of 100 of being wrong, that a difference in the obtained direction would be found if we tested the whole population from which our samples were drawn. For instance, if in the sample tested the boys had obtained a significantly higher

mean than the girls on a mechanical comprehension test, we could conclude that the boys would also excel in the total population.

THE RELIABILITY COEFFICIENT. Correlation coefficients have many uses
in the analysis of psychometric data. The measurement of test reliability
represents one application of such coefficients. An example of a reliability
coefficient, computed by the Pearson Product-Moment method, is to be
found in Figure 10. In this case, the scores of 104 persons on two equivalent
forms of a Word Fluency test[1] were correlated. In one form, the examinees
were given five minutes to write as many words as they could that began
with a given letter. The second form was identical, except that a different
letter was employed. The two letters were chosen by the test authors as
being approximately equal in difficulty for this purpose.

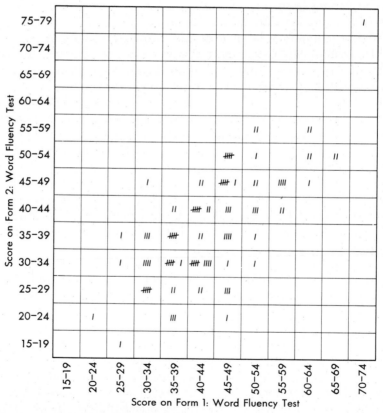

FIG. 10. A Reliability Coefficient of .72.
(Data from Anastasi & Drake, 1954.)

[1] One of the subtests of the SRA Tests of Primary Mental Abilities for Ages 11 to 17.
The data were obtained in an investigation by Anastasi and Drake (1954).

The correlation between the number of words written in the two forms of this test was found to be .72. This correlation is high and significant at the .01 level. With 104 cases, any correlation of .25 or higher is significant at this level. Nevertheless, the obtained correlation is somewhat lower than is desirable for reliability coefficients, which usually fall in the .80s or .90s. An examination of the scatter diagram in Figure 10 shows a typical bivariate distribution of scores corresponding to a high positive correlation. It will be noted that the tallies cluster close to the diagonal extending from the lower left- to the upper right-hand corner; the trend is definitely in this direction, although there is a certain amount of scatter of individual entries. In the following section, the use of the correlation coefficient in computing different measures of test reliability will be considered.

TYPES OF RELIABILITY

TEST-RETEST RELIABILITY. The most obvious method for finding the reliability of test scores is by repeating the identical test on a second occasion. The reliability coefficient (r_{tt}) in this case is simply the correlation between the scores obtained by the same persons on the two administrations of the test. The error variance corresponds to the random fluctuations of performance from one test session to the other. These variations may result in part from uncontrolled testing conditions, such as extreme changes in weather, sudden noises and other distractions, or a broken pencil point. To some extent, however, they arise from changes in the condition of the examinee himself, as illustrated by illness, fatigue, emotional strain, worry, recent experiences of a pleasant or unpleasant nature, and the like. Retest reliability shows the extent to which scores on a test can be generalized over different occasions; the higher the reliability, the less susceptible the scores are to the random daily changes in the condition of the examinee or of the testing environment.

When retest reliability is reported in a test manual, the interval over which it was measured should always be specified. Since retest correlations decrease progressively as this interval lengthens, there is not one but an infinite number of retest reliability coefficients for any test. It is also desirable to give some indication of relevant intervening experiences of the persons on whom reliability was measured, such as educational or job experiences, counseling, psychotherapy, and so forth.

Apart from the desirability of reporting length of interval, what considerations should guide the choice of interval? Illustrations could readily be cited of tests showing high reliability over periods of a few days or weeks, but whose scores reveal an almost complete lack of correspondence when the interval is extended to as long as ten or fifteen years. Many preschool intelligence tests, for example, yield moderately stable measures within the preschool period, but are virtually useless as predictors of late childhood or adult IQs. In actual practice, however, a simple distinction can usually be made. Short-range, random fluctuations that occur during intervals ranging from a few hours to a few months are generally included under the error variance of the test score. Thus, in checking this type of test reliability, an effort is made to keep the interval short. In testing young children, the period should be even shorter than for older persons, since at early ages progressive developmental changes are discernible over a period of a month or even less. For any type of person, the interval between retests should rarely exceed six months.

Any additional changes in the relative test performance of individuals that occur over longer periods of time are apt to be cumulative and progressive rather than entirely random. Moreover, they are likely to characterize a broader area of behavior than that covered by the test performance itself. Thus, one's general level of scholastic aptitude, mechanical comprehension, or artistic judgment may have altered appreciably over a ten-year period, owing to unusual intervening experiences. The individual's status may have either risen or dropped appreciably in relation to others of his or her own age, because of circumstances peculiar to the individual's own home, school, or community environment, or for other reasons such as illness or emotional disturbance.

The extent to which such factors can affect an individual's psychological development provides an important problem for investigation. This question, however, should not be confused with that of the reliability of a particular test. When we measure the reliability of the Stanford-Binet, for example, we do not ordinarily correlate retest scores over a period of ten years, or even one year, but over a few weeks. To be sure, long-range retests have been conducted with such tests, but the results are generally discussed in terms of the predictability of adult intelligence from childhood performance, rather than in terms of the reliability of a particular test. The concept of reliability is generally restricted to short-range, random changes that characterize the test performance itself rather than the entire behavior domain that is being tested.

It should be noted that different behavior functions may themselves vary in the extent of daily fluctuation they exhibit. For example, steadiness of delicate finger movements is undoubtedly more susceptible to slight changes in the person's condition than is verbal comprehension. If we wish to obtain an overall estimate of the individual's habitual finger steadiness, we would probably require repeated tests on several days, whereas a single test session would suffice for verbal comprehension. Again we must fall back on an analysis of the purposes of the test and on a thorough understanding of the behavior the test is designed to predict.

Although apparently simple and straightforward, the test-retest technique presents difficulties when applied to most psychological tests. Practice will probably produce varying amounts of improvement in the retest scores of different individuals. Moreover, if the interval between retests is fairly short, the examinees may recall many of their former responses. In other words, the same pattern of right and wrong responses is likely to recur through sheer memory. Thus, the scores on the two administrations of the test are not independently obtained and the correlation between them will be spuriously high. The nature of the test itself may also change with repetition. This is especially true of problems involving reasoning or ingenuity. Once the examinee has grasped the principle involved in the problem, or once he has worked out a solution, he can reproduce the correct response in the future without going through the intervening steps. Only tests that are not appreciably affected by repetition lend themselves to the retest technique. A number of sensory discrimination and motor tests would fall into this category. For the large majority of psychological tests, however, retesting with the identical test is not an appropriate technique for finding a reliability coefficient.

ALTERNATE-FORM RELIABILITY. One way of avoiding the difficulties encountered in test-retest reliability is through the use of alternate forms of the test. The same persons can thus be tested with one form on the first occasion and with another, comparable form on the second. The correlation between the scores obtained on the two forms represents the reliability coefficient of the test. It will be noted that such a reliability coefficient is a measure of both temporal stability and consistency of response to different item samples (or test forms). This coefficient thus combines two types of reliability. Since both types are important for most testing purposes, however, alternate-form reliability provides a useful measure for evaluating many tests.

The concept of item sampling, or *content sampling*, underlies not only alternate-form reliability but also other types of reliability to be discussed shortly. It is therefore appropriate to examine it more closely. Everyone has probably had the experience of taking a course examination in which he felt he had a "lucky break" because many of the items covered the very topics he happened to have studied most carefully. On another occasion, he may have had the opposite experience, finding an unusually large number of items on areas he had failed to review. This familiar situation illustrates error variance resulting from content sampling. To what extent do scores on this test depend on factors *specific* to the particular selection of items? If a different investigator, working independently, were to prepare another test in accordance with the same specifications, how much would an individual's score differ on the two tests?

Let us suppose that a 40-item vocabulary test has been constructed as a measure of general verbal comprehension. Now suppose that a second list of 40 different words is assembled for the same purpose, and that the items

Gerardo González

are constructed with equal care to cover the same range of difficulty as the first test. The differences in the scores obtained by the same individuals on these two tests illustrate the type of error variance under consideration. Owing to fortuitous factors in the past experience of different individuals, the relative difficulty of the two lists will vary somewhat from person to person. Thus, the first list might contain a larger number of words unfamiliar to individual A than does the second list. The second list, on the other hand, might contain a disproportionately large number of words unfamiliar to individual B. If the two individuals are approximately equal in their overall word knowledge (i.e., in their "true scores"), B will nevertheless excel A on the first list, while A will excel B on the second. The relative standing of these two persons will therefore be reversed on the two lists, owing to chance differences in the selection of items.

Like test-retest reliability, alternate-form reliability should always be accompanied by a statement of the length of the interval between test administrations, as well as a description of relevant intervening experiences. If the two forms are administered *in immediate succession,* the resulting correlation shows reliability across forms only, not across occasions. The error variance in this case represents fluctuations in performance from one set of items to another, but not fluctuations over time.

In the development of alternate forms, care should, of course, be exercised to ensure that they are truly parallel. Fundamentally, parallel forms of a test should be independently constructed tests designed to meet the same specifications. The tests should contain the same number of items, and the items should be expressed in the same form and should cover the same type of content. The range and level of difficulty of the items should also be equal. Instructions, time limits, illustrative examples, format, and all other aspects of the test must likewise be checked for comparability.

It should be added that the availability of parallel test forms is desirable for other reasons besides the determination of test reliability. Alternate forms are useful in follow-up studies or in investigations of the effects of some intervening experimental factor on test performance. The use of several alternate forms also provides a means of reducing the possibility of coaching or cheating.

Although much more widely applicable than test-retest reliability, alternate-form reliability also has certain limitations. In the first place, if the behavior functions under consideration are subject to a large practice effect, the use of alternate forms will reduce but not eliminate such an effect. To be sure, if all examinees were to show the same improvement with repetition, the correlation between their scores would remain unaffected, since adding a constant amount to each score does not alter the correlation coefficient. It is much more likely, however, that individuals will differ in amount of improvement, owing to extent of previous practice with similar material, motivation in taking the test, and other factors. Under these conditions, the practice effect represents another source of variance that will tend to reduce the correlation between the two test forms. If the practice effect is small, reduction will be negligible.

Another related question concerns the degree to which the nature of the test will change with repetition. In certain types of ingenuity problems, for example, any item involving the same principle can be readily solved by most persons once they have worked out the solution to the first. In such a case, changing the specific content of the items in the second form would not suffice to eliminate this carry-over from the first form. Finally, it should be added that alternate forms are unavailable for many tests, because of the practical difficulties of constructing comparable forms. For all these reasons, other techniques for estimating test reliability are often required.

SPLIT-HALF RELIABILITY. From a single administration of one form of 'a test it is possible to arrive at a measure of reliability by various split-half procedures. In such a way, two scores are obtained for each person by dividing the test into comparable halves. It is apparent that split-half reliability provides a measure of consistency with regard to content sampling. Temporal stability of the scores does not enter into such reliability, because only one test session is involved. This type of reliability coefficient is sometimes called a coefficient of internal consistency, since only a single administration of a single form is required.

To find split-half reliability, the first problem is how to split the test in order to obtain the most nearly comparable halves. Any test can be divided in many different ways. In most tests, the first half and the second half would not be comparable, owing to differences in nature and difficulty level of items, as well as to the cumulative effects of warming up, practice, fatigue, boredom, and any other factors varying progressively from the beginning to the end of the test. A procedure that is adequate for most purposes is to find the scores on the odd and even items of the test. If the items were originally arranged in an approximate order of difficulty, such a division yields very nearly equivalent half-scores. One precaution to be observed in making such an odd-even split pertains to groups of items dealing with a single problem, such as questions referring to a particular mechanical diagram or to a given passage in a reading test. In this case, a whole group of items should be assigned intact to one or the other half. Were the items in such a group to be placed in different halves of the test, the similarity of the half-scores would be spuriously inflated, since any single error in understanding of the problem might affect items in both halves.

Once the two half-scores have been obtained for each person, they may be correlated by the usual method. It should be noted, however, that this correlation actually gives the reliability of only a half-test. For example, if the entire test consists of 100 items, the correlation is computed between two sets of scores each of which is based on only 50 items. In both test-retest and alternate-form reliability, on the other hand, each score is based on the full number of items in the test.

Other things being equal, the longer a test, the more reliable it will be.[2] It is reasonable to expect that, with a larger sample of behavior, we can arrive at a more adequate and consistent measure. The effect that lengthening or shortening a test will have on its coefficient can be estimated by means of the Spearman-Brown formula, given below:

$$r_{nn} = \frac{nr_{tt}}{1 + (n-1)r_{tt}}$$

in which r_{nn} is the estimated coefficient, r_{tt} the obtained coefficient, and n is the number of times the test is lengthened or shortened. Thus, if the number of test items is increased from 25 to 100, n is 4; if it is decreased from 60 to 30, n is ½. The Spearman-Brown formula is widely used in determining reliability by the split-half method, many test manuals reporting reliability in this form. When applied to split-half reliability, the formula always involves doubling the length of the test. Under these conditions, it can be simplified as follows:

$$r_{tt} = \frac{2r_{hh}}{1 + r_{hh}}$$

in which r_{hh} is the correlation of the half-tests.

An alternate method for finding split-half reliability was developed by Rulon (1939). It requires only the variance of the *differences* between each person's scores on the two half-tests (SD_d^2) and the variance of total scores (SD_x^2); these two values are substituted in the following formula, which yields the reliability of the whole test directly:

$$r_{tt} = 1 - \frac{SD_d^2}{SD_x^2}$$

It is interesting to note the relationship of this formula to the definition of error variance. Any difference between a person's scores on the two half-tests represents chance error. The variance of these differences, divided by the variance of total scores, gives the proportion of error variance in the scores. When this error variance is subtracted from 1.00, it gives the proportion of "true" variance, which is equal to the reliability coefficient.

KUDER-RICHARDSON RELIABILITY AND COEFFICIENT ALPHA. A fourth method for finding reliability, also utilizing a single administration of a single form,

---

[2] Lengthening a test, however, will increase only its consistency in terms of content sampling, not its stability over time (see Cureton, 1965).

is based on the consistency of responses to all items in the test. This *interitem consistency* is influenced by two sources of error variance: (1) content sampling (as in alternate-form and split-half reliability); and (2) heterogeneity of the behavior domain sampled. The more homogeneous the domain, the higher the interitem consistency. For example, if one test includes only multiplication items, while another comprises addition, subtraction, multiplication, and division items, the former test will probably show more interitem consistency than the latter. In the latter, more heterogeneous test, one examinee may perform better in subtraction than in any of the other arithmetic operations; another examinee may score relatively well on the division items, but more poorly in addition, subtraction, and multiplication; and so on. A more extreme example would be represented by a test consisting of 40 vocabulary items, in contrast to one containing 10 vocabulary, 10 spatial relations, 10 arithmetic reasoning, and 10 perceptual speed items. In the latter test, there might be little or no relationship between an individual's performance on the different types of items.

It is apparent that test scores will be less ambiguous when derived from relatively homogeneous tests. Suppose that in the highly heterogeneous 40-item test cited above, Smith and Jones both obtain a score of 20. Can we conclude that the performances of the two on this test were equal? Not at all. Smith may have correctly completed 10 vocabulary items, 10 perceptual speed items, and none of the arithmetic reasoning and spatial relations items. In contrast, Jones may have received a score of 20 by the successful completion of 5 perceptual speed, 5 spatial relations, 10 arithmetic reasoning, and no vocabulary items.

Many other combinations could obviously produce the same total score of 20. This score would have a very different meaning when obtained through such dissimilar combinations of items. In the relatively homogeneous vocabulary test, on the other hand, a score of 20 would probably mean that the examinee had succeeded with approximately the first 20 words, if the items were arranged in ascending order of difficulty. He or she might have failed two or three easier words and correctly responded to two or three more difficult items beyond the 20th, but such individual variations are slight in comparison with those found in a more heterogeneous test.

A highly relevant question in this connection is whether the criterion that the test is trying to predict is itself relatively homogeneous or heterogeneous. Although homogeneous tests are to be preferred because their scores permit fairly unambiguous interpretation, a single homogeneous test is obviously not an adequate predictor of a highly heterogeneous criterion. Moreover, in the prediction of a heterogeneous criterion, the heterogeneity of test items would not necessarily represent error variance. Traditional intelligence tests provide a good example of heterogeneous tests designed to predict heterogeneous criteria. In such a case, however, it may be desirable to construct several relatively homogeneous tests, each measuring a different phase of the heterogeneous criterion. Thus, unambiguous interpretation of test scores could be combined with adequate criterion coverage.

The most common procedure for finding interitem consistency is that developed by Kuder and Richardson (1937). As in the split-half methods, interitem consistency is found from a single administration of a single test. Rather than requiring two half-scores, however, this technique is based on an examination of performance on each item. Of the various formulas derived in the original article, the most widely applicable, commonly known as "Kuder-Richardson formula 20," is the following:

$$r_{tt} = \left(\frac{n}{n-1} \right) \frac{SD_t^2 - \Sigma pq}{SD_t^2}$$

In this formula, r_{tt} is the reliability coefficient of the whole test, n is the number of items in the test, and SD_t the standard deviation of total scores on the test. The only new term in this formula, Σpq, is found by tabulating the proportion of persons who pass (p) and the proportion who do not pass (q) each item. The product of p and q is computed for each item, and these products are then added for all items, to give Σpq. Since in the process of test construction p is often routinely recorded in order to find the difficulty level of each item, this method of determining reliability involves little additional computation.

It can be shown mathematically that the Kuder-Richardson reliability coefficient is actually the mean of all split-half coefficients resulting from different splittings of a test (Cronbach, 1951).[3] The ordinary split-half coefficient, on the other hand, is based on a planned split designed to yield equivalent sets of items. Hence, unless the test items are highly homogeneous, the Kuder-Richardson coefficient will be lower than the split-half reliability. An extreme example will serve to highlight the difference. Suppose we construct a 50-item test out of 25 different kinds of items such that items 1 and 2 are vocabulary items, items 3 and 4 arithmetic reasoning, items 5 and 6 spatial orientation, and so on. The odd and even scores on this test could theoretically agree quite closely, thus yielding a high split-half reliability coefficient. The homogeneity of this test, however, would be very low, since there would be little consistency of performance among the entire set of 50 items. In this example, we would expect the Kuder-Richardson reliability to be much lower than the split-half reliability. It can be seen that the difference between Kuder-Richardson and split-half reliability coefficients may serve as a rough index of the heterogeneity of a test.

The Kuder-Richardson formula is applicable to tests whose items are scored as right or wrong, or according to some other all-or-none system.

[3] This is strictly true only when the split-half coefficients are found by the Rulon formula, not when they are found by correlation of halves and Spearman-Brown formula (Novick & Lewis, 1967).

Some tests, however, may have multiple-scored items. On a personality inventory, for example, the respondent may receive a different numerical score on an item, depending on whether he or she checks "usually," "sometimes," "rarely," or "never." For such tests, a generalized formula has been derived, known as coefficient alpha (Cronbach, 1951; Kaiser & Michael, 1975; Novick & Lewis, 1967). In this formula, the value Σpq is replaced by $\Sigma(SD_i^2)$, the sum of the variances of item scores. The procedure is to find the variance of all individuals' scores for each item and then to add these variances across all items. The complete formula for coefficient alpha is given below:

$$r_{tt} = \left(\frac{n}{n-1}\right)\frac{SD_t^2 - \Sigma(SD_i^2)}{SD_t^2}$$

A clear description of the computational layout for finding coefficient alpha can be found in Ebel (1965, pp. 328–330).

SCORER RELIABILITY. It should now be apparent that the different types of reliability vary in the factors they subsume under error variance. In one case, error variance covers temporal fluctuations; in another, it refers to differences between sets of parallel items; and in still another, it includes any interitem inconsistency. On the other hand, the factors *excluded* from measures of error variance are broadly of two types: (*a*) those factors whose variance should remain in the scores, since they are part of the true differences under consideration; and (*b*) those irrelevant factors that can be experimentally controlled. For example, it is not customary to report the error of measurement resulting when a test is administered under distracting conditions or with a longer or shorter time limit than that specified in the manual. Timing errors and serious distractions can be empirically eliminated from the testing situation. Hence, it is not necessary to report special reliability coefficients corresponding to "distraction variance" or "timing variance."

Similarly, most tests provide such highly standardized procedures for administration and scoring that error variance attributable to these factors is negligible. This is particularly true of group tests designed for mass testing and computer scoring. With such instruments, we need only to make certain that the prescribed procedures are carefully followed and adequately checked. With clinical instruments employed in intensive individual examinations, on the other hand, there is evidence of considerable "examiner variance." Through special experimental designs, it is possible to separate this variance from that attributable to temporal fluctuations in the examinee's condition or to the use of alternate test forms.

One source of error variance that can be checked quite simply is scorer variance. Certain types of tests—notably tests of creativity and projective tests of personality—leave a good deal to the judgment of the scorer. With such tests, there is as much need for a measure of scorer reliability as there is for the more usual reliability coefficients. Scorer reliability can be found by having a sample of test papers independently scored by two examiners. The two scores thus obtained by each examinee are then correlated in the usual way, and the resulting correlation coefficient is a measure of scorer reliability. This type of reliability is commonly computed when subjectively scored instruments are employed in research. Test manuals should also re-port it when appropriate.

OVERVIEW. The different types of reliability coefficients discussed in this section are summarized in Tables 8 and 9. In Table 8, the operations fol-

TABLE 8
Techniques for Measuring Reliability, in Relation to Test Form and Testing Session

Testing Sessions Required	Test Forms Required	
	One	Two
One	Split-Half Kuder-Richardson	Alternate-Form (Immediate)
Two	Test-Retest	Alternate-Form (Delayed)

lowed in obtaining each type of reliability are classified with regard to number of test forms and number of testing sessions required. Table 9 shows the sources of variance treated as error variance by each procedure.

TABLE 9
Sources of Error Variance in Relation to Reliability Coefficients

Type of Reliability Coefficient	Error Variance
Test-Retest	Time sampling
Alternate-Form (Immediate)	Content sampling
Alternate-Form (Delayed)	Time sampling and content sampling
Split-Half	Content sampling
Kuder-Richardson and Coefficient Alpha	Content sampling and content heterogeneity
Scorer	Interscorer differences

Any reliability coefficient may be interpreted directly in terms of the *percentage of score variance* attributable to different sources. Thus, a reliability coefficient of .85 signifies that 85% of the variance in test scores depends on true variance in the trait measured, and 15% depends on error variance (as operationally defined by the specific procedure followed). The statistically sophisticated reader may recall that it is the *square* of a correlation coefficient that represents proportion of common variance. Actually, the proportion of true variance in test scores is the square of the correlation between scores on a single form of the test and true scores, free from chance errors. This correlation, known as the index of reliability,[4] is equal to the square root of the reliability coefficient ($\sqrt{r_{tt}}$). When the index of reliability is squared, the result is the reliability coefficient (r_{tt}), which can therefore be interpreted directly as the percentage of true variance.

Experimental designs that yield more than one type of reliability coefficient for the same group permit the analysis of total score variance into different components. Let us consider the following hypothetical example. Forms A and B of a creativity test have been administered with a two-month interval to 100 sixth-grade children. The resulting alternate-form reliability is .70. From the responses on either form, a split-half reliability coefficient can also be computed.[5] This coefficient, stepped up by the Spearman-Brown formula, is .80. Finally, a second scorer has rescored a random sample of 50 papers, from which a scorer reliability of .92 is obtained. The three reliability coefficients can now be analyzed to yield the error variances shown in Table 10 and Figure 11. It will be noted that by subtracting the

TABLE 10
Analysis of Sources of Error Variance in a Hypothetical Test

From delayed alternate-form reliability: $\quad 1 - .70 = .30$ (time sampling plus content sampling)

From split-half, Spearman-Brown reliability: $\quad 1 - .80 = .20^*$ (content sampling)

Difference $\quad .10^*$ (time sampling)

From scorer reliability: $\quad 1 - .92 = .08^*$ (interscorer difference)

Total Measured Error Variance* $= .20 + .10 + .08 = .38$
True Variance $= 1 - .38 = .62$

[4] Derivations of the index of reliability, based on two different sets of assumptions, are given by Gulliksen (1950, Chs. 2 and 3).
[5] For a better estimate of the coefficient of internal consistency, split-half correlations could be computed for each form and the two coefficients averaged by the appropriate statistical procedures.

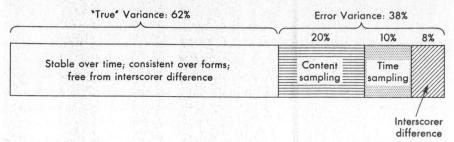

FIG. 11. Percentage Distribution of Score Variance in a Hypothetical Test.

error variance attributable to content sampling alone (split-half reliability) from the error variance attributable to both content and time sampling (alternate-form reliability), we find that .10 of the variance can be attributed to time sampling alone. Adding the error variances attributable to content sampling (.20), time sampling (.10), and interscorer difference (.08) gives a total error variance of .38 and hence a true variance of .62. These proportions, expressed in the more familiar percentage terms, are shown graphically in Figure 11.

RELIABILITY OF SPEEDED TESTS

Both in test construction and in the interpretation of test scores, an important distinction is that between the measurement of speed and of power. A pure *speed test* is one in which individual differences depend entirely on speed of performance. Such a test is constructed from items of uniformly low difficulty, all of which are well within the ability level of the persons for whom the test is designed. The time limit is made so short that no one can finish all the items. Under these conditions, each person's score reflects only the speed with which he or she worked. A pure *power test,* on the other hand, has a time limit long enough to permit everyone to attempt all items. The difficulty of the items is steeply graded, and the test includes some items too difficult for anyone to solve, so that no one can get a perfect score.

It will be noted that both speed and power tests are designed to prevent the achievement of perfect scores. The reason for such a precaution is that perfect scores are indeterminate, since it is impossible to know how much higher the individual's score would have been if more items, or more difficult items, had been included. To enable each individual to show fully what she or he is able to accomplish, the test must provide adequate ceiling, either in number of items or in difficulty level. An exception to this rule is found in mastery testing, as illustrated by the criterion-referenced tests discussed in Chapter 4. The purpose of such testing is not to establish the limits of what the individual can do, but to determine whether a preestablished performance level has or has not been reached.

In actual practice, the distinction between speed and power tests is one of degree, most tests depending on both power and speed in varying proportions. Information about these proportions is needed for each test in order not only to understand what the test measures but also to choose the proper procedures for evaluating its reliability. Single-trial reliability coefficients, such as those found by odd-even or Kuder-Richardson techniques, are inapplicable to speeded tests. To the extent that individual differences in test scores depend on speed of performance, reliability coefficients found by these methods will be spuriously high. An extreme example will help to clarify this point. Let us suppose that a 50-item test depends entirely on speed, so that individual differences in score are based wholly on number of items attempted, rather than on errors. Then, if individual A obtains a score of 44, he will obviously have 22 correct odd items and 22 correct even items. Similarly, individual B, with a score of 34, will have odd and even scores of 17 and 17, respectively. Consequently, except for accidental careless errors on a few items, the correlation between odd and even scores would be perfect, or +1.00. Such a correlation, however, is entirely spurious and provides no information about the reliability of the test.

An examination of the procedures followed in finding both split-half and Kuder-Richardson reliability will show that both are based on the consistency in *number of errors* made by the examinee. If, now, individual differences in test scores depend, not on errors, but on speed, the measure of reliability must obviously be based on consistency in *speed of work*. When test performance depends on a combination of speed and power, the single-trial reliability coefficient will fall below 1.00, but it will still be spuriously high. As long as individual differences in test scores are appreciably affected by speed, single-trial reliability coefficients cannot be properly interpreted.

What alternative procedures are available to determine the reliability of significantly speeded tests? If the test-retest technique is applicable, it would be appropriate. Similarly, equivalent-form reliability may be properly employed with speed tests. Split-half techniques may also be used, provided that the split is made in terms of time rather than in terms of items. In other words, the half-scores must be based on separately timed parts of the test. One way of effecting such a split is to administer two equivalent halves of the test with separate time limits. For example, the odd and even items may be separately printed on different pages, and each set of items given with one-half the time limit of the entire test. Such a procedure is tantamount to administering two equivalent forms of the test in immediate succession. Each form, however, is half as long as the test proper, while the examinees' scores are normally based on the whole test. For this reason, either the Spearman-Brown or some other appropriate formula should be used to find the reliability of the whole test.

If it is not feasible to administer the two half-tests separately, an alternative procedure is to divide the total time into quarters, and to find a score for each of the four quarters. This can easily be done by having the examinees mark the item on which they are working whenever the examiner gives a prearranged signal. The number of items correctly completed within the first and fourth quarters can then be combined to represent one half-score, while those in the second and third quarters can be combined to yield the other half-score. Such a combination of quarters tends to balance out the cumulative effects of practice, fatigue, and other factors. This method is especially satisfactory when the items are not steeply graded in difficulty level.

When is a test appreciably speeded? Under what conditions must the special precautions discussed in this section be observed? Obviously, the mere employment of a time limit does not signify a speed test. If all examinees finish within the given time limit, speed of work plays no part in determining the scores. Percentage of persons who fail to complete the test might be taken as a crude index of speed versus power. Even when no one finishes the test, however, the role of speed may be negligible. For example, if everyone completes exactly 40 items of a 50-item test, individual differences with regard to speed are entirely absent, although no one had time to attempt all the items.

The essential question, of course, is: "To what extent are individual differences in test scores attributable to speed?" In more technical terms, we want to know what proportion of the total variance of test scores is speed variance. This proportion can be estimated roughly by finding the variance of number of items completed by different persons and dividing it by the variance of total test scores (SD_c^2 / SD_t^2). In the example cited above, in which every individual finishes 40 items, the numerator of this fraction would be zero, since there are no individual differences in number of items completed ($SD_c^2 = 0$). The entire index would thus equal zero in a pure power test. On the other hand, if the total test variance (SD_t^2) is attributable to individual differences in speed, the two variances will be equal and the ratio will be 1.00. Several more refined procedures have been developed for determining this proportion, but their detailed consideration falls beyond the scope of this book.

An example of the effect of speed on single-trial reliability coefficients is provided by data collected in an investigation of the first edition of the SRA Tests of Primary Mental Abilities for Ages 11 to 17 (Anastasi & Drake, 1954). In this study, the reliability of each test was first determined by the usual odd-even procedure. These coefficients are given in the first row of Table 11. Reliability coefficients were then computed by correlating scores on separately timed halves. These coefficients are shown in the second row of Table 11. Calculation of speed indexes showed that the Verbal Meaning test was primarily a power test, while the Reasoning test was somewhat more dependent on speed. The Space and Number tests proved to be highly

TABLE 11
Reliability Coefficients of Four of the SRA Tests of Primary Mental
Abilities for Ages 11 to 17 (1st Edition)

(Data from Anastasi & Drake, 1954)

Reliability Coefficient Found by:	Verbal Meaning	Reasoning	Space	Number
Single-trial odd-even method	.94	.96	.90	.92
Separately timed halves	.90	.87	.75	.83

speeded. It will be noted in Table 11 that, when properly computed, the reliability of the Space test is .75, in contrast to a spuriously high odd-even coefficient of .90. Similarly, the reliability of the Reasoning test drops from .96 to .87, and that of the Number test drops from .92 to .83. The reliability of the relatively unspeeded Verbal Meaning test, on the other hand, shows a negligible difference when computed by the two methods.

DEPENDENCE OF RELIABILITY COEFFICIENTS ON THE SAMPLE TESTED

VARIABILITY. An important factor influencing the size of a reliability coefficient is the nature of the group on which reliability is measured. In the first place, any correlation coefficient is affected by the range of individual differences in the group. If every member of a group were nearly alike in spelling ability, then the correlation of spelling with any other ability would be close to zero in that group. It would obviously be impossible, within such a group, to predict an individual's standing in any other ability from a knowledge of her or his spelling score.

Another, less extreme, example is provided by the correlation between two aptitude tests, such as a verbal comprehension and an arithmetic reasoning test. If these tests were administered to a highly homogeneous sample, such as a group of 300 college sophomores, the correlation between the two would probably be very low. Because of restriction of range, there is little relationship, within such a selected sample of college students, between any individual's verbal ability and his or her numerical reasoning ability. On the other hand, were the tests to be given to a heterogeneous sample of 300 persons, ranging from mental retardates to college graduates, a high correlation would undoubtedly be obtained between the two tests. The mentally retarded would obtain poorer scores than the college graduates on *both* tests, and similar relationships would hold for other subgroups within this highly heterogeneous sample.

Examination of the hypothetical scatter diagram given in Figure 12 will

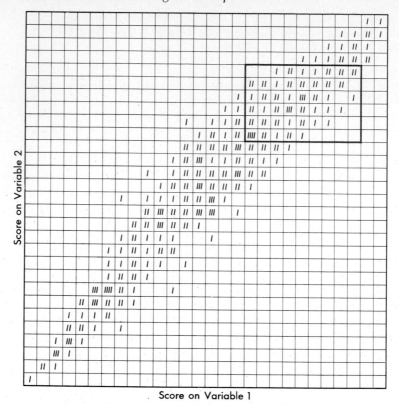

FIG. 12. The effect of Restricted Range upon a Correlation Coefficient.

further illustrate the dependence of correlation coefficients on the variability, or extent of individual differences, within the group. This scatter diagram shows a high positive correlation in the entire, heterogeneous group, since the entries are closely clustered about the diagonal extending from lower left- to upper right-hand corners. If, now, we consider only the subgroup falling within the small rectangle in the upper right-hand portion of the diagram, it is apparent that the correlation between the two variables is close to zero. Individuals falling within this restricted range in both variables represent a highly homogeneous group, as did the college sophomores mentioned above.

Like all correlation coefficients, reliability coefficients depend on the variability of the sample within which they are found. Thus, if the reliability coefficient reported in a test manual was determined in a group ranging from fourth-grade children to high school students, it cannot be assumed that the reliability would be equally high within, let us say, an eighth-grade sample. When a test is to be used to discriminate individual differences within a more homogeneous sample than the standardization group, the reliability coefficient should be redetermined on such a sample. Formulas for estimating the reliability coefficient to be expected when the standard deviation of the group is increased or decreased are available in elementary statistics textbooks. It is preferable, however, to recompute the reliability coefficient empirically on a group comparable to that on which the test is to be used. For tests designed to cover a wide range of age or ability, the test manual should report separate reliability coefficients for relatively homogeneous subgroups within the standardization sample.

ABILITY LEVEL. Not only does the reliability coefficient vary with the extent of individual differences in the sample, but it may also vary between groups differing in average ability level. These differences, moreover, cannot usually be predicted or estimated by any statistical formula but can be discovered only by empirical tryout of the test on groups differing in age or ability level. Such differences in the reliability of a single test may arise in part from the fact that a slightly different combination of abilities is measured at different difficulty levels of the test. Or it may result from the statistical properties of the scale itself, as in the Stanford-Binet (Pinneau, 1961, Ch. 5). Thus, for different ages and for different IQ levels, the reliability coefficient of the Stanford-Binet varies from .83 to .98. In other tests, reliability may be relatively low for the younger and less able groups, since their scores are unduly influenced by guessing. Under such circumstances, the particular test should not be employed at these levels.

It is apparent that every reliability coefficient should be accompanied by a full description of the type of group on which it was determined. Special attention should be given to the variability and the ability level of the sample. The reported reliability coefficient is applicable only to samples similar to that on which it was computed. A desirable and growing practice in test construction is to fractionate the standardization sample into more homogeneous subgroups, with regard to age, sex, grade level, occupation, and the like, and to report separate reliability coefficients for each subgroup. Under these conditions, the reliability coefficients are more likely to be applicable to the samples with which the test is to be used in actual practice.

STANDARD ERROR OF MEASUREMENT

INTERPRETATION OF INDIVIDUAL SCORES. The reliability of a test may be expressed in terms of the standard error of measurement ($\sigma_{meas.}$), also called the standard error of a score. This measure is particularly well suited to the interpretation of individual scores. For many testing purposes, it is therefore more useful than the reliability coefficient. The standard error of measurement can be easily computed from the reliability coefficient of the test, by the following formula:

$$\sigma_{meas.} = SD_t\sqrt{1 - r_{tt}}$$

in which SD_t is the standard deviation of the test scores and r_{tt} the reliability coefficient, both computed on the same group. For example, if deviation IQs on a particular intelligence test have a standard deviation of 15 and a reliability coefficient of .89, the $\sigma_{meas.}$ of an IQ on this test is: $15\sqrt{1-.89} = 15\sqrt{.11} = 15(.33) = 5$.

To understand what the $\sigma_{meas.}$ tells us about a score, let us suppose that we had a set of 100 IQs obtained with the above test by a single child, Janet. Because of the types of chance errors discussed in this chapter, these scores vary, falling into a normal distribution around Janet's true score. The mean of this distribution of 100 scores can be taken as the true score and the standard deviation of the distribution can be taken as the $\sigma_{meas.}$. Like any standard deviation, this standard error can be interpreted in terms of the normal curve frequencies discussed in Chapter 4 (see Figure 3). It will be recalled that between the mean and $\pm 1\sigma$, there are approximately 68% of the cases in a normal curve. Thus, we can conclude that the chances are roughly 2:1 (or 68:32) that Janet's IQ on this test will fluctuate between $\pm 1\sigma_{meas.}$ or 5 points on either side of her true IQ. If her true IQ is 110, we would expect her to score between 105 and 115 about two-thirds (68%) of the time.

If we want to be more certain of our prediction, we can choose higher odds than 2:1. Reference to Figure 3 in Chapter 4 shows that $\pm 3\sigma$ covers 99.7% of the cases. It can be ascertained from normal curve frequency tables that a distance of 2.58σ on either side of the mean includes exactly 99% of the cases. Hence, the chances are 99:1 that Janet's IQ will fall within $2.58\sigma_{meas.}$, or $(2.58)(5) = 13$ points, on either side of her true IQ. We can thus state at the 99% confidence level (with only one chance of error out of 100) that Janet's IQ on any single administration of the test will lie between 97 and 123 $(110 - 13$ and $110 + 13)$. If Janet were given 100 equivalent tests, her IQ would fall outside this band of values only once.

In actual practice, of course, we do not have the true scores, but only the scores obtained in a single test administration. Under these circumstances, we can apply the above reasoning in the reverse direction. If an individual's obtained score is unlikely to deviate by more than $2.58\sigma_{meas.}$ from her true score, we could argue that her *true* score must lie within $2.58\sigma_{meas.}$ of her *obtained* score. Although we cannot assign a probability to this statement for any given obtained score, we *can* say that the statement would be correct for 99% of all the cases. On the basis of this reasoning Gulliksen (1950, pp. 17–20) proposed that the standard error of measurement be used as illustrated above to estimate the reasonable limits of the true score for persons with any given obtained score. It is in terms of such "reasonable limits" that the error of measurement is customarily interpreted in psychological testing and it will be so interpreted in this book.

The standard error of measurement and the reliability coefficient are obviously alternative ways of expressing test reliability. Unlike the reliability coefficient, the error of measurement is independent of the variability of the group on which it is computed. Expressed in terms of individual scores, it remains unchanged when found in a homogeneous or a heterogeneous group. On the other hand, being reported in score units, the error of measurement will not be directly comparable from test to test. The usual problems of comparability of units would thus arise when errors of measurement are reported in terms of arithmetic problems, words in a vocabulary test, and the like. Hence, if we want to compare the reliability of *different tests,* the reliability coefficient is the better measure. To interpret *individual scores,* the standard error of measurement is more appropriate.

Neither reliability coefficients nor errors of measurement, however, can be assumed to remain constant when *ability level* varies widely. The differences in reliability coefficients discussed in the preceding section remain when errors of measurement are computed at, for example, different age or ability levels of the Stanford-Binet. A comprehensive solution for this problem is provided by the latent trait models cited in Chapter 4. Spanning a wide ability range, these models offer a means of expressing the measurement accuracy of a test as a function of the level of ability. The procedure yields a *test information curve* which depends only on the items included in the test and permits an estimation of the error of measurement at each ability level.

INTERPRETATION OF SCORE DIFFERENCES. It is particularly important to consider test reliability and errors of measurement when evaluating the *differences* between two scores. Thinking in terms of the range within which each score may fluctuate serves as a check against overemphasizing small differences between scores. Such caution is desirable both when comparing test scores of different persons and when comparing the scores of the same individual in different abilities. Similarly, changes in scores following instruction or other experimental variables need to be interpreted in the light of errors of measurement.

A frequent question about test scores concerns the individual's relative standing in different areas. Is Doris more able along verbal than along numerical lines? Does Tom have more aptitude for mechanical than for verbal activities? If Doris scored higher on the verbal than on the numerical subtests on an aptitude battery and Tom scored higher on the mechanical than on the verbal, how sure can we be that they would still do so on a retest with another form of the battery? In other words, could the score differences have resulted merely from the chance selection of specific items in the particular verbal, numerical, and mechanical tests employed?

Because of the growing interest in the interpretation of score profiles, test publishers have been developing report forms that permit the evaluation of scores in terms of their errors of measurement. An example is the Individual Report Form for use with the Differential Aptitude Tests, reproduced in

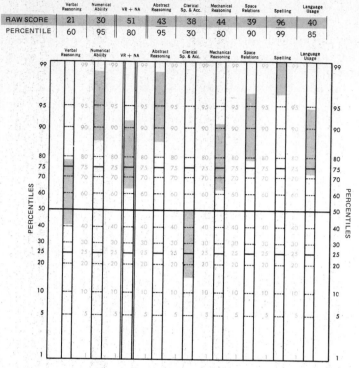

	Verbal Reasoning	Numerical Ability	VR + NA	Abstract Reasoning	Clerical Sp. & Acc.	Mechanical Reasoning	Space Relations	Spelling	Language Usage
RAW SCORE	21	30	51	43	38	44	39	96	40
PERCENTILE	60	95	80	95	30	80	90	99	85

FIG. 13. Score Profile on the Differential Aptitude Tests, Illustrating Use of Percentile Bands.

(Fig. 2, Fifth Edition Manual, p. 73. Reproduced by permission. Copyright © 1973, 1974 by The Psychological Corporation, New York, N.Y. All rights reserved.)

Figure 13. On this form, percentile scores on each subtest of the battery are plotted as one-inch bars, with the obtained percentile at the center. Each percentile bar corresponds to a distance of approximately 1½ to 2 standard errors on either side of the obtained score.[6] Hence the assumption that the individual's "true" score falls within the bar is correct about 90% of the time. In interpreting the profiles, test users are advised not to attach importance to differences between scores whose percentile bars overlap, especially if they overlap by more than half their length. In the profile illustrated in Figure 13, for example, the difference between the Verbal Reasoning and Numerical Ability scores probably reflects a genuine difference in ability level; that between Mechanical Reasoning and Space Relations probably does not; the difference between Abstract Reasoning and Mechanical Reasoning is in the doubtful range.

It is well to bear in mind that the standard error of the difference be-

---

[6] Because the reliability coefficient (and hence the $\sigma_{meas.}$) varies somewhat with subtest, grade, and sex, the actual ranges covered by the one-inch lines are not identical, but they are sufficiently close to permit uniform interpretations for practical purposes.

tween two scores is larger than the error of measurement of either of the two scores. This follows from the fact that this difference is affected by the chance errors present in *both* scores. The standard error of the difference between two scores can be found from the standard errors of measurement of the two scores by the following formula:[7]

$$\sigma_{diff.} = \sqrt{\sigma^2{}_{meas._1} + \sigma^2{}_{meas._2}}$$

in which $\sigma_{diff.}$ is the standard error of the difference between the two scores, and $\sigma_{meas._1}$ and $\sigma_{meas._2}$ are the standard errors of measurement of the separate scores. By substituting $SD\sqrt{1 - r_{11}}$ for $\sigma_{meas._1}$ and $SD\sqrt{1 - r_{22}}$ for $\sigma_{meas._2}$, we may rewrite the formula directly in terms of reliability coefficients, as follows.

$$\sigma_{diff.} = SD\sqrt{2 - r_{11} - r_{22}}$$

In this substitution, the same SD was used for tests 1 and 2, since their scores would have to be expressed in terms of the same scale before they could be compared.

We may illustrate the above procedure with the Verbal and Performance IQs on the Wechsler Adult Intelligence Scale—Revised (WAIS-R). The split-half reliabilities of these scores are .97 and .93, respectively. WAIS-R deviation IQs are expressed on a scale with a mean of 100 and an SD of 15. Hence the standard error of the difference between these two scores can be found as follows:

$$\sigma_{diff.} = 15\sqrt{2 - .97 - .93} = 4.74$$

To determine how large a score difference could be obtained by chance at the .05 level, we multiply the standard error of the difference (4.74) by 1.96. The result is 9.29, or approximately 10 points. Thus, the difference between an individual's WAIS-R Verbal and Performance IQ should be at least 10 points to be significant at the .05 level.[8]

RELIABILITY OF CRITERION-REFERENCED TESTS

It will be recalled from Chapter 4 that criterion-referenced tests usually (but not necessarily) evaluate performance in terms of mastery rather than degree of achievement. A major statistical implication of mastery testing is

[7] This formula should not be confused with the formula for the standard error of a difference between two *group means*, which includes a correlation term when the two variables to be compared are correlated. *Errors of measuremnt* in two variables are random errors and hence uncorrelated.

[8] More precise estimates can be obtained by using the actual reliabilities and SDs found within each age group. When thus computed, the minimum significant Verbal–Performance difference at the .05 level, as reported in the test manual, ranges from 8.83 to 12.04. Most of the values, however, are close to 10.

a reduction in variability of scores among persons. Theoretically, if everyone continues training until the skill is mastered, variability is reduced to zero. In an earlier section of this chapter, we saw that *any* correlation, including reliability coefficients, is affected by the variability of the group in which it is computed. As the variability of the sample decreases, so does the correlation coefficient. Obviously, then, it would be inappropriate to assess the reliability of most criterion-referenced tests by applying the usual procedures to a group of persons after they have reached the preestablished mastery level. Under these conditions, even a highly stable and internally consistent test could yield a reliability coefficient near zero.

This apparent difficulty in the assessment of reliability arises from a failure to consider what the criterion-referenced tests are designed to measure. In actual practice, these tests are used essentially to differentiate between those persons who have and those who have not acquired the skills and knowledge required for a designated activity. The specific purpose for which the test is administered may vary widely, from obtaining a driver's license or assignment to an occupational specialty to advancing to the next unit in an individualized instructional program or admission to a particular course of study. Nevertheless, in all such situations, the fact that a test is used at all implies the expectation of variability in performance among individuals. A major portion of this variability reflects individual differences in amount of prior training in the relevant functions.

It follows that available statistical techniques *can* be employed in assessing the reliability of criterion-referenced tests, provided they are applied to the appropriate data. And the appropriate data are the scores of persons with varying amounts of training. Thus, alternate-form or split-half reliability coefficients can be computed with the test scores of persons who have had different amounts of prior training. Such scores can be obtained at different stages in the course of an instructional program, including a preinstruction test, a postinstruction test, and tests administered at several intermediate points (Ebel, 1973; Shaycoft, 1979).

Other procedures can be applied to simple pass–fail (or mastery–nonmastery) scoring. For instance, in the use of criterion-referenced tests to identify persons ready for specific job assignments and those requiring further training, examinees can be tested twice within a short interval. To assess the consistency of results, we can find the percentage of persons for whom the same decision (pass or fail) is reached on both occasions (Berk, 1980, Part III; Hambleton & Novick, 1973; Panell & Laabs, 1979; Swezey & Perlstein, 1975). These data can be further evaluated by computing appropriate indexes of agreement and significance values. Among the measures that have been used for this purpose are the phi coefficient, chi square, and a more precise index, the kappa coefficient (J. Cohen, 1968; Panell & Laabs, 1979).

Chapter 6

Validity: Basic Concepts

T HE VALIDITY of a test concerns *what* the test measures and *how well* it does so. It tells us what can be inferred from test scores. In this connection, we should guard against accepting the test name as an index of what the test measures. Test names provide short, convenient labels for identification purposes. Most test names are far too broad and vague to furnish meaningful clues to the behavior area covered, although increasing efforts are being made to use more specific and operationally definable test names. The trait measured by a given test can be defined only through an examination of the objective sources of information and empirical operations utilized in establishing its validity (Anastasi, 1950). Moreover, the validity of a test cannot be reported in general terms. No test can be said to have "high" or "low" validity in the abstract. Its validity must be established with reference to the particular use for which the test is being considered.

Fundamentally, all procedures for determining test validity are concerned with the relationships between performance on the test and other independently observable facts about the behavior characteristics under consideration. The specific methods employed for investigating these relationships are numerous and have been described by various names. In the *Standards for Educational and Psychological Tests* (1974), these procedures are classified under three principal categories: content, criterion-related, and construct validity. Each of these types of validation procedures will be considered in one of the following sections, and the relations among them will be examined in a concluding section. Techniques for analyzing and interpreting validity data with reference to practical decisions will be discussed in Chapter 7.

CONTENT VALIDATION

NATURE. Content validation involves essentially the systematic examination of the test content to determine whether it covers a representative sample of the behavior domain to be measured. Such a validation procedure is commonly used in evaluating achievement tests. This type of test is designed to measure how well the individual has mastered a specific skill or course of study. It might seem that mere inspection of the content of the test should suffice to establish its validity for such a purpose. A test of multiplication, spelling, or bookkeeping would seem to be valid by definition if it consists of multiplication, spelling, or bookkeeping items, respectively.

The solution, however, is not so simple as it appears to be. One difficulty is that of adequately sampling the item universe. The behavior domain to be tested must be systematically analyzed to make certain that all major aspects are covered by the test items, and in the correct proportions. For example, a test can easily become overloaded with those aspects of the field that lend themselves more readily to the preparation of objective items. The domain under consideration should be fully described in advance, rather than being defined after the test has been prepared. A well-constructed achievement test should cover the objectives of instruction, not just its subject matter. Content must therefore be broadly defined to include major objectives, such as the application of principles and the interpretation of data, as well as factual knowledge. Moreover, content validity depends on the relevance of the individual's test responses to the behavior area under consideration, rather than on the apparent relevance of item content. Mere inspection of the test may fail to reveal the processes actually used by examinees in taking the test.

It is also important to guard against any tendency to overgeneralize regarding the domain sampled by the test. For instance, a multiple-choice spelling test may measure the ability to recognize correctly and incorrectly spelled words. But it cannot be assumed that such a test also measures ability to spell correctly from dictation, frequency of misspellings in written compositions, and other aspects of spelling ability (Ahlström, 1964; Knoell & Harris, 1952). Still another difficulty arises from the possible inclusion of irrelevant factors in the test scores. For example, a test designed to measure proficiency in mathematics or mechanics may be unduly influenced by the ability to understand verbal directions or by speed of performing simple, routine tasks.

SPECIFIC PROCEDURES. Content validity is built into a test from the outset through the choice of appropriate items. For educational tests, the preparation of items is preceded by a thorough and systematic examination of relevant course syllabi and textbooks, as well as by consultation with subject-matter experts. On the basis of the information thus gathered, *test specifications* are drawn up for the item writers. These specifications should show the content areas or topics to be covered, the instructional objectives or processes to be tested, and the relative importance of individual topics and processes. On this basis, the number of items of each kind to be prepared on each topic can be established. A convenient way to set up such specifications is in terms of a two-way table, with processes across the top and topics in the left-hand column (see Table 30, Ch. 14). Not all cells in such a table, of course, need to have items, since certain processes may be unsuitable or irrelevant for certain topics. It might be added that such a specification table will also prove helpful in the preparation of teacher-made examinations for classroom use in any subject.

The discussion of content validity in the manual of an educational achievement test should include a description of the procedures followed in ensuring that the test content is appropriate and representative. If subject-matter experts participated in the test-construction process, their number and professional qualifications should be stated. If they served as judges in classifying items, the directions they were given should be reported, as well as the extent of agreement among judges. Because curricula and course content change over time, it is particularly desirable to give the dates when subject-matter experts were consulted. Information should likewise be provided about number and nature of course syllabi and textbooks surveyed, including publication dates.

A number of empirical procedures are also commonly followed in order to supplement the content validation of an educational achievement test. Both total scores and performance on individual items can be checked for grade progress. In general, those items are retained that show the largest gains in the percentages of children passing them from the lower to the upper grades.

The end product of these test-development procedures consists of the items actually included in the final version of the test. The manual should provide information on the content areas and the skills or instructional objectives covered by the test, together with some indication of the number of items in each category. Figure 14 illustrates one way of reporting this information. It shows a portion of a table prepared for the third edition of the Sequential Tests of Educational Progress (STEP-III), a wide-range battery of educational achievement tests. The material reproduced in Figure 14 pertains to the Reading test for Levels G to J, which span Grades 5 through 12. Data are provided for two parallel forms, Form X and Form Y. In the upper section of the table, each item is listed by number in one of three reading skill categories, namely, vocabulary in context, literal comprehension, and inference. In the lower section, the same items are classified in eight content categories, such as narrative, poem, science, or newspaper article.

Other supplementary procedures that may be employed, when appropriate, include analyses of types of errors commonly made on a test and observation of the work methods employed by examinees. The latter could be done by testing students individually with instructions to "think aloud" while solving each problem. The contribution of speed can be checked by noting how many persons fail to finish the test or by one of the more refined methods discussed in Chapter 5. To detect the possible irrelevant influence of ability to read instructions on test performance, scores on the test can be correlated with scores on a reading comprehension test. On the other hand, if the test is designed to measure reading comprehension, giving the ques-

Reading Skill	Level G Form X	Level G Form Y	Level H Form X	Level H Form Y	Level I Form X	Level I Form Y	Level J Form X	Level J Form Y
A. Vocabulary in Context	13,16,22 28-35,40 42,45,49 50	11,15,20 21,25 28-35,44 47,50	5,7,10 14,15,22 28-35,36 46	9,12,15 23,24 28-35 36,48,49	1,11,20-24 30,33-36 38,42,44 50	1,13,14,17 24,26,29 30,35,40 41,44,45 47,49,50	1,3,7,9 15,16,19 20,22,25 29,33,35 37,45,47	5,6,9,10 12,14,15 17,19,20 22,27,28 31,43,49
B. Literal Comprehension	2-4,15 17-19,23 24,27,37 41,43 46-48	2,6,7,17 18,23,24 26,36,38 41-43,45 46,48	2,6,8 11-13,21 23-26,37 38,41,42 47	1,3,6-8 10,11,13 16,17,37 38,43-46	2,3,6,7 12,16,18 25,26,31 32,39,41 43,47,48	2,3,8-11 16,19,21 28,31,33 34,39,42 48	4,6,8,12 13,17,18 21,24, 26-28,30 32,34,46	4,7,13,16 18,21,25 29,33, 37-40 45-47
C. Inference	1,5-12 14,20,21 25,26,36 38,39,44	1,3-5 8-10 12-14,16 19,22,27 37,39,40 49	1,3,4,9 16-20,27 39,40 43-45 48-50	2,4,5,14 18-22, 25-27 39-42,47 50	4,5,8-10 13-15,17 19,27-29 37,40,45 46,49	4-7,12 15,18,20 22,23,25 27,32 36-38,43 46	2,5,10,11 14,23,31 36,38-44 48-50	1-3,8,11 23,24,26 30-32 34-36,41 42,44,48 50
Content Area *(Item Numbers)*								
1. Narrative	41-45	45-50	6-10	10-15 16-22	41-46	30-35	37-43	6-11
2. Social Science	16-21 36-40	40-44 22-27	1-5 16-21	5-9	29-35 22-28	23-29 41-45	6-10	31-37
3. Poem	5-11	6-11	46-50	23-27	11-15	46-50	11-15	38-43
4. Play	12-15	12-15	22-27	47-50	47-50	12-15	30-36	12-15
5. Science	22-27	16-21	41-45	41-46	6-10	6-11	16-22	16-23
6. Practical	1-4 46-50	1-5 36-39	11-15	1-4	16-21 36-40	16-22 36-40	1-5 23-29	1-5 24-30
7. Newspaper Article			36-40	36-40	1-5	1-5		
8. Humanities							44-50	44-50

Fig. 14. Data on Content Validity, as Illustrated by a Portion of Content Description Table from STEP-III, Reading Tests, Levels G to J, Grades 5–12. (From *STEP: Test Development and Content Description*, p. 13. Copyright © 1978 by Educational Testing Service. Reprinted by permission.)

134

tions without the reading passage on which they are based will show how many could be answered simply from the examinees' prior information or other irrelevant cues (Scherich & Hanna, 1977).

APPLICATIONS. Especially when bolstered by such empirical checks as those illustrated above, content validation provides an adequate technique for evaluating achievement tests. It permits us to answer two questions that are basic to the validity of educational and occupational achievement tests: (1) Does the test cover a representative sample of the specified skills and knowledge? (2) Is test performance reasonably free from the influence of irrelevant variables? Content validation is particularly appropriate for the criterion-referenced tests described in Chapter 4. Because performance on those tests is interpreted in terms of content meaning, it is obvious that content validation is a prime requirement for their effective use.

Content validation is also applicable to certain occupational tests designed for employee selection and classification, to be discussed in Chapter 15. This type of validation is suitable when the test is an actual job sample or otherwise calls for the same skills and knowledge required on the job. In such cases, a thorough job analysis should be carried out in order to demonstrate the close resemblance between the job activities and the test. A clear, step-by-step account of the application of these validation procedures to the development of an industrial reading test is given by Schoenfeldt, Schoenfeldt, Acker, and Perlson (1976). Working closely with job incumbents and supervisors, the investigators surveyed the reading requirements of entry-level jobs in a large manufacturing company in terms of both subject matter and comprehension skills. Test items were then constructed to match these requirements. This approach is used widely in developing tests for government employees at federal and state levels (Hardt, Eyde, Primoff, & Tordy, 1981; Menne, McCarthy, & Menne, 1976; Primoff, 1975; Tordy, Eyde, Primoff, & Hardt, 1976).

For aptitude and personality tests, on the other hand, content validation is usually inappropriate and may, in fact, be misleading. Although considerations of relevance and representativeness of content must obviously enter into the initial stages of constructing any test, eventual validation of aptitude or personality tests requires empirical verification by the procedures to be described in the following sections. These tests bear less intrinsic resemblance to the behavior domain they are trying to sample than do achievement tests. Consequently, the content of aptitude and personality tests can do little more than reveal the hypotheses that led the test constructor to choose a certain type of content for measuring a specified trait. Such hypotheses need to be empirically confirmed to establish the validity of the test.

Unlike achievement tests, aptitude and personality tests are not based on a specified course of instruction or uniform set of prior experiences from which test content can be drawn. Hence, in the latter tests, individuals are likely to vary more in the work methods or psychological processes employed in responding to the same test items. The identical test might thus measure different functions in different persons. Under these conditions, it would be virtually impossible to determine the psychological functions measured by the test from an inspection of its content. For example, college graduates might solve a problem in verbal or mathematical terms, while a mechanic would arrive at the same solution in terms of spatial visualization. Or a test measuring arithmetic reasoning among high school freshmen might measure only individual differences in speed of computation when given to college students.

FACE VALIDITY. Content validity should not be confused with face validity. The latter is not validity in the technical sense; it refers, not to what the test actually measures, but to what it appears superficially to measure. Face validity pertains to whether the test "looks valid" to the examinees who take it, the administrative personnel who decide on its use, and other technically untrained observers. Fundamentally, the question of face validity concerns rapport and public relations. Although common usage of the term validity in this connection may make for confusion, face validity itself is a desirable feature of tests. For example, when tests originally designed for children and developed within a classroom setting were first extended for adult use, they frequently met with resistance and criticism because of their lack of face validity. Certainly if test content appears irrelevant, inappropriate, silly, or childish, the result will be poor cooperation, regardless of the actual validity of the test. Especially in adult testing, it is not sufficient for a test to be objectively valid. It also needs face validity to function effectively in practical situations.

Face validity can often be improved by merely reformulating test items in terms that appear relevant and plausible in the particular setting in which they will be used. For example, if a test of simple arithmetic reasoning is constructed for use with machinists, the items should be worded in terms of machine operations rather than in terms of "how many oranges can be purchased for 86 cents" or other traditional schoolbook problems. Similarly, an arithmetic test for naval personnel can be expressed in naval terminology, without necessarily altering the functions measured. To be sure, face validity should never be regarded as a substitute for objectively determined validity. It cannot be assumed that improving the face validity of a test will improve its objective validity. Nor can it be assumed that when a test is modified so as to increase its face validity, its objective validity remains unaltered. The validity of the test in its final form should always be directly checked.

CRITERION-RELATED VALIDATION

Criterion-related validation procedures indicate the effectiveness of a test in predicting an individual's behavior in specified situations. For this purpose, performance on the test is checked against a *criterion,* i.e., a direct and independent measure of that which the test is designed to predict. Thus, for a mechanical aptitude test, the criterion might be subsequent job performance as a machinist; for a scholastic aptitude test, it might be college grades; and for a neuroticism test, it might be associates' ratings or other available information regarding the individual's behavior in various life situations.

CONCURRENT AND PREDICTIVE VALIDATION. The criterion measure against which test scores are validated may be obtained at approximately the same time as the test scores or after a stated interval. The APA test *Standards* (1974) differentiate between concurrent and predictive validity on the basis of these time relations between criterion and test. The term "prediction" can be used in the broader sense, to refer to prediction from the test to any criterion situation, or in the more limited sense of prediction over a time interval. It is in the latter sense that it is used in the expression "predictive validity." The information provided by predictive validation is most relevant to tests used in the selection and classification of personnel. Hiring job applicants, selecting students for admission to college or professional schools, and assigning military personnel to occupational training programs represent examples of the sort of decisions requiring a knowledge of the predictive validity of tests. Other examples include the use of tests to screen out applicants likely to develop emotional disorders in stressful environments and the use of tests to identify psychiatric patients most likely to benefit from a particular therapy.

In a number of instances, concurrent validation is employed merely as a substitute for predictive validation. It is frequently impracticable to extend validation procedures over the time required for predictive validation or to obtain a suitable preselection sample for testing purposes. As a compromise solution, therefore, tests are administered to a group on whom criterion data are already available. Thus, the test scores of college students may be compared with their cumulative grade-point average at the time of testing, or those of employees compared with their current job success.

For certain uses of psychological tests, on the other hand, concurrent validation is the most appropriate type and can be justified in its own right. The logical distinction between predictive and concurrent validation is based, not on time, but on the objectives of testing. Concurrent validation is relevant to tests employed for *diagnosis* of existing status, rather than prediction of future outcomes. The difference can be illustrated by asking:

"Is Smith neurotic?" (concurrent validation) and "Is Smith likely to become neurotic?" (predictive validation).

Because the criterion for concurrent validation is always available at the time of testing, we might ask what function is served by the test in such situations. Basically, such tests provide a simpler, quicker, or less expensive substitute for the criterion data. For example, if the criterion consists of continuous observation of a patient during a two-week hospitalization period, a test that could sort out normals from neurotic and doubtful cases would appreciably reduce the number of persons requiring such extensive observation.

CRITERION CONTAMINATION. An essential precaution in finding the validity of a test is to make certain that the test scores do not themselves influence any individual's criterion status. For example, if a college instructor or a supervisor in an industrial plant knows that a particular individual scored very poorly on an aptitude test, such knowledge might influence the grade given to the student or the rating assigned to the worker. Or a high-scoring person might be given the benefit of the doubt when academic grades or on-the-job ratings are being prepared. Such influences would obviously raise the correlation between test scores and criterion in a manner that is entirely spurious or artificial.

This possible source of error in test validation is known as criterion contamination, since the criterion ratings become "contaminated" by the rater's knowledge of the test scores. To prevent the operation of such an error, it is absolutely essential that no person who participates in the assignment of criterion ratings have any knowledge of the examinees' test scores. For this reason, test scores employed in "testing the test" must be kept strictly confidential. It is sometimes difficult to convince teachers, employers, military officers, and other line personnel that such a precaution is essential. In their urgency to utilize all available information for practical decisions, such persons may fail to realize that the test scores must be put aside until the criterion data mature and validity can be checked.

COMMON CRITERIA. A test may be validated against as many criteria as there are specific uses for it. Any method for assessing behavior in any situation could provide a criterion measure for some particular purpose. The criteria employed in finding the validities reported in test manuals, however, fall into a few common categories. Among the criteria most frequently employed in validating intelligence tests is some index of *academic achievement*. It is for this reason that such tests have often been more precisely described as measures of scholastic aptitude. The specific indices used as criterion measures include school grades, achievement test scores, promotion and graduation records, special honors and awards, and teachers' or instructors' ratings for "intelligence." Insofar as such ratings given within an academic setting are likely to be heavily colored by the individual's scholastic performance, they may be properly classified with the criterion of academic achievement.

The various indices of academic achievement have provided criterion data at all educational levels, from the primary grades to college and graduate school. Although employed principally in the validation of general intelligence tests, they have also served as criteria for certain multiple-aptitude and personality tests. In the validation of any of these types of tests for use in the selection of college students, for example, a common criterion is freshman grade-point average. This measure is the average grade in all courses taken during the freshman year, each grade being weighted by the number of course points for which it was received.

A variant of the criterion of academic achievement frequently employed with out-of-school adults is the amount of education the individual completed. It is expected that in general the more intelligent individuals continue their education longer, while the less intelligent drop out of school earlier. The assumption underlying this criterion is that the educational ladder serves as a progressively selective influence, eliminating those incapable of continuing beyond each step. Although it is undoubtedly true that college graduates, for example, represent a more highly selected group than elementary school graduates, the relation between amount of education and scholastic aptitude is far from perfect. Especially at the higher educational levels, economic, social, motivational, and other nonintellectual factors may influence the continuation of the individual's education. Moreover, with such concurrent validation, it is difficult to disentangle cause-and-effect relations. To what extent are the obtained differences in intelligence test scores simply the result of the varying amount of education? And to what extent could the test have predicted individual differences in subsequent educational progress? These questions can be answered only when the test is administered before the criterion data have matured, as in predictive validation.

In the development of special aptitude tests, a frequent type of criterion is based on *performance in specialized training*. For example, mechanical aptitude tests may be validated against final achievement in shop courses. Various business school courses, such as typing or bookkeeping, provide criteria for aptitude tests in these areas. Similarly, performance in music or art schools has been employed in validating music or art aptitude tests. Several professional aptitude tests have been validated in terms of achievement in schools of law, medicine, dentistry, engineering, and other areas. In the case of custom-made tests, designed for use within a specific testing program, training records are a frequent source of criterion data. An outstanding illustration is the validation of Air Force pilot-selection tests against performance in basic flight training. Performance in training programs is also commonly used as a criterion for test validation in other military occupational specialties and in some industrial validation studies.

Among the specific indices of training performance employed for criterion purposes may be mentioned achievement tests administered on completion of training, formally assigned grades, instructors' ratings, and successful completion of training versus elimination from the program. Multiple aptitude batteries have often been checked against grades in specific high school or college courses, in order to determine their validity as differential predictors. For example, scores on a verbal comprehension test may be compared with grades in English courses, spatial visualization scores with geometry grades, and so forth.

In connection with the use of training records in general as criterion measures, a useful distinction is that between intermediate and ultimate criteria. In the development of an Air Force pilot-selection test or a medical aptitude test, for example, the ultimate criteria would be combat performance and eventual achievement as a practicing physician, respectively. Obviously, it would require a long time for such criterion data to mature. It is doubtful, moreover, whether a truly ultimate criterion is ever obtained in actual practice. Finally, even were such an ultimate criterion available, it would probably be subject to many uncontrolled factors that would render it relatively useless. For example, it would be difficult to evaluate the relative degree of success of physicians practicing different specialties and in different parts of the country. For these reasons, such intermediate criteria as performance records at some stage of training are frequently employed as criterion measures.

For many purposes, the most satisfactory type of criterion measure is that based on follow-up records of actual *job performance*. This criterion has been used to some extent in the validation of general intelligence as well as personality tests, and to a larger extent in the validation of special aptitude tests. It is a common criterion in the validation of custom-made tests for specific jobs. The "jobs" in question may vary widely in both level and kind, including work in business, industry, the professions, and the armed services. Most measures of job performance, although probably not representing ultimate criteria, at least provide good intermediate criteria for many testing purposes. In this respect, they are to be preferred to training records. On the other hand, the measurement of job performance does not permit as much uniformity of conditions as is possible during training. Moreover, since it usually involves a longer follow-up, the criterion of job performance is likely to entail a loss in the number of available participants. Because of the variation in the nature of nominally similar jobs in different organizations, test manuals reporting validity data against job criteria should describe not only the specific criterion measures employed but also the job duties performed by the workers.

Validation by the method of *contrasted groups* generally involves a composite criterion that reflects the cumulative and uncontrolled selective influences of everyday life. This criterion is ultimately based on survival within a particular group versus elimination therefrom. For example, the validity

of a musical aptitude or a mechanical aptitude test may be checked by comparing the scores obtained by students enrolled in a music school or an engineering school, respectively, with the scores of unselected high school or
college students. Of course, contrasted groups could be selected on the basis
of any criterion, such as school grades, ratings, or job performance, by
simply choosing the extremes of the distribution of criterion measures. The
contrasted groups included in the present category, however, are distinct
groups that have gradually become differentiated through the operation of
the multiple demands of daily living. The criterion under consideration is
thus more complex and less clearly definable than those previously discussed.

The method of contrasted groups is used quite commonly in the validation
of personality tests. Thus, in validating a test of social traits, the test performance of salesmen or executives, on the one hand, may be compared with
that of clerks or engineers, on the other. The assumption underlying such a
procedure is that, with reference to many social traits, individuals who have
entered and remained in such occupations as selling or executive work will
as a group excel persons in such fields as clerical work or engineering. Similarly, college students who have engaged in many extracurricular activities
may be compared with those who have participated in none during a comparable period of college attendance. Occupational groups have frequently
been used in the development and validation of interest tests, such as the
Strong-Campbell Interest Inventory, as well as in the preparation of attitude
scales. Other groups sometimes employed in the validation of attitude scales
include political, religious, geographical, or other special groups generally
known to represent distinctly different points of view on certain issues.

In the empirical validation of criterion-referenced tests, several adaptations of the method of contrasted groups have been employed, in addition
to the usual content-validation procedures. For this purpose, groups differing in amount of relevant instruction are compared in test performance. If
mastery scoring is employed, a 2×2 analysis can be made, in which the proportion of pass and fail scores in the preinstruction group is compared with
the proportion of pass and fail scores in the postinstruction group (Panell &
Laabs, 1979). Similar comparisons can be made if the test is administered
to schoolchildren in one grade below and one grade above the grade where
the particular concept or skill assessed by the test is taught. If scores are
available after several different periods of instruction, a correlation can be
found between actual performance and amounts of instruction (Hambleton,
1980; Shaycoft, 1979, Ch. 6).

In the development of certain personality tests, *psychiatric diagnosis* is
used both as a basis for the selection of items and as evidence of test validity. Psychiatric diagnosis may serve as a satisfactory criterion provided
that it is based on prolonged observation and detailed case history, rather
than on a cursory psychiatric interview or examination. In the latter case,
there is no reason to expect the psychiatric diagnosis to be superior to the

test score itself as an indication of the individual's emotional condition. Such a psychiatric diagnosis could not be regarded as a criterion measure, but rather as an indicator or predictor whose own validity would have to be determined.

Mention has already been made, in connection with other criterion categories, of certain types of *ratings* by school teachers, instructors in specialized courses, and job supervisors. To these can be added ratings by officers in military situations, ratings of students by school counselors, and ratings by co-workers, classmates, fellow club-members, and other groups of associates. The ratings discussed earlier represented merely a subsidiary technique for obtaining information regarding such criteria as academic achievement, performance in specialized training, or job success. We are now considering the use of ratings as the very core of the criterion measure. Under these circumstances, the ratings themselves define the criterion. Moreover, such ratings are not restricted to the evaluation of specific achievement but involve a personal judgment by an observer regarding any of the variety of traits that psychological tests attempt to measure. Thus, the examinees in the validation sample might be rated on such characteristics as dominance, mechanical ingenuity, originality, leadership, or honesty.

Ratings have been employed in the validation of almost every type of test. They are particularly useful in providing criteria for personality tests, since objective criteria are much more difficult to find in this area. This is especially true of distinctly social traits, in which ratings based on personal contact many constitute the most logically defensible criterion. Although ratings may be subject to many judgmental errors, when obtained under carefully controlled conditions they represent a valuable source of criterion data. Techniques for improving the accuracy of ratings and for reducing common types of errors will be considered in Chapter 20.

Finally, correlations between a new test and *previously available tests* are frequently cited as evidence of validity. When the new test is an abbreviated or simplified form of a currently available test, the latter can properly be regarded as a criterion measure. Thus, a paper-and-pencil test might be validated against a more elaborate and time-consuming performance test whose validity had previously been established. Or a group test might be validated against an individual test. The Stanford-Binet, for example, has repeatedly served as a criterion in validating group tests. In such a case, the new test may be regarded at best as a crude approximation of the earlier one. It should be noted that unless the new test represents a simpler or shorter substitute for the earlier test, the use of the latter as a criterion is indefensible.

VALIDITY GENERALIZATION. Criterion-related validity is most appropriate for local validation studies, in which the effectiveness of a test for a specific program is to be assessed. This is the approach followed, for example, when a given company wishes to evaluate a test for selecting applicants for one of its jobs or when a given college wishes to determine how well an academic aptitude test can predict the course performance of its students. Criterion-related validity can be best characterized as the practical validity of a test in a specified situation.

When standardized aptitude tests were correlated with performance on presumably similar jobs in industrial validation studies, the validity coefficients were found to vary widely (Ghiselli, 1959, 1966). Similar variability among validity coefficients was observed when the criteria were grades in various school courses (Bennett, Seashore, & Wesman, 1974). Such findings led to widespread pessimism regarding the generalizability of test validity to different situations. Until the mid-1970s, "situational specificity" of psychological requirements was generally regarded as a serious limitation in the usefulness of standardized tests in personnel selection (Guion, 1976). In a sophisticated statistical analysis of the problem, however, Schmidt, Hunter, and their associates demonstrated that much of the variance among obtained validity coefficients may be a statistical artifact resulting from small sample size, criterion unreliability, and restriction of range in employee samples.[1]

The industrial samples available for test validation are generally too small to yield a stable estimate of the correlation between predictor and criterion. For the same reason, the obtained coefficients may be too low to reach statistical significance in the sample employed and may thus fail to provide evidence of the test's validity. It has been estimated that about half of the validation samples used in industrial studies include no more than 40 or 50 cases (Schmidt, Hunter, & Urry, 1976). With such small samples, the application of criterion-related validation is not technically feasible.

Applying their newly developed techniques to data from many samples drawn from a large number of occupational specialties, Schmidt, Hunter, and their co-workers were able to show that the validity of tests of verbal, numerical, and reasoning aptitudes can be generalized far more widely across occupations than had heretofore been recognized. The variance of validity coefficients typically found in earlier industrial studies proved to be no greater than would be expected by chance. This was true even when the particular job functions appeared to be quite dissimilar across jobs. Evidently, the successful performance of a wide variety of occupational tasks depends to a significant degree on a common core of cognitive skills. The tests included in these studies cover chiefly the type of content and skills sampled in traditional intelligence and scholastic aptitude tests. It would seem that this cluster of cognitive skills and knowledge is broadly predictive

---

[1] This work is part of a continuing research program reported in many articles and monographs. The publications most relevant to the present topic include Pearlman, Schmidt, and Hunter (1980); Schmidt and Hunter (1977); Schmidt, Gast-Rosenberg, and Hunter (1980); Schmidt, Hunter, and Pearlman (1981); and Schmidt, Hunter, Pearlman, and Shane (1979).

of performance in both academic and occupational activities demanded in advanced technological societies.[2]

CONSTRUCT VALIDATION

The construct validity of a test is the extent to which the test may be said to measure a theoretical construct or trait. Examples of such constructs are intelligence, mechanical comprehension, verbal fluency, speed of walking, neuroticism, and anxiety. Each construct is developed to explain and organize observed response consistencies. It derives from established inter-relationships among behavioral measures (Cronbach & Meehl, 1955; Messick, 1975, 1980b). Focusing on a broader, more enduring, and more abstract kind of behavioral description than the previously discussed validation procedures, construct validation requires the gradual accumulation of information from a variety of sources. Any data throwing light on the nature of the trait under consideration and the conditions affecting its development and manifestations are grist for this validity mill. Illustrations of specific techniques that contribute to construct validation are considered below.

DEVELOPMENTAL CHANGES. A major criterion employed in the validation of a number of intelligence tests is *age differentiation*. Such tests as the Stanford-Binet and most preschool tests are checked against chronological age to determine whether the scores show a progressive increase with advancing age. Since abilities are expected to increase with age during childhood, it is argued that the test scores should likewise show such an increase, if the test is valid. The very concept of an age scale of intelligence, as initiated by Binet, is based on the assumption that "intelligence" increases with age, at least until maturity.

The criterion of age differentiation, of course, is inapplicable to any functions that do not exhibit clear-cut and consistent age changes. In the area of personality measurement, for example, it has found limited use. Moreover, it should be noted that, even when applicable, age differentiation is a necessary but not a sufficient condition for validity. Thus, if the test scores fail to improve with age, such a finding probably indicates that the test is not a valid measure of the abilities it was designed to sample. On the other hand, to prove that a test measures something that increases with age does not define the area covered by the test very precisely. A measure of height or weight would also show regular age increments, although it would obviously not be designated as an intelligence test.

A final point should be emphasized regarding the interpretation of the age

[2] Applications and adaptations of validation procedures especially suitable for occupational tests will be discussed more specifically in Chapter 15.

criterion. A psychological test validated against such a criterion measures behavior characteristics that increase with age under the conditions existing in the type of environment in which the test was standardized. Because different cultures may stimulate and foster the development of dissimilar behavior characteristics, it cannot be assumed that the criterion of age differentiation is a universal one. Like all other criteria, it is circumscribed by the particular cultural setting in which it is derived.

Developmental analyses are also basic to the construct validation of the Piagetian ordinal scales cited in Chapter 4. A fundamental assumption of such scales is the *sequential patterning* of development, such that the attainment of earlier stages in concept development is prerequisite to the acquisition of later conceptual skills. There is thus an intrinsic hierarchy in the content of these scales. The construct validation of ordinal scales should therefore include empirical data on the sequential invariance of the successive steps. This involves checking the performance of children at different levels in the development of any tested concept, such as conservation or object permanence. Do children who demonstrate mastery of the concept at a given level also exhibit mastery at the lower levels?

CORRELATIONS WITH OTHER TESTS. Correlations between a new test and similar earlier tests are sometimes cited as evidence that the new test measures approximately the same general area of behavior as other tests designated by the same name, such as "intelligence tests" or "mechanical aptitude tests." Unlike the correlations found in criterion-related validity, these correlations should be moderately high, but not too high. If the new test correlates too highly with an already available test, without such added advantages as brevity or ease of administration, then the new test represents needless duplication.

Correlations with other tests are employed in still another way to demonstrate that the new test is relatively free from the influence of certain irrelevant factors. For example, a special aptitude test or a personality test should not have a high correlation with tests of general intelligence or scholastic aptitude. Similarly, reading comprehension should not appreciably affect performance on such tests. Accordingly, correlations with tests of general intelligence, reading, or verbal comprehension are sometimes reported as indirect or negative evidence of validity. In these cases, high correlations would make the test suspect. Low correlations, however, would not in themselves ensure validity. It will be noted that this use of correlations with other tests is similar to one of the supplementary techniques described under content validation.

FACTOR ANALYSIS. Developed as a means of identifying psychological traits, factor analysis is particularly relevant to construct validation. Essentially, factor analysis is a refined statistical technique for analyzing the interrelationships of behavior data. For example, if 20 tests have been given to 300 persons, the first step is to compute the correlations of each test with every other. An inspection of the resulting table of 190 correlations may itself reveal certain clusters among the tests, suggesting the location of common traits. Thus, if such tests as vocabulary, analogies, opposites, and sentence completion have high correlations with each other and low correlations with all other tests, we could tentatively infer the presence of a verbal comprehension factor. Because such an inspectional analysis of a correlation table is difficult and uncertain, however, more precise statistical techniques have been developed to locate the common factors required to account for the obtained correlations. These techniques of factor analysis will be examined further in Chapter 13, together with multiple aptitude tests developed by means of factor analysis.

In the process of factor analysis, the number of variables or categories in terms of which each individual's performance can be described is reduced from the number of original tests to a relatively small number of factors, or common traits. In the example cited above, five or six factors might suffice to account for the intercorrelations among the 20 tests. Each individual might thus be described in terms of her or his scores in the five or six factors, rather than in terms of the original 20 scores. A major purpose of factor analysis is to simplify the description of behavior by reducing the number of categories from an initial multiplicity of test variables to a few common factors, or traits.

After the factors have been identified, they can be utilized in describing the factorial composition of a test. Each test can thus be characterized in terms of the major factors determining its scores, together with the weight or loading of each factor and the correlation of the test with each factor. Such a correlation is known as the *factorial validity* of the test. Thus, if the verbal comprehension factor has a weight of .66 in a vocabulary test, the factorial validity of this vocabulary test as a measure of the trait of verbal comprehension is .66. It should be noted that factorial validity is essentially the correlation of the test with whatever is common to a group of tests or other indices of behavior. The set of variables analyzed can, of course, include both test and nontest data. Ratings and other criterion measures can thus be utilized, along with other tests, to explore the factorial composition of a particular test and to define the common traits it measures.

INTERNAL CONSISTENCY. In the published descriptions of certain tests, especially in the personality domain, the statement is made that the test has been validated by the method of internal consistency. The essential characteristic of this method is that the criterion is none other than the total score on the test itself. Sometimes an adaptation of the contrasted group method is used, extreme groups being selected on the basis of the total test score.

The performance of the upper criterion group on each test item is then compared with that of the lower criterion group. Items that fail to show a significantly greater proportion of "passes" (or keyed responses) in the upper than in the lower criterion group are considered invalid, and are either eliminated or revised. Correlational procedures may also be employed for this purpose. For example, the biserial correlation between "pass-fail" on each item and total test score can be computed. Only those items yielding significant item-test correlations would be retained. A test whose items were selected by this method can be said to show internal consistency, since each item differentiates among respondents in the same direction as does the entire test.

Another application of the criterion of internal consistency involves the correlation of subtest scores with total score. Many intelligence tests, for instance, consist of separately administered subtests (such as vocabulary, arithmetic, picture completion, etc.) whose scores are combined in finding the total test score. In the construction of these tests, the scores on each subtest are often correlated with total score, and any subtest whose correlation with total score is too low is eliminated. The correlations of the remaining subtests with total score are then reported as evidence of the internal consistency of the entire instrument.

It is apparent that internal consistency correlations, whether based on items or subtests, are essentially measures of homogeneity. Because it helps to characterize the behavior domain or trait sampled by the test, the degree of homogeneity of a test has some relevance to its construct validity. Nevertheless, the contribution of internal consistency data to test validation is limited. In the absence of data external to the test itself, little can be learned about what a test measures.

CONVERGENT AND DISCRIMINANT VALIDATION. In a thoughtful analysis of construct validation, D. T. Campbell (1960) pointed out that, in order to demonstrate construct validity, we must show not only that a test correlates highly with other variables with which it should theoretically correlate, but also that it does not correlate significantly with variables from which it should differ. In an earlier article, Campbell and Fiske (1959) described the former process as convergent validation and the latter as discriminant validation. Correlation of a quantitative reasoning test with subsequent grades in a math course would be an example of convergent validation. For the same test, discriminant validity would be illustrated by a low and insignificant correlation with scores on a reading comprehension test, since reading ability is an irrelevant variable in a test designed to measure quantitative reasoning.

It will be recalled that the requirement of low correlation with irrelevant variables was discussed in connection with supplementary and precautionary procedures followed in content validation. Discriminant validation is also especially relevant to the validation of personality tests, in which irrelevant variables may affect scores in a variety of ways.

Campbell and Fiske (1959) proposed a systematic experimental design for the dual approach of convergent and discriminant validation, which they called the *multitrait-multimethod matrix*. Essentially, this procedure requires the assessment of two or more traits by two or more methods. A hypothetical example provided by Campbell and Fiske will serve to illustrate the procedure. Table 12 shows all possible correlations among the scores obtained when three traits are each measured by three methods. The three traits could represent three personality characteristics, such as (A) dominance, (B) sociability, and (C) achievement motivation. The three methods could be (1) a self-report inventory, (2) a projective technique, and (3) peer ratings. Thus, A_1 would indicate dominance scores on the self-report inventory, A_2 dominance scores on the projective test, C_3 peer ratings on achievement motivation, and so forth.

The hypothetical correlations given in Table 12 include reliability coeffi-

TABLE 12

A Hypothetical Multitrait-Multimethod Matrix

(From Campbell & Fiske, 1959, p. 82. Copyright 1959 by the American Psychological Association. Reprinted by permission.)

	Traits	Method 1			Method 2			Method 3		
		A_1	B_1	C_1	A_2	B_2	C_2	A_3	B_3	C_3
Method 1	A_1	(.89)								
	B_1	.51	(.89)							
	C_1	.38	.37	(.76)						
Method 2	A_2	**.57**	.22	.09	(.93)					
	B_2	.22	**.57**	.10	.68	(.94)				
	C_2	.11	.11	**.46**	.59	.58	(.84)			
Method 3	A_3	**.56**	.22	.11	**.67**	.42	.33	(.94)		
	B_3	.23	**.58**	.12	.43	**.66**	.34	.67	(.92)	
	C_3	.11	.11	**.45**	.34	.32	**.58**	.58	.60	(.85)

Note. Letters A, B, C refer to traits, subscripts 1, 2, 3 to methods. Validity coefficients (monotrait-heteromethod) are the three diagonal sets of boldface numbers; reliability coefficient (monotrait-monomethod) are the numbers in parentheses along principal diagonal. Solid triangles enclose heterotrait-monomethod correlations; broken triangles enclose heterotrait-heteromethod correlations.

cients (in parentheses, along principal diagonal) and validity coefficient (in boldface, along three shorter diagonals). In these validity coefficients, the scores obtained for the same trait by different methods are correlated; each measure is thus being checked against other, independent measures of the same trait, as in the familiar validation procedure. The table also includes correlations between *different* traits measured by the *same* mehod (in solid triangles) and correlations between *different* traits measured by *different* methods (in broken triangles). For satisfactory construct validity, the validity coefficients should obviously be higher than the correlations between different traits measured by different methods; they should also be higher than the correlations between different traits measured by the same method. For example, the correlation between dominance scores from a self-report inventory and dominance scores from a projective test should be higher than the correlation between dominance and sociability scores from a self-report inventory. If the latter correlation, representing common method variance, were high, it might indicate, for example, that a person's scores on this inventory are unduly affected by some irrelevant common factor such as ability to understand the questions or desire to make oneself appear in a favorable light on all traits.

It might be noted that within the framework of the multitrait-multimethod matrix, reliability represents agreement between two measures of the same trait obtained through maximally similar methods, such as parallel forms of the same test; validity represents agreement between two measures of the same trait obtained by maximally different methods, such as test scores and supervisor's ratings. Since similarity and difference of methods are matters of degree, theoretically reliability and validity can be regarded as falling along a single continuum. Ordinarily, however, the techniques actually employed to measure reliability and validity correspond to easily identifiable regions of this continuum.

Fiske (1973) proposed still another set of correlations that should be analyzed, and this analysis has been employed in several investigations of personality measures (Fiske, 1973, 1976; Huba & Hamilton, 1976; Rezmovic & Rezmovic, 1980). In general, Fiske maintained that two measures of the same construct should yield the same pattern of correlations with measures of other personality traits. For example, peer ratings for dominance and self-report inventory scores for dominance should show approximately the same pattern of correlations with measures of endurance, affiliation, autonomy, or other traits assessed by these two methods.

The results actually obtained in these studies, however, revealed only a partial similarity of intertrait relationships, with appreciable differences attributable to method. Moreover, different correlational patterns may occur even within a single general method. Such differences have been found, for example, among independently constructed self-report inventories which differed in format (true-false, paired comparisons, checklist) or in the specific item content the investigator used to operationalize the construct.

Nevertheless, a substantial proportion of the variance assessed by different instruments may still represent a psychologically meaningful construct that is generalizable across methods. It is a question to be investigated for particular instruments and constructs. Essentially, these analyses provide one more approach to clarifying and refining the meaning of the constructs under consideration.

EXPERIMENTAL INTERVENTIONS. A further source of data for construct validation is provided by experiments on the effect of selected variables on test scores. In checking the validity of a criterion-referenced test for use in an individualized instructional program, for example, one approach is through a comparison of pretest and posttest scores. The rationale of such a test calls for low scores on the pretest, administered before the relevant instruction, and high scores on the posttest. This relationship can also be checked for individual items in the test (Popham, 1971). Ideally, the largest proportion of examinees should fail an item on the pretest and pass it on the posttest. Items that are commonly failed on both tests are too difficult, and those passed on both tests too easy, for the purposes of such a test. If a sizable proportion of examinees pass an item on the pretest and fail it on the posttest, there is obviously something wrong with the item, or the instruction, or both.

A test designed to measure anxiety-proneness can be administered to subjects who are subsequently put through a situation designed to arouse anxiety, such as taking an examination under distracting and stressful conditions. The initial anxiety test scores can then be correlated with physiological and other indices of anxiety expression during and after the examination. A different hypothesis regarding an anxiety test could be evaluated by administering the test before and after an anxiety-arousing experience and seeing whether test scores rise significantly on the retest. Positive findings from such an experiment would indicate that the test scores reflect current anxiety level. In a similar way, experiments can be designed to test any other hypothesis regarding the trait measured by a given test.

CONTRIBUTIONS FROM COGNITIVE PSYCHOLOGY. The 1970s witnessed a rapprochement of experimental psychology and psychometrics, which is beginning to yield significant contributions to our understanding of the constructs assessed by tests of intelligence and other broadly defined aptitudes. Some of the investigations in this area represent the work of psychologists trained in both fields; others resulted from the auspicious collaboration of specialists in the two fields.

As early as the 1950s, cognitive psychologists began to apply the concepts of information processing to the study of human problem-solving. Some investigators designed computer programs that carry out these processes and thereby simulate human thought. Programs can be written to simulate the performance of persons at different levels of skill, and with such programs it is possible to predict the number and kinds of errors made and the time required for different responses. In designing a program, the investigator usually begins with a task analysis that may include introspecting about one's own method of solving the problem, having subjects think aloud, or using more refined observational procedures. By comparing the performance of the computer with that of children or adults in solving the same problem, investigators can test their hypotheses regarding what persons do in carrying out the tasks. On the basis of the findings, the program can be modified and refined to improve the accuracy of the simulation. Examples of the tasks investigated by these methods include conventional puzzles, problems in logic, chess games, algebra word problems, and the spelling of English words (Simon, 1976).

The variables identified by these procedures consist of processes and knowledge. The cognitive models specify the intellectual processes used to perform the task, the way the processes are organized, the relevant knowledge store, and how this knowledge is represented in memory and retrieved when needed. A distinction is usually made among short-term, intermediate-term, and long-term memory. Increasing attention is also being given to what has been called an executive process or metacognition, which refers to the control the individual exercises over his or her own choice of processes, representations, and strategies for carrying out the task.

In the 1970s, a few psychologists began to apply these information-processing and computer-simulation techniques to an exploration of what intelligence tests measure (Resnick, 1976). Individual investigators approached this problem from several different angles. E. Hunt and his coworkers correlated subjects' performance on information-processing parameters from laboratory tasks with their scores from psychometric tests (E. Hunt, 1976; Hunt, Frost, & Lunneborg, 1973). Simon (1976) and his associates conducted many studies with computer programs written to simulate human problem-solving. Although this research was not directed specifically to the understanding of intelligence, some of the tasks investigated play an important part in common intelligence tests. A major example is provided by sequential pattern tasks, which are involved in such tests as number series completion and Raven's Progressive Matrices.

One of the most ambitious and systematic efforts to relate intelligence test performance to cognitive psychology is to be found in the research of Sternberg (1977, 1979) on what he calls componential analysis. This type of analysis has been applied to tasks that resemble complex intelligence test materials more closely than do the usual simplified and somewhat artificial laboratory tasks. The tasks employed by Sternberg include such familiar types as analogies, classifications, series completions, and syllogisms. His experimental procedures involve the manipulation, or systematic alteration, of both task variables and subject variables. An example of the latter is provided by age differences in performance on the same task. The experimental manipulation of task variables can be illustrated by task decomposition, whereby parts of tasks are presented separately or in succession. For instance, the first two premises of a syllogism are given in the first part of a trial and the full problem in the second part. In another example, the full task consists of a syllogism in which the height of three persons is compared; in the partial task, only two persons are included. The effects of such manipulations on the response time and error data are then compared with the effects predicted from the information-processing model.

What can we conclude regarding the contribution that cognitive psychology has made thus far to construct validation? While still in an early, exploratory stage, information-processing approaches have contributed heuristic concepts to guide further research. They have clearly focused attention on *response processes*, in contrast to the traditional concentration on the end products of thought in psychometric research. Analyzing test performance in terms of basic cognitive processes should certainly strengthen and enrich our understanding of what the tests measure. Moreover, analyzing individuals' performance at the level of elementary component processes should eventually make it possible to pinpoint each person's sources of weakness and strength and thereby enhance the diagnostic use of tests (Estes, 1974; Pellegrino & Glaser, 1979; Sternberg 1979; Sternberg & Weil, 1980). This, in turn, should facilitate the tailoring of training programs to the individual's needs.

OVERVIEW

COMPARISON OF VALIDATION PROCEDURES. We have considered several ways of asking, "How valid is this test?" To point up the distinctive features of the different validation procedures, let us apply each in turn to a test consisting of 50 assorted arithmetic problems. Four ways in which this test might be employed, together with the type of validation procedure appropriate to each, are illustrated in Table 13. This example highlights the fact that the choice of validation procedure depends on the use to be made of the test scores. The same test, when employed for different purposes, should be validated in different ways. If an achievement test is used to predict subsequent performance at a higher educational level, as when selecting high school students for college admission, it needs to be evaluated against the criterion of subsequent college performance rather than in terms of its content validity.

INCLUSIVENESS OF CONSTRUCT VALIDATION. The examples given in Table 13 focus on the differences among the various types of validation procedures. Further consideration of these procedures, however, shows that content,

TABLE 13
Validation of a Single Arithmetic Test for Different Purposes

Testing Purpose	Illustrative Question	Type of Validation
Achievement test in elementary school arithmetic	How much has Dick learned in the past?	Content
Aptitude test to predict performance in high school mathematics	How well will Jane learn in the future?	Criterion-related: predictive
Technique for diagnosing learning disabilities	Does Bill's performance show specific disabilities?	Criterion-related: concurrent
Measure of quantitative reasoning	How can we characterize Helen's cognitive processes?	Construct

criterion-related, and construct validation do not correspond to distinct or logically coordinate categories. On the contrary, construct validity is a comprehensive concept, which includes the other types. All the specific techniques for establishing content and criterion-related validity, discussed in earlier sections of this chapter, could have been listed again under construct validity. Comparing the test performance of contrasted groups, such as neurotics and normals, is one way of checking the construct validity of a test designed to measure emotional adjustment, anxiety, or other postulated traits. The correlations of a mechanical aptitude test with performance in shop courses and in a wide variety of jobs contribute to our understanding of the construct measured by the test.

Validity against various practical criteria is commonly reported in test manuals to aid the potential user in understanding what a test measures. Although he or she may not be directly concerned with the prediction of any of the specific criteria employed, by examining such criteria the test user is able to build up a concept of the behavior domain sampled by the test. If we follow this thinking a bit further, we can see that all test use and all interpretation of test scores imply construct validity, a fact that is being increasingly recognized (Guion, 1977; Messick, 1980b; Tenopyr, 1977). Since tests are rarely, if ever, used under conditions that are identical with those under which validity data were gathered, some degree of generalizability of results is inevitably involved. The interpretive meaning of test scores is always based on constructs, which may vary widely in breadth or generalizability with regard to behavior domains, populations, and situations.

Messick (1980b) has argued convincingly that the term validity, insofar as it designates the interpretive meaningfulness of a test, should be reserved for construct validity. Other procedures with which the term validity has been traditionally associated should, he maintains, be designated by more specifically descriptive labels. Thus, content validity can be labeled content relevance and content coverage, to refer to domain specifications and domain representativeness, respectively. Criterion-related validity can be labeled predictive utility and diagnostic utility, to correspond to predictive and concurrent validation. Substitute labels are likewise proposed for several, less well-known "types" of validity. The more clearly descriptive labels undoubtedly contribute to a better understanding of what the various procedures actually accomplish. It is likely, however, that the traditional terms will linger through a lengthy transition period because of their long-established usage and their general occurrence in available test manuals.

CONSTRUCT VALIDITY: EFFECTS AND SIDE EFFECTS. The term "construct validity" was officially introduced into the psychometrist's lexicon in 1954 in the *Technical Recommendations for Psychological Tests and Diagnostic Techniques,* which constituted the first edition of the current APA test *Standards* (1974). The first detailed exposition of construct validity appeared the following year in an article by Cronbach and Meehl (1955). The discussions of construct validation that followed—and that are continuing with renewed vigor—have served to make the implications of its procedures more explicit and to provide a systematic rationale for their use. Construct validation has focused attention on the role of psychological theory in test construction and on the need to formulate hypotheses that can be proved or disproved in the validation process. Construct validation has also stimulated the search for novel ways of gathering validity data. Although several of the techniques employed in investigating construct validity had long been familiar, the field of operation has been expanded to admit a wider variety of procedures.

On the negative side, superficial adoption of the concept of construct validity presents certain hazards. If loosely applied, it may open the way for subjective, unverified assertions about test validity. Because construct validity is a broad and complex concept, it has not always been clearly understood by those who employed the term. Some apparently regarded it as content validity expressed in terms of psychological trait names. Hence, they presented as construct validity purely subjective accounts of what they believed (or hoped) a test measured.

A further source of possible confusion arises from a statement that construct validation "is involved whenever a test is to be interpreted as a measure of some attribute or quality which is not 'operationally defined'" (Cronbach & Meehl, 1955, p. 282). Appearing in the first detailed published analysis of the concept of construct validity, this statement was often incorrectly accepted as justifying a claim for construct validity in the absence of data. That the authors of the statement did not intend such an interpretation is illustrated by their own insistence, in the same article, that "unless the network makes contact with observations . . . construct validation cannot be claimed" (p. 291). In the same connection, they criticized tests for which "a finespun network of rationalizations has been offered as if it were validation" (p. 291).

Actually, the theoretical construct, trait, or behavior domain measured by a particular test can be adequately defined only in the light of data gathered in the process of validating that test. Such a definition should take into account the variables with which the test correlated significantly, as well as the conditions found to affect its scores and the groups that differ significantly in such scores. These procedures are entirely in accord with the positive contributions made by the concept of construct validity. It is only through the empirical investigation of the relationships of test scores to other external data that we can discover what a test measures.

CHAPTER 7

Validity:
Measurement
and Interpretation

CHAPTER 6 was concerned with different concepts of validity and their appropriateness for various testing functions; this chapter deals with quantitative expressions of validity and their interpretation. Test users are concerned with validity at either or both of two stages. First, when considering the suitability of a test for their purposes, they examine available validity data reported in the test manual or other published sources. Through such information, they arrive at a tentative concept of what psychological functions the test actually measures, and they judge the relevance of such functions to their proposed use of the test. In effect, when test users rely on published validation data, they are dealing with construct validity, regardless of the specific procedures used in gathering the data. As we have seen in Chapter 6, the criteria employed in published studies cannot be assumed to be identical with those the test user wants to predict. Jobs bearing the same title in two different companies are rarely identical. Two courses in freshman English taught in different colleges may be quite dissimilar.

Because of the diversity of testing needs, test users may wish to check the validity of any chosen test against local criteria. Although published data may strongly suggest that a given test should have high validity in a particular situation, direct corroboration is desirable when technically feasible. The determination of validity against specific local criteria represents the second stage in the test users's evaluation of validity. The techniques to be discussed in this chapter are especially relevant to the analysis of validity data obtained by test users themselves. Most of them are also useful, however, in understanding and interpreting the validity data reported in test manuals.

VALIDITY COEFFICIENT AND ERROR OF ESTIMATE

MEASUREMENT OF RELATIONSHIP. A validity coefficient is a correlation between test score and criterion measure. Because it provides a single numerical index of test validity, it is commonly used in test manuals to report the validity of a test against each criterion for which data are available. The data used in computing any validity coefficient can also be expressed in the form of an expectancy table or expectancy chart, illustrated in Chapter 4. In fact, such tables and charts provide a convenient way to show what a validity coefficient means for the person tested. It will be recalled that expectancy charts give the probability that an individual who obtains a certain score on the test will attain a specified level of criterion performance. For example, with Table 6 (Ch. 4), if we know a student's score on the DAT Verbal Reasoning test, we can look up the chances that he or she will earn a particular grade in a high school course. The same data yield a validity coefficient of .66. When both test and criterion variables are continuous, as in this example, the familiar Pearson Product-Moment Correlation Coefficient is applicable. Other types of correlation coefficients can be computed when the data are expressed in different forms, as when a twofold pass-fail criterion is employed (e.g., Fig. 7, Ch. 4). The specific procedures for computing these different kinds of correlations can be found in any standard statistics text.

CONDITIONS AFFECTING VALIDITY COEFFICIENTS. As in the case of reliability, it is essential to specify the *nature of the group* on which a validity coefficient is found. The same test may measure different functions when given to individuals who differ in age, sex, educational level, occupation, or any other relevant characteristic. Persons with different experiential backgrounds, for example, may utilize different work methods to solve the same test problem. Consequently, a test could have high validity in predicting a particular criterion in one population, and little or no validity in another. Or it might be a valid measure of different functions in the two populations. Tests designed for use with diverse populations should cite appropriate data on population generalizability in their technical manuals.

The question of *sample heterogeneity* is relevant to the measurement of validity, as it is to the measurement of reliability, since both characteristics are commonly reported in terms of correlation coefficients. It will be recalled that, other things being equal, the wider the range of scores, the higher will be the correlation. This fact should be kept in mind when interpreting the validity coefficients given in test manuals.

A special difficulty encountered in many validation samples arises from *preselection.* For example, a new test that is being validated for job selection may be administered to a group of newly hired employees on whom criterion measures of job performance will eventually be available. It is likely, however, that such employees represent a superior selection of all those who applied for the job. Hence, the range of such a group in both test scores and criterion measures will be curtailed at the lower end of the distribution. The effect of such preselection will therefore be to lower the validity coefficient. In the subsequent use of the test, when it is administered to all applicants for selection purposes, the validity can be expected to be somewhat higher.

Validity coefficients may also change over time because of changing selection standards. An example is provided by a comparison of validity coefficients computed over a 30-year interval with Yale students (Burnham, 1965). Correlations were found between a predictive index based on College Board tests and high school records, on the one hand, and average freshman grades, on the other. This correlation dropped from .71 to .52 over the 30 years. An examination of the bivariate distributions clearly revealed the reason for this drop. Because of higher admission standards, the later class was more homogeneous than the earlier class in both predictor and criterion performance. Consequently, the correlation was lower in the later group, although the accuracy with which individuals' grades were predicted showed little change. In other words, the observed drop in correlation did *not* indicate that the predictors were less valid than they had been 30 years earlier. Had the differences in group homogeneity been ignored, it might have been wrongly concluded that this was the case.

For the proper interpretation of a validity coefficient, attention should also be given to the *form of the relationship* between test and criterion. The computation of a Pearson correlation coefficient assumes that the relationship is linear and uniform throughout the range. Research on the relationship of test scores to job performance has shown that these conditions are generally met (Schmidt, Hunter, McKenzie, & Muldrow, 1979, pp. 616–617). Nevertheless, special circumstances may alter this relationship, and the test user should be alert to such possibilities. For example, a particular job may require a minimum level of reading comprehension, to enable employees to read instruction manuals, labels, and the like. Once this minimum is exceeded, however, further increments in reading ability may be unrelated to degree of job success. This would be an example of a nonlinear relation between test and job performance. An examination of the bivariate distribution or scatter diagram obtained by plotting reading comprehension scores against criterion measures would show a rise in job performance up to the minimal required reading ability and a leveling off beyond that point. Hence, the entries would cluster around a curve rather than a straight line.

In other situations, the line of best fit may be a straight line, but the individual entries may deviate farther around this line at the upper than at the lower end of the scale. Suppose that performance on a scholastic aptitude test is a necessary but not a sufficient condition for successful achievement in a course. That is, the low-scoring students will perform poorly in the course; but among the high-scoring students, some will perform well in the course and others will perform poorly because of low motivation, lack of interest, or other adverse conditions. In this situation, there will be wider variability of criterion performance among the high-scoring than among the low-scoring students. This condition in a bivariate distribution is known as heteroscedasticity. The Pearson correlation assumes homoscedasticity or equal variability throughout the range of the bivariate distribution. In the present example, the bivariate distribution would be fan-shaped—wide at the upper end and narrow at the lower end. An examination of the bivariate distribution itself will usually give a good indication of the nature of the relationship between test and criterion. Expectancy tables and expectancy charts also correctly reveal the relative effectiveness of the test at different levels.

MAGNITUDE OF A VALIDITY COEFFICIENT. How high should a validity coefficient be? No general answer to this question is possible, since the interpretation of a validity coefficient must take into account a number of concomitant circumstances. The obtained correlation, of course, should be high enough to be *statistically significant* at some acceptable level, such as the .01 or .05 levels discussed in Chapter 5. In other words, before drawing any conclusions about the validity of a test, we should be reasonably certain that the obtained validity coefficient could not have arisen through chance fluctuations of sampling from a true correlation of zero.

Having established a significant correlation between test scores and criterion, however, we need to evaluate the size of the correlation in the light of the uses to be made of the test. If we wish to predict an individual's exact criterion score, such as the grade-point average a student will receive in college, the validity coefficient may be interpreted in terms of the *standard error of estimate*, which is analogous to the error of measurement discussed in connection with reliability. It will be recalled that the error of measurement indicates the margin of error to be expected in an individual's score as a result of the unreliability of the test. Similarly, the error of estimate shows the margin of error to be expected in the individual's predicted criterion score, as a result of the imperfect validity of the test.

The error of estimate is found by the following formula:

$$\sigma_{est.} = SD_y\sqrt{1 - r_{xy}^2}$$

in which r_{xy}^2 is the square of the validity coefficient and SD_y is the standard deviation of the criterion scores. It will be noted that if the validity were perfect ($r_{xy} = 1.00$), the error of estimate would be zero. On the other hand, with a test having zero validity, the error of estimate is as large as the standard deviation of the criterion distribution ($\sigma_{est.} = SD_y\sqrt{1 - 0} = SD_y$). Under these conditions, the prediction is no better than a guess; and the range of prediction error is as wide as the entire distribution of criterion scores. Between these two extremes are to be found the errors of estimate corresponding to tests of varying validity.

Reference to the formula for $\sigma_{est.}$ will show that term $\sqrt{1 - r_{xy}^2}$ serves to indicate the size of the error *relative to the error that would result from a mere guess,* i.e., with zero validity. In other words, if $\sqrt{1 - r_{xy}^2}$ is equal to 1.00, the error of estimate is as large as it would be if we were to guess the individual's criterion score. The predictive improvement attributable to the use of the test would thus be nil. If the validity coefficient is .80, then $\sqrt{1 - r_{xy}^2}$ is equal to .60, and the error is 60% as large as it would be by chance. To put it differently, the use of such a test enables us to predict the individual's criterion performance with a margin of error that is 40% smaller that it would be if we were to guess.

It would thus appear that even with a validity of .80, which is unusually high, the error of predicted scores is considerable. If the primary function of psychological tests were to predict each individual's exact position in the criterion distribution, the outlook would be quite discouraging. When examined in the light of the error of estimate, most tests do not appear very efficient. In most testing situations, however, it is not necessary to predict the specific criterion performance of individual cases, but rather to determine which individuals will exceed a certain minimum standard of performance, or cutoff point, in the criterion. What are the chances that Mary Greene will graduate from medical school, that Tom Higgins will pass a course in calculus, or that Beverly Bruce will succeed as an astronaut? Which applicants are likely to be satisfactory clerks, insurance agents, or machine operators? Such information is useful not only for group selection but also for individual career planning. For example, it is advantageous for a student to know that she has a good chance of passing all courses in law school, even if we are unable to estimate with certainty whether her grade average will be 74 or 81.

A test may appreciably improve predictive efficiency if it shows *any* significant correlation with the criterion, however low. Under certain circumstances, even validities as low as .20 or .30 may justify inclusion of the test in a selection program. For many testing purposes, evaluation of tests in terms of the error of estimate is unrealistically stringent. Consideration must be given to other ways of evaluating the contribution of a test, which take into account the types of decisions to be made from the scores. Some of these procedures will be illustrated in the following section.

TEST VALIDITY AND DECISION THEORY

BASIC APPROACH. Let us suppose that 100 applicants have been given an aptitude test and followed up until each could be evaluated for success on a

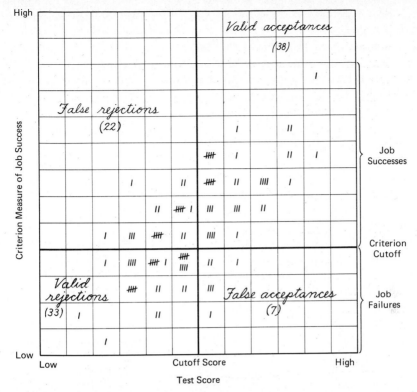

FIG. 15. Increase in the Proportion of "Successes" Resulting from the Use of a Selection Test.

certain job. Figure 15 shows the bivariate distribution of test scores and measures of job success for the 100 employees. The correlation between these two variables is slightly below .70. The minimum acceptable job performance, or criterion cutoff point, is indicated in the diagram by a heavy horizontal line. The 40 cases falling below this line would represent job failures; the 60 above the line, job successes. If all 100 applicants are hired, therefore, 60% will succeed on the job. Similarly, if a smaller number were hired at random, without reference to test scores, the proportion of successes would probably be close to 60%. Suppose, however, that the test scores are used to select the 45 most promising applicants out of the 100 (selection ratio = .45). In such a case, the 45 individuals falling to the right of the heavy vertical line would be chosen. Within this group of 45, it can be seen that there are 7 job failures, or *false acceptances*, falling below the heavy horizontal line, and 38 job successes. Hence, the percentage of job successes is now 84 rather than 60 (i.e., 38/45 = .84). This increase is attributable to the use of the test as a screening instrument. It will be noted that errors in predicted criterion score that do not affect the decision can be ignored. Only those prediction errors that cross the cutoff line and hence place the individual in the wrong category will reduce the selective effectiveness of the test.

For a complete evaluation of the effectiveness of the test as a screening instrument, another category of cases in Figure 15 must also be examined. This is the category of *false rejections,* comprising the 22 persons who score below the cutoff point on the test but above the criterion cutoff. From these data, we would estimate that 22% of the total applicant sample are potential job successes who will be lost if the test is used as a screening device with the present cutoff point. These false rejects in a personnel selection situation correspond to the *false positives* in clinical evaluations. This term has been adopted from medical practice, in which a test for a pathological condition is reported as positive if the condition is present and negative if the patient is normal. A false positive thus refers to a case in which the test erroneously indicates the presence of a pathological condition, as when brain damage is indicated in an individual who is actually normal. This terminology is likely to be confusing unless we remember that in clinical practice a positive result on a test denotes pathology and unfavorable diagnosis, whereas in personnel selection a positive result conventionally refers to a favorable prediction regarding job performance, academic achievement, and the like.

In setting a cutoff score on a test, attention should be given to the percentage of false rejects (or false positives) as well as to the percentages of successes and failures within the selected group. In certain situations, the cutoff point should be set sufficiently high to exclude all but a few possible failures. This would be the case when the job is of such a nature that a poorly qualified worker could cause serious loss or damage. An example would be a commercial airline pilot. Under other circumstances, it may be more important to admit as many qualified persons as possible, at the risk of including more failures. In the latter case, the number of false rejects can be reduced by the choice of a lower cutoff score. Other factors that normally determine the position of the cutoff score include the available personnel supply, the number of job openings, and the urgency or speed with which the openings must be filled.

In many personnel decisions, the selection ratio is determined by the practical demands of the situation. Because of supply and demand in filling job openings, for example, it may be necessary to hire the top 40% of applicants in one case and the top 75% in another. When the selection ratio is not externally imposed, the cutting score on a test can be set at that point giving the maximum differentiation between criterion groups. This can be done roughly by comparing the distribution of test scores in the two criterion groups. More precise mathematical procedures for setting optimal cutting scores have also been worked out (Darlington & Stauffer, 1966; Guttman & Raju, 1965; Rorer, Hoffman, La Forge, & Hsieh, 1966). These procedures make it possible to take into account other relevant parameters, such as the relative seriousness of false rejections and false acceptances.

In the terminology of decision theory, the example given in Figure 15 illustrates a simple *strategy,* or plan for deciding which applicants to accept and which to reject. In more general terms, a strategy is a technique for utilizing information in order to reach a decision about individuals. In this case, the strategy was to accept the 45 persons with the highest test scores. The increase in percentage of successful employees from 60 to 84 could be used as a basis for estimating the net benefit resulting from the use of the test.

Statistical decision theory was developed by Wald (1950) with special reference to the decisions required in the inspection and quality control of industrial products. Many of its implications for the construction and interpretation of psychological tests have been systematically worked out by Cronbach and Gleser (1965). Essentially, decision theory is an attempt to put the decision-making process into mathematical form, so that available information may be used to arrive at the most effective decision under specified circumstances. The mathematical procedures employed in decision theory are often quite complex, and their application to practical testing problems has been proceeding slowly. Some of the basic concepts of decision theory are proving helpful in the reformulation and clarification of certain questions about tests. A few of these ideas were introduced into testing before the formal development of statistical decision theory and were later recognized as fitting into that framework.

PREDICTION OF OUTCOMES. A precursor of decision theory in psychological testing is to be found in the Taylor-Russell tables (1939), which permit a determination of the net gain in selection accuracy attributable to the use of the test. The information required includes the validity coefficient of the test, the proportion of applicants who must be accepted (selection ratio), and the proportion of successful applicants selected without the use of the test (base rate). A change in any of these three factors can alter the predictive efficiency of the test.

For purposes of illustration, one of the Taylor-Russell tables has been reproduced in Table 14. This table is designed for use when the base rate, or percentage of successful applicants selected prior to the use of the test, is 60. Other tables are provided by Taylor and Russell for other base rates. Across the top of the table are given different values of the selection ratio, and along the side are the test validities. The entries in the body of the table indicate the proportion of successful persons selected after the use of the test. Thus, the difference between .60 and any one table entry shows the increase in proportion of successful selections attributable to the test.

Obviously if the selection ratio were 100%, that is, if all applicants had to be accepted, no test, however valid, could improve the selection process. Reference to Table 14 shows that, when as many as 95% of applicants must be admitted, even a test with perfect validity ($r = 1.00$) would raise the

TABLE 14

Proportion of "Successes" Expected Through the Use of Test of Given Validity and Given Selection Ratio, for Base Rate .60.

(From Taylor and Russell, 1939, p. 576)

Validity	Selection Ratio										
	.05	.10	.20	.30	.40	.50	.60	.70	.80	.90	.95
.00	.60	.60	.60	.60	.60	.60	.60	.60	.60	.60	.60
.05	.64	.63	.63	.62	.62	.62	.61	.61	.61	.60	.60
.10	.68	.67	.65	.64	.64	.63	.63	.62	.61	.61	.60
.15	.71	.70	.68	.67	.66	.65	.64	.63	.62	.61	.61
.20	.75	.73	.71	.69	.67	.66	.65	.64	.63	.62	.61
.25	.78	.76	.73	.71	.69	.68	.66	.65	.63	.62	.61
.30	.82	.79	.76	.73	.71	.69	.68	.66	.64	.62	.61
.35	.85	.82	.78	.75	.73	.71	.69	.67	.65	.63	.62
.40	.88	.85	.81	.78	.75	.73	.70	.68	.66	.63	.62
.45	.90	.87	.83	.80	.77	.74	.72	.69	.66	.64	.62
.50	.93	.90	.86	.82	.79	.76	.73	.70	.67	.64	.62
.55	.95	.92	.88	.84	.81	.78	.75	.71	.68	.64	.62
.60	.96	.94	.90	.87	.83	.80	.76	.73	.69	.65	.63
.65	.98	.96	.92	.89	.85	.82	.78	.74	.70	.65	.63
.70	.99	.97	.94	.91	.87	.84	.80	.75	.71	.66	.63
.75	.99	.99	.96	.93	.90	.86	.81	.77	.71	.66	.63
.80	1.00	.99	.98	.95	.92	.88	.83	.78	.72	.66	.63
.85	1.00	1.00	.99	.97	.95	.91	.86	.80	.73	.66	.63
.90	1.00	1.00	1.00	.99	.97	.94	.88	.82	.74	.67	.63
.95	1.00	1.00	1.00	1.00	.99	.97	.92	.84	.75	.67	.63
1.00	1.00	1.00	1.00	1.00	1.00	1.00	1.00	.86	.75	.67	.63

Note. A full set of tables can be found in Taylor and Russell (1939) and in McCormick and Ilgen (1980), Appendix B.

proportion of successful persons by only 3% (.60 to .63). On the other hand, when only 5% of applicants need to be chosen, a test with a validity coefficient of only .30 can raise the percentage of successful applicants selected from 60 to 82. The rise from 60 to 82 represents the *incremental validity* of the test (Sechrest, 1963), or the increase in predictive validity attributable to the test. It indicates the contribution the test makes to the selection of individuals who will meet the minimum standards in criterion performance. In applying the Taylor-Russell tables, of course, test validity should be computed on the same sort of group used to estimate percentage of prior successes. In other words, the contribution of the test is not evaluated against chance success unless applicants were previously selected by chance —a most unlikely circumstance. If applicants had been selected on the basis of previous job history, letters of recommendation, and interviews, the contribution of the test should be evaluated on the basis of what the test adds to these previous selection procedures.

The incremental validity resulting from the use of a test depends not only on the selection ratio but also on the base rate. In the previously illustrated job selection situation, the base rate refers to the proportion of successful employees prior to the introduction of the test for selection purposes. Table 14 shows the anticipated outcomes when the base rate is .60. For other base rates, we need to consult the other appropriate tables in the cited reference (Taylor & Russell, 1939). Let us consider an example in which test validity is .60 and the selection ratio is 40%. Under these conditions, what would be the contribution or incremental validity of the test if we begin with a base rate of 50%? And what would be the contribution if we begin with more extreme base rates of 10% and 90%? Reference to the appropriate Taylor-Russell tables for these base rates shows that the percentage of successful employees would rise from 50 to 75 in the first case; from 10 to 21 in the second; and from 90 to 99 in the third. Thus, the improvement in percentage of successful employees attributable to the use of the test is 25 when the base rate was 50, but only 11 and 9 when the base rates were more extreme.

The implications of extreme base rates are of special interest in clinical psychology, where the base rate refers to the frequency of the pathological condition to be diagnosed in the population tested (Buchwald, 1965; Cureton, 1957a; Meehl & Rosen, 1955; J. S. Wiggins, 1973). For example, if 5% of the intake population of a clinic has organic brain damage, then 5% is the base rate of brain damage in this population. Although the introduction of any valid test will improve predictive or diagnostic accuracy, the improvement is greatest when the base rates are closest to 50%. With the extreme base rates found with rare pathological conditions, however, the improvement may be negligible. Under these conditions, the use of a test may prove to be unjustified when the cost of its administration and scoring is taken into account. In a clinical situation, this cost would include the time of professional personnel that might otherwise be spent on the treatment of additional cases (Buchwald, 1965). The number of false positives, or normal individuals incorrectly classified as pathological, would of course increase this overall cost in a clinical situation.

When the seriousness of a rare condition makes its diagnosis urgent, tests of moderate validity may be employed in an early stage of sequential decisions. For example, all cases might first be screened with an easily administered test of moderate validity. If the cutoff score is set high enough (high scores being favorable), there will be few false negatives but many false positives, or normals diagnosed as pathological. The latter can then be detected through a more intensive individual examination given to all cases diagnosed as positive by the test. This solution would be appropriate, for instance, when available facilities make the intensive individual examination of all cases impracticable.

RELATION OF VALIDITY TO PRODUCTIVITY. In many practical situations, what is wanted is an estimate of the effect of the selection test, not on percentage of persons exceeding the minimum performance, but on overall productivity of the selected persons. How does the actual level of job proficiency or criterion achievement of the workers hired on the basis of the test compare with that of the total applicant sample that would have been hired without the test? Following the work of Taylor and Russell, several investigators addressed themselves to this question. Brogden (1946b) first demonstrated that the expected increase in output is directly proportional to the validity of the test. Thus, the improvement resulting from the use of a test of validity .50 is 50% as great as the improvement expected from a test of perfect validity.

The relation between test validity and expected rise in criterion achievement can be readily seen in Table 15.[1] Expressing criterion scores as standard scores with a mean of zero and an *SD* of 1.00, this table gives the expected mean criterion score of workers selected with a test of given validity and with a given selection ratio. In this context, the base output mean, corresponding to the performance of applicants selected without use of the test, is given in the column for zero validity. Using a test with zero validity is equivalent to using no test at all. To illustrate the use of the table, let us assume that the highest scoring 20% of the applicants are hired (selection ratio = .20) by means of a test whose validity coefficient is .50. Reference to Table 15 shows that the mean criterion performance of this group is .70 *SD* above the expected base mean of an untested sample. With the same 20% selection ratio and a perfect test (validity coefficient = 1.00), the mean criterion score of the accepted applicants would be 1.40, just twice what it would be with the test of validity .50. Similar direct linear relations will be found if other mean criterion performances are compared within any row of Table 15. For instance, with a selection ratio of 60%, a validity of .25 yields a mean criterion score of .16, while a validity of .50 yields a mean of .32. Again, doubling the validity doubles the output rise.

The analysis of productivity in relation to test validity was carried further by Schmidt and his associates (Schmidt, Hunter, McKenzie, & Muldrow, 1979). Using the job of computer programmer in the federal government as an illustration, these investigators estimated the dollar value of the productivity increase resulting from one year's use of a computer aptitude test (validity = .76) in selecting new hires. They arrived at their estimates through the application of innovative decision-theoretic techniques to data available in the U.S. Office of Personnel Management. Expected gains were

---

[1] A table including more values for both selection ratios and validity coefficients was prepared by Naylor and Shine (1965).

TABLE 15
Mean Standard Criterion Score of Accepted Cases in Relation to Test Validity and Selection Ratio

(From Brown and Ghiselli, 1953, p. 342)

Selection Ratio	Validity Coefficient																				
	.00	.05	.10	.15	.20	.25	.30	.35	.40	.45	.50	.55	.60	.65	.70	.75	.80	.85	.90	.95	1.00
.05	.00	.10	.21	.31	.42	.52	.62	.73	.83	.94	1.04	1.14	1.25	1.35	1.46	1.56	1.66	1.77	1.87	1.98	2.08
.10	.00	.09	.18	.26	.35	.44	.53	.62	.70	.79	.88	.97	1.05	1.14	1.23	1.32	1.41	1.49	1.58	1.67	1.76
.15	.00	.08	.15	.23	.31	.39	.46	.54	.62	.70	.77	.85	.93	1.01	1.08	1.16	1.24	1.32	1.39	1.47	1.55
.20	.00	.07	.14	.21	.28	.35	.42	.49	.56	.63	.70	.77	.84	.91	.98	1.05	1.12	1.19	1.26	1.33	1.40
.25	.00	.06	.13	.19	.25	.32	.38	.44	.51	.57	.63	.70	.76	.82	.89	.95	1.01	1.08	1.14	1.20	1.27
.30	.00	.06	.12	.17	.23	.29	.35	.40	.46	.52	.58	.64	.69	.75	.81	.87	.92	.98	1.04	1.10	1.16
.35	.00	.05	.11	.16	.21	.26	.32	.37	.42	.48	.53	.58	.63	.69	.74	.79	.84	.90	.95	1.00	1.06
.40	.00	.05	.10	.15	.19	.24	.29	.34	.39	.44	.48	.53	.58	.63	.68	.73	.77	.82	.87	.92	.97
.45	.00	.04	.09	.13	.18	.22	.26	.31	.35	.40	.44	.48	.53	.57	.62	.66	.70	.75	.79	.84	.88
.50	.00	.04	.08	.12	.16	.20	.24	.28	.32	.36	.40	.44	.48	.52	.56	.60	.64	.68	.72	.76	.80
.55	.00	.04	.07	.11	.14	.18	.22	.25	.29	.32	.36	.40	.43	.47	.50	.54	.58	.61	.65	.68	.72
.60	.00	.03	.06	.10	.13	.16	.19	.23	.26	.29	.32	.35	.39	.42	.45	.48	.52	.55	.58	.61	.64
.65	.00	.03	.06	.09	.11	.14	.17	.20	.23	.26	.28	.31	.34	.37	.40	.43	.46	.48	.51	.54	.57
.70	.00	.02	.05	.07	.10	.12	.15	.17	.20	.22	.25	.27	.30	.32	.35	.37	.40	.42	.45	.47	.50
.75	.00	.02	.04	.06	.08	.11	.13	.15	.17	.19	.21	.23	.25	.27	.30	.32	.33	.36	.38	.40	.42
.80	.00	.02	.04	.05	.07	.09	.11	.12	.14	.16	.18	.19	.21	.22	.25	.26	.28	.30	.32	.33	.35
.85	.00	.01	.03	.04	.05	.07	.08	.10	.11	.12	.14	.15	.16	.18	.19	.20	.22	.23	.25	.26	.27
.90	.00	.01	.02	.03	.04	.05	.06	.07	.08	.09	.10	.11	.12	.13	.14	.15	.16	.17	.18	.19	.20
.95	.00	.01	.01	.02	.02	.03	.03	.04	.04	.05	.05	.06	.07	.07	.08	.08	.09	.09	.10	.10	.11

computed for nine selection ratios ranging from .05 to .80, and for five validity coefficients of prior selection procedures ranging from zero (random selection) to .50.

The results indicated impressive gains in productivity from the use of the test under all these conditions. When use of the test was compared with random selection, the dollar gain ranged from $97.2 million for a selection ratio of .05 to $16.5 million for a selection ratio of .80. With prior selection validity of .50, the corresponding gains ranged from $33.3 million to $5.6 million. These gains would be spread over the expected tenure of the newly hired employees, which for computer programmers in the federal government averaged slightly under 10 years. It should also be noted that the estimates are based on the assumption that selection proceeds from the top-scoring applicants downward, until the specified selection ratio is reached. In other words, the procedure assumes optimum use of the selection process.

Using census data to assess the number of persons employed as computer programmers in the entire population of the United States, the investigators also worked out corresponding estimates of the effect of using the given test on the national level. In a still broader subsequent study, Hunter and Schmidt (1981) explored the possible application of the same statistical techniques to the entire national work force, across all occupations. While admittedly crude and tentative, these preliminary estimates strongly suggest that effective methods for allocating people to jobs can contribute substantially to national productivity.

THE ROLE OF VALUES IN DECISION THEORY. It is characteristic of decision theory that tests are evaluated in terms of their effectiveness in a particular situation. Such evaluation takes into account not only the validity of the test in predicting a particular criterion but also a number of other parameters, including base rate and selection ratio. Another important parameter is the relative *utility* of expected outcomes, the judged favorableness or unfavorableness of each outcome. The lack of adequate systems for assigning values to outcomes in terms of a uniform utility scale has been one of the chief obstacles to the application of decision theory. In industrial decisions, a dollar value can frequently be assigned to different outcomes. Even in such cases, however, certain outcomes pertaining to goodwill, public relations, and employee morale are difficult to assess in monetary terms. Educational decisions must take into account institutional goals, social values, and other relatively intangible factors. Individual decisions, as in counseling, must consider the individual's preferences and value system. It has been repeatedly pointed out, however, that decision theory did not introduce the problem of values into the decision process, but merely made it explicit. Value systems have always entered into decisions, but they were not heretofore clearly recognized or systematically handled.

Advances in procedures for the assignment of values in decision models are illustrated in the productivity research by Schmidt, Hunter, and their associates cited in the preceding section. Although concerned with the dollar value of the goods and services provided by workers, the techniques developed in that research are applicable to the measurement of other values. Being based on the quantification of human judgments, the same procedures can be used with any arbitrary numerical scale, provided that the scale is clearly defined and consistently applied. It should be noted that the estimates required by decision models pertain only to the relative, not the absolute, values of different outcomes.

The specific procedure employed in the computer programmer study involved the analysis of estimates obtained from experienced supervisors through a carefully constructed questionnaire. Each supervisor was asked to estimate the yearly dollar value to the organization of the products and services provided by an average programmer. The same estimate was requested for a "superior" performer, defined as a programmer at the 85th percentile, and for a "low-performing" programmer, defined as one at the 15th percentile. As an aid in placing a dollar value on these three performance levels, supervisors were asked "to consider what the cost would be of having an outside firm provide these products and services" (Schmidt, Hunter, McKenzie, & Muldrow, 1979, p. 621).

Estimates from 105 supervisors were averaged; these in turn provided two estimates of the standard deviation of the job-performance distribution in dollars, one corresponding to the difference between the average and the 85th percentile, the other to the difference between the average and the 15th percentile. The two estimates were not significantly different, indicating that the distribution was at least approximately normal. The average of these two estimates was the *SD* used in the subsequent calculations. This procedure is much simpler and less costly than standard cost-accounting methods; it can be adapted for use with values not measured in dollar units; and in some respects, it may provide more accurate estimates than have been obtained in studies using cost-accounting procedures (Schmidt et al., 1979, pp. 618–621).

EXPECTED UTILITY OF A SELECTION STRATEGY. In choosing a decision strategy, the goal is to maximize expected utilities across all outcomes. Reference to the schematic representation of a simple decision strategy in Figure 16 will help to clarify the procedure. This diagram shows the decision strategy illustrated in Figure 15, in which a single test is administered to a group of applicants and the decision to accept or reject an applicant is made on the basis of a cutoff score on the test. There are four possible outcomes, including valid and false acceptances and valid and false rejections. The probability of each outcome can be found from the number of persons in each of the four sections of Figure 15. Since there were 100 applicants in that

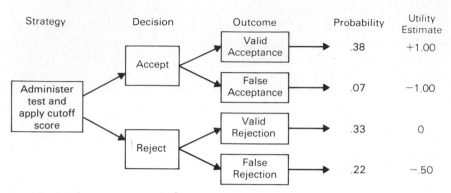

FIG. 16. A Simple Decision Strategy.

example, these numbers divided by 100 give the probabilities of the four outcomes listed in Figure 16.

The other data needed are the utilities of the different outcomes, expressed on a common scale. These are given in the last column of Figure 16. The expected overall utility of the strategy can be found by multiplying the probability of each outcome by the utility of the outcome, adding these products for the four outcomes, and subtracting a value corresponding to the cost of testing. This last term highlights the fact that a test of low validity is more likely to be retained if it is short, inexpensive, easily administered by relatively untrained personnel, and suitable for group administration. An individual test requiring a trained examiner or expensive equipment would need a higher validity to justify its use. In the hypothetical example illustrated in Figure 16, cost of testing is estimated as .10 on the utility scale. The total expected utility (EU) for this decision strategy is:

$$EU = (.38)(1.00) + (.07)(-1.00) + (.33)(0) + (.22)(-.50) - .10 = +.10.$$

This EU can then be compared with other EUs found with different cutoff points, with different tests (differing in validity and cost), or with a battery of tests, as well as with different decision strategies.[2]

SEQUENTIAL STRATEGIES AND ADAPTIVE TREATMENTS. In some situations, the effectiveness of a test may be increased through the use of more complex decision strategies which take still more parameters into account. Two examples will serve to illustrate these possibilities. First, tests may be used to make *sequential* rather then terminal decisions. With the simple decision strategy illustrated in Figures 15 and 16, all decisions to accept or reject are

[2] Examples of several decision strategies, showing all computational steps, can be found in J. S. Wiggins (1973), Ch. 6.

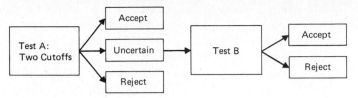

F**IG. 17.** A Sequential Decision Strategy.

treated as terminal. Figure 17, on the other hand, shows a two-stage sequential decision. Test A could be a short and easily administered screening
test. On the basis of performance on this test, individuals would be sorted
into three categories, including those clearly accepted or rejected, as well
as an intermediate "uncertain" group to be examined further with more
intensive techniques, represented by Test B. On the basis of the second-
stage testing, this group would be sorted into accepted and rejected categories.

Such sequential testing can also be employed within a single testing session, to maximize the effective use of testing time (Linn, Rock, & Cleary,
1969; Weiss, 1976). Although applicable to paper-and-pencil printed group
tests, sequential testing is particularly well suited for computer testing. Essentially, the sequence of items or item groups within the test is determined by the examinee's own performance. For example, everyone might
begin with a set of items of intermediate difficulty. Those who score poorly
are routed to easier items; those who score well, to more difficult items.
Such branching may occur repeatedly at several stages. The principal effect
is that each examinee attempts only those items suited to her or his ability
level, rather than trying all items. Sequential testing models will be discussed further in Chapter 11, in connection with the utilization of computers in group testing.

Another strategy, suitable for the diagnosis of psychological disorders, is
to use only two categories, but to test further *all* cases classified as positives
(i.e., possibly pathological) by the preliminary screening test. This is the
strategy cited earlier in this section, in connection with the use of tests to
diagnose pathological conditions with very low base rates.

It should also be noted that many personnel decisions are in effect sequential, although they may not be so perceived. Incompetent employees
hired because of prediction errors can usually be discharged after a probationary period; failing students can be dropped from college at several
stages. In such situations, it is only adverse selection decisions that are terminal. To be sure, incorrect selection decisions that are later rectified may
be costly in terms of several value systems. But they are often less costly
than terminal wrong decisions.

A second condition that may alter the effectiveness of a psychological test
is the availability of alternative treatments and the possibility of *adapting*

treatments to individual characteristics. An example would be the utilization of different training procedures for workers at different aptitude levels, or the introduction of remedial instruction programs for students with certain educational disabilities. Under these conditions, the decision strategy followed in individual cases should take into account available data on the interaction of initial test score and differential treatment. When adaptive treatments are utilized, the success rate is likely to be substantially improved. Because the assignment of individuals to alternative treatments is essentially a classification rather than a selection problem, more will be said about the required methodology in a later section on classification decisions.

The examples cited illustrate a few of the ways in which the concepts and rationale of decision theory can assist in the evaluation of psychological tests for specific testing purposes. Essentially, decision theory has served to focus attention on the complexity of factors that determine the contribution a given test can make in a particular situation. The validity coefficient alone cannot indicate whether or not a test should be used, since it is only one of the factors to be considered in evaluating the impact of the test on the efficacy of the total decision process.[3]

MODERATOR VARIABLES. The validity of a test for a given criterion may vary among subgroups differing in personal characteristics. The classic psychometric model assumes that prediction errors are characteristic of the test rather than of the person and that these errors are randomly distributed among persons. The flexibility of approach ushered in by decision theory stimulated some exploration of prediction models involving interaction between persons and tests. Such interaction would imply that the same test may be a better predictor for certain classes or subsets of persons than it is for others. For example, a given test may be a better predictor of criterion performance for men than for women, or a better predictor for applicants from a lower than for applicants from a higher socioeconomic level. In these examples, sex and socioeconomic level are known as *moderator variables*, since they moderate the validity of the test (Saunders, 1956).

Interests and motivation may function as moderator variables. Thus, if an applicant has little interest in a job, he will probably perform poorly regardless of his scores on relevant aptitude tests. Among such persons, the correlation between aptitude test scores and job performance would be low. For individuals who are interested and highly motivated, on the other hand, the correlation between aptitude test score and job success may be quite high.

The 1950s and 1960s witnessed a flurry of research on a wide variety of possible moderator variables. A series of studies by Ghiselli (1956, 1960, 1963, 1968) were concerned with the prediction of job performance. Other investigators tested hypotheses regarding the role of personality variables,

[3] For a fuller discussion of the implications of decision theory for test use, see J. S. Wiggins (1973), Ch. 6, and at a more technical level, Cronbach and Gleser (1965).

particularly in the prediction of college achievement (Frederiksen & Gilbert, 1960; Frederiksen & Melville, 1954; Grooms & Endler, 1960; Stricker, 1966).

One relatively consistent finding is a sex difference in the predictability of academic grades. Surveys covering several hundred correlation coefficients from many sources report higher correlations for women than for men between aptitude test scores and grades (Gross, Faggen, & McCarthy, 1974; Schmitt, Mellon, & Bylenga, 1978; Seashore, 1962). The same trend was found in high school and college, although the trend was more pronounced at the college level. The data do not indicate the reason for this sex difference in the predictability of academic achievement, but it may be interesting to speculate about it in the light of other known sex differences. If women students in general tend to be more conforming and more inclined to accept the values and standards of the school situation, their class achievement will probably depend largely on their abilities. If, on the other hand, men students tend to concentrate their efforts on those activities (in or out of school) that arouse their individual interests, these interest differences would introduce additional variance in their course achievement and would make it more difficult to predict achievement from aptitude test scores. It should be noted, however, that the sex differences in these validity coefficients, although fairly consistent, were generally small. Moreover, there is some indication that the differences tended to be smaller in the later studies, a finding that could reflect changing attitudes of women in the late 1960s and the 1970s.

In general, earlier expectations about the contribution of moderator variables were not fulfilled (Abrahams & Alf, 1972; Pinder, 1973; Zedeck, 1971). Methodological analyses revealed many pitfalls. Cross-validation in new samples frequently failed to corroborate initial findings. And it did not appear likely that the use of moderators would substantially improve the prediction that could be achieved through other means. In the light of present knowledge, no variable can be *assumed* to moderate validities in the absence of explicit evidence for such an effect. The concept of moderator variables may nevertheless have heuristic value in furthering the understanding of individual behavior, as in clinical case studies, and in suggesting fresh hypotheses that should be investigated with proper methodological controls.

COMBINING INFORMATION FROM DIFFERENT TESTS

For the prediction of practical criteria, not one but several tests may often be required. Most criteria are complex, the criterion measure depending on a number of different traits. A single test designed to measure such a criterion would thus have to be highly heterogeneous. It has already been pointed out, however, that a relatively homogeneous test, measuring largely a single trait, is more satisfactory because it yields less ambiguous scores

(Ch. 5). Hence, it is usually preferable to use a combination of several relatively homogeneous tests, each covering a different aspect of the criterion, rather than a single test consisting of a hodgepodge of many different kinds of items.

When a number of specially selected tests are employed together to predict a single criterion, they are known as a *test battery*. The chief problem arising in the use of such batteries concerns the way in which scores on the different tests are to be combined in arriving at a decision regarding each individual. The statistical procedures followed for this purpose are of two major types, namely, multiple regression equation and multiple cutoff scores.

When tests are administered in the intensive study of individual cases, as in clinical diagnosis, counseling, or the evaluation of high-level executives, it is a common practice for the examiner to utilize test scores without further statistical analysis. In preparing a case report and in making recommendations, the examiner relies on judgment, past experience, and theoretical rationale to interpret score patterns and integrate findings from different tests. Such clinical use of test scores will be discussed further in Chapter 16.

MULTIPLE REGRESSION EQUATION. The multiple regression equation yields a predicted criterion score for each individual on the basis of his or her scores on all the tests in the battery. The following regression equation illustrates the application of this technique to predicting a student's achievement in high school mathematics courses from his or her scores on verbal (V), numerical (N), and reasoning (R) tests:

$$\text{Mathematics Achievement} = .21\,V + .21\,N + .32\,R + 1.35$$

In this equation, the student's stanine score on each of the three tests is multiplied by the corresponding weight given in the equation. The sum of these products, plus a constant (1.35), gives the student's predicted stanine position in mathematics courses.

Suppose that Bill Jones receives the following stanine scores:

Verbal	6
Numerical	4
Reasoning	8

The estimated mathematics achievement of this student is found as follows:

$$\text{Math. Achiev.} = (.21)(6) + (.21)(4) + (.32)(8) + 1.35 = 6.01$$

Bill's predicted stanine is approximately 6. It will be recalled (Ch. 4) that a stanine of 5 represents average performance. Bill would thus be expected to do somewhat better than average in mathematics courses. His very superior performance in the reasoning test ($R = 8$) and his above-average score on the verbal test ($V = 6$) compensate for his poor score in speed and accuracy of computation ($N = 4$).

Specific techniques for the computation of regression equations can be found in texts on psychological statistics (e.g., Guilford & Fruchter, 1978). Essentially, such an equation is based on the correlation of each test with the criterion, as well as on the intercorrelations among the tests. Obviously, those tests that correlate higher with the criterion should receive more weight. It is equally important, however, to take into account the correlation of each test with the other tests in the battery. Tests correlating highly with each other represent needless duplication, since they cover to a large extent the same aspects of the criterion. The inclusion of two such tests will not appreciably increase the validity of the entire battery, even though both tests may correlate highly with the criterion. In such a case, one of the tests would serve about as effectively as the pair; only one would therefore be retained in the battery.

Even after the most serious instances of duplication have been eliminated, however, the tests remaining in the battery will correlate with each other to varying degrees. For maximum predictive value, tests that make a more nearly unique contribution to the total battery should receive greater weight than those that partly duplicate the functions of other tests. In the computation of a multiple regression equation, each test is weighted in direct proportion to its correlation with the criterion and in inverse proportion to its correlations with the other tests. Thus, the highest weight will be assigned to the test with the highest validity and the least amount of overlap with the rest of the battery.

The validity of the entire battery can be found by computing the multiple correlation (R) between the criterion and the battery. This correlation indicates the highest predictive value that can be obtained from the given battery, when each test is given optimum weight for predicting the criterion in question. The optimum weights are those determined by the regression equation.

It should be noted that these weights are optimum only for the particular sample in which they were found. Because of chance errors in the correlation coefficients used in deriving them, the regression weights may vary from sample to sample. Hence, the battery should be cross-validated by correlating the predicted criterion scores with the actual criterion scores in a new sample. Formulas are available for estimating the amount of *shrinkage* in a multiple correlation to be expected when the regression equation is applied to a second sample, but empirical verification is preferable whenever possible. The larger the sample on which regression weights were derived, the smaller the shrinkage will be.[4]

In certain situations, the predictive validity of a battery may be improved by including in the regression equation a test having a zero correlation with the criterion but a high correlation with another test in the battery. This

---

[4] Under certain conditions, unit weights or other alternatives may be preferable to the regression weights. For a brief overview of research on various weighting schemes, see Dunnette and Borman (1979).

curious situation arises when the test that is uncorrelated with the criterion acts as a *suppressor variable* to eliminate or suppress the irrelevant variance in the other test (Conger & Jackson, 1972; Horst, 1941). For example, reading comprehension might correlate highly with scores on a mathematical or a mechanical aptitude test, because the test problems require the understanding of complicated written instructions. If reading comprehension is irrelevant to the job behavior to be predicted, the reading comprehension required by the tests introduces error variance and lowers the predictive validity of the tests. Administering a reading comprehension test and including scores on this test in the regression equation will eliminate this error variance and raise the validity of the battery. The suppressor variable appears in the regression equation with a negative weight. Thus, the higher an individual's score on reading comprehension, the more is deducted from his or her score on the mathematical or mechanical test. In any situation, however, the more direct procedure of revising a test to eliminate the irrelevant variance is preferable to the indirect statistical elimination of such variance through a suppressor variable. When changes in the test are not feasible, the investigation of suppressor variables should be considered. In such cases, the effect of the suppressor variable should always be checked in a new sample.

MULTIPLE CUTOFF SCORES. An alternative strategy for combining test scores utilizes multiple cutoff points. Briefly, this procedure involves the establishment of a minimum cutoff score on each test. Every individual who falls below such a minimum score on *any one* of the tests is rejected. Only those persons who reach or exceed the cutoff scores in all tests are accepted.

In choosing appropriate tests and establishing cutoff scores for a given occupation, it is customary to consider more than test validities. If only tests yielding significant validity coefficients were taken into account, one or more essential abilities in which all workers in the occupation excel might be overlooked. Hence the need for considering also those aptitudes in which workers excel as a group, even when individual differences beyond a certain minimum are unrelated to degree of job success. The multiple cutoff method is preferable to the regression equation in situations such as these, in which test scores may not be linearly related to the criterion. In some jobs, moreover, workers may be so homogeneous in a key trait that the range of individual differences is too narrow to yield a significant correlation between test scores and criterion.

The multiple cutoff method can be illustrated with the General Aptitude Test Battery (GATB) developed by the United States Employment Service for use in the occupational counseling program of its state employment service offices (U.S. Department of Labor, 1970a). Of the nine aptitude scores yielded by this battery, those to be considered for each occupation were chosen on the basis of criterion correlations, as well as means and standard

TABLE 16

Illustrative Data Used to Establish Cutoff Scores for Bank Tellers on the GATB

(From U.S. Department of Labor, 1975, p. 11)

Aptitude	Mean	SD	Criterion Correlation
G General Learning Ability	103.2	16.4	.157*
V Verbal Aptitude	104.4	15.7	.168*
N Numerical Aptitude	104.7	16.5	.235*
S Spatial Aptitude	102.6	17.9	.009
P Form Perception	118.6	19.6	.182*
Q Clerical Perception	125.6	16.8	.201*
K Motor Coordination	117.3	15.8	.054
F Finger Dexterity	105.5	20.9	.067
M Manual Dexterity	105.6	19.8	.100

Note. All GATB scores are expressed as standard scores with mean of 100 and *SD* of 20.
* significant at .01 level.

deviations of workers in that occupation and the qualitative observations of job analysts.

The development of GATB occupational standards for bank tellers is illustrated in Tables 16 and 17. The quantitative data, including means, standard deviations, and criterion correlations, are given in Table 16. In the summary presented in Table 17, the quantitative data are considered together with the job analysts' judgments of the relevance and importance of each ability. It might be of interest to note that Form Perception was rated important by the job analysts because bank tellers should be able "to note in detail the markings, shapes, and shadings on bills in order to detect counterfeit currency." The object of the summary evaluation is to permit the selection of two to four aptitudes, with appropriate cutting scores, for each occupation. The requirements established for bank tellers are as follows (U.S. Department of Labor, 1975, 1980b):

Numerical Aptitude	85
Form Perception	105
Clerical Perception	110

The strongest argument for the use of multiple cutoffs rather than a regression equation centers around the question of compensatory qualifications. With the regression equation, an individual who rates low in one test may receive an acceptable total score because he or she rates very high in some other test in the battery. A marked deficiency in one skill may thus be compensated for by outstanding ability along other lines. It is possible, however, that certain types of activity may require essential skills for which

TABLE 17

Summary of Quantitative and Qualitative Data for Bank Teller Validation Sample

(From U.S. Department of Labor, 1975, p. 12)

Type of Evidence	Aptitudes								
	G	V	N	S	P	Q	K	F	M
"Critical" on basis of job analysis									
"Important" on basis of job analysis	x		x	x	x	x	x		
"Irrelevant" on basis of job analysis									
Relatively high mean				x	x	x			
Relatively low standard deviation									
Significant criterion correlation	x	x	x		x	x			
Aptitudes considered for inclusion in battery	G	V	N		P	Q	K		

there is no substitute. In such cases, individuals falling below the required minimum in the essential skill will fail, regardless of their other abilities. An opera singer, for example, cannot afford to have poor pitch discrimination, regardless of how well he or she meets the other requirements of such a career. Similarly, operators of sound-detection devices in submarines need good auditory discrimination. Those persons incapable of making the necessary discriminations cannot succeed in such an assignment, regardless of superior mechanical aptitude, general intelligence, or other traits in which they may excel. With a multiple cutoff strategy, individuals lacking any essential skill would always be rejected, while with a regression equation they might be accepted.

When the relation between tests and criterion is linear and additive, on the other hand, a higher proportion of correct decisions will be reached with a regression equation than with multiple cutoffs. Another important advantage of the regression equation is that it provides an estimate of each person's criterion score, thereby permitting the relative evaluation of all individuals. With multiple cutoffs, no further differentiation is possible among those accepted or among those rejected. In many situations, the best strategy may involve a combination of both procedures. Thus, the multiple cutoff may be applied first, in order to reject those falling below minimum standards on any test, and predicted criterion scores may then be computed for the remaining acceptable cases by the use of a regression equation. If enough is known about the particular job requirements, the preliminary screening may be done in terms of only one or two essential skills, prior to the application of the regression equation. It might be added that extensive research with the USES General Aptitude Test Battery provides strong evidence for the linearity of correlation between test scores and criterion performance (Hawk, 1970). Under these conditions, selecting individuals on the basis of the actual magnitude of their test scores yields better criterion performance than does accepting all those who exceed a minimum cutoff score.

USE OF TESTS FOR CLASSIFICATION DECISIONS

THE NATURE OF CLASSIFICATION. Psychological tests may be used for purposes of selection, placement, or classification. In *selection*, each individual is either accepted or rejected. Deciding whether or not to admit a student to college, to hire a job applicant, or to accept an army recruit for officer training are examples of selection decisions. When selection is done sequentially, the earlier stages are often called "screening," the term "selection" being reserved for the more intensive final stages. "Screening" may also be used to designate any rapid, rough selection process even when not followed by further selection procedures.

Both placement and classification differ from selection in that no one is rejected, or eliminated from the program. All individuals are assigned to appropriate "treatments" so as to maximize the effectiveness of outcomes. In *placement*, the assignments are based on a single score. This score may be derived from a single test, such as a mathematics achievement test. If a battery of tests has been administered, a composite score computed from a single regression equation would be employed. Examples of placement decisions include the sectioning of college freshmen into different mathematics classes on the basis of their achievement test scores, assigning applicants to clerical jobs requiring different levels of skill and responsibility, and placing psychiatric patients in "more disturbed" and "less disturbed" wards. It is evident that in each of these decisions only one criterion is employed and that placement is determined by the individual's position along a single predictor scale.

Classification, on the other hand, always involves two or more criteria. In a military situation, for example, classification is a major problem, since each individual in an available personnel pool must be assigned to the military specialty where he or she can serve most effectively. Classification decisions are likewise required in industry, when new employees are assigned to training programs for different kinds of jobs. Other examples include the counseling of students regarding choice of college curriculum (science, liberal arts, etc.), as well as field of concentration. Counseling is based essentially on classification, since the client is told her or his chances of succeeding in different academic programs or occupations. Clinical diagnosis is likewise a classification problem, the major purposes of each diagnosis being a decision regarding the most appropriate type of therapy.

Although placement can be done with either one or more predictors, classification requires multiple predictors whose validity is individually determined against each criterion. A classification battery requires a different regression equation for each criterion. Some of the tests may have weights in all the equations, although of different values; others may be included in only one or two equations, having zero or negligible weights for some of the criteria. Thus, the combination of tests employed out of the total battery, as well as the specific weights, differs with the particular criterion. An example of such a classification battery is that developed by the Air Force for assignment of personnel to different training programs. This battery, consisting of both paper-and-pencil and apparatus tests, provided stanine scores for pilots, navigators, bombardiers, and a few other air-crew specialties. By finding an individual's estimated criterion scores from the different regression equations, it was possible to predict whether, for example, he was better qualified as a pilot than as a navigator.

DIFFERENTIAL VALIDITY. In the evaluation of a classification battery, the major consideration is its differential validity against the separate criteria. The object of such a battery is to predict the *difference* in each person's performance in two or more jobs, training programs, or other criterion situations. Tests chosen for such a battery should yield very different validity coefficients for the separate criteria. In a two-criterion classification problem, for example, the ideal test would have a high correlation with one criterion and a zero correlation (or preferably a negative correlation) with the other criterion. General intelligence tests are relatively poor for classification purposes, since they predict success about equally well in most areas. Hence, their correlations with the criteria to be differentiated would be too similar. An individual scoring high on such a test would be classified as successful for either assignment, and it would be impossible to predict in which he or she would do better. In a classification battery, we need some tests that are good predictors of criterion A and poor predictors of criterion B, and other tests that are poor predictors of A and good predictors of B.

Statistical procedures have been developed for selecting tests so as to maximize the differential validity of a classification battery (Brogden, 1946a, 1951, 1954; Horst, 1954; Mollenkopf, 1950b; Thorndike, 1949). When the number of criteria is greater than two, however, the problem becomes very complex. In practice, various empirical approaches have been followed to approximate the desired goals.

MULTIPLE DISCRIMINANT FUNCTIONS. An alternative way of handling classification decisions is by means of the multiple discriminant function (French,

1966). Essentially, this is a mathematical procedure for determining how closely the individual's scores on a whole set of tests approximate the scores typical of persons in a given occupation, curriculum, psychiatric syndrome, or other category. A person would then be assigned to the particular group he or she resembles most closely. Although the regression equation permits the prediction of degree of success in each field, the multiple discriminant function treats all persons in one category as of equal status. Group membership is the only criterion data utilized by this method. The discriminant function is useful when criterion scores are unavailable and only group membership can be ascertained. Some tests, for instance, are validated by administering them to persons in different occupations, although no measure of degree of job success is available for individuals within each field.

The discriminant function is also appropriate when there is a nonlinear relation between the criterion and one or more predictors. For example, in certain personality traits there may be an optimum range for a given occupation. Individuals having either more or less of the trait in question would thus be at a disadvantage. It seems reasonable to expect, for instance, that salespersons showing a moderately high amount of social dominance would be most likely to succeed, and that the chances of success would decline as scores move in either direction from this region. With the discriminant function, we would tend to select individuals falling within this optimum range. With the regression equation, on the other hand, the more dominant the score, the more favorable would be the predicted outcome. If the correlation between predictor and criterion were negative, of course, the regression equation would yield more favorable predictions for the low scorers. But there is no direct way whereby an intermediate score would receive maximum credit. Although in many instances the two techniques would lead to the same choices, there are situations in which persons would be differently classified by regression equations and discriminant functions. For most psychological testing purposes, regression equations provide a more effective technique. Under certain circumstances, however, the discriminant function is better suited to yield the required information.

MAXIMIZING THE UTILIZATION OF TALENT. Differential prediction of criteria with a battery of tests permits a fuller utilization of available human resources than is possible with a single general test or with a composite score from a single regression equation. As we saw in the Taylor-Russell tables and elsewhere in this chapter, the effectiveness of any test in selecting personnel for a given job depends on the selection ratio. In classification decisions, we work with a smaller selection ratio and are thus able to assign better qualified persons to each job. If out of 100 applicants, 10 were needed to fill each of two different jobs, the selection ratio is 10% for each job, when separate predictors are employed for each. If a single predictor (such as a general intelligence test) were used to select applicants for both jobs, the selection ratio would be 20%, since we could do no better than take the top 20 applicants.

Even when predictors for the two jobs are highly correlated, so that some of the same applicants will qualify for both jobs, there is considerable gain from the use of separate predictors. This situation is illustrated in Table 18,

TABLE 18

Mean Standard Criterion Score of Persons Placed on Two Jobs by Selection or Classification Strategies

(Adapted from Brogden, 1951, p. 182)

Selection Ratio for Each Job	Selection: Single Predictor	Classification: Two predictors whose intercorrelation is				
		0	.20	.40	.60	.80
5%	.88	1.03	1.02	1.01	1.00	.96
10	.70	.87	.86	.84	.82	.79
20	.48	.68	.67	.65	.62	.59
30	.32	.55	.53	.50	.46	.43
40	.18	.42	.41	.37	.34	.29
50	.00	.31	.28	.25	.22	.17

which shows the mean standard criterion score of workers selected for each of two jobs by a selection strategy (single predictor) and by a classification strategy involving two different predictors, each validated against its own job criterion. If workers were assigned by chance, with no selection, the mean standard score in this scale would be zero. This would be the case if the selection ratio were 50% for each job, so that 100% of the applicants would have to be hired. Note that even under these conditions, job performance would be improved by the use of two predictors, as shown in the last row of the table. With two uncorrelated predictors, mean job performance would be .31 (approximately ⅓ of a standard deviation above the chance value). As the correlation between the predictors increases, the job effectiveness of the selected employees decreases; but it remains better than chance even when the correlation is .80. With lower selection ratios, we can of course obtain better qualified personnel. As can be seen in Table 18, however, for each selection ratio, mean job performance is better when applicants are chosen through classification than through selection strategies.

A practical illustration of the advantages of classification strategies is provided by the use of Aptitude Area scores in the assignment of personnel to military occupational specialties in the U.S. Army (Maier & Fuchs, 1972). Each Aptitude Area corresponds to a group of Army jobs requiring a similar pattern of aptitudes, knowledge, and interests. From a 13-test classification battery, combinations of three to five tests were used to find the individual's score in each Aptitude Area. Figure 18 shows the results of an investigation

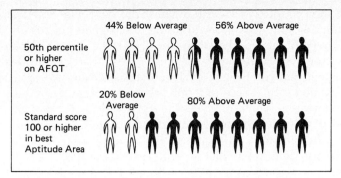

Fɪɢ. 18. Percentages Scoring Above Average on AFQT and on Best Aptitude Area of Army Classification Battery in a Sample of 7,500 Applicants for Enlistment.

(Data from U.S. Army Research Institute for the Behavioral and Social Sciences, Courtesy J. E. Uhlaner, 1974.)

of 7,500 applicants for enlistment in which the use of Aptitude Area scores was compared with the use of a global screening test, the Armed Forces Qualification Test (AFQT). It will be noted that only 56% of this group reached or exceeded the 50th percentile on the AFQT, while 80% reached or exceeded the average standard score of 100 on their best Aptitude Area. Thus, when individuals are allocated to specific jobs on the basis of the aptitudes required for each job, a very large majority are able to perform as well as the average of the entire sample or better. This apparent impossibility, in which nearly everyone could be above average, can be attained by capitalizing on the fact that nearly everyone excels in *some* aptitude.

The same point is illustrated with a quite different population in a study of gifted children by Feldman and Bratton (1972). For demonstration purposes, 49 children in two fifth-grade classes were evaluated on each of 19 measures, all of which had previously been used to select students for special programs for the gifted. Among these measures were global scores on a group intelligence test and on an educational achievement battery, tests of separate aptitudes and separate academic areas such as reading and arithmetic, a test of creative thinking, grades in music and art, and teachers' nominations of the most "gifted" and the most "creative" children in each class. When the five highest ranking children selected by each criterion were identified, they included 92% of the group. Thus, it was again shown that nearly all members of a group will excel when multivariate criteria are employed.

STATISTICAL ANALYSES OF TEST BIAS

ᴛʜᴇ ᴘʀᴏʙʟᴇᴍ. If we want to use tests to predict outcomes in some future situation, such as an applicant's performance in college or on a job, we need tests with high predictive validity against the particular criterion. This requirement is commonly overlooked in the development of so-called culture-fair tests (to be discussed further in Ch. 12). In the effort to include in such tests only functions common to different cultures or subcultures, we may choose content that has little relevance to any criterion we wish to predict. A better solution is to choose criterion-relevant content and then investigate possible population differences in the effectiveness of the test for its intended purpose. Validity coefficients, regression weights, and cutoff scores may vary as a function of differences in the examinees' experiential backgrounds. These values should therefore be checked within subgroups for whom there is reason to expect such effects. These possible subgroup differences will be recognized as a special case of the role of moderator variables discussed in a preceding section. And it will be recalled that the search for significant and stable moderator effects has proved disappointing. In the present section, we shall examine specific applications of this type of analysis to minority populations in the United States.

It should be noted that the predictive characteristics of test scores are less likely to vary among cultural groups when the test is intrinsically relevant to criterion performance. If a verbal test is employed to predict nonverbal job performance, a fortuitous validity may be found in one cultural group because of traditional associations of past experiences within that culture. In a group with a different experiential background, however, the validity of the test may disappear. On the other hand, a test that directly samples criterion behavior, or one that measures essential prerequisite skills, is likely to retain its validity in different groups.

Since the mid-1960s, there has been a rapid accumulation of research on possible ethnic differences in the predictive meaning of test scores.[5] The large majority of studies conducted thus far have dealt with black Americans, although a few have included other ethnic minorities. The problems investigated are generally subsumed under the heading of *test bias*. In this context, the term "bias" is employed in its well-established statistical sense, to designate constant or systematic error as opposed to chance error. This is the same sense in which we speak of a biased sample, in contrast to a random sample. The principal questions that have been raised regarding test bias pertain to validity coefficients (slope bias) and to the relationship between group means on the test and on the criterion (intercept bias). These questions will be examined in the next two sections.

SLOPE BIAS. To facilitate an understanding of the technical aspects of test bias, let us begin with a scatter diagram, or bivariate distribution, such

[5] Only a few representative studies can be cited from this voluminous literature. A comprehensive survey of relevant research results can be found in Jensen (1980), Ch. 10. References to many individual studies can also be obtained from several more specialized surveys to be cited below.

as those illustrated in Chapter 5 (Figs. 8, 9, 10; see especially Fig. 10, p. 108). For the present purpose, the horizontal axis (X) represents scores on a test and the vertical axis (Y) represents criterion scores, such as college grade-point average or an index of job performance. It will be recalled that the tally marks, showing the position of each individual on both test and criterion, indicate the direction and general magnitude of the correlation between the two variables. The line of best fit drawn through these tally marks is known as the regression line, and its equation is the regression equation. In this example, the regression equation would have only one predictor. The multiple regression equations discussed earlier in this chapter have several predictors, but the principle is the same.

When both test and criterion scores are expressed as standard scores ($SD = 1.00$), the *slope* of the regression line equals the correlation coefficient. For this reason, if a test yields a significantly different validity coefficient in the two groups, this difference is described as slope bias. This type of group difference is often designated as "differential validity." Several investigators have also employed the term "single-group validity" to refer to a test whose validity coefficient reached statistical significance in one group but failed to do so in another.

Figure 19 provides schematic illustrations of regression lines for several bivariate distributions.[6] The ellipses represent the region within which the tally marks of each sample would fall. Case 1 shows the bivariate distribution of two groups with different means in the predictor, but with identical regression lines between predictor and criterion. In this case, there is no test bias, since any given test score (X) corresponds to the identical criterion score (Y) in both groups. Case 2 illustrates slope bias, with a lower validity coefficient in the minority group.

In differential validity studies, certain methodological precautions should be observed. For example, the use of ratings as a criterion in this type of study may yield results that are out of line with those obtained with more objective criteria (Bass & Turner, 1973; Campbell, Crooks, Mahoney, & Rock, 1973; Kirkpatrick, Ewen, Barrett, & Katzell, 1968). A second example involves the comparison of ethnic samples from different institutions. In such cases, ethnic and institutional factors are likely to be confounded in the results (Kirkpatrick et al., 1968).

A common difficulty arises from the fact that in several studies the number of cases in the minority sample was much smaller than in the majority sample. Under these conditions, the same validity coefficient could be statistically significant in the majority sample and not significant in the mi-

---

[6] The type of analysis of test bias illustrated in Fig. 19 has come to be known as the "Cleary model" because it was used by Cleary (1968) in a widely cited study of College Board Scholastic Aptitude Test scores of minority students. The mathematical procedures were developed by Gulliksen and Wilks (1950), and their application to ethnic and sex comparisons was suggested by Humphreys (1952). The diagrams in Fig. 19 were adapted from a study by M. A. Gordon (1953) conducted in the U.S. Air Force under Humphreys' direction.

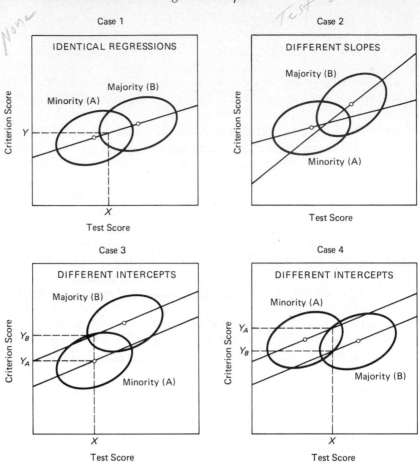

Fig. 19. Slope and Intercept Bias in Predicting Criterion Scores. The ellipses show the regions within which members of each group fall when their test scores are plotted against their criterion performance.

(Cases 1, 2, and 3 adapted from M. A. Gordon, 1953, p. 3.)

nority sample (so-called single-group validity). With 100 cases, for example, a correlation of .27 is clearly significant at the .01 level; with 30 cases, the same correlation falls far short of the minimum value required for significance even at the .05 level. For this reason, the proper procedure to follow in such differential validation studies is to evaluate the difference between the two validity coefficients, rather than testing each separately for significance (Humphreys, 1973; *Standards*, 1974, E9). By the latter procedure, one could easily "demonstrate" that a test is valid for, let us say, whites and not valid for blacks. All that would be needed for this purpose is a large enough group of whites and a small enough group of blacks! Cross-validation of results in a second pair of independent samples is also desirable, to check whether the group yielding higher validity in the first study still does so in the second.

A sophisticated statistical analysis of the results of 19 published studies reporting validity coefficients for black and white employment samples casts serious doubt on the conclusions reached in some of the earlier studies (Schmidt, Berner, & Hunter, 1973). Taking into account the obtained validities and the size of samples in each study, the investigators demonstrated that the discrepancies in validity coefficients found between blacks and whites did not differ from chance expectancy. This conclusion was corroborated in a later, more comprehensive analysis covering 39 studies (Hunter, Schmidt, & Hunter, 1979). The topic of differential validity for minority and nonminority job applicants elicited continuing discussion through the decade of the 1970s.[7] Some investigators observed that, because of methodological limitations, the results were merely inconclusive. It is noteworthy, however, that no evidence of differential validity was found in well-designed, large-scale studies on industrial samples (Campbell et al., 1973) and army personnel (Maier & Fuchs, 1973). In general, the methodologically sounder studies proved to be those less likely to find differential validity.

Similar results have been obtained in numerous investigations of black and white college students (Breland, 1979). Validity coefficients of the College Board Scholastic Aptitude Test and other college admission tests for black students were generally as high as those obtained for white students, or higher. These relationships were found when the black and white samples were attending the same colleges, as well as when they were attending separate colleges. Working at a very different level, Mitchell (1967) studied the validities of two educational readiness tests against end-of-year achievement test scores of first-grade schoolchildren. In the large samples of black and white children tested, validities of total scores and of subtests were very similar for the two ethnic groups, although tending to run somewhat higher for the blacks. These findings were consistently corroborated in later studies of black and white children, as well as in comparisons of children classified by father's occupational level and by indices of educational and socioeconomic level of the community.[8]

INTERCEPT BIAS. Even when a test yields the same validity coefficients for two groups, it may show intercept bias. The intercept of a regression line refers to the point at which the line intersects the axis. A test exhibits intercept bias if it systematically underpredicts or overpredicts criterion performance for a particular group. Let us look again at Case 1 in Figure 19, in

---

[7] Overviews of these discussions are provided by Hunter and Schmidt (1978) and Linn (1978).

[8] Summaries of these studies can be obtained from the test publisher, The Psychological Corporation.

which majority and minority samples show identical regressions. Under these conditions, there is neither slope nor intercept bias. Although the groups differ significantly in mean test scores, they show a corresponding difference in criterion performance. In Case 3, on the other hand, the two groups have regression lines with the same slope but different intercepts. In this case, the majority group (B) has a higher intercept than the minority group (A), that is, the majority regression line intersects the Y axis at a higher point than does the minority regression line. Although the validity coefficients computed within each group are equal, any test score (X) will correspond to different criterion scores in the two groups, as shown by points Y_A and Y_B. The same test score thus has a different predictive meaning for the two groups. In this situation, the majority mean again exceeds the minority mean in both test and criterion, as it did in Case 1. Because of the intercept difference, however, the use of the majority regression line for both groups would *overpredict* the criterion performance of minority group members. If a single cutoff score (X) were applied to both groups, it would discriminate in favor of the minority group. Intercept bias discriminates against the group with the higher intercept.

Psychologists who are concerned about the possible unfairness of tests for minority group members visualize a situation illustrated in Case 4. Note that, in this case, the majority excels on the test, but majority and minority perform equally well on the criterion. The minority group now has the higher intercept. Selecting all applicants in terms of a test cutoff established for the majority group would thus discriminate unfairly against the minority. Under these conditions, use of the majority regression line for both groups *underpredicts* the criterion performance of minority group members. This situation is likely to occur when a large proportion of test variance is irrelevant to criterion performance and measures functions in which the majority excels the minority. A thorough job analysis and satisfactory test validity provide safeguards against the choice of such a test.

Reilly (1973) has demonstrated mathematically that Case 3 will occur if the two groups differ in a third variable (e.g., sociocultural background) which correlates positively with both test and criterion. Under these conditions, the test overpredicts the performance of minority group members and the use of the same cutoff scores for both groups favors the minority. The findings of empirical studies do in fact support this expectation. Well-controlled studies have found either no significant differences or, more often, a tendency for the tests to overpredict the criterion performance of minority groups and hence to favor the members of minority groups in selection decisions. Such results have been obtained in the prediction of college grades (Breland, 1979), law school grades (Linn, 1975), performance in Army and Air Force training programs (M. A. Gordon, 1953; Maier & Fuchs, 1973; Shore & Marion, 1972), and a wide variety of industrial criteria (Campbell et al., 1973; Gael, Grant, & Ritchie, 1975a, 1975b; Grant & Bray, 1970; Ruch, 1972).

It is interesting to note that the same results have been obtained when comparisons were made between groups classified according to educational or socioeconomic level. The Army Classification Battery tended to overpredict the performance of high school dropouts and underpredict the performance of college graduates in training programs for military occupational specialties (Maier, 1972). Similarly, the college grades of students whose fathers were in the professions were underpredicted from various academic aptitude tests, while the grades of students from lower occupational levels tended to be overpredicted (Hewer, 1965). In all these studies, comparisons of higher-scoring and lower-scoring groups revealed either no significant difference in intercepts or a slight bias in favor of the groups scoring lower on the tests.

The problem of intercept bias relates most closely to what is commonly designated as "test fairness." Although the terms "test fairness" and "test bias" are sometimes used broadly and interchangeably to cover all aspects of test use with cultural minorities, it has become customary to identify test fairness (or unfairness) with intercept bias. This usage is followed in the *Uniform Guidelines on Employee Selection Procedures* (Appendix B). In the section on *Fairness* (14B), the defining statement reads:

> When members of one race, sex, or ethnic group characteristically obtain lower scores on a selection procedure than members of another group, and the differences in scores are not reflected in differences in a measure of job performance, use of the selection procedure may unfairly deny opportunities to members of the group that obtains the lower scores.

DECISION MODELS FOR FAIR USE OF TESTS. In the mid-1970's, the focus of research began to shift from the evaluation of test bias to the design of selection strategies for fair test use with cultural minorities. If a selection strategy follows the regression (or Cleary) model illustrated in Figure 19, individuals will be chosen (for college admission, employment, etc.) solely on the basis of their predicted criterion scores. This strategy will maximize overall criterion performance, without regard to other objectives of the selection process. According to this strategy, a fair use of tests in selection is one that is based only on the best estimate of criterion performance for each individual.

Several other decision models were proposed which have the effect of selecting larger proportions of persons from the lower-scoring group.[9] When first described, these alternative models appeared to follow quite different procedures than did the regression model. It was later demonstrated, how-

[9] The literature on the various decision models for fair test use is extensive, and much of it is quite technical and complicated. For simple summaries of the distinguishing features and implications of different models, see Dunnette and Borman (1979, pp. 497–500) and Gross and Su (1975, pp. 350–351). Fuller explanations can be found in Hunter and Schmidt (1976), Hunter, Schmidt, and Rauschenberger (1977), and Jensen (1980, Ch. 9).

ever, that they could all be expressed as variants of one comprehensive model (Darlington, 1971; Gross & Su, 1975; Petersen, 1974; Petersen & Novick, 1976). The differences among the various models can be explained in terms of the value judgments implicit in each model. The role of values in decision strategies was illustrated earlier in this chapter (see Fig. 16). It will be recalled that the assignment of a relative *utility* to each outcome requires a judgment of the degree of favorableness or unfavorableness of that outcome. These value judgments, together with the probability of each outcome, are used in computing the total expected utility (EU) of the decision strategy.

The decision-theoretic analyses of fair test use demonstrated that the proposed models differ in their definition of fairness, insofar as they implicitly assign different values to acceptance and rejection of potential successes and failures within minority and nonminority populations. The expected utility model makes the underlying social values explicit. This approach calls for an overt statement of utilities, which cannot be reached through statistical means but requires open discussion and successive approximations to balance conflicting goals (Darlington, 1976; Messick, 1980b). Among the goals to be reconciled are those of providing equality of opportunity for all individuals, maximizing achievement and productivity, and extending preferential treatment to groups disadvantaged by past inequities.

The concept of experiential disadvantage itself raises a fundamental psychological question. How should "disadvantage" be defined for purposes of test use as well as preferential treatment? Ethnic categories are far too broad and heterogeneous to serve as effective moderator variables in sorting persons into subgroups for these purposes. Any one "race," "color," or popularly recognized subculture covers a vast number of experiential differences whose combination varies from person to person. Narrower, more clearly defined experiential variables should prove more productive.

This problem is clearly recognized in a thoughtful and provocative article by Novick and Ellis (1977). Approaching the question from both psychological and legal viewpoints, these investigators propose that psychometrics broaden its assessment scope to include measures of individual disadvantage and individual utility as standard variables in decision making. The former would characterize individuals with reference to their need for compensatory treatment, the latter with reference to the social value of their potential contribution resulting from such treatment.

Finally, it should be emphasized that statistical adjustments in test scores, cutoffs, and prediction formulas hold little promise as a means of correcting social inequities. More constructive solutions are suggested by other approaches discussed earlier in this chapter. One is illustrated by multiple aptitude testing and classification strategies, which permit the fullest utilization of the diverse aptitude patterns fostered by different cultural backgrounds. Another approach is through adaptive treatments, such as individualized training programs. In order to maximize the fit of such programs to individual characteristics, it is essential that tests reveal as fully and accurately as possible the person's present level of development in the requisite abilities. Comprehensive decision models provide a framework for combining a diversity of approaches and value systems and assessing the overall effectiveness of each solution.

CHAPTER 8

Item Analysis

AMILIARITY with the basic concepts and techniques of item analysis, like knowledge about other phases of test construction, can help test users in their evaluation of published tests. In addition, item analysis is particularly relevant to the construction of informal, local tests, such as the quizzes and examinations prepared by teachers for classroom use. Some of the general guidelines for effective item writing, as well as the simpler statistical techniques of item analysis, can materially improve classroom tests and are worth using even with small groups.

Items can be analyzed qualitatively, in terms of their content and form, and quantitatively, in terms of their statistical properties. Qualitative analysis includes the consideration of content validity, discussed in Chapter 6, and the evaluation of items in terms of effective item-writing procedures, to be discussed in Chapter 14. Quantitative analysis includes principally the measurement of item difficulty and item discrimination. Both the validity and the reliability of any test depend ultimately on the characteristics of its items. High reliability and validity can be built into a test in advance through item analysis. Tests can be improved through the selection, substitution, or revision of items.

Item analysis makes it possible to shorten a test and at the same time to increase its validity and reliability. Other things being equal, a longer test is more valid and reliable than a shorter one. The effect of lengthening or shortening a test on the reliability coefficient was discussed in Chapter 5, where the Spearman-Brown formula for estimating this effect was also introduced. These estimated changes in reliability occur when the discarded items are equivalent to those that remain, or when equivalent new items are added to the test. Similar changes in validity will result from the deletion or addition of items of equivalent validity. All such estimates of change in reliability or validity refer to the lengthening or shortening of tests through a *random* selection of items, without item analysis. When a test is shortened by eliminating the least satisfactory items, however, the short test may be more valid and reliable than the original longer instrument.

ITEM DIFFICULTY

PERCENTAGE PASSING. For most testing purposes, the difficulty of an item is defined in terms of the percentage (or proportion) of persons who answer it correctly. The easier the item, the larger will this percentage be. A word that is correctly defined by 70% of the standardization sample ($p = .70$) is regarded as easier than one that is correctly defined by only 15% ($p = .15$). It is customary to arrange items in order of difficulty, so that examinees begin with relatively easy items and proceed to items of increasing difficulty. This arrangement gives the examinees confidence in approaching the test and also reduces the likelihood of their wasting much time on items beyond their ability to the neglect of easier items they can correctly complete.

In the process of test construction, a major reason for measuring item difficulty is to choose items of suitable difficulty level. Most standardized ability tests are designed to assess as accurately as possible each individual's level of attainment in the particular ability. For this purpose, if no one passes an item, it is excess baggage in the test. The same is true of items that everyone passes. Neither of these types of items provides any information about individual differences. Since such items do not affect the variability of test scores, they contribute nothing to the reliability or validity of the test. The closer the difficulty of an item approaches 1.00 or 0, the less differential information about examinees it contributes. Conversely, the closer the difficulty level approaches .50, the more differentiations the item can make. Suppose out of 100 persons, 50 pass an item and 50 fail it ($p = .50$). This item enables us to differentiate between each of those who passed it and each of those who failed it. We thus have 50×50 or 2,500 paired comparisons, or bits of differential information. An item passed by 70% of the persons provides 70×30 or 2,100 bits of information; one passed by 90% provides 90×10 or 900; one passed by 100% provides 100×0 or 0. The same relationships would hold for harder items, passed by fewer than 50%.

For maximum differentiation, then, it would seem that one should choose all items at the .50 difficulty level. The decision is complicated, however, by the fact that items within a test tend to be intercorrelated. The more homogeneous the test, the higher will these intercorrelations be. In an extreme case, if all items were perfectly intercorrelated and all were of .50 difficulty level, the same 50 persons out of 100 would pass each item. Consequently, half of the examinees would obtain perfect scores and the other half zero scores. Because of item intercorrelations, it is best to select items with a moderate spread of difficulty level, but whose average difficulty is .50. Moreover, the higher the item intercorrelations (or the correlations of items with total score), the wider should be the spread of item difficulty.

Another consideration in the choice of appropriate item difficulty pertains to the probability of guessing in multiple-choice items. To allow for the fact that a certain proportion of examinees will select the correct option by guessing, the desired proportion of correct responses is set higher than would be the case for a free response item. For a five-option multiple-choice item, for example, the average proportion correct should be approximately .69 (Lord, 1952).

INTERVAL SCALES. The percentage of persons passing an item expresses item difficulty in terms of an ordinal scale; that is, it correctly indicates the rank order or relative difficulty of items. For example, if Items 1, 2, and 3 are passed by 30%, 20%, and 10% of the cases, respectively, we can conclude that Item 1 is the easiest and Item 3 is the hardest of the three. But we cannot infer that the difference in difficulty between Items 1 and 2 is equal to that between Items 2 and 3. Equal percentage differences would correspond to equal differences in difficulty only in a rectangular distribution, in which the cases were uniformly distributed throughout the range. This problem is similar to that encountered in connection with percentile scores, which are also based on percentages of cases. It will be recalled from Chapter 4 that percentile scores do not represent equal units, but differ in magnitude from the center to the extremes of the distribution (Fig. 4, Ch. 4).

If we assume a normal distribution of the trait measured by any given item, the difficulty level of the item can be expressed in terms of an equal-unit interval scale by reference to a table of normal curve frequencies. In Chapter 4 we saw, for example, that approximately 34% of the cases in a normal distribution fall between the mean and a distance of 1σ in either direction (Fig. 3, Ch. 4). With this information, we can examine Figure 20, which shows the difficulty level of an item passed by 84% percent of the cases. Since it is the persons in the upper part of the distribution who pass and those in the lower part who fail, this 84% includes the upper half (50%) plus 34% of the cases from the lower half (50 + 34 = 84). Hence, the item falls 1σ *below* the mean, as shown in Figure 20. An item passed by 16% of

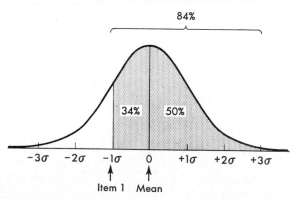

FIG. 20. Relation between Percentage of Persons Passing an Item and the Item Difficulty in Normal Curve Units.

the cases would fall 1σ *above* the mean, since above this point there are 16% of the cases ($50 - 34 = 16$). An item passed by exactly 50% of the cases falls at the mean and would thus have a 0 value on this scale. The more difficult items have plus values, the easier items minus values. The difficulty value corresponding to any percentage passing can be found by reference to a normal curve frequency table, given in any standard statistics text.

Because item difficulties expressed in terms of normal curve σ-units involve negative values and decimals, they are usually converted into a more manageable scale. One such scale, employed by Educational Testing Service in its test development, uses a unit designated by the Greek letter *delta* (Δ). The relation between Δ and normal curve σ-values (z) is shown below:

$$\Delta = 13 + 4z$$

The constants 13 and 4 were chosen arbitrarily in order to provide a scale that eliminates negative values and yields a range of integers wide enough to permit the dropping of decimals. An item passed by nearly 100% of the cases (99.87%), falling at -3σ, would have a Δ of: $13 + (4)(-3) = 1$. This is the lowest value likely to be found in most groups. At the other extreme, an item passed by less than 1% (0.13%) of the cases, would have a value of $+3\sigma$ and a Δ of: $13 + (4)(3) = 25$. An item falling at the mean will have a 0 σ-value and a Δ of: $13 + (4)(0) = 13$. The Δ scale is thus a scale in which practically all items fall between 1 and 25, and the mean difficulty value within any given group corresponds to 13.

A practical advantage of the Δ scale over other possible conversions is that a table is available (Fan, 1952) from which Δ can be found by simply entering the value of p (proportion of persons passing the item). The table eliminates the necessity of looking up normal curve σ-values and transforming these values to Δ's. For most practical purposes, an ordinal measure of item difficulty, such as percentage passing, is adequate. For more precise statistical analyses, requiring the measurement of difficulty on an interval scale, Δ values can be obtained with little additional effort.

THURSTONE ABSOLUTE SCALING. Indexes of item difficulty expressed as percentages or normal curve units are limited to the ability range covered by the sample from which they were obtained. For several purposes, however, there is need for a measure of item difficulty applicable across different samples varying in ability level. In educational achievement tests, for example, it is advantageous to be able to compare a child's score over several successive grades on a uniform scale. Yet it would obviously be impracticable to scale the items appropriate for all grades by administering them to a single group, since some items would be too difficult and some too easy for nearly everyone in the group.

Another example is provided by large-scale testing programs that require many equivalent forms to be administered at different times, such as college admission programs. This problem was considered in Chapter 4 as it affects the interpretation of total scores on such instruments as the Scholastic Aptitude Test. The solution described in that case was to use a fixed, standard reference group to define the scale units and origin and then to convert all subsequent scores to that scale. This conversion requires a set of anchor or linkage items that are included in the tests administered to any pair of groups. The items constitute a minitest, in that they are representative of the whole test in content and form. A different set of linkage items can be shared by different pairs of groups. Each new form is linked to one or two earlier forms, which in turn are linked to other forms through a chain of minitests extending back to the original reference group.

The same general method can be used to measure the difficulty of individual items on a uniform scale that is applicable to any number of interlocking groups. The statistical procedure, known as absolute scaling, was developed by Thurstone (1925, 1947a) and has been widely employed in test development (e.g., Angoff, 1971a; STEP, 1980). Essentially, this procedure involves two steps. First, we find scale values of items separately within each group, by converting the percentage passing each item into normal curve z units. Second, we translate all these scale values into corresponding values for *one* of the groups, chosen as a standard or reference group. Any group can be chosen as a reference group, such as the first group tested, the youngest group, a group in the middle of the range, or some other convenient group. What is required is a set of common, anchor items administered to two or more groups and scaled within each group.

The scale values of the same items in two (or more) groups serve to define the relation between the groups and permit the transmutation of all item difficulty values from one group to another. This relation is illustrated schematically in Figure 21, showing the σ-distance (z) of the same item (i) in two adjacent groups A and B. The same item (i) is passed by a larger

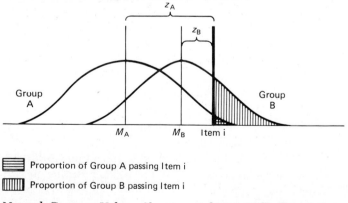

Fig. 21. Normal Curve z Values Showing Relative Difficulty of Same Item in Groups A and B.

proportion of persons in Group B than in Group A. Its distance from the mean is accordingly smaller in Group B (z_B) than in Group A (z_A). The corresponding Group A and Group B values for all the *common items* provide the basis for the conversion formula whereby *all items* given to Group B can be converted to Group A difficulty values or vice versa. A simple approximation can be obtained by plotting the Group A z values against the Group B z values and drawing a straight line through the points. This line can then be used to find z_A values for all other items administered to Group B.

The same conversion procedure can be extended to any number of groups by working with pairs of adjacent overlapping groups. For example, in a test designed for Grades 1 through 8, the eighth-grade scale values can be transmuted into the seventh–grade scale, the seventh-grade into the sixth, and so on down to the first grade. Adjacent grade groups are usually sufficiently similar to be able to share a large segment of the test for linkage purposes. Any one grade, however, would share different segments with the next higher and the next lower grades.

DISTRIBUTION OF TEST SCORES. The difficulty of the test as a whole is, of course, directly dependent on the difficulty of the items that make up the test. A comprehensive check of the difficulty of the total test for the population for which it is designed is provided by the distribution of total scores. If the standardization sample is a representative cross section of such a population, then it is generally expected that the scores will fall roughly into a normal distribution curve.

Let us suppose, however, that the obtained distribution curve is not normal but clearly skewed, as illustrated in Figure 22, Parts A and B. The first of these distributions, with a piling of scores at the low end, suggests that the test has too high a floor for the group under consideration, lacking a sufficient number of easy items to discriminate properly at the lower end of the range. The result is that persons who would normally scatter over a considerable range obtain zero or near-zero scores on this test. A peak at the low end of the scale is therefore obtained. This artificial piling of scores is illustrated schematically in Figure 23, in which a normally distributed group yields a skewed distribution on a particular test. The opposite skewness is illustrated in Part B of Figure 22, with the scores piled at the upper end, a finding that suggests insufficient test ceiling. Administering a test designed for the general population to selected samples of college or graduate students will usually yield such a skewed distribution, a number of students obtaining nearly perfect scores. With such a test, it is impossible to measure individual differences among the more able students in the group. If more difficult items had been included in the test, some individuals would undoubtedly have scored higher than the present test permits.

When the standardization sample yields a markedly nonnormal distribu-

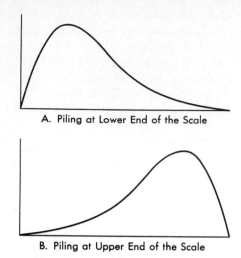

A. Piling at Lower End of the Scale

B. Piling at Upper End of the Scale

FIG. 22. Skewed Distribution Curves.

tion on a test, the difficulty level of the test is ordinarily modified until a normal curve is approximated. Depending on the type of deviation from normality that appears, easier or more difficult items may be added, other items eliminated or modified, the position of items in the scale altered, or the scoring weights assigned to certain responses revised. Such adjustments are continued until the distribution becomes at least roughly normal. Under these conditions, the most likely score, obtained by the largest number of persons, usually corresponds to about 50% correct items. To one who is unfamiliar with the methods of psychological test construction, a 50% score may seem shockingly low. It is sometimes objected, on this basis, that the examiner has set too low a standard of passing on the test. Or the inference is drawn that the group tested is a particularly poor one. Both conclusions, of course, are totally meaningless when viewed in the light of the procedures followed in developing psychological tests. Such tests are deliberately con-

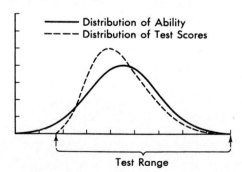

———— Distribution of Ability
– – – – Distribution of Test Scores

Test Range

FIG. 23. Skewness Resulting from Insufficient Test Floor.

structed and specifically modified so as to yield a mean score of approximately 50% correct. Only in this way can the maximum differentiation between individuals at all ability levels be obtained with the test. With a mean of approximately 50% correct items, there is the maximum opportunity for a normal distribution, with individual scores spreading widely at both extremes.[1]

RELATING ITEM DIFFICULTY TO TESTING PURPOSE. Standardized psychological tests have generally been designed to elicit maximum differentiation among individuals at all levels. Our discussion of item difficulty thus far has been directed to this type of test. In the construction of tests to serve special purposes, however, the choice of appropriate item difficulties, as well as the optimal form of the distribution of test scores, depends upon the type of discrimination sought. Accordingly, tests designed for screening purposes should utilize items whose difficulty values come closest to the desired selection ratio. For example, to select the upper 20% of the cases, the best items are those clustering around a p of .20 (or somewhat higher to allow for guessing in objective items). Since in a screening test no differentiation is required *within* the accepted or rejected groups, the most effective use of testing time is obtained when items cluster near the critical cutoff. It follows, for instance, that if a test is to be used to screen scholarship applicants from a college population, the items should be considerably more difficult than the average for that population. Similarly, if slow learners are being selected for a remedial training program, items that are much easier than average would be desirable.

Another illustration is provided by the National Assessment of Educational Progress (Womer, 1970). Designed as an attempt to obtain direct information on the outcomes of education throughout the United States, this project examined carefully chosen representative samples of the population at four age levels: 9-, 13-, and 17-year-olds and young adults between the ages of 26 and 35. The project was not concerned with the achievement of individuals. Its aim was to describe the knowledge, understanding, and skills manifested by the American population at the specified age levels. Within each of the content areas and each of the age groups tested, achievement was assessed in terms of three questions: (1) What do *almost all* persons know? (2) What does the *typical or average* person know? (3) What do the *most able*

---

[1] Actually, the normal curve provides finer discrimination at the ends than at the middle of the scale. Equal discrimination at all points of the scale would require a rectangular distribution. The normal curve, however, has an advantage if subsequent statistical analyses of scores are to be conducted, because many current statistical techniques assume approximate normality of distribution. For this and other reasons, it is likely that most tests designed for general use will continue to follow a normal-curve pattern for some time to come.

persons know? To answer these questions, exercises[2] were prepared at three difficulty levels: one third of the exercises were "easy" (.90); one third were "average" (.50); and one third were "difficult" (.10). The actual percentages of persons passing each exercise varied somewhat around these values. But the goal of the test constructors was to approximate the three values as closely as possible.

A third example of the choice of item difficulty levels in terms of special testing goals is to be found in mastery testing. It will be recalled (Ch. 4) that mastery testing is often associated with criterion-referenced testing. If the purpose of the test is to ascertain whether an individual has adequately mastered the basic essentials of a skill or whether he or she has acquired the prerequisite knowledge to advance to the next step in a learning program, then the items should probably be at the .80 or .90 difficulty level. Under these conditions, we would expect the majority of those taking the examination to complete nearly all items correctly. Thus, the very easy items (even those passed by 100% of the cases), which are discarded as nondiscriminative in the usual standardized test, are the very items that would be included in a mastery test. Similarly, a pretest, administered prior to a learning unit to determine whether any of the students have already acquired the skills to be taught, will yield very low percentages of passing for each item. In this case, items with very low or even zero p values should not be discarded, since they reveal what remains to be learned.

It is apparent from these examples that the appropriate difficulty level of items depends upon the purpose of the test. Although in most testing situations items clustering around a medium difficulty (.50) yield the maximum information about the individual's performance level, decisions about item difficulty cannot be made routinely, without knowing how the test scores will be used.

ITEM DISCRIMINATION

CHOICE OF CRITERION. Item discrimination refers to the degree to which an item differentiates correctly among examinees in the behavior that the test is designed to measure. When the test as a whole is to be evaluated by means of criterion-related validation, the items may themselves be evaluated and selected on the basis of their relationship to the same external criterion. This procedure has been followed especially in the development of certain personality and interest tests, to be discussed in Chapters 17 and 18. It is also the method generally followed in choosing items for inclusion in bio-

---

[2] Because of the nature of many of the tests, the term "exercise" was considered more appropriate than "item." For purposes of the present discussion, they can be regarded as items.

graphical inventories, which typically cover a heterogeneous collection of background facts about the individual.

In all these instruments, there is no a priori basis for grading a response as right or wrong, or assigning it a scoring weight, except by comparison with the criterion status of persons who give that response. From an initial pool of items, those items are retained that best differentiate among persons classified in different criterion categories, such as various occupations or psychiatric syndromes. Frequently, the criterion groups consist of successes and failures in an academic course, a training program, or a type of job.

In the criterion-referenced mastery testing described in Chapter 4, items can be evaluated by comparing the item performance of individuals who have had varying amounts of instruction in the relevant functions (Panell & Laabs, 1979; Shaycoft, 1979, Ch. 3). Usually the comparison is between the proportion of persons who give the correct item response in a pre-instruction and a postinstruction group. Because these tests are used to determine whether individuals have reached a specified level of mastery, individual differences in overall performance on a single occasion are minimized. Hence, internal item analyses will not be meaningful and an external criterion, such as amount of relevant instruction, is needed.

In other types of achievement tests, as in many aptitude tests, item discrimination is usually investigated against total score on the test itself.[3] For educational achievement tests, an external criterion is not typically available. For aptitude tests, the increasing emphasis on construct validation makes total score an appropriate criterion for item selection. In the initial stages of test development, the total score provides a first approximation to a measure of the ability, trait, or construct under investigation.

Let us examine further the implications of choosing items on the basis of an external criterion and on the basis of total test score. The former tends to maximize the validity of the test against the external criterion, the latter to maximize the internal consistency or homogeneity of the test. Under certain conditions, the two approaches may lead to opposite results, the items chosen on the basis of external validity being the very ones rejected on the basis of internal consistency. Let us suppose that the preliminary form of a scholastic aptitude test consists of 100 arithmetic items and 50 vocabulary items. In order to select items from this initial pool by the method of internal consistency, some index of agreement between performance on each item and total score on the 150 items will be computed. It is apparent that such an index would tend to be higher for the arithmetic than for the vocabulary items, since the total score is based on twice as many arithmetic items. If it is desired to retain the 75 "best" items in the final form

---

[3] Item-test correlations will be somewhat inflated by the common specific and error variance in the item and the test of which it is a part. Formulas are available to correct for this part-whole effect (Guilford & Fruchter, 1978, pp. 465–467).

of the test, it is likely that most of these items will prove to be arithmetic problems. In terms of the external criterion of scholastic achievement, however, the vocabulary items might have been more valid predictors than the arithmetic items. If such is the case, the item analysis will have served to lower rather than raise the validity of the test.

The practice of rejecting items that have low correlations with total score provides a means of purifying or homogenizing the test. By such a procedure, the items with the highest average intercorrelations will be retained. This method of selecting items will increase test validity only when the original pool of items measures a single trait and when this trait is present in the criterion. Some types of tests, however, measure a combination of traits required by a complex criterion. Purifying the test in such a case may reduce its criterion coverage and thus lower validity.

The selection of items to maximize criterion-related test validity may be likened to the selection of tests that will yield the highest validity for a battery. It will be recalled (Ch. 7) that the test contributing most toward battery validity is one having the highest correlation with the criterion and the lowest correlation with the other tests in the battery. If this principle is applied to the selection of items, it means that the most satisfactory items are those with the highest external validities and the lowest coefficients of internal consistency. Thus, an item that has a high correlation with the external criterion but a relatively low correlation with total score would be preferred to one correlating highly with both criterion and test score, since the first item presumably measures an aspect of the criterion not adequately covered by the rest of the test.

It might seem that items could be selected by the same methods used in choosing tests for inclusion in a battery. Thus, each item could be correlated with the external criterion and with every other item. The best items chosen by this method could then be weighted by means of a regression equation. Such a procedure, however, is neither feasible nor theoretically defensible. Not only would the computation labor be excessive, but inter-item correlations are also subject to wide sampling fluctuation, and the resulting regression weights would be too unstable to provide a satisfactory basis for item selection. An even more serious objection, however, is that the resulting test would be so heterogeneous in content as to preclude meaningful interpretation of the test score.

External validation and internal consistency are both desirable objectives of test construction. The relative emphasis to be placed on each varies with the nature and purpose of the test. For many testing purposes, a satisfactory compromise is to sort the relatively homogeneous items into separate tests or subtests, each of which covers a different aspect of the external criterion. Thus, breadth of coverage is achieved through a variety of tests, each yielding a relatively unambiguous score, rather than through heterogeneity of items within a single test. By such a procedure, items with low indices of internal consistency would not be discarded but would be segregated. As a result, fairly high internal consistency would be attained within each subtest or item group.

STATISTICAL INDICES OF ITEM DISCRIMINATION. Since item responses are generally recorded as right or wrong, the measurement of item discrimination usually involves a dichtomous variable (the item) and a continuous variable (the criterion). In certain situations, the criterion, too, may be dichotomous, as in graduation versus nongraduation from college, or success versus failure on a job. Moreover, a continuous criterion may be dichotomized for purposes of analysis.

Over fifty different indices of item discrimination have been developed and used in test construction. One difference among them pertains to their applicability to dichotomous or continuous measures. Among those applicable to dichotomous variables, moreover, some assume a continuous and normal distribution of the underlying trait on which the dichotomy has been artificially imposed; others assume a true dichotomy. Another difference concerns the relation of item difficulty to discrimination. Certain indices measure item discrimination independently of item difficulty. Others yield higher discrimination values for items close to the .50 difficulty level than for those at the extremes of difficulty.

Despite differences in procedure and assumptions, most item discrimination indices provide closely similar results (Henrysson, 1971; Oosterhof, 1976). Although the numerical values of the indices may differ, the items that are retained and those that are rejected on the basis of different discrimination indices are largely the same. In fact, the variation in item discrimination data from sample to sample is generally greater than that among different methods. For this reason, the choice of method is often based on the amount of computational labor required and the availability of special computational aids. Among the published computational aids are a number of abacs or nomographs. These are computing diagrams with which, for example, the value of an item–criterion correlation can be read directly if the percentages of persons passing the item in high and low criterion groups are known (Fan, 1952; Guilford & Fruchter, 1978, pp. 462–465; Jurgensen, 1947).

USE OF EXTREME GROUPS. A common practice in item analysis is to compare the proportion of cases who pass an item in contrasting criterion groups. When the criterion is measured along a continuous scale, as in the case of course grades, job ratings, output records, or total scores on the test, upper (U) and lower (L) criterion groups are selected from the extremes of the distribution. Obviously, the more extreme the groups the sharper will be the differentiation. But the use of very extreme groups, such as upper and lower 10%, would reduce the reliability of the results because of the small number of cases utilized. In a normal distribution, the optimum point at which these two conditions balance is reached with the upper and lower 27% (Kelley, 1939). When the distribution is flatter than the normal curve, the optimum percentage is slightly greater than 27 and approaches 33 (Cureton, 1957b). With small groups, as in an ordinary classroom, the sampling error of item statistics is so large that only rough results can be obtained. Under these conditions, therefore, we need not be too concerned about the exact percentage of cases in the two contrasted groups. Any convenient number between 25% and 33% will serve satisfactorily.

With the large and normally distributed samples employed in the development of standardized tests, it has been customary to work with the upper and lower 27% of the criterion distribution. Many of the tables and abacs prepared to facilitate the computation of item discrimination indices are based on the assumption that the "27% rule" has been followed. As high-speed computers become more generally available, it is likely that the various labor-saving procedures developed to facilitate item analysis will be gradually replaced by more exact and sophisticated methods. With computer facilities, it is better to analyze the results for the entire sample, rather than working with upper and lower extremes.

SIMPLE ANALYSIS WITH SMALL GROUPS. Because item analysis is frequently conducted with small groups, such as the students who have taken a classroom quiz, we shall consider first a simple procedure especially suitable for this situation. Let us suppose that in a class of 60 students we have chosen the 20 students (33%) with the highest and the 20 with the lowest test scores. We now have three groups of papers which we may call the Upper (U), Middle (M), and Lower (L) groups. First, we need to tally the correct responses to each item given by students in the three groups. This can be done most readily if we list the item numbers in one column and prepare three other columns headed U, M, and L. As we come to each student's paper, we simply place a tally next to each item he or she answered correctly. This is done for each of the 20 papers in the U group, then for each of the 20 in the M group, and finally for each of the 20 in the L group. We are now ready to count up the tallies and record totals for each group as shown in Table 19. For illustrative purposes, the first seven items have been entered. A rough index of the discriminative value of each item can be found by subtracting the number of persons answering it correctly in the L group from the number answering it correctly in the U group. These U–L differences are given in the last column of Table 19. A measure of item difficulty can be obtained with the same data by adding the number passing each item in all three criterion groups (U + M + L).

Examination of Table 19 reveals four questionable items that have been identified for further consideration or for class discussion. Two items, 2 and 7, have been singled out because one seems to be too easy, having been

TABLE 19
Simple Item Analysis Procedure: Number of Persons Giving Correct
Response in Each Criterion Group

Item	U (20)	M (20)	L (20)	Difficulty (U + M + L)	Discrimina- tion (U − L)
1	15	9	7	31	8
2	20	20	16	56*	4
3	19	18	9	46	10
4	10	11	16	37	− 6*
5	11	13	11	35	0*
6	16	14	9	39	7
7	5	0	0	5*	5
.					
.					
.					
.					
75					

* Items chosen for discussion.

passed by 56 out of 60 students, and the other too difficult, having been
passed by only 5. Items 4 and 5, while satisfactory with regard to difficulty
level, show a negative and a zero discriminative value, respectively. We
would also consider in this category any items with a very small positive
U–L difference, of roughly three or less when groups of approximately this
size are being compared. With larger groups, we would expect larger differences to occur by chance in a nondiscriminating item.

The purpose of item analysis in a teacher-made test is to identify deficiencies either in the test or in the teaching. Discussing questionable items
with the class is often sufficient to diagnose the problem. If the wording of
the item was at fault, it can be revised or discarded in subsequent testing.
Discussion may show, however, that the item was satisfactory, but the point
being tested had not been properly understood. In that case, the topic may
be reviewed and clarified. In narrowing down the source of the difficulty,
it is often helpful to carry out a supplementary analysis, as shown in Table
20, with at least some of the items chosen for discussion. This tabulation
gives the number of students in the U and L groups who chose each option
in answering the particular items.

Although Item 2 has been included in Table 20, there is little more we
can learn about it by tabulating the frequency of each wrong option,
since only 4 persons in the L group and none in the U group chose wrong
answers. Discussion of the item with the students, however, may help to
determine whether the item as a whole was too easy and therefore of little
intrinsic value, whether some defect in its construction served to give away

TABLE 20
Response Analysis of Individual Items

Item	Group	Response Options[a]				
		1	2	3	4	5
2	Upper	0	0	0	*20*	0
	Lower	2	0	1	*16*	1
4	Upper	0	*10*	9	0	1
	Lower	2	*16*	2	0	0
5	Upper	2	3	2	*11*	2
	Lower	1	3	3	*11*	2
7	Upper	*5*	3	5	4	3
	Lower	*0*	5	8	3	4

[a] Correct options have been italicized.

the right answer, or whether it is a good item dealing with a point that happened to have been effectively taught and well remembered. In the first case, the item would probably be discarded, in the second it would be revised, and in the third it would be retained unchanged.

The data on Item 4 suggest that the third option had some unsuspected implications that led 9 of the better students to prefer it to the correct alternative. The point could easily be settled by asking those students to explain why they chose it. In Item 5, the fault seems to lie in the wording either of the stem or of the correct alternative, because the students who missed the item were uniformly distributed over the four wrong options. Item 7 is an unusually difficult one which was answered incorrectly by 15 of the U and all of the L group. The slight clustering of responses on incorrect option 3 suggests a superficial attractiveness of this option, especially for the more easily misled L group. Similarly, the lack of choices of the correct response (option 1) by any of the L group suggests that this alternative was so worded that superficially, or to the uninformed, it seemed wrong. Both of these features, of course, are desiderata of good test items. Class discussion might show that Item 7 is a good item dealing with a point that few class members had actually learned.

THE INDEX OF DISCRIMINATION. If the numbers of persons passing each item in U and L criterion groups are expressed as percentages, the difference between these two percentages provides an index of item discrimination that can be interpreted independently of the size of the particular sample in which it was obtained. This index has been repeatedly described in the psychometric literature (see, e.g., Ebel, 1965, 1979; A. P. Johnson, 1951; Oosterhof, 1976) and has been variously designed as *U–L, ULI, ULD,* or simply *D.* Despite its simplicity, it has been shown to agree quite closely with other, more elaborate measures of item discrimination (Engelhart, 1965; Oosterhof, 1976). The computation of *D* can be illustrated by reference to the data previously reported in Table 19. First, the numbers of persons passing each item in the U and L groups are changed to percentages. Because the number of cases in each group is 20, we could divide each number by 20 and multiply the result by 100. It is easier, however, to divide 100 by 20, which gives 5, and then multiply each number by that constant. Thus, for Item 1, $15 \times 5 = 75$ (U group) and $7 \times 5 = 35$ (L group). For this item, then, *D*, is $75 - 35 = 40$. The remaining values for the seven items are given in Table 21.[4]

TABLE 21
Computation of Index of Discrimination

Item	Percentage Passing		Difference (Index of Discrimination)
	Upper Group	Lower Group	
1	75	35	40
2	100	80	20
3	95	45	50
4	50	80	−30
5	55	55	0
6	80	45	35
7	25	0	25

Data from Table 19.

D can have any value between $+100$ and -100. If all members of the U group and none of the L group pass an item, *D* equals 100. Conversely, if all members of the L group and none of the U group pass it, *D* equals -100. If the percentages of both groups passing an item are equal, *D* will be zero. *D* has several interesting properties. It has been demonstrated (Ebel, 1965; Findley, 1956) that *D* is directly proportional to the difference between the numbers of correct and incorrect discriminations made by an item. Correct discriminations are based on the number of passes in the U group versus the number of failures in the L group; incorrect discriminations are based on the number of failures in the U group versus the number of

---

[4] The alert reader may have noticed that the same result can be obtained by simply multiplying the differences in the last column of Table 19 by the constant. 5.

passes in the L group. Ebel (1967) has also shown that there is a close relation between the mean D index of the items and the reliability coefficient of the test. The higher the mean D, the higher the reliability.

Another noteworthy characteristic of D is one it shares with several other indices of item discrimination. The values of D are not independent of item difficulty but are biased in favor of intermediate difficulty levels. Table 22

TABLE 22
Relation of Maximum Value of D to Item Difficulty

Percentage Passing Item	Maximum Value of D
100	0
90	20
70	60
50	100
30	60
10	20
0	0

shows the maximum possible value of D for items with different percentages of correct responses. If either 100% or 0% of the cases in the total sample pass an item, there can be no difference in percentage passing in U and L groups; hence D is zero. At the other extreme, if 50% pass an item, it would be possible for all the U cases and none of the L cases to pass it, thus yielding a D of 100 ($100 - 0 = 100$). If 70% pass, the maximum value that D could take can be illustrated as follows: (U) 50/50 = 100%; (L) 20/50 = 40%; $D = 100 - 40 = 60$. It will be recalled that, for most testing purposes, items closer to the 50% difficulty level are preferable. Hence, item discrimination indices that favor this difficulty level are often appropriate for item selection.

PHI COEFFICIENT. Many indices of item discrimination report the relationship between item and criterion in the form of a correlaton coefficient. One of these is the phi coefficient (ϕ). Computed from a fourfold table, ϕ is based on the proportions of cases passing and failing an item in U and L criterion groups. Like all correlation coefficients, it yields values between +1.00 and −1.00. The ϕ coefficient assumes a genuine dichotomy in both item response and criterion variable. Consequently, it is strictly applicable only to the dichotomous conditions under which it was obtained and cannot be generalized to any underlying relationship between the traits measured by item and criterion. Like the D index, ϕ is biased toward the middle diffi-

culty levels—that is, it yields the highest possible correlations for dichoto-
mies closest to a 50–50 split.

Several computational aids are available for finding ϕ coefficients. When
the number of cases in U and L criterion groups is equal, ϕ can be found
with the Jurgensen tables (1947) by simply entering the percentages passing
the item in U and L groups. Since in conducting an item analysis it is usually feasible to select U and L groups of equal size, the Jurgensen tables are
widely used for this purpose. When the two criterion groups are unequal, ϕ
can be found with another set of tables, prepared by Edgerton (1960),
although their application is slightly more time-consuming.

The significance level of a ϕ coefficient can be readily computed through
the relation of ϕ to both chi square and the normal curve ratio. Applying
the latter, we can identify the minimum value of ϕ that would reach statistical significance at the .05 or .01 levels with the following formulas:

$$\phi_{.05} = \frac{1.96}{\sqrt{N}}$$

$$\phi_{.01} = \frac{2.58}{\sqrt{N}}$$

In these formulas, N represents the total number of cases in both criterion
groups combined. Thus, if there were 50 cases in U and 50 in L groups, N
would be 100 and the minimum ϕ significant at the .05 level would be $1.96 \div
\sqrt{100} = .196$. Any item whose ϕ reached or exceeded .196 would thus be
valid at the .05 level of significance.

BISERIAL CORRELATION. As a final example of a commonly used measure
of item discrimination, we may consider the biserial correlation coefficient
(r_{bis}), which contrasts with ϕ in two major respects. First, r_{bis} assumes a
continuous and normal distribution of the trait underlying the dichotomous
item response. Second, it yields a measure of item-criterion relationship
that is independent of item difficulty. To compute r_{bis} directly from the data,
we would need the mean criterion score of those who pass and those who
fail the item, as well as the proportion of cases passing and failing the item
in the entire sample and the standard deviation of the criterion scores.

Computing all the needed terms and applying the r_{bis} formula for each
item can be quite time-consuming. Tables have been prepared from which
r_{bis} can be estimated by merely entering the percentages passing the item
in the upper and lower 27% of the criterion group (Fan, 1952, 1954). These
are the previously mentioned tables obtainable from Educational Testing
Service. With these tables it is possible by entering the percentage passing
in U and L groups to find three values: an estimate of p, the percentage who
pass the item in the entire sample; the previously described Δ, a measure
of item difficulty on an interval scale; and r_{bis} between item and criterion.

These tables are only applicable when exactly 27% of the cases are placed in U and L groups.

There is no way of computing exact significance levels for these estimated biserial correlations, but it has been shown that their standard errors are somewhat larger than those of biserial correlations computed from all the data in the usual way. That is, the r_{bis} estimated from the Fan tables fluctuates more from sample to sample than does the r_{bis} computed by formula. With this information, one could use the standard error of r_{bis} to estimate approximately how large the correlation should be for statistical significance.[5] It should be reiterated that, with computer facilities, biserial correlations can be readily found from the responses of the total sample; and this is the preferred procedure.

ITEM RESPONSE THEORY

ITEM-TEST REGRESSION. Both item difficulty and item discrimination can be represented simultaneously in item-test regression graphs. For purposes of illustration, let us consider a hypothetical 12-item test calling for short answers of the free-response type, such as the vocabulary tests in individually administered intelligence scales. Table 23 gives the proportion of persons at each total score level who responded correctly to each of two items. These data have been plotted in Figure 24.

TABLE 23
Hypothetical Data Illustrating Item-Test Regression

Total Score	Proportion Correct	
	Item 7	Item 13
12	1.00	.95
11	.82	.62
10	.87	.53
9	.70	.16
8	.49	.05
7	.23	.00
6	.10	.00
5	.06	.00
4	.03	.00
3	.00	.00
2	.00	.00
1	.00	.00

5 The formula for the standard error of r_{bis}, as well as for r_{bis} itself, can be found in any standard statistics text, such as Guilford and Fruchter (1976, pp. 304–306).

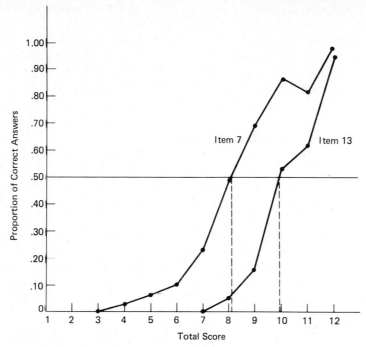

Fig. 24. Item-Test Regression for Items 7 and 13.
(Data from Table 23.)

The difficulty level of each item can be defined as its 50% threshold, as is customary in establishing sensory thresholds in psychophysics. This has been done in Figure 24 by dropping perpendiculars from the points where the two item curves cross the 50% line to the horizontal axis, where the corresponding total scores are located. It is thereby shown that persons with total scores of approximately 8 have a 50–50 chance of passing Item 7, as do those with scores of approximately 10 in the case of Item 13. The discriminative power of each item is indicated by the steepness of the curve: the steeper the curve, the higher the correlation of item performance with total score and the higher the discriminative index. By inspection, the discriminative power of Items 7 and 13 appears roughly similar.

An examination of item-score regressions, as illustrated in Figure 24, enables us to visualize how effectively an item functions. Such graphs not only combine information on item difficulty and item discrimination but also provide a complete picture of the relation between item performance and total score. For instance, Item 7 shows a reversal, insofar as the proportion of persons with scores of 10 who passed the item is greater than the proportion of those with scores of 11 who did so. If these results were based on a small sample, this reversal would probably be negligible; but it illustrates the kind of information that such an analysis of item data can bring to light.

For purposes of mathematical treatment and of precise evaluation and selection of items, however, such a graph is crude and quite limited. This approach has served as the starting point for the development of highly sophisticated and complicated types of item analysis, which have attracted increasing attention in the 1970s and early 1980s. A reason for their growing popularity is undoubtedly to be found in the rapidly expanding availability of high-speed computers, without which the computational tasks required by such analyses would be prohibitive. With the preparation of computer programs for several proposed models of item analysis, the practical application of these refined procedures became feasible.

Major features of this approach will be described below. Most of the publications dealing with the actual mathematical procedures are quite technical. In the late 1970s, however, articles began to appear that provided simple introductions to this methodology, and these may be consulted for fuller explanations and critical evaluations (e.g., Baker, 1977; Hambleton, 1979; Hambleton & Cook, 1977; Weiss & Davison, 1981). A comprehensive, detailed, technical treatment of the whole approach can be found in Lord (1980). A brief overview at an intermediate level of difficulty is provided by Allen and Yen (1979, Ch. 11). Wright and Stone (1979) give a clear introduction to the use of the Rasch model, a relatively simple variant of this approach.

ITEM RESPONSE THEORY: BASIC FEATURES. The mathematical approach under consideration has been variously designated as latent trait theory, item response theory, and item characteristic curve (ICC) theory. A fundamental feature of this approach is that item performance is related to the estimated amount of the respondent's "latent trait," symbolized by the Greek letter θ (theta). As used in this context, a "latent trait" refers to a statistical construct; there is no implication that it is a psychological or physiological entity with an independent existence. In cognitive tests, the latent trait is generally called the ability measured by the test. Total score on the test is often taken as an initial estimate of that ability.

Item characteristic curves are plotted from mathematically derived functions, rather than from the empirical data used in item-test regression curves. Different latent trait models utilize different mathematical functions, based on diverse sets of assumptions. Some models use normal ogive functions (i.e., cumulative normal distributions); others use logistic functions, which take advantage of some mathematically convenient properties of logarithmic relations. In general, the results obtained with the various models are substantially similar, provided their assumptions are met in the particular situations. Figure 25 shows item characteristic curves for three hypothetical items. The horizontal axis gives the ability scale (θ), estimated from total test score and other information available about test responses in a particular sample. The vertical axis gives $P_i(\theta)$, the probability of a correct response to Item i as a function of the person's position on the ability

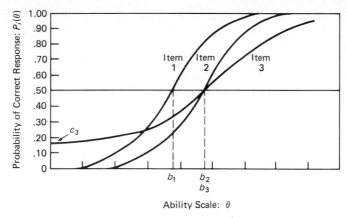

FIG. 25. Hypothetical Item Characteristic Curves for Three Items.

scale (θ). This probability is derived from data on the proportion of persons at different ability levels who passed the item.

In the complete, three-parameter model, each ICC is described by three parameters derived mathematically from the empirical data. The item discrimination parameter (a_i) indicates the slope of the curve. It is inversely related to the distance one must travel along the ability continuum (θ) in order to increase $P_i(\theta)$. The higher the value of a_i the steeper the slope. In Figure 25, Items 1 and 2 have the same a_i, or discriminative value; Item 3 has a lower a_i, since its curve rises more slowly. The item difficulty parameter (b_i) corresponds to the location on the ability axis at which the probability of a correct response, $P_i(\theta)$, is .50. It will be seen that Items 2 and 3 have the same b_i, while Item 1 is easier, requiring less ability for a .50 probability of correct response. Latent trait models designed to deal with multiple-choice items often include a third parameter, the so-called guessing parameter (c_i).[6] It represents the probability that a correct response occurs by chance. In a multiple-choice item, even examinees at very low ability levels have a higher than zero probability of giving a correct response. This is illustrated by Item 3 in Figure 25, whose lower asymptote is considerably above zero.

Estimates of both item parameters and ability are typically computed by iterative or successive-approximation procedures; the approximations are repeated until the values stabilize. In addition to yielding mathematically refined indices of item difficulty and item discrimination, ICC techniques provide several other benefits. An important feature of this approach is its treatment of reliability and error of measurement through *item information functions*. These functions, which are computed for each item, provide a

[6] Some investigators recommended that c_i be called simply a lower-asymptote parameter for the ICC, because three-parameter models treat c_i as independent of ability, whereas guessing is a function of ability.

sound basis for choosing items in test construction. The item information function takes all item parameters into account and shows the measurement efficiency of the item at different ability levels.

The most widely publicized contribution of latent trait models pertains to the sample-free nature of their results, technically described as *invariance of item parameters*. It is a basic concept of latent trait theory that item parameters should be invariant when computed in groups differing in ability. This means that a uniform scale of measurement can be provided for use in different groups. It also means that groups as well as individuals can be tested with a different set of items, appropriate to their ability levels, and their scores will be directly comparable. Whether the anticipated invariance occurs in fact requires empirical verification. Some supportive findings have been obtained under especially favorable conditions, as in the testing of very large samples with a test of a narrowly defined and stable trait (Lord, 1970b). But such conditions are not typical of test construction situations.

When many different samples are to be tested, one procedure is to work with a large item pool or item bank that has been precalibrated on a large random sample. When the ability range is very wide, as in achievement test series overlapping many school grades, it is necessary to use common items (variously called anchor, linkage, or calibration items), in order to bridge the gaps across groups. Once the items in the pool are calibrated, any subset of items can be administered to any group or individual, and the resulting scores will be comparable.

OTHER LATENT TRAIT MODELS. In the preceding section, we have examined a three-parameter model. Two-parameter models, which omit the chance-response parameter (c_i), are appropriate when the effects of guessing on test performance can be regarded as negligible. A one-parameter model, based only on the difficulty (b_i) of a set of items, was developed by Rasch (1966) and has been adapted and strongly championed by some investigators (e.g., Wright, 1968, 1977; Wright & Stone, 1979). This model is based on the assumption that both guessing and item differences in discrimination are negligible. In constructing tests, the proponents of the Rasch model frequently discard those items that do not meet these assumptions. It has been argued, too, that latent trait models are quite "robust," in the statistical sense, meaning that various assumptions may be violated within limits, without distortion of results. This, of course, is a matter for empirical verification.

The models considered thus far assume *unidimensionality* of the test; that is, it is assumed that item responses can be attributed to a single trait. More general models, applicable to multidimensional tests, have also been designed, but the computational procedures are more laborious. Still other variants have been developed to handle graded (rather than dichotomous or right–wrong) item responses (Samejima, 1969), or to analyze the different response options in multiple-choice items (Bock, 1972).

CURRENT STATUS. Item response theory is still at a formative stage. The relative merits of alternative models are being vigorously debated. There is need for much more checking of mathematically derived values, not only with artificial data and computer simulation, but also with live data. The invariance of item parameters needs especially to be widely investigated in realistic situations. Some psychometricians question the very applicability of ICC techniques to psychological tests on theoretical grounds. For example, unidimensionality cannot be demonstrated by the usual factor-analytic procedures, since item intercorrelations are likely to be curvilinear. Moreover, the same items may involve a different mix of abilities when performed by persons with different experiential backgrounds or by the same person at different stages of learning.

The application of ICC procedures to practical testing problems is proceeding slowly. Most studies published thus far report what are essentially demonstrations, rather than full-scale operational uses. Nevertheless, these techniques are beginning to influence several aspects of testing. They are particularly appropriate for certain newly emerging types of testing, such as individually tailored testing (to be discussed in Chapter 11). In such testing, each examinee may respond to a different set of items, but all are to be scored on a uniform scale.

ITEM ANALYSIS OF SPEEDED TESTS

Whether or not speed is relevant to the function being measured, item indices computed from a speeded test may be misleading. Except for items that all or nearly all examinees have had time to attempt, the item indices found from a speed test will reflect the *position* of the item in the test rather than its intrinsic difficulty or discriminative power. Items that appear late in the test will be passed by a relatively small percentage of the total sample, because only a few persons have time to reach these items. Regardless of how easy the item may be, if it occurs late in a speeded test, it will appear difficult. Even if the item merely asked for one's name, the percentage of persons who passed it might be very low if the item were placed toward the end of a speeded test.

Similarly, item discrimination indices tend to be overestimated for those items that have not been reached by all examinees. Because the more proficient individuals tend to work faster, they are more likely to reach one of the later items in a speed test. Thus, regardless of the nature of the item itself, some correlation between the item and the criterion would be obtained if the item occurred late in a speed test.

To avoid some of these difficulties, we could limit the analysis of each item to those persons who have reached the item. This is not a completely satisfactory solution, however, unless the number of persons failing to reach the item is small. Such a procedure would involve the use of a rapidly shrinking number of cases and would thus render the results on the later items quite unreliable. Moreover, the persons on whom the later items are analyzed would probably constitute a selected sample and hence would not be comparable to the larger samples used for the earlier items. As has already been pointed out, the faster performers tend also to be the more proficient. The later items would thus be analyzed on a superior sample of individuals. One effect of such a selective factor would be to lower the apparent difficulty level of the later items, since the percentage passing would be greater in the selected superior group than in the entire sample. It will be noted that this is the opposite error from that introduced when the percentage passing is computed in terms of the entire sample. In that case, the apparent difficulty of items is spuriously raised.

The effect of the above procedure on indices of item discrimination is less obvious, but nonetheless real. It has been observed, for example, that some low-scoring examinees tend to hurry through the test, marking items almost at random in their effort to try all items within the time allowed. This tendency is much less common among high-scoring examinees. As a result, the sample on which a late-appearing item is analyzed is likely to consist of some very poor respondents, who will perform no better than chance on the item, and a larger number of very proficient and fast respondents, who are likely to answer the item correctly. In such a group, the item–criterion correlation will probably be higher than it would be in a more representative sample. In the absence of such random respondents, on the other hand, the sample on which the later items are analyzed will cover a relatively narrow range of ability. Under these conditions, the discrimination indices of the later items will tend to be lower than they would be if computed on the entire unselected sample.

The anticipated effects of speed on indices of item difficulty and item discrimination have been empirically verified, both when item statistics are computed with the entire sample (Wesman, 1949) and when they are computed with only those persons who attempt the item (Mollenkopf, 1950a). In the latter study, comparable groups of high school students were given two forms of a verbal test and two forms of a mathematics test. Each of the two forms contained the same items as the other, but items occurring early in one form were placed late in the other. Each form was administered with a short time limit (speed conditions) and with a very liberal time limit (power conditions). Various intercomparisons were thus possible between forms and timing conditions. The results clearly showed that the position of an item in the speed tests affected its indices of difficulty and discrimination. When the same item occurred later in a speeded test, it was passed by a greater percentage of those attempting it, and it yielded a higher item–criterion correlation.

The difficulties encountered in the item analysis of speeded tests are fundamentally similar to those discussed in Chapter 5 in connection with the reliability of speeded tests. Various solutions, both empirical and statistical, have been developed for meeting these difficulties. One empirical solution is to administer the test with a long time limit to the group on which item analysis is to be carried out. This solution is satisfactory provided that speed itself is not an important aspect of the ability to be measured by the test. Apart from the technical problems presented by specific tests, however, it is well to keep in mind that item-analysis data obtained with speeded tests are suspect and call for careful scrutiny.

CROSS-VALIDATION

MEANING OF CROSS-VALIDATION. It is essential that test validity be computed on a different sample of persons from that on which the items were selected. This independent determination of the validity of the entire test is known as cross-validation. Any validity coefficient computed on the same sample that was used for item-selection purposes will capitalize on random sampling errors within that particular sample and will consequently be spuriously high. In fact, a high validity coefficient could result under such circumstances even when the test has no validity at all in predicting the particular criterion.

Let us suppose that out of a sample of 100 medical students, the 30 with the highest and the 30 with the lowest medical school grades have been chosen to represent contrasted criterion groups. If, now, these two groups are compared in a number of traits actually irrelevant to success in medical school, certain chance differences will undoubtedly be found. Thus, there might be an excess of private-school graduates and of red-haired persons within the upper criterion group. If we were to assign each individual a score by crediting her or him with one point for private-school graduation and one point for red hair, the mean of such scores would undoubtedly be higher in the upper than in the lower criterion group. This is not evidence for the validity of the predictors, however, since such a validation process is based on a circular argument. The two predictors were chosen in the first place on the basis of the chance variations that characterized this particular sample. And the *same* chance differences are operating to produce the mean differences in total score. When tested in another sample, however, the chance differences in frequency of private-school graduation and red hair are likely to disappear or be reversed. Consequently, the validity of the scores will collapse.

AN EMPIRICAL EXAMPLE. A classic demonstration of the need for cross-validation is provided by an early investigation conducted with the Rorschach inkblot test (Kurtz, 1948). In an attempt to determine whether the Rorschach could be of any help in selecting sales managers for life insurance agencies, this test was administered to 80 such managers. These managers had been carefully chosen from several hundred employed by eight life insurance companies, so as to represent an upper criterion group of 42 considered very satisfactory by their respective companies, and a lower criterion group of 38 considered unsatisfactory. The 80 test records were studied by a Rorschach expert, who selected a set of 32 signs, or response characteristics, occurring more frequently in one criterion group than in the other. Signs found more often in the upper criterion group were scored +1 if present and 0 if absent; those more common in the lower group were scored −1 or 0. Since there were 16 signs of each type, total scores could range theoretically from −16 to +16.

When the scoring key based on these 32 signs was reapplied to the original group of 80 persons, 79 of the 80 were correctly classified as being in the upper or lower group. The correlation between test score and criterion would thus have been close to 1.00. However, when the test was cross-validated on a second comparable sample of 41 managers, 21 in the upper and 20 in the lower group, the validity coefficient dropped to a negligible .02. It was thus apparent that the key developed in the first sample had no validity for selecting such personnel.

AN EXAMPLE WITH CHANCE DATA. That the use of a single sample for item selection and test validation can produce a completely spurious validity coefficient under pure chance conditions was vividly demonstrated by Cureton (1950). The criterion to be predicted was the grade-point average of each of 29 students registered in a psychology course. This criterion was dichotomized into grades of B or better and grades below B. The "items" consisted of 85 tags, numbered from 1 to 85 on one side. To obtain a test score for each student, the 85 tags were shaken in a container and dropped on the table. All tags that fell with numbered side up were recorded as indicating the presence of that particular item in the student's performance. A complete record for each student was thus obtained from 29 throws of the 85 tags, showing the presence or absence of each item or response sign in that student's performance. Because of the procedure followed in generating these chance scores, Cureton facetiously named the test the "B-Projective Psychokinesis Test."

An item analysis was then conducted, with each student's grade-point average as the criterion. On this basis, 24 "items" were selected out of the 85. Of these, 9 occurred more frequently among the students with an average grade of B or better and received a weight of +1; 15 occurred more frequently among the students with an average grade below B and received a weight of −1. The sum of these item weights constituted the total score for each student. Despite the known chance derivation of these "test scores," their correlation with the grade criterion in the original group of 29 students proved to be .82. Such a finding is similar to that obtained with the Rorschach scores in the previously cited study. In both instances, the apparent correspondence between test score and criterion resulted from the utilization of the same chance differences both in selecting items and in determining validity of total test scores.

CONDITIONS AFFECTING VALIDITY SHRINKAGE. The amount of shrinkage of a validity coefficient in cross-validation depends in part on the size of the original item pool and the proportion of items retained. When the number of original items is large and the proportion retained is small, there is more opportunity to capitalize on chance differences and thus obtain a spuriously high validity coefficient. Another condition affecting amount of shrinkage in cross-validation is size of sample. Since spuriously high validity in the initial sample results from an accumulation of sampling errors, smaller groups (which yield larger sampling errors) exhibit greater validity shrinkage.

If items are chosen on the basis of previously formulated hypotheses, derived from psychological theory or from past experience with the criterion, validity shrinkage in cross-validation will be minimized. For example, if a particular hypothesis required that the answer "Yes" be more frequent among successful students, then the item would *not* be retained if a significantly larger number of "Yes" answers were given by the *unsuccessful* students. The opposite, blindly empirical approach would be illustrated by assembling a miscellaneous set of questions with little regard to their relevance to the criterion behavior, and then retaining all items yielding significant positive or negative correlations with the criterion. Under the latter circumstances, we would expect much more shrinkage than under the former. In summary, shrinkage of test validity in cross-validation will be greatest when samples are small, the initial item pool is large, the proportion of items retained is small, and items are assembled without previously formulated rationale.

ITEM-BY-GROUP INTERACTION

RESEARCH ON ITEM BIAS. As one approach to the investigation of test bias for minority groups, the analysis of item bias has received considerable attention. Such analysis is concerned essentially with the *relative difficulty* of individual test items for groups with dissimilar cultural or experiential backgrounds. A comprehensive survey of studies on this topic can be found in Jensen (1980, pp. 552–580). Data have been gathered with a large number of individual and group tests of general intelligence and scholastic aptitude, as well as with some educational and occupational achievement tests. Research covering specifically college admission tests has been summarized by Breland (1979). Most of the studies were conducted with black and white samples in the United States; other minorities have been investigated in much smaller numbers. The specific procedures employed for item analysis range widely, from subjective assessment of items by representatives of cultural minorities and simple statistical comparisons of the proportion of persons passing each item in different groups, to analysis of variance and applications of item response theory.

The findings have been largely negative. For widely used, standardized aptitude or achievement tests, few items have emerged as significantly biased. There is also little consistency in the items identified as biased by the different procedures (Ironson & Subkoviak, 1979; Sandoval & Whelan, 1979). Moreover, when significant differences in item difficulty did appear, they were more closely associated with differences in performance level on the test as a whole than with cultural group membership.

When evaluated in the light of recent methodological advances in item analysis, the accumulated research on item bias can best be characterized as inconclusive because of methodological problems. Several investigators have argued that the usual procedures, including the comparison of item difficulties by means of percentage passing or normal curve delta values obtained in different groups, are subject to various statistical artifacts (Hunter, 1975; Pine, 1977). Consequently, spurious evidence of item bias may appear when such bias is absent, or bias may fail to be detected when present. Spurious differences in the relative difficulty of an item may result from group differences in overall ability on the test, or in the discriminative power of the item, or in the extent of guessing. Group comparisons will also be affected by lack of homogeneity or unidimensionality of the items.

To meet these methodological difficulties, item bias can be investigated by the methods of item response theory, which permit the measurement of item difficulty independently of other item parameters. A few illustrative applications of these methods have been reported. Some involve a direct comparison of the ICCs of individual items in different cultural groups (Lord, 1976). Others compare the difficulty parameter (b_i) for each test item derived in different groups (Pine, 1977).

Figure 26 illustrates a cross-plot of item difficulties (b_i) for a multiple-choice vocabulary test administered to 58 black and 168 white high school students. The items had been tested for unidimensionality by factor analysis of item intercorrelations within both groups, and they were found to meet this condition satisfactorily. If the items were equally difficult for both groups, they would cluster about the broken diagonal line. The fact that they cluster about the lower, solid line demonstrates that they are more difficult for the black students. Item bias is indicated by divergence from this lower straight line. For example, Item x in Figure 26 was easier for the black than for the white respondents, falling at a difficulty value of 0 in the black sample and approximately +0.5 in the white sample. The reverse group

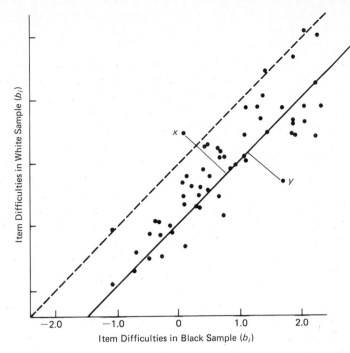

FIG. 26. Bivariate Distribution of Item Difficulties (b₁) in Black and White Samples of High School Students.

(Adapted from Pine, 1977, p. 42.)

difference is indicated for Item y, with difficulty values of approximately $+1.75$ for blacks and -0.5 for whites. The overall degree of correspondence between the relative difficulty of items in the two groups is shown by a correlation of .86, indicating a high degree of linear relationship in the test as a whole.

It should be borne in mind that this example was reported simply to demonstrate procedure. The samples used were small, and the test was developed and administered for research purposes only. If an operational test were being evaluated, the deviation of individual items from the solid regression line would be assessed for statistical significance, and items deviating beyond an acceptable limit would be carefully scrutinized and would probably be either eliminated or revised.

ITEM SELECTION TO MINIMIZE OR MAXIMIZE GROUP DIFFERENCES. In the construction of certain tests, item × group interactions have been used as one basis for the selection of items. In the development of the Stanford-Binet, for example, an effort was made to exclude any item that favored either sex significantly, on the assumption that such items might reflect purely fortuitous and irrelevant differences in the experiences of the two sexes (McNemar, 1942, Ch. 5). Owing to the limited number of items available for each age level, however, it was not possible to eliminate all sex-differentiating items. In order to rule out sex differences in total score, therefore, the remaining sex-differentiating items were balanced, approximately the same number favoring boys and girls.

No generalization can be made regarding the elimination of sex differences, or any other group differences, in the selection of test items. While certain tests, like the Stanford-Binet, have sought to equalize the performance of the two sexes, others have retained such differencs and report separate norms for the two sexes. This practice is relatively common in the case of special aptitude tests, in which fairly large differences in favor of one or the other sex have been consistently found.

Under certain circumstances, moreover, items may be chosen, not to minimize, but to maximize, sex differentiation. An example of the latter procedure is to be found in the masculinity–femininity scales developed for use with several personality inventories (to be discussed in Ch. 17). Since the purpose of these scales was to measure the degree to which an individual's responses agreed with those characteristic of men or of women in a particular culture, only those items that differentiated significantly between the sexes in that culture were retained.

A similar diversity of procedure can be found with reference to other group differences in item performance. In the development of a socioeconomic status scale for the Minnesota Multiphasic Personality Inventory, only those items were retained that differentiated significantly between the responses of high school students in two contrasted socioeconomic groups (Gough, 1948). Cross-validation of this status scale on a new sample of high school students yielded a correlation of .50 with objective indices of socioeconomic status. The object of this test was to determine the degree to which an individual's emotional and social responses resembled those characteristic of persons in upper or lower socioeconomic levels, respectively. Hence, those items showing the maximum differentiation between social classes were included in the scale, and those showing little or no differentiation were discarded. This procedure is similar to that followed in the development of masculinity–femininity scales. It is apparent that in both types of tests the group differentiation constitutes the criterion in terms of which the test is validated. In such cases, socioeconomic level and sex, respectively, represent the most relevant variables on the basis of which items can be chosen.

Examples of the opposite approach to socioeconomic or cultural differentials in test responses can also be found. An extensive project on such cultural differentials in intelligence test items was conducted at the University of Chicago (Eells, et al., 1951). These investigators believed that most intelligence tests might be unfair to children from lower socioeconomic levels, since many of the test items presuppose information, skills, or interests typical of middle-class children. To obtain evidence for such a hypothesis, a detailed item analysis was conducted on eight widely used group intelligence tests. For each item, the frequencies of correct responses by children in higher and lower socioeconomic levels were compared. Following this investigation, two members of the research team prepared a special test designed to be "fair" to lower-class urban American children. In the construction of this test, an effort was made to exclude the types of items previously found to favor middle-class children. Known as the Davis-Eells Games, this test was subsequently discontinued because it proved unsatisfactory in a number of ways, including low validity in predicting academic achievement and other practical criteria. Moreover, the anticipated advantage of lower-class children on this test did not hold up in other samples.

As in the case of sex differences, no rigid policy can be laid down regarding items that exhibit cultural differentiation. Certain basic facts of test construction and interpretation should, however, be noted. First, whether items that differentiate significantly between certain groups are retained or discarded should depend on the purpose for which the test is designed. If the criteria to be predicted show significant differences between the sexes, socioeconomic groups, or other categories of persons, then it is to be expected that the test items will also exhibit such group differences. To eliminate items showing these differences might serve only to lower the validity of the test for predicting the given criteria. In the second place, tests designed to measure an individual's resemblance to one or another group should obviously magnify the differentiation between such groups. For these tests, items showing the largest group differences in response should be chosen, as in the case of the masculinity–femininity and social status scales cited above.

The third point is of primary concern, not to the test constructor, but to the test user and the general student of psycholgy who wishes to interpret test results properly. Tests whose items have been selected with reference to the responses of any special groups cannot be used to compare such groups. For example, the statement that boys and girls do not differ significantly in Stanford-Binet IQ provides no information whatever regarding sex differences. Since sex differences were deliberately eliminated in the process of selecting items for the test, their absence from the final scores merely indicates that this aspect of test construction was successfully executed. Similarly, lack of socioeconomic differences on a test constructed so as to eliminate such differences would provide no information on the relative performance of groups varying in socioeconomic status.

Tests designed to maximize group differentiation, such as the masculinity–femininity and social status scales, are equally unsuitable for group comparisons. In these cases, the sex or socioeconomic differentiation in personality characteristics would be artificially magnified. To obtain an unbiased estimate of the existing group differences, the test items must be selected without reference to the responses of such groups. The principal conclusion to be drawn from the present discussion is that proper interpretation of scores on any test requires a knowledge of the basis on which items were selected for that test.

PART THREE

Tests of
General Intellectual Level

Chapter 9

Individual Tests

IN PART TWO, we were concerned with the major principles of psychological testing. We are now ready to apply these principles to the evaluation of specific tests. We now know what questions to ask about each test and where to look for the answers. The test manuals, the *Mental Measurements Yearbooks,* and other sources described in Chapter 1 may be consulted to obtain information regarding any of the tests cited.

The purpose of the remaining parts of the book is twofold. One objective is to afford an opportunity to observe the application of testing principles to a wide variety of tests. Another is to acquaint the reader with a few outstanding tests in each of the major areas. No attempt will be made to provide a comprehensive survey of available tests within any area. Such a survey would be outside the scope of this book. Moreover, it would probably be outdated before publication, because of the rapidity with which new or revised tests appear. For these reasons, the discussion will concentrate on a few representative tests in each category, chosen either because of their widespread use or because they illustrate important developments in testing procedure. We shall consider tests of general intellectual level in Part Three, tests of separate abilities in Part Four, and personality tests in Part Five.

A classified list of representative tests in all areas covered in this text will be found in Appendix E. This list includes not only all currently available tests cited in the text, but also some additional examples of well-known tests in each category. With each test, the table gives the name of the publisher and the entry number in the latest *Mental Measurements Yearbook* where information about the test can be located. Unless otherwise indicated, all data about tests discussed in the text are taken from the test manual or technical supplements supplied by the test publishers. As a further aid to the reader's own evaluation of tests, Appendix C contains a suggested outline for test evaluation. The APA *Standards* (1974) provide more detailed guidelines for this purpose.

Traditionally called "intelligence tests," the types of tests to be discussed in Part Three are the direct descendants of the original Binet scales. Such tests are designed for use in a wide variety of situations and are validated against relatively broad criteria. They characteristically provide a single score, such as an IQ, indicating the individual's general intellectual level. A typical approach is to arrive at this global estimate of intellectual performance by "the sinking of shafts at critical points" (Terman & Merrill, 1937, p. 4). In other words, a wide variety of tasks is presented to the examinee in the expectation that an adequate sampling of important intellectual functions will thus be covered. In actual practice, the tests are usually overloaded with certain functions, such as verbal ability, and completely omit others.

Because so many intelligence tests are validated against measures of academic achievement, they are often designated as tests of scholastic aptitude. Intelligence tests are frequently employed as preliminary screening instruments, to be followed by tests of special aptitudes. This practice is especially prevalent in the testing of normal adolescents or adults for educational and occupational counseling, personnel selection, and similar purposes. Another common use of general intelligence tests is to be found in clinical testing, especially in the identification and classification of the mentally retarded. For clinical purposes, individual tests are generally employed. Among the most widely used individual intelligence tests are the Stanford-Binet and Wechsler scales discussed in this chapter. Because the Stanford-Binet is the first test to be covered in this text, it is discussed more fully than are other tests throughout the book. This is done in order to illustrate at the outset the kinds of information to be considered in evaluating a test.

STANFORD-BINET INTELLIGENCE SCALE

EVOLUTION OF THE SCALES. The original Binet-Simon scales have already been described briefly in Chapter 1. It will be recalled that the 1905 scale consisted simply of 30 short tests, arranged in ascending order of difficulty. The 1908 scale was the first age scale; and the 1911 scale introduced minor improvements and additions. The age range covered by the 1911 revision extended from 3 years to the adult level. Among the many translations and adaptations of the early Binet tests were a number of American revisions, of which the most viable has been the Stanford-Binet.[1]

The first Stanford revision of the Binet-Simon scales, prepared by Terman and his associates at Stanford University, was published in 1916 (Terman, 1916). This revision introduced so many changes and additions as to represent virtually a new test. Over one third of the items were new, and a number of old items were revised, reallocated to different age levels, or discarded. The entire scale was restandardized on an American sample of approximately 1,000 children and 400 adults. Detailed instructions for administering and scoring each test[2] were provided, and the IQ was employed for the first time in any psychological test. The second Stanford revision, ap-

---

[1] A detailed account of the Binet-Simon scales and of the development, use, and clinical interpretation of the Stanford-Binet can be found in Sattler (1982).

[2] The items in the Binet scales are commonly called "tests," since each is separately administered and may contain several parts.

pearing in 1937, consisted of two equivalent forms, L and M (Terman & Merrill, 1937). In this revision, the scale was greatly expanded and completely restandardized on a new sample of the U.S. population. The 3,184 examinees employed for this purpose included approximately 100 children at each half-year interval from 1½ to 5½ years, 200 at each age from 6 to 14, and 100 at each age from 15 to 18. Despite serious efforts to obtain a representative cross section of the population, however, the sampling was somewhat higher than the U.S. population in socioeconomic level, contained an excess of urban cases, and included only native-born whites.

A third revision, published in 1960, provided a single form (L-M) incorporating the best items from the two 1937 forms (Terman & Merrill, 1960). Without introducing any new content, it was thus possible to eliminate obsolescent items and to relocate items whose difficulty level had altered during the intervening years owing to cultural changes. In preparing the 1960 Stanford-Binet, the authors were faced with a common dilemma of psychological testing. On the one hand, frequent revisions are desirable in order to profit from technical advances and refinements in test construction and from prior experience in the use of the test, as well as to keep test content up to date. The last-named consideration is especially important for information items and for pictorial material, which may be affected by changing fashions in dress, household appliances, cars, and other common articles. The use of obsolete test content may seriously undermine rapport and may alter the difficulty level of items. On the other hand, revision may render much of the accumulated data inapplicable to the new form. Tests that have been widely used for many years have acquired a rich body of interpretive material, which should be carefully weighed against the need for revision. It was for these reasons that the authors of the Stanford-Binet chose to condense the two earlier forms into one, thereby steering a course between the twin hazards of obsolescence and discontinuity. The loss of a parallel form was not too great a price to pay for accomplishing this purpose. By 1960, there was less need for an alternate form than there had been in 1937, when no other well-constructed individual intelligence scale was available.

In the preparation of the 1960 Stanford-Binet, items were selected from forms L and M on the basis of the performance of 4,498 examinees, aged 2½ to 18 years, who had taken either or both forms of the test between 1950 and 1954. The examinees were drawn from six states situated in the Northeast, in the Midwest, and on the West Coast. Although these cases did not constitute a representative sampling of American schoolchildren, care was taken to avoid the operation of major selective factors.[3] The 1960 Stanford-Binet did *not* involve a restandardization of the normative scale. The new samples were utilized only to identify changes in item

[3] For special statistical analyses, there were two additional samples of California children, including 100 6-year-olds stratified with regard to father's occupation and 100 15-year-olds stratified with regard to both father's occupation and grade distribution.

difficulty over the intervening, period. Accordingly, the difficulty of each item was redetermined by finding the percentage of children passing it at successive *mental ages* on the 1937 forms. Thus, for purposes of item analysis, the children were grouped, not according to their chronological age, but according to the mental age they had obtained on the 1937 forms. Consequently, mental ages and IQs on the 1960 Form L-M were still expressed in terms of the 1937 normative sample.

The next stage was the 1972 restandardization of Form L-M (Terman & Merrill, 1973, Part 4). This time the test content remained unchanged,[4] but the norms were derived from a new sample of approximately 2,100 cases tested during the 1971–1972 academic year. To achieve national representativeness despite the practical impossibility of administering individual tests to very large samples, the test publishers took advantage of a sample of approximately 20,000 children at each age level, employed in the standardization of a group test (Cognitive Abilities Test). This sample of some 200,000 schoolchildren in Grades 3 through 12 was chosen from communities stratified in terms of size, geographical region, and economic status, and included black, Mexican-American, and Puerto Rican children.

The children to be tested with the Stanford-Binet were identified through their scores on the verbal battery of the Cognitive Abilities Test, so that the distribution of scores in this subsample corresponded to the national distribution of the entire sample. The only cases excluded were those for whom the primary language spoken in the home was not English. To cover ages 2 to 8, the investigators located siblings of the group-tested children, choosing each child on the basis of the Cognitive Abilities Test score obtained by his or her older sibling. Additional cases at the upper ages were recruited in the same way. The Stanford-Binet sample included approximately 100 cases in each half-year age group from 2 to 5½ years, and 100 at each year group from 6 to 18.

In comparison with the 1937 norms, the 1972 norms are based on a more representative sample, as well as being updated and hence reflecting any effects of intervening cultural changes on test performance. It is interesting to note that the later norms show some improvement in test performance at all ages. The improvement is substantial at the preschool ages, averaging about 10 IQ points. The test authors attribute this improvement to the impact of the mass media on young children and the increasing literacy and educational level of parents, among other cultural changes. There is a smaller but clearly discernible improvement at ages 15 and over, which, as the authors suggest, may be associated with the larger proportion of students who continued their education through high school in the 1970s than in the 1930s. On the basis of both cross-sectional and longitudinal comparisons, Thorndike (1977) explored these normative changes further and pro-

---

[4] With only two very minor exceptions: the picture on the "doll card" at age II was updated; and the word "charcoal" was permitted as a substitute for "coal" in the Similarities test at age VII.

posed still other contributing factors, including the introduction of special television programs designed to stimulate intellectual development in preschool-age children.

Rising test norms from the 1930s or 1940s to the 1970s have also been found in other tests of general intellectual level (Herman, 1979). From the standpoint of the test user, an important implication of such findings is that individuals or groups examined with the earlier and later forms will appear to decline in ability because their performance is evaluated against a higher standard in the later form. The examiner should be aware of this possible artifact in interpreting scores.

ADMINISTRATION AND SCORING. The materials needed to administer the Stanford-Binet are shown in Figure 27. They include a box of standard toy objects for use at the younger age levels, two booklets of printed cards, a record booklet for recording responses, and a test manual. The tests are grouped into age levels extending from age II to superior adult. Between the ages of II and V, the test proceeds by half-year intervals. Thus, there is a level corresponding to age II, one to age II-6, one to age III, and so forth. Because progress is so rapid during these early ages, it proved feasible and desirable to measure change over six-month intervals. Between V and XIV, the age levels correspond to yearly intervals. The remaining levels are designated as Average Adult level and Superior Adult levels I, II, and III. Each age level contains six tests, with the exception of the Average Adult level, which contains eight.

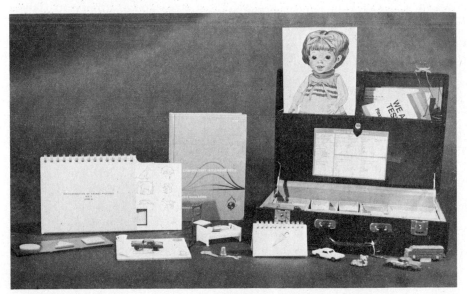

FIG. 27. Test Materials Employed in Administering the Stanford-Binet.
(Courtesy of The Riverside Publishing Company.)

The tests within any one age level are of approximately uniform difficulty and are arranged without regard to such residual differences in difficulty as may be present. An *alternate* test is also provided at each age level. Being of approximately equivalent difficulty, the alternate may be substituted for any of the tests in the level. Alternates are used if one of the regular tests must be omitted because special circumstances make it inappropriate for the individual or because some irregularity interfered with its standardized administration.

Four tests in each year level were selected on the basis of validity and representativeness to constitute an *abbreviated scale* for use when time does not permit the administration of the entire scale. These tests are marked with an asterisk on the record booklets. Comparisons between full-scale and abbreviated-scale IQs on a variety of groups show a close correspondence between the two, the correlations being approximately as high as the reliability coefficient of the full scale (Himelstein, 1966; Sattler, 1982; Terman & Merrill, 1973, pp. 61–62). The mean IQ, however, tends to run slightly lower on the short scale. This discrepancy is also found when the numbers of persons scoring higher on each version are compared. Over 50% of the cases receive lower IQs on the short version, while only 30% score higher.

In common with most individual intelligence tests, the Stanford-Binet requires a highly trained examiner. Both administration and scoring are fairly complicated for many of the tests. Considerable familiarity and experience with the scale are therefore required for a smooth performance. Hesitation and fumbling may be ruinous to rapport. Slight inadvertent changes in wording may alter the difficulty of items. A further complication is presented by the fact that tests must be scored as they are administered, since the subsequent conduct of the examination depends on the child's performance on previously administered levels.

Many clinicians regard the Stanford-Binet not only as a standardized test, but also as a clinical interview. The very characteristics that make this scale so difficult to administer also create opportunities for interaction between examiner and examinee and provide other sources of clues for the experienced clinician. Even more than most other individual tests, the Stanford-Binet makes it possible to observe the person's work methods, his or her approach to a problem, and other qualitative aspects of performance. The examiner may also have an opportunity to judge certain personality characteristics, such as activity level, self-confidence, persistence, and ability to concentrate. Any qualitative observations made in the course of Stanford-Binet administration should, of course, be clearly recognized as such and ought not to be interpreted in the same manner as objective test scores. The value of such qualitative observations depends to a large extent on the skill, experience, and psychological sophistication of the examiner, as well as on his or her awareness of the pitfalls and limitations inherent in this type of observation. The types of clinical observations that can be made during an individual intelligence examination are richly illustrated by Moriarty (1960, 1961, 1966), who sees in the testing session an opportunity to investigate the child's behavior in meeting a challenging, demanding, difficult, or frustrating situation.

In taking the Stanford-Binet, no one examinee tries all items. Each individual is tested only over a range of age levels suited to her or his own intellectual level. Testing usually requires no more than 30 to 40 minutes for younger children and not more than one hour and a half for older examinees. The standard procedure is to begin testing at a level slightly below the expected mental age of the examinee. Thus, the first tests given should be easy enough to arouse confidence, but not so easy as to cause boredom and annoyance. If the individual fails any test within the year level first administered, the next lower level is given. This procedure continues until a level is reached at which all tests are passed. This level is known as the *basal age*. Testing is then continued upward to a level at which all tests are failed, designated as the *ceiling age*. When this level is reached, the test is discontinued.

Individual Stanford-Binet items, or tests, are scored on an all-or-none basis. For each test, the minimal performance that constitutes "passing" is specified in the manual. For example, in identifying objects by use at year level II-6, the child passes if he or she correctly identifies three out of six designated objects; in answering comprehension questions at year level VIII, any four correct answers out of six represent a passing performance. Certain tests appear in identical form at different year levels, but are scored with a different standard of passing. Such tests are administered only once, the individual's performance determining the year level at which they are credited. The vocabulary test, for example, may be scored anywhere from level VI to Superior Adult III, depending on the number of words correctly defined.

The items passed and failed by any one individual will show a certain amount of *scatter* among adjacent year levels. We do not find that examinees pass all tests at or below their mental age level and fail all tests above such a level. Instead, the successfully passed tests are spread over several year levels, bounded by the examinee's basal age at one extreme and his or her ceiling age at the other. Mental age on the Stanford-Binet is found by crediting the individual with his or her basal age and adding to that age further months of credit for every test passed beyond the basal level. In the half-year levels between II and V, each of the six tests counts as one month; between VI and XIV, each of the six tests corresponds to two months of credit. Since each of the adult levels (AA, SA I, SA II, and SA III) covers more than one year of mental age, the months of credit for each test are adjusted accordingly. For example, the Average Adult level includes eight tests, each of which is credited with two months; the Superior Adult I level contains six tests, each receiving four months.

The highest mental age theoretically attainable on the Stanford-Binet is

22 years and 10 months. Such a score is not, of course, a true mental age, but a numerical score indicating degree of superiority above the Average Adult performance. It certainly does not correspond to the achievement of the average 22-year-old; according to the 1972 norms, the average 22-year-old obtains a mental age of 16–8. For any adult over 18 years of age, a mental age of 16–8 yields an IQ of 100 on this scale. In fact, above 13 years, mental ages cease to have the same significance as they do at lower levels, since it is just beyond 13 that the mean MA begins to lag behind CA on this scale. The Stanford-Binet is not suitable for adult testing, especially within the normal and superior range. Despite the three Superior Adult levels, there is insufficient ceiling for most superior adults or even for very superior adolescents (Kennedy et al., 1960). In such cases, it is often impossible to reach a ceiling age level at which all tests are failed. Moreover, most of the Stanford-Binet tests have more appeal for children than for adults, the content being of relatively little interest to most adults.

NORMATIVE INTERPRETATION. A major innovation introduced in the 1960 Stanford-Binet was the substitution of deviation IQs for the ratio IQs used in the earlier forms. These deviation IQs are standard scores with a mean of 100 and an SD of 16. As explained in Chapter 4, the principal advantage of this type of IQ is that it provides comparable scores at all age levels, thus eliminating the vagaries of ratio IQs. Despite the care with which the 1937 scales were developed in the effort to obtain constant IQ variability at all ages, the SDs of ratio IQs on these scales fluctuated from a low of 13 at age VI to a high of 21 at age II-6. Thus, an IQ of 113 at age VI corresponded to an IQ of 121 at age II-6. Special correction tables were developed to adjust for the major IQ variations in the 1937 scales (McNemar, 1942, pp. 172–174). All these difficulties were circumvented in the 1960 form through the use of deviation IQs, which automatically have the same SD throughout the age range.

As an aid to the examiner, Pinneau prepared tables in which deviation IQs can be looked up by entering MA and CA in years and months. These Pinneau tables are reproduced in the Stanford-Binet manual (Terman & Merrill, 1973). The latest manual includes both the 1972 and the 1937 normative IQ tables. For most testing purposes, the 1972 norms are appropriate, showing how the child's performance compares with that of others of his own age in his generation. To provide comparability with IQs obtained earlier, however, the 1937 norms are more suitable. They would thus be preferred in a continuing longitudinal study, or in comparing an individual's IQ with the IQ he obtained on the Stanford-Binet at a younger age. When used in this way, the 1937 standardization sample represents a fixed reference group, just as the students taking the College Board Scholastic Aptitude Test in 1941 provide a fixed reference group for that test (see Ch. 4).

Although the deviation IQ is the most convenient index for evaluating an individual's standing in his or her age group, the MA itself can serve a useful function. To say that a 6-year-old child performs as well as a typical 8-year-old usually conveys more meaning to a layperson than saying the child has an IQ of 137. A knowledge of the child's MA level also facilitates an understanding of what can be expected of that child in terms of educational achievement and other developmental norms of behavior. It should be noted, however, that the MAs obtained on the Stanford-Binet are still expressed in terms of the 1937 norms. It is only the IQ tables that incorporate the updated 1972 norms. Reference to these tables will show, for example, that if a child whose CA is 5–0 obtains an MA of 5–0, his or her IQ is *not* 100. To receive an IQ of 100 with the 1972 norms, this child would need an MA of 5–6.

One of the advantages of the Stanford-Binet derives from the mass of interpretive data and clinical experience that have been accumulated regarding this test. For many clinicians, educators, and others concerned with the evaluation of general ability level, the Stanford-Binet IQ has become almost synonymous with intelligence. Much has been learned about what sort of behavior can be expected from a child with an IQ of 50 or 80 or 120 on this test. The distributions of IQs in the successive standardization samples (1916, 1937, 1972) have provided a common frame of reference for the interpretation of IQs.

Because of the size of the error of measurement of a Stanford-Binet IQ, it is customary to allow approximately a 10-point band on either side of the obtained IQ for chance variation. Thus, any IQ between 90 and 110 is considered equivalent to the average IQ of 100. IQs above 110 represent superior deviations, those below 90 inferior deviations. There is no generally accepted frame of reference for classifying superior IQs. It may be noteworthy, however, that in the classical, long-term investigation of gifted children by Terman and his co-workers, a minimum IQ of 140 was required for inclusion in the principal part of the project (Terman & Oden, 1959).

At the other end of the scale, a widely used educational classification of mental retardates recognizes the educable, trainable, and custodial categories. In general, it is estimated that the educable group, in the IQ range from 50 to 75, is likely to advance to at least the third grade in academic work—and possibly as high as the sixth grade—if taught in a specially adapted classroom situation. The trainable group, with IQs between 25 and 50, can be taught self-care and social adjustment in a protected environment. Those below IQ 25 generally require custodial and nursing care, although increasing efforts are under way to provide effective learning experiences for such children.[5]

In its manual on terminology and classification, the American Association on Mental Deficiency (AAMD) lists four levels of mental retardation, de-

---

[5] See Robinson and Robinson (1976) for a comprehensive survey of definitions and classifications in mental retardation (Ch. 2) and for an overview of the education and training of retarded children (Ch. 18).

Table 24

Levels of Mental Retardation as Defined in Manual of American Association on Mental Deficiency

(Data in first two columns from Grossman, 1973, p. 18. Reprinted by permission of the American Association on Mental Deficiency)

Level	Cutoff Points (in SD units from Mean)	Range of Stanford-Binet IQ (SD = 16)	Percentage of Cases
Mild	−2	68–52	2.14
Moderate	−3	51–36	0.13
Severe	−4	35–20	0.003
Profound	−5	19 and below	0.00003

fined more precisely in terms of SD units. This classification is given in Table 24, together with the Stanford-Binet IQ ranges corresponding to each level and the expected percentage of cases. It will be noted that the classification is based on a division of the lower portion of the normal distribution curve into steps of 1 SD each, beginning at −2 SD. The advantage of such a classification is that it can be readily translated into standard scores or deviation IQs in any scale. Since the Stanford-Binet deviation IQ scale has an SD of 16, the mild level, extending from −2 SD down to −3 SD, ranges from 68 ($100 - 2 \times 16$) to 52 ($100 - 3 \times 16$). The other IQ ranges can be found in a similar manner. The percentages of cases at each level are those expected in a normal distribution (see Fig. 6, Ch. 4). They agree quite closely with the percentages of persons at these IQ levels found empirically in the general population. The frequency of mental retardation in the general population is usually estimated as close to 2%. The Stanford-Binet manual contains still another classification of levels of mental retardation, based on somewhat different IQ limits, which has been widely used as an interpretive frame of reference by clinical psychologists (Terman & Merrill, 1973, p. 18).

The use of such classifications of IQ levels, although of unquestionable help in standardizing the interpretation of test performance, carries certain dangers. Like all classifications of persons, it should not be rigidly applied, nor used to the exclusion of other data about the individual. There are, of course, no sharp dividing lines between the "mentally retarded" and the "normal" or between the "normal" and the "gifted." Individuals with IQs of 60 have been known to make satisfactory adjustments to the demands of daily living, while some with IQs close to 100 may require special care and guidance.

Decisions regarding admission to special treatment and training programs for mental retardates must take into account not only IQ but also social maturity, emotional adjustment, physical condition, and other circumstances of the individual case. The AAMD defines mental retardation as "significantly subaverage general intellectual functioning existing concurrently with deficits in adaptive behavior, and manifested during the developmental period" (Grossman, 1973, p. 11). This definition is further explicated in the stipulation that a child should not be classified as mentally retarded unless he or she is deficient in *both* intellectual functioning, as indicated by IQ level, and in adaptive behavior, as measured by such instruments as the Vineland Social Maturity Scale or the AAMD Adaptive Behavior Scales (to be discussed in Chapter 10).

Nor is high IQ synonymous with genius. Persons with IQs of 160 do occasionally lead undistinguished lives, while some with IQs much closer to 100 may make outstanding contributions. High-level achievement in specific fields may require special talents, originality, persistence, singleness of purpose, and other propitious emotional and motivational conditions.

RELIABILITY. The reliability of the 1937 Stanford-Binet was determined by correlating IQs on Forms L and M administered to the standardization group within an interval of one week or less. Such reliability coefficients are thus measures of both short-term temporal stability and equivalence of content across the two item samples. An exceptionally thorough analysis of the reliability of this test was carried out with reference to age and IQ level of examinees (McNemar, 1942, Ch. 6). In general, the Stanford-Binet tends to be more reliable for the older than for the younger ages, and for the lower than for the higher IQs. Thus, at ages 2½ to 5½, the reliability coefficients range from .83 (for IQ 140–149) to .91 (for IQ 60–69); for ages 6 to 13, they range from .91 to .97, respectively, for the same IQ levels; and for ages 14 to 18, the corresponding range of reliability coefficients extends from .95 to .98.

The increasing reliability of scores with increasing age is characteristic of tests in general. It results in part from the better control of conditions that is possible with older children (especially in comparison with the preschool ages). Another factor is the slowing down of developmental rate with age. When reliability is measured by retesting, individuals who are undergoing less change are also likely to exhibit less random fluctuation over short periods of time (Pinneau, 1961, Ch. 5).

The higher reliability obtained with lower IQ levels at any given CA, on the other hand, appears to be associated with the specific structural characteristics of the Stanford-Binet. It will be recalled that because of the difference in number of items available at different age levels, each item receives a weight of one month at the lowest levels, a weight of two months at the intermediate levels, and weights of four, five, or six months at the highest levels. This weighting tends to magnify the error of measurement at the upper levels, because the chance passing or failure of a single item makes a larger difference in total score at these levels than it does at lower levels. Since at any given CA, individuals with higher IQs are tested with higher

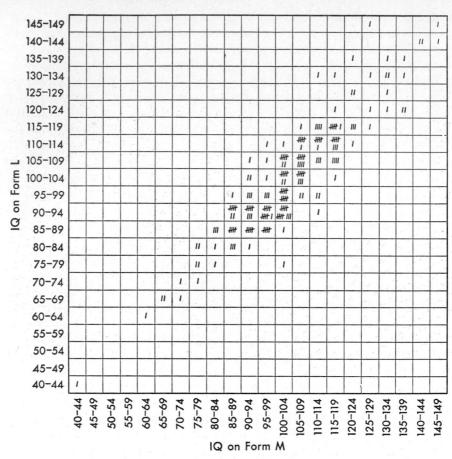

Fig. 28. Parallel-Form Reliability of the Stanford-Binet: Bivariate Distribution of IQ's Obtained by Seven-Year-Old Children on Forms L and M.

(From Terman & Merrill, 1937, p. 45. Reproduced by permission of Houghton Mifflin Company.)

age levels on the scale, their IQs will have a larger error of measurement and lower reliability (Pinneau, 1961, Ch. 5). The relationship between IQ level and reliability of the Stanford-Binet is also illustrated graphically in Figure 28, showing the bivariate distribution of IQs obtained by 7-year-old children on Forms L and M. It will be observed that the individual entries fall close to the diagonal at lower IQ levels and spread farther apart at the higher levels. This indicates closer agreement between L and M IQs at lower levels and wider discrepancies between them at upper levels. With such a fan-shaped scatter diagram, a single correlation coefficient is misleading. For this reason, separate reliability coefficients have been reported for different portions of the IQ range.

On the whole, the data indicate that the Stanford-Binet is a highly reliable test, most of the reported reliability coefficients for the various age and IQ levels being over .90. Such high reliability coefficients were obtained despite the fact that they were computed separately within each age group. It should be noted that all cases in the standardization sample were tested within a month of a birthday or half-year birthday. This narrowly restricted age range would tend to produce lower reliability coefficients than found for most tests, which employ more heterogeneous samples. Translated in terms of individual IQs, a reliability coefficient of .90 and an *SD* of 16 give an error of measurement of approximately 5 IQ points (see Ch. 5). In other words, the chances are about 2:1 that a child's true Stanford-Binet IQ differs by 5 points or less from the IQ obtained in a single testing, and the chances are 95 out of 100 that it varies by no more than 10 points ($5 \times 1.96 = 9.8$). Reflecting the same differences found in the reliability coefficients, these errors of measurement will be somewhat larger for younger than for older children, and somewhat larger for high performers than for low performers within age levels.

VALIDITY. Some information bearing on the *content validity* of the Stanford-Binet is provided by an examination of the tasks to be performed by the examinee in the various tests. These tasks run the gamut from simple manipulation to abstract reasoning. At the earliest age levels, the tests require chiefly eye-hand coordination, perceptual discrimination, and ability to follow directions, as in block building, stringing beads, comparing lengths, and matching geometric forms. A relatively large number of tests at the lower levels also involve the identification of common objects presented in toy models or in pictures.

Several tests occurring over a wide age range call for practical judgment or common sense. For example, the child is asked, "What should you do if you found on the streets of a city a three-year-old baby that was lost from its parents?" In other tests, the examinee is asked to explain why certain practices are commonly followed or certain objects are employed in daily living. A number of tests calling for the interpretation of pictorially or verbally presented situations, or the detection of absurdities in either pictures or brief stories, also seem to fall into this category. Memory tests are found throughout the scale and utilize a wide variety of materials. The individual is required to recall or recognize objects, pictures, geometric designs, bead patterns, digits, sentences, and the content of passages. Several tests of spatial orientation occur at widely scattered levels. These include maze tracing, paper folding, paper cutting, rearrangement of geometric figures, and directional orientation. Skills acquired in school, such as reading and arithmetic, are required for successful performance at the upper year levels.

The most common type of test, especially at the upper age levels, is that employing verbal content. In this category are to be found such well-known tests as vocabulary, analogies, sentence completion, disarranged sentences, defining abstract terms, and interpreting proverbs. Some stress verbal fluency, as in naming unrelated words as rapidly as possible, giving rhymes, or building sentences containing three given words. It should also be noted that many of the tests that are not predominantly verbal in content nevertheless require the understanding of fairly complex verbal instructions. That the scale as a whole is heavily weighted with verbal ability is indicated by the correlations obtained between the 45-word vocabulary test and mental ages on the entire scale. These correlations were found to be .71, .83, .86, and .83 for groups of examinees aged 8, 11, 14, and 18 years, respectively (McNemar, 1942, pp. 139–140; see also A. J. Edwards, 1963).[6] The correlations are at least as high as those normally found between tests designed to measure the same functions, and they fall within the range of common reliability coefficients.

Insofar as all the functions listed are relevant to what is commonly regarded as "intelligence," the scale may be said to have content validity. The preponderance of verbal content at the upper levels is defended by the test authors on theoretical grounds. Thus, they wrote:

At these levels the major intellectual differences between subjects reduce largely to differences in the ability to do conceptual thinking, and facility in dealing with concepts is most readily sampled by the use of verbal tests. Language, essentially, is the shorthand of the higher thought processes, and the level at which this shorthand functions is one of the most important determinants of the level of the processes themselves. (Terman & Merrill, 1937, p. 5)

It should be added that clinical psychologists have developed several schemes for classifying Stanford-Binet tests, as aids in the qualitative description of the individual's test performance (Sattler, 1982). Pattern analysis of the examinee's successes and failures in different functions may provide helpful clues for further clinical exploration. The results of such analyses, however, should be regarded as tentative and interpreted with caution. Most functions are represented by too few tests to permit reliable measurement, and the coverage of any one function varies widely from one year level to another.

Data on the *criterion-related validity* of the Stanford-Binet, both concurrent and predictive, have been obtained chiefly in terms of academic achievment. Since the publication of the original 1916 Scale, many correlations have been computed between Stanford-Binet IQ and school grades, teachers' ratings, and achievement test scores. Most of these correlations fall between .40 and .75. School progress was likewise found to be related to Stanford-Binet IQ. Children who were accelerated by one or more grades averaged considerably higher in IQ than did those at normal age-grade loca-

---

[6] Since these are part-whole correlations, they are spuriously raised by the inclusion of the vocabulary test in the determination of MA. This effect is slight, however, since the vocabulary test constitutes less than 5% of the total number of test items (McNemar, 1942, p. 140).

tion; and children who were retarded by one or more grades averaged considerably below (McNemar, 1942, Ch. 3).

Like most intelligence tests, the Stanford-Binet correlates highly with performance in nearly all academic courses, but its correlations are highest with the predominantly verbal courses, such as English and history. Correlations with achievement test scores show the same pattern. In a study of high school sophomores, for example, Form L IQs correlated .73 with Reading Comprehension scores, .54 with Biology scores, and .48 with Geometry scores (Bond, 1940). Correlations in the .50s and .60s have been found with college grades. Among college students, both selective factors and insufficient test ceiling frequently lower the correlations.

There have been relatively few validation studies with the 1960 Form L-M (see Himelstein, 1966). Kennedy, Van de Reit, and White (1963) report a correlation of .69 with total score on the California Achievement Test in a large sample of black elementary school children. Correlations with scores on separate parts of the same battery were: Reading, .68; Arithmetic, .64; and Language, .70.

In interpreting the IQ, it should be borne in mind that the Stanford-Binet —like most so-called intelligence tests—is largely a measure of scholastic aptitude and that it is heavily loaded with verbal functions, especially at the upper levels. Individuals with a language handicap, as well as those whose strongest abilities lie along nonverbal lines, will thus score relatively low on such a test. Similarly, there are undoubtedly a number of fields in which scholastic aptitude and verbal comprehension are not of primary importance. Obviously, to apply any test to situations for which it is inappropriate will only reduce its effectiveness. Because of the common identification of Stanford-Binet IQ with the very concept of intelligence, there has been a tendency to expect too much from this one test.

Data on the *construct validity* of the Stanford-Binet come from many sources. Continuity in the functions measured in the 1916, 1937, and 1960 scales was ensured by retaining in each version only those items that correlated satisfactorily with mental age on the preceding form. Hence, the information that clinicians have accumulated over the years regarding typical behavior of individuals at different MA and IQ levels can be utilized in their interpretation of scores on this scale.

Age differentiation represents the major criterion in the selection of Stanford-Binet items. Thus, there is assurance that the Stanford-Binet measures abilities that increase with age during childhood and adolescence in our culture. In each form, internal consistency was a further criterion for item selection. That there is a good deal of functional homogeneity in the Stanford-Binet, despite the apparent variety of content, is indicated by a mean item-scale correlation of .66 for the 1960 revision. The predominance of verbal functions in the scale is shown by the higher correlation of verbal than nonverbal items with performance on the total scale (Terman & Merrill, 1973, pp. 33–34).

Further data pertaining to construct validity are provided by several independent factor analyses of Stanford-Binet items. If IQs are to be comparable at different ages, the scale should have approximately the same factorial composition at all age levels. For an unambiguous interpretation of IQs, moreover, the scale should be highly saturated with a single common factor. The latter point has already been discussed in connection with homogeneity in Chapter 5. If the scores were heavily weighted with two group factors, such as verbal and numerical aptitudes, an IQ of, let us say, 115 obtained by different persons might indicate high verbal ability in one case and high numerical ability in the other.

McNemar (1942, Ch. 9) conducted separate factorial analyses of Stanford-Binet items at 14 age levels, including half-year groups from 2 to 5 and year groups at ages 6, 7, 9, 11, 13, 15, and 18. The number of cases employed in each analysis varied from 99 to 200, and the number of items ranged from 19 to 35. In each of these analyses, tetrachoric correlations were computed between the items, and the resulting correlations were factor analyzed. By including items from adjacent year levels in more than one analysis, some evidence was obtained regarding the identity of the common factor at different ages. The factor loadings of tests that recur at several age levels provided further data on this point. In general, the results of these analyses indicated that performance on Stanford-Binet items is largely explicable in terms of a single common factor. Evidence of additional group factors was found at a few age levels, but the contribution of these factors was small. It was likewise demonstrated that the common factor found at adjacent age levels was essentially the same, although this conclusion may not apply to more widely separated age levels. In fact, there was some evidence to suggest that the common factor becomes increasingly verbal as the higher ages are approached. The common factor loading of the vocabulary test, for example, rose from .59 at age 6 to .91 at age 18.

Other factor-analytic studies of both the 1937 and the 1960 forms have used statistical techniques designed to bring out more fully the operation of group factors (L. V. Jones, 1949, 1954; Ramsey & Vane, 1970; Sattler, 1982; Stott & Ball, 1965). Among the factors thus identified were several verbal, memory, reasoning, spatial visualization, and perceptual abilities. In general, the results suggest that there is much in common in the scale as a whole—a characteristic that is largely built into the Stanford-Binet by selecting items that have high correlations with total scores. At the same time, performance is also influenced by a number of special abilities whose composition varies with the age level tested.

WECHSLER ADULT INTELLIGENCE SCALE

The rest of this chapter is concerned with the intelligence scales prepared by David Wechsler. Although administered as individual tests and designed for many of the same uses as the Stanford-Binet, these scales differ in several important ways from the earlier test. Rather than being organized into age levels, all items of a given type are grouped into subtests and arranged in increasing order of difficulty within each subtest. In this respect the Wechsler scales follow the pattern established for group tests, rather than that of the Stanford-Binet. Another characteristic feature of these scales is the inclusion of verbal and performance subtests, from which separate verbal and performance IQs are computed.

Besides their use as measures of general intelligence, the Wechsler scales have been investigated as a possible aid in psychiatric diagnosis. Beginning with the observation that brain damage, psychotic deterioration, and emotional difficulties may affect some intellectual functions more than others, Wechsler and other clinical psychologists argued that an analysis of the individual's relative performance on different subtests should reveal specific psychiatric disorders. The problems and results pertaining to such a profile analysis of the Wechsler scales will be analyzed in Chapter 16, as an example of the clinical use of tests.

The interest aroused by the Wechsler scales and the extent of their use is attested by over 3,000 publications appearing to date about these scales. In addition to the usual test reviews in the *Mental Measurements Yearbooks,* research pertaining to the Wechsler scales has been surveyed periodically in journals (Guertin et al., 1956, 1962, 1966, 1971; Littell, 1960; Rabin & Guertin, 1951; Zimmerman & Woo-Sam, 1972) and has been summarized in several books (Glasser & Zimmerman, 1967; Kaufman, 1979; Matarazzo, 1972; Wechsler, 1958; Zimmerman, Woo-Sam, & Glasser, 1973).

ANTECEDENTS OF THE WECHSLER INTELLIGENCE SCALES. The first form of the Wechsler scales, known as the Wechsler-Bellevue Intelligence Scale, was published in 1939. One of the primary objectives in its preparation was to provide an intelligence test suitable for adults. In first presenting this scale, Wechsler (1939) pointed out that previously available intelligence tests had been designed primarily for schoolchildren and had been adapted for adult use by adding more difficult items of the same kinds. The content of such tests was often of little interest to adults. Unless the test items have a certain minimum of face validity, rapport cannot be properly established with adult examinees. Many intelligence test items, written with special reference to the daily activities of the schoolchild, clearly lack face validity for most adults.

The overemphasis on speed in most tests also tends to handicap the older person. Similarly, Wechsler believed that relatively routine manipulation of words received undue weight in the traditional intelligence test. He likewise called attention to the inapplicability of mental age norms to adults and pointed out that few adults had previously been included in the standardization samples for individual intelligence tests.

It was to meet these various objections that the original Wechsler-Bellevue was developed. In form and content, this scale was closely similar to the more recent Wechsler Adult Intelligence Scale (WAIS) which supplanted it in 1955. The earlier scale had a number of technical deficiencies, particularly with regard to size and representativeness of normative sample and reliability of subtests, which were largely corrected in the later revisions. The latest edition is the Wechsler Adult Intelligence Scale—Revised (WAIS-R), published in 1981.

DESCRIPTION. The WAIS-R comprises eleven subtests. Six subtests constitute the Verbal Scale and five the Performance Scale. These subtests are listed and briefly described below. They are numbered in the order of their administration, in which verbal and performance tests are alternated.

VERBAL SCALE

1. *Information:* 29 questions covering a wide variety of information that adults have presumably had an opportunity to acquire in our culture. An effort was made to avoid specialized or academic knowledge. It might be added that questions of general information have been used for a long time in informal psychiatric examinations to establish the individual's intellectual level and practical orientation.

3. *Digit Span:* Orally presented lists of three to nine digits are to be orally reproduced. In the second part, the examinee must reproduce lists of two to eight digits backwards.

5. *Vocabulary:* 35 words of increasing difficulty are presented both orally and visually. The examinee is asked what each word means.

7. *Arithmetic:* 14 problems similar to those encountered in elementary school arithmetic. Each problem is orally presented and is to be solved without the use of paper and pencil.

9. *Comprehension:* 16 items, in each of which the examinee explains what should be done under certain circumstances, why certain practices are followed, the meaning of proverbs, etc. Designed to measure practical judgment and common sense, this test is similar to the Stanford-Binet Comprehension items; but its specific content was chosen so as to be more consonant with the interests and activities of adults.

11. *Similarities:* 14 items requiring the examinee to say in what way two things are alike.

PERFORMANCE SCALE

2. *Picture Completion:* 20 cards, each containing a picture from which some part is missing. Examinee must tell what is missing from each picture.

4. *Picture Arrangement:* Each of the 10 items consists of a set of cards containing pictures to be rearranged in the proper sequence so as to tell a story.

Figure 29 shows one set of cards in the order in which they are presented to the examinee.

6. *Block Design:* This subtest uses a set of 9 cards containing designs in red and white and a set of identical one-inch blocks whose sides are painted red, white, and red-and-white. The examinee is shown one design at a time, which he must reproduce by choosing and assembling the proper blocks.

8. *Object Assembly:* In each of the four parts of this subtest, cutouts are to be assembled to make a flat picture of a familiar object (see Fig. 30).

10. *Digit Symbol:* This is a version of the familiar code-substitution test which has often been included in nonlanguage intelligence scales. The key contains 9 symbols paired with the 9 digits. With this key before him, the examinee has 1½ minutes to fill in as many symbols as he can under the numbers on the answer sheet.

Both speed and correctness of performance influence the score on the Arithmetic, Picture Arrangement, Block Design, Object Assembly, and Digit Symbol subtests.

FIG. 29. Easy item from WAIS-R Picture Arrangement Test.

(Reproduced by permission. Copyright © 1976 by The Psychological Corporation, New York, N.Y. All rights reserved.)

Since the publication of the original Wechsler-Bellevue scale, a large number of *abbreviated scales* have been proposed. These scales are formed simply by omitting some of the subtests and prorating scores to obtain a Full Scale IQ comparable to the published norms. The fact that several subtest combinations, while effecting considerable saving in time, correlate over .90 with Full Scale IQs has encouraged the development and use of abbreviated scales for rapid screening purposes. Extensive research has been conducted to identify the most effective combinations of two, three, four, and five subtests in predicting Verbal, Performance, and Full Scale IQs (Matarazzo, 1972, pp. 252–255). A comparative analysis of a single four-subtest combination at different age levels from 18–19 to 75 and over yielded correlations of .95 to .97 with Full Scale IQs. Equally close correspondences have been found in several studies of abbreviated scales formed by reducing the number of items within subtests. Much of this research has utilized the WAIS standardization data; but similar studies have been conducted on mental retardates and psychiatric patients.

FIG. 30. Administration of WAIS-R Object Assembly Test.
(Courtesy of The Psychological Corporation.)

Although an excessive amount of energy seems to have been expended in assembling and checking short forms of the Wechsler scales, it is probably inadvisable to use such abbreviated versions except as rough screening devices. Many of the qualitative observations made possible by the administration of an individual scale are lost when abbreviated scales are used. Moreover, the assumption that the original Full Scale norms are applicable to prorated total scores on short scales may not always be justified.

NORMS. The WAIS-R standardization sample was chosen with exceptional care to ensure its representativeness. The normative sample consisted of 1,880 cases, including an equal number of men and women distributed over nine age levels from 16–17 to 70–74 years. Participants were selected so as to match as closely as possible the proportions in the 1970 United States Census (updated through more recent available reports), with regard to geographical region, urban–rural residence, race (white versus nonwhite), occupational level, and education. The standardization sample was designed so as to include only "normal adults." Institutionalized mental retardates, as well as persons with known brain damage, severe behavioral or emotional problems, or physical defects that would restrict their ability to respond to test items, were excluded from the sample. Persons whose primary language was other than English were tested only if they were able to speak and understand English. Examiners were instructed not to test more than one member of a family.

Raw scores on each WAIS-R subtest are transmuted into standard scores with a mean of 10 and an SD of 3. These scaled scores were derived from a reference group of 500 cases which included all persons between the ages of 20 and 34 in the standardization sample. All subtest scores are thus expressed in comparable units and in terms of a fixed reference group. Verbal, Performance, and Full Scale scores are found by adding the scaled scores on the six Verbal subtests, the five Performance subtests, and all eleven subtests, respectively. By reference to appropriate tables provided in the manual, these three scores can be expressed as deviation IQs with a mean of 100 and an *SD* of 15. Such IQs, however, are found with reference to the individual's own age group. They therefore show the individual's standing in comparison with persons of his or her own age level.

In the interpretation of WAIS-R IQs, the relative magnitude of IQs obtained on the Wechsler scales and on other intelligence tests should also be taken into account. It has been repeatedly found that above-average examinees tend to score higher on the Stanford-Binet than on the Wechsler scales, while below-average examinees score higher on the Wechsler than on the Stanford-Binet. For example, studies of college freshmen show significantly higher mean IQs on the Stanford-Binet than on the Wechsler, while the reverse is generally found among the mentally retarded. To some extent, the difference in standard deviation of Wechsler and Stanford-Binet IQs may account for the differences between the IQs obtained with the two scales. It will be recalled that the *SD* of the Stanford-Binet IQ is 16, while that of the Wechsler IQ is 15. The discrepancies in individual IQs, however, are larger than would be expected on the basis of such a difference. Another difference between the two scales is that the Wechsler has less floor and ceiling than the Stanford-Binet and hence does not discriminate as well at the extremes of the IQ range.

The relationship between Stanford-Binet and Wechsler IQs depends not only on IQ level but also on age. Other things being equal, older persons tend to obtain higher IQs on the Wechsler than on the Stanford-Binet, while the reverse is true of younger subjects. One explanation for such a trend is obviously provided by the use of a declining standard in the computation of the Wechsler IQs of older persons. On the Stanford-Binet, on the other hand, all adults are evaluated in terms of the average peak age on that scale, viz., 18 years. It is also possible that, since the Stanford-Binet was standardized primarily on children and the Wechsler on adults, the content of the former tends to favor children while that of the latter favors older persons.

RELIABILITY. For each of the eleven subtests, as well as for Verbal, Performance, and Full Scale IQs, reliability coefficients were computed within each of the nine age groups. Split-half reliability coefficients (corrected for full test length by the Spearman-Brown formula) were employed for every subtest except Digit Span and Digit Symbol. This technique was inappropriate for Digit Span, because it is administered as two separate subtests, and for Digit Symbol, because it is a speeded test. For these two tests, alternate-form reliability coefficients were found on special samples examined with the WAIS-R and WAIS, or with the WAIS-R and WISC-R, depending on age level.

Reliabilities for Full Scale IQ ranged from .96 to .98. The range for Verbal IQ was .95 to .97, and for Performance IQ, .88 to .94. As would be expected, the individual subtests had lower reliabilities, ranging from .52 for Object Assembly at age 16–17 to .96 for Vocabulary at six of the nine age levels. For the entire span of age levels, however, only five of the 89 coefficients for the 11 subtests fell below .70. It is particularly important to consider these subtest reliabilities when evaluating the significance of differences between subtest scores obtained by the same individual, as in profile analysis.

The WAIS-R manual also reports standard errors of measurement for the three IQs and for subtest scores. For Verbal IQ, such errors varied between 2.50 and 3.30 points among the age groups; for Performance IQ, from 3.69 to 5.18; and for Full Scale IQ, they were all below 3. We may thus conclude, for example, that the chances are roughly 2:1 that an individual's true Full Scale IQ falls within 3 points of his or her obtained Full Scale IQ. Some data were also obtained on the stability of WAIS-R scores over time. The WAIS-R was administered twice over an interval of 2 to 7 weeks to two groups: 71 persons in the 25–34 year group and 48 persons in the 45–54 year group. In both groups, stability coefficients were in the .90s for Verbal, Performance, and Full Scale IQs. For the individual subtests, they fell mostly in the .80 and .90s, with none below .67. This retest study also revealed a tendency for IQs to rise on the second test, the mean gain in the two groups being 6 and 7 points for Full Scale IQ. Such an expected practice effect, although slight, should be taken into account when retesting individuals after a short time interval.

VALIDITY. Any discussion of validity of the WAIS-R must draw on research done with the earlier Wechsler adult scales. Since all changes introduced in the later revisions represent improvements (in reliability, ceiling, normative sample, and so on) and since the nature of the test remained substantially the same, it is reasonable to suppose that validity data obtained on the earlier editions underestimate rather than overestimate the validity of the WAIS.

The WAIS-R manual itself contains no validity data, but several aspects of validity are covered in the books by Wechsler (1958) and by Matarazzo (1972). Wechsler (1958, Ch. 5) argued that the psychological functions tapped by each of the 11 chosen subtests fit the definition of intelligence, that similar tests have been successfully employed in previously developed intelligence scales, and that such tests have proved their worth in clinical experience. The test author himself places the major emphasis on this approach to validity. The treatment is essentially in terms of *content validity,* although it has overtones of construct validity without supporting data. Much of the discussion in Matarazzo's book is of the same nature, dealing with the construct of global intelligence, but having only a tenuous relation to the evaluation of the WAIS as a measuring instrument.

Some empirical data on *concurrent criterion-related validity* are summarized in the two books (Matarazzo, 1972, p. 284; Wechsler, 1958, Ch. 14). These data include mean IQ differences among various educational and occupational groups, as well as a few correlations with job-performance ratings and academic grades. Most group differences, though small, are in the expected directions. Persons in white-collar jobs of different kinds and levels averaged higher in Verbal than in Performance IQ, but skilled workers averaged higher in Performance than in Verbal. In studies of industrial executives and psychiatric residents, Verbal IQ correlated in the .30's with overall performance ratings. Both groups, of course, were already preselected in terms of the abilities measured by these tests. Correlations in the .40s and .50s have been found between Verbal IQ and college or engineering school grades. In all these groups, the Verbal Scale yielded somewhat higher correlations than the Full Scale; correlations with the Performance Scale were much lower. Even the correlations with the Verbal Scale, however, were not appreciably higher than those obtained with the Stanford-Binet and with well-known group tests. In studies of mental retardates, WAIS IQs have proved to be satisfactory predictors of institutional release rate and subsequent work adjustment (Guertin et al., 1966).

The Wechsler scales have been repeatedly correlated with the Stanford-Binet as well as with other well-known tests of intelligence (Guertin et al., 1971; Matarazzo, 1972; Wechsler, 1958). Correlations with the Stanford-Binet in unselected adolescent or adult groups and among mental retardates cluster around .80. Within more homogeneous samples, such as college students, the correlations tend to be considerably lower. Group tests yield somewhat lower correlations with the Wechsler scales, although such correlations vary widely as a function of the particular test and the nature and heterogeneity of the sample. For both Stanford-Binet and group scales, correlations are nearly always higher with the Wechsler Verbal Scale than with the Full Scale, while correlations with the Performance Scale are much lower than either. On the other hand, Performance IQs correlate more highly than Verbal IQs with tests of spatial abilities. For example, a correlation of '.72 was found between Performance IQ and the Minnesota Paper Form Board Test in a group of 16-year-old boys and girls (Janke & Havighurst, 1945). In other studies, Performance IQs correlated .70 with Raven's Progressive Matrices (Hall, 1957) and .35 with the Bennett Mechanical Comprehension Test (Wechsler, 1958, p. 228).

Of some relevance to the *construct validity* of the Wechsler scales are the intercorrelations of subtests, as well as factorial analyses of the scores. In the process of standardizing the WAIS-R, intercorrelations of the 11 subtests and of the Verbal and Performance Scale scores were computed on each of the nine age groups. When these correlations were averaged across the age groups, the Verbal and Performance Scales correlated .74. Intercorrelations of separate subtests were generally higher among Verbal than among Performance subtests. The correlations between Performance and Verbal subtests were not substantially lower than those of the Performance subtests with each other. The average correlations ranged from .46 to .81 among Verbal subtests, from .38 to .63 among Performance subtests, and from .33 to .56 between Verbal and Performance subtests. Both individual subtest correlations and correlations between total Verbal and Performance Scale scores suggest that the two scales have much in common and that the allocation of tests to one or the other scale may be somewhat arbitrary.

Factorial analyses of the Wechsler scales have been conducted with a variety of groups ranging from eighth-grade students to a special old-age sample and including both normal and abnormal groups. They have also employed different statistical procedures and have approached the analysis from different points of view. Some have been directly concerned with age changes in the factorial organization of the Wechsler subtests, but the findings of different investigators are inconsistent in this regard. As an example, we may examine the factorial analyses of the WAIS conducted by J. Cohen (1957a, 1957b) with the intercorrelations of subtests obtained on four age groups in the standardization sample (18–19, 25–34, 45–54, and 60–75+). The major results of this study are in line with those of other investigations using comparable procedures, as well as with the findings of later studies by Cohen and his associates on different populations (Guertin et al., 1962, 1966).

That all 11 subtests have much in common was demonstrated in Cohen's study by the presence of a single general factor that accounted for about 50% of the total variance of the battery. In addition, three major group factors were identified. One was a *verbal comprehension* factor, with large weights in the Vocabulary, Information, Comprehension, and Similarities subtests. A *perceptual organization* factor was found chiefly in Block Design and Object Assembly. This factor may actually represent a combination of the perceptual speed and spatial visualization factors repeatedly found in factorial analyses of aptitude tests. The results of an earlier investigation by P. C. Davis (1956), in which "reference tests" measuring various factors were included with the Wechsler subtests, support this composite interpretation of the perceptual organization factor.

The third major group factor identified by Cohen was described as a *memory* factor. Found principally in Arithmetic and Digit Span, it apparently includes both immediate rote memory for new material and recall of previously learned material. Ability to concentrate and to resist distraction may be involved in this factor. Of special interest is the finding that the memory factor increased sharply in prominence in the old-age sample. At that age level it had significant loadings, not only in Arithmetic and Digit Span, but also in Vocabulary, Information, Comprehension, and Digit Symbol. Cohen pointed out that in old age memory begins to deteriorate at different ages and rates in different persons. Individual differences in memory thus come to play a more prominent part in intellectual functioning than had been true at earlier ages. Many of the Wechsler subtests require memory at all ages. Until differential deterioration sets in, however, individual differences in the retentive ability required in most of the subtests are insignificant.

WECHSLER INTELLIGENCE SCALE FOR CHILDREN

DESCRIPTION. The Wechsler Intelligence Scale for Children (WISC) was first prepared as a downward extension of the original Wechsler-Bellevue (Seashore, Wesman, & Doppelt, 1950). Many items were taken directly from the adult test; and easier items of the same types were added to each test. A revised edition, WISC-R, was published in 1974. The WISC-R consists of 12 subtests, of which 2 are used only as alternates or as supplementary tests if time permits. The materials used in administering the WISC-R are pictured in Figure 31; and Figure 32 shows a child working on one of

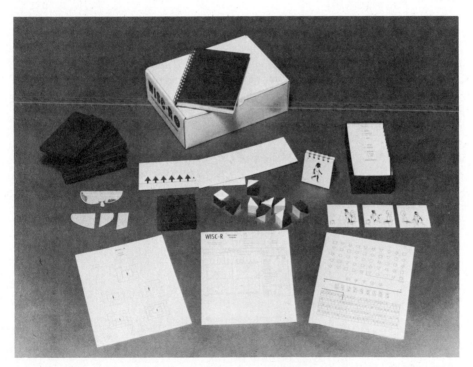

FIG. 31. Materials Used with the Wechsler Intelligence Scale for Children—Revised.

(Courtesy of The Psychological Corporation.)

the easier items of the Picture Completion subtest. As in the other Wechsler scales, the subtests are classified into a Verbal and a Performance scale and are administered in alternating order, as shown below.

VERBAL SCALE   PERFORMANCE SCALE

  1. Information   2. Picture Completion

  3. Similarities   4. Picture Arrangement

  5. Arithmetic   6. Block Design

  7. Vocabulary   8. Object Assembly

  9. Comprehension   10. Coding (or Mazes)

(Digit Span)

The Mazes subtest, which requires more time, may be substituted for Coding if the examiner so prefers. Any other substitution, including the substitution of Mazes for any other subtest and the substitution of Digit Span for any of the Verbal subtests, should be made only if one of the regular subtests must be omitted because of special handicaps or accidental disruption of testing procedure. The supplementary tests may always be

FIG. 32. The Picture Completion Test of the Wechsler Intelligence Scale for Children—Revised.

(Courtesy of The Psychological Corporation.)

administered in addition to the regular battery and their inclusion is advised because of the qualitative and diagnostic information provided. In such cases, however, their scores are not used in finding IQs.

With regard to content, the only subtest that does not appear in the adult scale is Mazes. This test consists of nine paper-and-pencil mazes of increasing difficulty, to be completed within designated time limits and scored in terms of errors. The Coding subtest corresponds to the Digit Symbol subtest of the WAIS, with an easier part added. The remaining subtests represent downward extensions of the adult tests. The development of the WISC was somewhat paradoxical, since Wechsler embarked upon his original enterprise partly because of the need for an adult scale that would *not* be a mere upward extension of available children's scales. The first edition of the WISC was, in fact, criticized because its content was not sufficiently child-oriented.

In the revised edition (WISC-R), special efforts were made to replace or modify adult-oriented items so as to bring their content closer to common childhood experiences. In the Arithmetic subtest, for instance, "cigars" was changed to "candy bars" and items about a taxi and a card game were replaced. Other changes included the elimination of items that might be differentially familiar to particular groups of children and the inclusion of more female and black persons in the pictorial content of the subtests. Several of the subtests were lengthened in order to increase reliability; and improvements were introduced in administration and scoring procedures.

As in the case of the WAIS, there has been considerable experimentation with abbreviated scales of the WISC. The correlations of these short forms with Full Scale IQs run lower than in the WAIS. With scales consisting of five or six subtests from both Verbal and Performance sets, correlations in the .80s have been found with Full Scale IQs. It should be noted, however, that these data were obtained with the earlier form of WISC. With the increased length and improved reliability of the WISC-R subtests, the correlations of abbreviated scales with Full Scale IQs will undoubtedly be higher. Using the WISC standardization data and a procedure that takes subtest reliability into account, Silverstein (1970) identified the ten best combinations of two, three, four, and five WISC subtests. A widely used two-test combination consists of Vocabulary and Block Design. The same cautions mentioned regarding the use of WAIS short forms can be repeated here.

NORMS. The treatment of scores on the WISC-R follows the same procedures used in the adult scale, with minor differences. Raw scores on each subtest are first transmuted into normalized standard scores *within the child's own age group*. Tables of such scaled scores are provided for every four-month interval between the ages of 6–0 and 16–11 years. As in the adult scales, the subtest scaled scores are expressed in terms of a distribution with a mean of 10 and an *SD* of 3 points. The scaled subtest scores are added and converted into a deviation IQ with a mean of 100 and an *SD* of 15. Verbal, Performance, and Full Scale IQs can be found by the same method.

Although a mental age is not needed to compute a deviation IQ, the WISC-R provides data for interpreting performance on individual subtests in terms of age norms. For each subtest, the manual gives the mean raw score found in the standardization sample for each age from 6–2 to 16–10 at intervals of four months. A child's *test age* can be found by looking up the age corresponding to her or his raw score. A mean or median test age on the entire scale can be computed if desired.

The standardization sample for the WISC-R included 100 boys and 100 girls at each year of age from 6½ through 16½, giving a total of 2,200 cases. Each child was tested within six weeks of his or her midyear. For example, the 8-year-olds ranged from 8-years 4-months 15-days to 8-years 7-months 15-days. The sample was stratified on the basis of the 1970 U.S. Census with respect to geographic region, urban-rural residence, occupation of head of household, and race (white-nonwhite). Bilinguals were included if they could speak and understand English. Institutionalized mental retardates and children with severe emotional disorders were excluded. Testing was conducted in 32 states (including Hawaii) and Washington, D.C. In many respects, the WISC-R standardization sample is more nearly representative of the U.S. population within the designated age limits than is any other sample employed in standardizing individual tests.

Unlike the earlier WISC, the WISC-R yields means IQs that are very close to Stanford-Binet IQs (1972 norms). The increased similarity in IQ may be attributed in part to the previously mentioned improvements in content, administration, and scoring procedures in the WISC-R, and in part to the closeness in time when the norms were gathered for the two scales. That the time when normative samples were examined is an important factor is borne out by a comparison of the 1949 WISC with the 1974 WISC-R. At all ages, the later WISC-R has higher norms than the WISC (Kaufman, 1979, pp. 125–129).

RELIABILITY. Both split-half and retest coefficients were computed for WISC-R subtests,[7] as well as for Verbal, Performance, and Full Scale IQs. Odd-even reliabilities were computed separately within each of the 11 age groups; retest coefficients were found within three age groups (6½–7½, 10½–11½, 14½–15½), the tests being readministered after approximately a one-month interval. Average split-half reliabilities for Verbal, Performance, and Full Scale IQs were .94, .90, and .96. The corresponding retest coefficients were .93, .90, and .95. Some practice effect was observed on the re-

---

[7] Only retest coefficients are reported for Coding and Digit Span, for which split-half coefficients would be inappropriate.

test, with mean gains of 3½ IQ points on the Verbal Scale, 9½ on the Performance Scale, and 7 on the Full Scale. Such a practice effect should be taken into account when retesting children after short intervals of time.

Subtest reliabilities are generally satisfactory and higher than in the earlier form. Split-half reliabilities averaged across age groups range from .70 to .86; and mean retest coefficients range from .65 to .88. A noteworthy feature of the manual is the inclusion of tables giving the standard error of measurement for subtests and for Verbal, Performance, and Full Scale IQs within each age group, as well as the minimum difference between scores required for significance at specified levels. In comparisons of Verbal and Performance IQs, a difference of 11 or 12 points is significant at the .05 level. The standard error of the Full Scale IQ is approximately 3 points. Thus the chances are 95 out of 100 that a child's true WISC-R IQ differs from his or her obtained IQ by no more than ±6 points ($3 \times 1.96 = 5.88$).

VALIDITY. No discussion of validity is included in the WISC-R manual. To be sure, normative tables of standard score equivalents for each subtest provide evidence of age differentiation, but no evaluation of the data in terms of this criterion is given. A number of independent investigators have found concurrent validity coefficients between the earlier WISC and achievement tests or other academic criteria of intelligence clustering between .50 and .60 (Littell, 1960; Zimmerman & Woo-Sam, 1972). As would be expected, the Verbal Scale tended to correlate higher than the Performance Scale with such criteria. When children in the WISC standardization sample were classified according to father's occupational level, the usual hierarchy of mean IQs was found (Seashore, Wesman, & Doppelt, 1950). The difference tended to be slightly larger in Verbal than in Performance IQ and to decrease somewhat with age, possibly because of exposure to relatively uniform education (B. W. Estes, 1953, 1955).

The WISC-R manual reports correlations with 1972 Stanford-Binet IQs within homogeneous age groups. The mean correlation with Full Scale IQ is .73. The Verbal Scale again correlates more highly with the Stanford-Binet than does the Performance Scale (.71 versus .60). Among the subtests, Vocabulary yields the highest mean correlation (.69) and Coding the lowest (.26).

Additional information provided in the WISC-R manual includes intercorrelations among the individual subtests, as well as the correlation of each subtest with Verbal, Performance, and Full Scale scores, and of these three composite scores with each other. All correlations are given separately for the 200 cases in each of the 11 age groups in the standardization sample. The correlations between total Verbal and Performance scores ranged from .60 to .73 within age groups, averaging .67. Thus, the two parts of the scale have much in common, although the correlations between them are low enough to justify the retention of the separate scores.

Factorial analyses of the earlier WISC subtests identified factors quite similar to those found in the adult scales, namely, general, verbal comprehension, perceptual–spatial, and memory (or freedom from distractibility) factors (see Littell, 1960; Zimmerman & Woo-Sam, 1972). In a more recent study (Silverstein, 1973), the WISC subtests were factor-analyzed separately in groups of 505 English-speaking white, 318 black, and 487 Mexican-American children aged 6 to 11 years. The results revealed a verbal comprehension factor having substantial correlations with the five verbal tests; and a perceptual organization factor having substantial correlations with Block Design and Object Assembly. A major finding of this study was the similarity of factor structure across the three ethnic groups, suggesting that the tests measure the same abilities in these groups.

A factor analysis of the WISC-R scores of the standardization sample at 11 age levels between 6½ and 16½ years yielded clear evidence of three major factors at each age level (Kaufman, 1975a). These factors corresponded closely to the previously described factors of verbal comprehension, perceptual organization, and freedom from distractibility. The same factorial structure was found in a study of intellectually gifted children, especially with regard to the first two factors (Karnes & Brown, 1980). Comparative studies of the WISC-R performance of Mexican-American and Anglo-American children revealed the same three factors and similar factorial composition of the subtests in the two populations. Reliability and predictive validity of subtests and IQ scales were likewise found to be similar in the samples investigated from these two populations (Dean, 1977, 1979, 1980). Factorial analyses of the WISC-R performance of black and white children from the standardization sample again corroborated the similarity of factor structure in the two ethnic groups, and supported the comparability of construct validity and score interpretation across such groups (Gutkin & Reynolds, 1981).

WECHSLER PRESCHOOL AND PRIMARY SCALE OF INTELLIGENCE

DESCRIPTION. In more than one sense, the Wechsler Preschool and Primary Scale of Intelligence (WPPSI) is the baby of the series. Designed for ages 4 to 6½ years, it was the last of the Wechsler scales to be developed. WPPSI includes 11 subtests, only 10 of which are used in finding the IQ. Eight of the subtests are downward extensions and adaptations of WISC subtests; the other three were newly constructed to replace WISC subtests that proved unsuitable for a variety of reasons. As in the WISC and WAIS, the subtests are grouped into a Verbal and a Performance scale, from which Verbal, Performance, and Full Scale IQs are found. As in the latest versions of the other Wechsler scales, the administration of Verbal and Performance subtests is alternated. Total testing time ranges from 50 to 75 minutes, in one or two testing sessions.

In the following list, the new subtests have been starred:

VERBAL SCALE	PERFORMANCE SCALE
1. Information	2. *Animal House
3. Vocabulary	4. Picture Completion
5. Arithmetic	6. Mazes
7. Similarities	8. *Geometric Design
9. Comprehension	10. Block Design

*Sentences (Supplementary Test)

"Sentences" is a memory test, substituted for the WISC Digit Span. The child repeats each sentence immediately after oral presentation by the examiner. This test can be used as an alternate for one of the other verbal tests; or it can be administered as an additional test to provide further information about the child, in which case it is not included in the total score in calculating the IQ. "Animal House" is basically similar to the WAIS Digit Symbol and the WISC Coding test. A key at the top of the board has pictures of dog, chicken, fish, and cat, each with a differently colored cylinder (its "house") under it. The child is to insert the correctly colored cylinder in the hole beneath each animal on the board (see Fig. 33). Time, errors, and omissions determine the score. "Geometric Design" requires the copying of 10 simple designs with a colored pencil.

The possibility of using short forms seems to have aroused as much interest for WPPSI as it had for WAIS and WISC. Some of the same investigators have been concerned with the derivation of such abbreviated scales at all three levels, notably Silverstein (1968a, 1968b, 1970, 1971). In a particularly well-designed study, Kaufman (1972) constructed a short form consisting of two Verbal subtests (Arithmetic and Comprehension) and two Performance subtests (Block Design and Picture Completion). Within individual age levels, this battery yielded reliability coefficients ranging from .91 to .94 and correlations with Full Scale IQ ranging from .89 to .92. Half the WPPSI standardization sample of 1,200 cases was used in the selection of the tests; the other half was used to cross-validate the resulting battery. Kaufman reiterated the customary caution to use the short form only for screening purposes when time does not permit the administration of the entire scale.

NORMS. The WPPSI was standardized on a national sample of 1,200 children: 100 boys and 100 girls in each of six half-year age groups from 4 to 6½. Children were tested within six weeks of the required birthday or

FIG. 33. The Animal House Test of the Wechsler Preschool and Primary Scale of Intelligence.
(Courtesy of The Psychological Corporation.)

midyear date. The sample was stratified against 1960 census data with reference to geographical region, urban-rural residence, proportion of whites and nonwhites, and father's occupational level. Raw scores on each subtest are converted to normalized standard scores with a mean of 10 and an *SD* of 3 within each quarter-year group. The sums of the scaled scores on the Verbal, Performance, and Full Scale are then converted to deviation IQs with a mean of 100 and an *SD* of 15. Although Wechsler argues against the use of mental age scores because of their possible misinterpretations, the manual provides a table for converting raw scores on each subtest to "test ages" in quarter-year units.

RELIABILITY. For every subtest except Animal House, reliability was found by correlating odd and even scores and applying the Spearman-Brown formula. Since scores on Animal House depend to a considerable extent on speed, its reliability was found by a retest at the end of the testing session. Reliability coefficients were computed separately within each half-year age group in the standardization sample. While varying with subtest and age level, these reliabilities fell mostly in the .80s. Reliability of the Full Scale IQ varied between .92 and .94; for Verbal IQ, it varied between .87 and .90; and for Performance IQ, between .84 and .91. Standard errors of measurement are also provided in the manual, as well as tables for evaluating the significance of the difference between scores. From these data, it is suggested that a difference of 15 points or more between Verbal and Performance IQs is sufficiently important to be investigated.

Stability over time was checked in a group of 50 kindergarten children retested after an average interval of 11 weeks. Under these conditions, reliability of Full Scale IQ was .92; for Verbal IQ it was .86; and for Performance IQ, .89.

VALIDITY. As is true of the other two Wechsler scales, the WPPSI manual contains no section labeled "validity," although it does provide some data of tangential relevance to the validity of the instrument. Intercorrelations of the 11 subtests within each age level in the standardization sample fall largely between .40 and .60. Correlations between Verbal and Performance subtests are nearly as high as those within each scale. The overlap between the two scales is also indicated by an average correlation of .66 between Verbal and Performance IQs.

The manual reports a correlation of .75 with Stanford-Binet in a group of 98 children aged 5 to 6 years. As in the case of the WISC, the Stanford-Binet correlates higher with the Verbal IQ (.76) than with the Performance IQ (.56). This finding was corroborated in subsequent studies by other investigators working with a variety of groups. In the studies surveyed by Sattler (1982), median correlations of WPPSI with Stanford-Binet IQ were .82, .81, and .67 for Full Scale, Verbal, and Performance IQs, respectively. Correlations have also been found with a number of other general ability tests (for references, see Sattler, 1982). Data on predictive validity, however, are meager (Kaufman, 1973a).

A carefully designed reanalysis of the standardization sample of 1,200 cases (Kaufman, 1973b) provided information on the relation of WPPSI scores to socioeconomic status (as indicated by father's occupational level), urban versus rural residence, and geographic region. For each of these three variables, WPPSI Verbal, Performance, and Full Scale IQs were compared between samples matched on all the other stratification variables (including the other two variables under investigation plus sex, age, and color).

Socioeconomic status yielded significant differences only at the extremes of the distribution. Children with fathers in the professional and technical categories averaged significantly higher than all other groups (Mean IQ = 110); and children whose fathers were in the unskilled category averaged significantly lower than all other groups (Mean IQ = 92.1). Geographic region showed no clear relation to scores. No significant difference was found between matched urban and rural samples, unlike earlier studies with the WISC (Seashore, Wesman, & Doppelt, 1950) and the Stanford-Binet (McNemar, 1942). Kaufman attributed the discrepancy principally to the contribution of other variables, which were controlled in this study but not in the earlier studies. Another major difference, however, is in the time when the data were gathered. The intervening 25 or 30 years have witnessed marked changes both in population movements between urban and rural environments and in the educational and cultural facilities available in those environments. It is reasonable to expect that such sociocultural changes could have cancelled out the earlier differences in intelligence test performance characterizing children in these two types of environment.

Since the publication of the WPPSI, several investigators have factor-analyzed the subtest scores on samples of diverse populations (see Sattler, 1982). A comprehensive study (Hollenbeck & Kaufman, 1973) applied several factor-analytic techniques to three separate age groups in the WPPSI standardization sample. The results provided consistent evidence of a general factor in the battery as a whole, together with two broad group factors: a verbal factor with substantial loadings in the six verbal subtests in each age group; and a performance factor with substantial loadings in the five performance tests in the two older groups and somewhat lower but still appreciable loadings in the youngest group (ages 4 to 4½ years). The separation of the two group factors was generally less clear-cut in the youngest group, a finding that is in line with much of the earlier research on the organization of abilities in young children. When subtest scores were factor analyzed separately for black and white children in the standardization sample, the results in both groups were closely similar to those obtained in the total sample (Kaufman & Hollenbeck, 1974).

CONCLUDING REMARKS ON THE WECHSLER SCALES. The successive editions of the three Wechsler scales reflect an increasing level of sophistication and experience in test construction, corresponding to the decades when they were developed. In comparison with other individually administered tests, their principal strengths stem from the size and representativeness of the standardization samples, particularly for adult and preschool populations, and the technical quality of their test construction procedures. The treatment of reliability and errors of measurement is especially commendable. The weakest feature of all three scales is the dearth of empirical data on validity. The factor-analytic studies contribute to a clarification of the constructs in terms of which performance on the Wechsler scales may be described; but these studies would have been more informative if they had included more indices of behavior external to the scales themselvs.

ASSESSMENT OF COMPETENCE

INTELLIGENCE TESTS IN THE CONTEXT OF INDIVIDUAL ASSESSMENT. Tests such as the Stanford-Binet and the Wechsler scales are fundamentally individual, clinical instruments. The clinical approach to testing implies an intensive study of the individual, in which the test (or tests) administered represents only one of several sources of data. It also implies an examiner who is knowledgeable in psychology and who can draw upon insights from available research and theory (Kaufman, 1979).

The use of intelligence tests within such a clinical framework will be examined further in Chapter 16, concerned specifically with clinical testing. It is nevertheless well to recognize that these instruments, while individually administered by specially trained examiners, are sometimes interpreted in a hasty and routine manner. Taking IQs at face value in classifying children, for example, may lead to incorrect conclusions in the absence of the needed supplementary observations and background data. This superficial use of tests, often resulting from time pressure and heavy case loads, is likely to be especially misleading when the examinees differ substantially in experiential background. In recognition of these possible hazards in large-scale uses of intelligence test scores, certain safeguards have been developed. These safeguards may be regarded as attempts to systematize and facilitate for large-scale usage the procedures followed by the well-trained clinical psychologist in the intensive case study of an individual.

This approach to testing has sometimes been designated as the assessment of competence (Sundberg, Snowden, & Reynolds, 1978). It focuses on the knowledge, skills, and attitudes the individual can utilize to function effectively in specified environments and situations. The variety of data sources required for proper assessment and recommendations in individual cases was illustrated earlier in this chapter with reference to the examining of mentally retarded children. Any important life decision, at all intellectual levels, demands a similar breadth of information. This approach has also been described quite simply as "intelligent testing," or the intelligent use of intelligence tests (Kaufman, 1979; Wesman, 1968). And it has been advocated as a reunification of testing and psychology (Anastasi, 1967).

SYSTEM OF MULTICULTURAL PLURALISTIC ASSESSMENT. A specific effort to bridge the gap between mass testing and individual assessment, with particular reference to the testing of cultural minorities, is illustrated by the work of Mercer (1973, 1978, 1979). Mercer's long-term research project led to the development of the System of Multicultural Pluralistic Assessment: SOMPA (Lewis & Mercer, 1978; Mercer & Lewis, 1978). Mercer was particularly concerned about the misclassification of children from culturally and linguistically diverse backgrounds as mentally retarded simply on the basis of intelligence test scores. This is certainly a misuse of tests. A test score can tell us only *what* an individual is able to do at the time. No test can tell us *why* the individual performs as he or she does.

SOMPA is a comprehensive assessment program, suitable for ages 5 to 11, which includes the WISC (or WPPSI for younger children), together with other standardized measures and supplementary data about the child's physical condition and social competence within his or her own environment. Another major feature of SOMPA is the provision of empirically established subgroup norms, thus far available for black, Hispanic, and Anglo (white) samples. The child's intelligence test performance can thus be evaluated within his or her own ethnic group, as well as in terms of the "school culture" to which the child needs to adapt in order to enjoy the benefits of the core culture. The general norms from the WISC standardization sample are employed as representative of the school or core culture. The test scores are further analyzed with reference to the child's assessed position on four sociocultural scales, including family size, family structure, socioeconomic status, and urban acculturation.

The data-gathering procedures utilized in SOMPA include a one-hour parent interview and an individual examination of the child, conducted over two or more testing sessions. SOMPA combines data from three separate assessment models, designated as medical, social system, and pluralistic models. The *medical model* is concerned with perceptual-motor development and health conditions that may be related to learning difficulties. A health history is included in the parent interview. During the individual examination of the child, data are obtained on weight by height, visual and auditory acuity, and physical dexterity. Also included is the Bender Visual Motor Gestalt Test, a clinical instrument widely used to assess perceptual-motor development and to detect possible neurological impairment (discussed in Ch. 16).

The *social system model* evaluates the child's adaptive behavior in family, school, and community roles. The WISC (or WPPSI) is used to assess the child's adaptive behavior in the school or student role. Adaptive performance in family and community roles is measured by a specially developed Adaptive Behavior Inventory for Children (ABIC), which is also administered during the parent interview. This instrument is similar to the adaptive behavior and social maturity scales mentioned earlier in this chapter and described in Chapter 10.

The *pluralistic model* measures important aspects of the child's sociocultural background, also derived from information obtained during the parent interview. These measures are used in arriving at an estimate of the child's "learning potential." The Estimated Learning Potential (ELP), expressed as a standard score, is based on a comparison of the child's obtained WISC-R score and the WISC-R score predicted through regression equations for children having the same sociocultural and ethnic background. Two special cautions in the interpretations of ELPs are mentioned in the Student Assessment Manual (Mercer & Lewis, 1978, p. 54). First, ELPs do *not* predict how well a child will succeed in mainstream public school instructional programs. What they *are* designed to predict is "the extent to which a child is likely to benefit from an educational program that takes appropriate account of his or her sociocultural background." Second, the published ELP tables are based on the California population sampled in the standardization of SOMPA. Although there is some evidence suggesting that these values are fairly stable across geographical regions, it is recommended that users develop local norms, with the corresponding regression equations, and a procedure for so doing is clearly described in the Technical Manual (Mercer, 1979, pp. 144–145).

In summary, SOMPA provides a prefabricated assessment program of the sort required in a thorough, personalized clinical case study. It is less flexible than the latter, but it certainly offers a powerful corrective for the routine, superficial misuse of test scores in isolation. In addition, it provides empirical norms on the performance of children classified with reference to a number of significant experiential variables.

CHAPTER 10

Tests for Special Populations

THE TESTS brought together in this chapter include both individual and group scales. They were developed primarily for use with persons who cannot be properly or adequately examined with traditional instruments, such as the individual scales described in the preceding chapter or the typical group tests to be considered in the next chapter. Historically, the kinds of tests surveyed in this chapter were designated as performance, nonlanguage, or nonverbal tests.

Performance tests, on the whole, involve the manipulation of objects, with a minimal use of paper and pencil. *Nonlanguage tests* require no language on the part of either examiner or examinee. The instructions for these tests can be given by demonstration, gesture, and pantomime, without the use of oral or written language. A prototype of nonlanguage group tests was the Army Examination Beta, developed for testing foreign-speaking and illiterate recruits during World War I (Yerkes, 1921). Revisions of this test were subsequently prepared for civilian use. For most testing purposes, it is not necessary to eliminate all language from test administration, since the examinees usually have some knowledge of a common language. Moreover, short, simple instructions can usually be translated or given successively in two languages without appreciably altering the nature or difficulty of the test. None of these tests, however, requires examinees themselves to use either written or spoken language.

Still another related category is that of *nonverbal tests,* more properly designated as nonreading tests. Most tests for primary school and preschool children fall into this category, as do tests for illiterates and nonreaders at any age level. While requiring no reading or writing, these tests make extensive use of oral instructions and communication on the part of the examiner. Moreover, they frequently measure verbal comprehension, such as vocabulary and the understanding of sentences and short paragraphs, through the use of pictorial material supplemented with oral instructions to accompany each item. Unlike the nonlanguage tests, they would thus be unsuited for foreign-speaking or deaf persons.

Although the traditional categories of performance, nonlanguage, and nonverbal tests contribute to an understanding of the purposes that different tests may serve, the distinctions have become somewhat blurred as more and more test batteries were developed that cut across these categories. The combination of verbal and performance tests in the Wechsler scales is a classical example.

In the present chapter, tests have been classified, not in terms of their content or administrative procedures, but with reference to their principal uses. Four major categories can be recognized from this viewpoint: tests for the infant and preschool level; tests employed for a comprehensive assessment of mental retardates; tests for persons with diverse sensory and motor handicaps; and tests designed for use across cultures or subcultures. Such a classification must remain flexible, however, since several of the tests have proved useful in more than one context. This is especially true of some of the instruments originally designed for cross-cultural testing, which are now more commonly used in clinical examinations.

Finally, although some of the tests covered in this chapter were designed as group tests, they are frequently administered individually. A few are widely used in clinical testing to supplement the usual type of intelligence test and thus provide a fuller picture of the individual's intellectual functioning. Several permit the kind of qualitative observations associated with individual testing and may require considerable clinical sophistication for a detailed interpretation of test performance. On the whole, they are closer to the individual tests illustrated in Chapter 9 than to the group tests to be surveyed in Chapter 11.

INFANT AND PRESCHOOL TESTING

All tests designed for infants and preschool children require individual administration. Some kindergarten children can be tested in small groups with the types of tests constructed for the primary grades. In general, however, group tests are not applicable until the child has reached school age. Most tests for children below the age of 6 are either performance or oral tests. A few involve rudimentary manipulation of paper and pencil.

It is customary to subdivide the first five years of life into the infant period and the preschool period. The first extends from birth to the age of approximately 18 months; the second, from 18 to 60 months. From the viewpoint of test administration, it should be noted that the infant must be tested while either lying down or supported on a person's lap. Speech is of little use in giving test instructions, although the child's own language development provides relevant data. Many of the tests deal with sensorimotor development, as illustrated by the infant's ability to lift his or her head, turn over, reach for and grasp objects, and follow a moving object with the eyes. The preschool child, on the other hand, can walk, sit at a table, use her or his hands in manipulating test objects, and communicate by language.

At the preschool level, the child is also much more responsive to the examiner as a person, whereas for the infant the examiner serves primarily as a means of providing stimulus objects. Preschool testing is a more highly interpersonal process—a feature that augments both the opportunities and the difficulties presented by the test situation.

The proper psychological examination of young children requires coverage of a broad spectrum of behavior, including motor and social as well as cognitive traits. This orientation is reflected in some of the instruments discussed in this chapter. It has also been reaffirmed in recent analyses of the field by specialists in early childhood education (Anderson & Messick, 1974). Typical scales, designed for infancy and early childhood and representing a diversity of approaches, are considered in this section. The Wechsler Preschool and Primary Scale of Intelligence also belongs in this category but was covered in Chapter 9 in order to maintain the continuity of the Wechsler series.

GESELL DEVELOPMENTAL SCHEDULES. Following a series of longitudinal studies of the normal course of behavior development in the infant and preschool child, Gesell and his associates at Yale prepared the Gesell Developmental Schedules. When first published (Gesell et al., 1940), these schedules represented a pioneer attempt to provide a systematic, empirically based method of assessing the behavior development of young children. Over the years, they have been used widely by psychologists and pediatricians, in both research and practice. In their latest version,[1] these schedules cover five major fields of behavior: adaptive, gross motor, fine motor, language, and personal-social behavior. They provide a standardized procedure for observing and evaluating the course of behavior development in the child's daily life. Although a few may be properly described as tests, most of the items in these schedules are purely observational. Data are obtained through the direct observation of the child's responses to standard toys and other stimulus objects and are supplemented by information provided by the mother. In evaluating the child's responses, the examiner is aided by very detailed verbal descriptions of the behavior typical of different age levels, together with drawings such as those reproduced in Figure 34. While extending from the age of 4 weeks to 5 years, the Gesell schedules typify the approach followed in infant testing. Items from these schedules have been incorporated in several other developmental scales designed for the infant level.

Although both observational and scoring procedures are less highly

---

[1] Detailed instructions for data gathering and interpretation are given in Knobloch and Pasamanick (1974). Another updated treatment of the entire series of developmental schedules can be found in Gesell, Ilg, and Ames (1974). New behavioral norms for ages 2½ to 6, by half-year intervals, are provided by Ames, Gillespie, Haines, and Ilg (1979).

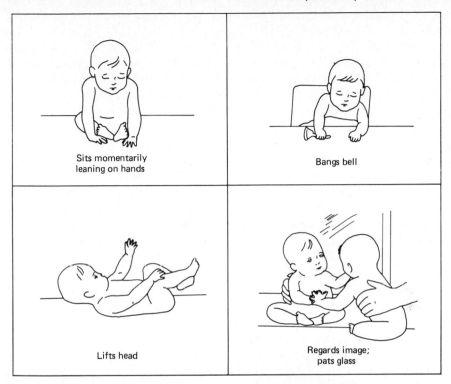

Sits momentarily
leaning on hands

Bangs bell

Lifts head

Regards image;
pats glass

FIG. 34. Drawings Employed with the Gesell Developmental Schedules to Illustrate Typical Behavior at 28 Weeks of Age.

(From Knobloch & Pasamanick, 1974. Copyright © 1974 by Harper & Row. Reproduced by permission.)

standardized in the Gesell schedules than in the usual psychological test, there is evidence that, with adequate training, examiner reliabilities over .95 can be attained (Knobloch & Pasamanick, 1974, pp. 141–142). In general, these schedules may be regarded as a refinement and elaboration of the qualitative observations routinely made by pediatricians and other specialists concerned with infant development. They appear to be most useful as a supplement to medical examinations for the identification of neurological defect and organically caused behavioral abnormalities in early life (Knobloch & Pasamanick, 1974).

BAYLEY SCALES OF INFANT DEVELOPMENT. The decades of the 1960s and the 1970s witnessed an upsurge of interest in tests for infants and preschool children. One contributing factor was the rapid expansion of educational programs for mentally retarded children. Another was the widespread development of preschool programs of compensatory education for culturally disadvantaged children. To meet these pressing practical needs, new tests have appeared and considerable research has been conducted on innovative approaches to assessment.

An especially well-constructed test for the earliest age levels is the Bayley Scales of Infant Development, illustrated in Figure 35. Incorporating some items from the Gesell schedules and other infant and preschool tests, these scales represent the end product of many years of research by Bayley and her co-workers, including the longitudinal investigations of the Berkeley Growth Study.

The Bayley scales provide three complementary tools for assessing the developmental status of children between the ages of 2 months and 2½ years: the Mental Scale, the Motor Scale, and the Infant Behavior Record. The Mental Scale samples such functions as perception, memory, learning, problem solving, vocalization, the beginnings of verbal communication, and rudimentary abstract thinking. The Motor Scale provides measures of gross motor abilities, such as sitting, standing, walking, and stair climbing, as well as manipulatory skills of hands and fingers. At the infant level, locomotor and manipulatory development plays an important part in the child's inter-actions with the environment and hence in the development of his or her mental processes. The Infant Behavior Record is a rating scale completed

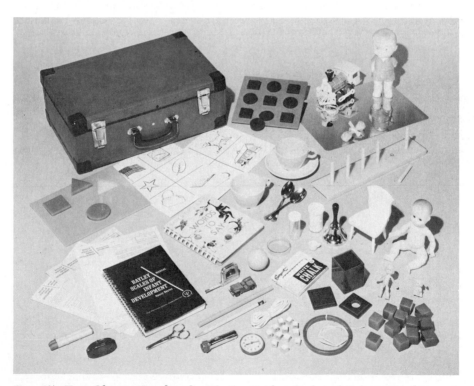

FIG. 35. Test Objects Employed with the Bayley Scales of Infant Development. (Courtesy of The Psychological Corporation.)

by the examiner after the other two parts have been administered. It is designed to assess various aspects of personality development, such as emotional and social behavior, attention span, persistence, and goal directedness.

In the technical quality of their test-construction procedures, the Bayley scales are clearly outstanding among tests for the infant level. Norms were established on 1,262 children, about equally distributed between the ages of 2 and 30 months. The standardization sample was chosen so as to be representative of the U.S. population in terms of urban-rural residence, major geographic region, sex ratio, race (white-nonwhite), and education of head of household. Institutionalized children, premature babies, and children over the age of 12 months from bilingual homes were excluded. Mental and Motor scales yield separate developmental indexes, expressed as normalized standard scores with a mean of 100 and an *SD* of 16 (as in Stanford-Binet deviation IQs). These developmental indexes are found within the child's own age group, classified by half-month steps from 2 to 6 months and by one-month steps from 6 to 30 months.

Split-half reliability coefficients within separate age groups ranged from .81 to .93, with a median value of .88, for the Mental Scale; and from .68 to .92, with a median of .84, for the Motor Scale. These coefficients compare favorably with the reliabilities usually found in testing infants. The manual reports standard errors of measurement and minimum differences between indexes on the Mental and Motor scales required for statistical significance. Data on tester–observer agreement and on retest reliability after a one-week interval are also encouraging.

Bayley observed that these scales, like all infant tests, should be used principally to assess current developmental status rather than to predict subsequent ability levels. Development of abilities at these early ages is susceptible to so many intervening influences as to render long-term predictions of little value. The scales can be most helpful in the early detection of sensory and neurological defects, emotional disturbances, and environmental deficits.[2]

MCCARTHY SCALES OF CHILDREN'S ABILITIES. At the preschool level, a well-constructed instrument is the McCarthy Scales of Children's Abilities (MSCA), suitable for children between the ages of 2½ and 8½ years. It consists of 18 tests, grouped into six overlapping scales: Verbal, Perceptual-Performance, Quantitative, General Cognitive, Memory, and Motor. Figure 36 illustrates the Conceptual Grouping Test from the Perceptual-Performance Scale. In this test, the child is shown red, yellow, and blue circles and squares in two sizes and asked to find the pieces with stated characteristics. The General Cognitive score comes closest to the traditional global measure

[2] For a history of infant intelligence tests and a discussion of their uses and limitations, see Lewis (1976a), especially Chapters 1 and 2.

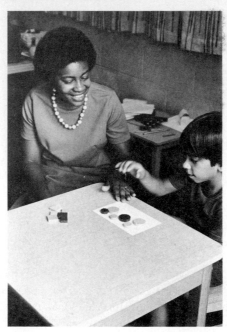

Fig. 36. Examiner Administering the Conceptual Grouping Test of the McCarthy Scales of Children's Abilities.

(Courtesy of The Psychological Corporation.)

of intellectual development. It is found from the sum of the scores on the first three scales, which do not overlap each other but which do contain all the Memory tests and all but three of the Motor tests. The General Cognitive score is thus based on 15 of the 18 tests in the entire battery.

Scores on the General Cognitive Scale are expressed as a General Cognitive Index (GCI), which is a normalized standard score with a mean of 100 and an *SD* of 16, found within each 3-month age group. The manual makes it clear that, although the GCI is reported in the same units as traditional IQs, the term IQ was deliberately avoided because of its many misleading connotations. The GCI is described as an index of the child's functioning at the time of testing, with no implications of immutability or etiology. Scores on the separate scales are normalized standard scores with a mean of 50 and an *SD* of 10 in terms of the same age groups.

The standardization sample of 1,032 cases included approximately 100 children at each of 10 age levels, by half-year steps between 2½ and 5½ and by one-year steps between 5½ and 8½. At each age level, the sample contained an equal number of boys and girls and was stratified by race (white–nonwhite), geographic region, father's occupational level, and (approximately) urban-rural residence, in accordance with the 1970 U.S. Census. Institutionalized mental retardates and children with severe behavioral or emotional disorders, brain damage, or obvious physical defects were excluded; bilinguals were tested only if they could speak and understand English.

Split-half reliability for the General Cognitive Index averaged .93 within age levels; average coefficients for the other five scales ranged from .79 to .88. The manual also reports standard errors of measurement and minimum differences between scale scores required for significance at the .05 level. Retest reliabilities over a one-month interval for 125 children classified into three age groups averaged .90 for GCI and ranged from .69 to .89 for the separate scales.

With regard to validity, the manual cites suggestive but meager data on predictive validity against an educational achievement battery administered at the end of the first grade. The initial selection of tests and their grouping into scales was based on a combination of clinical experience, findings of developmental psychology, and the results of factor-analytic research. In the course of developing the scales, a somewhat longer series of tests was factor-analyzed separately within three age levels on about 60% of the standardization sample (Kaufman & Hollenbeck, 1973). General cognitive, memory, and motor factors were identified at all ages; other factors showed developmental trends, suggesting that different abilities might be utilized in performing the same tasks at different ages. For example, drawing tests had a large motor component at the younger ages but were predominantly conceptual at the older ages. The results of the preliminary factor analyses were susbtantially corroborated in subsequent factor analyses of the final version of the battery on the entire standardization sample (Kaufman, 1975b).

Other studies have investigated differences in MSCA performance in relation to sex, race (black-white), and socioeconomic status (father's occupational level). No significant sex differences were found in either GCI or any of the separate scale indexes (Kaufman & Kaufman, 1973b). Ethnic comparisons (Kaufman & Kaufman, 1973a) revealed few significant differences: in favor of blacks on the Motor Scale in the youngest age group (4–5½), and in favor of whites on the other scales in the oldest age group (6½–8½). Moreover, investigations of paternal occupational level within both ethnic groups suggest that socioeconomic status may be more important than race as a concomitant of performance on the McCarthy scales (Kaufman & Kaufman, 1975).

PIAGETIAN SCALES. Although applicable well beyond the preschool level, the scales modeled on the developmental theories of Jean Piaget have thus far found their major applications in early childhood. All such scales are in an experimental form; few are commercially available. Most have been developed for use in the authors' own research programs, although some of these scales are available to other research workers. At this stage, the major contribution of Piagetian scales to the psychological testing of children consists in their providing a theoretical framework that focuses on developmental sequences and a procedural approach characterized by flexibility and qualitative interpretation.

Some of the features of Piagetian scales, with special reference to normative interpretation of performance, were discussed in Chapter 4. Basically, Piagetian scales are ordinal in the sense that they presuppose a uniform sequence of development through successive stages. These stages, spanning the period from infancy to adolescence and beyond, are designated as the sensorimotor, the preoperational, the concrete operational, and the formal operational stages. The scales are also content-referenced, insofar as they provide qualitative descriptions of what the child is actually able to do. Piagetian tasks focus on the long-term development of specific concepts or cognitive schemata,[3] rather than on broad traits. With regard to administration, the major object of Piagetian scales is to elicit the child's explanation for an observed event and the reasons that underlie her or his explanation. Scoring is characteristically based on the quality of the responses to a relatively small number of problem situations presented to the child, rather than on the number or difficulty of successfully completed items. For this purpose, the child's misconceptions revealed by the incorrect responses are of primary interest. The examiner concentrates more on the process of problem solving than on the product.

Because of its highly individualized procedures, Piagetian testing is well suited for clinical work. It has also attracted the attention of educators because it permits the integration of testing and teaching.[4] Its most frequent use, however, is still in research on developmental psychology. The three sets of tests described below have been selected in part because of their present or anticipated availability for use outside of the authors' own research, and in part because of their detailed description in published sources.

At the University of Montreal, Laurendeau and Pinard have been engaged in an unusually comprehensive, long-term research project designed to replicate Piaget's work under standardized conditions, with large representative samples, and in a different cultural milieu (Laurendeau & Pinard, 1962, 1970; Pinard & Laurendeau, 1964). A byproduct of this research is the construction of scales of mental development that may eventually be available to other investigators. At this time, however, the authors feel it would be premature to release their scale of mental development until they have completed much more research with their tests.

In the course of their investigations, Laurendeau and Pinard administered a battery of 57 tests to 700 children ranging in age from 2 to 12 years. The

---

[3] "Schemata" is the plural of "schema," a term commonly encountered in Piagetian writings and signifying essentially a framework into which the individual fits incoming sensory data.

[4] An example of such an application is "Let's Look at Children," to be discussed in Chapter 14.

tests for children under 4 were newly constructed or adapted from conventional scales, although all were chosen to assess characteristics that Piaget attributed to this developmental period. Twenty-five of the tests, designed chiefly for ages 4 and up, were modeled directly after Piagetian tasks. Thus far, the results obtained with 10 of these tests have been reported in detail in two books (Laurendeau & Pinard, 1962, 1970). Five tests deal with *causality*, including the child's explanations of the nature and causes of dreams, the differences between animate and inanimate objects, what makes it dark at night, what causes the movements of clouds, and why some objects float and others sink. These tests are administered almost entirely through oral questionnaires, which fall about midway between Piaget's unstructured *"méthode clinique"* and the completely controlled techniques of traditional tests. All questions are standardized; but depending upon the child's initial responses, the examiner follows alternative routes in the further exploration of the child's thinking processes.

The other five tests are concerned with the child's concepts of *space*. They include such tasks as recognizing objects by touch and identifying them among visually presented drawings of the same objects; arranging a set of toy lampposts in a straight line between two toy houses; placing a toy man in the same spots in the child's landscape that he occupies in the examiner's identical landscape; designating right and left on the child's own body, on the examiner in different positions, and in the relation of objects on the table; and problems of perspective, in which the child indicates how three toy mountains look to a man standing in different places. Several of these spatial tests deal with the "egocentrism" of the young child's thinking, which makes it difficult for him to regard objects from viewpoints other than his own.

The complete protocol of the child's responses to each test is scored as a unit, in terms of the developmental level indicated by the quality of the responses. Laurendeau and Pinard have subjected their tests to extensive statistical analyses. Their standardization sample of 700 cases included 25 boys and 25 girls at each six-month interval from 2 to 5 years, and at each one-year interval from 5 to 12. The children were selected so as to constitute a representative sample of the French Canadian population of Montreal with regard to father's occupational level and school grade (or number of children in the family, at the preschool ages). Besides providing normative age data, the authors analyzed their results for ordinality, or uniformity of sequence in the attainment of response levels by different children. They also investigated the degree of similarity in the developmental stages reached by each child in the different tests. Intercorrelations of scores on the five causality tests ranged from .59 to .78; on the five space tests, the correlations ranged from .37 to .67 (Laurendeau & Pinard, 1962, p. 236; 1970, p. 412).

The Ordinal Scales of Psychological Development prepared by Užgiris and Hunt (1975) are designed for a much younger age level than are those of Laurendeau and Pinard, extending from the age of 2 weeks to 2 years. These ages cover approximately what Piaget characterizes as the sensorimotor period and within which he recognizes six levels. In order to increase the sensitivity of their instruments, Užgiris and Hunt classified the responses into more than six levels, the number varying from 7 to 14 in the different scales. The series includes six scales, designated as follows:

1. *Object Permanence*—the child's emerging notion of independently existing objects is indicated by visual following of an object and searching for an object after it is hidden with increasing degrees of concealment.

2. *Development of Means* for achieving desired environmental ends—use of own hands in reaching for objects and of other means such as strings, stick, support, etc.

3. *Imitation*—including both gestural and vocal imitation.

4. *Operational Causality*—recognizing and adapting to objective causality, ranging from visual observation of one's own hands to eliciting desired behavior from a human agent and activating a mechanical toy.

5. *Object Relations in Space*—coordination of schemata of looking and listening in localizing objects in space; understanding such relations as container, equilibrium, gravity.

6. *Development of Schemata* for relating to objects—responding to objects by looking, feeling, manipulating, dropping, throwing, etc., and by socially instigated schemata appropriate to particular objects (e.g., "driving" toy car, building with blocks, wearing beads, naming objects).

No norms are provided, but the authors collected data on several psychometric properties of their scales by administering them to 84 infants, including at least four at each month of age up to one year and at least four at each two months of age between one and two years. Most of the infants were children of graduate students and staff at the University of Illinois. Both observer agreement and test-retest agreement after a 48-hour interval are reported. In general, the tests appear quite satisfactory in both respects. An index of ordinality, computed for each scale from the scores of the same 84 children, ranged from .802 to .991. The authors report that .50 is considered minimally satisfactory evidence of ordinality with the index employed.[5]

Užgiris and Hunt clearly explain that these are only provisional scales, although they are available to other investigators for research purposes. Apart from journal articles reporting specific studies in which the scales were employed, the authors describe the tests in a book (Užgiris & Hunt, 1975) and also provide six sound films demonstrating their use. The scales were originally designed to measure the effects of specific environmental conditions on the rate and course of development of infants. Studies of

---

[5] Procedures for the measurement of ordinality and the application of scalogram analysis to Piagetian scales are still controversial, a fact that should be borne in mind in interpreting any reported indices of ordinality (see Hooper, 1973; Wohlwill, 1970).

infants reared under different conditions (Paraskevopoulos & Hunt, 1971) and on infants participating in intervention programs (Hunt, Paraskevopoulos, Schickedanz, & Užgiris, 1975) have thus far indicated significant effects of these environmental variables on the mean age at which children attain different steps in the developmental scales (Hunt, 1976).

Unlike the first two examples of Piagetian scales, the Concept Assessment Kit—Conservation is a published test which may be purchased on the same basis as other psychological tests. Designed for ages 4 to 7 years, it provides a measure of one of the best-known Piagetian concepts. Conservation refers to the child's realization that such properties of objects as weight, volume, or number remain unchanged when the objects undergo transformations in shape, position, form, or other attributes. The authors (Goldschmid & Bentler, 1968b) focused on conservation as an indicator of the child's transition from the preoperational to the concrete operational stage of thinking, which Piaget places roughly at the age of 7 or 8 years.

Throughout the test, the procedure is essentially the same. The child is shown two identical objects; then the examiner makes certain transformations in one of them and interrogates the child about their similarity or difference. After answering, the child is asked to explain his or her answer. In each item, one point is scored for the correct judgment of equivalence and one point for an acceptable explanation. For example, the examiner begins with two standard glasses containing equal amounts of water (continuous quantity) or grains of corn (discontinuous quantity) and pours the contents into a flat dish or into several small glasses. In another task, the examiner shows the child two equal balls of Playdoh and then flattens one into a pancake and asks whether the ball is as heavy as the pancake.

Three forms of the test are available. Forms A and B are parallel, each providing six tasks: Two-Dimensional Space, Number, Substance, Continuous Quantity, Weight, and Discontinuous Quantity. The two forms were shown to be closely equivalent in means and SDs and their scores correlated .95. Form C includes two different tasks, Area and Length; it correlates .76 and .74 with Forms A and B, respectively. Administration is facilitated by printing all essential directions on the record form, including diagrams of the materials, directions for manipulating materials, and verbal instructions.

Norms were established on a standardization sample of 560 boys and girls between the ages of 4 and 8, obtained from schools, daycare centers, and Head Start centers in the Los Angeles, California area. The sample included both blacks and whites and covered a wide range of socioeconomic level, but with a slight overrepresentation of the lower-middle class. Percentile norms are reported for each age level. These norms, of course, must be regarded as tentative in view of the small number of cases at each age and the limitations in representativeness of the sample. Mean scores for each age show a systematic rise with age, with a sharp rise between 6 and 8 years, as anticipated from Piagetian theory.

Both in the process of test construction and in the evaluation of the final forms, the authors carried out various statistical analyses to assess: scorer reliability; Kuder-Richardson, parallel-form, and retest reliability; scalability, or ordinality; and factorial composition (see also Goldschmid & Bentler, 1968a). Although based on rather small samples, the results indicate generally satisfactory reliability and give good evidence of ordinality and of the presence of a large common factor of conservation throughout the tasks.

Comparative studies in seven countries suggest that the test is applicable in widely diverse cultures, yielding high reliabilities and showing approximately similar age trends (Goldschmid et al., 1973). Differences among cultures and subcultures, however, have been found in the mean ages at which concepts are acquired, i.e., the age curves may be displaced horizontally by one or two years (see also Figurelli & Keller, 1972; Wasik & Wasik, 1971). Training in conservation tasks has been found to improve scores significantly (see also Goldschmid, 1968; Zimmerman & Rosenthal, 1974a, 1974b). The manual cites several studies on small groups that contribute suggestive data about the construct validity of the test. Some evidence of predictive validity is provided by significant correlations in the .30s and .40s with first-grade achievement, the correlation being highest with arithmetic grades (.52).

A major obstacle encountered in all these ordinal scales is what Piagetian researchers call *"décalage,"* or inconsistencies in the anticipated sequences. There is a growing body of data that casts doubt on the implied continuities and regularities of intellectual development. Too often the stage corresponding to a given individual's performance varies with the task, not only when different processes are required for its solution, but also when the same process is applied to different contents (Dasen, 1977; Goodnow, 1976; Horn, 1976; J. McV. Hunt, 1976; Tuddenham, 1971; Ward, 1972). It might also be noted that Piagetian scales have been found to correlate substantially with standardized intelligence tests (Gottfried & Brody, 1975; Kaufman, 1971), and to correlate about as high with school achievement of first-grade children as did a group intelligence test (Kaufman & Kaufman, 1972). What these findings suggest is that, despite pronounced differences in methodology, Piagetian scales, standardized intelligence tests, and school achievement have much in common in the overall assessment of children that they provide. The Piagetian scales are more difficult to administer and much more time-consuming, but they yield a much richer picture of what the child can do and how he or she does it.

COMPREHENSIVE ASSESSMENT OF THE MENTALLY RETARDED

The testing of children with either mental or physical handicaps has undergone a conspicuous spurt of growth in the United States following the enactment in 1977 of the Education for All Handicapped Children Act

(P.L. 94-142).[6] The implementation of this law requires four basic procedures: (1) all handicapped children must be identified through preliminary screening instruments; (2) the children thus identified are to be evaluated by a team of specialists to determine each child's educational needs; (3) the school must develop an individualized educational program to meet these needs; and (4) each child is to be reevaluated periodically in the course of the program. Tests suitable for use in educational programs that meet the requirements of P.L. 94-142 are discussed in several portions of this book, including Chapters 9 and 16, as well as in this and the following section of the present chapter.

In Chapter 9, reference was made to the need for a comprehensive assessment of individual competence, especially in the planning of appropriate educational and therapeutic programs for mentally retarded children. The System of Multicultural Pluralistic Assessment (SOMPA) was described as an illustration of this approach. SOMPA combines the WISC-R with several other sources of information about the characteristics of the child and of his or her home environment. Assessment programs for the mentally retarded typically include an examination of motor development (also incorporated in infant scales) and some measure of adaptive behavior in everyday-life situations. The prototypes of scales designed to assess these two areas of behavior development are the Oseretsky Tests of Motor Proficiency and the Vineland Social Maturity Scale.

The Oseretsky Tests of Motor Proficiency were originally published in Russia in 1923. They were subsequently translated into several languages and used in a number of European countries. In 1946, Doll (1946), then Director of Research for the Vineland Training School, sponsored and edited an English translation of these tests. A scale of motor development is especially useful in testing the mentally retarded, who are also frequently retarded in motor functions. Other applications of the Oseretsky tests are found in the testing of children with motor handicaps, minimal brain dysfunction, or learning disabilities, particularly in connection with the administration of individualized training programs. The original Oseretsky tests extended from 4 to 16 years, the tests being grouped into year levels as in the Stanford-Binet. The Oseretsky scale was designed to cover all major types of motor behavior, from postural reactions and gross bodily movements to finger coordination and control of facial muscles.

Further revisions of the Oseretsky scales have been developed, the most recent being the Bruininks-Oseretsky Test of Motor Proficiency, published in 1978. Requiring from 45 to 60 minutes, the complete battery comprises 46 items grouped into eight substests. It yields three scores: a Gross Motor Composite measuring performance of the large muscles of shoulders, trunk, and legs; a Fine Motor Composite measuring performance of the small

---

[6] *Federal Register*, Vol. 42, No. 163, August 23, 1977. Some educational implications of this law are discussed by R. E. Paul in Lidz (1981, Ch. 8).

muscles of the fingers, hands, and forearm; and a total Battery Composite. There is also a 14-item Short Form, requiring 15 to 20 minutes and providing a single index of general motor proficiency. Performance can be expressed in terms of age-based standard scores, percentile ranks, and stanines. Age-equivalents are also available for each subtest. The battery was standardized on a sample of 765 children between the ages of 4½ and 14½, chosen so as to be nationally representative in age, sex, race, community size, and geographic region. Test-retest reliability of the composite scores, over intervals of 7 to 12 days, cluster in the .80s. Validity was investigated in several ways, including factor analysis of items, age differentiation, and a comparison of normal children with retarded and with learning disabled children.

The Vineland Social Maturity Scale[7] (Doll, 1953, 1965) is a developmental schedule concerned with the individual's ability to look after his or her practical needs and to take responsibility. Although covering a range from birth to over 25 years, this scale has been found most useful at the younger age levels, and particularly with the mentally retarded. The entire scale consists of 117 items grouped into year levels. The information required for each item is obtained, not through test situations, but through an interview with an informant or with the examinee himself. The scale is based on what the individual has actually done in his daily living. The items fall into eight categories: general self-help, self-help in eating, self-help in dressing, self-direction, occupation, communication, locomotion, and socialization. A social age (SA) and a social quotient (SQ) can be computed from the person's record on the entire scale.

The Vineland scale was standardized on 620 cases, including 10 males and 10 females at each year from birth to 30 years. These norms undoubtedly need updating. Moreover, the sample contained too few cases at each age and was not sufficiently representative of the general population, most of the cases coming from middle-class homes. A retest reliability of .92 is reported for 123 cases, the retest intervals varying from one day to nine months. The use of different examiners or informants did not appreciably affect results in this group, as long as all informants had had an adequate opportunity to observe the examinees. Validity of the scale was determined chiefly on the basis of age differentiation, comparison of normals with mental retardates, and correlation of scores with judgments of observers who knew the examinees well. Correlations between the Vineland scale and the Stanford-Binet vary widely but are sufficiently low, in general, to indicate that different facets of behavior are being tapped by the two scales.

A newer and more comprehensive instrument is the Adaptive Behavior Scale (ABS), prepared by a committee of the American Association on Mental Deficiency. Designed primarily for mental retardates, this scale can

---

[7] A revision of this scale is in progress and is scheduled for publication in 1982.

also be used with emotionally maladjusted and other handicapped persons. Adaptive behavior is defined as "the effectiveness of an individual in coping with the natural and social demands of his or her environment" (American Association on Mental Deficiency, 1974). In its 1974 revision, this scale provides a single form applicable from the age of 3 years on. Like the Vineland, it is based on observations of everyday behavior and may be completed by parents, teachers, ward personnel, or others who have been in close contact with the examinee. The information may also be obtained through questioning or interviewing one or more observers.

The ABS consists of two parts. Part 1 is a developmental scale covering 10 behavior domains, several of which are divided into subdomains as indicated below:

Independent Functioning: eating, toilet use, cleanliness, appearance, care of clothing, dressing and undressing, travel, general independent functioning

Physical Development: sensory development, motor development

Economic Activity: money handling and budgeting, shopping skills

Language Development: expression, comprehension, social language development

Numbers and Time

Domestic Activity: cleaning, kitchen duties, other domestic activities

Vocational Activity

Self-direction: initiative, perseverance, leisure time

Responsibility

Socialization

Specific items with multiple responses are provided under each domain or subdomain. Special instructions are included for handling questions about activities that the individual may have had no opportunity to perform (e.g., shopping, restaurant eating).

Part 2 is designed to assess maladaptive behavior related to personality and behavior disorders. It covers 14 behavior domains, such as violent and destructive behavior, withdrawal, and hyperactive tendencies. In each of the 14 categories, specific items of behavior (e.g., "bites others," "attempts to set fires") are rated 1 if they occur occasionally and 2 if they occur frequently.

Instructions for administering and scoring are clearly set forth on the form itself and explained further in the manual. The scale yields a summary profile of percentile scores in each of the 24 behavior domains. Norms were obtained on institutionalized mental retardates of both sexes between the ages of 3 and 69 years. Percentile equivalents are reported for 11 age levels, grouped by one-year intervals at the youngest ages and by 2, 3, 10, and 20 years at the older ages. Cases were drawn from institutions through-out the United States, the numbers at each age level ranging from about 100 to slightly over 500.

In the interpretation of scores, the authors emphasize the importance of considering the individual's ability to remain and to function adequately in his or her own setting, community, or neighborhood. Preliminary data on rater reliability and on concurrent and construct validity are promising. The authors refer to several lines of research under way, including the application of the scale to noninstitutionalized mental retardates and to emotionally disturbed but nonretarded persons, longitudinal studies of change in scores during treatment and training programs, and investigations of various psychometric features of the instrument itself.

Other instruments, designed especially to assess the competency of trainable mentally retarded (TMR) individuals, are the Cain-Levine Social Competency Scales and the T.M.R. School Competency Scales. The Cain-Levine scales are concerned primarily with basic social competency skills in moderately or severely retarded children between the ages of 5 and 13. Information is obtained through a structured interview with a parent or other knowledgeable observer. The scales yield scores in self-help, initiative, social skills, and communication, as well as a total social competency score. The T.M.R. scales are essentially an extension of the Cain-Levine scales to include higher-level skills needed if the mentally retarded child is to function in the school situation. Designed for ages 5 through 17 and over, these scales yield scores in five areas of competence: perceptual-motor, initiative-responsibility, cognition, personal-social, and language. They are useful in identifying specific strengths and weaknesses for planning individual training programs, as well as in measuring progress in the course of training.

TESTING THE PHYSICALLY HANDICAPPED

DEAFNESS. Owing to their general retardation in linguistic development, deaf children are usually handicapped on verbal tests, even when the verbal content is presented visually. In fact, the testing of deaf children was the primary object in the development of some of the earliest performance scales, such as the Pintner-Paterson Performance Scale and the Arthur Performance Scale. Special adaptations of the Wechsler scales are sometimes employed in testing deaf persons. The verbal tests can be administered if the oral questions are typed on cards. Various procedures for communicating the instructions for the performance tests have also been worked out (see Sattler, 1982, Ch. 9). With such modifications of standard testing procedures, however, one cannot assume that reliability, validity, and norms remain unchanged. Nonlanguage group tests, such as the Army Beta, are also used in testing the deaf.

Whether or not they require special procedural adaptations, all the tests mentioned thus far were standardized on hearing persons. For many purposes, it is of course desirable to compare the performance of the deaf with general norms established on hearing persons. At the same time, norms obtained on deaf children are also useful in a number of situations pertaining to the educational development of these children.

To meet this need, the Hiskey-Nebraska Test of Learning Aptitude was developed and standardized on deaf and hard-of-hearing children. This is an individual test suitable for ages 3 to 16. Speed was eliminated, since it is difficult to convey the idea of speed to young deaf children. An attempt was also made to sample a wider variety of intellectual functions than those covered by most performance tests. Pantomime and practice exercises to communicate the instructions, as well as intrinsically interesting items to establish rapport, were considered important requirements for such a test. All were chosen with special reference to the limitations of deaf children, the final item selection being based chiefly on the criterion of age differentiation.

The Hiskey-Nebraska Test consists of twelve subtests:

1. Bead Patterns
2. Memory for Color
3. Picture Identification
4. Picture Associations
5. Paper Folding (Patterns)
6. Visual Attention Span
7. Block Patterns
8. Completion of Drawings
9. Memory for Digits
10. Puzzle Blocks
11. Picture Analogies
12. Spatial Reasoning

The manual provides parallel instructions for testing deaf and hearing children. Norms were derived separately from 1,079 deaf and 1,074 hearing children between the ages of 3 and 17 years, tested in 10 states. Split-half reliabilities in the .90s are reported for deaf and hearing groups. Intercorrelations of the 12 subtests range from the .30s to the .70s among younger children (ages 3 to 10) and from the .20s to the .40s among older children (ages 11 to 17). Correlations of .78 to .86 were found between the Hiskey-Nebraska and either the Stanford-Binet or the Wechsler Intelligence Scale for Children in small groups of hearing children. Further evidence of validity was provided by substantial correlations with achievement tests among deaf children. The manual contains a discussion of desirable practices to be followed in testing deaf children.

BLINDNESS. Testing the blind presents a very different set of problems from those encountered with the deaf. Oral tests can be most readily adapted for blind persons, while performance tests are least likely to be applicable. In addition to the usual oral presentation by the examiner, other suitable testing techniques have been utilized, such as phonograph records and tape or wire recordings. Some tests are also available in braille. The latter technique is somewhat limited in its applicability, however, by the greater bulkiness of materials printed in braille as compared with inkprint, by the slower reading rate for braille, and by the number of blind persons who are not facile braille readers. The examinee's responses may likewise be recorded in braille or on a typewriter. Specially prepared embossed answer sheets or cards are also available for use with true-false, multiple-choice, and other objective-type items. In many individually administered tests, of course, oral responses can be obtained.

Among the principal examples of general intelligence tests that have been adapted for blind persons are the Binet and the Wechsler. The first Hayes-Binet revision for testing the blind was based on the 1916 Stanford-Binet. In 1942, the Interim Hayes-Binet[8] was prepared from the 1937 Stanford-Binet (Hayes, 1942, 1943). All items that could be administered without the use of vision were selected from both Form L and Form M. This procedure yielded six tests for each year level from VIII to XIV, and eight tests at the Average Adult level. In order to assemble enough tests for year levels III to VI, it was necessary to draw on some of the special tests devised for use in the earlier Hayes-Binet. Most of the tests in the final scale are oral, a few requiring braille materials. A retest reliability of .90 and a split-half reliability of .91 are reported by Hayes. Correlations with braille editions of standard achievement tests ranged from .82 to .93. The validity of this test was also checked against school progress.

The Wechsler scales have also been adapted for blind examinees. These adaptations consist essentially in using the verbal tests and omitting the performance tests. A few items inappropriate for the blind have also been replaced by alternates. When tested under these conditions, blind persons as a group have been found to equal or excel the general seeing norms.

A number of group intelligence tests have likewise been adapted for use with the visually handicapped and are available in either large-type or braille editions, or both. Examples include the School and College Ability Tests (SCAT), the College Board Scholastic Aptitude Test (SAT), and the Aptitude Test of the Graduate Record Examinations (GRE). Research with a tactile form of the Progressive Matrices has shown it to have promise as a nonverbal intelligence test for blind children between the ages of 9 and 15 years (Rich & Anderson, 1965). The Blind Learning Aptitude Test incorporates some items from the Progressive Matrices together with other nonverbal items in a tactile test employing an embossed format. The emphasis is on the learning process rather than on the products of past learning, in which the blind child may have been handicapped. Reliability data and norms compare favorably with those usually available for instruments designed for special populations. Information regarding validity is meager and requires further research.

---

[8] Originally designated as an interim edition because of the tentative nature of its standardization, this revision has come to be known by this name in the literature.

Some efforts have also been made to develop adaptive behavior scales suitable for blind children. Examples include an adaptation of the Vineland Social Maturity Scale for blind preschool children (Maxfield & Buchholz, 1957) and the Developmental Checklists (Zimmerman & Bornstein, undated).[9]

ORTHOPEDIC HANDICAPS. Although usually able to receive auditory and visual stimulation, the orthopedically handicapped may have such severe motor disorders as to make either oral or written responses impracticable. The manipulation of formboards or other performance materials would likewise meet with difficulties. Working against a time limit or in strange surroundings often increases the motor disturbance in the orthopedically handicapped. Their greater susceptibility to fatigue makes short testing sessions necessary.

Some of the severest motor handicaps are found among the cerebral palsied. Yet surveys of these cases have frequently employed common intelligence tests such as the Stanford-Binet or the Arthur Performance Scale. In such studies, the most severely handicapped were usually excluded as untestable. Frequently, informal adjustments in testing procedure were made in order to adapt the test to the child's response capacities. Both of these procedures, of course, are makeshifts.

A more satisfactory approach lies in the development of testing instruments suitable for even the most severely handicapped individuals. A number of specially designed tests or adaptations of existing tests are now available for this purpose, although their normative and validity data are often meager. Several of the tests to be discussed in the next section, originally designed for use in cross-cultural testing, have also proved applicable to the handicapped. Adaptations of the Leiter International Performance Scale and the Porteus Mazes, suitable for administration to cerebral-palsied children, have been prepared (Allen & Collins, 1955; Arnold, 1951). In both adapted tests, the examiner manipulates the test materials, while the examinee responds only by appropriate head movements. A similar adaptation of the Stanford-Binet has been proposed (E. Katz, 1958). The Progressive Matrices provide a promising tool for this purpose. Since this test is given with no time limit, and since the response may be indicated orally, in writing, or by pointing or nodding, it appears to be especially appropriate for the orthopedically handicapped. Despite the flexibility and simplicity of its response indicator, this test covers a wide range of difficulty and provides a fairly high test ceiling. Successful use of this test has been reported in studies of cerebral-palsied children and adults (Allen & Collins, 1955; Holden, 1951; Tracht, 1948).

Another type of test that permits the utilization of a simple pointing response is the *picture vocabulary test*. These tests provide a rapid measure

9 See also *Eighth Mental Measurements Yearbook*, #321.

of "use" vocabulary, especially applicable to persons unable to vocalize well (such as the cerebral-palsied) and to the deaf. Since they are easy to administer and can be completed in about 15 minutes, they are also useful as a rapid screening device in situations where no trained examiner is available but individual testing is needed.

The Peabody Picture Vocabulary Test is typical of these instruments. Its current revision (PPVT-R) consists of a series of 175 plates, each containing four pictures. As each plate is presented, the examiner provides a stimulus word orally; the examinee responds by pointing to or in some other way designating the picture on the plate that best illustrates the meaning of the stimulus word. Although the entire test covers a range from the preschool to the adult level, each individual is given only the plates appropriate to his or her own performance level, as determined by a specified run of successes at one end and failures at the other. Raw scores can be converted to standard scores ($M = 100$, $SD = 15$), percentile ranks, and stanines. These derived scores are plotted on a chart with confidence bands covering $\pm$ SEM (Standard error of measurement). Age-equivalent scores are also provided, with instructions for computing the appropriate confidence bands. The PPVT-R is untimed, but requires from 10 to 20 minutes. It is available in two parallel forms, each using a different set of cards and different stimulus words.

The PPVT-R was standardized on a national sample of 4,200 children and adolescents between the ages of 2½ and 18 years. The sample included 100 males and 100 females at each age level, and was representative of the population of the United States with regard to geographical region, parental occupational category, community size, and ethnic group. Additional adult norms were obtained on 828 persons aged 19 through 40, selected so as to be nationally representative in geographical region and major occupational groups. Reliability coefficients within single age groups were found by several procedures. Internal consistency coefficients fell mostly in the .70s and .80s, with medians in the low .80s. Alternate form reliabilities with immediate retest yielded similar values, with a median of .82. With retest intervals ranging from 9 to 31 days, alternate form reliabilities had a median value of .78.

The PPVT-R has been published too recently to permit a significant accumulation of direct validity data. Because of the basic similarity of the two editions, however, and because of a median correlation of .70 between scores on the two editions, validity data gathered with the first edition can contribute substantially toward an interim evaluation of the PPVT-R. A survey of over 300 studies using the PPVT yielded high correlations with other vocabulary tests, moderate correlations with tests of verbal intelligence and scholastic aptitude, and promising relations with performance on educational achievement tests (Dunn & Dunn, 1981). Correlations were similar in diverse populations, including physically handicapped, mentally retarded, and economically disadvantaged groups. Children participating in compensatory education programs showed more improvement on this test than on the Stanford-Binet (Howard & Plant, 1967; Klaus & Gray, 1968; Milgram, 1971), and their gains tended to be larger than those of nondisadvantaged pupils attending regular schools (Dunn & Dunn, 1981). Scores on the PPVT reflect in part the respondent's degree of cultural assimilation and exposure to Standard American English.

Similar procedures of test administration have been incorporated in *pictorial classification tests,* as illustrated by the Columbia Mental Maturity Scale (CMMS). Originally developed for use with cerebral-palsied children, this scale comprises 92 items, each consisting of a set of three, four, or five drawings printed on a large card. The examinee is required to identify the drawing that does not belong with the others, indicating his choice by pointing or nodding (see Fig. 37). To heighten interest and appeal, the cards and drawings are varicolored. The objects depicted were chosen to be within the range of experience of most American children. Scores are expressed as Age Deviation Scores, which are normalized standard scores within age groups, with a mean of 100 and an *SD* of 16. Percentile and stanine equivalents for these scores are also provided. To meet the demand for developmental norms, the manual includes a Maturity Index, indicating the age group in the standardization sample whose test performance is most similar to that of the child.

The standardization sample for the CMMS comprised 2,600 children, including 100 boys and 100 girls in each of 13 six-month age groups between the ages of 3–6 and 9–11. The sample was stratified in terms of the 1960 U.S. Census with regard to parental occupational level, race, and geographical region; proportion of children living in metropolitan and nonmetropolitan areas was also approximately controlled. Split-half reliabilities within single age groups ranged from .85 to .91. Standard errors of measurement of the Age Deviation Scores are between 5 and 6 points. Retest of three age groups after an interval of 7 to 10 days yielded reliabilities of .84 to .86. A correla-

Fɪɢ. 37. Examiner Administering Columbia Mental Maturity Scale to Child.

(From Columbia Mental Maturity Scale: Guide for Administering and Interpreting, 1972, p. 11. Copyright © 1972 by Harcourt Brace Jovanovich, Inc. Reproduced by permission.)

tion of .67 with Stanford-Binet was found in a group of 52 preschool and first-grade children. Correlations with achievement test scores in first- and second-grade samples fell mostly between the high .40s and the low .60s. More extensive data on validity and on applicability to various handicapped groups are available for an earlier form of the test.

CROSS-CULTURAL TESTING

THE PROBLEM. The testing of persons with highly dissimilar cultural backgrounds has received increasing attention since midcentury. Tests are needed for the maximum utilization of human resources in the newly developing nations in Africa and elsewhere. The rapidly expanding educational facilities in these countries require testing for admission purposes as well as for individual counseling. With increasing industrialization, there is a mounting demand for tests to aid in the job selection and placement of personnel, particularly in mechanical, clerical, and professional fields.

In America the practical problems of cross-cultural testing have been associated chiefly with subcultures or minority cultures within the dominant culture. There has been widespread concern regarding the applicability of available tests to culturally disadvantaged groups. It should be noted parenthetically that cultural disadvantage is a relative concept. Objectively, there is only cultural difference between any two cultures or subcultures. Each culture fosters and encourages the development of behavior that is adapted to its values and demands. When an individual must adjust to and compete within a culture or subculture other than that in which he or she was reared, then cultural difference is likely to become cultural disadvantage.

Although concern with cross-cultural testing has been greatly stimulated by recent social and political developments, the problem was recognized at least as early as 1910. Some of the earliest cross-cultural tests were developed for testing the large waves of immigrants coming to the United States at the turn of the century. Other early tests originated in basic research on the comparative abilities of relatively isolated cultural groups. These cultures were often quite primitive and had had little or no contact with Western civilization within whose framework most psychological tests had been developed.

Traditionally, cross-cultural tests have tried to rule out one or more parameters along which cultures vary. A well-known example of such a parameter is *language*. If the cultural groups to be tested spoke different languages, tests were developed that required no language on the part of either examiner or examinees. When educational backgrounds differed widely and illiteracy was prevalent, *reading* was ruled out. Oral language was not eliminated from these tests because they were designed for persons speaking a common language. Another parameter in which cultures or subcultures differ is that of *speed*. Not only the tempo of daily life, but also the motivation to hurry and the value attached to rapid performance vary widely among national cultures, among ethnic minority groups within a single nation, and between urban and rural subcultures (see, e.g., Kline-berg, 1928; Knapp, 1960). Accordingly, cross-cultural tests have often—though not always—tried to eliminate the influence of speed by allowing long time limits and giving no premium for faster performance.

Still other parameters along which cultures differ pertain to *test content*. Several nonlanguage and nonreading tests, for example, call for items of information that are specific to certain cultures. Thus, they may require the examinee to understand the function of such objects as violin, postage stamp, gun, pocketknife, telephone, piano, or mirror. Persons reared in certain cultures may lack the experiential background to respond correctly to such items. It was chiefly to control this type of cultural parameter that the classic "culture-free" tests were first developed. Following a brief examination of typical tests designed to eliminate one or more of the above parameters, we shall turn to an analysis of alternative approaches to cross-cultural testing.

TYPICAL INSTRUMENTS. In their efforts to construct tests applicable across cultures, psychometricians have followed a variety of procedures, some of which are illustrated by the four tests to be considered in this section. The Leiter International Performance Scale is an individually administered performance scale. It was developed through several years of use with different ethnic groups in Hawaii, including elementary and high school pupils. The scale was subsequently applied to several African groups by Porteus and to a few other national groups by other investigators. A later revision, issued in 1948, was based on further testing of American children, high school students, and army recruits during World War II. A distinctive feature of the Leiter scale is the almost complete elimination of instructions, either spoken or pantomime. Each test begins with a very easy task of the type to be encountered throughout that test. The comprehension of the task is treated as part of the test. The materials consist of a response frame, illustrated in Figure 38, with an adjustable card holder. All tests are administered by attaching the appropriate card, containing printed pictures, to the frame. The examinee chooses the blocks with the proper response pictures and inserts them into the frame.

The Leiter scale was designed to cover a wide range of functions, similar to those found in verbal scales. Among the tasks included may be mentioned: matching identical colors, shades of gray, forms, or pictures; copying a block design; picture completion; number estimation; analogies; series completion; recognition of age differences; spatial relations; footprint recognition; similarities; memory for a series; and classification of animals according to habitat. Administered individually, with no time limit, these tests

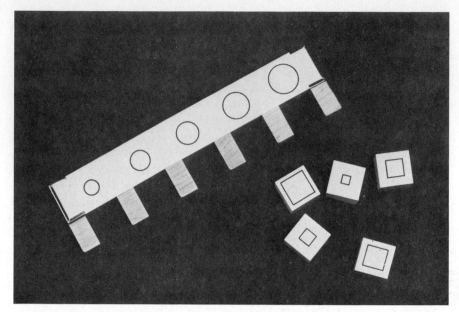

FIG. 38. Typical Materials for Use in the Leiter International Performance Scale. The test illustrated is the Analogies Progression Test from the Six-Year Level. (Courtesy of C. H. Stoelting Company.)

are arranged into year levels from 2 to 18. The scale is scored in terms of MA and ratio IQ, although there is no assurance that such an IQ retains the same meaning at different ages. In fact, the published data show considerable fluctuation in the standard deviation of the IQs at different age levels. Split-half reliabilities of .91 to .94 are reported from several studies, but the samples were quite heterogeneous in age and probably in other characteristics. Validation data are based principally on age differentiation and internal consistency. Some correlations are also reported with teachers' ratings of intelligence and with scores on other tests, including the Stanford-Binet and the WISC. These correlations range from .56 to .92, but most were obtained on rather heterogeneous groups.

The tests in year levels 2 to 12 are also available as the Arthur Adaptation of the Leiter International Performance Scale. This adaptation, considered most suitable for testing children between the ages of 3 and 8 years, was standardized by Grace Arthur in 1952. Its norms must be regarded as quite limited, being derived from a standardization sample of 289 children from a middle-class, midwestern metropolitan background. Like the original scale, the Arthur adaptation yields an MA and a ratio IQ.

The Culture Fair Intelligence Test, developed by R. B. Cattell and published by the Institute for Personality and Ability Testing (IPAT), is a paper-and-pencil test. This test is available in three levels: Scale 1, for ages 4 to 8 and mentally retarded adults; Scale 2, for ages 8 to 13 and average adults; and Scale 3, for Grades 10 to 16 and superior adults. Each scale has been prepared in two parallel forms, A and B. Scale 1 requires individual administration for at least some of the tests; the other scales may be given either as individual or as group tests. Scale 1 comprises eight tests, only four of which are described by the author as culture-fair. The other four involve both verbal comprehension and specific cultural information. It is suggested that the four culture-fair tests can be used as a subbattery, separate norms being provided for this abbreviated scale. Scales 2 and 3 are alike, except for difficulty level. Each consists of the following four tests, sample items from which are shown in Figure 39.

1. *Series:* Select the item that completes the series.

2. *Classification:* Mark the one item in each row that does not belong with the others.

3. *Matrices:* Mark the item that correctly completes the given matrix, or pattern.

4. *Conditions:* Insert a dot in one of the alternative designs so as to meet the same conditions indicated in the sample design. Thus, in the example reproduced in Figure 39, the dot must be in the two rectangles, but not in the circle. This condition can be met only in the third response alternative, which has been marked.

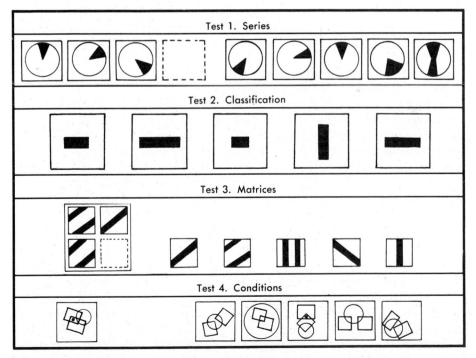

FIG. 39. Sample Items from Culture Fair Intelligence Test, Scale 2.

(Copyright by Institute of Personality and Ability Testing. Reproduced by permission.)

For Scale 1, only ratio IQs are provided. In Scales 2 and 3, scores can be converted into deviation IQs with an *SD* of 16 points. Scales 2 and 3 have been standardized on larger samples than Scale 1, but the representatives of the samples and the number of cases at some age levels still fall short of desirable test-construction standards. Although the tests are highly speeded, some norms are provided for an untimed version. Fairly extensive verbal instructions are required, but the author asserts that giving these instructions in a foreign language or in pantomime will not affect the difficulty of the test.

Internal consistency and alternate-form reliability coefficients are marginal, especially for Scale 3, where they fall mostly in the .50s and .60s. Validity is discussed chiefly in terms of saturation with a general intellective factor (*g*), having been investigated largely through correlation with other tests and through factor analysis. Scattered studies of concurrent and predictive validity show moderate correlations with various academic and occupational criteria. The Cattell tests have been administered in several European countries, in America, and in certain African and Asian cultures. Norms tended to remain unchanged in cultures moderately similar to that in which the tests were developed; in other cultures, however, performance fell considerably below the original norms. Moreover, black children of low socioeconomic level tested in the United States did no better on this test than on the Stanford-Binet (Willard, 1968).

The Progressive Matrices, developed in Great Britain by J. C. Raven, were also designed as a measure of Spearman's *g* factor. Requiring chiefly the eduction of relations among abstract items, this test is regarded by most British psychologists as the best available measure of *g*. It consists of 60 matrices, or designs, from each of which a part has been removed. The examinee chooses the missing insert from six or eight given alternatives. The items are grouped into five series, each containing 12 matrices of increasing difficulty but similar in principle. The earlier series require accuracy of discrimination; the later, more difficult series involve analogies, permutation and alternation of pattern, and other logical relations. Two sample items are reproduced in Figure 40. The test is administered with no time limit and can be given individually or in groups. Very simple oral instructions are required.

Percentile norms are provided for each half-year interval between 8 and 14 years, and for each five-year interval between 20 and 65 years. These norms are based on British samples, including 1,407 children, 3,665 men in military service tested during World War II, and 2,192 civilian adults. Closely similar norms were obtained by Rimoldi (1948) on 1,680 children in Argentina. Use of the test in several European countries likewise indicated the applicability of available norms. Studies in a number of non-European cultures, however, have raised doubts about the suitability of this test for groups with very dissimilar backgrounds. In such groups, moreover,

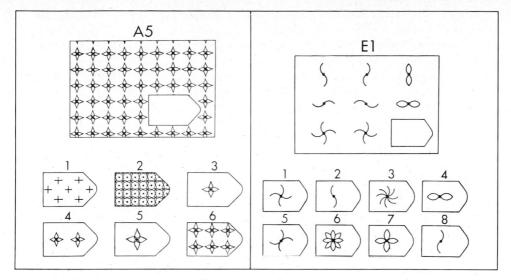

Fig. 40. Sample Items from the Progressive Matrices.
(Reproduced by permission of J. C. Raven.)

the test was found to reflect amount of education and to be susceptible to considerable practice effect.

The manual for the Progressive Matrices is quite inadequate, giving little information on reliability and none on validity. Many investigations have been published, however, that provide relevant data on this test. Research continues at a rapid pace, especially in America where this test has received growing recognition. The *Eighth Mental Measurements Yearbook* lists nearly 700 studies, many dealing with the use of this test with clinical patients.

Retest reliability in groups of older children and adults that were moderately homogeneous in age varies approximately between .70 and .90. At the lower score ranges, however, reliability falls considerably below these values. Correlations with both verbal and performance tests of intelligence range between .40 and .75, tending to be higher with performance than with verbal tests. Studies with the mentally retarded and with different occupational and educational groups indicate fair concurrent validity. Predictive validity coefficients against academic criteria run somewhat lower than those of the usual verbal intelligence tests. Several factorial analyses suggest that the Progressive Matrices are heavily loaded with a factor common to most intelligence tests (identified with Spearman's g by British psychologists), but that spatial aptitude, inductive reasoning, perceptual accuracy, and other group factors also influence performance.

An easier form, the Coloured Progressive Matrices, is available for children between the ages of 5 and 11 years and for mentally retarded adults.

A more advanced form has also been developed for superior adults, but its distribution is restricted to approved and registered users.

A still different approach is illustrated by the Goodenough Draw-a-Man Test, in which the examinee is simply instructed to "make a picture of a man; make the very best picture that you can." This test was in use without change from its original standardization in 1926 until 1963. An extension and revision was published in 1963 under the title of Goodenough-Harris Drawing Test (D. B. Harris, 1963). In the revision, as in the original test, emphasis is placed on the child's accuracy of observation and on the development of conceptual thinking, rather than on artistic skill. Credit is given for the inclusion of individual body parts, clothing details, proportion, perspective, and similar features. A total of 73 scorable items were selected on the basis of age differentiation, relation to total scores on the test, and relation to group intelligence test scores. Data for this purpose were obtained by testing samples of 50 boys and 50 girls at each grade level from kindergarten through the ninth grade in urban and rural areas of Minnesota and Wisconsin, stratified according to father's occupation.

In the revised scale, examinees are also asked to draw a picture of a woman and of themselves. The Woman scale is scored in terms of 71 items similar to those in the Man scale. The Self scale was developed as a projective test of personality, although available findings from this application are not promising. Norms on both Man and Woman scales were established on new samples of 300 children at each year of age from 5 to 15, selected so as to be representative of the United States population with regard to father's occupation and geographical region. Point scores on each scale are transmuted into standard scores with a mean of 100 and an *SD* of 15. Figure 41 shows three illustrative drawings produced by children aged 5–8, 8–8, and 12–11, together with the corresponding raw point scores and standard scores. An alternative, simplified scoring procedure is provided by the Quality scales for both Man and Woman drawings. Instead of the point scoring, the Quality scales utilize a global, qualitative assessment of the entire drawing, obtained by matching the child's drawing with the one it resembles most closely in a graded series of 12 samples.

The reliability of the Goodenough-Harris Drawing Test has been repeatedly investigated by a variety of procedures. In one carefully controlled study of the earlier form administered to 386 third- and fourth-grade schoolchildren, the retest correlation after a one-week interval was .68, and split-half reliability was .89 (McCarthy, 1944). Rescoring of the identical drawings by a different scorer yielded a scorer reliability of .90, and rescorings by the same scorer correlated .94. Studies with the new form (Dunn, 1967; D. B. Harris, 1963) have yielded similar results. Readministration of the test to groups of kindergarten children on consecutive days revealed no significant difference in performance on different days. Examiner effect was also found to be negligible, as was the effect of art training in school. The old and new scales are apparently quite similar; their scores correlate be-

Man: Raw Score 7	Woman: Raw Score 31	Man: Raw Score 66
CA 5–8	CA 8–8	CA 12–11
Standard Score 73	Standard Score 103	Standard Score 134

Fig. 41. Specimen Drawings Obtained in Goodenough-Harris Drawing Test. (Courtesy of Dale B. Harris.)

tween .91 and .98 in homogeneous age groups. The correlation of the Man and Woman scales is about as high as the split-half reliability of the Man scale found in comparable samples. On this basis, Harris recommends that the two scales be regarded as alternate forms and that the mean of their standard scores be used for greater reliability. The Quality scales, representing a quicker but cruder scoring method, yield interscorer reliabilities clustering in the .80's. Correlations of about the same magnitude have been found between Quality scale ratings and point scores obtained for the same drawings.

Apart from the item-analysis data gathered in the development of the scales, information regarding the construct validity of the test is provided by correlations with other intelligence tests. These correlations vary widely, but the majority are over .50. In a study with 100 fourth-grade children, correlations were found between the Draw-a-Man Test and a number of tests of known factorial composition (Ansbacher, 1952). Such correlations indicated that, within the ages covered, the Draw-a-Man Test correlates highest with tests of reasoning, spatial aptitude, and perceptual accuracy. Motor coordination plays a negligible role in the test at these ages. For kindergarten children, the Draw-a-Man Test correlated higher with numerical aptitude and lower with perceptual speed and accuracy than it did for fourth-grade children (D. B. Harris, 1963). Such findings suggest that the test may measure somewhat different functions at different ages.

The original Draw-a-Man Test has been administered widely in clinics as a supplement to the Stanford-Binet and other verbal scales. It has also been employed in a large number of studies on different cultural and ethnic groups, including several American Indian samples. Such investigations have indicated that performance on this test is more dependent on differences in cultural background than was originally assumed. In a review of studies pertaining to this test, Goodenough and Harris (1950, p. 399) expressed the opinion that "the search for a culture-free test, whether of intelligence, artistic ability, personal-social characteristics, or any other measurable trait is illusory." This view was reaffirmed by Harris in his 1963 book. Subsequently, Dennis (1966) analyzed comparative data obtained with this test in 40 widely different cultural groups, principally from 6-year-old children. Mean group scores appeared to be most closely related to the amount of experience with representational art within each culture. In the case of groups with little indigenous art, it was hypothesized that test performance reflects degree of acculturation to Western civilization.

Cultural differences in experiential background were again revealed in a well-designed comparative investigation of Mexican and American children with the Goodenough-Harris test (Laosa, Swartz, & Diaz-Guerrero, 1974). In studies of this test in Nigeria (Bakare, 1972) and Turkey (Uçman, 1972), mean scores increased consistently and significantly with the children's socioeconomic level. It should be added that these findings with the Goodenough-Harris test are typical of results obtained with all tests initially designed to be "culture-free" or "culture-fair" (Samuda, 1975, Ch. 6).

APPROACHES TO CROSS-CULTURAL TESTING. Theoretically, we can identify three approaches to the development of tests for persons reared in different cultures or subcultures, although in practice some features from all three may be combined. The first approach involves the choice of items common to many cultures and the validation of the resulting test against local criteria in many different cultures. This is the basic approach of the culture-fair tests, although their repeated validation in different cultures has often been either neglected altogether or inadequately executed. Without such a step, however, we cannot be sure that the test is relatively free from culturally restricted elements. Moreover, it is unlikely that any single test could be designed that would fully meet these requirements across a wide range of cultures.

On the other hand, cross-cultural assessment techniques are needed for basic research on some very fundamental questions. One of these questions pertains to the generality of psychological principles and constructs derived within a single culture (Anastasi, 1958, Ch. 18). Another question concerns the role of environmental conditions in the development of individual differences in behavior—a problem that can be more effectively studied within the wide range of environmental variation provided by highly dissimilar cultures. Research of this sort calls for instruments that can be administered under at least moderately comparable conditions in different cultures. Safeguards against incorrect interpretations of results obtained with such instruments should be sought in appropriate experimental designs and in the investigators' thorough familiarity with the cultures or subcultures under investigation.

A second major approach is to make up a test within one culture and administer it to individuals with different cultural backgrounds. Such a procedure would be followed when the object of testing is prediction of a local criterion within a particular culture. In such a case, if the specific cultural loading of the test is reduced, the test validity may also drop, since the criterion itself is culturally loaded. On the other hand, we should avoid the mistake of regarding any test developed within a single cultural framework as a universal yardstick for measuring "intelligence." Nor should we assume that a low score on such a test has the same causal explanation when obtained by a member of another culture as when obtained by a member of the test culture. What *can* be ascertained by such an approach is the cultural distance between groups, as well as the individual's degree of acculturation and her or his readiness for educational and vocational activities that are culture-specific.

From time to time, investigators have followed this approach in order to dramatize the fact that the cultural milieu in which an individual is reared affects the cognitive skills and knowledge he or she acquires. Early examples include a footprint recognition test standardized on aboriginal Australians (Porteus, 1931) and a Draw-a-Horse Test standardized on Pueblo Indian children (DuBois, 1939). In both cases, the cultural group on which the test was developed excelled in comparisons with other groups. A recent example followed a more extreme test-construction procedure to ensure large group differences. In The BITCH Test (Black Intelligence Test of Cultural Homogeneity), black and white respondents were compared in their understanding of typical in-group slang used by black Americans. In the development of this test, items were selected on the basis of empirical differences in black-white performance. Thus, the item-selection procedure was similar to that followed in the early masculinity-femininity scales and in the social status scale of the MMPI, discussed in Chapter 8. Such a test could serve as an index (albeit a very limited index) of the degree of one's assimilation to a particular culture at the time and place in which the test was constructed (see also Cronbach, 1978; Krauskopf, 1978).

As a third approach, *different* tests may be developed within each culture, validated against local criteria, and used only within the appropriate culture. This approach is exemplified by the many revisions of the original Binet scales for use in different European, Asian, and African cultures, as well as by the development of tests for industrial and military personnel within particular cultures. A current example is provided by the test-development program conducted in several developing nations of Africa, Asia, and Latin America by the American Institutes for Research, under the sponsorship of the United States Agency for International Development (Schwarz, 1964a, 1964b; Schwarz & Krug, 1972). Another example is the long-term testing program of the National Institute of Personnel Research in Johannesburg (Blake, 1972). In such instances, the tests are validated against the specific educational and vocational criteria they are designed to predict, and performance is evaluated in terms of local norms. Each test is applied only within the culture in which it was developed and no cross-cultural comparisons are attempted. If the criteria to be predicted are technological, however, "Western-type intelligence" is likely to be needed, and the tests will reflect the direction in which the particular culture is evolving rather than its prevalent cultural characteristics at the time (see also Vernon, 1969 Ch. 14).

Attention should also be called to the publication, in the late 1960s and early 1970s, of several handbooks concerned with cross-cultural testing and research, and with the use of tests in developing countries (Biesheuvel, 1969; Brislin, Lonner, & Thorndike, 1974; Schwarz & Krug, 1972). All provide information on recommended tests, adaptations of standardized tests, and procedural guidelines for the development and application of tests. Further indication of the widespread interest in cross-cultural testing can be found in the report of an international conference on Mental Tests and Cultural Adaptation held in 1971 in Istanbul, Turkey (Cronbach & Drenth, 1972). The papers presented at this conference reflect the wide diversity of interests and backgrounds of the participants. The topics range from methodological problems and evaluations of specific instruments to theoretical discussions and reports of empirical studies.

The principal focus in both the handbooks and the conference report is on major cultural differences, as found among nations and among peoples at very different stages in their cultural evolution. In addition, a vast amount of literature has accumulated in the decades of the 1960s and 1970s on the psychological testing of minorities in the United States, chiefly for educational purposes. In the present book, this material is treated wherever it can be most clearly presented. Thus, in Chapter 3, the focus was on social and ethical concerns and responsibilities in the use of tests with cultural minorities. The technical psychometric problems of test bias and item-group interactions were considered in Chapters 7 and 8. In the present chapter, attention was centered on instruments developed for cross-cultural ability testing. Problems in the interpretation of the results of cross-cultural testing will be considered in Chapter 12.

A final point should be reiterated about the instruments discussed in this section. Although initially developed for cross-cultural testing, several of these instruments have found a major application in the armamentarium of the clinical psychologist, both to supplement information obtained with such instruments as the Stanford-Binet and the Wechsler scales and in the testing of persons with various handicaps. This is especially true of the Goodenough-Harris Drawing Test, the Progressive Matrices, and the Arthur Adaptation of the Leiter scale.

Chapter 11

Group Testing

WHILE individual tests such as the Stanford-Binet and the Wechsler scales find their principal application in the clinic, group tests are used primarily in the educational system, government service, industry, and the military services. It will be recalled that mass testing began during World War I with the development of the Army Alpha and the Army Beta for use in the United States Army. The former was a verbal test designed for general screening and placement purposes. The latter was a nonlanguage test for use with men who could not properly be tested with the Alpha owing to foreign-language background or illiteracy. The pattern established by these tests was closely followed in the subsequent development of a large number of group tests for civilian application.

Revisions of the civilian forms of both original army tests continued in use for several decades. In the armed services, the Armed Forces Qualification Test (AFQT) was subsequently developed as a preliminary screening instrument, followed by multiple-aptitude classification batteries for assignment to occupational specialties. The AFQT provided a single score based on an equal number of vocabulary, arithmetic, spatial relations, and mechanical ability items.

In this chapter, major types of group tests in current use will be surveyed. First, we shall consider the principal differences between group and individual tests. This will be followed by an overview of emerging procedures for individually tailored group testing and computer utilization in testing programs. Then, we shall discuss the characteristics of current multilevel batteries designed to cover a wide age or grade range, with typical illustrations from different levels. Finally, group tests designed for use at the college level and beyond will be examined.

GROUP TESTS VERSUS INDIVIDUAL TESTS

ADVANTAGES OF GROUP TESTING. Group tests are designed primarily as instruments for mass testing. In comparison with individual tests, they have both advantages and disadvantages. On the positive side, group tests can be administered simultaneously to as many persons as can be fitted comfortably into the available space and reached through a microphone. Large-scale testing programs were made possible by the development of group testing techniques. By utilizing only printed items and simple responses that can be recorded on a test booklet or answer sheet, the need for a one-to-one relationship between examiner and examinee was eliminated.

A second way in which group tests facilitated mass testing was by greatly simplifying the examiner's role. In contrast to the extensive training and experience required to administer the Stanford-Binet, for example, most group tests require only the ability to read simple instructions to the examinees and to keep accurate time. Some preliminary training sessions are desirable, of course, since inexperienced examiners are likely to deviate inadvertently from the standardized procedure in ways that may affect test results. Because the examiner's role is minimized, however, group testing can provide more uniform conditions than does individual testing. The use of tapes, records, and film in test administration offers further opportunities for standardizing procedure and eliminating examiner variance in large-scale testing.

Scoring is typically more objective in group testing and can be done by a clerk. Most group tests can also be scored by computers through several available test-scoring services. Moreover, whether hand-scored or machine-scored, group tests usually provide separate answer sheets and reusable test booklets. Since in these tests all responses are written on the answer sheet, the test booklets can be used indefinitely until they wear out, thereby effecting considerable economy. Answer sheets also take up less room than test booklets and hence can be more conveniently filed for large numbers of examinees.

From another angle, group tests characteristically provide better established norms than do individual tests. Because of the relative ease and rapidity of gathering data with group tests, it is customary to test very large, representative samples in the standardization process. In the most recently standardized group tests, it is not unusual for the normative samples to number between 100,000 and 200,000, in contrast to the 2,000 to 4,000 cases laboriously accumulated in standardizing the most carefully developed individual intelligence scales.

Group tests necessarily differ from individual tests in form and arrangement of items. Although open-ended questions calling for free responses could be used—and were used in the early group tests—today the typical group test employs *multiple-choice items*. This change was obviously required for uniformity and objectivity of scoring, whether by hand or machine. With regard to arrangement of items, whereas the Binet type of scale groups items into age levels, group tests characteristically group items of similar content into *separately timed subtests*. Within each subtest, items are usually arranged in increasing order of difficulty. This arrangement ensures that each examinee has an opportunity to try each type of item (such as vocabulary, arithmetic, spatial, etc.) and to complete the easier items of each type before trying the more difficult ones on which he or she might otherwise waste a good deal of time.

A practical difficulty encountered with separate subtests, however, is that the less experienced or less careful examiners may make timing errors. Such errors are more likely to occur and are relatively more serious with several short time limits than with a single long time limit for the whole test. To reconcile the use of a single time limit with an arrangement permitting all examinees to try all types of items at successively increasing difficulty levels, some tests utilize the *spiral-omnibus format.* One of the earliest tests to introduce this format was the Otis Self-Administering Tests of Mental Ability, which, as its name implies, endeavored to reduce the examiner's role to a minimum. The same arrangement is followed in the Otis-Lennon School Ability Test, from the fourth-grade level up. In a spiral-omnibus test, the easiest items of each type are presented first, followed by the next easiest of each type, and so on in a rising spiral of difficulty level, as illustrated below:

1. The opposite of hate is: Answer
   1. enemy,   2. fear,   3. love,   4. friend,   5. joy .... ( )

2. If 3 pencils cost 25 cents, how many pencils can be bought for 75
   cents? .... ( )

3. A bird does not always have:
   1. wings,   2. eyes,   3. feet,   4. a nest,   5. a bill .... ( )

4. The opposite of honor is:
   1. glory,   2. disgrace,   3. cowardice,   4. fear,   5. defeat ...... ( )

In order to avoid the necessity of repeating instructions in each item and to reduce the number of shifts in instructional set required of the examinees, some tests apply the spiral-omnibus arrangement not to single items but to blocks of 5 to 10 items.

DISADVANTAGES OF GROUP TESTING. Although group tests have several desirable features and serve a well-nigh indispensable function in present-day testing, their limitations should also be noted. In group testing, the examiner has much less opportunity to establish rapport, obtain cooperation, and maintain the interest of examinees. Any temporary condition of the examinee, such as illness, fatigue, worry, or anxiety, that may interfere with test performance is less readily detected in group than in individual testing. In general, persons unaccustomed to testing may be somewhat more handicapped on group than on individual tests. There is also some evidence suggesting that emotionally disturbed children may perform better on individual than on group tests (Bower, 1969; Willis, 1970).

From another angle, group tests have been attacked because of the restrictions imposed on the examinee's responses. Criticisms have been directed particularly against multiple-choice items and against such standard item types as analogies, similarities, and classification (Hoffman, 1962; LaFave, 1966). Some of the arguments are ingenious and provocative. One contention is that such items may penalize a brilliant and original thinker who sees unusual implications in the answers. It should be noted parenthetically that if this happens, it must be a rare occurrence, in view of the item analysis and validity date. If it does occur in one or two items in an individual's test, moreover, it would hardly have an appreciable effect on that examinee's total score. Some critics have focused on the importance of analyzing errors and inquiring into the reasons why an individual chooses a particular answer, as in the typical Piagetian approach (Sigel, 1963). It is undoubtedly true that group tests provide little or no opportunity for direct observations of the examinee's behavior or for identifying the causes of atypical performance. For this and other reasons, when important decisions about individuals are to be made, it is desirable to supplement group tests either with individual examination of doubtful cases or with additional information from other sources.

Still another limitation of traditional group testing is its lack of flexibility, insofar as every examinee is ordinarily tested on all items. Available testing time could be more effectively utilized if each examinee concentrated on items appropriate to her or his ability level. Moreover, such a procedure would avoid boredom from working on too easy items, at one extreme, and mounting frustration and anxiety from attempting items beyond the individual's present ability level, at the other. It will be recalled that in some individual tests, such as the Stanford-Binet and the Peabody Picture Vocabulary Test, the selection of items to be presented by the examiner depends upon the examinee's prior responses. Thus, in these tests, the examinee is given only items within a difficulty range appropriate to his or her ability level.

COMPUTER UTILIZATION AND ADAPTIVE TESTING

INDIVIDUALLY TAILORED TESTS. In the effort to combine some of the advantages of individual and group testing, several innovative techniques are being explored. Major interest thus far has centered on ways of adjusting item coverage to the response characteristics of individual examinees. In the rapidly growing literature on the topic, this approach has been variously designated as adaptive, sequential, branched, tailored, individualized, programmed, dynamic, or response-contingent testing (Baker, 1971; Glaser & Nitko, 1971; Weiss & Betz, 1973). Although it is possible to design paper-and-pencil group tests that incorporate such adaptive procedures (Cleary,

Linn, & Rock, 1968; Lord, 1971a), these techniques lend themselves best to computerized test administration.

Adaptive testing can follow a wide variety of procedural models (De-Witt & Weiss, 1974; Larkin & Weiss, 1974; Weiss, 1974; Weiss & Betz, 1973). A simple example involving two-stage testing is illustrated in Figure 42. In this hypothetical test, all examinees take a 10-item routing test, whose items cover a wide difficulty range. Depending on his or her performance on the routing test, each examinee is directed to one of the three 20-item measurement tests at different levels of difficulty. Thus, each person takes only 30 items, although the entire test comprises 70 items. A different arrangement is illustrated in the pyramidal test shown in Figure 43. In this case, all examinees begin with an item of intermediate difficulty. If an individual's response to this item is correct, she or he is routed upward to the next more difficult item; if the response is wrong, he or she moves downward to the next easier item. This procedure is repeated after each item response, until the individual has given 10 responses. The illustration shows a 10-stage test, in which each examinee is given 10 items out of the total pool of 55 items in the test. The heavy line shows the route followed by one examinee whose responses are listed as + (Right) or − (Wrong) along the top.

Several variants of both of these adaptive testing models have been tried,

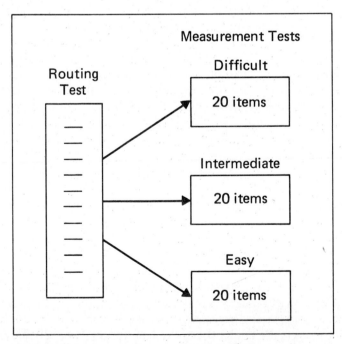

Fig. 42. Two-Stage Adaptive Testing with Three Measurement Levels. Each examinee takes routing test and one measurement test.

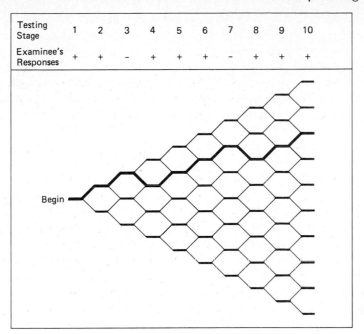

Testing Stage	1	2	3	4	5	6	7	8	9	10
Examinee's Responses	+	+	−	+	+	+	−	+	+	+

FIG. 43. Pyramidal Testing Model. Heavy line shows route of examinee whose item scores are listed across top.

with both paper-and-pencil and computer forms. More complex models, which do not use preestablished, fixed patterns of item sequences, are feasible only when a computer is available (Urry, 1977; Weiss, 1973, 1976). These computerized testing procedures utilize the item response theory (IRT) techniques described in Chapter 8 for assembling the item pool, for testing individuals, and for scoring individual performance. For each item in the pool, there is an estimate of the ability level, or amount of "latent trait," required for a 50–50 chance of passing that item. This ability estimate is the score the individual receives for passing that item. It reflects the difficulty level, discriminative value, and probability of guessing correctly that are associated with that item. Also available for each item is the standard error of this ability estimate. Following each item response, the computer selects the next item, on the basis of the individual's total response history, so as to effect the maximum reduction in this error of estimate. Testing continues with the addition of new items until the error of estimate, or accuracy of measurement, reaches a preestablished standard. It is also possible to adjust the entry point, or initial item, to the individual's ability level. The selection of entry point utilizes prior data about the individual, such as other tests and school grades, or information obtained from the examinee at the beginning of the testing session.

The individual's score is based, not on the number of items answered correctly, but on the difficulty level and other psychometric characteristics of those items. The total test score is derived from the ability estimates corresponding to each item passed. This ability estimate is readjusted and refined as each new item is added, until the predetermined measurement accuracy is reached. Such scores will be comparable for all persons examined with the item pool, regardless of the particular set of items given to each individual.

In general, research by various methods indicates that individualized adaptive testing can achieve the same reliability and validity as conventional tests, with a much smaller number of items and less testing time. It also provides greater precision of measurement for individuals at the upper and lower extremes of the ability range covered by the test (Lord, 1970b, 1971b, 1971c; Weiss & Betz, 1973). Adaptive testing is especially appropriate for use in the individualized instructional programs cited in Chapter 4, in which students proceed at their own pace and may therefore require test items at widely different difficulty levels. Computerized testing makes it possible to stop testing as soon as the individual's responses provide enough information for a decision about his or her content mastery.

Other uses of computerized adaptive testing are being actively investigated and developed in several settings. One such prototype system has been developed at Educational Testing Services and is being evaluated empirically for use in schools (Kreitzberg & Jones, 1980). With a computer-stored pool of verbal aptitude items, it can provide individually tailored tests covering a range of ability from the fifth grade to the graduate school. Similar exploratory research is in progress in the armed services and in civilian government service for the selection and classification of persons with regard to occupational specialties (Gorham, 1975; McBride, 1979; Urry, 1977; Urry & Dorans, in press).

OTHER APPLICATIONS OF COMPUTERS. Besides providing the opportunity to adapt testing to the abilities and needs of individual examinees, computers can help to circumvent other limitations of traditional group tests (Baker, 1971; Glaser & Nitko, 1971; B. F. Green, 1970). One potential contribution is the analysis of wrong responses, in order to identify types of error in individual cases. Another is the use of response modes that permit the examinee to try alternative responses in turn, with immediate feedback, until the correct response is chosen. Still another possibility is the development of special response procedures and item types to investigate the examinee's problem-solving techniques. For instance, following the initial presentation of the problem, examinees may have to ask the computer for further information needed to proceed at each step in the solution; or they may be required to respond by indicating the steps they follow in arriving at the solution. This approach has been employed in medical education to test the diagnostic and therapeutic decision-making skills of medical school students and graduates (Friedman, 1973).

MULTILEVEL BATTERIES

OVERVIEW. Unlike individual scales of the Binet type and computerized or other adaptive tests, traditional group tests present the same items to all examinees, regardless of their individual responses. For this reason, any given group test must cover a relatively restricted range of difficulty, suitable for the particular age, grade, or ability level for which it is designed. To provide comparable measures of intellectual development over a broader range, series of overlapping multilevel batteries have been constructed. Thus, any one individual is examined only with the level appropriate to her or him, but other levels can be used for retesting the same person in subsequent years, or for comparative evaluations of different age groups. The fact that successive batteries overlap provides adequate floor and ceiling for individuals at the extremes of their own age or grade distributions. It should be recognized, of course, that the match between item difficulty and examinee ability provided by multilevel batteries is at best approximate. Unlike the individualized procedures described in the preceding section, moreover, the match is based on prior knowledge about the examinees, such as their age or school grade, rather than on their own test responses.

Multilevel batteries are especially suitable for use in the schools, where comparability over several years is highly desirable. For this reason the levels are typically described in terms of grades. Most multilevel batteries provide a reasonable degree of continuity with regard to content or intellectual functions covered. Scores are expressed in terms of the same scale of units throughout. The normative samples employed at different levels are also more nearly equivalent than would be true of independently standardized tests. Individual levels usually cover from one to three grades. The total range that can be uniformly tested with a given multilevel battery, on the other hand, may extend from kindergarten to college entrance.

Most of the batteries provide deviation IQs or similar standard scores. Some batteries furnish several types of norms, including percentiles, stanines, or grade equivalents, as well as deviation IQs. In addition to a total, global score, most batteries also yield separate verbal and quantitative, or linguistic and nonlinguistic scores. This breakdown is in line with the finding that an individual's performance in verbal and in other types of subtests may be quite dissimilar, especially at the upper levels.

The names of the batteries are also of interest. Such terms as "intelligence," "general ability," "mental ability," "mental maturity," "academic potential," and "school ability" are used to designate essentially the same type of test. In the psychometrician's vocabulary, these terms are virtually synonymous and interchangeable. It is noteworthy that, in the most recently developed or revised batteries, the term 'intelligence" has been replaced by more specific designations. This change reflects the growing recognition that the term "intelligence" has acquired too many excess meanings, which may lead to misinterpretations of test scores. The multilevel batteries sample major intellectual skills found to be prerequisite for schoolwork and other important activities of daily life. Their primary function is to assess the individual's readiness for school learning at each stage in the educational process.

To illustrate the nature and scope of current multilevel ability batteries, three batteries will be discussed. These batteries were chosen because of the recency of their latest revisions, as well as for the high quality of their test-construction procedures. Still another noteworthy feature of these three batteries is that each was standardized concurrently with a multilevel battery of educational achievement tests for the same grades, to be described in Chapter 14. By administering both types of instruments to the same standardization samples, it is possible to establish correspondences between the two sets of scores. As a result, the two instruments can be used jointly to permit a fuller exploration of the child's educational development and of the conditions that influence it.

PRIMARY LEVEL. The youngest age at which it has proved feasible to employ group tests is the kindergarten and first-grade level. At the preschool ages, individual testing is required in order to establish and maintain rapport, as well as to administer the oral and performance type of items suitable for such children. By the age of 5 or 6, however, it is possible to administer printed tests to small groups of no more than 10 or 15 children. In such testing, the examiner must still give considerable individual attention to the children to make sure that directions are followed, see that pages are turned properly in the test booklets, and supervise other procedural details. With one or two assistant examiners, somewhat larger groups may be tested if necessary.

Group tests for the primary level generally cover kindergarten and the first two or three grades of elementary school. In such tests, each child is provided with a booklet on which are printed the pictures and diagrams constituting the test items. All instructions are given orally and are usually accompanied by demonstrations. Fore-exercises are frequently included in which examinees try one or two sample items and the examiner or proctor checks the responses to make certain that the instructions were properly understood. The child marks his or her responses on the test booklet with a crayon or soft pencil. Most of the tests require only marking the correct picture out of a set. A few call for simple motor coordination, as in drawing lines that join two dots. Obviously, tests for the primary level can require no reading or writing on the part of the examinee.

Most multilevel ability batteries include tests suitable for the primary level. To illustrate the nature of tests at this level, we shall examine the Primary Level of the Otis-Lennon School Ability Test. The current edition of this test, published in 1979–1980, is available in two equivalent forms, R and S, at all levels, from Grade 1 through Grade 12. The Primary Level actually consists of two levels, Primary I for Grade 1 and Primary II for Grades 2 and 3. The two levels are essentially similar in content, except for the slightly higher difficulty range of the items in Primary II. There are also minor format differences to facilitate understanding and hold the interest of younger children at Primary I. For instance, pages and rows are designated by numbers and letters at Primary II, while at Primary I they are designated by tiny pictures of familiar objects, such as buttons, balloons, or spoons. In both levels, the child indicates his or her response by filling in the circle under the chosen picture, as illustrated in Figure 44. All instructions are given orally by the examiner. The total test at these two levels requires 80 minutes and is administered in two or three sessions at Primary I and in two sessions at Primary II.

The items are grouped into three parts: I. Classification, II. Analogies, and III. Omnibus. In Part III, the task varies from item to item, and the examiner gives specific instructions for each item. These Omnibus items measure such functions as following directions, quantitative reasoning, and verbal comprehension. Figure 44 shows two of the sample items for each of the three parts. These are relatively simple items employed to familiarize the children with the item types they will encounter in the test. The explanations given in Figure 44 are a highly condensed version of the oral instructions accompanying each item.

Norms for all levels of the Otis-Lennon battery were established on a national sample of approximately 130,000 students from 70 school systems. This standardization sample was closely representative of the entire school population of the United States, with regard to size and type of school system, geographic region, socioeconomic variables, and ethnic composition. At each level, scores are expressed as a "School Ability Index," which is in effect a deviation IQ or standard score with a mean of 100 and an *SD* of 16. Percentile ranks and stanines can also be found with reference to both age and grade norms. Scores can be further interpreted in combination with the child's performance on the Metropolitan Achievement Tests, since both batteries were normed concurrently.

Kuder-Richardson reliability coefficients of the Otis-Lennon battery are in the .90s within each grade or age level. Retests within six months yielded reliability coefficients between .84 and .92. Both concurrent and predictive validity against achievement test scores and end-of-year grades in different school subjects cluster in the .50s, ranging mostly between .40 and .60. With regard to all these psychometric properties, the results are substantially uniform for all ages and grades covered by the battery. With well-constructed tests, satisfactory reliability and validity can be obtained as early as the first grade.

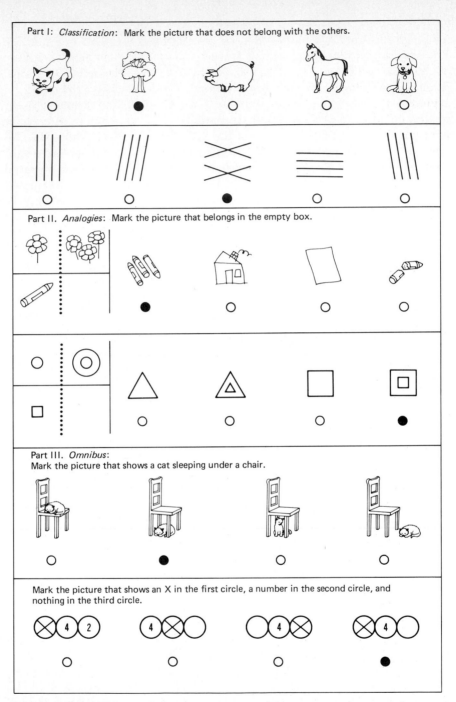

Fig. 44. Some Sample Items Used in the Otis-Lennon School Ability Test, Primary I and Primary II Levels.

ELEMENTARY SCHOOL LEVEL. Group tests of academic intelligence or scholastic ability designed for use from the fourth grade of elementary school through high school have much in common in both content and general design. Since functional literacy is presupposed at these levels, the tests are predominantly verbal in content; most also include arithmetic problems or other numerical tests. In addition, a few batteries provide nonreading tests designed to assess the same abstract reasoning abilities in children with foreign language background, reading disabilities, or other educational handicaps.

As an example of tests for the elementary school grades, we shall consider some of the intermediate levels of the Cognitive Abilities Test. The entire series includes two primary levels (for kindergarten through the third

---

1. *Vocabulary:* find the one word that means the same or nearly the same as the word in dark type at the beginning of the line.

   impolite   A unhappy   B angry   C faithless   D rude   E talkative

---

2. *Sentence Completion:* pick the one word that best fits the empty space in the sentence.

   Mark was very fond of his science teacher, but he did not ‿‿‿‿ his mathematics teacher.

   A obey   B discuss   C regard   D desire   E like

---

3. *Verbal Classification:* think in what way the words in dark type go together. Then find the word in the line below that goes with them.

   dove   hawk   sparrow

   A moth   B bat   C gull   D bee   E squirrel

---

4. *Verbal Analogies:* figure out how the first two words are related to each other. Then from the five words on the line below find the word that is related to the third word in the same way.

   pea → bean : peach →

   A pit   B tree   C eat   D skin   E apple

FIG. 45. Typical Items from Verbal Battery of Cognitive Abilities Test. Answers: 1–D, 2–E, 3–C, 4–E.

(Reproduced by courtesy of Robert L. Thorndike and Elizabeth Hagen.)

grade) and a Multilevel Edition covering Grades 3 through 12. The Multilevel Edition comprises eight levels (A–H) printed in a single booklet. Examinees taking different levels start and stop with different sets of items, or modules. The test is designed so that most examinees will be tested with items that are at intermediate difficulty for them, where discrimination will be most effective.

All eight levels of the Multilevel Edition contain the same 10 subtests, grouped into three batteries as follows:

Verbal Battery—Vocabulary, Sentence Completion, Verbal Classification, Verbal Analogies.

Quantitative Battery—Quantitative Relations, Number Series, Equation Building.

Nonverbal Battery—Figure Classification, Figure Analogies, Figure Synthesis. These subtests use no words or numbers, but only geometric or figural elements; the items bear relatively little relation to formal school instruction.

Each subtest is preceded by practice exercises, the same set being used for all levels. In Figures 45, 46, and 47 will be found a typical item from each of the 10 subtests, with highly condensed instructions. In difficulty level, these items correspond to items given in Grades 4 to 6. The authors recommend that all three batteries be given to each child, in three testing sessions. For most children, the Nonverbal Battery does not predict school achievement as well as do the Verbal and Quantitative batteries. However, a com-

---

1. *Quantitative Relations:* If the amount or quantity in Column I is more than in Column II, mark A; if it is less, mark B; if they are equal, mark C.

Column I	Column II
5×0	5

---

2. *Number Series:* the numbers at the left are in a certain order. Find the number at the right that should come next.

18   16   14   12   10   →   A 7   B 8   C 9   D 10   E 12

---

3. *Equation Building:* Arrange the numbers and signs below to make true equations and then choose the number at the right that gives you a correct answer.

1   8   9   +   –   A 0   B 3   C 8   D 9   E 18

Fig. 46. Typical Items from Quantitative Battery of Cognitive Abilities Test. Answers: 1–B, 2–B, 3–A.

(Reproduced by courtesy of Robert L. Thorndike and Elizabeth Hagen.)

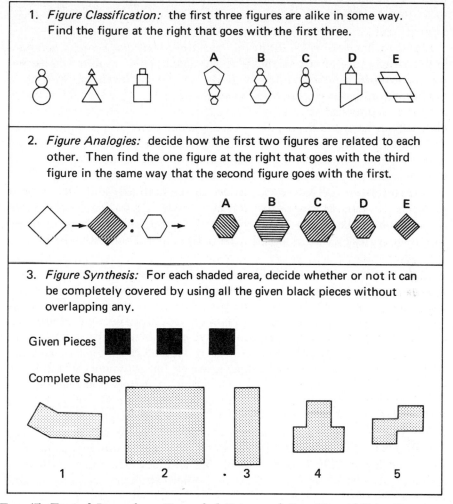

1. *Figure Classification:* the first three figures are alike in some way. Find the figure at the right that goes with the first three.

2. *Figure Analogies:* decide how the first two figures are related to each other. Then find the one figure at the right that goes with the third figure in the same way that the second figure goes with the first.

3. *Figure Synthesis:* For each shaded area, decide whether or not it can be completely covered by using all the given black pieces without overlapping any.

Given Pieces

Complete Shapes

Fig. 47. Typical Items from Nonverbal Battery of Cognitive Abilities Test. Answers: 1–B, 2–D, 3–3 & 4.

(Reproduced by courtesy of Robert L. Thorndike and Elizabeth Hagen.)

parison of performance on the three batteries may provide useful information regarding special abilities or disabilities.

The standardization sample, including approximately 18,000 cases in each of the 10 grade groups, was carefully chosen to represent the school population of the country, with regard to socioeconomic and ethnic categories, among others. Raw scores on each battery are translated into a uniform scale across all levels to permit continuity of measurement and comparability of scores in different grades. For normative interpretations, the scores on each battery can be expressed as normalized standard scores

within each age, with a mean of 100 and an *SD* of 16. Percentiles and stanines can also be found, within ages and within grades. The manual advises
against combining scores from the three batteries into a single index.

Kuder-Richardson reliabilities of the three battery scores, computed
within grades, are mostly in the .90s. The manual also reports standard errors of measurement for different grades and score levels, as well as the
minimum interbattery score differences that can be regarded as having statistical and practical significance. Investigation of long-term stability with
alternate forms over a six-month interval yielded correlations in the .70s and
.80s. Retest correlations after two and three years were somewhat lower and
more variable. In general, the Verbal Battery proved to be more stable over
time than did either the Quantitative or the Nonverbal batteries.

Intercorrelations of battery scores are in the high .60s and .70s; intercorrelations of subtests are also unusually high. Factor analyses likewise
showed the presence of a large general factor through the three batteries,
probably representing principally the ability to reason with abstract and
symbolic content.

The Cognitive Abilities Test was standardized on the same normative sample as two achievement batteries, the Iowa Tests of Basic Skills for kindergarten to Grade 9 and the Tests of Achievement and Proficiency for Grades
9 to 12. Concurrent validity of the Cognitive Abilities Test against these two
achievement batteries fell mostly in the .70s and .80s. As is generally found
with academic criteria, the Verbal Battery yielded the highest correlations
with achievement in all school subjects, except for arithmetic, which tended
to correlate slightly higher with the Quantitative Battery. Correlations with
the Nonverbal Battery were uniformly lower than with the other two batteries. Correlations with achievement tests over a three-year interval are of
about the same magnitude as the concurrent correlations. Predictive validity
coefficients against school grades obtained from one to three years later run
somewhat lower, falling mostly in the .50s and .60s. These correlations are
probably attenuated by unreliability and other extraneous variance in grading procedures.

HIGH SCHOOL LEVEL. It should be noted that the high school levels of
multilevel batteries, as well as other tests designed for high school students,
are also suitable for testing general, unselected adult groups. Short screening tests of general academic intelligence, designed especially for job applicants, will be considered in Chapter 15.

An example of an academic aptitude test for the high school level is provided by the Advanced Level of the School and College Ability Tests
(SCAT-III), designed for Grades 9 to 12. The entire battery extends from
the end of Grade 3, through Grade 12, in three levels. At all levels, the
SCAT tests are available in two alternate forms, X and Y. Oriented specifically toward the prediction of academic achievement, all levels yield a
Verbal, a Quantitative, and a Total score. The Verbal score is based on a

verbal analogies test. The items in this test, however, differ from the traditional analogies items in that the respondent must choose both words in the second pair, rather than just the fourth word. The Quantitative score is derived from a quantitative comparison test designed to assess the examinee's understanding of fundamental number operations. Covering both numerical and geometric content, these items require a minimum of reading and emphasize insight and resourcefulness rather than traditional computational procedures. Figure 48 shows Verbal and Quantitative items typical of those found at the high school level of SCAT. At all levels, testing time is 40 minutes, 20 minutes for each part.

In line with current trends in testing theory, SCAT undertakes to measure developed abilities. This is simply an explicit admission of what is more or less true of all intelligence tests, namely that test scores reflect the nature and amount of schooling the individual has received rather than measuring "capacity" independently of relevant prior experiences. Accordingly, SCAT draws freely on word knowledge and arithmetic processes learned in the appropriate school grades. In this respect, SCAT does not really differ from other academic intelligence tests, especially those designed for the high school and college levels; it only makes overt a condition sometimes unrecognized in other tests.

Verbal, Quantitative, and Total scores from all SCAT levels are expressed on a common scale which permits direct comparison from one level to another. These scores can in turn be converted into percentile ranks or stanines for the appropriate grade. A particularly desirable feature of SCAT scores is the provision of a *percentile band* in addition to a single percentile for each obtained score. Representing a distance of approximately one standard error of measurement on either side of the corresponding percentile, the percentile band gives the 68% confidence interval, or the range within which are found 68% of the cases in a normal curve. In other words, if we conclude that an individual's true score lies within the given percentile band, the chances of our being correct are 68 out of 100 (roughly 2:1 ratio). As explained in Chapter 5, the error of measurement provides a concrete way of taking the reliability of a test into account when interpreting an individual's score.

If two percentile bands overlap, the difference between the scores can be ignored; if they do not overlap, the difference can be regarded as significant. Thus, if two students were to obtain Total SCAT scores that fall in the percentile bands 52–58 and 63–79, we could conclude with fair confidence that the second actually excels the first and would continue to do so on a retest. Percentile bands likewise help in comparing a single individual's relative standing on Verbal and Quantitative parts of the test. If a student's Verbal and Quantitative scores correspond to the percentile bands 71–91 and 65–88, respectively, we would conclude that he or she is *not* significantly better in verbal than in quantitative abilities, because the percentile bands for these two scores overlap.

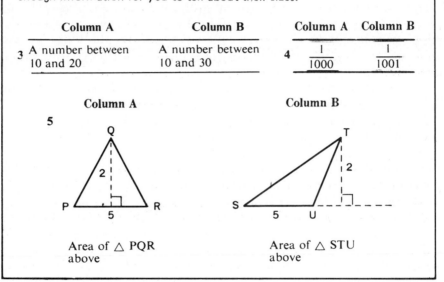

Part I — *Verbal*: each item begins with two words that go together in a certain way. Find the two other words that go together in about the same way.

1 tool : hammer ::
    A table : chair
    B toy : doll
    C weapon : metal
    D sleigh : bell

2 braggart : humility ::
    A traitor : repentance
    B radical : conventionality
    C precursor : foresight
    D sophisticate : predisposition

Part II — *Quantitative*: each item is made up of two amounts or quantities, one in Column A and one in Column B. You have four choices: A, B, C, or D. Choose A if the quantity in Column A is greater, B if that in Column B is greater, C if the quantities are equal, or D if there is not enough information for you to tell about their sizes.

Column A	Column B
3 A number between 10 and 20	A number between 10 and 30

	Column A	Column B
4	$\dfrac{1}{1000}$	$\dfrac{1}{1001}$

Column A

5

Area of △ PQR above

Column B

Area of △ STU above

FIG. 48. Items Typical of Those Used in School and College Ability Tests (SCAT) for Grades 9 to 12. Answers: 1—**B**, 2—**B**, 3—**D**, 4—**A**, 5—**C**.

The SCAT standardization sample of over 50,000 cases was selected so as to constitute a representative cross section of the national school population in Grades 4 through 12. For this purpose, a three-stage sampling procedure was employed, in which the units to be sampled were school systems (public and private), schools, and classrooms, respectively. SCAT-III was standardized jointly with the current edition of an achievement battery, the Sequential Tests of Educational Progress (STEP), thereby permitting cross-comparisons of scores on the two instruments.

Reliability coefficients for Verbal, Quantitative, and Total scores were separately computed within single grade groups by the Kuder-Richardson technique. The reported reliabilities are uniformly high. Within separate grade groups, from Grade 4 to 12, Total score reliabilities are all above .90. Verbal and Quantitative reliabilities cluster around .90. Correlations between alternate forms administered in immediate succession, in groups tested with the Advanced (high school) level, are in the .80s for Verbal and Quantitative scores, and approximately .90 for Total scores.

In view of the stated purpose for which SCAT was developed, its predictive validity against academic achievement is of prime relevance. Correlations with the Sequential Tests of Educational Progress generally fall between .60 and .80. Quantitative scores tend to correlate higher than Verbal scores with mathematics achievement; and Verbal scores tend to correlate higher than Quantitative scores with achievement in all other subjects. Total SCAT scores, however, generally yield validity coefficients as high as those of either of the two part scores or higher. Thus, the effectiveness of Verbal and Quantitative scores as differential predictors of academic achievement remains uncertain. Some data are also available on correlations between SCAT scores and grade-point average, as well as grades in different school subjects. Although running lower in general magnitude, these correlations follow the same pattern with regard to Verbal, Quantitative, and Total SCAT scores as do the SCAT–STEP correlations.

It is noteworthy in this connection that the Verbal and Quantitative scores are themselves highly correlated. These correlations are mostly in the .70s. Such close similarity may result from the item types employed in the two tests, which involve largely the ability to detect and utilize relations in symbolic and abstract content. Like other tests discussed in this chapter, SCAT was designed principally as a measure of general intellectual development and only secondarily as an indicator of intraindividual aptitude differences.

For college-bound high school students, another application of SCAT scores is of particular interest. SCAT scores obtained in the 9th, 10th, and 11th grades can be used to predict the student's chances of scoring at or above specified levels on the College Board's Scholastic Aptitude Test (SAT), to be described in the following section. On the basis of data gathered during the SCAT-III standardization regarding the correlation of SCAT and SAT scores, tables were constructed that permit this type of estimate. For each of these three grade levels, the tables report the chances in 100 that a student with a given SCAT Verbal and SCAT Quantitative score would obtain an SAT Verbal and Mathematical score that equals or exceeds 350, 450, 550, and 650.

TESTS FOR THE COLLEGE LEVEL AND BEYOND

COLLEGE ADMISSION. A number of tests have been developed for use in the admission, placement, and counseling of college students. An outstanding example is the Scholastic Aptitude Test (SAT) of the College Entrance Examination Board. Several new forms of this test are prepared each year, a different form being employed in each administration. Separate scores are reported for the Verbal and Mathematical Sections of the test. Figures 49 and 50 contain brief descriptions of the verbal and mathematical item types, with illustrations. The items reproduced are among those given in the orientation booklet distributed to prospective examinees (College Entrance Examination Board, 1981).

First incorporated into the CEEB testing program in 1926, the SAT has undergone continuing development and extensive research of high technical quality. One of the reviewers in the *Seventh Mental Measurements Year-*

Antonyms: choose the lettered word or phrase that is most nearly *opposite* in meaning to the word in capital letters.

1. SUBSEQUENT: (A) primary   (B) recent   (C) contemporary
    (D) prior   (E) simultaneous

Analogies: select the lettered pair that best expresses a relationship similar to that expressed in the original pair.

2. KNIFE : INCISION ::   (A) bulldozer : excavation
    (B) tool : operation   (C) pencil : calculation
        (D) hose : irrigation   (E) plow : agriculture

Sentence Completions: choose the one word or set of words that, when inserted in the sentence, *best* fits the meaning of the sentence as a whole.

3. The excitement does not ---- but ---- his senses, giving him a keener perception of a thousand details.
    (A) show . . diverts   (B) blur . . sharpens   (C) overrule . . constricts
    (D) heighten . . aggravates   (E) forewarn . . quickens

Reading Comprehension: examinee reads a passage and answers multiple-choice questions assessing his or her understanding of its content.

FIG. 49. Illustrative Verbal Items from College Board Scholastic Aptitude Test. Instructions have been highly condensed. Answers: 1—D, 2—A, 3—B.

(From *Taking the SAT*, College Entrance Examination Board, 1981. Sample test questions reprinted by permission of Educational Testing Service, copyright owner.)

Standard Multiple-Choice Questions: drawing upon elementary arithmetic, algebra, and geometry taught in the ninth grade or earlier, these items emphasize insightful reasoning and the application of principles.

1. If $16 \times 16 \times 16 = 8 \times 8 \times P$, then $P =$
   (A) 4   (B) 8   (C) 32   (D) 48   (E) 64

Quantitative Comparisons: mark (A) if the quantity in Column A is greater, (B) if the quantity in column B is greater, (C) if the two quantities are equal, (D) if the relationship cannot be determined from the information given.

Column A	Column B
2.	$(37) \frac{1}{43} (58)$	$(59) \frac{1}{43} (37)$

FIG. 50. Illustrative Mathematical Items from College Board Scholastic Aptitude Test. Instructions have been highly condensed. Answers: 1—**E**, 2—**B**.

(From *Taking the SAT*, College Entrance Examination Board, 1981. Sample test questions reprinted by permission of Educational Testing Service, the copyright owner.)

book wrote, "Technically, the SAT may be regarded as highly perfected— possibly reaching the pinnacle of the current state of the art of psychometrics" (DuBois, 1972). Another commented, "The system of pretesting of items, analysis, and standardization of new forms exemplifies the most sophisticated procedures in modern psychometrics" (Wallace, 1972). Several aspects of the SAT research have been cited in different chapters of this book to illustrate specific procedures. A detailed account of methodology and results can be found in the technical report edited by Angoff (1971a).[1] A shorter comparable form, known as the Preliminary SAT, has also been in use since 1959. Generally taken at an earlier stage, this test provides a rough estimate of the high school student's aptitude for college work and has been employed for educational counseling and other special purposes. Both tests are restricted to the testing program administered by the College Entrance Examination Board on behalf of member colleges. All applicants to these colleges take the SAT. Some colleges also require one or more achievement tests in special fields, likewise administered by CEEB.

Another nationwide program, launched in 1959, is the American College Testing Program (ACT). Originally limited largely to state university systems, this program has grown rapidly and is now used by many colleges throughout the country. The Academic Tests of the ACT Assessment program comprise four tests: English Usage, Mathematics Usage, Social Studies Reading, and Natural Sciences Reading. Reflecting the point of view of its founder, E. F. Lindquist, the examination provides a set of work samples of

---

[1] A revision of this report is in progress, with anticipated publication date in 1982.

college work. It overlaps traditional aptitude and achievement tests, focusing on the basic intellectual skills required for satisfactory performance in college.

Technically, the ACT does not come up to the standards set by the SAT. Reliabilities are generally lower than desirable for individual decisions, although they have improved in the later editions of the tests. The separate scores are somewhat redundant insofar as the four parts are heavily loaded with reading comprehension and highly intercorrelated. On the other hand, validity data compare favorably with those found for other instruments in similar settings. Correlations between composite scores on the whole battery and college grade-point averages cluster between .40 and .50. Most of these validity data were obtained through research services made available to member colleges by the ACT program staff. The program also provides extensive normative and interpretive data and other ancillary services.

It should be noted that tests such as the SAT and the ACT are not intended as substitutes for high school grades in the prediction of college achievement. High school grades can predict college grades as well as most tests or slightly better. When test scores are combined with high school grades, however, the prediction of college performance is significantly improved. In part, this improvement stems from the fact that a uniform, objective test serves as a corrective for the variability in grading standards among different high schools. Moreover, such tests are not subject to the influence of irrelevant variables and possible personal biases that may enter into the assignment of course grades.

GRADUATE SCHOOL ADMISSION. The practice of testing applicants for admission to college was subsequently extended to include graduate and professional schools.[2] Most of the tests designed for this purpose represent a combination of general intelligence and achievement tests. A well-known example is the Graduate Record Examinations (GRE). This series of tests originated in 1936 in a joint project of the Carnegie Foundation for the Advancement of Teaching and the graduate schools of four eastern universities. Now greatly expanded, the program is conducted by Educational Testing Service, under the general direction of the Graduate Record Examinations Board. Students are tested at designated centers prior to their admission to graduate school. The test results are used by the universities to aid in making admission and placement decisions and in selecting recipients for scholarships, fellowships, and special appointments. The GRE include an Aptitude Test and an Advanced Test in the student's field of specialization. The latter is available in many fields, such as biology, English literature, French, mathematics, political science, and psychology.

The Aptitude Test is essentially a scholastic aptitude test suitable for ad-

---

[2] The testing of applicants to professional schools will be discussed in Chapter 15, in connection with occupational tests.

vanced undergraduates and graduate students. Like many such tests, it yields separate Verbal and Quantitative scores. The verbal items require verbal reasoning and comprehension of reading passages taken from several fields. The quantitative items require mathematical reasoning, as well as the interpretation of graphs, diagrams, and descriptive data. Following extensive research on various item types, a new section on Analytical Ability was added to the Aptitude Test in 1977 (Conrad, Trismen, & Miller, 1977; Wild, 1979). Employing both verbal content and diagrams, the item types chosen for this section are designed to measure such functions as recognizing logical relations (e.g., between evidence and hypotheses, or between premises and conclusion); drawing conclusions from a complex series of statements; using a sequential procedure to eliminate incorrect choices in order to reach a conclusion; and determining relationships between independent or interdependent categories or groups. In most psychometric characteristics, such as reliability, the new section compares favorably with the Verbal and Quantitative sections. While demonstrating an acceptable degree of independence of Verbal and Quantitative scores, the Analytical scores correlate higher with the other two scores than those scores correlate with each other. Research is under way to assess the predictive validity of the Analytical scores against performance in graduate school.

Scores on all GRE tests are reported in terms of a single standard score scale with a mean of 500 and an *SD* of 100. These scores are directly comparable for all tests, having been anchored to the Aptitude Test scores of a fixed reference group of 2,095 seniors examined in 1952 at 11 colleges. A score of 500 on an Advanced Physics Test, for example, is the score expected from physics majors whose Aptitude Test score equals the mean Aptitude Test score of the reference group. Since graduate school applicants are a selected sample with reference to academic aptitude, the means of most groups actually taking each Advanced Test in the graduate student selection program will be considerably above 500. Moreover, there are consistent differences in the intellectual caliber of students majoring in different subjects. For normative interpretation, therefore, the current percentiles given for specific groups are more relevant and local norms are still better.

The reliability and validity of the GRE have been investigated in a number of different student samples (*Guide for the Use of the GRE,* 1980). Kuder-Richardson reliabilities of the Verbal, Quantitative, and Analytical scores of the Aptitude Test and of total scores on the Advanced Tests are consistently at or above .90. Several Advanced Tests also report scores in two or three major subdivisions of the field, such as experimental and social psychology. The reliabilities of these subscores are mostly in the .80s. The lower reliabilities, as well as the high intercorrelations among the parts, call for caution in the interpretation of subscores.

Predictive validity has been checked against such criteria as graduate school grade-point average, performance on departmental comprehensive examinations, overall faculty ratings, and attainment of the PhD (Conrad et al., 1977; Willingham, 1974). In general, the GRE composite score, including Aptitude and Advanced tests, proved to be more valid than undergraduate grade-point average as a predictor of graduate school performance. Depending upon the criterion used, the difference in favor of the GRE varied from slight to substantial. Consistent with expectation, GRE–Q was a better predictor than GRE–V in those scientific fields in which mathematical ability is of major importance; the reverse was true of such fields as English. The GRE Advanced Test was the most generally valid single predictor among those investigated. Illustrative data from three fields can be seen in Figure 51, showing the percentage of students attaining the PhD in successive intervals of Advanced Test scores. The three coefficients given in Figure 51 are biserial correlations between GRE Advanced Test scores and attainment or nonattainment of the PhD.

The highest validities were obtained with weighted composites of undergraduate grade-point average and one or more GRE scores. These multiple

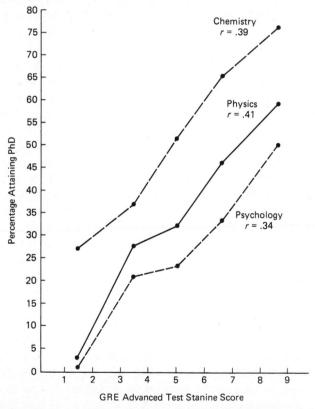

Fig. 51. Percentage of Students at Various Levels of GRE Advanced Test Scores Who Attained the PhD within 10 Years.

(From Willingham, 1974, p. 276; data from Creager, 1965. Copyright © 1974 by the American Association for the Advancement of Science.)

correlations fell mostly between .40 and .45 for various criteria and for different fields. It should be noted that the narrow range of talent covered by graduate school applicants necessarily results in lower correlations than are obtained with the SAT among college applicants. This finding does not imply that the GRE is intrinsically less valid than the SAT; rather, it means that finer discriminations are required within the more narrowly restricted graduate school population.

Another widely used test for the selection of graduate students is the Miller Analogies Test. Consisting of complex analogies items whose subject matter is drawn from many academic fields, this test has an unusually high ceiling. Although a 50-minute time limit is imposed, the test is primarily a power test. The Miller Analogies Test was first developed for use at the University of Minnesota, but later forms were made available to other graduate schools and it was subsequently published by the Psychological Corporation. Its administration, however, is restricted to licensed centers in universities or business organizations. The test is used both in the selection of graduate students and in the evaluation of personnel for high-level jobs in industry. It is available in five parallel forms, one of which is reserved for reexaminations.

Percentile norms on the Miller Analogies Test are given for graduate and professional school students in several fields and for groups of industrial employees and applicants. Over half of these groups contained 500 or more cases and none had less than 100. Marked variations in test performance are found among these different samples. The median of one group, for example, corresponds to the 90th percentile of another. Means and *SD*s for additional, smaller industrial samples are also reported as further aids in normative interpretation.

Odd-even reliability coefficients of .92 to .95 were found in different samples, and alternate-form reliabilities ranged from .85 to .90. Correlations with several individual and group tests of general intelligence and academic aptitudes fall almost entirely between the .50s and the .70s. Over 100 validity coefficients are reported for graduate and professional student groups and for a few industrial samples. These coefficients vary widely. Slightly over a third are between .30 and .60. About an equal number are clearly too low to be significant. The field of specialization, the nature of the criteria employed, and the size, heterogeneity, and other characteristics of the samples are obvious conditions affecting these coefficients. Means and *SD*s of several contrasting groups in different settings provide some additional promising validity data. It is evident that the validity of this test must be evaluated in terms of the specific context in which it is to be used.

INTELLECTUALLY GIFTED ADULTS. Any test designed for college or graduate students is also likely to be suitable for examining intellectually superior adults for occupational assessment, research, or other purposes. The use of the Miller Analogies Test for the selection and evaluation of high-level industrial personnel has already been mentioned. Another test that provides sufficient ceiling for the examination of highly gifted adults is the Concept Mastery Test (CMT). Originating as a byproduct of Terman's extensive longitudinal study of gifted children, Form A of the Concept Mastery Test was developed for testing the intelligence of the gifted group in early maturity (Terman & Oden, 1947). For a still later follow-up, when the gifted subjects were in their mid-40s, Form T was prepared (Terman & Oden, 1959). This form, which is somewhat easier than Form A, was subsequently released for more general use.

The Concept Mastery Test consists of both analogies and synonym–antonym items. Like the Miller Analogies Test, it draws on concepts from many fields, including physical and biological sciencies, mathematics, history, geography, literature, music, and others. Although predominantly verbal, the test incorporates some numerical content in the analogies items.

Percentile norms are given for approximately 1,000 cases in the Stanford gifted group, tested at a mean age of 41 years, as well as for smaller samples of graduate students, college seniors applying for Ford Foundation Fellowships in Behavioral Sciences, and engineers and scientists in a navy electronics laboratory. To provide further interpretive data, the manual (with 1973 supplement) reports means and SDs of some 20 additional student and occupational samples.

Alternate-form reliabilities of the CMT range from .86 to .94. Scores show consistent rise with increasing educational level and yield correlations clustering around .60 with predominantly verbal intelligence tests. Significant correlations with grade-point averages were found in seven college samples, the correlations ranging from .26 to .59. Some suggestive findings in other contexts are also cited. For example, in two groups of managers participating in advanced management training programs, CMT scores correlated .40 and .45 with peer ratings of ability to think critically and analytically. And in a group of 200 experienced elementary and secondary school teachers, CMT correlated .54 with a scale designed to measure teachers' attitude toward gifted children. Evidently, the teachers who themselves scored higher on this test had more favorable attitudes toward gifted children.

Because of its unique features, the Concept Mastery Test can undoubtedly serve a useful function for certain testing purposes. On the other hand, it is clearly not an instrument that can be used or interpreted routinely. A meaningful interpretation of CMT scores requires a careful study of all the diverse data accumulated in the manual, preferably supplemented by local norms.

CHAPTER 12

Psychological Issues in Intelligence Testing

PSYCHOLOGICAL tests should be regarded as tools. Like all tools, their effectiveness depends on the knowledge, skill, and integrity of the user. A hammer can be employed to build a crude kitchen table or a fine cabinet—or as a weapon of assault. Since psychological tests are measures of behavior, the interpretation of test results requires knowledge about human behavior. Psychological tests cannot be properly applied outside the context of psychological science. Familiarity with relevant behavioral research is needed not only by the test constructor but also by the test user.

An inevitable consequence of the expansion and growing complexity of any scientific endeavor is an increasing specialization of interests and functions among its practitioners. Such specialization is clearly apparent in the relationship of psychological testing to the mainstream of contemporary psychology (Anastasi, 1967). Specialists in psychometrics have raised techniques of test construction to truly impressive pinnacles of quality. While providing technically superior instruments, however, they have given relatively little attention to ensuring that test users had the psychological information needed for the proper use of such instruments. As a result, outdated interpretations of test performance all too often survived without reference to the results of pertinent behavioral research. This partial isolation of psychological testing from other fields of psychology—with its consequent misuses and misinterpretations of tests—accounts in part for the growing public discontent with psychological testing that began in the 1950s and rose to a strident crescendo in the late 1970s. The topics chosen for discussion in this chapter illustrate ways in which the findings of psychological research can contribute to the effective use of intelligence tests and help to correct popular misconceptions about the IQ and similar scores.

LONGITUDINAL STUDIES OF CHILDREN'S INTELLIGENCE

An important approach to the understanding of the construct, "intelligence," is through longitudinal studies of the same individuals over long periods of time. Although such investigations may be regarded as contributing to the long-term predictive validation of specific tests, they have broader implications for the nature of intelligence and the meaning of an IQ. When intelligence was believed to be largely an expression of hereditary potential, each individual's IQ was expected to remain very nearly constant throughout life. Any observed variation on retesting was attributed to weaknesses in the measuring instrument—either inadequate reliability or poor selection of functions tested. With increasing research on the nature of intelligence, however, has come the realization that intelligence itself is both complex and dynamic. In the following sections, we shall examine typical findings of longitudinal studies of intelligence and shall inquire into the conditions making for both stability and instability of the IQ.

STABILITY OF THE IQ. An extensive body of data has accumulated showing that, over the elementary, high school, and college period, intelligence test performance is quite stable (see Anastasi, 1958, pp. 232–238; McCall, Appelbaum, & Hogarty, 1973). In a Swedish study of a relatively unselected population, for example, Husén (1951) found a correlation of .72 between the test scores of 613 third-grade school boys and the scores obtained by the same persons 10 years later on their induction into military service. In a later Swedish study, Härnqvist (1968) reports a correlation of .78 between tests administered at 13 and 18 years of age to over 4,500 young men. Even preschool tests show remarkably high correlations with later retests. In a longitudinal study of 140 children conducted at Fels Research Institute (Sontag, Baker, & Nelson, 1958), Stanford-Binet scores obtained at 3 and at 4 years of age correlated .83. The correlation with the 3-year tests decreased as the interval between retests increased, but by age 12 it was still as high as .46. Of special relevance to the Stanford-Binet is the follow-up conducted by Bradway, Thompson, and Cravens (1958) on children originally tested between the ages of 2 and 5½ as part of the 1937 Stanford-Binet standardization sample. Initial IQs correlated .65 with 10-year retests and .59 with 25-year retests. The correlation between the 10-year retest (mean age = 14 years) and 25-year retest (mean age = 29 years) was .85.

As would be expected, retest correlations are higher, the shorter the interval between tests. With a constant interval between tests, moreover, retest correlations tend to be higher the older the children. The effects of age and retest interval on retest correlations exhibit considerable regularity and are themselves highly predictable (Thorndike, 1933, 1940). One explanation for the increasing stability of the IQ with age is provided by the cumulative nature of intellectual development. The individual's intellectual skills and knowledge at each age include all his or her earlier skills and knowedge plus an increment of new acquisitions. Even if the annual increments bear no relation to each other, a growing consistency of performance level would emerge, simply because earlier acquisitions constitute an increasing proportion of total skills and knowledge as age increases. Predictions of IQ from age 10 to 16 would thus be more accurate than from 3 to 9, because scores at 10 include over half of what is present at 16, while scores at 3 include a much smaller proportion of what is present at 9.

Anderson (1940) described this relationship between successive scores as the *overlap hypothesis*. He maintained that, "Since the growing individual does not lose what he already has, the constancy of the IQ is in large measure a matter of the part-whole or overlap relation" (p. 394). In support of this hypothesis, Anderson computed a set of correlations between initial and terminal "scores" obtained with shuffled cards and random numbers. These correlations, which depended solely on the extent of overlap between successive measures, agreed closely with empirical test-retest correlations in intelligence test scores found in three published longitudinal studies. In fact, the test scores tended to give somewhat *lower* correlations, a difference Anderson attributed to such factors as errors of measurement and change in test content with age.

Although the overlap hypothesis undoubtedly accounts for some of the increasing stability of the IQ in the developing individual, two additional conditions merit consideration. The first is the *environmental stability* characterizing the developmental years of most individuals. Children tend to remain in the same family, the same socioeconomic level, and the same cultural milieu as they grow up. They are not typically shifted at random from intellectually stimulating to intellectually retarding environments. Hence, whatever intellectual advantages or disadvantages they had at one stage in their development tend to persist in the interval between retests.

A second condition contributing to the general stability of the IQ pertains to the role of *prerequisite learning skills* on subsequent learning. Not only does the individual retain prior learning, but much of her or his prior learning provides tools for subsequent learning. Hence, the more progress a child has made in the acquisition of intellectual skills and knowledge at any one point in time, the better able he or she is to profit from subsequent learning experiences. The concept of readiness in education is an expression of this general principle. The sequential nature of learning is also implied in the previously discussed Piagetian approach to mental development, as well as in the various individualized instructional programs.

Applications of the same principle underlie Project Head Start and other compensatory educational programs for culturally disadvantaged preschool children (Bloom, Davis, & Hess, 1965; Gordon & Wilkerson, 1966; Sigel, 1973; Stanley, 1972, 1973; Zigler & Valentine, 1980). Insofar as children from disadvantaged backgrounds lack some of the essential prerequisites for effective school learning, they would only fall farther and farther behind in academic achievement as they progressed through the school grades. It should be added that learning prerequisites cover not only such intellectual skills as the acquisition of language and of quantitative concepts, but also attitudes, interests, motivation, problem-solving styles, reactions to frustration, self-concepts, and other personality characteristics.

The object of compensatory educational programs is to provide the learning prerequisites that will enable children to profit from subsequent schooling. In so doing, of course, these programs hope to disrupt the "stability" of IQs that would otherwise have remained low. Compensatory education programs provide one example of the interaction between initial score and treatment in the prediction of subsequent score, discussed in Chapter 7.

INSTABILITY OF THE IQ. Correlation studies on the stability of the IQ provide actuarial data, applicable to group predictions. For the reasons given above, IQs tend to be quite stable in this actuarial sense. Studies of individuals, on the other hand, reveal large upward or downward shifts in IQ.[1] Sharp rises or drops in IQ may occur as a result of major environmental changes in the child's life. Drastic changes in family structure or home conditions, adoption into a foster home, severe or prolonged illness, and therapeutic or remedial programs are examples of the type of events that may alter the child's subsequent intellectual development. Even children who remain in the same environment, however, may show large increases or decreases in IQ on retesting. These changes mean, of course, that the child is developing at a faster or a slower rate than that of the normative population on which the test was standardized. In general, children in culturally disadvantaged environments tend to lose and those in superior environments to gain in IQ with age. Investigations of the specific characteristics of these environments and of the children themselves are of both theoretical and practical interest.

Typical data on the magnitude of individual IQ changes are provided by the California Guidance Study. In an analysis of retest data from 222 cases in this study, Honzik, Macfarlane, and Allen (1948) reported individual IQ changes of as much as 50 points. Over the period from 6 to 18 years, when retest correlations are generally high, 59% of the children changed by 15 or more IQ points, 37% by 20 or more points, and 9% by 30 or more. Nor are most of these changes random or erratic in nature. On the contrary, children exhibit consistent upward or downward trends over several consecutive years; and these changes are related to environmental characteristics. In the California Guidance Study, detailed investigation of home conditions and parent-child relationships indicated that large upward or downward shifts

[1] See, e.g., Bayley (1955), Bayley and Schaefer (1964), Bradway (1945), Bradway and Robinson (1961), Honzik, Macfarlane, and Allen (1948), Kagan and Freeman (1963), Kagan, Sontag, Baker, and Nelson (1958), McCall, Appelbaum, and Hogarty (1973), Moriarty (1966), Rees and Palmer (1970), Sontag, Baker, and Nelson (1958), Wiener, Rider, and Oppel (1963). Pinneau (1961) prepared tables showing the median and range of individual IQ changes found in the Berkeley Growth Study for each age at test and retest from 1 month to 17 years.

in IQ were associated with the cultural milieu and emotional climate in which the child was reared. A further follow-up conducted when the participants had reached the age of 30 still found significant correlations between test scores and family milieu as assessed at the age of 21 months (Honzik, 1967). Parental concern with the child's educational achievement emerged as an important correlate of subsequent test performance, as did other variables reflecting parental concern with the child's general welfare.

In the previously mentioned follow-up of the 1937 Stanford-Binet standardization sample, Bradway (1945) selected for special study the 50 children showing the largest IQ changes from the preschool to the junior high school period. Results of home visits and interviews with parents again indicated that significant rises or drops in IQ over the 10-year period were related to various familial and home characteristics.

In a reanalysis of results obtained in five published longitudinal studies, including some of those cited directly in this chapter, Rees and Palmer (1970) found changes in IQ between 6 and 12 years to be significantly related to socioeconomic status as indicated by father's educational and occupational level. A similar relationship was observed by Härnqvist (1968) in his Swedish study. In their 10- and 25-year follow-ups of children who had taken the Stanford-Binet at preschool ages, Bradway and Robinson (1961) computed an index based on parents' education, father's occupation, and occupation of both grandfathers. Although they labeled this measure an ancestral index, rather than an index of socioeconomic status, their results are consistent with those of other investigators: the index yielded significant correlations of approximately .30 with IQs in both follow-ups. Several longitudinal studies have demonstrated a relation between amount and direction of change in intelligence test scores and amount of formal schooling that the examinees themselves had completed in the interval between test and retest (see Härnqvist, 1968). The score differences associated with schooling are larger than those associated with socioeconomic status of the family.

Some investigators have concentrated more specifically on the personality characteristics associated with intellectual acceleration and deceleration. At the Fels Research Institute, 140 children were included in an intensive longitudinal study extending from early infancy to adolescence and beyond (Kagan & Freeman, 1963; Kagan, Sontag, Baker, & Nelson, 1958; Sontag, Baker, & Nelson, 1958). Within this group, those children showing the largest gains and those showing the largest losses in IQ between the ages of 4½ and 6 were compared in a wide variety of personality and environmental measures; the same was done with those showing the largest IQ changes between 6 and 10. During the preschool years, emotional dependency on parents was the principal condition associated with IQ loss. During the school years, IQ gains were associated chiefly with high achievement drive, competitive striving, and curiosity about nature. Suggestive data were likewise obtained regarding the role of parental attitudes and child-rearing practices in the development of these traits.

A later analysis of the same sample, extending through age 17, focused principally on patterns of IQ change over time (McCall, Appelbaum, & Hogarty, 1973). Children exhibiting different patterns were compared with regard to child-rearing practices as assessed through periodic home visits. A typical finding is that the parents of children whose IQs showed a rising trend during the preschool years presented "an encouraging and rewarding atmosphere, but one with some structure and enforcement of policies" (McCall et al., 1973, p. 54). A major condition associated with rising IQs is described as accelerational attempt, or the extent to which "the parent deliberately trained the child in various mental and motor skills which were not yet essential" (p. 52).

Another approach to an understanding of IQ changes is illustrated by a longitudinal study of coping and defense mechanisms in children (Moriarty, 1966). These mechanisms pertain to contrasting personality styles in dealing with problems and frustrations. Coping mechanisms in general represent an objective, constructive, realistic approach; defense mechanisms are characterized by withdrawal, denial, rationalization, and distortion. In this study, 65 children were tested from two to four times between infancy and the early teens. On the basis of IQ changes, the children were classified into four categories: (a) relatively constant—40%; (b) accelerative spurts in one or more areas of functioning—25%; (c) slow, delayed, or inhibited development—9%; (d) erratic score changes, inconsistent performance in different functions, or progressive IQ decline—26%. Intensive case studies of the individual children in these four categories led Moriarty to hypothesize that characteristic differences in the child's reliance on coping or defense mechanisms constitute a major factor in the observed course of IQ over time.

Research on the factors associated with increases and decreases in IQ throws light on the conditions determining intellectual development in general. It also suggests that prediction of subsequent intellectual status can be improved if measures of the individual's emotional and motivational characteristics and of his or her environment are combined with initial test scores. From still another viewpoint, the findings of this type of research point the way to the kind of intervention programs that can effectively alter the course of intellectual development in the desired directions.

INTELLIGENCE IN EARLY CHILDHOOD

The assessment of intelligence at the two extremes of the age range presents special theoretical and interpretive problems. One of these problems pertains to the functions that should be tested. What constitutes intelligence for the infant and the preschool child? What constitutes intelligence for the older adult? The second problem is not entirely independent of the first. Unlike the schoolchild, the infant and preschooler have not been exposed to the standardized series of experiences represented by the school curriculum. In developing tests for the elementary, high school, and college levels, test constructors have a large fund of common experiential material from which they can draw test items. Prior to school entrance, on the other hand, the child's experiences are far less standardized, despite certain broad cultural uniformities in child-rearing practices. Under these conditions, both the construction of tests and the interpretation of test results are much more difficult. To some extent, the same difficulty is encountered in testing older adults, whose schooling was completed many years earlier and who have since been engaged in highly diversified activities. In this and the next section, we shall examine some of the implications of these problems for early childhood and adult testing, respectively.

PREDICTIVE VALIDITY OF INFANT AND PRESCHOOL TESTS. The conclusion that emerges from longitudinal studies is that preschool tests (especially when administered after the age of 2 years) have moderate validity in predicting subsequent intelligence test performance, but that infant tests have virtually none (Bayley, 1970; Lewis, 1973; McCall, Hogarty, & Hurlburt, 1972). Combining the results reported in eight studies, McCall and his associates computed the median correlations between tests administered during the first 30 months of life and childhood IQ obtained between 3 and 18 years (McCall et al., 1972). Their findings are reproduced in Table 25.

TABLE 25
Median Correlations between Infant Tests and Childhood IQ

(From McCall, Hogarty, & Hurlburt, 1972. Copyright 1972 by the American Psychological Association. Reprinted by permission.)

Childhood Age in Years (Retest)	Infant Age in Months (Initial Test)			
	1–6	7–12	13–18	19–30
8–18	.01	.20	.21	.49
5–7	.01	.06	.30	.41
3–4	.23	.33	.47	.54

Several trends are apparent in this table. First, tests given during the first year of life have little or no long-term predictive value. Second, infant tests show some validity in predicting IQ at preschool ages (3–4 years), but the correlations exhibit a sharp drop beyond that point, after children reach school age. Third, after the age of 18 months, validities are moderate and stable. When predictions are made from these ages, the correlations seem to be of the same order of magnitude regardless of the length of the retest interval.

The lack of long-term predictive validity of infant tests needs to be evaluated further with regard to other related findings. First, a number of clinicians have argued that infant tests *do* improve the prediction of subsequent development, but only if interpreted in the light of concomitant clinical observations (Donofrio, 1965; Escalona, 1950; Knobloch & Pasamanick, 1960). Predictions might also be improved by a consideration of developmental trends through repeated testing, a procedure originally proposed by Gesell with reference to his Developmental Schedules.

In the second place, several investigators have found that infant tests have much higher predictive validity within nonnormal, clinical populations than within normal populations. Significant validity coefficients in the .60s and .70s have been reported for children with initial IQs below 80, as well as for groups having known or suspected neurological abnormalities (Ireton, Thwing, & Gravem, 1970; Knobloch & Pasamanick, 1963, 1966, 1967; Werner, Honzik, & Smith, 1968). Infant tests appear to be most useful as aids in the diagnosis of defective development resulting from organic pathology of either hereditary or environmental origin. In the absence of organic pathology, the child's subsequent development is determined largely by the environment in which he or she is reared. This the test cannot be expected to predict. In fact, parental education and other characteristics of the home environment are better predictors of subsequent IQ than are infant test scores; and beyond 18 months, prediction is appreciably improved if test scores are combined with indices of familial socioeconomic status (Bayley, 1955; McCall et al., 1972; Pinneau, 1961; Werner, Honzik, & Smith, 1968).

NATURE OF EARLY CHILDHOOD INTELLIGENCE. Several investigators have concluded that, while lacking predictive validity for the general population, infant intelligence tests are valid indicators of the child's cognitive abilities at the time (Bayley, 1970; Stott & Ball, 1965; Thomas, 1970). According to this view, a major reason for the negligible correlations between infant tests and subsequent performance is to be found in the changing nature and composition of intelligence with age. Intelligence in infancy is qualitatively different from intelligence at school age; it consists of a different combination of abilities.

This approach is consistent with the concept of developmental tasks proposed by several psychologists in a variety of contexts (Erikson, 1950; Havighurst, 1953; Super et al., 1957). Educationally and vocationally, as well as in other aspects of human development, the individual encounters typical behavioral demands and problems at different life stages, from infancy to senescence. Although both the problems and the appropriate reactions vary somewhat among cultures and subcultures, modal requirements can be specified within a given cultural setting. Each life stage makes characteristic demands on the individual. Mastery of the developmental tasks of earlier stages influences the individual's handling of the behavioral demands of the next.

Within the more circumscribed area of cognitive development, Piagetian stages provide a framework for examining the changing nature of intelligence. McCall and his associates at the Fels Research Institute (McCall, 1976; McCall et al., 1972) have explored the interrelations of infant behavior in terms of such a Piagetian orientation. Through sophisticated statistical analyses involving intercorrelations of different skills within each age as well as correlations among the same and different skills across ages, these investigators looked for precursors of later development in infant behavior. Although the findings are presented as highly tentative and only suggestive, the authors describe the major component of infant intelligence at each six-month period during the first 2 years of life. These descriptions bear a rough resemblance to Piagetian developmental sequences. The main developmental trends at 6, 12, 18, and 24 months, respectively, are summarized as follows: (1) manipulation that produces contingent perceptual responses; (2) imitation of fine motor and social-vocal-verbal behavior; (3) verbal labeling and comprehension; (4) further verbal development, including fluent verbal production and grammatical maturity.

Apart from a wealth of provocative hypotheses, one conclusion that emerges clearly from the research of McCall and his co-workers is that the predominant behavior at different ages exhibits qualitative shifts, which represent orderly and reasonable transitions. The findings fail to support the conception of a "constant and pervasive" general intellectual ability (McCall et al., 1972, p. 746). The same conclusion was reached by Lewis (1973; 1976b) on the basis of both his own research and his survey of published studies. Lewis describes infant intelligence test performance as being neither stable nor unitary. Negligible correlations may be found over intervals even as short as three months; and correlations with performance on the same or different scales at the age of two years and beyond are usually insignificant. Moreover, there is little correlation among different scales administered at the same age. These results have been obtained with both standardized instruments such as the Bayley Scales of Infant Development and with ordinal scales of the Piagetian type (Gottfried & Brody, 1975; King & Seegmiller, 1973; Lewis, 1976a; Lewis & McGurk, 1972). In place of the traditional model of a "developmentally constant general intelligence," Lewis proposes an interactionist view, emphasizing both the role of experience in cognitive development and the specificity of intellectual skills.

IMPLICATIONS FOR INTERVENTION PROGRAMS. The late 1960s and early 1970s witnessed some disillusionment and considerable confusion regarding the purposes, methods, and effectiveness of compensatory preschool educational programs, such as Project Head Start (Payne, Mercer, Payne, & Davison, 1973). Designed principally to enhance the academic readiness of children from disadvantaged backgrounds, these programs differed widely in procedures and results. Most were crash projects, initiated with inadequate planning for either implementation or evaluation. Only a few could demonstrate substantial improvements in the children's performance—and such improvements were often limited and short-lived.

Against this background, the Office of Child Development of the U.S. Department of Health, Education, and Welfare sponsored a conference of a panel of experts to try to define "social competency" in early childhood (Anderson & Messick, 1974). The panel agreed that social competency includes more than the traditional concept of general intelligence. After working through a diversity of approaches and some thorny theoretical issues, the panel drew up a list of 29 components of social competency, which could serve as possible goals of early intervention programs. Including emotional, motivational, and attitudinal as well as cognitive variables, these components ranged from self-care and a differentiated self-concept to verbal and quantitative skills, creative thinking, and the enjoyment of humor, play, and fantasy. Assessment of these components requires not only a wide variety of tests but also other measurement techniques, such as ratings, records, and naturalistic observations. Few if any intervention programs could undertake to implement all the goals. But the selection of goals should be explicit and deliberate; and it should guide both intervention procedures and program evaluation.

The importance of evaluating the effectiveness of an intervention program in terms of the specific skills (cognitive or noncognitive) that the program was designed to improve is emphasized by Lewis (1973). In line with the previously cited specificity of behavioral development in early childhood, Lewis urges the measurement of specific skills rather than the use of an IQ or other broad developmental indices. Training in sensorimotor functions should not be expected to improve verbal skills; training in the development of object permanence should be assessed by a test of object permanence, and so forth. In addition, the content of the intervention program should be tailored to fit the needs of the individual child, with reference to the prior development attained in specific skills.

Sigel (1973) gives an incisive analysis of preschool programs against the background of current knowledge regarding both child development and educational techniques. In line with available knowledge about developmental processes, he, too, recommends the use of specific achievement tests to assess progress in the skills developed by the educational programs, instead of such global scores as IQs. He also emphasizes the importance of process, interrelation of changes in different functions, and patterns of development, as in the characteristic Piagetian approach. And he urges the reformulation of the goals of early childhood education in more realistic terms.

It should be added that evaluating the effectiveness of intervention programs is not simple; it calls for considerable methodological sophistication. Apart from questions of experimental design, statistical artifacts associated with the psychometric properties of the assessment instruments may yield spurious positive or negative results (Bejar, 1980). Differences in either the difficulty or the discriminative value of test items between treated and control groups, or between pretest and posttest performance of the same group, may lead to incorrect conclusions regarding the success or failure of the program. The use of tests developed and scored on the basis of item characteristic curve (ICC) techniques (Ch. 8) and individually tailored to the examinees (Ch. 11) avoids some of these difficulties.

The late 1970s witnessed a revival of interest in early childhood programs for the educationally disadvantaged, as well as some renewed optimism about their effectiveness (B. Brown, 1978; Consortium, 1978; Day & Parker, 1977; J. McV. Hunt, 1975; Peleg & Adler, 1977; Zigler & Valentine, 1980). Promising results were obtained in long-term follow-ups of children who had participated in a few relatively well-designed, high-quality intervention projects. The more recently initiated programs benefited from the rapidly growing data base in the educational technology of early childhood. Several focused on intensive training in the cognitive skills prerequisite for effective school learning. Parental involvement proved beneficial as a means of supplementing the preschool experiences at home and ensuring their continuation after the program terminates. Daycare and home tutoring programs directed at the infant level represent another promising approach.

PROBLEMS IN THE TESTING OF ADULT INTELLIGENCE

AGE DECREMENT. A distinctive feature introduced by the Wechsler scales for measuring adult intelligence (Ch. 9) was the use of a declining norm to compute deviation IQs. It will be recalled that raw scores on the WAIS subtests are first transmuted into standard scores with a mean of 10 and an SD of 3. These scaled scores are expressed in terms of a fixed reference group consisting of 500 persons between the ages of 20 and 34 years included in the standardization sample. The sum of the scaled scores on the 11 subtests is used in finding the deviation IQ in the appropriate age table. If we examine the sums of the scaled scores directly, however, we can compare the performance of different age groups in terms of a single, continuous scale. Figure 52 shows the means of these total scaled scores for the age levels included in the national standardization sample and for a more limited "old-age sample" of 475 persons aged 60 years and over (Doppelt & Wallace, 1955).

As can be seen in Figure 52, the scores reach a peak between the ages of 20 and 34 and then decline slowly until 60. A sharper rate of decline was found after 60 in the old-age sample. The deviation IQ is found by referring an individual's total scaled score to the norm for his or her own age group. Thus, if the examinee shows the same decline in performance with age as does the normative sample, his or her IQ should remain constant. Wechsler's original rationale for this procedure was that it is "normal" for a person's

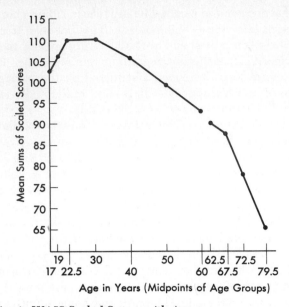

Fig. 52. Decline in WAIS Scaled Scores with Age.

(From Doppelt & Wallace, 1955, p. 323. Copyright 1955 by the American Psychological Association. Reprinted by permission.)

tested ability to decline with age beyond the 30s.

In the interpretation of the age decline illustrated in Figure 52, however, we must consider an essential feature of the samples employed in test standardization. Because every standardization sample is a *normative* sample, it should reflect existing population characteristics at each age level (Anastasi, 1956). It follows that, when the educational level of the general population has been rising over several decades, older groups at any one point in time will have received less education than have younger groups. This educational difference is clearly reflected in the standardization samples of both the WAIS (tested between 1953 and 1954) and the WAIS-R (tested between 1976 and 1980). In both samples, the maximum years of schooling are found in the 20- to 34-year levels, and educational level drops consistently in the older groups. Although the later, WAIS-R sample received much more education as a group than did the WAIS sample, the age decline in years of schooling is just as pronounced within the later as it is within the earlier standardization sample. And the corresponding age decline in WAIS-R scaled scores closely parallels that found with the earlier WAIS and illustrated in Figure 52.

Age differences in amount of education are inevitable if a test standardization sample is to be truly representative of the population of the country at the time the norms are established. Nevertheless, the educational differences complicate the interpretation of the observed score decrements. The older groups in the standardization sample may have performed more poorly on the test, not because they were growing old, but because they had received less education than the younger groups.

The results obtained with the standardization samples of the Wechsler scales are typical of the findings of all cross-sectional studies of adult intelligence. Cross-sectional comparisons, in which persons of different ages are examined at the same time, are likely to show an apparent age decrement because cultural changes are confounded with the effects of aging. Amount of formal education is only one of many variables in which age groups may differ. Other cultural changes have occurred in our society during the past half century which make the experiential backgrounds of 20-year-olds and 70-year-olds quite dissimilar. Certainly changes in communication media, such as radio and television, and in transportation facilities have greatly increased the range of information available to the developing individual. Improvements in nutrition and medical care would also indirectly influence behavior development.

Longitudinal studies, based on retests of the same persons over periods of 5 to 40 years, have generally revealed the opposite trend, the scores tending to improve with age. Several of these longitudinal investigations have been conducted with intellectually superior groups, such as college graduates or individuals initially chosen because of high IQs (Bayley & Oden, 1955; Burns, 1966; D. P. Campbell, 1965; Nisbet, 1957; Owens, 1953, 1966). For this reason, some writers have argued that the findings may be restricted to persons in the higher intellectual or educational levels and do not apply to the general population. However, similar results have been obtained in other longitudinal studies with normals (Charles & James, 1964; Eisdorfer, 1963; Tuddenham, Blumenkrantz, & Wilkin, 1968), as well as with mentally retarded adults outside of institutions (Baller, Charles, & Miller, 1967; Bell & Zubek, 1960; Charles, 1953).

Neither cross-sectional nor longitudinal studies alone can provide a conclusive interpretation of observed age changes. Several excellent analyses of the methodological difficulties inherent in each approach, together with the required experimental designs, have been published (Baltes, 1968; Buss, 1973; Goulet & Baltes, 1970; Nesselroade & Reese, 1973; Schaie, 1965). Basically, what is needed in order to tease out the effect of cultural changes is a combination of cross-sectional and longitudinal approaches. On the one hand, age differences in educational level may produce a spurious age decrement in test performance in cross-sectional studies. On the other hand, as individuals grow older, they are themselves exposed to cultural changes that may improve their performance on intelligence tests.

A few studies provide data that permit at least a partial analysis of the contributing factors. Owens (1966) in his 40-year retest of Iowa State University students and D. P. Campbell (1965) in his 25-year retest of University of Minnesota students also tested *present* freshmen in the respective colleges. Thus, multiple comparisons could be made between the performance of the two groups tested at the same age 25 or 40 years apart, and the performance of a single group tested before and after the same time intervals. In both studies, the initial group improved over its own earlier performance but performed about on a par with the younger group tested at the later date. Such findings suggest that it is cultural changes and other experiential factors, rather than age per se, that produce both the rises and declines in scores obtained with the more limited experimental designs.

A particularly well-designed study utilizing this combined approach was conducted on a more nearly representative sample of the adult population (Schaie & Strother, 1968). A specially selected battery of tests[2] was administered to a stratified-random sample of 500 persons. The population from which this sample was drawn consisted of approximately 18,000 members of a prepaid medical plan, whose membership was fairly representative of the census figures for a large metropolitan area. The sample included 25 men and 25 women at each five-year age interval from 20 to 70. Seven years later, all the original participants who could be located were contacted and 302 of them were given the same tests again. This subsample was shown to be closely comparable to the original group in age, sex ratio, and socioeconomic level.

The design of this study permits two types of comparisons: (1) a cross-sectional comparison among different age groups from 20 to 70 tested at the same time, and (2) a longitudinal comparison within the same individuals, initially tested at ages ranging from 20 to 70 and retested after seven years. The results of the cross-sectional comparisons showed significant intergeneration differences on all tests. In other words, those born and reared more recently performed better than those born and reared at an earlier time period. Longitudinal comparisons, on the other hand, showed a tendency for mean scores either to rise or remain unchanged when individuals were retested. The one major exception occurred in two highly speeded tests, in which performance was significantly poorer after the seven-year interval.

The contrast between the results of the cross-sectional and longitudinal approaches is illustrated in Figure 53, showing the trends obtained with four of the tests.[3] Similar results were found in a second seven-year retest of 161 of the original participants (Schaie & Labouvie-Vief, 1974). Further corroboration was provided by a still different approach involving the testing of three independent age-stratified samples drawn from the same population in 1956, 1963, and 1970 (Schaie, Labouvie, & Buech, 1973).[4]

In general, the results of the better-designed studies of adult intelligence

2 The SRA Primary Mental Abilities Test and Schaie's Test of Behavioral Rigidity.

3 These are the tests that most closely resemble intelligence tests in their content. Of these four tests, only Reasoning showed a barely significant ($p < .05$) relation to age in the longitudinal study. The magnitude of the decline, however, is much smaller than in the cross-sectional comparison.

4 For a bit of controversy regarding the theoretical interpretation of these results, see Horn and Donaldson (1976) and Baltes and Schaie (1976).

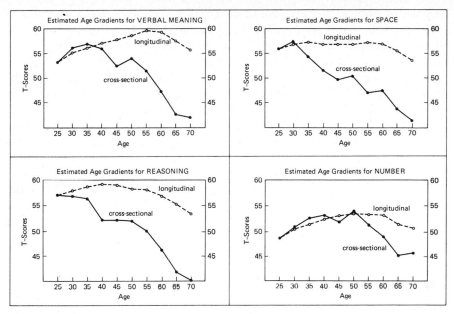

Fig. 53. Differences in Adult Intelligence as Assessed by Cross-Sectional and Longitudinal Analyses.

(From Schaie & Strother, 1968, pp. 675, 676. Copyright © 1968 by the American Psychological Association. Reprinted by permission.)

strongly suggest that the ability decrements formerly attributed to aging are predominantly intergeneration or intercohort differences, probably associated with cultural changes in our society. Genuine ability decrements are not likely to be manifested until well over the age of 60. Moreover, any generalization, whether pertaining to age decrement or cohort differences, must be qualified by a recognition of the wide individual variability found in all situations. Individual differences within any one age level are much greater than the average difference between age levels. As a result, the distributions of scores obtained by persons of different ages overlap extensively. This simply means that large numbers of older persons can be found whose performance equals that of younger persons. Moreover, the best performers within the older groups excel the poorest performers within the younger groups. Nor is such overlapping limited to adjacent age levels; the ranges of performance still overlap when extreme groups are compared. Thus some 80-year-olds will do better than some 20-year-olds.

What is even more relevant to the present topic, however, is that the *changes* that occur with aging vary with the individual. Thus, between the ages of 50 and 60, for example, some persons may show a decrease, some no appreciable change, and some an increase in test performance. The amount of change, whether it be a drop or a rise, will also vary widely among individuals. Moreover, intensive studies of persons of advanced age, extending into the seventh, eighth, and ninth decades of life, indicate that intellectual functioning in more closely related to the individual's health status than to chronological age (Birren, 1968; Palmore, 1970; Schaie & Gribbin, 1975).

NATURE OF ADULT INTELLIGENCE. Within the life span, intelligence testing has been oriented chiefly toward the schoolchild and the college student. At these levels, the test constructor can draw on the large common pool of experiences that have been organized into academic curricula. Most intelligence tests measure how well the individual has acquired the intellectual skills taught in our schools; and they can in turn predict how well he or she is prepared for the next level in the educational hierarchy. Tests for adults, including the Wechsler scales, draw largely on this identifiable common fund of experience. As the individual grows older and his or her own formal educational experiences recede farther into the past, this fund of common experience may become increasingly less appropriate to assess her or his intellectual functioning. Adult occupations are more diversified than childhood schooling. The cumulative experiences of adulthood may thus stimulate a differential development of abilities in different persons.

Because intelligence tests are closely linked to academic abilities, it is not surprising to find that longitudinal studies of adults show larger age increments in score among those individuals who have continued their education longer (D. P. Campbell, 1965; Härnqvist, 1968; Husén, 1951; Lorge, 1945; Owens, 1953). Similarly, persons whose occupations are more "academic" in content, calling into play verbal and numerical abilities, are likely to maintain their performance level or show improvement in intelligence test scores over the years, while those engaged in occupations emphasizing mechanical activities or interpersonal relations may show a loss. Some suggestive data in support of this hypothesis are reported by Williams (1960), who compared the performance of 100 persons, ranging in age from 65 to over 90, on a series of verbal and nonverbal tests. Rather striking correspondences were found between the individual's occupation and his or her relative performance on the two types of tasks. Longitudinal investigations of adults have also found suggestive relationships between total IQ changes and certain biographical inventory items (Charles & James, 1964; Owens, 1966).

Each time and place fosters the development of skills appropriate to its characteristic demands. Within the life span, these demands differ for the infant, the schoolchild, the adult in different occupations, and the retired septuagenarian (Baltes, Reese, & Lipsitt, 1980). An early demonstration of the implications of this fact for intelligence testing was provided by Demming and Pressey (1957). These investigators began with a task analysis of typical adult functions, conducted through informal surveys of reading matter and of reported daily activities and problems. On this basis, they prepared preliminary forms of some 20 tests "indigenous" to the older years. The tests emphasized practical information, judgment, and social perception. Results with three of these tests, administered together with standard verbal and nonverbal tests to samples of different ages, showed that the older persons excelled the younger on the new tests while the reverse relationship held for the traditional tests. All these types of research suggest that whether intelligence test scores rise or decline with increasing age in adulthood depends largely on what experiences the individual undergoes during those years and on the relationship between these experiences and the functions covered by the tests.

POPULATION CHANGES IN INTELLIGENCE TEST PERFORMANCE

RISING SCORES. What happens to the intelligence test performance of a population over long time periods? This is a question we have already encountered in several connections. In the preceding section, it was seen that, as the educational level of the adult population increased over the decades, mean intelligence test performance rose accordingly. As a result, the older members of the normative sample, who had completed less education on the average than had the younger members, scored lower on the test than did the younger. In Chapter 9, we found a similar phenomenon in the standardization sample of tests for children. In both the restandardization of the Stanford-Binet and the development of the WISC-R, the later standardization sample performed substantially better than the earlier sample. The result was that any one child would receive a lower IQ if tested with the revised edition than he or she would on the earlier edition, simply because his or her performance was evaluated against higher norms. The higher educational level of the parents of children tested in the later sample was one of the conditions mentioned for this rise in tested intelligence.

This type of comparison may be designated as the longitudinal study of populations. The usual application of the longitudinal method in psychological research involves the repeated testing of the same individuals over time. In the longitudinal study of populations, however, the population is sampled at different time periods. The comparison is between cohorts of persons born at different times but tested at the same ages. Several large-scale investigations conducted during the first five decades of the twentieth century revealed a rising intelligence in the population as measured by standardized intelligence tests (Anastasi, 1958, pp. 209–211). With increasing literacy, higher educational levels, and other cultural changes, it was evident that the mean tested intelligence of the general population of all ages showed a steady rise for several decades.

Various procedures have been employed in these comparative studies. One procedure is to administer the identical test after a lapse of time, as was done in surveys of 11-year-old Scottish children in 1932 and 1947 (Scottish Council, 1949). Another procedure is to give two tests to a representative sample of persons in order to establish the correspondence between the two sets of scores and thereby "translate" performance from one test to the other. This was done in a comparison of the performance of soldiers in the U.S. Army in World Wars I and II, who had been examined with the Army Alpha and the Army General Classification Test, respectively (Tudden- ham, 1948). A third and technically sounder approach is based on the es- tablishment of an absolute, sample-free score scale through the use of anchor items, as is done with the College Board tests. The application of latent trait theory and ICC technique (Chs. 4 and 7) represents a further refine- ment of this approach.

DECLINING SCORES. Whether the intelligence test scores of a given popula- tion rise, decline, or remain stable over time depends on many conditions. The *time period* covered, with its concomitant cultural changes, is clearly a prime factor. The *age* of the persons examined also makes a difference. For instance, a rising educational level of the population will directly affect the test performance of adults; but it will only indirectly influence children's performance, since the children in the samples compared have had the same amount of education when tested. Another important consideration, par- ticularly when examining a selected subpopulation, is any change in the *degree of selection* at different time periods. For example, if a larger propor- tion of the population attended high school in 1960 than in 1910, as was undoubtedly the case, then the 1910 high school students represent a more highly selected sample of the general population of their own time than do the 1960 high school students.

The number and complexity of conditions that may account for a popula- tion rise or decline in tested intelligence are well illustrated by an analysis of the highly publicized score decline on the College Board's Scholastic Apti- tude Test, or SAT (Wirtz, 1977). Between 1963 and 1977, the mean SAT Verbal score fell from 478 to 429, and the mean SAT Mathematical score fell from 502 to 470. In an effort to understand this steady 14-year score decline, a specially appointed panel commissioned 38 studies by experts in various areas and considered an impressive array of causal hypotheses.

A major conclusion reached by the panel was that the causal pattern var- ied from the first to the second half of the 14-year period. During the first 7 years, the score decline resulted predominantly from a compositional change in the group taking the SAT. Because of a continuing increase in the proportion of high school graduates going to college over this period, the sampling became progressively less selected in the cognitive skills meas- ured by the test. During the second 7 years, however, the college-going population had become stabilized, and sampling selection accounted for a much smaller portion of the score decline. For this period, the explanation had to be sought principally in conditions in the home, the school, and society at large. The panel observed that the available data do not permit a determination of the relative contribution of different cultural changes to the score decline. Among the many factors cited as probably significant, however, were a diminished emphasis on academic standards, grade inflation and automatic promotions, reduced homework assignment, increased school absenteeism, diminished attention to mastery of skills and knowledge, excessive TV watching, and the social upheavals of the period as well as other distractions in the lives of students.

It should be added that the score decline, while most thoroughly investigated with reference to the SAT, was not limited to this instrument. Not only did it occur in other college admission tests, such as those of the ACT program, but there is also evidence of a corresponding decline in test performance at the high school and elementary school levels. It is these score declines, coupled with observations of declining ability to apply basic verbal and quantitative skills in daily life, that aroused public concern in the late 1970s and early 1980s and created demands for minimum competency testing as a requirement for high school graduation. These broader educational and societal problems are clearly beyond the scope of this book. From the standpoint of good testing practice, what is relevant is the substantial influence of cultural conditions on the individual's performance on tests of academic intelligence or scholastic aptitude. The implications are twofold: (1) test norms require frequent updating, and (2) experiential variables should be taken into account in interpreting test scores.

PROBLEMS IN CROSS-CULTURAL TESTING

The use of tests with persons of diverse cultural backgrounds has already been considered from various angles in earlier parts of this book. Chapter 3 was concerned with the social and ethical implications of such testing, particularly with reference to minority groups within a broader national culture. Technical problems pertaining to test bias and to item-group interaction were analyzed in Chapters 7 and 8. And in Chapter 10 we examined typical tests designed for various transcultural applications. In this section, we shall present some basic theoretical issues about the role of culture in behavior, with special reference to the interpretation of intelligence test scores.

LEVELS OF CULTURAL DIFFERENTIALS. Cultural differences may operate in many ways to bring about group differences in behavior. The level at which cultural influences are manifested varies along a continuum extending from superficial and temporary effects to those that are basic, permanent, and far-reaching. From both a theoretical and a practical standpoint, it is important to inquire at what level of this continuum any observed behavioral difference falls. At one extreme, we find cultural differences that may affect only responses on a particular test and thus reduce its validity for certain groups. There are undoubtedly test items that have no diagnostic value when applied to persons from certain cultures because of lack of familiarity with specific objects or other relatively trivial experiential differences.

Most cultural factors that affect test responses, however, are also likely to influence the broader behavior domain that the test is designed to sample. In an English-speaking culture, for example, inadequate mastery of English may handicap a child not only on an intelligence test but also in schoolwork, contact with associates, play activities, and other situations of daily life. Such a condition would thus interfere with the child's subsequent intellectual and emotional development and would have practical implications that extend far beyond immediate test performance. At the same time, deficiencies of this sort can be remedied without much difficulty. Suitable language training *can* bring the individual up to an effective functioning level within a relatively short period.

The language an individual has been taught to speak was chosen in the above example because it provides an extreme and obvious illustration of several points: (1) it is clearly not a hereditary condition; (2) it can be altered; (3) it can seriously affect performance on a test administered in a different language; and (4) it will similarly affect the individual's educational, vocational, and social activities in a culture that uses an unfamiliar language. Many other examples can be cited from the middle range of the continuum of cultural differentials. Some are cognitive differentials, such as reading disability or ineffective strategies for solving abstract problems; others are attitudinal or motivational, such as lack of interest in intellectual activities, hostility toward authority figures, low achievement drive, or poor self-concept. All such conditions can be ameliorated by a variety of means, ranging from functional literacy training to personal counseling and psychotherapy. All are likely to affect both test performance and the daily life activities of the child and adult.

As we move along the continuum of cultural differentials, we must recognize that the longer an environmental condition has operated in the individual's lifetime, the more difficult it becomes to reverse its effects. Conditions that are environmentally determined are not necessarily remediable. Adverse experiential factors operating over many years may produce intellectual or emotional damage that can no longer be eliminated by the time intervention occurs. It is also important to bear in mind, however, that the permanence or irremediability of a psychological condition is no proof of hereditary origin.

An example of cultural differentials that may produce permanent effects on individual behavior is provided by research on complications of pregnancy and parturition (Knobloch & Pasamanick, 1966; Pasamanick & Knobloch, 1966). In a series of studies on large samples of blacks and whites, prenatal and perinatal disorders were found to be significantly related to mental retardation and behavior disorders in the offspring. An important source of such irregularities in the process of childbearing and birth is to be found in deficiencies of maternal nutrition and other conditions associated with low socioeconomic status. Analysis of the data revealed a much higher frequency of all such medical complications in lower than in higher socioeconomic levels, and a higher frequency among blacks than among whites. Here then is an example of cultural differentials producing organic disorders that in turn may lead to behavioral deficiencies. The effects of this type of cultural differential cannot be completely reversed within the lifetime of the individual; they require more than one generation for their elimination. Again, it needs to be emphasized, however, that such a situation does not imply hereditary defect, nor does it provide any justification for failure to improve the environmental conditions that brought it about.

CULTURAL DIFFERENCES AND CULTURAL HANDICAP. When psychologists began to develop instruments for cross-cultural testing in the first quarter of this century, they hoped it would be at least theoretically possible to measure "hereditary intellectual potential" independently of the impact of cultural experiences. The individual's behavior was thought to be overlaid with a sort of cultural veneer whose penetration became the objective of what were then called "culture-free" tests. Subsequent developments in genetics and psychology have demonstrated the fallacy of this concept. We now recognize that hereditary and environmental factors operate jointly at all stages in the organism's development and that their effects are inextricably intertwined in the resulting behavior. For humans, culture permeates nearly all environmental contacts. Since all behavior is thus affected by the cultural milieu in which the individual is reared and since psychological tests are but samples of behavior, cultural influences will and should be reflected in test performance. It is therefore futile to try to devise a test that is *free* from cultural influences. The present objective in cross-cultural testing is rather to construct tests that presuppose only experiences that are *common* to different cultures. For this reason, such terms as "culture-common," "culture-fair," and "cross-cultural" have replaced the earlier "culture-free" label.

No single test can be universally applicable or equally "fair" to all cultures. There are as many varieties of culture-fair tests as there are parameters in which cultures differ. A nonreading test may be culture-fair in one situation, a nonlanguage test in another, a performance test in a third, and a translated adaptation of a verbal test in a fourth. The varieties of available cross-cultural tests are not interchangeable but are useful in different types of cross-cultural comparisons.

It is unlikely, moreover, that any test can be equally "fair" to more than one cultural group, especially if the cultures are quite dissimilar. While reducing cultural differentials in test performance, cross-cultural tests cannot completely eliminate such differentials. Every test tends to favor persons from the culture in which it was developed. The mere use of paper and pencil or the presentation of abstract tasks having no immediate practical significance will favor some cultural groups and handicap others. Emotional and motivational factors likewise influence test performance. Among the many relevant conditions differing from culture to culture may be mentioned the intrinsic interest of the test content, rapport with the examiner, drive to do well on a test, desire to excel others, and past habits of solving problems individually or cooperatively. In testing children of low socioeconomic level, several investigators have found that the examinees rush through the test, marking answers almost at random and finishing before time is called (Eells et al., 1951). The same reaction has been observed among Puerto Rican schoolchildren tested in New York City and in Hawaii (Anastasi & Cordova, 1953; S. Smith, 1942). Such a reaction may reflect a combination of lack of interest in the relatively abstract test content and expectation of low achievement on tasks resembling school work. By hurrying through the test, the child shortens the period of discomfort.

Each culture and subculture encourages and fosters certain abilities and ways of behaving; and it discourages or suppresses others. It is therefore to be expected that, on tests developed within the majority American culture, for example, persons reared in that culture will generally excel. If a test were constructed by the same procedures within a culture differing markedly from ours, Americans would probably appear deficient in terms of test norms. Data bearing on this type of cultural comparison are meager. What evidence is available, however, suggests that persons from our culture may be just as handicapped on tests prepared within other cultures as members of those cultures are on our tests. A few examples of such reversals were cited in Chapter 10. Cultural differences become cultural handicaps when the individual moves out of the culture or subculture in which he or she was reared and endeavors to function, compete, or succeed within another culture. From a broader viewpoint, however, it is these very contacts and interchanges between cultures that stimulate the advancement of civilizations. Cultural isolation, while possibly more comfortable for individuals, leads to societal stagnation.

A related concept is that of cultural deprivation. Although this term has been used in many different senses, Feuerstein (1979, 1980) gives the concept a special meaning and makes it a focal point in his cognitive training program. He regards cultural deprivation as a state of reduced cognitive modifiability, produced by a lack of *mediated learning experience*. The transmission of the accumulated knowledge of the culture from one generation to the next is a distinctly human occurrence. In this process, the parent or other caregiver acts as a *mediating agent* in selecting and organizing the stimuli encountered by the child. Feuerstein considers such mediated learning essential for the child's cognitive development, insofar as it fosters the establishment of learning sets, orientations, and other behavior patterns that facilitate subsequent learning. Children who, for whatever reason, have failed to experience such mediated learning lack the prerequisites for high-level cognitive functioning. By contrast, those who have had mediated learning experiences within their own culture have developed the prerequisite skills and habits for continued modifiability, and they can adapt to the demands of a new culture after a relatively brief transition period.

LANGUAGE IN TRANSCULTURAL TESTING. Most cross-cultural tests utilize nonverbal content in the hope of obtaining a more nearly culture-fair measure of the same intellectual functions measured by verbal intelligence tests. Both assumptions underlying this approach are questionable. First, it cannot be assumed that nonverbal tests measure the same functions as verbal tests, however similar they may appear. A spatial analogies test is not merely a nonverbal version of a verbal analogies test. Some of the early nonlanguage tests, such as the Army Beta, were heavily loaded with spatial visualization and perceptual abilities, which are quite unrelated to verbal and numerical abilities. Even in tests like the Progressive Matrices and other nonlanguage tests deliberately designed to tap reasoning and abstract conceptualization, factorial analyses have revealed a large contribution of nonverbal factors to the variance of test scores (e.g., Das, 1963).

From a different angle, there is a growing body of evidence suggesting that nonlanguage tests may be more culturally loaded than language tests. Investigations with a wide variety of cultural groups in many countries have found larger group differences in performance and other nonverbal tests than in verbal tests (Anastasi, 1961; Irvine, 1969a, 1969b; Jensen, 1968; Ortar, 1963, 1972; Vernon, 1969). In a provocative analysis of the problem, Ortar (1963, pp. 232–233) wrote:

On the basis of our results it appears that, both from the practical point of view and on theoretical grounds, the verbal tests and items are better suited as intercultural measuring instruments than any other kind. They must, of course, be translated and adapted, but this adaptation is infinitely easier and more reliable than the well-nigh impossible task of "translating" and adapting a performance test. The "language" of performance is the cultural perception, but its "words" and grammar and syntax are not even completely understood, let alone organized in national entities. We do not know how to "translate" a picture into the representational language of a different culture, but we are thoroughly familiar with the technique and requirements of translating verbal contents. . . . A concept that is non-existent in a certain language simply cannot be translated into this language, a factor which acts as a safeguard against mechanical use of a given instrument when adapting it for a different culture.

Among the examples cited by Ortar is the observation that, when presented with a picture of a head from which the mouth was missing, Oriental immigrant children in Israel said the body was missing. Unfamiliar with the convention of considering the drawing of a head as a complete picture, these children regarded the absence of the body as more important than the omission of a mere detail like the mouth. The use of pictorial representation itself may be unsuitable in cultures unaccustomed to representative drawing. A two-dimensional reproduction of an object is not an exact replica of the original; it simply presents certain cues which, as a result of past experience, lead to the perception of the object. If the cues are highly reduced, as in a simplified or schematic drawing, and if the necessary past experience is absent, the correct perception may not follow. There is now a considerable body of empirical data indicating marked differences in the perception of pictures by persons in different cultures (Miller, 1973; Segall, Campbell, & Herskovits, 1966).

From still another angle, nonverbal, spatial-perceptual tests frequently require relatively abstract thinking processes and analytic cognitive styles characteristic of middle-class Western cultures (Berry, 1972; R. A. Cohen, 1969). Persons reared in other cultural contexts may be much less accustomed to such problem-solving approaches. Cultures differ in the value they place on generalization and on the search for common features in disparate experiences. In some cultures, behavior is typically linked to contexts and situations. The response to a question may depend on who asks the question and on what type of content is involved (Cole & Bruner, 1971; Goodnow, 1976; Neisser, 1976, 1979).

It should be added that nonverbal tests have fared no better in the testing of minority groups and persons of low socioeconomic status within the United States. On the WISC, for instance, black children usually find the Performance tests as difficult as the Verbal tests, or more difficult; this pattern is also characteristic of children from low socioeconomic levels (Caldwell & Smith, 1968; Cole & Hunter, 1971; Goffeney, Henderson, & Butler, 1971; Hughes & Lessler, 1965; Teahan & Drews, 1962). The same groups tend to do better on the Stanford-Binet than on either Raven's Progressive Matrices (Higgins & Sivers, 1958) or Cattell's Culture Fair Intelligence Test (Willard, 1968).

There is of course no procedural difficulty in administering a verbal test across cultures speaking a common language. When language differences necessitate a translation of the test, problems arise regarding the comparability of norms and the equivalence of scores. It should also be noted that a simple translation would rarely suffice. Some adaptation and revision of content is generally required. Of interest in this connection is the procedure developed in equating the scales of the CEEB Scholastic Aptitude Test (SAT) and the Prueba de Aptitud Académica (PAA)—a Spanish version of the SAT (Angoff & Modu, 1973). The PAA was developed for local use in Puerto Rico. With this objective in mind, an exploratory project in scale equating was undertaken. This project provides a demonstration of a method applicable to other situations requiring testing in multiple languages.

Essentially, the procedure consists of two steps. The first step is the selection of a common set of anchor items judged to be equally appropriate for both groups of students. These items are administered in English to the

English-speaking students and in Spanish to the Spanish-speaking students. The performance of these groups provides the data for measuring the difficulty level (Δ value) and discriminative power (r_{bis} with total test score) of each item. For the final set of anchor items, any items showing appreciable item-group interaction are discarded.[5] These would be the "biased" items that are likely to have a psychologically different meaning for the two groups. The final anchor items are those having approximately the same *relative* difficulty for the English-speaking and the Spanish-speaking samples, in addition to meeting the specifications for difficulty level and discriminative power.

The second step is to include these anchor items in a regular administration of the SAT and the PAA and to use the scores on the anchor items as a basis for converting all test scores to a single scale. This step involves the same equating procedure regularly followed in converting scores on successive forms of the SAT to a uniform scale.

NATURE OF INTELLIGENCE

MEANING OF AN IQ. For the general public, the IQ is not identified with a particular type of score on a particular test, but is often a shorthand designation for intelligence. So prevalent has this usage become, that it cannot be merely ignored or deplored as a popular misconception. To be sure, when considering the numerical value of a given IQ, we should always specify the test from which it was derived. Different intelligence tests that yield an IQ do in fact differ in content and in other ways that affect the interpretation of their scores. Some of these differences among tests sharing the common label of "intelligence test" were apparent in the examples considered in the preceding chapters. Nonetheless, there is a need to reexamine the general connotations of the construct "intelligence," as symbolized by the IQ. It might be added that the prevalent conception of intelligence has been shaped to a considerable degree by the characteristics of the Stanford-Binet scale, which for many years provided the only instrument for the intensive measurement of intelligence and which was often used as a criterion for validating new tests.

First, intelligence should be regarded as a descriptive rather than an explanatory concept. An IQ is an expression of an individual's ability level at a given point in time, in relation to the age norms. No intelligence test can indicate the reasons for one's performance. To attribute inadequate performance on a test or in everyday-life activities to "inadequate intelligence" is a tautology and in no way advances our understanding of the individual's handicap. In fact, it may serve to halt efforts to explore the causes of the handicap in the individual's history.

---

5 The more refined ICC procedures described in Chapter 8 may be employed in identifying such items, but the experimental design would be the same.

Intelligence tests, as well as any other kind of tests, should be used not to label individuals but to help in understanding them (Hobbs, 1975a, 1975b). To bring persons to their maximum functioning level we need to start where they are at the time; we need to assess their strengths and weaknesses and plan accordingly. If a reading test indicates that a child is retarded in reading, we do not label the child as a nonreader and stop; nor do we administer a nonverbal test to conceal the handicap. Instead we concentrate on teaching the child to read.

An important goal of contemporary testing, moreover, is to contribute to self-understanding and personal development. The information provided by tests is being used increasingly to assist individuals in educational and career planning and in making decisions about their own lives. The attention being given to effective ways of communicating test results to the individual attests to the growing recognition of this application of testing.

A second major point to bear in mind is that intelligence is not a single, unitary ability, but a composite of several functions. The term is commonly used to cover that combination of abilities required for survival and advancement within a particular culture. It follows that the specific abilities included in this composite, as well as their relative weights, vary with time and place. In different cultures and at different historical periods within the same culture, the qualifications for successful achievement differ. The changing composition of intelligence can also be recognized within the life of the individual, from infancy to adulthood. One's relative ability tends to increase with age in those functions whose value is emphasized by one's culture or subculture; and one's relative ability tends to decrease in those functions whose value is deemphasized.

Typical intelligence tests designed for use with school-age children or adults measure largely verbal abilities; to a lesser degree, they also cover abilities to deal with numerical and other abstract symbols. These are the abilities that predominate in school learning. Most intelligence tests can therefore be regarded as measures of scholastic aptitude or academic intelligence. The IQ is both a reflection of prior educational achievement and a predictor of subsequent educational performance. Because the functions taught in the educational system are of basic importance in modern, technologically advanced cultures, the score on a test of academic intelligence is also an effective predictor of performance in many occupations and other activities of daily life.

It should be noted, of course, that there are many important psychological functions that intelligence tests have never undertaken to measure. Mechanical, motor, musical, and artistic aptitudes are obvious examples. Motivational, emotional, and attitudinal variables are important determiners of achievement in all areas. Creativity research is identifying both cognitive and personality variables that are associated with creative productivity. All this implies, of course, that both individual and institutional decisions should be based on as much relevant data as can reasonably be gathered. To base decisions on tests alone, and especially on one or two tests alone, is clearly a misuse of tests. Decisions must be made by persons. Tests represent one source of data utilized in making decisions; they are not themselves decision-making instruments.

Much of our information about what intelligence tests measure comes from practical studies of the validity of the tests in predicting educational and vocational achievement. At a more theoretical level, the late 1970s and early 1980s witnessed a strong upsurge of interest in the construct of intelligence, as measured by intelligence tests (Humphreys, 1979; Resnick, 1976; Sternberg, 1977, 1979; Sternberg & Detterman, 1979). Efforts to understand what intelligence tests measure have included not only the standard statistical procedures of construct validation, such as factor analysis, but also the application of information-processing techniques to the tasks presented in intelligence tests (see Ch. 6). The latter approach focuses on the elementary processes whereby an examinee arrives at the answer to a test question, rather than considering only the correctness of the answer. This type of analysis should contribute substantially to the diagnostic use of tests and to the development of training programs to meet specific individual needs (Estes, 1974; Pellegrino & Glaser, 1979; Sternberg, 1979; Sternberg & Weil, 1980).

HERITABILITY AND MODIFIABILITY. Much confusion and controversy have resulted from the application of heritability estimates to intelligence test scores. A well-known example is an article by Jensen (1969), which engendered great furor and led to many heated arguments. Although there are several aspects to this controversy and the issues are complicated, a major substantive source of controversy pertains to the interpretation of heritability estimates. Specifically, a heritability index shows the proportional contribution of genetic or hereditary factors to the total variance of a particular trait in a given population under existing conditions. For example, the statement that the heritability of Stanford-Binet IQ among urban American high school students is .70 would mean that 70% of the variance found in these scores is attributable to hereditary differences and 30% is attributable to environment.

Heritability indexes have been computed by various formulas (see, e.g., Jensen, 1969; Loehlin, Lindzey, & Spuhler, 1975), but their basic data are measures of familial resemblance in the trait under consideration. A frequent procedure is to utilize intelligence test correlations of monozygotic (identical) and dizygotic (fraternal) twins. Correlations between monozygotic twins reared together and between monozygotic twins reared apart in foster homes have also been used.

Several points should be noted in interpreting heritability estimates. First, the empirical data on familial resemblances are subject to some distortion because of the unassessed contributions of environmental factors. For instance, there is evidence that monozygotic twins share a more closely similar environment than do dizygotic twins (Anastasi, 1958, pp. 287–288; Koch, 1966). Another difficulty is that twin pairs reared apart are not assigned at random to different foster homes, as they would be in an ideal experiment; it is well known that foster home placements are selective with regard to characteristics of the child and the foster family. Hence, the foster home environments of the twins within each pair are likely to show sufficient resemblance to account for some of the correlation between their test scores. There is also evidence that twin data regarding heritability may not be generalizable to the population at large because of the greater susceptibility of twins to prenatal trauma leading to severe mental retardation. The inclusion of such severely retarded cases in a sample may greatly increase the twin correlation in intelligence test scores (Nichols & Broman, 1974).

Apart from questionable data, heritability indexes have other intrinsic limitations (see, Anastasi, 1971; Hebb, 1970). It is noteworthy that in the early part of the previously cited article, Jensen (1969, pp. 33–46) clearly listed these limitations among others. First, the concept of heritability is applicable to populations, not individuals. For example, in trying to establish the etiology of a particular child's mental retardation, the heritability index would be of no help. Regardless of the size of the heritability index in the population, the child's mental retardation could have resulted from a defective gene, as in phenylketonuria (PKU), from prenatal brain damage, or from extreme experiential deprivation.

Second, heritability indexes refer to the population on which they were found at the time. Any change in either hereditary or environmental conditions would alter the heritability index. For instance, an increase in inbreeding, as on an isolated island, would reduce the variance attributable to heredity and hence lower the heritability index; increasing environmental homogeneity, on the other hand, would reduce the variance attributable to environment and hence raise the heritability index. Furthermore, a heritability index computed within one population is not applicable to an analysis of the differences in test performance between two populations, such as different ethnic groups.

Third, heritability does not indicate the degree of modifiability of a trait. Even if the heritability index of a trait in a given population is 100%, it does not follow that the contribution of environment to that trait is unimportant. An extreme example may help to clarify the point. Suppose in a hypothetical adult community everyone has the identical diet. All receive the same food in identical quantities. In this population, the contribution of food to the total variance of health and physical condition would be zero, since food variance accounts for none of the individual differences in health and physique. Nevertheless, if the food supply were suddenly cut off, the entire community would die of starvation. Conversely, improving the quality of the diet could well result in a general rise in the health of the community.

Regardless of the magnitude of heritability indexes found for IQs in various populations, one empirical fact is well established: the IQ is not fixed and unchanging; and it is amenable to modification by environmental interventions. Some evidence for this conclusion was examined earlier in this chapter, in connection with longitudinal studies. There has been some progress in identifying characteristics of accelerating and decelerating environments. Rises and drops in IQ may also result from both fortuitous environmental changes occurring in a child's life and planned environmental interventions. Major changes in family structure, sharp rises or drops in family income level, or adoption into a foster home may produce conspicuous increases or decreases in IQ.

Research on the effects of planned interventions at the infant and preschool levels was cited in an earlier section of this chapter. There is a growing body of evidence demonstrating the effectiveness of such interventions at later life stages. Although on a smaller scale than those directed at the preschool level, programs for school-age children have yielded encouraging results (Bloom, 1976; Jacobs & Vandeventer, 1971; Olton & Crutchfield, 1969; Resnick & Glaser, 1976). Some investigators have focused on still older age levels, working with college and professional school students; and they, too, report significant improvement in both academic achievement and scholastic aptitude test performance (Bloom & Broder, 1950; Whimbey, 1975, 1977, 1980). Research on elderly persons has also yielded evidence of learning and transfer effects following training interventions (Willis, Blieszner, & Baltes, 1981). Still other investigators have concentrated on educable mentally retarded children and adolescents, again with significant improvements (Babad & Budoff, 1974; Budoff & Corman, 1974; Feuerstein, 1980; Hamilton & Budoff, 1974; Rand, Tannenbaum, & Feuerstein, 1979).[6]

These programs provide training in widely applicable cognitive skills, problem-solving strategies, and efficient learning habits. Of special interest is the emphasis on self-monitoring or autocriticism as a condition for effective performance (Flavell, 1979; Owings, Petersen, Bransford, Morris, & Stein, 1980; Whimbey, 1975). The evaluation of one's own performance and the recognition of what one understands and what one does not understand represent an important first step toward improving performance. All too often, the unsuccessful learner is unable to differentiate between true understanding and inaccurate or superficial understanding. There is evidence that children with learning disabilities are especially deficient in autocriticism and in monitoring their own cognition (Kotsonis & Patterson, 1980).

Other examples of the type of cognitive skills taught in these intellectual development programs were cited in Chapter 2. In that chapter, such training in widely applicable intellectual skills was contrasted with narrowly limited coaching on test items. As was observed in that connection, a crucial question to investigate in evaluating intellectual development programs is

---

[6] Several of these investigators have also been exploring the use of the child's responsiveness to brief training interventions as part of a comprehensive assessment program (see Lidz, 1981, Ch. 3).

the extent of transfer or generalizability of the effects of training beyond the types of content and settings in which the training occurred. A related question pertains to the durability of the improvement. A further consideration is the time required by the older child or the adult to accumulate the content knowledge that is also a part of intelligence and contributes to the person's readiness to learn more advanced material. Although the older person, armed with efficient learning techniques, can build up this content store more quickly than he or she would have as a child, it is unrealistic to expect this to occur during a short training program. The older the person, the larger the knowledge gap to be filled. Failure to recognize this point may lead to disappointment and weaken confidence in the efficacy of all such training programs.

MOTIVATION AND INTELLIGENCE. Although it is customary and convenient to classify tests into separate categories, it should be recognized that all such distinctions are superficial. In interpreting test scores, personality and aptitudes cannot be kept apart. An individual's performance on an aptitude test, as well as his or her performance in school, on the job, or in any other context, is influenced by his or her achievement drive, persistence, value system, freedom from handicapping emotional problems, and other characteristics traditionally classified under the heading of "personality."

There is an increasing recognition of the role of students' motivation in school learning (Bloom, 1976, Ch. 4; Nichols, 1979). The individual's interests, attitudes, and self-concept as a school learner influence his or her openness to a learning task, the desire to learn it well, the attention given to the teacher, and the time actively devoted to the task. And there is evidence that these individual reactions are significantly related to educational achievement.

Even more important is the cumulative effect of personality characteristics on the direction and extent of the individual's intellectual development. Some of the evidence for this effect, collected through longitudinal studies of children and adults, was summarized earlier in this chapter. Other investigations on groups ranging from preschool children to college students have been surveyed by Dreger (1968). Although some of the research on young children utilized a longitudinal approach, data from older persons were gathered almost exclusively through concurrent correlations of personality test scores with intelligence test scores and indices of academic achievement. The data assembled by Dreger indicate the importance of considering appropriate personality variables as an aid in understanding an individual's intelligence test performance and in predicting her or his academic achievement.

It would thus seem that prediction of a child's subsequent intellectual development could be improved by combining information about the child's emotional and motivational characteristics with his or her scores on ability tests. A word should be added, however, regarding the assessment of "motivation." In the practical evaluation of schoolchildren, college students, job applicants, and other categories of persons, psychologists are often asked for a measure of the individual's "motivation." When thus worded, this is a meaningless request, since motivation is specific. What is needed is an indication of the individual's value system and the intensity with which he or she will strive toward specific goals. The strength of these specific motives will interact with situational factors, as well as with aptitudes, to determine the individual's actual performance in given situations.

The relation between personality and intellect is reciprocal. Not only do personality characteristics affect intellectual development, but intellectual level also affects personality development. Suggestive data in support of this relation are provided in a study by Plant and Minium (1967). Drawing upon the data gathered in five available longitudinal investigations of college-bound young adults, the authors selected the upper and lower 25% of each sample in terms of intelligence test scores. These contrasted groups were then compared on a series of personality tests that had been administered to one or more of the samples. The personality tests include measures of attitudes, values, motivation, and interpersonal and other noncognitive traits. The results of this analysis revealed a strong tendency for the high-aptitude groups to undergo substantially more "psychologically positive" personality changes than did the low-aptitude groups.

The success an individual attains in the development and use of his or her aptitudes is bound to influence that person's emotional adjustment, interpersonal relations, and self-concept. In the self-concept, we can see most clearly the mutual influence of aptitudes and personality traits. The child's achievement in school, on the playground, and in other situations helps to shape her or his self-concept; and this self-concept at any given stage influences her or his subsequent performance, in a continuing spiral. In this regard, the self-concept operates as a sort of private self-fulfilling prophecy.

On the basis of 25 years of research on achievement motivation, J. W. Atkinson (1974) and his co-workers formulated a comprehensive schema representing the interrelationships of abilities, motivation, and environmental variables. The approach is dynamic in that it implies systematic change rather than constancy in the individual's lifetime. It also incorporates the reciprocal effects of aptitudes and motivational variables; and it emphasizes the contribution of motivational variance to test performance. To illustrate the application of this conceptual schema, computer simulations were employed, showing how ability and motivation can jointly influence both intelligence test performance and cumulative achievement. Some supporting empirical data are also cited regarding the high school grade-point average of boys as predicted from earlier intelligence test scores and a measure of achievement motivation (Atkinson & Birch, 1978, Ch. 4; Atkinson, O'Malley & Lens, 1976).

A diagram of Atkinson's conceptual schema is reproduced in Figure 54.

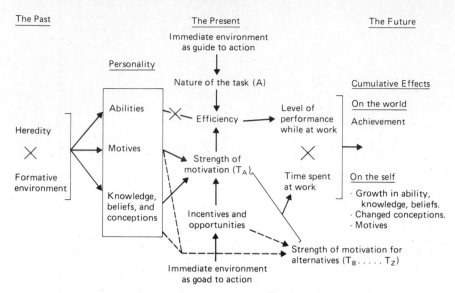

FIG. 54. Schema Illustrating Interaction of Cognitive and Noncognitive Factors in Cumulative Achievement and Individual Development.

(From Atkinson, O'Malley, & Lens, 1976. Copyright © 1976 by Academic Press. Reproduced by permission.)

Beginning at the left, this figure shows the combined operation of heredity and past formative environment in the development of both cognitive and noncognitive aspects of the total personality. The present environment provides the immediate task and contributes to motivational strength for this task relative to the competing motivational strengths of alternative actions. Motivation affects both the efficiency with which the task is performed and the time spent on it (e.g., studying, carrying out a job-related activity). Efficiency reflects the relationship between nature of task and current motivation. Level of performance results from the individual's relevant abilities (e.g., as assessed by test scores) and the efficiency with which he or she applies those abilities to the current task. The final achievement or product shows the combined effects of level of performance while at work and time spent at work. Another and highly important consequent of level of performance × time spent at work is the lasting cumulative effects of this activity or experience on the individual's own cognitive and noncognitive development. This last step represents a feedback loop to the individual's personality, whose effects are likely to be reflected in his or her future test scores. Many implications of this approach for the interpretation of test scores are spelled out in the original sources cited above, which should be examined for further details. The schema provides a promising orientation for the more effective utilization of tests and for the better understanding of the conditions underlying human achievement.

PART FOUR

Tests of Separate Abilities

Chapter 13

Measuring Multiple Aptitudes

RADITIONAL intelligence tests were designed primarily to yield a single, global measure of the individual's general level of cognitive development, such as an IQ. Both practical and theoretical developments, however, soon drew attention to certain differentiable aptitudes within the loose conglomerate represented by early intelligence tests. These developments led to the construction of separate tests for the measurement of a few widely applicable aptitudes. At the same time, they led to a refined definition and a fuller understanding of what the intelligence tests themselves measured.

A number of events contributed to the growing interest in the measurement of different aptitudes. First, there was an increasing recognition of intraindividual variation in performance on intelligence tests. Crude attempts to compare the individual's relative standing on different subtests or item groups antedated the development of multiple aptitude batteries by many years. Intelligence tests, however, were not designed for this purpose. The subtests or item groups were often too unreliable to justify intraindividual comparisons. In the construction of intelligence tests, moreover, items or subtests are generally chosen to provide a unitary and internally consistent measure. In such a selection, an effort is therefore made to minimize, rather than maximize, intraindividual variation. Subtests or items that correlate very low with the rest of the scale would, in general, be excluded. Yet these are the very parts that would probably have been retained if the emphasis had been on the differentiation of abilities. Because of the way in which intelligence tests are constructed, it is unlikely that performance on these tests can be significantly differentiated into more than two categories, such as verbal and nonverbal, or linguistic and quantitative.

The development of multiple aptitude batteries was further stimulated by the gradual realization that so-called general intelligence tests are in fact less general than was originally supposed. It soon became apparent that many such tests were primarily measures of verbal comprehension. Certain areas, such as that of mechanical abilities, were usually untouched, except in some of the performance and nonlanguage scales. As these limitations of intelligence tests became evident, psychologists began to qualify the term "intelligence." Distinctions between "academic" and "practical" intelligence were suggested by some. Others spoke of "abstract," "mechanical," and "social" intelligence. Tests of "special aptitudes" were likewise constructed, to supplement the intelligence tests. But closer analysis showed that the intelligence tests themselves could be said to measure a certain combination of special aptitudes, such as verbal and numerical abilities.

A strong impetus to differential aptitude testing was also provided by the growing activities of psychologists in career counseling, as well as in the selection and classification of industrial and military personnel. The early development of specialized tests in clerical, mechanical, and other vocational areas is a reflection of such interests. The assembling of test batteries for the selection of applicants for admission to schools of medicine, law, engineering, dentistry, and other professional fields represents a similar development which has been in progress for many years. Moreover, a number of differential aptitude batteries, such as those prepared by the armed services and by the United States Employment Service, were the direct result of occupational selection or classification work.

Finally, the application of factor analysis to the study of trait organization provided the theoretical basis for the construction of multiple aptitude batteries. Through factor-analytic techniques, the different abilities loosely grouped under "intelligence" could be more systematically identified, sorted, and defined. Tests could then be selected so that each represented the best available measure of one of the traits or factors identified by factor analysis.

FACTOR ANALYSIS

THE FACTOR MATRIX. The principal object of factor analysis is to simplify the description of data by reducing the number of necessary variables, or dimensions. Thus, if we find that five factors are sufficient to account for all the common variance in a battery of 20 tests, we can for most purposes substitute 5 scores for the original 20 without sacrificing any essential information. The usual practice is to retain from among the original tests those providing the best measures of each of the factors.

All techniques of factor analysis begin with a complete table of intercorrelations among a set of tests. Such a table is known as a correlation matrix. Every factor analysis ends with a factor matrix, i.e., a table showing the weight or loading of each of the factors in each test. A hypothetical factor matrix involving only two factors is shown in Table 26. The factors are listed across the top and their weights in each of the 10 tests are given in the appropriate rows.

Several different methods for analyzing a set of variables into common factors have been derived. As early as 1901, Pearson (1901) pointed the way for this type of analysis; and Spearman (1904, 1927) developed a

TABLE 26
A Hypothetical Factor Matrix

Test	Factor I	Factor II
1. Vocabulary	.74	.54
2. Analogies	.64	.39
3. Sentence Completion	.68	.43
4. Disarranged Sentences	.32	.23
5. Reading Comprehension	.70	.50
6. Addition	.22	−.51
7. Multiplication	.40	−.50
8. Arithmetic Problems	.52	−.48
9. Equation Relations	.43	−.37
10. Number Series Completion	.32	−.25

precursor of modern factor analysis. Kelley (1935) and Thurstone (1947b) in America and Burt (1941) in England did much to advance the method. Alternative procedures, modifications, and refinements have been developed by many others. The availability of high-speed computers is leading to the adoption of more refined and laborious techniques. Although differing in their initial postulates, most of these methods yield similar results.[1] For simple introductions to the specific procedures of factor analysis, the reader is referred to Kim and Mueller (1978a, 1978b) and Gorsuch (1974). A comprehensive and much more advanced treatment can be found in Harman (1976).

It is beyond the scope of this book to cover the mathematical basis or the computational procedures of factor analysis. An understanding of the results of factor analysis, however, need not be limited to those who have mastered its specialized methodology. Even without knowing how the factor loadings were computed, it is possible to see how a factor matrix is utilized in the identification and interpretation of factors. For an intelligent reading of reports of factor-analytic research, however, familiarity with a few other concepts and terms is helpful.

THE REFERENCE AXES. It is customary to represent factors geometrically as reference axes in terms of which each test can be plotted. Figure 55 illustrates this procedure. In this graph, each of the 10 tests from Table 26 has been plotted against the two factors, which correspond to axes I and II.

---

[1] The factor matrix shown in Table 26 is typical of those obtained with the centroid method, which was widely used prior to the advent of high-speed computers. Though crude, this method yields results that closely approximate those of the more refined and currently popular method of principal axes.

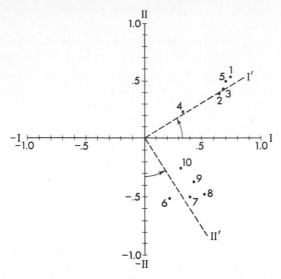

FIG. 55. A Hypothetical Factor Pattern, Showing Weights of Two Group Factors in Each of Ten Tests.

Thus, the point representing Test 1 is located by moving .74 of the distance along axis I and .54 of the distance along axis II. The points corresponding to the remaining 9 tests are plotted in the same way, using the weights given in Table 26. Although all the weights on Factor I are positive, it will be noted that on Factor II some of the weights are positive and some negative. This can also be seen in Figure 55, where Tests 1 to 5 cluster in one part of the graph and Tests 6 to 10 in another.

In this connection it should be noted that the position of the reference axes is not fixed by the data. The original correlation table determines only the position of the tests (points in Figure 55) *in relation to each other.* The same points can be plotted with the reference axes in any position. For this reason, factor analysts usually rotate axes until they obtain the most satisfactory and easily interpretable pattern. This is a legitimate procedure, somewhat analogous to measuring longitude from, let us say, Chicago rather than Greenwich.

The reference axes in Figure 55 were rotated to positions I' and II', shown by the broken lines.[2] This rotation was carried out in accordance with Thurstone's criteria of *positive manifold* and *simple structure.* The former requires the rotation of axes to such a position as to eliminate all significant negative weights. Most psychologists regard negative factor loadings as inapplicable to aptitude tests, since such a loading implies that the higher

[2] The reader may feel that rotated axis II' should have been labeled −II', to correspond to the unrotated axis −II. Which pole of the axis is labeled plus and which minus, however, is an arbitrary matter. In the present example, the rotated axis II' has been "reflected" in order to eliminate negative weights.

the individual rates in the particular factor, the poorer will be his or her performance on the test. The criterion of simple structure means that each test shall have loadings on as few factors as possible. Both of these criteria are designed to yield factors that can be most readily and unambiguously interpreted. If a test has a high loading on a single factor and no significant loading on any other, we can learn something about the nature of the factor by examining the content of the test. If instead the test has moderate to low loadings on six factors, it can tell us little about the nature of any of these factors.

It will be seen that on the rotated axes in Figure 55 all the verbal tests (Tests 1 to 5) fall along or very close to axis I'. Similarly, the numerical tests (Tests 6 to 10) cluster closely around axis II'. The new factor loadings, measured along the rotated axes, are given in Table 27. The reader may easily verify these factor loadings by preparing a paper "ruler" with a scale of units corresponding to that in Figure 55. With this ruler, distances can be measured along the rotated axes. The factor loadings in Table 27 include no negative values except for very low, negligible amounts attributable to sampling errors. All of the verbal tests have high loadings on Factor I' and practically zero loadings on Factor II'. The numerical tests, on the other hand, have high loadings on Factor II' and low, negligible loadings on Factor I'. The identification and naming of the two factors and the description of the factorial composition of each test have thus been simplified by the rotation of reference axes. In actual practice, the number of factors is often greater than two—a condition that complicates the geometrical representation and the statistical analysis, but does not alter the basic procedure. The fact that factor patterns are rarely as clear-cut as the one illustrated in Figure 55 adds further to the difficulty of rotating axes and of identifying factors.

TABLE 27
Rotated Factor Matrix

(Data from Figure 55)

Test	Factor I'	Factor II'
1. Vocabulary	.91	−.06
2. Analogies	.75	.02
3. Sentence Completion	.80	.00
4. Disarranged Sentences	.39	−.02
5. Reading Comprehension	.86	−.04
6. Addition	−.09	.55
7. Multiplication	.07	.64
8. Arithmetic Problems	.18	.68
9. Equation Relations	.16	.54
10. Number Series Completion	.13	.38

Some factor analysts use a theoretical model as a guide in the rotation of axes. Invariance, or the corroboration of the same factors in independent but comparable investigations, is also taken into account. The rotated patterns resulting from such procedures usually exhibit simple structure (Guilford & Hoepfner, 1971).

INTERPRETATION OF FACTORS. Once the rotated factor matrix has been computed, we can proceed with the interpretation and naming of factors. This step calls for psychological insight rather than statistical training. To learn the nature of a particular factor, we simply examine the tests having high loadings on that factor and we try to discover what psychological processes they have in common. The more tests there are with high loadings on a given factor, the more clearly we can define the nature of the factor. In Table 27, for example, it is apparent that Factor I′ is verbal and Factor II′ is numerical.

The factor loadings given in Table 27 also represent the correlation of each test with the factor.[3] It will be recalled that this correlation is the factorial validity of the test (Ch. 6). From Table 27 we can say, for instance, that the factorial validity of the Vocabulary test as a measure of the verbal factor is .91. The factorial validity of the Addition test, in terms of the numerical factor, is .55. Obviously, the first five tests have negligible validity as measures of the numerical factor, and the last five have practically no validity as measures of the verbal factor. The concept of factorial validity is especially relevant to the type of tests to be discussed in this chapter.

FACTORIAL COMPOSITION OF A TEST. One of the basic theorems of factor analysis states that the total variance of a test is the sum of the variances contributed by the common factors (shared with other tests) and the specific factors (occurring in that test alone), plus the error variance. We have already encountered error variance in the analysis of test scores (Ch. 5). If, for instance, the reliability coefficient of a test is .83, we conclude that 17% of the variance of scores on this test is error variance $(1.00 - .83 = .17)$. Through factor analysis, we can further subdivide the sources of variance contributing toward performance on any test.

Let us consider the two tests listed in Table 28. For each test, we have its factor loading in Verbal (V), Numerical (N), and Reasoning (R) factors, as well as its reliability coefficient. Since each factor loading also represents the correlation between the test and the factor, the square of the factor loading gives us the proportion of common variance between the test and

---

[3] This is true only when an orthogonal rotation of axes is applied. With oblique rotation, to be defined in a later section of this chapter, factor loadings and factor correlations bear a simple relation to each other and each can be found from the other by appropriate computations.

TABLE 28
Source of Variance of Test Scores

Test	Common Factor Loadings			Reliability Coefficient	Proportional Contribution				
	V	N	R		V	N	R	Specific	Error
1. Arithmetic Reasoning	.40	.55	.60	.90	.16	.30	.36	.08	.10
2. Multiplication	.10	.70	.30	.85	.01	.49	.09	.26	.15

that factor. In the last section of the table, each factor loading has been squared to show the proportional contribution of that factor to the total variance of test scores. Thus, we find that in the Arithmetic Reasoning test 16% of the variance is attributable to the Verbal factor, 30% to the Numerical factor, and 36% to the Reasoning factor. The error variance in the last column is found by simply subtracting the reliability coefficient from the total variance $(1.00 - .90 = .10)$. Whatever is left represents the specificity of this test, i.e., that portion of its "true" variance it does not share with any other test with which it was factor analyzed. For the Arithmetic Reasoning test, we have:

$$.16 + .30 + .36 + .10 = .92$$
$$1.00 - .92 = .08$$

Figure 56 provides a pictorial breakdown of the sources of variance for the two tests of Table 28.

Any individual's performance on these two tests depends on the amounts of each of the relevant abilities or factors he or she possesses, as well as the relative weights of these factors in the particular test. Thus, if we had the

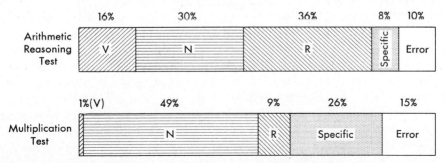

FIG. 56. Percentage of Common, Specific, and Error Variance in Two Hypothetical Tests.

(Data from Table 28.)

individual's score in the V, N, and R factors, expressed in the same units, we could weight each score by multiplying it by the corresponding factor loading. The sum of these products would provide an estimate of the individual's score on the test. The smaller the contribution of specific and error factors to the test, the more accurate would this estimate be.

In the example given in Table 28, if an individual rates very high in V, this would help her or him much more on the Arithmetic Reasoning than on the Multiplication test. In fact, it would help four times as much, since the weight of the V factor is four times as great in Arithmetic Reasoning as in Multiplication (.40 *vs.* .10). Of the three common factors, N would have the greatest effect on Multiplication (loading = .70) and R would have the greatest effect on Arithmetic Reasoning (loading = .60).

FACTOR LOADINGS AND CORRELATION. A second basic theorem of factor analysis concerns the relationship between factor loadings and the correlations among variables. The correlation between any two variables is equal to the sum of the cross-products of their common-factor loadings. Since specific and error factors are unique to each variable, they cannot contribute to the correlation between variables. The correlation between any two variables depends only on the factors that these two variables share. The larger the weights of these common factors in the two variables, the higher will be the correlation between the variables. The correlation between the two tests given in Table 28 can be found by multiplying the loadings of each of the three common factors in the two tests and adding the products, as shown below:

$$r_{12} = (.40)(.10) + (.55)(.70) + (.60)(.30) = .60$$

OBLIQUE AXES AND SECOND-ORDER FACTORS. The axes employed in Figure 55 are known as *orthogonal axes,* since they are at right angles to each other. Occasionally, the test clusters are so situated that a better fit can be obtained with *oblique axes.* In such a case, the factors would themselves be correlated. Some investigators have maintained that orthogonal, or uncorrelated, factors should always be employed, since they provide a simpler and clearer picture of trait relationships. Others insist that oblique axes should be used when they fit the data better, since the most meaningful categories need not be uncorrelated. An example cited by Thurstone is that of height and weight. Although it is well known that height and weight are highly correlated, they have proved to be useful categories in the measurement of physique.

When the factors are themselves correlated, it is possible to subject the intercorrelations among the factors to the same statistical analysis we employ with intercorrelations among tests. In other words, we can "factorize the factors" and derive *second-order factors.* This process has been followed in a number of studies with both aptitude and personality variables. Certain investigations with aptitude tests have yielded a single second-order general factor. As a rule, American factor analysts have proceeded by accounting for as much of the common variance as possible through group factors and then identifying a general factor as a second-order factor if the data justified it. British psychologists, on the other hand, usually begin with a general factor, to which they attribute the major portion of the common variance, and then resort to group factors to account for any remaining correlation. These procedural differences reflect differences in theoretical orientation to be discussed in the following section.

THEORIES OF TRAIT ORGANIZATION

THE TWO-FACTOR THEORY. The first theory of trait organization based on a statistical analysis of test scores was the two-factor theory developed by the British psychologist Charles Spearman (1904, 1927). In its original formulation, this theory maintained that all intellectual activities share a single common factor, called the *general factor*, or *g*. In addition, the theory postulated numerous *specifics*, or *s* factors, each being strictly specific to a single activity. Positive correlation between any two functions was thus attributed to the *g* factor. The more highly the two functions were "saturated" with *g*, the higher would be the correlation between them. The presence of specifics, on the other hand, tended to lower the correlation between functions.

Although two types of factors, general and specific, are posited by this theory, it is only the single factor *g* that accounts for correlation. In contrast to other theories of trait relations, therefore, it could be more precisely characterized as a single-factor theory, although the original designation has persisted. Figure 57 illustrates the basis for correlation among tests according to this theory. In this illustration, tests 1 and 2 would correlate highly with each other since each is highly saturated with *g*, as shown by the shaded areas. The white area in each test represents specific and error variance.

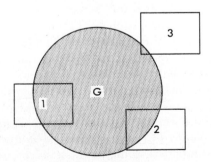

FIG. 57. Correlation Model Underlying Two-Factor Theory.

Test 3 would have low correlations with each of the other two tests, since it contains very little g.

It follows from the two-factor theory that the aim of psychological testing should be to measure the amount of each individual's g. If this factor runs through all abilities, it furnishes the only basis for prediction of the individual's performance from one situation to another. It would be futile to measure specific factors, since each by definition operates in only a single activity. Accordingly, Spearman proposed that a single test, highly saturated with g, be substituted for the heterogeneous collection of items found in intelligence tests. He suggested that tests dealing with abstract relations are probably the best measures of g and could be used for this purpose. Examples of tests constructed as measures of g include Raven's Progressive Matrices and Cattell's Culture Fair Intelligence Test, both discussed in Chapter 10.

From the outset, Spearman realized that the two-factor theory must be qualified. When the activities compared are very similar, a certain degree of correlation may result over and above that attributable to the g factor. Thus, in addition to general and specific factors, there might be another, intermediate class of factors, not so universal as g nor so strictly specific as the s factors. Such a factor, common to a group of activities but not to all, was designated as a *group factor*. In the early formulation of his theory. Spearman admitted the possibility of very narrow and negligibly small group factors. Following later investigations by several of his students, he included much broader group factors such as arithmetic, mechanical, and linguistic abilities.

MULTIPLE-FACTOR THEORIES. The prevalent contemporary American view of trait organization recognizes a number of moderately broad group factors, each of which may enter with different weights into different tests. For example, a verbal factor may have a large weight in a vocabulary test, a smaller weight in a verbal analogies test, and a still smaller weight in an arithmetic reasoning test. Figure 58 illustrates the intercorrelations among five tests in terms of a multiple-factor model. The correlations of Tests 1, 2, and 3 with each other result from their common loadings with the verbal factor (V). Similarly, the correlation between Tests 3 and 5 results from the Spatial factor (S), and that between Tests 4 and 5 from the Number factor (N). Tests 3 and 5 are factorially complex, each having appreciable loadings in more than one factor: V and S in Test 3, N and S in Test 5. From the second basic theorem of factor analysis, discussed in the preceding section, we can also tell something about the relative magnitude of the intercorrelations. For example, Test 3 will correlate higher with Test 5 than with Test 2 because the weights of the S factor in Tests 3 and 5 (represented by the overlapping areas) are larger than the weights of the V factor in Tests 2 and 3.

The publication of Kelley's *Crossroads in the Mind of Man* (1928) paved the way for a large number of studies in quest of particular group factors. Chief among the factors proposed by Kelley were manipulation of spatial

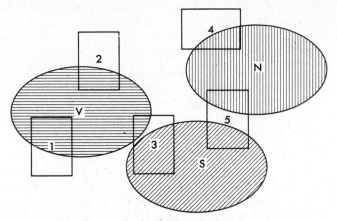

Fig. 58. Correlation Model Underlying Multiple-Factor Theories.

relationships, facility with numbers, facility with verbal material, memory, and speed. This list has been modified and extended by subsequent investigators employing the more modern methods of factor analysis discussed in the preceding section.

One of the leading exponents of multiple-factor theory was Thurstone. On the basis of extensive research by himself and his students, Thurstone proposed about a dozen group factors which he designated as "primary mental abilities." Those most frequently corroborated in the work of Thurstone and of other independent investigators (French, 1951; Harman, 1975; Thurstone, 1938; Thurstone & Thurstone, 1941) include the following:

V. *Verbal Comprehension:* The principal factor in such tests as reading comprehension, verbal analogies, disarranged sentences, verbal reasoning, and proverb matching. It is most adequately measured by vocabulary tests.

W. *Word Fluency:* Found in such tests as anagrams, rhyming, or naming words in a given category (e.g., boys' names, words beginning with the letter T).

N. *Number:* Most closely identified with speed and accuracy of simple arithmetic computation.

S. *Space:* This factor may represent two distinct factors, one covering perception of fixed spatial or geometric relations, the other manipulatory visualizations, in which changed positions or transformations must be visualized (McGee, 1979).

M. *Associative Memory:* Found principally in tests demanding rote memory for paired associates. There is some evidence to suggest that this factor may reflect the extent to which memory crutches are utilized (Christal, 1958). The evidence is against the presence of a broader factor through all memory tests. Other restricted memory factors, such as memory for temporal sequences and for spatial position, have been suggested by some investigations.

P. *Perceptual Speed:* Quick and accurate grasping of visual details, similarities, and differences. This factor may be the same as the speed factor identified by Kelley and other early investigators. This is one of several factors subsequently identified in perceptual tasks (Thurstone, 1944).

I. (or R). *Induction* (or *General Reasoning*): The identification of this factor was least clear. Thurstone originally proposed an inductive and a deductive factor. The latter was best measured by tests of syllogistic reasoning and the former by tests requiring the subject to find a rule, as in a number series completion test. Evidence for the deductive factor, however, was much weaker than for the inductive. Moreover, other investigators suggested a general reasoning factor, best measured by arithmetic reasoning tests.

It should be noted that the distinction between general, group, and specific factors is not so basic as may at first appear. If the number or variety of tests in a battery is small, a single general factor may account for all the correlations among them. But when the same tests are included in a larger battery with a more heterogeneous collection of tests, the original general factor may emerge as a group factor, common to some but not all tests. Similarly, a certain factor may be represented by only one test in the original battery, but may be shared by several tests in the larger battery. Such a factor would have been identified as a specific in the original battery, but would become a group factor in the more comprehensive battery. In the light of these considerations, it is not surprising to find that intensive factorial investigations of special areas have yielded many factors in place of the one or two primary mental abilities originally identified in each area. Such has been the case in studies of verbal, perceptual, memory, and reasoning tests.

Factorial research seems to have produced a bewildering multiplication of factors. The number of cognitive factors reported to date by different investigators is well over 100. A certain amount of order has been achieved by cross-identification of factors reported by different investigators and often given different names (French, 1951; Harman, 1975). Such cross-identification can be accomplished when there are several tests common to the investigations being compared. To facilitate this process, a group of factor analysts assembled a kit of "reference tests" measuring the principal aptitude factors so far identified. This kit, which is distributed by Educational Testing Service (Ekstrom, French, & Harman, 1976; *ETS*, 1976), makes it easier for different investigators planning factorial research to include some common tests in their batteries. The kit covers 23 cognitive factors, each represented by at least three tests.

It is apparent that even after these efforts at simplification and coordination, the number of factors remains large. Human behavior is varied and complex, and perhaps it is unrealistic to expect a dozen or so factors to provide an adequate description of it. For specific purposes, however, we can choose appropriate factors with regard to both nature and breadth. For example, if we are selecting applicants for a difficult and highly specialized mechanical job, we would probably want to measure fairly narrow perceptual and spatial factors that closely match the job requirements. In selecting college students, on the other hand, a few broad factors such as verbal comprehension, numerical facility, and general reasoning would be most relevant. Illustrations of the different ways in which factorial results have been utilized in test development will be given later in this chapter.

STRUCTURE-OF-INTELLECT MODEL. Some factor analysts have tried to simplify the picture of trait relationships by organizing the traits into a systematic schema. On the basis of more than two decades of factor-analytic research, Guilford (1967; Guilford & Hoepfner, 1971) has proposed a boxlike model which he calls the structure-of-intellect model (SI). Illustrated in Figure 59, this model classifies intellectual traits along three dimensions:

Operations—what the respondent does. These include cognition, memory, divergent production (prominent in creative activity), convergent production, and evaluation.

Contents—the nature of the materials or information on which operations are performed. These include figural, symbolic (e.g., letters, numbers), semantic (e.g., words), and behavioral (information about other persons' behavior, attitudes, needs, etc.).

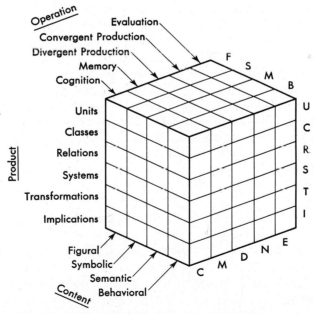

FIG. 59. Three-Dimensional Model of the Structure of Intellect.

(From Guilford, 1967, p. 63. Copyright © 1967 by McGraw-Hill. Reproduced by permission.)

Products—the form in which information is processed by the respondent. Products are classified into units, classes, relations, systems, transformations, and implications.

Since this classification includes $5 \times 4 \times 6$ categories, there are 120 cells in the model. In each cell, at least one factor or ability is expected; some cells may contain more than one factor. Each factor is described in terms of all three dimensions. Figure 59 gives both the names and letter symbols for each dimension. The code used by Guilford and his associates in describing each factor specifies Operation, Content, and Product, in that order. The well-known factor of verbal comprehension, for example, corresponds to cognition of semantic units (CMU) and is best measured by vocabulary tests. A memory span test utilizing series of unrelated letters or numbers assesses memory for symbolic units (MSU). Upon the completion of the Aptitudes Research Project—a 20-year coordinated program of research on the SI model—Guilford and his associates had identified 98 of the anticipated factors (Guilford & Hoepfner, 1971). The remaining unfilled cells provide a plan for further research. An alphabetical list and brief description of the many tests developed in the course of this 20-year project can be found in the book by Guilford and Hoepfner (1971, Appendix B).[4] It may also be noted that Meeker (1969) has applied the SI categories in classifying the items of the Stanford-Binet and Wechsler scales.

It should be borne in mind that the SI model, like all models of trait organization, provides one schema for representing the obtained correlations among variables. Its factors and dimensions do not correspond to basic or immutable entities. With regard to the SI model in particular, it has been demonstrated that, because of the method employed in the rotation of axes, the empirical corroboration of this model does not preclude other models (J. B. Carroll, 1972; Horn & Knapp, 1973). Essentially, the procedure was to write a target matrix to conform to the theoretical model and then rotate axes in each empirical factor matrix so as to approximate as closely as possible the solution specified in the target matrix. Different rotations of the same data could be found to fit other models equally closely.

HIERARCHICAL THEORIES.   An alternative schema for the organization of factors has been proposed by a number of British psychologists, including Burt (1949) and Vernon (1961), and by Humphreys (1962) in America. A diagram illustrating Vernon's application of this system is reproduced in Figure 60. At the top of the hierarchy, Vernon places Spearman's g factor. At the next level are two broad group factors, corresponding to verbal-educational (v:ed) and to practical-mechanical (k:m) aptitudes. These major factors may be further subdivided. The verbal-educational factor,

---

[4] About 30 of these tests have thus far been published and can be purchased by qualified persons from Sheridan Psychological Services.

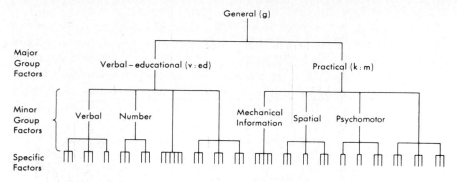

Fɪɢ. 60. Model of a Hierarchical Organization of Abilities.

(Adapted from Vernon, 1961, p. 22. Copyright © 1960, Methuen & Co., Ltd. Reproduced by permission.)

for example, yields verbal and numerical subfactors, among others. Similarly, the practical-mechanical factor splits into such subfactors as mechanical-information, spatial, and psychomotor abilities. Still narrower subfactors can be identified by further analysis, let us say, of the verbal tasks. At the lowest level of the hierarchy are the specific factors. Such a hierarchical structure thus resembles an inverted genealogical tree, with *g* at the top, *s* factors at the bottom, and progressively narrower group factors in between.

In a later elaboration of the model, Vernon (1969) included certain more complex interrelations and cross-contributions of factors at the third level, especially in connection with educational and vocational achievement. For example, scientific and technical abilities are linked to both spatial abilities and mechanical information; mathematical abilities are linked to both spatial and number abilities, as well as more directly to the *g* factor through an induction factor.

Humphreys (1962, 1970) also recommends a hierarchical model as a means of coping with the proliferation of factors. Rather than considering the first-order, narrower factors as primary, he suggests that each test constructor or user choose that level of the hierarchy that is most appropriate for her or his purposes. Humphreys recognizes, however, that a single test may be classified into more than one hierarchy, with reference to content, method, and other facets. To measure any one facet, he proposes that the test be made *heterogeneous* with regard to all other facets. For example, if we are interested in the person's ability to solve analogies problems, we should use a test that includes verbal, numerical, pictorial, and spatial analogies. If we wish to measure verbal ability, we should do so with a variety of item types, such as vocabulary, analogies, and series completion. This procedure contrasts with that followed by Guilford, who seeks separate factors (and tests) for each homogeneous cell in his three-way classification.

NATURE AND DEVELOPMENT OF FACTORS. That different investigators may arrive at dissimilar models of trait organization becomes less perplexing when we recognize that the traits identified through factor analysis are simply an expression of correlation among behavior measures. They are not underlying entities or causal factors, but descriptive categories. Hence, it is conceivable that different principles of classification may be applicable to the same data.

The concept of factors as descriptive categories was explicit in the writings of Thomson (1916, 1948), Burt (1941, 1944), and Vernon (1960) in England, and those of R. C. Tryon (1935) in America. All these writers called attention to the vast multiplicity of behavioral elements, which may become organized into clusters through either hereditary or experiential linkages. For example, persons in our culture are likely to develop a broad verbal-educational factor running through all activities learned in school. A narrower factor of numerical aptitude may result from the fact that all arithmetic processes are taught together by the same teacher in the same classroom. Hence, the child who is discouraged, antagonized, or bored during the arithmetic period will tend to fall behind in learning *all* these processes; the one who is stimulated and gratified in the arithmetic class will tend to learn well all that is taught in that class period and to develop attitudes that will advance his or her subsequent numerical learning.

There has been an increasing recognition of the role of experiential conditions in the formation of group factors. It is not only the level of performance in different abilities but also the way in which performance is organized into distinct traits that is influenced by experiential background. Differences in factor patterns have been found to be associated with different cultures or subcultures, socioeconomic levels, and types of school curricula (see Anastasi, 1970). Changes in factor patterns over time are also relevant. These include long-term changes—which may reflect the cumulative effect of everyday-life experiences—as well as short-term changes resulting from practice and other experimentally controlled learning experiences (Fleishman, 1972; Khan, 1970, 1972; Reinert, 1970). Research on animals has also yielded suggestive evidence regarding the experimental production of factors by the control of early experiences (Whimbey & Denenberg, 1966).

The factorial composition of the same objective task may differ among individuals with diverse experiential backgrounds. One reason for these individual differences may be found in the use of different methods to carry out the same task. Individuals with highly developed verbal abilities, for example, will tend to utilize verbal mediators to solve a mechanical or spatial problem; those whose experiences have been predominantly mechanical, on the other hand, will tend to follow a perceptual or spatial approach in solving the same problem. Relevant evidence was provided by French (1965), who found that the factorial composition of the same tests differed between groups of persons classified according to their typical problem-solving styles. Suggestive evidence can also be found in a study by C. H. Frederiksen (1969) on the cognitive strategies subjects use in memorizing words. In the course of learning, individuals may change their choice of strategy and thereby alter the factorial composition of the task as performed by them. Similar shifts in aptitude requirements have been shown to occur over longer periods of time in the course of instruction (Burns, 1980).

A mechanism for the emergence of factors is provided by the familiar concepts of learning set and transfer of training (J. B. Carroll, 1966; Ferguson, 1954, 1956; Whiteman, 1964). The establishment of learning sets enables the individual to learn more efficiently when presented with a new problem of the same kind. In Harlow's (1949, 1960) classic experiments with monkeys, after the animal had solved problems requiring the differentiation between certain shapes (like triangle and circle), it learned to discriminate between *other* shapes much more rapidly than did animals without such prior experience. The animal had established a learning set for differentiating shapes; it knew what to look for when faced with a new problem. The animal had thus "learned how to learn" this type of problem.

Similarly, many of the skills developed through formal schooling, such as reading and arithmetic computation, are applicable to a wide variety of subsequent learning situations. Efficient and systematic problem-solving techniques can likewise be applied to the solution of new problems. Individual differences in the extent to which these skills have been acquired will be reflected in the performance of a large number of different tasks; and in a factor analysis of these tasks, these widely applicable skills would emerge as broad group factors. The breadth of the transfer effect, or the variety of tasks to which a skill is applicable, would thus determine the breadth of the resulting group factor.

In summary, the factors or abilities identified through factor analysis are descriptive categories, reflecting the changing interrelationships of performance in a variety of situations. These factors are not static entities but are themselves the product of the individual's cumulative experiential history. Insofar as the interrelationships of experiences vary among individuals and groups, different factor patterns may be expected among them. As the individual's experiences change—through formal education, occupational functions, and other continuing activities—new traits may become differentiated or previously existing traits may merge into broader composites.

MULTIPLE APTITUDE BATTERIES

BATTERIES FOR GENERAL USE. One of the major effects of factor analysis on test construction can be seen in the development of multiple aptitude batteries. These batteries yield a profile of test scores in a set of relatively independent abilities identified through factor-analytic research. The Chicago Tests of Primary Mental Abilities (PMA) represent the first systematic effort to construct such a battery. Originally published in 1941, this battery was the direct outcome of Thurstone's previously described factor-analytic investigations. For each factor, Thurstone selected those tests with the highest validities. This battery, designed principally for the high school and college levels, required six testing sessions.

Later versions of the PMA tests, published by Science Research Associates, were characterized chiefly by reduction in length and extension to younger age levels. These tests were marred by a number of technical deficiencies, which have been fully discussed in a series of reviews in the *Mental Measurements Yearbooks,* as well as in other critical surveys (e.g., Super, 1958). The chief criticisms pertained to inadequacies of normative data, questionable types of scores (such as ratio IQs), unsupported interpretations of scores in terms of educational and vocational criteria, meager validity data, improper procedures for computing the reliability of speeded tests, excessive dependence of scores on speed, and low reliabilities of certain factor scores.

While several of these deficiencies were corrected in later editions, the PMA tests still fall short of the technical standards set by other contemporary instruments of the same type. The original Thurstone tests were based on extensive factor-analytic research and represented an important breakthrough in test construction. The expectations aroused by the initial experimental test series, however, were not realized in the commercially published batteries. As one reviewer expressed it:

While the history of PMA as a test has been one of steady decline, the history of primary mental abilities as a paradigm has been one of steady growth. The undergirding conceptual framework of PMA provided a common paradigm which not only generated competing multifactor instruments but also structured the "normal science" within which such tests are still being viewed and used. (Schutz, 1972, p. 1067)

One of the most widely used multiple aptitude batteries is the Differential Aptitude Tests (DAT). First published in 1947, the DAT was revised in 1962 and in 1972. This battery was designed principally for use in the educational and vocational counseling of students in Grades 8 to 12. Although not utilizing factor analysis in its construction, the authors of the DAT were guided in their choice of tests by the accumulated results of factorial research, as well as by practical counseling needs. Rather than striving for factorial purity, they included tests that might be factorially complex if they represented well-recognized vocational or educational areas. The DAT yields the following eight scores: Verbal Reasoning, Numerical Ability, Abstract Reasoning, Clerical Speed and Accuracy, Mechanical Reasoning, Space Relations, Spelling, and Language Usage. A sample item from each test is reproduced·in Figures 61A and 61B. The complete battery is available in two equivalent forms, S and T.

` The DAT manual provides a full account of the test-construction procedures followed in developing the battery. Norms were derived from over 64,000 students in 76 public and parochial school systems distributed over 33 states and the District of Columbia. The standardization sample was selected by a two-stage sampling procedure so as to be representative of the entire student population of the United States in Grades 8 to 12 with respect to socioeconomic level of the community, size of enrollment of the school district, and scholastic achievement and ethnic composition of the students.

With the exception of Clerical Speed and Accuracy, all DAT tests are essentially power tests. Reliability coefficients are high and permit interpretation of intertest differences with considerable confidence. By combining information on test reliabilities with the intercorrelations among tests, the test authors determined the proportion of differences in excess of chance between each pair of tests. These percentages ranged from 25 to 57, most falling in the 30s and 40s. In other words, for all possible test pairs, from one fourth to one half of the examinees in representative samples obtained larger score differences between tests than would be expected from errors of measurement.

Both percentile and stanine norms are provided. Individual percentile scores are plotted on normalized percentile charts, thereby eliminating the inequalities of percentile units. In order to facilitate the interpretation of score differences between tests, the profile charts show a percentile band for each score, such that the chances are approximately 90 out of 100 that the individual's "true" score lies within the band (see Fig. 13, Ch. 5). As was explained in Chapter 5, test·scores whose percentile bands do not overlap can be regarded as significantly different.

The amount of validity data available on the DAT is overwhelming, including several thousand validity coefficients. Most of these data are concerned with predictive validity in terms of high school achievement in both academic and vocational programs. Many of the coefficients are high, even with intervals as long as three years between test and criterion data. The results are somewhat less encouraging with regard to differential prediction. Although, in general, verbal tests correlate more highly with English courses and numerical tests with mathematics courses, there is evidence of a large general factor underlying performance in all academic work. Verbal Reasoning, for example, gives high correlations with most courses. It is chiefly for this reason that the VR + NA score was introduced as an index of scholastic aptitude. Being the sum of the raw scores on the Verbal Reasoning and Numerical Ability subtests, this index correlates in the .70s and .80s with composite criteria of academic achievement. Norms are provided for this index, which is one of the scores regularly included in the DAT profile (see Fig. 13, Ch. 5). The manual also provides regression equations

VERBAL REASONING

Choose the correct pair of words to fill the blanks. The first word of the pair goes in the blank space at the beginning of the sentence; the second word of the pair goes in the blank at the end of the sentence.

...... is to night as breakfast is to ......

    A. supper —— corner
    B. gentle —— morning
    C. door —— corner
    D. flow —— enjoy
    E. supper —— morning

The correct answer is E.

NUMERICAL ABILITY

Choose the correct answer for each problem.

Add 13		Subtract 30	
12	A 14	20	A 15
	B 25		B 26
	C 16		C 16
	D 59		D 8
	N none of these		N none of these

The correct answer for the first problem is B; for the second, N.

ABSTRACT REASONING

The four "problem figures" in each row make a series. Find the one among the "answer figures" that would be next in the series.

PROBLEM FIGURES   **ANSWER FIGURES**

The correct answer is D

CLERICAL SPEED AND ACCURACY

In each test item, one of the five combinations is underlined. Find the same combination on the answer sheet and mark it.

Fig. 61A. Sample Items from the Differential Aptitude Tests.

MECHANICAL REASONING

Which man has the heavier load? (If equal, mark C.)

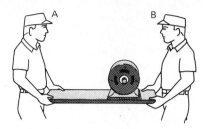

The correct answer is B.

SPACE RELATIONS

Which one of the following figures could be made by folding the pattern at the left? The pattern always shows the outside of the figure. Note the grey surfaces.

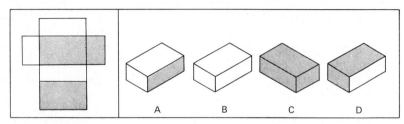

The correct answer is D.

SPELLING

Indicate whether each word is spelled right or wrong.

W. man

X. gurl

LANGUAGE USAGE

Decide which of the lettered parts of the sentence contains an error and mark the corresponding letter on the answer sheet. If there is no error, mark N.

X.   Ain't we / going to / the office / next week?
     A   B   C   D

FIG. 61B. Sample Items from the Differential Aptitude Tests.

for predicting the Verbal and Mathematical scores on the College Board's Scholastic Aptitude Test from appropriate combinations of three DAT subtests.

With regard to vocational criteria, there is some evidence for the predictive validity of individual DAT subtests, but the data are relatively meager. A four-year follow-up of 1,700 high school juniors and seniors and a seven-year follow-up of a somewhat smaller group revealed several profile differences among students who subsequently entered different educational curricula or occupations.

As an aid to educational and career counseling, there is also a DAT Career Planning Program which utilizes DAT scores and student responses to a Career Planning Questionnaire. In the questionnaire, students record their liking for various school subjects and other school activities, their educational and career goals, their general academic performance, and their interest in different fields of work and representative occupations. The DAT Career Planning Report is a computer printout including the student's DAT scores, with appropriate explanations, and interpretive statements that relate the DAT scores to the student's expressed interests and plans. The computer program was prepared by counseling psychologists on the basis of the available fund of information about job requirements and about the occupational validity of aptitude tests and interests. The manual for the DAT Career Planning Program (Super, 1973) gives a concise but clear description of the development of the program. Another counseling aid is provided by a casebook (*Counseling from Profiles*, 1977), giving actual case studies in which the DAT was used in counseling students. In each case study, DAT scores are considered in combination with scores from other tests, as well as with additional information available about the particular student. Some cases also include data from the Career Planning Program.

About a dozen multiple aptitude batteries have been developed for use in educational testing, counseling, and personnel classification. These instruments vary widely in approach, technical quality, and amount of available validation data. A common feature, however, is their disappointing performance with regard to *differential validity*. Yet it is in terms of differential validity that the distinctive contribution of multiple factor batteries should be evaluated. It is in connection with classification decisions that these batteries find their chief practical applications. Many have been designed explicitly for counseling purposes, in which classification decisions are preeminent. In a counseling situation, the profile of test scores is utilized to aid the counselee in choosing among several possible fields of educational or occupational specialization. Such a choice represents a typical classification decision. Institutional decisions regarding the assignment of personnel to different jobs or the admission of students to different educational curricula likewise involve a classification strategy. It will be recalled from our earlier discussion of validity (Ch. 7) that for classification instruments it is differential validity that is of prime importance. In terms of available data, however, multifactor batteries have fallen short of their initial promise.

To be sure, the academic criteria against which most multiple aptitude batteries have so far been predominantly validated may not be clearly differentiable on the basis of aptitudes. It is possible that differences in performance in specific courses depend principally on interests, motivation, and emotional factors. Unpredictable contingency factors, such as interpersonal relations between an individual student and a particular instructor, may also play a part. With regard to aptitudes, the large common contribution of verbal comprehension to achievement in all academic areas has been repeatedly demonstrated.

There is also a growing body of evidence indicating that traditional tests of "general intelligence" or "scholastic aptitude" yield fairly similar validity coefficients against a wide variety of educational and occupational criteria (Ghiselli, 1973; Pearlman, Schmidt, & Hunter, 1980; Schmidt, Hunter, Pearlman, & Shane, 1979). Such tests include essentially the same cluster of cognitive skills and knowledge assessed by the VR + NA score from the DAT. It may thus be more effective to test this particular aptitude cluster by available instruments, and then to supplement it with special aptitude tests selected to fit the needs of the specific individual or situation. Particular tests from a multifactor battery could, of course, be used in this fashion. An advantage of using tests selected from a single battery arises from the availability of comparable norms obtained on the same standardization sample.

BATTERIES FOR SPECIAL PROGRAMS. Factor analysis underlies the development of classification batteries widely employed in the armed services and in certain civilian agencies. The General Aptitude Test Battery (GATB) was developed by the United States Employment Service (USES) for use by employment counselors in the state employment service offices (U.S. Department of Labor, 1970a). Preliminary research included factor analyses of several overlapping sets of tests administered to different groups of men, most·of whom were trainees in vocational courses. On this basis, tests were selected for the final battery, which now includes 12 tests yielding a total of 9 factor scores, as listed below:

G. *Intelligence (General Learning Ability)*: Found by adding the scores on three tests also used to measure factors (Vocabulary, Arithmetic Reasoning, Three-Dimensional Space).

V. *Verbal Aptitude:* Measured by a Vocabulary test requiring examinee to indicate which two words in each set have either the same or opposite meaning.

N. *Numerical Aptitude:* Includes both Computation and Arithmetic Reasoning tests.

S. *Spatial Aptitude:* Measured by Three-Dimensional Space test, involving the ability to comprehend two-dimensional representation of three-dimensional objects and to visualize effects of movement in three dimensions.

P. *Form Perception:* Measured by two tests requiring the examinee to match identical drawings of tools in one test and of geometric forms in the other.

Q. *Clerical Perception:* Similar to P, but requiring the matching of names rather than pictures or forms.

K. *Motor Coordination:* Measured by a simple paper-and-pencil test requiring the examinee to make specified pencil marks in a series of squares.

F. *Finger Dexterity:* Two tests requiring the assembling and disassembling, respectively, of rivets and washers.

M. *Manual Dexterity:* Two tests requiring the examinee to transfer and reverse pegs in a board.

The four tests used for measuring factors F and M require simple apparatus; the other eight are paper-and-pencil tests. Alternate forms are available for the first seven tests, used for measuring factors G through Q. The entire battery requires approximately 2½ hours.

The nine factor scores on the GATB are converted into standard scores with a mean of 100 and an SD of 20. These standard score norms were derived from a sample of 4,000 cases representative of the 1940 working population of the United States in terms of age, sex, educational, occupational, and geographical distribution. This sample may thus be regarded as a fixed reference group to which the score scale is anchored. By testing many groups of employees, applicants, and trainees in different kinds of jobs, score patterns were subsequently established, showing the critical aptitudes and minimum standard scores required for each occupation.

In USES terminology, the aptitudes (with their appropriate cutoff scores) chosen for a specific occupation constitute a Special Aptitude Test Battery (SATB). The development of an SATB was illustrated in Chapter 7. The procedure followed with each group includes job analysis, selection of suitable criterion data (output records, supervisors' ratings, training performance, etc.), and administration of the 12-test battery. The significant aptitudes are chosen on the basis of their criterion correlations, as well as the means and SDs of scores on each aptitude and the qualitative job-analysis information. For example, if workers on the job under consideration average considerably above the normative sample in a particular aptitude and also show relatively low variability in their scores, that aptitude would probably be included in the SATB even if it fails to show a significant criterion correlation. Such a situation could occur if employees on a certain job were a highly selected group with regard to that aptitude.

To facilitate the use of score patterns in counseling, specific occupations having similar aptitude requirements have been grouped into a relatively small number of job families. Cutoff scores were then established in the three most significant aptitudes for each family. The resulting score patterns are designated as OAPs (Occupational Ability Patterns). By 1979, 66 OAPs had been prepared, covering several thousand occupations (U.S. Department of Labor, 1979b, 1980a). The GATB is used regularly in state employment service offices in the counseling and job referral of a vast number of persons. In addition, the battery may be obtained by nonprofit organizations such as secondary schools, colleges, Veterans' Administration hospitals, and prisons, under arrangements with the appropriate state employment service.[5]

Through the facilities of the USES and the various state offices, an extensive body of data has been accumulated on the GATB, and a continuing research program is in progress. Despite the brevity of individual tests, reliabilities of the factor scores are generally satisfactory. Both equivalent-form and retest correlations cluster in the .80s and low .90s, although the reliabilities of the motor tests tend to be somewhat lower.

A large amount of information on the validity of both SATBs and OAPs is reported in the GATB *Manual* (U.S. Department of Labor, 1970a; see also Bemis, 1968). Data were gathered through some 450 studies involving over 25,000 employees, applicants, apprentices, trainees, and students. Current validation studies include minority group representation and provide separate validities for minority and nonminority subsamples. Both predictive and concurrent validities have been investigated; but the large majority of the studies used only concurrent procedures. Most of the composite validities for the SATBs cluster around .40. Although cross-validation has not been systematically carried out and rather crude statistical procedures have been employed, the available cross-validation data are encouraging.

Certain limitations of the GATB should be noted. All tests are highly speeded. Coverage of aptitudes is somewhat limited. No mechanical comprehension test is included, nor are tests of reasoning and inventiveness well represented. The factorial structure of the battery rests on a series of early exploratory studies. A more comprehensive investigation with a large sample and a wider variety of tests would provide a more solid foundation. The consistent reliance on a multiple-cutoff strategy, rather than on regression equations, is also open to question. Although it is probable that certain occupations require critical skills whose lack cannot be compensated by other aptitudes, there is no empirical evidence that this is true of all aptitudes required for all occupations. As for nonlinear relations between aptitudes and job criteria, these too can be handled by regression equations, although the computation of the equation is admittedly more complicated in such cases. The principal justification for the exclusive use of the multiple-cutoff strategy with the GATB is based on practical limitations in the time

[5] The GATB is part of a coordinated career counseling system, which also includes an Interest Inventory (U.S. Department of Labor, 1981), the *Dictionary of Occupational Titles* (U.S. Department of Labor, 1977), and the *Guide for Occupational Exploration* (U.S. Department of Labor, 1979a). With the *Guide,* the counselor can integrate data on aptitudes and interests with job requirements, and can explore types of jobs that would be suitable for an individual (U.S. Department of Labor, 1981).

and technical training of the personnel interpreting the scores. With the increasing availability of computers, however, this argument loses much of its cogency.

Mention should also be made of the many activities undertaken by the USES to facilitate the testing and job placement of culturally and educationally disadvantaged applicants. Several test orientation procedures have been introduced, including materials and discussion plans designed to allay anxiety and correct misunderstandings about the nature and purpose of testing; booklets giving hints for doing well on tests; and practice exercises with items and answer sheets similar to those used on the GATB. Another innovation was the development of the Basic Occupational Literacy Test (BOLT) for assessing literacy skills of educationally deficient adults. Covering vocabulary, reading comprehension, arithmetic computation, and arithmetic reasoning, this battery is available in four levels. A short, wide-range preliminary test is used to choose the level appropriate for each examinee. The scores on the BOLT are evaluated in terms of occupational literacy requirements rather than school grades.

A major effort to adapt testing procedures to the needs of educationally and culturally disadvantaged adults was the construction of the Nonreading Aptitude Test Battery (NATB) (U.S. Department of Labor, 1970b). This battery was designed to yield the same nine aptitude scores as the GATB, but requires no reading or writing. Although introduced on a trial basis and subjected to continuing research and revision, the nonreading battery proved disappointing (Steckler, 1973; Tuckman, 1978). In its original form, the NATB was not widely adopted, probably because it took longer and was more difficult to administer than the GATB. It also did not correlate highly enough with the GATB to permit equivalent interpretation of scores. And educationally deficient persons who took both tests scored about as well on the GATB as on the NATB. As a result, alternative procedures for testing educationally disadvantaged persons are being explored, and the NATB is likely to be discontinued.

The armed services make extensive use of multiple aptitude batteries. These batteries are given for classification purposes after preliminary screening with more general instruments. Although the Air Force pioneered in the development of classification batteries, all branches of the armed services eventually prepared multifactor batteries for assigning personnel to military occupational specialties. The use of the Aptitude Area scores, derived from an early Army Classification Battery, was illustrated in Chapter 7. More recently, the various batteries were replaced by the Armed Services Vocational Aptitude Battery (ASVAB), a composite selection and classification battery developed jointly for use in all the armed services (Bayroff & Fuchs, 1970; Jensen, Massey, & Valentine, 1977). Each service combines and uses the scores from this battery to fit its particular personnel classification needs. Three subtests serve as the basic qualification component across services. One form of the ASVAB is also available to high schools for testing and counseling students, although the available reliability and validity data are still meager for such operational uses.

On the whole, both the GATB and the various multifactor batteries developed for military use have proved relatively successful as classification instruments. Both differ from the general batteries discussed in the preceding section in that they have been validated chiefly against occupational rather than academic criteria. To be sure, training criteria have sometimes been substituted for actual job performance, but the training programs were job-oriented and quite unlike schoolwork. Both training and job activities of airplane pilots, bakers, beauticians, and the many other kinds of workers included in these testing programs are far removed from traditional academic tasks. With criteria differing more widely from each other and from the verbally loaded academic criteria, there is more room for differential validity.

Another advantage enjoyed by some military batteries is that the number of occupational fields to be covered is smaller than in a general counseling battery. This was especially true of the Aircrew Classification Battery, first developed and employed during World War II for selecting pilots and other flight personnel. An expectancy chart showing pilot stanine scores on this battery in relation to performance in basic flight training was reproduced in Chapter 4 (Fig. 7). In the development of this battery, it was possible to work with relatively narrow group factors, which specifically matched the criterion requirements. In the Air Force research, a large number of different sensorimotor, perceptual, and spatial factors were identified and utilized in test construction. A general counseling battery, on the other hand, must concentrate on a few broad group factors, each of which is common to many jobs. With such broad factors, distinctions are blurred and differential validity drops.

MEASUREMENT OF CREATIVITY

RESEARCH ON CREATIVE TALENT. A significant development in psychological testing since midcentury concerns the measurement of creativity. This development is itself only one aspect of an upsurge in research on the nature and cultivation of creative talent (Barron, 1969; Bloomberg, 1973; Dellas & Gaier, 1970; Stein, 1974, 1975; Taylor, 1972; Taylor & Barron, 1963; Torrance, 1962; Wallach & Wing, 1969; Welsh, 1975b). Psychologists and educators generally recognize that creative talent is not synonymous with academic intelligence and is rarely covered by tests yielding an "IQ." In an early paper, Thurstone (1951) emphasized this distinction and provided a provocative analysis of the possible role of ideational fluency, inductive reasoning, and certain perceptual tendencies in creative behavior. He also called special attention to the contribution of nonintellectual, temperamental factors to creative activity. He observed that creativity is encouraged by a receptive as contrasted to a critical attitude toward novel ideas and that creative solutions are more likely to occur during periods of relaxed, dispersed attention than during periods of active concentration on a problem.

The investigation of creativity received considerable impetus in the 1950s and 1960s from the growing demand for research scientists, engineers, and high-level executives. Studies of scientific talent became increasingly concerned with creative abilities. Interest shifted from the individual who is merely a dependable, accurate, and critical thinker to the one who also displays ingenuity, originality, and inventiveness. Thus, creativity, long regarded as the prime quality in artistic production, came to be widely recognized as a basis for scientific achievement as well.

Investigations of the variables associated with creative achievement followed a variety of approaches. Some researchers concentrated on the creative person's biographical history and antecedent experiences; others analyzed the situational variables conducive to creative productivity. Some investigators conducted intensive clinical studies of highly eminent scientists. Still others combined a clinical with a psychometric approach through the use of a variety of personality-testing techniques and controlled observational procedures. This approach is exemplified by the long-term research conducted by MacKinnon (1962) and his associates at the University of California's Institute of Personality Assessment and Research (IPAR). In both the IPAR investigations and other research projects, large and significant differences in a number of personality traits have been found between creative and noncreative groups (Welsh, 1975).

Standardized tests of creative aptitudes have been produced chiefly in the course of large-scale research projects on the nature of creativity. Two major batteries, to be considered below, are the University of Southern California tests, developed by Guilford and his colleagues in the Aptitudes Research Project, and the Torrance Tests of Creative Thinking. Although commercially available, all these tests are still in experimental form and not ready for operational use. The items in creativity tests are typically open-ended, thus precluding objective scoring. For this reason, it is imperative to ascertain scorer reliability for all such instruments. Norms are generally tentative, being based on small scattered groups chosen primarily because of availability. Data on reliability and validity vary among individual tests but are usually quite limited. At this stage, the chief application of these tests is in research. The availability of uniform, standardized testing instruments assures a reasonable degree of comparability among different investigations. Eventually, some of these tests may be ready for use in clinical, counseling, educational, or occupational situations.

TESTS FROM THE UNIVERSITY OF SOUTHERN CALIFORNIA APTITUDES RESEARCH PROJECT (ARP). Earlier in this chapter, we discussed the factor-analytic research conducted by Guilford and his associates at the University of

Southern California. Extending over more than two decades, this research led to the formulation of the structure-of-intellect model (SI). While this model encompasses all intellectual functions, a major contribution of the ARP was in the divergent-production section, about which relatively little prior research was available. In fact, the ARP began primarily as an investigation of reasoning, creativity, and problem-solving.

In the course of his factor-analytic investigations, Guilford developed the categories of divergent and convergent thinking. Convergent thinking leads to a single correct solution determined by the given facts. Divergent thinking, on the other hand, is "the kind that goes off in different directions" (Guilford, 1959, p. 381). Such thinking is less restricted by given facts; it permits changes of direction in problem-solving and leads to a diversity of solutions or products. Figure 62 shows the location of the divergent-produc-

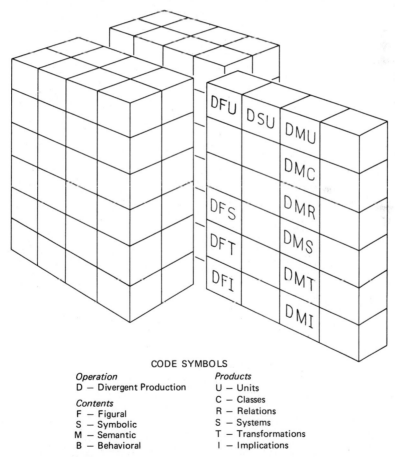

CODE SYMBOLS

Operation	*Products*
D — Divergent Production	U — Units
	C — Classes
Contents	R — Relations
F — Figural	S — Systems
S — Symbolic	T — Transformations
M — Semantic	I — Implications
B — Behavioral	

FIG. 62. Tests of Divergent Thinking from Aptitudes Research Project, Placed within the Structure-of-Intellect Model.

tion slab of the SI model, together with the individual cells for which tests have thus far been published. These tests are described below, along with the code letters of the principal SI factor measured by each. It will be recalled that this code always gives the Operation, Content, and Product in that order. For example, DSU stands for "divergent production of symbolic units."

ARP TESTS OF DIVERGENT THINKING[6]

Word Fluency (DSU)—write words containing a specified letter. E.g., "O": load, over, pot . . . .

Ideational Fluency (DMU)—name things that belong in the given class. E.g., "Fluids that will burn": gasoline, kerosene, alcohol . . . .

Associational Fluency (DMR)—write words similar in meaning to the given word. E.g., "Hard": difficult, solid, tough . . . .

Expressional Fluency (DMS)—write four-word sentences, each word to begin with a given letter. E.g., "K——u——y——i——.": Keep up your interest. Kill useless yellow insects.

Alternate Uses (DMC)—list possible uses for a specified object, other than its common use. E.g., "Newspaper (used for reading)": Start a fire. Stuffing to pack boxes . . . .

Simile Interpretations (DMS)—complete in several different ways sentences that contain similes. E.g., "A woman's beauty is like the autumn; it——.": . . . passes before it can be fully appreciated . . . .

Plot Titles (DMU, DMT)—write titles for short-story plots. E.g., "A new clerk in a department store, in anticipation of winter, ordered 10 dozen gloves, but forgot to specify that they should be in pairs. The store now has 100 left-handed gloves.": Southpaw's Delight. Left with a Lot of Lefts . . . . Two scores: total number of titles (ideational fluency—DMU); number of "clever" titles, such as those illustrated (originality—DMT).

Consequences (DMU, DMT)—list different consequences of a given hypothetical event. E.g., "What would be the results if people no longer needed or wanted sleep?": Get more work done. Alarm clocks not necessary . . . . Two scores: number of "obvious" responses (ideational fluency—DMU); number of "remote" responses (originality—DMT).

Possible Jobs (DMI)—list possible jobs that might be symbolized by a given emblem. E.g., "Light bulb": electrical engineer, light-bulb manufacturer, a bright student . . . .

Making Objects (DFS)—draw specified objects using only a set of given figures, like circle, triangle, etc. Any given figure may be used repeatedly for the same object and may be changed in size, but no other figures or lines may be added. Figure 63 shows a demonstration item employed as a fore-exercise in this test.

[6] The illustrations are parts of sample items, used in explaining instructions in each test. Copyright, Sheridan Psychological Services, and reproduced by permission.

Sketches (DFU)—each test page contains a set of identical figures, such as circles; make as many different sketches of recognizable objects as possible by elaborating on each figure.

Match Problems (DFT)—remove a specified number of matchsticks, leaving a specified number of squares or triangles. Figure 64 shows part of one of the demonstration items used with this test.

Decorations (DFI)—outline drawings of common objects are to be decorated with as many different designs as possible.

It should be noted that the first nine tests listed require verbal (semantic) responses, while the last four employ figural content. These published tests represent only some of the divergent-thinking instruments developed in the Aptitudes Research Project (Guilford & Hoepfner, 1971).[7]

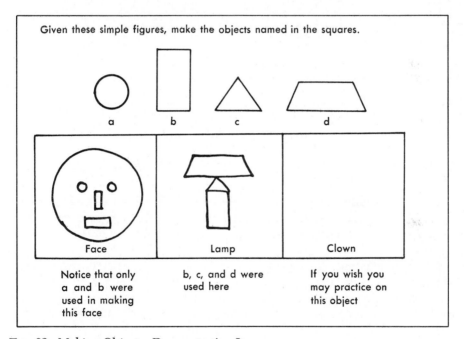

FIG. 63. Making Objects: Demonstration Item.
(Reproduced by permission of Sheridan Psychological Services, Inc.)

In the preliminary manuals, Guilford and his co-workers provide tentative norms in terms of percentiles and standard scores. For most of the tests, these norms are given for groups of adults, or ninth-grade students, or both. The tests are generally applicable at the high school level and above. Scorer

[7] All published tests from this project are included in *Tests in Print—II*. Those listed in Appendix E are also included in the *Eighth Mental Measurements Yearbook*.

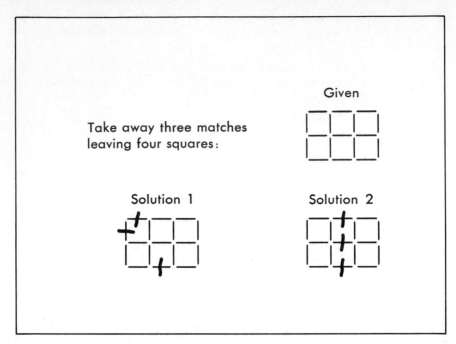

FIG. 64. Match Problems: Part of Demonstration Item.
(Reproduced by permission of Sheridan Psychological Services, Inc.)

reliability is not reported in the manuals, but other investigators who have employed these tests in research have obtained coefficients around .90. With a reasonable amount of practice in following the instructions and studying the examples in the manuals, such tests can probably be scored with satisfactory consistency, although the scoring process is quite laborious and time-consuming.

Split-half reliability coefficients reported in the manuals run lower than would be desirable, ranging from the .60s to the .80s. For all these tests, factorial validity is reported in terms of the SI factors. Such validity data are based on the extensive research that preceded the publication of each test. Information on criterion-related validity, however, is lacking except for a few scattered independent investigations. A possible limitation of all these tests is their heavy reliance on speed of responses.

A parallel series, *Creativity Tests for Children,* has also been developed in the same project. Consisting of ten tests, it includes five verbal (semantic) and five figural tests. Seven of the ten tests are adaptations of adult tests for the same factors. Norms are provided for Grades 4 through 6. The standardization sample consisted of 1,300 middle-class children from four school systems in California and one in Florida. Substantial proportions of black and Mexican-American children were included in the sample. Psychometric properties of these tests are quite similar to those of the adult tests. No factor analyses, however, were conducted directly with children. The tests were constructed and classified in terms of the factors identified in the adult research.

TORRANCE TESTS OF CREATIVE THINKING. While the ARP tests were a by-product of factor-analytic research on the nature of intellect, the Torrance tests were developed within an educational context, as part of a long-term research program emphasizing classroom experiences that foster and stimulate creativity (Torrance, 1962, 1963, 1965). Some of the Torrance tests are adaptations of techniques employed in the ARP tests. Moreover, the scores derived from the complete batteries are based on factors identified in Guilford's research, namely, Fluency, Flexibility, Originality, and Elaboration. In this connection, Torrance explains that he did not seek factorially pure tests. Rather, he tried to contrive situations that provide models of the creative process in its natural complexity. Each test is therefore scored in terms of two, three, or all four of the above factors.

The Torrance Tests of Creative Thinking comprise 12 tests, grouped into a verbal, a pictorial, and an auditory battery. The first battery is labeled *Thinking Creatively with Words,* the second *Thinking Creatively with Pictures,* and the third *Thinking Creatively with Sounds and Words.* In an effort to eliminate threat and to induce a comfortable and stimulating psychological climate, the tests are called "activities" and the instructions place much emphasis on "having fun." The tests are described as suitable from kindergarten to graduate school, although below the fourth grade they have to be administered individually and orally. Two equivalent forms of each battery are available.

In *Thinking Creatively with Words,* the first three activities (Ask-and-Guess) utilize a rather intriguing picture to which the examinee responds by (1) writing all the questions he would need to ask to find out what is happening; (2) listing possible causes of the action depicted; and (3) listing possible consequences of the action. Activity 4 is concerned with ways of improving a given toy so that children will have more fun playing with it. Activity 5 calls for a list of unusual uses for a common object, as in Guilford's Alternate Uses. Activity 6 requires unusual questions that could be asked about the same object. Activity 7, modeled after Guilford's Consequences, asks for all the things that would happen if a given improbable situation were true. The entire battery yields a total score in each of three traits: Fluency, Flexibility, and Originality.

Thinking Creatively with Pictures consists of three activities. In Picture Construction, a brightly colored curved shape is pasted by the examinee on a blank sheet in a position of his or her choice and is used as a starting point for drawing an unusual picture "that tells an interesting and exciting story." In Picture Completion, each item provides a few lines as a start for drawing a picture. The instructions for this test stress unusual ideas, and the scoring is based on aspects of creativity rather than on artistic quality. The last activity provides pairs of short parallel lines (Form A) or circles (Form B), with which as many different pictures as possible are to be produced. Four total scores are obtained from the pictorial battery: Fluency, Flexibility, Originality, and Elaboration.

The most recent addition to the series, *Thinking Creatively with Sounds and Words*, consists of two tests administered by means of long-playing records, which provide both the instructions and the stimuli. The first test, Sounds and Images, utilizes both familiar and unfamiliar sound effects as stimuli. The second, Onomatopoeia and Images, utilizes onomatopoeic words, i.e., words such as "crunch" or "pop" that imitate the natural sound associated with the object or action involved. In both tests, the responses are verbal: after listening to each stimulus, the examinee writes down what it suggests to her or him. Respondents are urged to give free rein to their imagination. The first test consists of four sound sequences, presented three times; the second consists of ten words, presented four times. Examinees are instructed to give a different association each time. Responses in each test are scored only for Originality, on the basis of empirically established infrequency of occurrence. Thus, uncommon responses receive more credit than common responses.

The manuals accompanying the Torrance batteries provide detailed scoring guides, with many examples. The technical manuals cite the results of several studies of scorer reliability, with interscorer correlations falling mostly in the .80s and .90s. In the verbal and pictorial batteries, Originality proved to be the most difficult trait to score, having yielded the only scorer reliabilities under .80. Scattered studies of alternate-form reliabilities over short time intervals, as well as odd-even reliabilities, found coefficients that usually ranged from the .70s to the .90s. In general, the verbal scores show higher reliabilities than the figural scores. Tentative norms for each of the three verbal, four figural, and two auditory scores are given as standard scores in terms of available groups of schoolchildren and adults. Means and *SD*s of several other groups are also included for comparative purposes.

As in the ARP tests, speed is an integral part of performance on the Torrance tests, a characteristic common to virtually all current creativity tests. The technical manuals summarize a number of investigations in which the Torrance tests were employed for a variety of research purposes. All these unrelated studies contribute toward the construct validation of the tests, but no clear picture emerges as yet. Most of the studies were conducted on schoolchildren, although some data on high school and college students and on occupational adult groups are also cited. Many suggestive relationships have been found between Torrance scores and interests, attitudes, and other personality traits measured by tests, ratings, or other assessment procedures. Significant improvement in Torrance scores has also been observed as a result of educational experiences designed to stimulate creative thinking, but no external evidence is provided to indicate whether such improvement extends to other, nontest situations.

In general, evidence of relation between the Torrance tests and everyday-life criteria of creative achievement is meager. There is need for comprehensive, systematic validation studies showing the relation of these tests to measures of other intellectual traits as well as to practical criteria. The use of Fluency, Flexibility, Originality, and Elaboration scores that cut across the individual tests is questionable. A factor analysis of the performance of about 800 fifth-grade children on the Torrance tests gave no support to the interpretation of these scores in terms of single constructs (Yamamoto & Frengel, 1966). On the contrary, the factors identified were task-specific. The intercorrelations of different scores derived from a single test were higher than the intercorrelations of similarly labeled scores (e.g., Fluency) derived from different tests. The two Originality scores obtained from the third battery yield correlations in the .30s and .40s with each other and still lower correlations with Originality scores from the verbal and figural batteries. It would thus seem inadvisable to derive more than one score from any one test or to treat similarly labeled scores from different tests as measures of a single trait.

CREATIVE ACHIEVEMENT. Although tests of divergent production, such as those of Guilford and Torrance, probably come close to measuring essential aspects of creativity, other abilities are undoubtedly needed for effective creative achievement, especially in the sciences. In their zeal to counteract the earlier concentration on comprehension and memory, as represented by traditional intelligence tests, some investigators may have swung too far in the opposite direction. For genuine creative achievement, the uninhibited divergent-production phase must eventually be followed by critical evaluation. In the technique popularly known as "brainstorming," for example, creativity is stimulated by the temporal separation of the productive and evaluative phases of creative activity. A critical, evaluative attitude at an early stage of creative production may seriously thwart the development of new ideas. But critical evaluation is to be only temporarily deferred, not permanently abolished.

Several cognitive and evaluative aptitudes usually classified under reasoning have emerged from the Guilford research. Some of the published tests from the Aptitudes Research Project measure these factors.[8] A number of other reasoning tests, also developed through factor analysis, are included in the previously described *Kit of Factor-Referenced Cognitive Tests* (*ETS*, 1976). Another test covering several aspects of effective reasoning is the

[8] E.g., Ship Destination Test, Logical Reasoning, and Pertinent Questions, all distributed by Sheridan Psychological Services and included in the *Mental Measurements Yearbooks*.

Watson-Glaser Critical Thinking Appraisal. Designed for high school and college levels, this test contains five parts, dealing with inference, recognition of assumptions, deduction, interpretation, and evaluation of arguments.

In discussing creative productivity in the arts, Guilford (1957, 1967) suggested that several of the divergent-production factors so far identified may play an important part. Those in the verbal area, with which many of the available tests are concerned, are probably related to creative writing. Corresponding factors pertaining to visual, auditory, or even kinesthetic figural content—many of which have not yet been identified—may play an equally important part in the graphic arts, music, and choreography. In addition, creative productivity in the arts, as in the sciences, undoubtedly requires a certain minimum proficiency in relevant comprehension and memory factors, such as verbal comprehension, spatial orientation, visual or auditory memory, and the like.

It is thus apparent that creative achievement—whether in science, engineering, art, music, or other fields of human endeavor—requires a complex pattern of aptitudes and personality traits appropriate to the particular field. Current tests of creativity concentrate on certain elements of this pattern that had heretofore been largely neglected in psychometrics. But they are not intended to replace other types of available tests.

CHAPTER 14

Educational Testing

N EARLY every type of available test is utilized in the schools. Intelligence, special aptitude, multiple aptitude, and personality tests can all be found in the repertory of the educational counselor and the school psychologist. Teachers and educational administrators frequently have to act on the results obtained with several different kinds of tests. Certain types of tests, however, have been specifically developed for use in educational contexts, predominantly at the elementary and high school levels. It is with these tests that the present chapter is concerned. They include both predictive instruments designed for specific educational purposes and many varieties of educational achievement tests.

ACHIEVEMENT TESTS: THEIR NATURE AND USES

NATURE. Surpassing all other types of standardized tests in sheer numbers, achievement tests are designed to measure the effects of a specific program of instruction or training. It has been customary to contrast achievement tests with aptitude tests, the latter including general intelligence tests, multiple aptitude batteries, and special aptitude tests. From one point of view, the difference between achievement and aptitude testing is a difference in the degree of uniformity of relevant antecedent experience. Thus achievement tests measure the effects of relatively standardized sets of experiences, such as a course in elementary French, trigonometry, or computer programming. In contrast, aptitude test performance reflects the cumulative influence of a multiplicity of experiences in daily living. We might say that aptitude tests measure the effects of learning under relatively uncontrolled and unknown conditions, while achievement tests measure the effects of learning that occurred under partially known and controlled conditions.

A second distinction between aptitude and achievement tests pertains to their respective uses. Aptitude tests serve to predict subsequent performance. They are employed to estimate the extent to which the individual will profit from a specified course of training, or to forecast the quality of his or her achievement in a new situation. Achievement tests, on the other hand, generally represent a terminal evaluation of the individual's status on the completion of training. The emphasis in such tests is on what the individual can do at the time. This difference is perhaps most clearly illustrated by the procedures for estimating the validity of achievement tests, as contrasted with those followed in validating aptitude tests. Although predictive criterion-oriented validity is the most direct way of assessing aptitude tests, achievement tests are characteristically evaluated in terms of their content validity (Ch. 6).

It should be recognized, however, that no distinction between aptitude and achievement tests can be rigidly applied. Some aptitude tests may depend on fairly specific and uniform prior learning, while some achievement tests cover relatively broad and unstandardized educational experiences. Similarly, an achievement test may be used as a predictor of future learning. As such it serves the same purpose as an aptitude test. For example, the progress a student has made in arithmetic, as determined by her or his present achievement test score, may be employed to predict that student's subsequent success in algebra. Achievement tests on premedical courses can serve as predictors of performance in medical school. Whenever different individuals have had the same or closely similar courses of study, achievement tests based on such courses may provide efficient indices of future performance. When used for predictive purposes, of course, achievement tests should be evaluated in terms of their criterion correlations.

In differentiating between aptitude and achievement tests, we should especially guard against the naive assumption that achievement tests measure the effects of learning, while aptitude tests measure "innate capacity" independent of learning. This misconception was fairly prevalent in the early days of psychological testing, but has been largely corrected in the subsequent clarification of psychometric concepts. It should be obvious that all psychological tests measure the individual's current behavior, which inevitably reflects the influence of prior learning. The fact that every test score has a "past" does not, however, preclude its having a "future." While revealing the effects of past learning, test scores may, under certain conditions, serve as predictors of future learning.[1]

A useful concept that is coming to replace the traditional categories of aptitude and achievement in psychometrics is that of *developed abilities*. All ability tests—whether they be designed as general intelligence tests, multiple aptitude batteries, special aptitude tests, or achievement tests—measure the level of development attained by the individual in one or more abilities. No test reveals how or why the individual reached that level. Existing tests of developed abilities may be ordered along a continuum in terms of the specificity of experiential background that they presuppose. This continuum is illustrated in Figure 65. At one extreme are the course-

---

[1] For a further discussion of the distinction between aptitude and achievement tests, from many viewpoints, see the conference report edited by D. R. Green (1974), especially the chapters by Humphreys (Ch. 8) and Ebel (Ch. 10), and the review of this report by Anastasi (1975). See also Anastasi (1980).

Specificity ———————————————————————————————— Generality

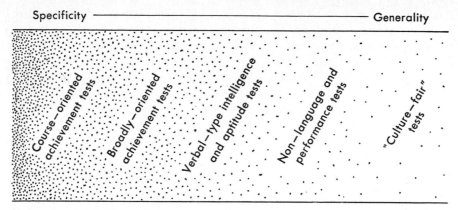

FIG. 65. Tests of Developed Abilities: Continuum of Experiential Specificity.

oriented achievement tests covering narrowly defined technical skills or factual information. A test in Russian vocabulary or television maintenance would fall at this end of the continuum. Many of the achievement tests employed for personnel selection or classification in industry or the armed services are of this type. Teacher-made classroom examinations also belong in this category.

Next in the continuum come the broadly oriented achievement tests commonly used today to assess the attainment of major, long-term educational goals. Here we find tests focusing on the understanding and application of scientific principles, the interpretation of literature, or the appreciation of art. Still boarder in orientation are tests of basic cognitive skills that affect the individual's performance in a wide variety of activities. These skills may themselves be rather narrowly defined, as in certain common work-study skills (e.g., interpretation of tables, use of indexes and dictionaries). Or they may be broader, such as reading comprehension and arithmetic computation. At the broadest level, we find achievement tests designed to measure the effects of education on logical thinking, critical evaluation of conclusions, problem-solving techniques, and imagination. It is apparent that at this point achievement tests fuse imperceptibly with traditional intelligence and aptitude tests. This overlapping of "aptitude" and "achievement" tests can easily be demonstrated empirically. An examination of the content of several current instruments classified as intelligence tests and as achievement tests reveals close similarity of content. It has long been known, moreover, that intelligence tests correlate about as highly with achievement tests as different intelligence tests correlate with each other (Coleman & Cureton, 1954; Kelley, 1927, pp. 193–209). In some instances, in fact, the correlation between achievement and intelligence tests is as high as the reliability coefficients of each test.

Further reference to Figure 65 shows a wide disparity among traditional intelligence or aptitude tests with regard to the experiential or educational specificity of their content. The predominantly verbal intelligence or aptitude tests, such as the Stanford-Binet or the Differential Aptitude Tests, are closest to the achievement tests. Next come nonlanguage and performance tests, and finally the "culture-fair" tests designed for use with persons of widely varied experiential backgrounds (Ch. 10). As a safeguard against possible misinterpretation of either aptitude or achievement test scores, this schematic continuum should be kept constantly in mind.

Labeling some instruments as "aptitude tests" and others as "achievement tests" has led to certain misuses of test results. A common example is the practice of identifying as underachievers those children whose achievement test scores are lower than their scholastic aptitude or intelligence test scores. Actually, such intraindividual differences in test scores reflect the universal fact that no two tests (or other performance indicators such as course grades) correlate perfectly with each other. The question of under- or overachievement can be more accurately formulated as overprediction or underprediction from the first to the second test. Among the reasons for the prediction errors in individual cases are the unreliability of the measuring instruments, differences in content coverage, the varied effects of attitudinal and motivational factors on the two measures, and the impact of such intervening experiences as remedial instruction or a long illness.[2]

It should be noted that underprediction and overprediction will occur regardless of the type of test used, i.e., if an intelligence test is used to predict subsequent achievement test performance, or if an achievement test is used to predict subsequent intelligence test performance; and they will occur in estimating scores on the later test from scores on the earlier test or vice versa. Finally, the administration of alternate forms or different levels of an achievement test before and after a course of instruction permits a more accurate analysis of individual accomplishment than does the use of two different tests. To take an extreme example, if achievement in reading comprehension is predicted from a nonverbal intelligence test that is heavily loaded with spatial aptitude, the children with higher spatial than verbal aptitude will look like underachievers, while those with higher verbal than spatial aptitude will look like overachievers.

USES. The many roles that achievement tests can play in the educational process have long been recognized. As an aid in the assignment of grades— or in any other assessment of achieved competence—achievement tests have the advantages of objectivity and uniformity. If properly constructed, they have other merits, such as adequacy of content coverage and reduction of the operation of irrelevant and chance factors in marking procedures.

---

[2] For a comprehensive analysis of methodological problems in the measurement of underachievement, see Thorndike (1963).

Achievement tests also constitute an important feature of remedial teaching programs. In this connection, they are useful both in the identification of students with special educational disabilities and in the measurement of progress in the course of remedial work.

For all types of learners, the periodic administration of well-constructed and properly chosen achievement tests serves to facilitate learning. Such tests reveal weaknesses in past learning, give direction to subsequent learning, and motivate the learner. The incentive value of "knowledge of results" has been repeatedly demonstrated by psychological experiments in many types of learning situations, with learners of widely varying age and education. The effectiveness of such self-checking is generally heightened by immediacy. Thus, when achievement examinations are employed primarily as a learning aid, it is desirable for the students to become aware of their errors as soon after taking the tests as possible.

From another angle, achievement tests provide a means of adapting instruction to individual needs. Teaching can be most fruitful when it meets the learner at whatever stage he or she happens to be. Ascertaining what individuals are already able to do and what they already know about a subject is thus a necessary first step for effective teaching. The growth of fall testing programs points up the increasing use of test results as a basis for planning what is to be taught to a class as a whole and what modifications and adjustments need to be made in individual cases. By giving tests at the beginning of the school year, constructive steps can be taken to fill the major gaps in knowledge revealed by the test results. Further examples of the role of achievement tests in the teaching process can be found in connection with criterion-referenced testing, individually tailored instructional systems, and computer-aided learning procedures, discussed in Chapter 4.

Finally, achievement tests may be employed as aids in the evaluation and improvement of teaching and in the formulation of educational goals. Achievement tests can provide information on the adequacy with which essential content and skills are actually being taught. They can likewise indicate how much of the course content is retained and for how long. Are certain types of material retained longer than others? What are the most common errors and misunderstandings encountered? How well can the learners apply their knowledge to new situations? By focusing attention on such questions and by providing concrete facts, achievement tests stimulate an analysis of training objectives and encourage a critical examination of the content and methods of instruction. Public demands for educational accountability require the proper use of well-constructed achievement tests to assess the results of the educational process (Gronlund, 1974; Wrightstone, Hogan, & Abbott, 1972). It is especially important for this purpose to recognize the many conditions that affect both test performance and school learning, including the cumulative effects of antecedent and continuing experiences outside of the school environment.

ESSAY VERSUS OBJECTIVE QUESTIONS. Historically, the traditional school examination began as a set of questions to be answered either orally or in writing. In either case, the examinee composed and formulated the response. The term "essay question" has come to be used broadly to cover all free-response questions, including not only those demanding a lengthy essay but also those requiring the examinee to produce a short answer or to work out the solution for a mathematical problem. Objective questions, by contrast, call for the choice of a correct answer out of several provided for each question. This feature is especially clear in multiple-choice questions, although the recognition of the correct choice is also the major response given in true-false, matching, rearrangement, and other variants. The introduction of multiple-choice items into achievement tests was followed by extensive discussion and some well-designed research comparing the merits of the new item types with those of the traditional essay questions.

As objective items came to be widely accepted, there was a tendency to take them for granted—possibly as a necessary evil of large-scale testing programs—and to lose sight of both the logical arguments and the empirical data in support of their use. Some recent attacks on standardized tests have focused on alleged deficiencies of objective items while ignoring the available evidence. It is therefore appropriate to reexamine the relevant arguments and research findings.

Two points may be noted at the outset. First, objective items are *not* used only for convenience in large-scale testing; they have other advantages as well. Second, their advantages are *not* based solely on logical arguments; they are also supported by empirical evidence. The advantages traditionally cited in favor of essay questions are that they test the individual's ability to select, relate, and organize material, as well as his or her ability to express ideas clearly and accurately. Unfortunately, the time available to the examinee in answering essay questions is usually too short to measure these particular skills. It is possible, in fact, that essay examinations may be partly responsible for the habits of unclear and careless writing developed by many students. Apart from lack of time for effective organization and good writing, the student answering essay questions writes for an instructor who knows more about the subject than the student does. Confident in the expectation that even obscure answers will be understood and duly credited, the student rarely takes the trouble to communicate clearly.

From another angle, many of the abilities formerly believed to be amenable only to essay questions are proving to be testable by objective items. It is only the inexperienced item writer who concentrates on trivial points involving rote memory for facts. Such items require less thought and effort to prepare. With training and practice, however, items can be written to tap complex thinking processes, reasoning, evaluation of arguments, and the application of knowledge to new situations. Several well-constructed standardized achievement tests provide excellent examples of these types of items.

A major advantage of objective items is that each item requires much less of the examinee's time than does a typical essay question. Consequently, objective items permit a fuller coverage of content and hence reduce an important source of chance error and individual unfairness in test scores. Some early research demonstrated that the more items there are in a test, the smaller is the contribution of chance or luck to the total score (Posey, 1932; Ruch, 1929, p. 56).

A widely recognized and extensively investigated advantage of objective items pertains to ease, rapidity, and uniformity of scoring. The fact that objective items can be scored by a properly trained clerk or—increasingly—by computers contributes greatly to their usefulness in large-scale testing programs, especially when scores must be available within a short time after test administration. From the standpoint of the individual examinee, however, the greater accuracy and objectivity of the scores are a far more important consideration. There is a fairly extensive series of empirical investigations documenting the low scorer reliabilities found when the same essays are evaluated by two or more readers (Finlaysson, 1951; Starch & Elliott, 1912, 1913a, 1913b; Vernon & Millican, 1954). Equally large inconsistencies occurred when the same essay papers were graded by the same readers after an interval of two months (Hulten, 1925). Although much of this research pertained to essays in English composition, similar results were obtained when evaluating essay questions in other content areas.

To obtain an adequate and reliable assessment of an individual's performance on essay questions—and especially an index of his or her ability to write clearly and correctly—one needs several essays on different topics, written on different days, and preferably read by different examiners. This goal can be approximated in a course of study, where it represents a highly desirable instructional procedure; but it cannot be achieved during an examination. It is interesting to note in this connection that if we have a well-established criterion measure of writing performance gathered during a course, objective tests correlate higher with such a criterion than do essay tests. In other words, objective tests prove to be more valid predictors of the quality of essays written under proper conditions than do essay tests (Breland, 1977; Hartson, 1930; Huddleston, 1954; McKee, 1934; Stalnaker, 1933).

In summary, objective items have largely replaced essay questions in standardized testing programs, not only because of time restriction in test scoring, but also—and more importantly—because they provide broader subject-matter coverage, yield more reliable and more valid scores, and are fairer to individuals. Essay writing should be encouraged and developed primarily as an instructional procedure to foster clear, correct, and effective communication in all content areas.

GENERAL ACHIEVEMENT BATTERIES

NATURE AND SCOPE. Several batteries are available for measuring general educational achievement in the areas most commonly covered by academic curricula. This type of test can be used from the primary grades to the adult level, although its major application has been in the elementary school. Typically, these batteries provide profiles of scores on individual subtests or in major academic areas. An advantage of such batteries as against independently constructed achievement tests is that they may permit horizontal or vertical comparisons, or both. Thus, an individual's relative standing in different subject-matter areas or educational skills can be compared in terms of a uniform normative sample. Or the child's progress from grade to grade can be reported in terms of a single score scale. The test user should check whether a particular battery was so standardized as to yield either or both kinds of comparability.

To provide an overview of the nature and grade range of general achievement batteries, some representative examples have been listed in Table 29, together with the grade levels covered by each. It will be noted that some of these batteries are designed for the elementary grades, others for the high

TABLE 29
Representative Achievement Batteries

Battery	Grade Range													
	K	1	2	3	4	5	6	7	8	9	10	11	12	13
California Achievement Tests	x	x	x	x	x	x	x	x	x	x	x	x	x	
Iowa Tests of Basic Skills	x	x	x	x	x	x	x	x	x	x				
Iowa Tests of Educational Development										x	x	x	x	
Metropolitan Achievement Tests	x	x	x	x	x	x	x	x	x	x	x	x	x	
SRA Achievement Series	x	x	x	x	x	x	x	x	x	x	x	x	x	
Sequential Tests of Educational Progress—Series III (STEP III)[a]					x	x	x	x	x	x	x	x	x	
Stanford Achievement Test[a]		x	x	x	x	x	x	x	x	x				
Stanford Test of Academic Skills (TASK)										x	x	x	x	x
Tests of Achievement and Proficiency (TAP)										x	x	x	x	

[a] CIRCUS extends STEP III to the preschool level; the Stanford Early School Achievement Test (SESAT) extends the Stanford series to the beginning of kindergarten. Both early childhood tests are discussed in the last section of this chapter.

school; but most span a broad range extending into both levels and occasionally even into the junior or community college. Although a few provide a single battery for the grade range covered, the large majority have several overlapping batteries for use at different grade levels. Some separately listed batteries for the elementary and high school levels actually form a coordinated series, permitting comparable measurement from Grades 1 through 12. One such combination is the Iowa Tests of Basic Skills and the Tests of Achievement and Proficiency; another is the Stanford Achievement Test and the Stanford Test of Academic Skills.

A noteworthy feature of some achievement batteries is that they were concurrently normed with a test of academic intelligence or scholastic aptitude. Major examples include achievement batteries that were paired with three academic aptitude tests illustrated in Chapter 11, namely, Metropolitan Achievement Tests with Otis-Lennon School Ability Test, Iowa Tests of Basic Skills and Tests of Achievement and Proficiency with Cognitive Abilities Test, and STEP III with SCAT III. The use of the same standardization sample in these cases permits direct comparisons of the scores any student obtains on the two types of tests. Usually, the two tests correlate highly, and individuals will obtain closely similar scores on them. For students who score substantially higher on either type of test, it is desirable to explore possible reasons for the discrepancy. The achievement battery measures largely what the individual has learned in basic school courses; the academic aptitude test assesses broader cognitive skills and knowledge learned both in and out of school. Any significant performance discrepancy could reflect the influence of specific abilities or disabilities, or of such noncognitive factors as motivation, interests, and attitudes. The individual's experiential background often provides clues to the conditions leading to unusual discrepancies in test performance.

Available batteries differ in their relative emphasis on basic cognitive skills and on knowledge of content. A primary focus on skills is characteristic of the California Achievement Tests and the Iowa Tests of Basic Skills. These tests generally assess performance in reading; mathematics; spelling and language usage; and such work–study skills as reading tables, graphs, and maps, and use of index, dictionary, and other reference sources. When achievement in different subject-matter areas is to be measured—particularly at the high school level where specialized courses are common—some batteries may concentrate on the student's ability to understand passages from each content area. The Iowa Tests of Educational Development, for example, include tests on the ability to interpret reading materials in literature, the social studies, and the natural sciences. Most batteries provide separate tests of basic skills and of content knowledge in science and social studies. The facts and concepts covered in the content areas, however, are not tied to specific curricular material, but can be acquired in different types of courses. Moreover, the emphasis is on the application of knowledge to the solution of new problems rather than on simple recall.

METROPOLITAN ACHIEVEMENT TESTS. As an example of a widely used and recently revised achievement battery, we may consider the Metropolitan Achievement Tests (MAT). First developed in the 1930s, this battery has undergone extensive changes in successive editions, the latest appearing in 1978. A major feature of this edition is the inclusion of a Survey Battery, to be described in this section, and three Instructional Batteries for diagnostic purposes, to be discussed in a later section of this chapter. The Survey Battery extends from kindergarten to Grade 12 in eight overlapping batteries. All batteries are available in two parallel forms. There is also a practice booklet containing typical items, which can be administered a few days before the test proper.

To illustrate the content of the MAT, we may examine the Elementary Level, spanning Grades 3.5 to 4.9. The Survey Battery at this level comprises the following five tests:

Reading: a series of graded reading passages with questions to be answered on each; measures word meaning in context, as well as literal, inferential, and evaluative comprehension.

Mathematics: covers numeration, geometry and measurement, solving verbally presented problems, numerical operations with whole numbers, and laws and properties of operations that contribute to an understanding of computation (e.g., division is the opposite of multiplication).

Language: including both oral and written parts, this test covers listening comprehension, punctuation and capitalization, usage, grammar and syntax, spelling, and study skills.

Science: items are designed to test knowledge, comprehension, inquiry skills, and critical analysis in three content areas, viz., physical science, earth and space science, and life science.

Social Studies: The same four cognitive skills listed under Science are applied to geography, sociology, economics, political science, history, anthropology, and psychology.

Typical items from three of these tests are illustrated in Figure 66. At all levels, the complete Survey Battery extends over several sessions. At the Elementary Level, it is administered over seven sittings of from 25 to 50 minutes each, although they need not all be given on separate days.

Both fall and spring norms are available for each of the five tests, as well as for the basic skills subtotal (Reading, Mathematics, Language) and for the total score on the entire battery. Several kinds of scores are provided, including percentile ranks and stanines within grades, as well as grade equivalents. The last were undoubtedly added because of continuing user demand; but it is gratifying to find in the manual the statement, "Grade equivalents are losing the popularity they once had as a way of interpreting

Mathematics

If someone mixes up the marbles in the box and asks you to take out one marble without looking, what is the probability that the marble will have a stripe?

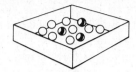

$\frac{3}{11}$ $\frac{1}{2}$ $\frac{6}{11}$ $\frac{1}{11}$

Ⓐ   Ⓑ   Ⓒ   Ⓓ

Language

(Listening Comprehension Item: Examiner reads instructions and story.)
Mark the letter for the picture that shows what the word <u>it</u> refers to.

"Instead of making a snowman, Betsy made a snowdog. Betsy's little sister came over and patted it on the head."

Ⓐ   Ⓑ   Ⓒ

Science

You have dissolved some sugar in a pan of water and left the pan in a warm place. When the water evaporates, the sugar will—

Ⓐ   break down into molecules of carbon and water
Ⓑ   evaporate too
Ⓒ   melt
Ⓓ   still be in the pan

Fɪɢ. 66. Typical Items Illustrating Three of the Metropolitan Achievement Tests: Complete Survey Battery.
(Courtesy of Harcourt Brace Jovanovich, Inc.)

test performance" (Prescott, Balow, Hogan, & Farr, 1978, p. 31). Apparently the many deficiencies of grade-equivalent norms (see Ch. 4) are gradually coming to be recognized.

Metropolitan scores can also be converted to specially scaled scores which express preformance on a continuous scale and are directly comparable for all battery levels and forms. This feature permits an assessment of change in a student's performance over time and across grade levels. These scaled scores are not, however, directly comparable across tests, such as Reading and Mathematics. Percentile ranks or stanines can be used for that type of comparison.

The standardization program of the 1978 MAT, with all its component parts, involved the testing of over 550,000 pupils. Standardization samples were selected to represent the national school population closely with respect to size of school system, public versus nonpublic school affiliation, geographical region, socioeconomic status, and ethnic background. Test reliabilities were high for all levels. For the Elementary Level, a single-grade Kuder-Richardson reliability of .98 was found for total scores on the complete battery, while the reliabilities of the five test scores ranged from .88 to .96.

The procedures followed for establishing content validity were thorough and sophisticated. Beginning with extensive analyses of textbooks, syllabuses, state guidelines, and other curricular sources, test blueprints were prepared as guides to item writing. These blueprints included detailed instructional objectives within each subject and level. Empirical item tryouts on nationally representative samples permitted the selection of the most satisfactory items from the large initial pool. In addition to the customary editorial review, all items were also reviewed by panels of minority educators to detect possible cultural or sex biases and to recommend changes. Insofar as curricular content may vary locally, the MAT Teacher's Manual (Prescott et al., 1978, App. C-1) provides a detailed listing of all instructional objectives covered by each item in the final forms. An examination of this compendium for the appropriate levels and subjects should assist schools in judging the content validity of the tests for their own purposes.

TESTS OF MINIMUM COMPETENCY IN BASIC SKILLS

The late 1970s and early 1980s witnessed a mounting concern about the low competence level of many high school graduates in reading, writing, and arithmetic skills. This concern led to popular demands for competency tests in basic skills as a means of certifying the attainment of minimum competency and as a basis for awarding a high school diploma. Such demands aroused a storm of controversy; most of the objections centered on the likelihood of misuses and misinterpretations of minimum competency tests, and on the educational rigidities and bureaucratic controls that might ensue. While most states have established policies regarding minimum competency testing, their policies and procedures vary widely in the time and grade level at which the tests are administered, the particular use made of the results, and the nature and degree of local autonomy in the development or choice of tests. The appropriate tests may be developed by schools or school systems, often with the assistance of test publishers who can provide technically trained personnel and large item banks.

Even before the general dissatisfaction with the attainment of minimum competency through formal schooling, standardized tests for assessing competency in basic skills were being developed for a variety of uses with both children and adults. Most major test publishers prepared tests of this type, several of which are listed in Appendix E. While varying in quality, many of these tests are technically crude, having originated in crash programs to meet an immediate practical need. They are chiefly screening tests, designed to yield an all-or-none assessment of a specified competency level.

A concept underlying most of these instruments is "functional literacy" (Sticht, 1975), which can be extended to functional competence in the use of language in speaking and writing and in arithmetic computation. Functional competence is defined in terms of the demands of practical situations, such as the difficulty level and amount of reading required to perform particular jobs or, more broadly, the basic educational skills required to manage one's own life in a modern society. Several tests concentrate either wholly or in some subtests on the application of basic skills to common everyday-life activities, such as figuring change, comparing prices of merchandise, reading labels on containers, using classified newspaper ads, and filling out forms (e.g., Life Skills, Minimum Essentials Test).

Some tests center on school needs, being designed for use in assessing the minimum competencies of junior and senior high school students in reading, writing, and mathematics. An outstanding example is the Basic Skills Assessment, designed for Grades 7 through 12. This is a nationally available testing program developed by Educational Testing Service in collaboration with a national consortium of school districts. When administered in the seventh or eighth grades, such instruments provide an early-warning system that allows sufficient time for any needed remedial instruction. The entire battery comprises four parts: a writing sample calling for such practical writing activities as completing a form or writing a job application letter, and three multiple-choice tests in reading, writing skills, and mathematics. Typical items from the multiple-choice tests are shown in Figures 67, 68, and 69. This instrument meets high quality standards in such technical characteristics as item analysis, reliability, content validity, and score interpretation.

A few tests are designed as rapid screening instruments over a wide range of competence. Examples include the Peabody Individual Achievement Test and the Wide Range Achievement Test (WRAT), both of which are applicable from the preschool to the adult level. Both are individual, clinical instruments, in which each person is given only the items suitable to his or her performance level.

Still other competency tests in basic skills have been developed specially for adult job applicants with poor educational backgrounds. This type of test is illustrated by the USES Basic Occupational Literacy Test (BOLT), described in Chapter 13. Another example is the Reading-Arithmetic Index published by Science Research Associates. A relatively well-constructed

Questions 1-3 refer to the following medicine label.

RAMITOL: FOR TEMPORARY RELIEF
OF MILD SORE THROAT

Dosage: 3-6 years: ¼ teaspoon at 6-hour intervals

6-12 years: ½ teaspoon at 6-hour intervals

over 12 years: 1 teaspoon at 4-hour intervals

WARNING: Severe and persistent sore throat or sore throat accompanied by fever, headache, nausea, or vomiting may be serious. Consult a physician immediately. If rash or irritation develops stop use and consult a physician. Do not use more than 2 days or administer to children under 3 years of age unless directed by physician.

1. According to the directions, if you have a sore throat, fever, and a headache, you should

   (A) use Ramitol for more than 2 days
   (B) call a doctor as soon as you can
   (C) increase the amount of Ramitol you take
   (D) use other medicine to stop the pain

2. How much Ramitol should be given to a 7-year-old child?

   (A) ¼ teaspoon every 6 hours
   (B) ½ teaspoon every 6 hours
   (C) ½ teaspoon every 4 hours
   (D) 1 teaspoon every 4 hours

3. You should stop using Ramitol right away if you get a

   (A) headache   (B) fever   (C) rash   (D) sore throat

FIG. 67. Typical Items from Basic Skills Assessment: Reading.
(Reproduced by courtesy of Educational Testing Service.)

test in this category is the Adult Basic Learning Examination (ABLE). This is an achievement test specifically designed for use in connection with adult-education classes, educational programs conducted in penal institutions, and job-training programs. It is available in three levels corresponding approximately to Grades 1–4 (Level I), 5–8 (Level II), and 9–12 (Level III). At each level, there are two equivalent forms. Drawing largely from practical problems of adult daily life, ABLE consists of the following four tests:

1. *Vocabulary:* examinee chooses correct word to fit orally presented definitions.

2. *Reading:* paragraph comprehension, inference, and associated general information.

3. *Spelling:* writing words from dictation.

4. *Arithmetic:* number computation and problem-solving—requires no reading at Level I.

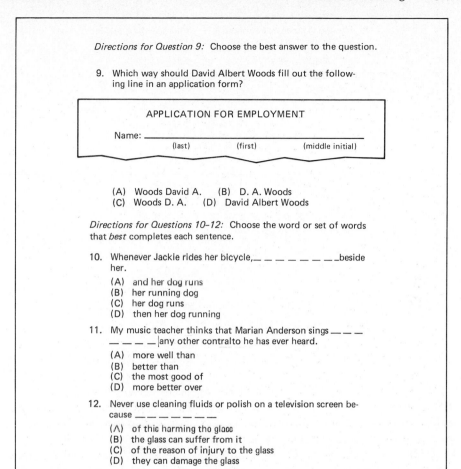

Directions for Question 9: Choose the best answer to the question.

9. Which way should David Albert Woods fill out the following line in an application form?

> APPLICATION FOR EMPLOYMENT
>
> Name: _____
>   (last)   (first)   (middle initial)

(A) Woods David A.   (B) D. A. Woods
(C) Woods D. A.   (D) David Albert Woods

Directions for Questions 10–12: Choose the word or set of words that *best* completes each sentence.

10. Whenever Jackie rides her bicycle,_ _ _ _ _ _ _beside her.

(A) and her dog runs
(B) her running dog
(C) her dog runs
(D) then her dog running

11. My music teacher thinks that Marian Anderson sings _ _ _ _ _ _ _|any other contralto he has ever heard.

(A) more well than
(B) better than
(C) the most good of
(D) more better over

12. Never use cleaning fluids or polish on a television screen because _ _ _ _ _ _ _

(A) of this harming the glass
(B) the glass can suffer from it
(C) of the reason of injury to the glass
(D) they can damage the glass

FIG. 68. Typical Items from Basic Skills Assessment: A Writer's Skills. (Reproduced by courtesy of Educational Testing Service.)

Scores on each of the four tests may be evaluated in terms of grade equivalents, established by administering both ABLE and the Stanford Achievement Test to samples of elementary and high school students. Percentile and stanine norms are also available from large groups enrolled in adult basic education programs and from military samples. Split-half and Kuder-Richardson reliabilities of each test in adult groups range from .80 to .96. Correlations between corresponding tests of ABLE and the Stanford Achievement Test in the elementary and high school samples range from the .60s to the .80s. Correlations of the same general magnitude were also found in several adult samples, both with the Stanford Achievement Test and with the Tests of General Educational Development.

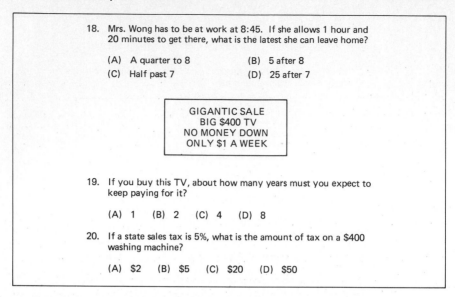

18. Mrs. Wong has to be at work at 8:45. If she allows 1 hour and 20 minutes to get there, what is the latest she can leave home?

   (A) A quarter to 8   (B) 5 after 8
   (C) Half past 7   (D) 25 after 7

   ```
   GIGANTIC SALE
   BIG $400 TV
   NO MONEY DOWN
   ONLY $1 A WEEK
   ```

19. If you buy this TV, about how many years must you expect to keep paying for it?

   (A) 1   (B) 2   (C) 4   (D) 8

20. If a state sales tax is 5%, what is the amount of tax on a $400 washing machine?

   (A) $2   (B) $5   (C) $20   (D) $50

FIG. 69. Typical Items from Basic Skills Assessment: Mathematics. (Reproduced by courtesy of Educational Testing Service.)

STANDARDIZED TESTS IN SEPARATE CONTENT AREAS

While the general achievement batteries have been focusing more and more on basic educational skills, there remains a need for well-constructed instruments to measure achievement in the many specialized areas included in educational curricula. This need increases progressively from the lower to the higher levels of the educational system, as students branch out from the common educational core. It should be noted, too, that nearly all achievement batteries make available separately printed parts covering particular areas. The most common are achievement tests in reading and in mathematics; but tests covering other broad content areas can also be obtained.

Separate standardized tests have been prepared for almost every subject, from American history to physical education, and from accounting to physics. The *Mental Measurements Yearbooks* cover this type of test quite fully, under the appropriate subject-matter categories. A noteworthy development has been the publication of tests in modern foreign languages that use tape recordings to test proficiency in reading, writing, listening, and speaking. Examples of these tests and of recently developed tests in other instructional areas are listed in Appendix E.

Of particular interest is the coordinated series of achievement tests for different high school subjects included in the annual testing program of the College Entrance Examination Board (1981a). A major feature of such a coordinated series is the provision of a single system of comparable scores for all tests. It is thus possible to make direct comparisons among scores obtained in different subject-matter areas. Unlike the achievement batteries discussed earlier in this chapter, however, these tests cannot be standardized on a single normative population. Moreover, it is likely that the standardization samples available for the various academic subjects differ appreciably in general scholastic aptitude. For example, students taking an examination in advanced mathematics are probably more highly selected than those taking an examination in American history. If scores on all these tests are evaluated with reference to the means of their respective normative samples, an individual might, for instance, appear to be more proficient in American history than in mathematics, simply because he or she was compared with an academically weaker normative sample in the former case.

The College Board tests employ a common standard score scale that is adjusted for the differences among normative samples for each test (Angoff, 1971a, 1971b). The scores on the Scholastic Aptitude Test, taken by all candidates, provide the basis for such adjustments. All raw scores on achievement tests are converted into a standard score scale having a mean of 500 and an *SD* of 100 in the fixed reference group. As explained in Chapter 4, this group consists of the 10,651 students who took the SAT in 1941. The scores obtained by the candidates taking any achievement test during subsequent years are expressed with reference to this group. The adjustment takes into account any differences in the distribution of SAT scores between the group taking an achievement test in a particular subject and the fixed reference group.

The availability of comparable achievement test scores across fields is desirable for many purposes. It is clear that some adjustment must be made to allow for the differences among the examinee populations in different fields. A word of caution is in order, however, regarding the interpretation of the system of scaled scores described above. Close comparability of scores can be attained only when the norming test and the anchor test correlate very highly with each other. It cannot be assumed that the relative status of different groups on a scholastic aptitude or general intelligence test is necessarily the same as their relative status on other tests. For example, if the candidates taking a physics test and those taking a Latin test were to obtain the same distribution of scholastic aptitude scores, they might still differ significantly in their aptitudes for Latin and for physics. In other words, we cannot assume that the Latin sample would have obtained the same scores in physics as the present physics sample, if both had pursued the same courses.

To be sure, such an assumption is not implied by the use of the above system of scaled scores. This system merely expresses all scores in terms of a fixed standard that can be precisely and operationally defined. But the test user with only a superficial knowledge of how the scores were derived could easily be misled into unwarranted interpretations. It must be borne in mind that the procedures followed in developing such a scoring system provide comparability of a sort. But they do not necessarily yield the identical norms that would be obtained if all students had been enrolled in the same courses of study and had been given all the tests in each series.

We may inquire where the type of achievement test discussed in this section fits into the total testing picture. Such tests are obviously well suited for use as end-of-course examinations. But they may serve other functions also. In comparison with the more broadly oriented tests of educational development, traditional achievement tests, which are more closely linked to specific courses, measure more nearly distinct skills and knowledge. For this reason, they are likely to yield lower correlations with scholastic aptitude or academic intelligence tests than have been found for broad achievement tests. If combined with scholastic aptitude tests, therefore, the specialized achievement tests will contribute more unique, nonoverlapping variance and may permit better prediction of subsequent outcomes.

There is also an increasing utilization of specialized achievement tests as college equivalency examinations. High school students with additional preparation in certain areas may take tests in the College Board's Advanced Placement Program (APP) to gain admission to college with advanced standing in one or more subjects. A related development is to be found in the College-Level Examination Program (CLEP), also administered by the College Board. The general purpose of this program is to facilitate the granting of college credit by examination and to provide a national system for evaluating college-level education acquired through independent study and other nontraditional procedures. A similar test series, the ACT Proficiency Examination Program, is administered by the American College Testing Program.

TEACHER-MADE CLASSROOM TESTS

Undoubtedly the largest number of tests covering the content of specific courses or parts of courses are prepared by instructors for use in their own classrooms. The vast diversity among courses on the same subject and with identical titles—particularly at the high school level and beyond—is well known. Under these conditions, no external standardized test could suffice. The preparation of local classroom tests, however, can be substantially improved by an application of the techniques and accumulated experience of professional test constructors. The development of classroom tests can be divided into three major steps: (1) planning the test, (2) item writing, and (3) item analysis. Some simple techniques of item analysis, suitable for use with small groups, were described in Chapter 7. An overview of the other two steps is given below.

The test constructor who plunges directly into item writing is likely to produce a lopsided test. Without an advance plan, some areas will be overrepresented while others may remain untouched. It is generally easier to prepare objective items on some topics than on others. And it is easier to prepare items that require the recall of simple facts than to devise items calling for critical evaluation, integration of different facts, or application of principles to new situations. Yet follow-up studies have shown that the factual details learned in a course are most likely to be forgotten, while the understanding of principles and their application to new situations show either no retention loss or an actual gain with time after completion of a course. Thus, the test constructed without a blueprint is likely to be over-loaded with relatively impermanent and less important material. Many of the popular criticisms of objective tests stem from the common overempha-sis of rote memory and trivial details in poorly constructed tests.

To guard against these fortuitous imbalances and disproportions of item coverage, *test specifications* should be drawn up before any items are pre-pared. For classroom examinations, such specifications should begin with an outline of both the instructional objectives of the course and the subject matter to be covered. Table 30 illustrates a two-way specification table for a 50-item examination in economics, covering the topic of money and bank-ing (Gronlund, 1978). In the left-hand column are listed four content areas

TABLE 30
Two-Way Specification Table for a 50-Item Economics Test on Money and Banking

(Adapted from Gronlund, 1978, p. 51. © Copyright 1978 by Norman E. Gronlund. Repro-duced by permission of Macmillan Publishing Co., Inc.)

Content Areas	Instructional Objectives				Total
	Knows Basic Terms	Understands Concepts and Principles	Applies Principles	Interprets Data	
Forms and functions of money	3	4	3		10
Operation of banks	4	3	5	3	15
Role of the Federal Reserve System	4	6	3	2	15
State regulation of banks	4	2	4		10
Total	15	15	15	5	50

or subject-matter categories to be covered. Across the top are four instructional objectives or types of learning to be tested. The entries in the body of the table give the desired number of items, classified by content and objective. These numbers should reflect the relative importance and scope of each topic and objective. When a particular objective or type of learning is inapplicable to a given topic, no items are listed in the corresponding cell. Column and row totals show the overall weight of each topic and type of learning in the entire examination. Frequently, only these column and row totals are established in advance, thereby controlling the relative coverage of topics and types of learning, but not specifying the cross-classification of individual items.

The test constructor must also decide on the most appropriate *item form* for the material. The relative advantages of essay questions and objective items were examined in an earlier section of this chapter with special reference to their use in large-scale, standardized testing programs. In the case of teacher-made tests for use in a single class, essay questions can serve useful functions for both instructional and assessment purposes. With small groups, it may not be worthwhile to prepare objective items, especially if the instructor is relatively inexperienced in the construction of such items. Under such circumstances, essay questions that are carefully formulated and scored may provide the most practicable solution. Or a combination of essay and objective items may be chosen. Essay items can be improved by full and explicit formulation of the question and by systematic scoring procedures. A common weakness of essay examinations arises from subjectivity of scoring. To minimize this source of error variance, it is advisable to list in advance the points to be covered by the answer and the credit to be assigned to each. Preparing sample answers also helps, especially when more than one person will do the scoring. In any event, it is important not to overgeneralize from a student's performance on a single essay question. Essay questions yield more valid and fairer estimates of an individual's knowledge when the assessment is based on multiple questions, covering a variety of topics and administered on different occasions.

For more complete content coverage and a more reliable evaluation of performance, the inclusion of at least some objective items is highly desirable. Among objective items, there is a choice of several specific forms, such as true-false, multiple-choice, completion, matching, and arrangement (in order of magnitude, chronological order, etc.). The content and type of learning to be tested would largely determine the most appropriate item form. Multiple-choice items have proved to be the most widely applicable. They are also easier to score than certain other forms, and reduce the chances of correct guessing by presenting several alternative responses.

Many practical rules for effective *item writing* have been formulated on the basis of years of experience in preparing items and empirical evaluation of responses. Anyone planning to prepare objective items would do well to consult one of the books summarizing these suggestions (e.g., Adkins, 1974; Ebel, 1979, Chs. 4–9; Gronlund, 1977 Chs. 5–7; 1981; Hopkins & Stanley, 1981, Ch. 9; Miller, Williams, & Haladyna, 1978; Thorndike & Hagen, 1977, Ch. 7).

To add one more summary of item-writing "rules" to the many already available would be redundant. However, a few examples will be given to suggest the kind of pitfalls that await the unwary item writer. Ambiguous or unclear items are a familiar difficulty. Misunderstandings are likely to occur because of the necessary brevity. It is difficult to write a single sentence that can stand alone with clarity and precision. In ordinary writing, any obscurity in one sentence can be cleared away by the sentences that follow; but it requires unusual skill to compose isolated sentences that can carry the whole burden unaided. The best test of clarity under these circumstances is to have the statement read by someone else. The writer, who knows the context within which he or she framed the item, may find it difficult to perceive other meanings in it. By rereading the item at a later time, however, the writer himself or herself may be able to spot ambiguities.

While students who feel they may have been cheated out of one or two score points by ambiguous items are quick to call it to the instructor's attention, the opposite type of error is less likely to be publicized. Yet many poorly constructed items give an advantage to the observant guesser. For example, one item may give away the answer to another occurring in a different part of the examination. Thus, one item may require the student to identify the name of the psychologist who developed the test of primary mental abilities, while another begins with the words, "In Thurstone's tests of primary mental abilities. . . ." Grammatical cues, such as differences in number or tense of verbs or the use of the indefinite article "a" instead of "an," may reveal the correct alternative in a multiple-choice item or may at least permit the student to eliminate one of the wrong alternatives.

In the effort to be clear, the inexperienced item writer frequently makes the correct alternative longer or qualifies it more fully than the other alternatives. Examinees soon learn that the odds are in their favor if they choose such an alternative when they do not know the correct answer. Still another example is provided by clang, or alliterative associations, as in the following vocabulary item:

(poor) illicit: secret illegal sexual ignorant daring
(good) illicit: secret unlawful sexual illiterate daring

In the first example, the individual who does not know the meaning of "illicit" could get the item right by choosing the word that sounds most nearly like it. Substituting "unlawful" for "illegal" in the second version has eliminated this cue. In addition, the alliterative cue in this version would mislead the guesser, since on this basis she or he would choose a wrong alternative, "illiterate."

DIAGNOSTIC AND CRITERION-REFERENCED TESTS

In contrast to the survey tests represented by both general achievement batteries and achievement tests in special areas, diagnostic tests are designed to analyze the individual's specific strengths and weaknesses in a subject and to suggest causes of his or her difficulties. Diagnostic tests have much in common with criterion-referenced tests. Although the latter are used for a variety of purposes, as described in Chapter 4, diagnosis is certainly one of their major functions. Like traditional diagnostic tests, criterion-referenced tests elicit information about the individual's performance in highly specific skills and relate this information to instructional prescriptions. Most published tests in both the diagnostic and the criterion-referenced categories deal with either reading or mathematics; several include other language functions, such as listening, speaking, and writing.

DIAGNOSTIC TESTS. There are currently a large number and variety of specialized reading tests. Reading disabilities attracted attention earlier and more extensively than did disabilities in other basic skills. The conspicuous role of reading, not only in education but also in most life activities in a modern society, undoubtedly helped to focus attention on this skill.

All the examples of reading tests listed in Appendix E have been classified under diagnostic tests, since they all have at least some diagnostic features. Available reading instruments vary widely in the type and extent of diagnostic analysis they provide. Some are individually administered series of diagnostic tests, permitting detailed observation of many aspects of the child's reading behavior, such as oral and silent reading, listening comprehension, visual and auditory discrimination of sounds, vocabulary recognition, and spelling. Through such measures, the examiner tries to assess the child's strengths and weaknesses, to identify faulty reading habits, and to recommend remedial procedures. This approach is illustrated by the Durrell Analysis of Reading Difficulty: Revised (1980) and the Diagnostic Reading Scales (1981 rev.). Another category of tests, designed for a different purpose and following a distinctly different approach, is the group survey test with limited diagnostic features. Examples from this category include the Gates-MacGinitie Reading Tests, the Nelson-Denny Reading Test, and the Nelson Reading Skills Test.

A relatively recent development is the inclusion of intensive diagnostic batteries for group administration as separate components of general achievement batteries. The diagnostic batteries may cover reading, mathematics, and language skills. Examples of this approach are provided by the Stanford Diagnostic Mathematics Test, the Stanford Diagnostic Reading Test, and the three batteries of Instructional Tests of the Metropolitan Achievement Tests.

The Survey Battery of the Metropolitan Achievement Tests was discussed in an earlier section of this chapter as an example of a general achievement battery. We shall now examine the Metropolitan Instructional Tests to illustrate diagnostic group tests in reading, mathematics, and language. The two sets of components, survey and instructional, are closely coordinated, having been developed and standardized concurrently. The items in the three skill tests of the Survey Battery (i.e., Reading, Mathematics, Language) represent a sampling of the items included in the corresponding Instructional Tests. The instructional objectives, however, are covered much more fully in the Instructional Tests.

At the Elementary Level, the Reading Instructional Tests of the Metropolitan include seven tests, each concerned with a different "learning strand," or aspect of reading behavior, appropriate for the level. The tests are as follows:

READING INSTRUCTIONAL TESTS

Reading Comprehension

Sight Vocabulary

Phoneme/Grapheme: Consonants (Fig. 70)

Phoneme/Grapheme: Vowels (Fig. 70)

Word Part Clues (Fig. 70)

Vocabulary in Context

Rate of Comprehension

Within each of these tests, there are items corresponding to highly specific objectives, such as those illustrated in Figure 70.[3] Each objective is represented by at least three items and some by as many as 30.

The Instructional Tests for Mathematics and for Language follow closely the structure described for the Reading Tests. At the Elementary Level, the following tests are included:

MATHEMATICAL INSTRUCTIONAL TESTS

Numeration

Geometry and Measurement (Fig. 71)

Problem Solving

Operations: Whole Numbers

Operations: Laws and Properties (Fig. 71)

LANGUAGE INSTRUCTIONAL TESTS

Listening Comprehension

Punctuation and Capitalization

Usage

Grammar and Syntax (Fig. 72)

Spelling

Study Skills (Fig. 72)

[3] The items reproduced in Figures 70, 71, and 72 are sample items, used only to introduce each test and demonstrate the required response. They are generally easier than the scored items in the test itself.

Phoneme/Grapheme: Consonants

Objective: Silent letters

(Find the word that has the same part *silent* as the part underlined in the
 key word)

knee

    Ⓐ   king
    Ⓑ   pink
    Ⓒ   knit
    Ⓓ   keen

Phoneme/Grapheme: Vowels

Objective: Long o

(Find the word that has the *same sound* as the underlined part of the key word)

boat

    Ⓐ   hole
    Ⓑ   land
    Ⓒ   shoe
    Ⓓ   got

Word Part Clues

Objective: Derivational suffix

(Find the word that best completes the sentence)

Mrs. King is our reading _____

    Ⓐ   teaching   Ⓒ   teacher
    Ⓑ   teaches   Ⓓ   teach

Objective: Identification of compound words

(In each sentence, find the compound word)

The pretty cupcakes were soon eaten.
    Ⓐ   Ⓑ   Ⓒ

Fig. 70. Sample Items from Three of the Metropolitan Reading Instructional
Tests. Directions are paraphrased and greatly shortened to fit this figure.
(Copyright © 1978 by Harcourt Brace Jovanovich, Inc. Reproduced by permission.)

Numeration
Objective: Associates number–words with numerals (through millions)

NINE

Which numeral names the number in the box?

     Ⓐ   9
     Ⓑ   90
     Ⓒ   8
     Ⓓ   900

Geometry and Measurement
Objective: Can tell time to the minute

This clock shows that the time is—

    Ⓐ   8:00   Ⓒ   9:00
    Ⓑ   9:30   Ⓓ   8:30

Operations: Laws and Properties
Objective: Can use commutative property of addition

Which statement below is true?

    Ⓔ $16 - 4 = 16 - 6$
    Ⓕ $4 + 16 = 14 + 16$
    Ⓖ $16 + 4 = 16 + 6$
    Ⓗ $16 + 4 = 4 + 16$

FIG. 71. Sample Items from Three of the Metropolitan Mathematics Instructional Tests.
(Copyright © 1978 by Harcourt Brace Jovanovich, Inc. Reproduced by permission.)

Like the Survey Battery, each battery of Instructional Tests is administered in several sittings distributed over different days. With regard to standardization sample and all other technical features of test construction, the Instructional Tests meet the same high standards as does the Survey Battery. A noteworthy feature of the Instructional Tests pertains to the coverage of objectives. Unusually thorough procedures were followed for identifying current instructional objectives in each skill area. Also characteristic of the specialized purpose of these batteries is the type of diagnostic information

Grammar and Syntax

Objectives: Can identify sentence fragments (Item 1)
Can identify plural nouns (Item 2)
Can identify adverbs (Item 3)

Heavily on tired feet

1. These words make—

    Ⓐ   a command   Ⓒ   a statement
    Ⓑ   a question   Ⓓ   an incomplete sentence

2. Which word is used as a plural noun?

    Ⓔ   Tired   Ⓖ   On
    Ⓕ   Heavily   Ⓗ   Feet

3. The word *heavily* is used as—

    Ⓐ   an adverb   Ⓒ   a singular noun
    Ⓑ   a verb   Ⓓ   an adjective

Study Skills

Objective: Can determine alphabetical order of words—third letter discrimination

Which word would come <u>first</u> in the dictionary?

Ⓐ   inn   Ⓒ   inch
Ⓑ   indeed   Ⓓ   insect

Fig. 72. Sample Items from Two of the Metropolitan Language Instructional Tests.

(Copyright © 1978 by Harcourt Brace Jovanovich, Inc. Reproduced by permission.)

provided. Performance on each test within the particular battery can be expressed as scaled scores, percentile ranks, and stanines. In addition, there is an analysis of performance on specific objectives within each test. The performance reports combine norm-referenced with criterion-referenced interpretations and include qualitative comments and teaching suggestions. Similar analyses can be provided for a class as for individual pupils. It is also possible to analyze responses to individual items, if desirable for special instructional purposes.

In connection with the use of all diagnostic tests, one point deserves special emphasis. The diagnosis of learning disabilities and the subsequent program of remedial teaching are the proper functions of a trained specialist. No battery of diagnostic tests can suffice for this purpose. The diagnosis and treatment of severe reading disabilities require an intensive clinical case study, including supplementary information on sensory capacities and motor development, medical and health history, complete educational history, data on home and family background, and a thorough investigation of possible emotional difficulties. In some cases, serious reading retardation proves to be only one symptom of a more basic psychological disturbance. Although survey and group diagnostic tests may serve to identify individuals in need of further attention, the diagnosis and therapy of reading disabilities often represent a problem for the clinician. This may also be true in cases of severe disabilities in other basic skills. The appropriate procedures will be considered further in Chapter 16, in connection with clinical testing.

CRITERION-REFERENCED TESTS. Several published criterion-referenced tests are now available for reading and mathematics. Some currently available examples are listed in Appendix E. At this stage, nearly all are designed for the elementary school grades. Items are described in terms of highly specific objectives, the number of such objectives varying from 30 to over 300 in any one test. Mastery scoring is used regularly, the individual's performance being judged as indicating mastery or nonmastery of each skill. The tests are diagnostic and prescriptive; the performance records are keyed to basic texts, workbooks, and supplementary instructional materials to which the student is directed. Usually, the instruments are organized into a continuing testing program, so that pupils can be examined after learning each skill.

A common pattern consists of a preliminary broad-range test, which may contain as few as one or two items for each objective, and several follow-up tests for the more intensive testing of a single objective or a group of closely related objectives. An example is the combination of Prescriptive Reading Inventory (PRI) and the PRI Interim Tests, and of Diagnostic Mathematics Inventory (DMI) and the DMI Interim Tests, both published by CTB/McGraw-Hill. Another is the Skills Monitoring System: Reading developed by the Psychological Corporation. At each grade level, this system includes a skill locator and some 30 one-page minitests consisting of 8 to 12 items on a single objective. An interesting feature of this particular system is that the minitests are self-scored and provide immediate feedback to the pupils. This is accomplished by the use of chemically treated crayons and latent images. When the examinee fills in the box next to the chosen answer, "Y" (yes) appears if the choice is correct; if "N" (no) appears, the examinee continues to mark other alternatives until he or she finds the correct answer.

Most test publishers have been grappling with the technical problems characteristic of criterion-referenced tests, with varying degrees of success. There is the three-headed problem of assessing a long list of narrowly defined objectives, including enough items to measure each objective reliably, and keeping the whole process within manageable length. There is the perennial problem of setting an acceptable performance level as a standard of mastery. And there are the special problems associated with the measurement of reliability and validity of such instruments.

It is unlikely, moreover, that a single set of highly specific instructional objectives would suit all users, except possibly at the most elementary stages of learning. It would seem that one of the intrinsic advantages of criterion-referenced testing stems from its being tailored to local needs. Some test publishers do, in fact, offer a "customized" service to schools or school districts, which permits a local choice of instructional objectives and corresponding test items from a large resource pool.[4] While affording greater flexibility than ready-made criterion-referenced tests, this alternative does not overcome all the difficulties associated with the use of such tests.

In the *Eighth Mental Measurements Yearbook,* the evaluations of commercially available criterion-referenced tests, including both "catalog" and "customized" versions, are generally unenthusiastic. It is likely that this approach to test administration and performance evaluation may serve best when employed as an integral component of an individualized instructional system. It will be recalled that this is the context in which current criterion-referenced tests originated (Ch. 4). For other educational purposes, the standardized diagnostic tests described in the preceding section, which combine a norm-referenced and a criterion-referenced approach, probably serve more effectively.

SPECIALIZED PROGNOSTIC TESTS

Certain types of tests designed for use in educational contexts are essentially predictive instruments. As such, they function as aptitude rather than as achievement tests. At the same time, they frequently resemble achievement tests closely in content, because what they undertake to predict is usually performance in a specific academic course. The extent to which individuals have acquired prerequisite knowledge and skills is a good predictor of their subsequent performance in such a course. How well they learn new material similar to that which they will encounter in the course is another. The latter approach is followed in the Orleans-Hanna Algebra Prognosis Test. In this test, students are provided with a set of short, simple "lessons" in algebra and are immediately tested on what they have learned. The test thus consists of worksamples, in which the students' later course learning is predicted from their performance in the sample learning tasks.

Another type of prognostic instrument is illustrated by the Modern Lan-

---

[4] See, e.g., descriptions of such services offered by CTB/McGraw-Hill, Science Research Associates, and Instructional Objectives Exchange in the *Eighth Mental Measurements Yearbook,* Nos. 278, 279, 766, 767.

guage Aptitude Test. Designed to assess the capacity of an English-speaking student for learning any foreign language, this test utilizes both paper-and-pencil and tape-recorded materials. It is suitable for high school, college, and adult groups. Two of its subtests require the learning of orally presented numbers and visually presented words in an artificial language. The other three parts test the person's sensitivity to English grammatical structure, as well as certain word recognition skills with visual and auditory materials. An elementary form of this test, suitable for Grades 3 to 6, is also available.

Percentile norms are reported for beginning language students in Grades 9, 10, 11, and 13, as well as for military and civilian personnel assigned to intensive foreign language training. Most of the normative samples are small, however, and may not be comparable at different grade levels. Split-half reliabilities for total scores are high, most of them exceeding .90. Data on predictive validity in college and high school groups appear promising. In an earlier experimental version, this test proved especially effective in predicting success in intensive language training courses conducted by the Foreign Service Institute of the Department of State, the Air Force, and the Army Language School.

Designed for the same general purpose, the Pimsleur Language Aptitude Test is applicable in Grades 6 to 12. The total score on this test is a weighted sum of the scores on four subtests, the student's grade-point average in academic areas other than foreign languages, and his or her self-rated interest in learning a foreign language. The four subtests provide measures of English vocabulary, ability to identify and correctly apply grammatical endings and word sequences in an artificial language (see Fig. 73), ability to learn

---

The list below contains words from a foreign language and the English equivalents of these words.

gade .... father, a father
shi .... horse, a horse
gade shir le .... Father sees a horse.

By referring to the above list, figure out how the following statement should be expressed in this language.

A horse sees Father.

(Correct answer: shi gader le.)

Fig. 73. Demonstration Item from Pimsleur Language Aptitude Test.

new phonetic distinctions and to recognize them in different contexts, and ability to associate sounds with their written symbols. The directions for all tests as well as the items for the last two tests are on tape.

Both percentile and stanine norms are given for students tested at the beginning of Grades 7, 8, and 9, as well as for students completing the first year of instruction in French or Spanish. Each normative sample includes from about 1,000 to about 3,000 students drawn from 5 to 13 states. Norms are available for total scores and for verbal and auditory scores, each of the latter being based on the sum of two subtests. Split-half reliabilities in the .80s were obtained for total scores within each grade level of the normative sample. A few medium to high correlations with terminal course grades and achievement test scores are reported. It is likely, however, that the parts of the battery should be combined with different weights for predicting different aspects of language mastery, such as listening comprehension, speaking, reading, and writing.

ASSESSMENT IN EARLY CHILDHOOD EDUCATION

Many new instruments for measuring the educational development of young children have been published since 1970. Several influences contributed both to the amount and nature of this activity. Research in early cognitive development, the burgeoning of programs for preschool education, and the widespread concern about the effects of cultural handicaps on the child's ability to profit from school instruction have all played major roles. The Piagetian approach and criterion-referenced orientations can be seen in several recently developed instruments. Some of the tests were designed principally to measure the outcomes of early childhood education and thus function as achievement tests. Others are presented as predictive or aptitude instruments to assess the child's readiness for first-grade instruction. The two types of instruments merge imperceptibly, however, and each can usually serve either purpose.

School readiness refers essentially to the attainment of prerequisite skills, knowledge, attitudes, motivations, and other appropriate behavioral traits that enable the learner to profit maximally from school instruction. These prerequisites are what Hunt and Kirk (1974) have called the "entry skills" that the child needs to cope with the teaching-learning situation encountered in the first grade. At one time, readiness was conceived largely in terms of maturation. To be sure, the development of certain minimum physical qualifications facilitates some kinds of learning. Unless children can make the necessary auditory discriminations, they cannot learn to speak by the usual procedures; without the ability for fine motor coordination, they are unable to manipulate a pencil in writing. Most school learning, however, is not so closely linked to sensorimotor development. In the mastery of educational tasks, the importance of prior learning is being increasingly recognized. More and more emphasis is now placed on the hierarchical development of knowledges and skills, whereby the acquisition of simple concepts equips the child for the learning of more complex concepts at any age.

Readiness tests are generally administered upon school entrance. While they have much in common with intelligence tests for the primary grades, readiness tests place more emphasis on the abilities found to be important in learning to read. Some attention is also given to the prerequisites of numerical thinking and to the sensorimotor control required in learning to write. Among the specific functions frequently covered are visual and auditory discrimination, motor control, aural comprehension, vocabulary, quantitative concepts, and general information.

A widely used readiness battery is the Metropolitan Readiness Tests (MRT). In its 1976 edition, this battery has two levels, one for the beginning and middle of kindergarten and one for the end of kindergarten and the beginning of Grade 1. Both levels are orally administered, requiring the child to make simple marks in the test booklet. A Practice Booklet is administered in advance to acquaint children with the materials and procedures they will encounter in the tests themselves. Level II contains the following eight tests, of which the last two are optional:

1. *Beginning Consonants:* child looks at four pictures in test booklet, while examiner names each; then child selects the one whose name begins with the same sound as a word pronounced by examiner but not pictured (Fig. 74).

2. *Sound-Letter Correspondence:* each item consists of a picture followed by four letters; after examiner names the picture, child selects the letter that stands for the sound at the beginning of the name.

3. *Visual Matching:* match what is shown at the beginning of each row with one of four choices which follow; includes letter series (nonwords), words, numerals, and letterlike forms (artificial letters).

4. *Finding Patterns:* designed to assess ability to "see" a given formation of letter groups, words, numerals, or artificial letters within a larger grouping; child must perceive the visual stimulus, then match it with its hidden counterpart amid distracting surroundings (Fig. 74).

5. *School Language:* tests child's understanding of some of the basic and some of the more complex grammatical structures and concepts of the usual language of school instruction (e.g., "Mark the picture that shows this: The car that is in front of the truck is turning the corner").

6. *Listening:* tests comprehension of vocabulary and structure of orally presented passages; some items call for inferences and conclusions.

7. *Quantitative Concepts* (optional): tests knowledge of concepts basic to an understanding of primary level mathematics, including size, shape, position, quantity, etc.

8. *Quantitative Operations* (optional): assessment of child's mastery of counting and simple mathematical operations.

Because many users are interested in assessing only reading readiness, the
manual provides norms for converting total score on the prereading skills
composite (Tests 1 to 6) to stanines or percentile ranks. These six tests are
always given. Tests 7 and 8, yielding a quantitative skill area score, are
optional, as is an additional, qualitatively scored copying test. Norms are
also available for interpreting several other subtest combinations, as well as
the total eight-test battery score.

The MRT norms were derived from a representative national sample of
about 100,000 kindergarten and first-grade children. Both split-half and alternate-form reliabilities are high. As is true of readiness tests generally, this
test shows considerable overlap with intelligence tests for the primary
grades. Several studies with the earlier edition of the MRT yielded corre-

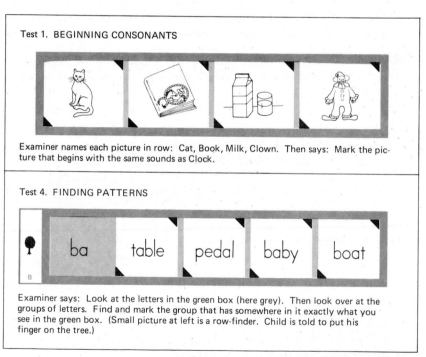

FIG. 74. Demonstration Items from the Metropolitan Readiness Tests. Throughout the battery, the child is instructed to mark the answer by drawing a line from
one black corner to the other, a procedure he/she was taught to follow in the
practice booklet and which is demonstrated anew on the chalkboard before the
administration of each test. This marking technique permits computer scoring of
the booklets.

(Copyright © 1974. Items reprinted by courtesy of Harcourt Brace Jovanovich, Inc.)

lations in the .70s with group intelligence tests. However, when checked against end-of-year achievement test scores, readiness tests yield consistently higher validities than do intelligence tests.[5] Since readiness tests are specifically designed to assess identifiable prerequisite skills, it is understandable that they are better predictors of school achievement than are the more generally oriented intelligence tests.

Some tests have combined a criterion-referenced approach with norm-referenced interpretations. Examples include the Tests of Basic Experiences (TOBE) and the Boehm Test of Basic Concepts. Of the two, TOBE has a broader scope, covering a rather heterogeneous collection of items grouped into four tests: Language, Mathematics, Science, and Social Studies. The Boehm Test was designed to serve a more narrowly circumscribed function. According to the author, its purpose is "to assess beginning school children's knowledge of frequently used basic concepts widely but sometimes mistakenly assumed to be familiar to children at their time of entry into kindergarten or first grade" (Manual, p. 3). Each of the two equivalent forms of the Boehm test contains 50 items, classified under Space (location, direction, orientation, dimensions), Quantity (including number), Time, and Miscellaneous. Four typical items are shown in Figure 75.

A well-designed class record form for the Boehm test facilitates the evaluation of test performance for both individuals and class in terms of total scores (norm-referenced) and individual items (criterion-referenced). A portion of this record form is reproduced in Figure 76. For each item, the form gives a key word identifying the concept and a letter indicating the broader classification. Each column shows the performance of the child whose name is written at the top. The child's total score and percentile rank are entered at the bottom of the column. Reading across each row permits the computation of the percentage of children in the group who answered each item correctly. For comparative purposes, the manual lists percentages of children in the standardization sample who passed each item in high, middle, and low socioeconomic levels within kindergarten, Grade 1, and Grade 2 groups. Suggestions for individual remediation and group instruction are included in the manual. An additional resource guide is available, which provides simple materials and directions for teaching basic concepts.

Several of the concepts assessed in both the Boehm test and the TOBE are reminiscent of Piagetian scales. A more direct application of Piagetian methods is demonstrated in a series of individually administered tests described by Hunt and Kirk (1974). Although not a published instrument, this test series is fully described by the authors, who offer it as a paradigm to illustrate the applicability of Piagetian procedures to the determination of school readiness. The concepts tested pertain to color, position, shape, and

[5] Unpublished data covering both MRT and other readiness tests. Assembled by Blythe C. Mitchell, Harcourt Brace Jovanovich (personal communication, July 1974).

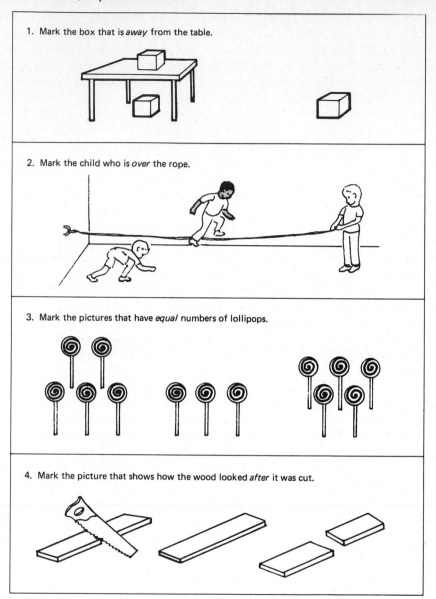

1. Mark the box that is *away* from the table.

2. Mark the child who is *over* the rope.

3. Mark the pictures that have *equal* numbers of lollipops.

4. Mark the picture that shows how the wood looked *after* it was cut.

FIG. 75. Typical Items from Boehm Test of Basic Concepts.

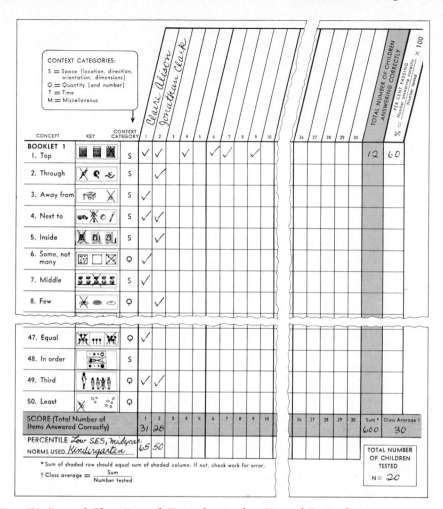

FIG. 76. Part of Class Record Form for Boehm Test of Basic Concepts.

number. Mastery of these concepts is tested through perceptual, listening, and spoken identification. For example, the child selects blocks that match a designated block in shape, in imitation of the examiner's demonstration; she responds to the examiner's naming of each shape by touching the correct block, giving it to the examiner, or carrying out other specified motor responses; and she herself names the shapes indicated by the examiner. A further test concerns the childs' ability to communicate these concepts orally to another child. Preliminary research with these tests revealed marked differences between the performance of culturally disadvantaged children in a Head Start Program and the performance of children in a middle-class nursery school. These findings support the hypothesis that children from different socioeconomic backgrounds vary substantially in their mastery of basic cognitive skills at the time of school entrance.

The Piagetian approach is also central to Let's Look at Children, a combined assessment and instructional program developed at Educational Testing Service. Originating in 1965 in a joint project of ETS and the New York City Board of Education dealing with first-grade children, the program was later extended downward to prekindergarten and upward to Grade 3. Let's Look at Children is highly flexible, comprising an unstructured set of procedures and materials that can be used as a whole or as separate components. It was designed principally to aid teachers in the continuing, day-by-day processes of observing, understanding, assessing, and fostering the intellectual development of young children. The teacher functions as an integral part of the program.

Essentially, this instrument consists of a two-part manual: Part I concentrates on the development of thought, Part II on the development of language and communication. Both provide theoretical background, chiefly from a Piagetian orientation, to guide the interpretation of children's classroom behavior and of their responses to assessment procedures. The same procedures often serve both an assessment and an instructional function, insofar as they provide experiences relevant to the development of the corresponding skills and understandings. All the needed materials are available in the ordinary classroom or can be easily prepared by the teacher. The procedures may be applied individually or with small groups of children.

Several recent developments in psychometrics, psychological research, and early childhood education converged in CIRCUS, a series of assessment instruments originally prepared by ETS for use with preschool and kindergarten children (*CIRCUS*, 1973). The instruments were later extended upward through Grade 3 in four levels (A–D). These levels of CIRCUS represent the first four levels of STEP III, cited earlier in this chapter. The entire series spans the period from the preschool through high school. Those parts of CIRCUS dealing with reading and prereading, mathematics, listening, and writing skills have been linked to the appropriate STEP III scale so that, in these areas, scores can be expressed along a common, continuous standard score scale. For other CIRCUS tests for which there are no corresponding STEP tests, performance is also expressed in terms of a comparable standard score scale that spans the CIRCUS levels.

The circus theme, which pervades the CIRCUS tests, was chosen because of its intrinsic appeal to all children, regardless of sex, race, geography, or socioeconomic status. At Level A, the entire series includes: 14 instruments for obtaining responses from children, only one of which requires oral responses and is therefore restricted to individual testing; two questionnaires for obtaining teacher ratings—one concerned with the child's habitual classroom behavior and the other with her or his behavior during the test situation; and an educational environment questionnaire, also filled out by the teacher, dealing with the child's familial and educational background, characteristics of the class and school environment, and the background, attitudes, and educational values of the teacher. In explaining the rationale for the last' three instruments, the authors emphasize the importance of interpreting the child's cognitive development in relation to his or her own personality characteristics, as revealed in day-by-day behavior, and in the light of the environmental contexts in which he or she functions and develops (Messick, 1973).

Below are a few examples of the 14 instruments requiring responses by the child at Level A, suitable for preschoolers and kindergarten entrants:

What Words Mean: designed to assess the child's receptive vocabulary, the task is to choose the picture that corresponds to a given noun, verb, or modifier.

How Much and How Many: understanding of quantitative concepts, e.g., "Mark the cone with the most ice cream in it." (See also Fig. 77.)

Fig. 77. Illustrative Items from CIRCUS: Level A. Instructions are given orally by the examiner.

Noises: child identifies picture that belongs with "real world" sounds from a tape cassette, e.g., baby's cry, crackling of a newspaper, dripping of a faucet, croaking of a frog.

How Words Work: discriminating verb forms, prepositions, negatives and positives, sentence orders. (See Fig. 77.)

Say and Tell: assesses productive as contrasted to receptive language skills, in three parts (individually administered):
   (a) *Descriptive Usage.* E.g., child is handed two pennies and asked to tell all about them. "Suppose someone didn't know what they are. . . ."
   (b) *Linguistic Structure.* E.g., "Here is a house. Here are two ———."
   (c) *Narrative Usage.* Teacher shows child a large colored picture, explaining that it is a picture out of a storybook and adding, "I don't have the story that was in the book, so I want you to make up a story to go with the picture."

Users may choose any of the CIRCUS instruments suited to their needs. All parts and levels of the program are designed for use by classroom teachers. A preliminary practice test is used to give children an opportunity to learn the mechanics of marking responses and moving from item to item. Performance can be described in both norm-referenced and criterion-referenced terms for individuals as well as groups. In addition to several types of carefully developed numerical scores, CIRCUS yields verbal "sentence reports," giving the child's strengths and weaknesses in specific functions. These verbal reports are especially useful for parents and teachers. The manual also provides a theoretical framework for each measure, to aid in the interpretation of results.

Chapter 15

Occupational Testing

Psychological tests are commonly employed as aids in occupational decisions, including both individual counseling decisions and institutional decisions concerning the selection and classification of personnel. Nearly every type of available test may be useful in occupational decisions. Special aptitude tests have often been developd primarily for occupational purposes. Multiple aptitude tests and interest tests are particularly appropriate in counseling situations. Discussions of the role of tests in counseling can be found in a number of sources (e.g., Goldman, 1971; Tyler, 1969). A highly informative overview of the use of tests in the selection and classification of personnel is provided by Dunnette and Borman (1979). Major aspects of such test uses are examined intensively in several chapters of the comprehensive handbook edited by Dunnette (1976, Chs. 11, 15, 17, 18, 20). McCormick and Ilgen (1980) consider the applications of tests in industry, with many examples from specific occupations. The Division of Industrial and Organizational Psychology of the American Psychological Association (APA, 1980) has prepared and adopted a set of principles for the validation and use of personnel selection procedures. While concerned with good practice in the choice, development, and evaluation of all personnel selection procedures, these principles are highly relevant to standardized tests. Also of interest to test users in personnel selection is a loose-leaf testing manual, which includes, among other items, copies of several sets of testing guidelines issued by government agencies and professional associations (Ramsay, 1981).

As in our treatment of educational tests in Chapter 14, we shall concentrate in this chapter on those tests specially designed for occupational purposes, over and above the more widely applicable instruments discussed in other chapters. We shall also examine the procedures typically followed in industrial settings to assemble and validate batteries of appropriate tests. In one section, we shall consider how tests are employed in career counseling and shall examine typical instruments developed specifically for this purpose. The last section will provide a brief look at the uses of tests in professional training programs and in certification.

VALIDATION OF INDUSTRIAL TESTS

From the standpoint of both employee and employer, it is obviously of prime importance that individuals be placed in jobs for which they have appropriate qualifications. Effective placement also implies that traits irrelevant to the requirements of the particular job should not affect selection decisions, either favorably or unfavorably. If a mechanical ability test requires a much higher level of reading comprehension than does the job, its use would not lead to the most effective utilization of personnel for that job. The simple psychometric fact that test validity must be ascertained for specific uses of the test has long been familiar. It has now acquired new urgency because of the widespread concern about the job placement of culturally and educationally disadvantaged minorities (see Ch. 3 and Appendix B). An invalid test or one that includes elements not related to the job under consideration may unfairly exclude minority group members who could have performed the job satisfactorily.

Another relevant concern, for both particular organizations and society at large, stems from the demonstrated relation between productivity and the validity of selection instruments. Procedures for assessing this relation and typical results were cited in Chapter 7. The estimated gains or losses in productivity associated with rises and drops in the validity of personnel selection procedures are substantial. In organizations hiring many employees, such as government agencies, the cumulative dollar value of such gains and losses is so large as to deserve close attention.

LOCAL CRITERION-RELATED VALIDATION. For several decades, the prevalent opinion in personnel psychology was that selection tests should undergo full-scale validation against local criteria of job performance. Specific procedures for such criterion-related validation were discussed in Chapters 6 and 7. In an industrial setting, this validation involves four principal steps:

1. Conducting a job analysis to identify the major job elements and specify the corresponding skills, knowledge, and other worker traits required by the job.

2. Selecting or constructing tests to assess the characteristics specified in Step 1.

3. Correlating each test with appropriate criteria of job performance and choosing tests for the final battery.

4. Formulating a strategy for personal decisions, i.e., determining how scores on the chosen tests will be used in making operational decisions.

The ideal procedure would further require the hiring of an unselected sample of applicants and their retention on the job for a period long enough to accumulate adequate and stable criterion data.

That such a full-scale, longitudinal validation study is unrealistic in the large majority of industrial situations is obvious. Even under unusually favorable conditions, with access to large employee samples, several practical limitations become apparent (see, e.g., Anastasi, 1972; Campbell, Crooks, Mahoney, & Rock, 1973). In Chapter 6, three principal reasons were given why such local investigations are likely to yield uninterpretable results: (1) unavailability of sufficiently reliable and inclusive criterion data; (2) inadequate number of employees performing the same or closely similar jobs; and (3) restriction of range through preselection, since not all applicants can be hired and followed up.

If time restrictions or other conditions necessitate the use of present employees rather than applicants, several additional features of the experimental design are sacrificed. Attrition over time will not only shrink sample size but will also further reduce variability with a corresponding lowering of validity coefficients. Present employees will also have had varying amounts of job experience, which may be reflected in their test performance and thereby confound the relations between test score and criterion. Furthermore, when employees are given tests "for research purposes only," their motivation and test-taking attitudes may be quite unlike those of genuine job applicants; and these conditions are likely to be reflected in their test performance. In view of the practical difficulties in the way of full-scale local investigations of criterion-related validity, a number of alternative procedures have been explored. These procedures can be ordered along a continuum representing degree of resemblance between test content and job functions.

CONTENT VALIDATION: GLOBAL PROCEDURES. There is a growing interest in the application of content validation to personnel selection tests. In all its forms, this application of content validation depends on a thorough and systematic job analysis (McCormick, 1979). To be effective, a job analysis must be specific. A description in terms of vague generalities that would be equally applicable to most jobs is of little use for this purpose. The job analysis should identify any requirements that differentiate the particular job from other jobs. To obtain a well-rounded picture of job activities, the job analyst may draw upon several sources of information. He or she may consult published sources, including descriptions of similar jobs as well as training and operating manuals prepared for the particular job. Performance records may be examined, particularly those containing qualitative descriptions of common errors, learning difficulties, and reasons for failure on this job. Records of customer complaints may provide clues useful in the analysis of sales jobs. An important source of information for any kind of job is provided by interviews—with supervisors, job instructors, and workers of varying degrees of experience and job success.

One approach to personnel selection utilizes global assessment procedures that resemble the total job situation as closely as possible. This resemblance, however, can never be complete. A *probationary appointment* comes closest to being a true replica of the job. But even in this case, the shortness of the period and the knowledge that the appointment is probationary may influence worker behavior in a number of ways. The probationary appointment undoubtedly has a different effect on different persons because of individual differences in motivation, anxiety level, self-confidence, and other characteristics.

Job samples represent another attempt to approximate actual job performance. In the job sample, the task is actually a part of the work to be performed on the job, but the task and working conditions are uniform for all examinees. Some job-sample tests are custom-made to fit specific jobs. The representativeness of the work sample and the closeness with which the task duplicates actual job conditions are essential considerations. Familiar examples are tests for drivers, as well as several standardized tests for office skills, such as typing, filing, bookkeeping, and the operation of various business machines. For certain types of jobs, written or oral information tests fall into the same category. It should be noted, of course, that such information tests are not substitutes for performance tests in jobs requiring manipulative skills. Moreover, they must be carefully checked to ensure that they do not require a higher level of verbal comprehension than is demanded by the job.

Some tests employ *simulation* to reproduce the functions performed on the job. Simulators merge imperceptibly with job samples. Examples range from the operation of a miniature punch press to simulators for locomotive engineers and for airplane pilots. Simulators have been used for both training and testing purposes in the NASA space program, as well as in a number of military specialties. In a different context, simulation techniques have been applied to the design of tests for certain aspects of executive work (N. Frederiksen, 1962, 1966a, 1966b; Shapira & Dunbar, 1980). Known as the in-basket test, this technique has been adapted for testing Air Force officers in administrative positions, business executives, administrators in government agencies, and school principals. Simulating the familiar "in-basket" found on the administrator's desk, this test provides a carefully prepared set of incoming letters, memoranda, reports, papers to be signed, and similar items. Before taking the test, the examinee has an opportunity to study background materials for orientation and information regarding the hypothetical job. During the test proper, the task is to handle all the matters in the in-basket as the examinee would on the job. All actions must be recorded in writing but may include letters, memos, decisions, plans, directives, information to be obtained or transmitted by telephone, agenda for meetings, or any other notes.

To this list may also be added *assessment center techniques* (Finkle, 1976), which are used largely in evaluating managerial or administrative personnel. This approach was first developed for the selection of specialized military personnel during World War II. During the intervening years, it was used in personality research, principally at the Institute of Personality Assessment and Research (IPAR) of the University of California (Taft, 1959). More recently, it has been adopted by several large industrial organizations. In the typical assessment center, a small group of persons to be evaluated for the same type of job are brought together, usually for two or three days. During this period, multiple assessment techniques are utilized, including interviewing and a variety of ability and personality tests. A distinctive feature of this approach is the inclusion of situational tests, such as the previously cited in-basket test. The program usually employs specially designed job simulations, roleplaying, group problem-solving, and business games. Another common feature is the use of multiple assessors, often including one or more trained in clinical psychology. Frequent use is also made of peer ratings, usually through a nominating technique. Many of the traits evaluated pertain to motivation, interpersonal skills, and other personality variables.

Although depending at least in part on job resemblance as evidence of their "job relatedness," these global assessment procedures have also been evaluated by criterion-related validation. This is especially true of simulation and assessment-center techniques. Some research has been conducted on most of these procedures to obtain corroborative evidence of their relation to the job categories and job performance of the examinees.

CONTENT VALIDATION: JOB ELEMENT METHOD. An effective job analysis should concentrate on those aspects of performance that differentiate most sharply between the better and the poorer workers. In many jobs, workers of different levels of proficiency may differ little in the way they carry out most parts of their jobs—only certain features of the job may bring out the major differences between successes and failures. In his classic book on *Aptitude Testing*, Hull (1928) stressed the importance of these differentiating aspects of job performance, which he called "critical part-activities" (p. 286). Later, this concept was reemphasized by Flanagan (1949, 1954), under the name of "critical requirements." To implement the concept of critical requirements. Flanagan proposed the critical incident technique. Essentially, this technique calls for factual descriptions of specific instances of job behavior that are characteristic of either satisfactory or unsatisfactory workers. A record of such incidents is usually kept by the supervisor during a designated period, such as two weeks. Growing out of Air Force research during World War II, the critical incident technique has been employed with such varied groups as commercial airline pilots, research personnel in physical science laboratories, factory workers, dentists, and department store salesclerks.

The focus on critical job requirements led, through various routes, to the development of the job element method for constructing tests and demonstrating their content validity (Eyde, Primoff, & Hardt, 1981; Hardt, Eyde, Primoff, & Tordy, 1981; McCormick, 1976, 1979; McCormick, Jeanneret, &

Mecham, 1972; Menne, McCarthy, & Menne, 1976; Primoff, 1975; Tordy, Eyde, Primoff, & Hardt, 1976). This method has been fully developed and widely employed by Primoff and his associates at the U.S. Office of Personnel Management (formerly U.S. Civil Service Commission). In this agency, it is the required method for developing examinations for blue-collar workers in trades and industrial occupations, but it has also been used with various white-collar jobs. Similar procedures have been employed in developing written tests for a wide variety of jobs in state and local government agencies (Eyde et al., 1981; Menne et al., 1976). Essentially, job elements are the units describing critical work requirements. The job element statements are generated and rated by present job incumbents and supervisors, who are thoroughly familiar with the job. Job elements refer to those specific job behaviors that differentiate most clearly between marginal and superior workers. Relying ultimately on the observations and judgment of experienced workers, the job element method provides techniques for systematically gathering and quantifying these judgments.

Although various adaptations of the job element method differ in the details of procedure, all provide for the description of job activities in terms of specific behavioral requirements, from which test items can be directly formulated. The specific behavioral statements can, in turn, be grouped into broader categories, such as computational accuracy, dexterity of hands and arms, visual discrimination, or ability to work under pressure. There is a growing body of research aimed at the development of a general taxonomy of job performance (Fleishman, 1975; Pearlman, 1980). The job element method contributes to this goal and thereby facilitates the content validation of a test for many superficially different jobs. This is illustrated by the Position Analysis Questionnaire (PAQ), a job analysis instrument that permits the rating of jobs in terms of common behavioral requirements. The PAQ was developed through several years of research with job element techniques (McCormick et al., 1972).

The job element method is related to the concept of *synthetic validation.* Insofar as job elements identify skills, knowledge, and other performance requirements common to many different jobs, it should be possible to estimate the validity of a test for a particular job in the absence of local criterion-related validation. The concept of synthetic validity has been defined as "the inferring of validity in a specific situation from a systematic analysis of job elements, a determination of test validity for these elements, and a combination of elemental validities into a whole" (Balma, 1959, p. 395). Procedures have been developed for gathering the needed empirical data and for combining these data to obtain an estimate of synthetic validity for a particular complex criterion (see, e.g., Lawshe & Balma, 1966, Ch. 14; McCormick, 1959; Primoff, 1959). Essentially, the process involves three steps: (1) detailed job analysis to identify the job elements and their relative weights in a particular job; (2) analysis and empirical study of each test to determine the extent to which it measures proficiency in performing each of these job elements; and (3) finding the validity of each test for the given job synthetically from the weights of these elements in the job and in the test. A statistical procedure for computing this validity was developed by Primoff (1959; Urry, 1978). Designated as the J-coefficient (for job coefficient), this procedure is essentially an adaptation of multiple regression equations, discussed in Chapter 7. For each job element, its correlation with the job is multiplied by its weight in the test, and these products are added across all appropriate job elements.

Because of its concentration on job-relevant skills, the job element method should help in improving the employment opportunities of minority applicants and persons with little formal education. Similarly, the job element method can contribute substantially to the evaluation and accreditation of experiential learning as a substitute for formal training and paid experience. This application is illustrated in the development of a system to identify and assess the skills acquired by women through homemaking, child rearing, community service, and other life experiences. (Beier & Ekstrom, 1979). Such information is useful for women who wish to resume their education or to explore career opportunities.

BAYESIAN MODEL FOR TEST VALIDATION. Another approach to the validation of personnel selection tests is provided by the procedures developed by Schmidt and Hunter (1977). These procedures represent a special application of Bayesian statistics (Novick & Jackson, 1974). Essentially, the Bayesian model permits the utilization of *prior information* in assessing the validity of a test in a particular situation. Following a job analysis of the job under consideration, the investigator chooses a test (or a set of tests) found to predict the relevant job behaviors in earlier research. Statistical procedures are given for estimating the extent of variability in prior validity coefficients attributable to chance errors. As was explained in Chapter 6, these chance errors are associated with small sample size, criterion unreliability, and range restriction through preselection. From this analysis, it is possible to assess the degree of generalizability of prior validity findings to the present job situation. If the validity coefficient anticipated from such an analysis of prior data is high enough, no further local research is needed. If not, local criterion-related validation is conducted on the limited available sample. However, with a Bayesian approach, the data obtained in the present sample are interpreted *in combination* with the data accumulated in prior studies, thereby strengthening the confidence that can be placed in the results.

Schmidt, Hunter, and their co-workers applied these procedures to many samples of workers in several kinds of government jobs, as well as to approximately 700 published and unpublished studies of clerical workers (Pearlman, Schmidt, & Hunter, 1980; Schmidt, Gast-Rosenberg, & Hunter, 1980; Schmidt, Hunter, Pearlman, & Shane, 1979). The results showed much wider generalizability of validity across jobs and work settings than had heretofore been recognized. The Schmidt-Hunter model can be applied to industrial jobs if test validity data obtained in many different situations are available for combined analysis. Such an analysis can be conducted by utilizing data from various plants and divisions of a large company. In addition, cooperative validation studies undertaken by trade and industry associations are beginning to provide the necessary data on an industrywide basis (e.g., Bentz, 1980).

THE ROLE OF ACADEMIC INTELLIGENCE

"Intelligence" is a broad term, with many definitions. What constitutes intelligence undoubtedly varies in different cultures, during different historical epochs, and at different life stages (see Ch. 12). Traditional intelligence tests, however, cover a more narrowly limited, identifiable cluster of cognitive skills and knowledge. This cluster has proved to be widely predictive of performance in both academic and occupational activities demanded in modern, advanced technological societies. Because it deals largely with knowledge and skills developed in the course of formal schooling in such societies, this ability cluster is frequently described as academic intelligence or scholastic ability. Its content includes principally verbal comprehension, quantitative reasoning, and other aspects of abstract thinking.

The broadly generalizable validity of academic intelligence can be better understood if we think of these tests as contributing data on three levels. First, they permit a direct assessment of prerequisite intellectual skills demanded by many important tasks in our culture. Second, they assess the availability of a relevant store of knowledge or content also prerequisite for many educational and occupational tasks. Third, they provide an indirect index of the extent to which the individual has developed effective learning strategies, problem-solving techniques, and work habits and has utilized them in the past. The effectiveness of this past behavior is reflected in the fullness of the individual's current knowledge store and the readiness with which relevant knowledge can be retrieved. In at least these three ways, therefore, performance on such tests provides clues about the resources available to the individual for subsequent learning, problem solving, and related activities.

It is well known that performance on tests of academic intelligence correlates substantially with amount of education. It would thus seem that educational requirements could be established to cover the applicant's qualifications in this important cluster of cognitive skills and knowledge. There are difficulties, however, in the way of this solution. Amount of education is an indirect index of the individual's cognitive developmental status, and the correlation between the two is far from perfect. On the one hand,

mere exposure to formal schooling does not ensure equal learning of what
has been taught. On the other hand, the knowledge and cognitive skills
normally developed through schooling *can* be acquired in other ways by
some persons. It is therefore fairer to the individual to test his or her knowledge and cognitive skills directly rather than accepting or rejecting applicants on the basis of amount of formal education completed.

An example of the large-scale utilization of specially developed tests
within the academic-intelligence cluster is provided by the Professional and
Administrative Career Examination (PACE). This test battery was designed
for use in selecting applicants for entry-level positions in 120 professional,
administrative, and technical occupations in the federal government of the
United States (McKillip & Wing, 1980). The occupations are quite varied
in specific job activities; examples of the job titles include internal revenue
officer, computer specialist, writing and editing, and personnel management.
PACE was developed over a period of several years at the U.S. Office of
Personnel Management. It was the product of extensive research, including
the identification of the appropriate cognitive constructs, systematic job
analyses of the types of occupations to be covered, test development, and
corroboratove validation against several criteria of job performance. In its
present form, the PACE battery yields five scores: Deduction, Induction,
Judgment, Number, and Verbal Comprehension. These scores are differently
weighted for different groups of occupations within the set. Research is
continuing on various aspects of the nature and uses of PACE.

Among commercially published instruments, several short tests of academic intelligence have been specially developed for use in industry. An
example is the Wesman Personnel Classification Test. Like most current
intelligence tests, it yields Verbal, Numerical, and Total scores. The Verbal
score is based on an 18-minute verbal analogies test, in which each item
contains two blanks, as illustrated in Figure 78. The Numerical score is de-

Find two words that will make the following sentences true and sensible. Choose a
numbered word for the beginning of the sentence and a lettered word for the end.

Example 1.   . . . . is to water as eat is to *2C*

      1. continue   2. drink   3. foot   4. girl
      A. drive   B. enemy C. food D. industry

    2.   . . . . is to newspaper as manager is to . . . . . .   _____

      1. reporter   2. column   3. advertising 4. editor
      A. president B. publisher C. store   D. employer

FIG. 78. Sample Analogies Items from the Wesman Personnel Classification Test.

rived from a 10-minute arithmetic computation test whose items were designed so as to put a premium on ingenuity and ability to perceive numerical relations. Two parallel forms are available. Percentile norms on each of the three scores are reported for groups of students, job applicants, and employees, each group including from 93 to 1,476 cases. Parallel-form reliability coefficients for V, N, and Total scores fall mostly in the .80s. Correlations of V and N scores vary from .25 to .57, indicating that the overlap of the two parts is small enough to justify retention of separate scores.

Mean scores on the test show progressive rise with increasing educational and occupational level in the groups compared. Correlations with criteria of vocational success, usually based on supervisors' ratings, range from .29 to .62. From the nature of the items, as well as from the distribution of scores reported for various groups, it appears that this test is most suitable for white-collar employees, such as sales, clerical, supervisory, and managerial personnel.

To test applicants for many industrial jobs, a more appropriate instrument is the Personnel Tests for Industry (PTI). This battery includes a 5-minute Verbal Test, a 20-minute Numerical Test, and a 15-minute Oral Directions Test. The three tests may be used together or separately. The Oral Directions Test, administered by phonograph or tape recording, is suitable for applicants with limited schooling or with a foreign language background. It is also available in a Spanish edition.

Alternate-form reliabilities of the Verbal and Numerical Tests range from .73 to .92; split-half reliabilities of the Oral Directions Test range from .82 to .94. Norms for all three tests are reported for various industrial and educational samples. Older persons may be somewhat handicapped on the Oral Directions Test because of its dependence on auditory discrimination and speed. The test is rather heavily weighted with perceptual and spatial items and also depends to a considerable extent on immediate memory for auditory instructions. Available data suggest that it discriminates somewhat better at the lower intellectual levels and may be particularly useful in screening applicants for such jobs as general laborer, maintenance and service worker, and messenger. Reference may also be made to the adult tests for minimum competency in basic skills (Ch. 14), designed for similar populations but more specifically directed to the assessment of educational skills.

SPECIAL APTITUDE TESTS

Even prior to the development of multiple aptitude batteries, it was generally recognized that intelligence tests were limited in their coverage of abilities. Efforts were soon made to fill the major gaps by means of special aptitude tests. Among the earliest were those designed to measure mechanical aptitude. Since traditional intelligence tests concentrate chiefly on abstract functions involving the use of verbal or numerical symbols, a particular need was felt for tests covering the more concrete or practical abilities. Mechanical aptitude tests were developed partly to meet this need.

The demands of occupational selection and counseling likewise stimulated the development of tests to measure mechanical, clerical, musical, and artistic aptitudes. Tests of vision, hearing, and motor dexterity have also been widely utilized in the selection and classification of personnel for industrial and military purposes. It is thus apparent that a strong impetus to the construction of all special aptitude tests has been provided by the urgent problems of matching job requirements with the specific pattern of abilities characterizing each individual.

A word should be added about the concept of special aptitudes. The term originated at a time when the major emphasis in testing was placed on general intelligence. Mechanical, musical, and other special aptitudes were thus regarded as supplementary to the "IQ" in the description of the individual. With the advent of factor analysis, however, it was gradually recognized that intelligence itself comprises a number of relatively independent aptitudes, such as verbal comprehension, numerical reasoning, numerical computation, spatial visualization, associative memory, and the like. Moreover, several of the traditional special aptitudes, such as mechanical and clerical, are now incorporated in some of the multiple aptitude batteries.

What, then, is the role of special aptitude tests? First, there are certain areas, such as vision, hearing, motor dexterity, and artistic talents, that are rarely included in multiple aptitude batteries. The situations requiring tests in these areas are too specialized to justify the inclusion of such tests in standard batteries. Special aptitude tests are also employed, however, in areas that are covered in multiple aptitude batteries, such as clerical and mechanical aptitudes. In several testing programs, tests of academic intelligence are combined with specially selected tests of other relevant aptitudes. One reason for this practice is to be found in the extensive normative and validation data available for some widely used tests of special aptitudes. Another reason is undoubtedly the flexibility that this procedure provides, not only in the choice of relevant aptitudes but also in the fullness with which each aptitude is measured for specific purposes.

PSYCHOMOTOR SKILLS. Many tests have been devised to measure speed, coordination, and other characteristics of movement responses. Most are concerned with manual dexterity, but a few involve leg or foot movements that may be required in performing specific jobs. Some measure a combination of motor and perceptual, spatial, or mechanical aptitudes, thus overlapping the tests to be discussed in the next sections. Psychomotor tests are characteristically apparatus tests, although several paper-and-pencil adaptations have been designed for group administration. Examples can be found in the USES General Aptitude Test Battery, discussed in Chapter 13. Some of these printed motor tests may prove valid in their own right as predictors of practical criteria. Available evidence indicates, however, that there is little or no correlation between printed tests and apparatus tests designed to measure the same motor functions (Fleishman, 1958; Melton, 1947.)

The principal application of motor tests has been in the selection of industrial and military personnel. Frequently, they have been custom-made to meet the requirements of specific jobs. Many are constructed on the principle of simulation. This means that the test closely reproduces all or part of the movements required in the performance of the job itself. Specifically, to ensure validity, the test and the job should call for the use of the same muscle groups. Many examples of motor coordination tests, ranging from simple to very complex, are provided by the classification testing program conducted by the Air Force during World War II (Melton, 1947). While these tests are not commercially available, their published report represents a rich source of test material for the research worker and the test constructor.

A test requiring several simple manipulative skills is the Crawford Small Parts Dexterity Test, shown in Figure 79. In Part I of this test, the examinee uses tweezers to insert pins in close-fitting holes, and then places a small collar over each pin. In Part II, small screws are placed in threaded holes and screwed down with a screwdriver. The score is the time required to complete each part. Split-half reliability coefficients between .80 and .95 are reported for the two parts of this test. Despite the apparent similarity of the functions required by Parts I and II, the correlations between the two parts ranged from .10 to .50 in several industrial and high school samples, with a median correlation of .42.

FIG. 79. Crawford Small Parts Dexterity Test.
(Courtesy of The Psychological Corporation.)

Another widely used manual dexterity test which, however, utilizes no tools is the Purdue Pegboard. This test is said to provide a measure of two types of activity, one requiring gross movements of hands, fingers, and arms, and the other involving tip-of-the-finger dexterity needed in small assembly work. First, pins are inserted individually in small holes with the right hand, left hand, and both hands together, in successive trials. In another part of the test, pins, collars, and washers are assembled in each hole. The prescribed procedure for this activity involves the simultaneous use of both hands.

What can be said about the effectiveness of psychomotor tests as a whole? The most important point to note in evaluating such tests is the high degree of *specificity* of motor functions. Intercorrelations and factor analyses of large numbers of motor tests have failed to reveal broad group factors such as those found for intellectual functions. In extensive factor-analytic research, Fleishman (1975) identified 11 major factors in psychomotor functions. Examples include multilimb coordination, speed of arm movement, manual dexterity, finger dexterity, arm–hand steadiness, and aiming. Still other factors have been identified in gross bodily movements, as exemplified by tests of physical fitness (Fleishman, 1964, 1975). These include static strength (continued exertion of force up to a maximum), dynamic strength (muscular endurance requiring repeated exertion of force), explosive strength (mobilization of energy for bursts of muscular effort, as in sprints and jumps), trunk strength, extent flexibility, dynamic flexibility (repeated, rapid flexing movements), body coordination, gross body equilibrium, and stamina (capacity to sustain maximum effort).

In considering the validity of psychomotor tests, we need to differentiate between complex motor tests that closely resemble the particular criterion performance they are trying to predict and tests of simple motor functions designed for more general use. The former are well illustrated by some of the Air Force tests. Such complex, custom-made tests that reproduce the combination of motor aptitudes required by the criterion have shown fair validity. The Complex Coordination Test of the Air Force, for example, considerably improved the prediction of performance in pilot training. For most purposes, however, the use of such tests is not practicable, since a very large number of tests would have to be devised to match different criteria. With regard to commercially available motor tests, the functions they measure are very simple and their validities against most criteria are not high. For this reason, such tests can serve best as part of a selection battery, rather than as single predictors.

MECHANICAL APTITUDES. Mechanical aptitude tests, cover a variety of functions. Psychomotor factors enter into some of the tests in this category, either because the rapid manipulation of materials is required in the performance of the test, or because special subtests designed to measure motor dexterity are included in a paper-and-pencil test. In terms of the factors discussed in Chapter 13, perceptual and spatial aptitudes play an important part in many of these tests. Finally, mechanical reasoning and sheer mechanical information predominate in a number of mechanical aptitude tests.

It is important to recognize the diversity of functions subsumed under the heading of mechanical aptitude, since each function may be differently related to other variables. For example, mechanical information tests are much more dependent on past experience with mechanical objects than are abstract spatial or perceptual tests. Similarly, sex differences may be reversed from one of these functions to another. Thus, in manual dexterity and in perceptual discrimination tests, women generally excel; in abstract spatial tests, a small but significant average difference in favor of males is usually found; while in mechanical reasoning or information tests, men are markedly superior, the difference increasing with age (Anastasi, 1958, Ch. 14).

Among the aptitudes included in all multiple aptitude batteries is spatial aptitude. This is the ability measured by the Space Relations test of the DAT; it corresponds to the *S* factor in Thurstones' primary mental abilities and to the *k* factor in the British hierarchical model of intelligence. It has also been found to have a high loading in many performance and nonlanguage tests of general intelligence. One of the best single measures of this aptitude is the Revised Minnesota Paper Form Board Test. Available in two equivalent forms, this test was originally developed as a paper-and-pencil adaptation of the familiar formboard type of test. Two sample items are reproduced in Figure 80. Each item consists of a figure cut into two or more parts. The examinee must determine how the pieces would fit together into the complete figure; he or she then chooses the drawing that correctly shows this arrangement.

The manual for the Minnesota Paper Form Board provides extensive tables of norms based on large and well-defined educational and industrial

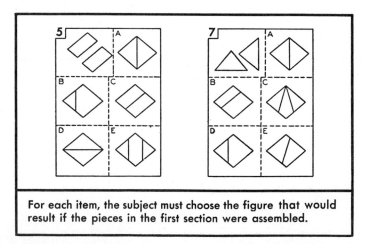

For each item, the subject must choose the figure that would result if the pieces in the first section were assembled.

FIG. 80. Sample Items from the Revised Minnesota Paper Form Board.

samples. Alternate-form reliability coefficients are in the .80s. An unusually large number of studies have been conducted with this test. The results indicate that it is one of the most valid available instruments for measuring the ability to visualize and manipulate objects in space. Among the criteria employed in this research were performance in shop courses, grades in engineering and in other technical and mechanical courses, supervisors' ratings, and objective production records. The test has also shown some validity in predicting the achievement of dentistry and art students.

Another major type of mechanical aptitude test is concerned with mechanical information, mechanical reasoning, or mechanical comprehension. While requiring some familiarity with common tools and mechanical relations, these tests assume no more technical knowledge than can be acquired through everyday experience in an industrial society such as ours. Some of the early tests in this field required the examinee to assemble common.mechanical objects from the given parts. For general testing purposes, paper-and-pencil group tests are now widely employed.

A well-known example of this type of test is the Bennett Mechanical Comprehension Test. Utilizing pictures about which short questions are to be answered, this test emphasizes the understanding of mechanical principles as applied to a wide variety of everyday-life situations. Two items employed in the fore-exercise of this test are reproduced in Figure 81.

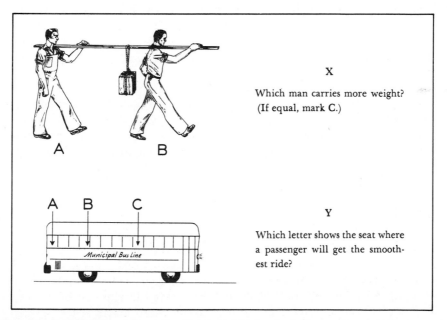

FIG. 81. Sample Items from the Bennett Mechanical Comprehension Test.

This test has been used widely for both military and civilian purposes. In its current revision, it is available in two equivalent forms, S and T. Covering a wide difficulty range, these forms are suitable for such groups as high school students, industrial and mechanical job applicants and employees, and candidates for engineering school. Percentile norms are provided for several groups, permitting the user to choose the most appropriate group in terms of educational level, specialized training, or prospective job category. Odd-even reliability coefficients of each form range from .81 to .93 in different groups.

With regard to validity, the manual gives some thirty correlations with training or job-performance criteria, most of which were obtained with earlier forms of the test. While varying widely, about two thirds are above .30 and extend to the .60s. Other published studies with both civilian and military forms provide good evidence of both concurrent and predictive validity for mechanical trades and engineering (Ghiselli, 1966). During World War II, this test proved to be one of the best predictors of pilot success (Guilford & Lacey, 1947, p. 843). Its validity for this purpose seems to have resulted chiefly from the contribution of a mechanical information factor and a spatial visualization factor, which together accounted for about 60% of the variance of its scores (Guilford & Lacey, 1947, pp. 336–339).

For examinees with limited reading skills, Forms S and T may be administered with tape recorded instructions and questions. Spanish versions are also available for both regular and oral administration. It should be added that the Mechanical Reasoning Test of the Differential Aptitude Tests (Ch. 13) is sufficiently similar to the Bennett Mechanical Comprehension Test to be regarded as another form of the same test.

CLERICAL APTITUDES. Tests designed to measure clerical aptitudes are characterized by a common emphasis on perceptual speed. A well-known example is the Minnesota Clerical Test, which consists of two separately timed subtests, Number Comparison and Name Comparison. In the first, the examinee is given 200 pairs of numbers, each containing from 3 to 12 digits. If the two numbers in the pair are identical, the examinee places a check mark between them. The task is similar in the second subtest, proper names being substituted for numbers. Sample items from both subtests are reproduced in Figure 82. Although a deduction is made for errors, the scores depend predominantly on speed. Performance on this test is influenced by the examinee's response set. Occasionally, a very careful worker will obtain a poor score because he or she proceeds slowly in order to avoid errors. By contrast, the examinee who emphasizes speed at the expense of accuracy will complete many more items and will be penalized only a few points as a result of errors. The possible effect of response set should therefore be taken into account when interpreting a low score, especially when such a score is obtained by an otherwise able or promising person.

When the two numbers or names in a pair are <u>exactly the same</u>, make a check mark on the line between them.

66273894 _____ 66273984

527384578 _____ 527384578

New York World _____ New York World

Cargill Grain Co. _____ Cargil Grain Co.

FIG. 82. Sample Items from the Minnesota Clerical Test.

(Reproduced by permission. Copyright © 1933–1959 by The Psychological Corporation, New York, N.Y. All rights reserved.)

Percentile norms on the Minnesota Clerical Test are reported for several large samples of clerical applicants and employed clerical workers, as well as for boys and girls in Grades 8 to 12. Retest reliability coefficients over intervals of several months fall mostly in the .70s and .80s. These values are probably underestimates, since the intervals were longer than those usually employed for estimating reliability.

Data on both concurrent and predictive validity of the Minnesota Clerical Test are provided by a number of independent studies. Moderately high correlations have been found between scores on this test and ratings by office supervisors or by commercial teachers, as well as performance records in courses and in various kinds of clerical jobs. Several studies employed the method of contrasted groups. Thus, comparisons are reported between different levels of clerks, between clerical workers and persons engaged in other occupations, and between employed and unemployed clerks. All these comparisons yielded significant differences in mean scores in the expected direction. A marked and consistent sex difference in favor of women has been found on this test, beginning in childhood and continuing into adulthood.

It is apparent, of course, that such a relatively homogeneous test as the Minnesota Clerical Test measures only one aspect of clerical work. Clerical jobs cover a multiplicity of functions. Moreover, the number and particular combination of duties vary tremendously with the type and level of job. Despite such a diversity of activities, however, job analyses of clerical work generally indicate that a relatively large proportion of time is spent in tasks requiring speed and accuracy in perceiving details. To be sure, many types of jobs besides that of clerk require perceptual speed and accuracy. Inspectors, checkers, packers, and a host of other factory workers obviously need this ability. It is interesting to note in this connection that the Minnesota

Clerical Test was also found to have some validity in predicting the performance of such workers (Dorcus & Jones, 1950). However, it is likely that higher validity may be obtained in such cases by designing a similar test with pictorial rather than with verbal or numerical material. It will be recalled that, in the GATB prepared by the United States Employment Service, separate tests are included for the Q and P factors. The Q factor appeared in number- and word-checking tests similar to those that make up the Minnesota Clerical Test. The P factor, on the other hand, occurred in tests requiring the perception of similarities and differences in spatial items, and is probably more closely related to the inspection of materials.

Several tests of clerical aptitude combine perceptual speed and accuracy with other functions required for clerical work. Among the measures used for the latter functions are job-sample types of tests for such activities as alphabetizing, classifying, coding, and the like. In addition, some measure of verbal and numerical ability may be included, to serve in lieu of a general intelligence test. Other clerical aptitude tests include such office skills as business vocabulary, business information, spelling, and language usage.

ARTISTIC APTITUDES. Successful achievement in the visual arts calls for a multiplicity of aptitudes and personality traits. Different combinations of these characteristics may be required by diverse specialties and art forms. The sculptor and the painter utilize different skills; among painters, the traditional portraitist and the surrealist artist undoubtedly differ in a number of significant ways. In pursuing a career in art, moreover, an individual may play any of several roles, each with its distinct set of qualifications. Thus, the creative artist, art teacher, critic, dealer, and museum administrator approach art with different patterns of skills, knowledge, interests, attitudes, and feelings.

Standardized tests of artistic aptitudes have traditionally concentrated on a few aptitudes considered to be basic to artistic activity, whatever its form. Among these tests, however, a distinction can be made between those concerned only with aesthetic appreciation and those measuring also productive skills. Obviously, a person may be a highly discriminating and sophisticated connoisseur of paintings without himself being able to paint. But artistic production, except at a routine and mechanical level, undoubtedly presupposes superiority in both appreciative and productive skills. Thus, tests of art appreciation have a broader applicability than tests of production.

Tests of artistic appreciation have generally followed a common pattern. In each item, the examinee is requested to express his preference regarding two or more variants of the same object. One variant is either an original by an eminent artist or a version preferred by the majority of a group of art experts. The other versions represent deliberate distortions designed to violate some accepted principle of art. Any controversial items, on which a clear consensus of experts cannot be obtained, are usually eliminated from such a test.

In the development of art appreciation tests, both original item selection and subsequent validation procedures depend heavily on the opinions of contemporary art experts within our culture. It is well to bear this fact in mind when interpreting scores. Essentially, such tests indicate the degree to which the individual's aesthetic taste agrees with that of contemporary art experts. The representativeness of the particular group of experts employed in developing the test is obviously an important consideration. Insofar as aesthetic standards or taste may change with time, the periodic rechecking of scoring key and item validities is likewise desirable.

A well-established and unusually viable test in the field of art appreciation is the Meier Art Judgment Test. First published in 1929 and revised in 1940, this test employs relatively timeless artworks, that will not readily go out of date. Most are paintings or drawings by acknowledged masters, while a few represent vases or designs suitable for pottery. All reproductions are in black and white. Each item contains only two versions, an original and a variation in which the symmetry, balance, unity, or rhythm has been altered. This test thus concentrates on the judgment of aesthetic organization, generally considered to be a key factor in artistic sensitivity. In order to rule out the contribution of perceptual accuracy, the examinee is told in what detail the two versions of each picture differ. An illustrative item is reproduced in Figure 83.

Percentile norms are given for junior and senior high school students and for adults. All norms are derived largely from students in art courses, whether in high school, college, or special art schools. Data were gathered in 25 schools scattered throughout the United States. Split-half reliability coefficients between .70 and .84 are reported for relatively homogeneous samples.

Most of the available evidence regarding validity of the Meier Art Judgment Test can be summarized under the headings of item selection and contrasted group performance, although a few correlations with independent criteria of artistic accomplishment have also been reported. Items were selected on the basis of several criteria, including: original artwork versus deliberate distortion; agreement among a group of art experts; choice of original version by large majority of a miscellaneous sample of about 1,000 persons; and internal consistency, i.e., correspondence between item choice and total score.

Performance on the Meier Art Judgment Test exhibits a sharp differentiation in terms of age, grade, and art training. Thus, art faculty score higher than nonart faculty, art students higher than comparable nonart students. The extent to which these group differences result from selection or from previous art training cannot be determined from available data.

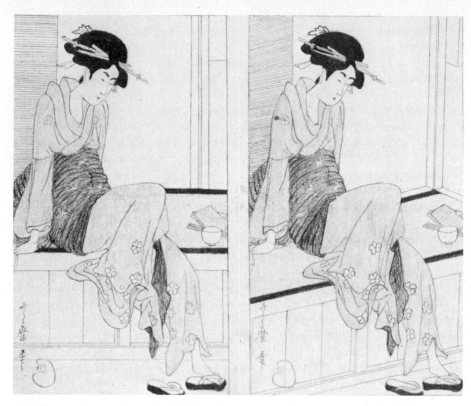

Fig. 83. Item Similar to Those Employed in the Meier Art Judgment Test. The difference between the two versions is in the angle at which the window seat crosses the picture.

(Courtesy of Norman C. Meier.)

Although no validity coefficients are given in the manual, a few are reported in other published sources. In several early studies, correlations ranging from .40 to .69 were found between scores on this test and art grades or ratings of artistic ability (H. A. Carroll, 1933; Morrow, 1938).

As in most artistic aptitude tests, the Meier Art Judgment Test has regularly shown negligible correlation with traditional intelligence tests, such as the Stanford-Binet or group verbal tests. This is simply an indication of discriminant validity (see Ch. 6) for a test designed to measure a special aptitude. It does not imply that abstract intelligence or scholastic aptitude is unrelated to success in an art career. In fact, research by Meier and his associates suggested that, for higher levels of artistic accomplishment, superior scholastic aptitude is a decided asset. In one study, for example, the mean IQ of successful artists was found to be 119 (Tiebout & Meier, 1936). Similarly, a group of artistically gifted children had IQs ranging from 111 to 166 (Meier, 1942).

MUSICAL APTITUDES. During the first four decades of this century, extensive research on the psychology of music was conducted at the University of Iowa under the direction of Carl E. Seashore (1938). One of the outcomes of these investigations was the preparation of the Seashore Measures of Musical Talents. In its present form, this series consists of six tests covering pitch, loudness, rhythm, time, timbre, and tonal memory. The Seashore tests are now available on both an LP record and a tape recording. Either or both of these modes of presentation are utilized in most current musical aptitude tests to permit group administration and to ensure uniformity of procedure.

Each item in the Seashore tests consists of a pair of tones or tonal sequences. In the pitch test, the examinee indicates whether the second tone is higher or lower than the first. The items are made progressively more difficult by decreasing the difference in pitch between the two tones in each pair. In the loudness test, the question is whether the second tone is stronger or weaker than the first. The rhythm test requires the comparison of rhythmic patterns that are either the same or different within each pair. In the time test, the examinee records whether the second tone in each pair is longer or shorter than the first. The timbre test calls for the discrimination of tone quality, the two tones in each pair being either the same or different in this respect. In the tonal memory test, short series of three to five tones are played twice in immediate succession. During the second playing, one note is changed, and the examinee must write the number of the altered note (i.e., first, second, etc.).

The Seashore tests are applicable from the fourth grade to the adult level. The testing of younger children by this procedure has not proved feasible because of the difficulty of sustaining interest and attention. Even above the age of 10, the scores on these tests may be lowered by inattention. The scores are not combined into a single total, but are evaluated separately in terms of percentile norms. Age changes are slight and sex differences are negligible. The tests are probably somewhat susceptible to practice and training, although studies of these effects have yielded conflicting results.

A more comprehensive approach to the measurement of musical aptitude was followed in a battery developed in England by Wing (1941, 1962). Applicable from the age of 8 on, the Wing tests depart from the "atomistic" sensory orientation of the Seashore tests and make use of musically meaningful content. Piano music is employed in each of the seven tests, which cover chord analysis, pitch discrimination, memory for pitch, harmony, intensity, rhythm, and phrasing. The first three tests require sensory discrimination, but at a somewhat more complex level than in the Seashore tests. In the other four, the examinee compares the aesthetic quality of two versions. Thus, the battery places considerable emphasis on music appreciation.

Presented on tape, the entire battery requires approximately one hour but may be administered in two sessions. Norms are provided for total scores on the seven-test battery, as well as for a subtotal on the first three tests only. It is suggested that the first three tests may be used as a short battery with younger children or as a preliminary screening instrument. Based on a standardization sample of over 8,000 cases, the norms are reported separately for each age from 8 to 17 (adult). For older children and adults, both retest and split-half reliabilities of total scores on the entire battery are in the .90s; but they drop to the .70s for younger children.

Preliminary studies of validity in small groups yielded correlations of .60 or higher with teachers' ratings of musical ability. Other validation studies on both children and adults give promising evidence of predictive validity in terms of performance in music training. The use of total scores is supported by the identification of a general factor of musical ability in factorial analyses of music tests (McLeish, 1950; Wing, 1941). This factor, described as the cognitive aspect of musical ability, accounted for 30% to 40% of the total test variances. The Wing tests have high ceilings and may find their greatest usefulness in the selection of musically talented children for further training.

A similar approach was followed by E. Gordon (1965, 1967) in the more recently developed Musical Aptitude Profile. The taped selections in this test use exclusively violin and cello, rather than piano as in the Wing tests. Some reviewers have objected that this choice of instruments makes the test monotonous for the listeners. The entire battery comprises seven tests, grouped under tonal imagery (two tests), rhythm imagery (two tests), and musical sensitivity (three tests). Separate scores may be found in the seven tests, the three sections, and the total battery. The first four tests require perception of similarity or difference between pairs of phrases, with regard to melody, harmony, tempo, and meter, respectively. The last three call for musical preference within each pair of selections; the selections differ in phrasing, balance, or style. Insofar as they involve aesthetic judgment or taste, these three tests resemble the last four of the Wing tests.

In test-construction procedures, the Gordon tests compare favorably with other music tests. Percentile norms for Grades 4 to 12 are reported for the seven tests, the three part scores, and the composite. These norms were derived from over 12,800 pupils enrolled in a national sample of school systems, stratified with respect to geographical region, community size, and socioeconomic level. Additional norms are provided for musically select groups within the standardization sample. Reliability is satisfactory: in the .70s for separate tests, in the .80s for the three part scores, and in the .90s for composite battery scores. Available validity data are encouraging. Concurrent validity coefficients cited in the manual, with teachers' ratings as criteria, range from the .70s to the .90s for total scores. In a later, well-designed longitudinal study of predictive validity, the battery was administered to fourth- and fifth-grade children and the scores were compared with their performance at the end of one, two, and three years of instrumental training (Gordon, 1967). Correlations with objective evaluations of performance ranged from .53 to .71; correlations with teachers' ratings were in the .30s. Predictive validity did not decline—and in fact tended to rise—as the interval between test and criterion performance increased.[1]

CAREER COUNSELING

Special aptitude tests, such as those in art, music, and mechanical abilities, are sometimes helpful in career counseling. The two types of instruments that are most directly applicable to career exploration, however, are the multiple aptitude batteries described in Chapter 13 and the interest inventories to be considered in Chapter 18. Choosing a career often implies the choice of a general lifestyle, with its characteristic set of values. Because interest inventories essentially assess the individual's value system, they are coming more and more to be regarded as focal in effective career planning.

In the present section, we shall examine two types of instruments that have been specially designed for career counseling, namely, comprehensive programs for career exploration and measures of career maturity. Both represent recent developments and are still at a preliminary stage. Although several published instruments are available for practical application, their evaluation must await the accumulation of more data through actual use.

COMPREHENSIVE PROGRAMS FOR CAREER EXPLORATION. Several multiple aptitude batteries have been incorporated in career guidance systems. An example is provided by the Differential Aptitude Tests (DAT), whose Career Planning Questionnaire and DAT Career Planning Report were described in Chapter 13. The latter integrates the DAT scores and the interest data from the questionnaire with job information.

Another example is the program developed by the United States Employment Service, whose General Aptitude Test Battery (GATB) was also discussed in Chapter 13. The core of the USES career counseling program is the *Guide for Occupational Exploration* (U.S. Department of Labor, 1979a)[2]. Intended for use both by counselors and by individuals themselves, this *Guide* groups the thousands of occupations in the world of work by major interest areas and by ability patterns and other traits required for successful performance. Included are 12 interest areas (such as scientific, humanitarian, mechanical, selling) and 66 work groups classified under the appropriate interest areas; specific jobs are in turn listed under each work group. The individual can use the *Guide* for preliminary career exploration by identifying those work groups in which he or she has a strong interest

---

[1] For fuller coverage of available music tests, see Lehman (1968), as well as the appropriate section of the latest *Mental Measurements Yearbook*. Music and art tests are grouped in separate sections of the MMY, under the general heading of Fine Arts.

[2] Revised edition in press, 1981.

and then checking the training and skills they require. The *Guide* also links the data available regarding job functions and qualifications with the aptitude scores obtained with the GATB and the information obtained with the newly developed USES Interest Inventory and Interest Checklist (U.S. Department of Labor, 1981).

Some programs have been developed completely as career exploration systems, rather than incorporating previously available instruments. An example of this approach is to be found in the Planning Career Goals (PCG) designed for students in Grades 8 to 12. This program is a product of a longitudinal study of a national sample of high school students. Known as Project TALENT, the study began in 1960 with the administration of a comprehensive battery of aptitude and achievement tests, as well as interest and personality inventories, to approximately 400,000 high school students (Flanagan, 1973; Flanagan, Shaycoft, Richards, & Claudy, 1971). The group was carefully chosen so as to yield a stratified sample of students enrolled in public, parochial, and private high schools throughout the country. In addition, in order to secure national norms for one complete age group, 15-year-olds not in high school were also tested. Follow-ups after 5 and 11 years included analyses of the initial test results of students classified according to the type of work they were doing. The occupations represented in the sample were classified into 12 career groups on the basis of similarities in training requirements and job functions. For each career group, a profile was prepared from the scores of the high school students who had later entered that field. The profile covers values, interests, job information, and abilities.

The PCG utilizes adaptations of those Project TALENT instruments that differentiated most clearly among members of different career groups. The program includes (1) a values inventory relating to life and career plans and goals; (2) an interest inventory covering occupational titles and activities, as well as current activities that are relevant to occupational functions; (3) an information measure sampling the knowledge the individual has acquired about each of the 12 career groups; and (4) a multiple aptitude battery yielding scores in 10 factors, such as reading comprehension, mechanical reasoning, quantitative reasoning, computation, and creativity. Results are reported in the form of score profiles for each of the 12 career groups. The student's scores can be compared with those obtained by high school students who later entered each of the 12 career groups. A narrative report synthesizing some of these findings is also included in the computerized report.

ASSESSMENT OF CAREER MATURITY. Another type of instrument specifically developed for use in career counseling is concerned with the individual's level of career maturity. This concept emerged from a long-term research project on career development conducted by Super and his associates

(Super, Crites, Hummel, Moser, Overstreet, & Warnath, 1957). Career maturity (or vocational maturity, as it was originally called) refers to individuals' mastery of the vocational tasks appropriate to their age level, and their effectiveness in coping with such tasks. The research itself comprised a 20-year longitudinal investigation of approximately 100 ninth-grade boys (Super et al., 1957; Super & Overstreet, 1960). The students were all attending a public high school in an urban community in New York State, chosen as typical of American cities in many socioeconomic indices. A mass of data was gathered through tests, questionnaires, and a series of interviews with each participant. Further data were obtained from records of school achievement, reports of extracurricular and community activities, peer ratings, interviews with parents, and other miscellaneous sources. Several indices of career development were formulated and applied to the group. The resulting measures were intercorrelated and factor-analyzed.

On the basis of these analyses, the following indices were identified as the best measures of the construct "vocational maturity" at this age level: concern with choice (awareness of need for choice and knowledge of factors affecting choice), acceptance of responsibility for choice and planning, specificity of planning for the preferred occupation, and use of resources in obtaining occupational information. The findings suggested that the major career-development task at the junior high school level is that of preparing to make career choices. For the ninth-grade boy, vocational maturity is shown, not by the wisdom or consistency of the ultimate career goal he chooses, but by the way he handles the preliminary planning and exploration required at this stage. Other research on career development, by both cross-sectional and longitudinal approaches, has been contributing data that help to fill out the picture (Crites, 1965a, 1965b, 1969; Gribbons & Lohnes, 1968, 1969; Jordaan & Heyde, 1979; Super, 1974, 1977, 1980).

One of the byproducts of the research on career development has been the construction of standardized measures of career maturity. An example is the Career Development Inventory prepared by Super. In its current School Form (Grades 8 to 12), this inventory consists of two parts. The first, Career Orientation, is concerned with what the student has done thus far toward career planning and exploration, his or her judgment about how to make career decisions, and the information he or she has acquired about the world of work. In the second part, Knowledge of Preferred Occupation, students first designate which of 20 occupational groups interests them most. They then answer a series of questions about this occupation, with regard to such characteristics as nature of the work, working conditions, ability requirements, interests, and values. A College and University Form of this inventory is in preparation, with anticipated publication date in 1982; an Adult Form is also under development.

The results obtained with such inventories serve to highlight any aspects of career orientation in which individual students need assistance. They are also useful in assessing the effects of training programs in career decision-making. Several training programs of this kind are now available, varying from simple workbooks to more extensive multimedia instructional systems (e.g., *Careers in Focus,* 1976) and individualized procedures utilizing interactive computer systems (e.g., *SIGI,* 1974, 1975; M. R. Katz, 1969, 1974).

TESTING IN THE PROFESSIONS

Standardized tests are used in many large-scale programs for the selection of professional personnel. Some of these programs are directed toward the selection of students for admission to professional training. Tests are administered to candidates for schools of medicine, dentistry, nursing, law, business, engineering, theology, architecture, and other professional fields. Although such testing programs emphasize aptitudes and the prediction of subsequent performance in specialized training, achievement tests on preprofessional courses constitute an important part of most batteries.

It should also be noted that in the selection of students for professional schools what is involved is not so much new types of tests as specially administered testing programs. There is no evidence that the various professional fields require any special aptitudes not already covered by available tests. The typical professional-school testing program includes a test of scholastic aptitude or general academic intelligence, one or more achievement tests on preprofessional training, and possibly tests of interests or other personality traits. Test results are often supplemented with biographical data, letters of recommendation, previous academic record, and interview ratings.

The intelligence test employed in such a program may be a standard scholastic aptitude test at an advanced level. More often it is specially designed so that the content can be slanted toward the particular professional field under consideration. Such a choice of content increases face validity, in addition to permitting better security control of test materials. There is also some evidence to suggest that the predictive validity of these special tests is a little higher than that of the intelligence or scholastic aptitude tests available for general use. The specialized scholastic aptitude tests often contain measures of reading comprehension for material similar to that which the student will encounter in professional school. Some of the tests yield separate verbal and quantitative scores. Spatial, mechanical, and motor aptitudes may also be separately tested when relevant to the field.

Another level at which standardized testing programs are making major inroads is that of specialty certification and the selection of job applicants following completion of training. Understandably these terminal testing programs draw much more heavily on achievement tests in specialized content areas; but more general types of tests are not excluded. Examples of major testing programs at this level include the National Teacher Examinations, constructed and administered by Educational Testing Service, and the various tests for nursing developed by the National League for Nursing (NLN). Educational Testing Service also works with several medical specialty boards and with the American Nurse's Association and other professional organizations in the development of certification examinations in the health professions. In the following sections, we shall look briefly at two programs illustrating the use of tests at pretraining and posttraining levels, respectively.

LAW SCHOOL ADMISSION TEST. The Law School Admission Test is administered to law school candidates on a national basis. In its present form, this test includes eight separately timed sections and yields two scores, designated as the LSAT score and the Writing Ability score. The sections yielding the LSAT score are designed to measure principally reading comprehension and logical reasoning with verbal and quantitative material. The content is drawn from a wide variety of sources, such as the humanities, science, business contexts, and popular writing or speech. No field of specialization receives a particular advantage. Although numerical data, tables, and graphs are included in the quantitative sections, these items nevertheless require careful reading of rather intricate verbal material. In view of the prime importance of verbal comprehension in legal practice, it is understandable that legal aptitude tests have always been predominantly verbal in content.

The *Law School Admission Bulletin,* distributed to all candidates who register for the examination, contains a full description of the test, with sample items, detailed explanations of how the correct responses are chosen, and suggestions for solving each type of problem. It also contains a complete sample test with an answer key. A major portion of this bulletin thus represents an effective test orientation procedure. Although the item types may vary somewhat from form to form, the following outline is representative of current content. Several of the item types are ingenious and illustrate the effective use of the multiple-choice format in tapping complex intellectual processes.

LSAT SCORE

    I. *Logical Reasoning:* passages followed by questions requiring various applications of logical and critical thinking (see Fig. 84).[3]

    II. *Practical Judgment:* each passage reports facts and conditions about a practical or business situation, as well as the goal to be achieved and possible solutions; two sets of questions follow, concerned with data evaluation and data application.

    III. *Data Interpretation:* obtaining and synthesizing quantitative information from graphic or tabular representations of data—requires no mathematics beyond early high school level.

[3] The illustrated items are relatively simple and short. Most LSAT items are more complex and considerably longer—too long to reproduce in a one-page illustration.

1. When you ask me, my fellow citizens, if I favor the special bond issue for schools, I reply that I have always been for better education. It is our hope for the future because better-educated youth means better-educated leaders for tomorrow. Education is the road to progress. And yet I would not deem it wise to bankrupt ourselves even to pay for better education. This is a serious question that you have wisely raised—so serious that I think each person should think it through for himself. That is one of the triumphs of our American democratic system—that each person has a right to determine for himself which way he will vote.

Of the following, which is the flaw in this politician's speech?

   (A) He fails to discuss the purpose of education.
   (B) He favors economy measures over educational reform.
   (C) His ideas about the democratic system are contradictory.
   (D) He fails to answer the question posed to him.
   (E) He dismisses the issue because it is not a serious one.

2. Janet: All Frenchmen are gourmets.
   Bill: That's not true. I know some Italians who live only to enjoy food.

   Bill's response shows that he has interpreted Janet's remark to mean that

   (A) French cooking is the best in the world
   (B) the French are superior to other peoples
   (C) only the French are gourmets
   (D) gourmets are people who enjoy food but not drink
   (E) Frenchmen are more likely to be gourmets than are persons of other nationalities

Fig. 84. Items Illustrating Logical Reasoning Section of Law School Admission Test. Answers: 1—**D**, 2—**C**.

(From *1980–81 Law School Admission Bulletin*, p. 48. Reproduced by permission of the Law School Admission Council and Educational Testing Service.)

IV. *Quantitative Comparisons:* comparing the relative magnitude of two given quantities presented in numerical, algebraic, or geometric form.

V. *Principles and Cases:* demands chiefly reading comprehension and logical reasoning; presents hypothetical legal situations, principles, and decisions, but presupposes no prior knowledge of law.

WRITING ABILITY SCORE

VI. *Error Recognition:* identify which type of writing error is illustrated, if any, in given sentence (e.g., poor diction, verbosity, faulty grammar).

VII. *Sentence Correction:* choose best of five given versions for each sentence.

VIII. *Usage:* indicate which underlined part of each sentence should be changed, if any.

The Writing Ability test was introduced principally on the basis of content validity, on the assumption that prospective lawyers should be competent in written communication. Its correlations with law school grades run slightly lower than those of LSAT (Schrader, 1977) and it adds little to the predictive validity of the battery (Pitcher, 1965, pp. 15–20).

The predictive validity of the LSAT score has been investigated in a continuing research program involving the joint participation of many law schools. In a summary of over 600 studies conducted in 150 law schools between 1948 and 1975, Schrader (1977) reports correlations between LSAT and first-year law school grades clustering around .40. These correlations tended to be higher than those between undergraduate grades and law school grades. As is generally found in such studies, the predictive validity was higher when LSAT and undergraduate grades were combined than when either was used alone.

It should be borne in mind, of course, that these correlations were all obtained with students who had been admitted to law school partly on the basis of LSAT scores. The correlations are therefore lowered by preselection. Over the period from 1948 to 1970, there was a steady rise in mean LSAT score and a decrease in both SDs and validity coefficients, thereby reflecting an increasing degree of preselection over this period. These changes do not affect the predictive efficacy of individual scores, as indicated by the error of estimate. Between 1971 and 1974, both SDs and validity coefficients tended to rise. This increasing heterogeneity of the admitted student population may have resulted from the increasing efforts of law schools to admit more minority students in the 1970s.

Comparative studies on blacks, Chicanos, and whites, as well as on men and women, revealed no consistent ethnic or sex differences in the predictive validity of the LSAT or the Writing Ability scores, and no statistical evidence of test bias against minorities or women (Linn & Pitcher, 1976; Pitcher, 1975, 1976; Powers, 1977). Some attention has also been given to predictive validity beyond first-year law school grades. In a study of over 5,000 candidates taking the bar examination in seven states (Carlson & Werts, 1976), LSAT scores correlated higher with performance on the bar examination than they did with law school grades.

CERTIFICATION AND LICENSURE OF PSYCHOLOGISTS. The use of tests in assessing the competence of professional personnel after the completion of training can be illustrated within the field of psychology. It has been customary in this field to differentiate between certification, concerned essentially with control of the title "psychologist," and licensing, designed to control the practice of psychology. Nearly all states now have laws of one type or the other and publish directories of licensed or certified psychologists. Although the majority of states began with certification laws, there was a strong movement to change to the more stringent licensing laws, which require a precise definition of the practice of psychology. Clearly, the licensing laws are more effective in protecting the public against charlatans and incompetent practitioners. Both types of laws are designed principally for psychologists who render professional services directly to individuals, organizations, or the public rather than as a part of their functions in a university, government agency, or similar institution.

While varying in details, the basic requirements for the certification or licensure of psychologists are similar across states. To be admitted to the psychologist examination, candidates must have a doctoral degree in psychology plus supervised experience (usually one or two years). A uniform national examination is now constructed semiannually by the Examination Committee of the American Association of State Psychology Boards, with the technical support of the Professional Examination Service (Carlson, 1978; Wiens, 1980). The examination is designed to assess knowledge of the major fields of psychology at a level that all licensed or certified psychologists should have attained regardless of their own specialty. Emphasis is on basic knowledge that has widespread application in the solution of problems encountered in all specialty areas. This examination is not designed to measure specific job skills or competency in practice. Rather it samples the common body of knowledge that defines the discipline of psychology and differentiates professional psychologists from other practitioners.

In its curent form, the Examination for Professional Practice in Psychology (EPPP) consists of approximately 200 multiple-choice items drawn from four major areas: (1) basic science of psychology, covering such standard topics as physiological and comparative psychology, perception, learning, motivation and emotion, developmental psychology, personality and social psychology, and behavior disorders; (2) methodology, including research design, statistics, test construction and validation, and program evaluation; (3) professional conduct and ethics, and professional affairs; and (4) applications of psychology to major professional specialties, including clinical, counseling, educational and school, and industrial-organizational psychology.

The examination is administered by the state boards,[4] and the answer sheets (with code numbers in place of names) are scored by the Professional Examination Service. General normative data are provided with the raw scores, but each state board sets its own passing score. At the candidate's request, scores may be sent to other states, thereby facilitating reciprocity of licensure among states and accommodating the mobility of practitioners. Only the EPPP is common across states. Other requirements, such as essay and oral examinations, interviews, and qualifications with regard to education and experience, are established by the state boards.

In the development of the EPPP, content validity is achieved through the various steps followed in the preparation and multiple review of items by subject-matter specialists and testing technicians. Continuing item analysis provides data on the psychometric properties of each item in the item bank.

---

[4] The EPPP is also used by some of the provinces of Canada (Wand, 1980).

There have also been a number of independent studies that contributed data toward the construct validation of the EPPP (Shrader, 1980). The construct that this examination undertakes to measure has been defined as mastery of the basic knowledge of psychology.

If the test does in fact assess this construct, its scores should be significantly related with other indices of the individual's mastery of this body of knowledge. This hypothesis is supported by the obtained relations between EPPP scores and such variables as undergraduates' grade-point average in psychology courses, number of psychology courses completed by undergraduate and graduate students, and quality of education and training received in different programs. The EPPP has also yielded high correlations with other tests such as the Graduate Record Examination Advanced Psychology Test and essay examinations given to licensure candidates. Other investigators have explored the internal structure of the test through factor analysis of items, and they have compared the performance on item clusters in particular domains with the examinees' credit hours and grade-point averages in the same domains. Currently, there is renewed interest in validation research on this test. Comprehensive and coordinated investigations are under way with regard to both content and construct validation (Richman, 1980; Shrader, 1980).

Generally, an individual is licensed or certified for the practice of psychology as a whole, rather than in a speciality. Moreover, these statutory procedures are concerned with the attainment of minimal competence for acceptable practice. A higher level of accreditation is provided by the American Board of Professional Psychology (ABPP), an independently incorporated board within the profession itself, originally established by the American Psychological Association. ABPP grants diplomas in four specialties: Clinical, Counseling, Industrial and Organizational, and School Psychology, Requirements include a PhD in the psychological specialty in which the diploma is sought, plus five years of experience in that specialty. In addition, ABPP now requires an oral examination in the individual's own specialty, which may include field observations of his or her professional work, or standardized skill assessments in simulated professional situations.

Chapter 16

Clinical Testing

C LINICAL psychologists employ a wide variety of tests, including most of the types already discussed. High in frequency of use are such individual intelligence tests as the Stanford-Binet and the Wechsler scales, as well as some of the nonverbal and performance tests discussed in Chapter 10. Many of the personality tests to be considered in the next four chapters are also prominent in the clinician's repertory. Certain diagnostic educational tests are appropriate in cases of learning disabilities or other school-related problems.

Clinicians typically draw upon multiple sources of data in the intensive study of individual cases. Information derived from interviewing and from the case history is combined with test scores to build up an integrated picture of the individual. The clinician thus has available certain safeguards against overgeneralizing from isolated test scores. This fact probably accounts at least in part for the continued use in clinical contexts of some tests whose psychometric properties are either weak or unproved. As long as such instruments serve primarily to suggest leads for the skilled clinician to follow up, their retention can be justified. There is a danger, of course, that a relatively inexperienced and overzealous clinician, unmindful of the limitations of an instrument, may place more confidence in its scores than is warranted.

The effectively functioning clinical psychologist engages in a continuing sequence of hypothesis formation and hypothesis testing about the individual case. Each item of information—whether it be an event recorded in the case history, a comment by the client, or a test score—suggests a hypothesis about the individual that will be either confirmed or refuted as other facts are gathered. Such hypotheses themselves indicate the direction of further lines of inquiry. It should be borne in mind that even highly reliable tests with well-established validity do not yield sufficiently precise results for individual diagnosis. Hence, it is understandable that clinicians as a group tend to be more receptive than other psychologists to psychometrically crude instruments, which may nevertheless provide a rich harvest of leads for further exploration.

In the present chapter, we shall consider a few types of tests used predominantly if not exclusively in clinical settings. For a comprehensive view of clinical testing, these instruments should be added to those mentioned in the opening paragraph. We shall also examine certain special procedures and problems characteristic of clinical testing.

DIAGNOSTIC USE OF INTELLIGENCE TESTS

When an alert and trained clinician is in active contact with an individual during the hour or so required to administer a test, he or she can hardly fail to learn more about that person than is conveyed by an IQ or some other single score. This is still true if the test itself is administered by a technician, provided that a complete record of the examinee's responses is retained, as is customary in individually administered tests. The literature of clinical psychology contains thousands of research reports and theoretical discussions designed to systematize, facilitate, and improve the utilization of these supplementary sources of data.

PATTERN ANALYSIS OF TEST SCORES. Besides using intelligence tests to assess an individual's general level of intellectual functioning, clinical psychologists also customarily explore the pattern, or profile, of test scores for possible indices of psychopathology. It is likely that pathological deterioration, as from brain damage or psychotic disorders, does not affect all intellectual functions uniformly. Some functions are believed to remain relatively unaffected, while others are considered to be more sensitive to particular pathological influences. Similarly, neurotic anxiety may seriously interfere with performance on certain types of tests, which require careful observation and concentration, while leaving performance on other tests unimpaired.

The Wechsler scales lend themselves especially well to such profile analyses, since all subtest scores are expressed in directly comparable standard scores. From the outset, Wechsler has described a number of diagnostic uses of his scales. Several other clinicians have recommended other techniques and modifications (Guertin et al., 1962, 1966; Kaufman, 1979; Matarazzo, 1972; Rapaport et al., 1968). Specifically, any one of three major procedures have been utilized. The first involves the amount of *scatter,* or extent of variation among the individual's scores on all subtests. The underlying rationale of scatter indices is that intertest variation should be larger in pathological than in normal cases. The second procedure is based on the computation of a *deterioration index* based on the difference between "hold" tests, allegedly resistant to deterioration from pathology or old age, and "don't hold" tests, considered to be susceptible to decline. The third approach is based on *score patterns* associated with particular clinical syndromes, such as brain damage, schizophrenia, anxiety states, and delinquency. Wechsler and other investigators have described patterns of high and low subtest scores characterizing each of these disorders, among others.

Three decades of research on these various forms of pattern analysis with the Wechsler scales have provided little support for their diagnostic value (Guertin et al., 1956, 1962, 1966, 1971; Matarazzo, 1972). Several methodological requirements must be considered in evaluating this research. First, it is obviously essential to ascertain what is the minimum statistically significant difference between any two test scores. It will be recalled (Ch. 5) that the probability of a difference exceeding chance depends on the reliability coefficients of the two tests. The data required for such statistical evaluation of score differences are now available in the Wechsler scale manuals, as well as in other pertinent publications (e.g., Field, 1960; Zimmerman, Woo-Sam, & Glasser, 1973). For instance, the minimum statistically significant difference between WAIS-R Verbal and Performance IQs is approximately 10 points at the .05 level and 13 points at the .01 level. The same limitations apply to comparisons among individual subtest scores, whose reliabilities are generally lower than those of the composite V and P IQs (see Ch. 9).

A second consideration is the base rate or frequency of occurrence of any given difference in the standardization sample (Field, 1960). Although a V–P difference of 15 or more IQ points is statistically significant and is generally regarded as clinically suspect, differences of this magnitude occurred in about 10% of the standardization sample. A third and related point, pertaining to differences between individual subtests, stems from the large number of possible paired comparisons between tests in any individual's record. As H. G. Jones (1956) observed, the 11 subtests yield 55 possible intertest differences. Hence, a difference expected in, let us say, 10% of the cases between any one pair of subtests will actually occur about five times in a single person's record (10% of 55 = 5.5). Rather than occurring in only 10% of normal persons, therefore, differences of such magnitude would be found, on the average, five times in *every* normal person's record.

A fourth important methodological requirement is the cross-validation of group differences in score patterns. Because of the large number of possible diagnostic signs, or pattern differences, the comparison of any single pathological sample with a normal control sample could easily yield a set of spurious differences through sampling error. When actually submitted to cross-validation, most of the initial findings in pattern analysis were not, in fact, corroborated.

A fifth problem arises from the multiplicity of conditions that may account for atypical variations among subtest scores. Such variations may result not only from pathology but also from differences in educational, occupational, cultural, or other background factors. Language handicap may account for lower Verbal than Performance scores. It will be recalled that skilled laborers tend to score higher on Performance than on Verbal Scales, unlike white-collar groups (Ch. 9). Socioeconomic and urban–rural differences in subtest pattern have likewise been noted. There is also evidence that education affects relative standing on Verbal and Performance Scales. In a study of psychiatric patients (A. Smith, 1966), as schooling decreased from over 12 years to under 5 years, the percentage of cases with higher Performance than Verbal IQs increased from 21 to 64. Sex differences and subcultural differences in subtest scores may likewise confound the interpretation of WAIS patterns (Levinson, 1959, 1963; Norman, 1966; Zimmerman, Woo-Sam, & Glasser, 1973).

A sixth point—especially emphasized by Matarazzo (1972)—pertains to the nature of the traditional diagnostic categories that provided the criteria for pattern analysis. In the large majority of studies, these categories were heterogeneous, unreliable, and crude. Such broad designations as brain damage or schizophrenia are probably associated with such varied and contradictory behavioral correlates in different subgroups as to be of little use in the identification of typical test patterns.

QUALITATIVE OBSERVATIONS AND INDIVIDUALIZED INTERPRETATION. Any individual intelligence test can provide information at various levels. At the most objective level, such scales yield an IQ with high reliability and fair evidence of validity for many purposes. At a less objective level, we find the innumerable attempts at semiquantitative, standardized pattern analysis. Both methodological evaluations and empirical results have thus far lent little or no support to the proposed interpretations. Even if well-designed future investigations should conclusively demonstrate a relationship between test response patterns and clearly defined diagnostic categories, the results would still indicate only group trends and would not be equally applicable to all individual cases. Such diagnostic signs, therefore, could not be employed routinely, by formula. They would still need to be interpreted in the light of other data about the individual.

At a purely qualitative level, any irregularity of performance should suggest avenues for further exploration. Applications of this approach to the Wechsler scales can be found in Glasser and Zimmerman (1967), Matarazzo (1972, Ch. 15); and Zimmerman, Woo-Sam, and Glasser (1973). For each subtest, these sources provide an interpretive framework, with summaries of relevant data and a discussion of the types of information a clinician may obtain with regard to both intellectual and personality characteristics. Similar guidelines have been prepared for the qualitative interpretation of the Stanford-Binet (see, e.g., Sattler, 1982, Chs. 8, 18).

Significant leads may emerge from the form as well as the content of test responses. Bizarreness, overelaboration, or excessive self-reference, for example, may indicate personality disorders. A qualitative analysis of both errors and correct responses may provide useful cues about problem-solving approaches, conceptual development, or cognitive styles. Atypical content of test responses is a further source of leads. As Wechsler (1958, p. 181) observed, if in the Vocabulary test one person defines "sentence" as a group of words and another as a penalty imposed by a judge, this difference may furnish a clue to important dissimilarities in experiential background or personality. Sattler cites an example of a sexually delinquent girl who, when given the Word Naming test of the Stanford-Binet, responded with 35 boys' names (Lejeune, cited in Sattler, 1974, p. 264). Still another source of qualitative data available during the administration of an individual intelligence test is the individual's general behavior in the testing situation. Examples include motor activities, speech, emotional responses, attitude toward examiner, and behavior toward the test materials and the testing environment.

Because of their idiosyncratic nature, such qualitative cues cannot be validated by quantitative methods adapted to the measurement of group trends. The validity of the inferences they suggest can only be tested for the individual case by the process of successive data gathering and verification characteristic of the clinical method.

A clear illustration of the sophisticated clinical use of intelligence tests, combining psychometric data with qualitative observations, is provided by Kaufman (1979). In a book entitled *Intelligent Testing with the WISC-R*, Kaufman demonstrates in detail how the clinician can integrate statistical information about test scores, such as the significance of differences between scores and the results of factor analyses, with knowledge about human development, personality theory, and other areas of psychological research. For an effective clinical evaluation of a child's performance on the WISC-R, the book describes a step-by-step procedure, from the interpretation of the total IQ and the Verbal–Performance discrepancy, through the examination of various subtest patterns, to a consideration of the skills and extraneous conditions that influence performance on each subtest. Kaufman also emphasizes the need for supplementary information, derived from other tests, case history, and clinical observations of behavior in the course of testing. Recognizing that the Wechsler subtests measure what the individual has learned, Kaufman observes that score patterns must be interpreted against the individual's experiential background.

The test scores, together with other data sources, lead to the formulation of hypotheses about the individual, which can be tested as more information is gathered to round out the picture. The most important feature of this approach is that it calls for individualized interpretations of test performance, in contrast to the uniform application of any one type of pattern analysis. The same score pattern may lead to quite different interpretations for different individuals. Similar procedures have been developed by Kaufman and his colleagues for use with other individual intelligence tests, such as the Stanford-Binet (Kaufman & Waterstreet, 1978) and the McCarthy scales (Kaufman & Kaufman, 1977).

The basic approach described by Kaufman undoubtedly represents a major contribution to the clinical use of intelligence tests. Nevertheless, it should be recognized that its implementation requires a sophisticated clinician who is well informed in several fields of psychology. Moreover, some of the proposed interpretations are still controversial and must be critically evaluated by the individual user (see, e.g., Sattler, 1981b).

NEUROPSYCHOLOGICAL TESTS

TESTS OF CEREBRAL DYSFUNCTION. A large number of tests have been specially designed as clinical instruments for assessing neuropsychological impairment (C. J. Golden, 1979, Ch. 8; Lezak, 1976). These tests are often designated as indicators of organicity or brain damage. Most available tests in this category, however, are broader in function and have been employed to detect intellectual deterioration or impairment arising from a variety of possible causes. Psychological tests of intellectual impairment are generally based on the premise of a differential deficit in different functions. Chief among the functions considered most sensitive to pathological processes are perception of spatial relations and memory for newly learned material. The assessment of these functions is illustrated by two well-known tests which have been in use for many years, namely, the Benton Visual Retention Test and the Bender-Gestalt Test.

The Benton test utilizes 10 cards, each containing one or more simple geometric figures. In the standard administration, each card is exposed for 10 seconds and the examinee is told to draw what was on the card immediately after its removal. The test thus requires spatial perception, immediate recall, and visuomotor reproduction of drawings. Performance is scored in terms of number of cards correctly reproduced and total number of errors. Interscorer reliability of the order of .95 is reported for these scores. Additional qualitative information can be obtained by classifying the errors as omissions (and additions), distortions, perseverations, rotations, misplacements, and size errors (see Fig. 85). Three equivalent forms of 10 drawings each are available. Reliability assessed by correlation of alternate forms is in the .80s.

The Benton test may also be administered with certain procedural variations. Of particular interest is the copying administration, in which the card remains in view while the examinee executes the drawing. This procedure thus permits a separation of perceptual from memory errors. In the interpretation of scores, both number of correct reproductions and number of errors may be compared with the expected "normal" score for each age and intellectual level. The latter can be determined from the IQ on any standard verbal intelligence test. Benton scores falling more than a designated number of points below the expected level for an individual are considered significant in the clinical sense. The manual makes it clear, however, that many conditions other than pathology could account for a deviant performance on this test. To reach a diagnosis, the clinician needs corrobo-

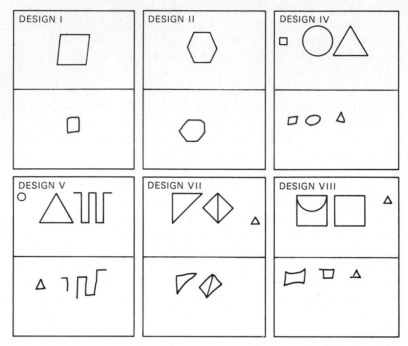

FIG. 85. Errors by a Brain-Injured Patient on Benton Visual Retention Test (Copying Administration). Upper design in each item is sample, lower is patient's copy. In addition to distortions and size errors, note omission of small peripheral figures in Designs V and VII.

(From Benton, 1974, p. 63. Reproduced by permission. Copyright 1955, 1963, © 1974 by The Psychological Corporation, New York, N.Y. All rights reserved.)

rative data from other appropriate tests, together with information about the individual's history and background.

Several investigations have yielded significant mean differences between brain-injured and control cases in both number of correct drawings and total number of errors. While overlapping in score distributions is always present, the frequency of correct differentiations appears promising. In one comparison of 100 brain-injured and 100 control cases, for example, a cutoff score of 3 points below expected number of correct drawings identified 57% of the patients, with only 4% false positives among the controls. When the cutoff was raised to 4 points below the expected score, 36% of the patients and none of the controls were identified as brain-injured (Benton, 1974, pp. 52–53). Although useful in detecting brain injury in children, the test does not differentiate as sharply when applied to children as when applied to adults. Suggestive data have also been reported on the performance of several other groups, such as schizophrenics, emotionally disturbed children, mental retardates, and persons over 65.

The Bender Visual Motor Gestalt Test, commonly known as the Bender-

Gestalt Test, is widely used by clinical psychologists, predominantly for the detection of brain damage. In this test, the nine simple designs shown in Figure 86 are presented one at a time on cards. The examinee is instructed to copy each design, with the sample before her or him. The designs were selected by Bender from a longer series originally employed by Wertheimer, one of the founders of the Gestalt school, in his studies of visual perception. The particular designs were constructed so as to illustrate certain principles of Gestalt psychology, and Bender's own analyses of the test results are formulated in terms of Gestalt concepts. Although for many years the test was administered by Bender and others to children and adults showing a variety of intellectual and emotional disorders, the data were not reported in objective and systematic form and were therefore difficult to evaluate.

While many clinicians still interpret the Bender-Gestalt Test through subjective intuitive procedures, several objective scoring systems have been developed for use with either adults or children (see Tolor & Brannigan, 1980; Tolor & Schulberg, 1963). In one of the most carefully developed of these scoring systems, Pascal and Suttell (1951) undertook a standardization and quantification of the Bender-Gestalt Test on an *adult population*. On the basis of the drawing errors that significantly differentiated between matched

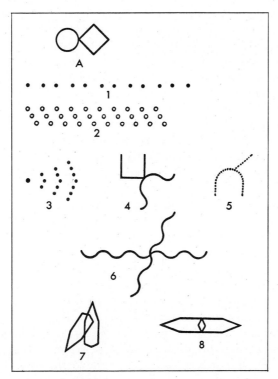

FIG. 86. The Bender-Gestalt Test.
(From Bender, 1938, p. 4; reproduced by permission of Lauretta Bender.)

samples of normals and abnormals, a relatively objective scoring key was developed. Cross-validation of this key on new samples of 474 nonpatients (or normal controls), 187 neurotics, and 136 psychotics yielded mean scores of 50, 68.2, and 81.8 respectively. These scores are standard scores with a mean of 50 and an *SD* of 10, the higher scores indicating more diagnostic errors. The biserial correlation of test scores against the criterion of patient versus nonpatient status was .74. This correlation may be regarded as a measure of concurrent criterion-related validity. There is also evidence that this adaptation of the test can significantly differentiate groups of organics from both normal and psychotic groups.

Retest reliabilities of about .70 were found in normal samples over a 24-hour interval. Scorer reliabilities of approximately .90 are reported for trained scorers. Performance on the test is apparently independent of drawing ability but is significantly related to amount of education. In this adaptation, the Bender-Gestalt Test appears to have promise as a rapid screening device, especially for detecting the more serious forms of disturbance. The normative sample, however, is rather restricted geographically, educationally, and in other ways.

Although the Pascal-Suttell scoring system is probably the most widely used for adults, there are many other modifications of the Bender-Gestalt test. These various forms employ the same test materials, while differing in administration procedure, scoring systems, or interpretive elaboration (e.g., Hutt, 1977). It should also be noted that there has been a continuing flow of research by independent investigators that provides supplementary normative and validity data. The *Eighth Mental Measurements Yearbook* lists over 1,000 publications on this test.

Koppitz (1964, 1975) carried out an extensive standardization of the Bender-Gestalt Test with *children*.[1] Providing norms on 1,104 kindergarten to fourth-grade children in midwestern and eastern public schools, this adaptation of the Bender-Gestalt Test was prepared as a nonverbal developmental scale for ages 5 to 10. Scorer reliability appears satisfactory, the interscorer correlations varying between .88 and .96. Retest reliability over a four-month interval within single-grade groups was rather low, with coefficients ranging from .547 to .659. Between the ages of 5 and 10 years, the scores show consistent improvement with age and moderate to high correlations with standard intelligence tests. Within single-year groups, correlations ranging from .48 to .79 were found between Bender-Gestalt scores and Stanford-Binet or WISC IQs. After the age of 10, the Bender-Gestalt no longer correlates significantly with either intelligence test scores or age, since normal persons beyond that age obtain virtually perfect scores.

Koppitz reports fairly high validities for the test in assessing school readiness and in predicting the subsequent educational achievement of first-grade children. Studies of first- and second-grade children also showed significant relationships between Bender-Gestalt scores and performance in

[1] Also known as the Bender-Gestalt Test for Young Children.

reading and arithmetic. Finally, evidence is given suggesting that among mentally retarded children the Bender-Gestalt developmental score has fairly high validity as a measure of intellectual level and as a predictor of academic achievement. All these analyses are based on small samples and need further verification.

Comparison of brain-injured with normal children between the ages of 5 and 10 showed significant group differences in total score on the Bender-Gestalt developmental scale. For a diagnosis of brain injury, however, Koppitz concluded that the total score should be supplemented with a number of additional observations of the child's performance, including time required, amount of space employed in reproducing the drawings, detailed analysis of individual errors, observations of the child's behavior, and inquiry into the child's awareness of his or her errors. All the uses of the Koppitz adaptation of the Bender-Gestalt discussed thus far are based on the developmental scoring scale. In addition, Koppitz presents a set of 10 "emotional indicators" applicable when the test is employed as a projective instrument for detecting emotional disturbances in children.

As screening instruments for the detection of brain damage, the Benton test and the Bender-Gestalt have proved to be among the most successful. In a survey of 94 studies using various instruments with adult psychiatric patients, these tests yielded a median percentage of correct classifications of approximately 75 (Heaton, Baade, & Johnson, 1978). This hit rate includes both brain-damaged and non-brain-damaged psychiatric cases that were correctly identified as such.

METHODOLOGICAL PROBLEMS IN THE DIAGNOSIS OF BRAIN DAMAGE. Knowledge about the behavioral effects of brain damage dates largely from the writings of Kurt Goldstein and his associates in the early 1920s (Goldstein & Scheerer, 1941). Following extensive observations of soldiers who had sustained brain injuries during World War I, Goldstein formulated his classic description of the intellectual impairment associated with brain damage. Among the principal symptoms were a diminution in the ability for abstract thought and a tendency to respond to extraneous stimuli that may disrupt normal perception.

Widespread concern with brain injury in children arose in the late 1930s and in the 1940s, following the research of Alfred Strauss and his associates (Strauss & Lehtinen, 1947; Werner & Strauss, 1941, 1943). These investigators identified a subgroup of mentally retarded children whose case histories showed evidence of brain injury due to trauma or infection occurring before, during, or shortly after birth. The behavioral description of these children represented an extension and elaboration of the adult syndrome formulated by Goldstein. It delineated a distinctive pattern of both intellectual and emotional disorders that was widely accepted as characteristic of *the* brain-injured child. Included in this pattern were specific perceptual and conceptual disorders combined with relatively high verbal ability, as well as overactivity, distractibility, and aggressiveness. For many years, both research and practice with brain-injured children was dominated by a unidimensional concept of "organicity." This approach led to a search for diagnostic tests of organic involvement as such and an attempt to devise remedial or educational programs suitable for brain-injured children as a whole.

Since midcentury, psychologists have increasingly recognized that brain injury may lead to a wide variety of behavioral patterns. No one symptom or set of symptoms need be common to all brain-injured cases. In fact, brain damage may produce the opposite behavior pattern in two individuals. Such findings are consistent with the wide diversity of the underlying organic pathology itself. A significant advance in the analysis of brain–behavior relationships was made by the research of Reitan and his co-workers at the Indiana University Medical Center (see Matarazzo, 1972, Ch. 13; Reitan, 1955, 1966). These investigations provide a good example of the importance of working with relatively homogeneous and clearly defined criterion groups.

In an initial attempt to sort out the variety of disorders loosely classified under "brain damage," Reitan selected for study three groups of patients: one with left-hemisphere lesions, one with right-hemisphere lesions, and one with diffuse brain damage involving both hemispheres. Diagnoses were based on neurological and neurosurgical data, utilizing electroencephalography and other sophisticated techniques. The three groups were approximately comparable in age and education. Although the samples were small, the principal findings have been corroborated in a number of subsequent investigations (Guertin et al., 1962, 1966; Matarazzo, 1972, p. 390). Essentially, the results showed that left-hemisphere lesions tend to be associated with lower Verbal than Performance IQ on the Wechsler scales ($V < P$). The opposite pattern ($V > P$) predominated in the groups with lesions in the right hemisphere and with diffuse brain damage. The latter score pattern corresponds to the classic diagnostic pattern of brain damage.

Research by Reitan and other investigators is continuing to sort out the complex interactions of other variables with the behavioral effects of brain pathology. There is a growing body of evidence indicating that *age* affects the behavioral symptoms resulting from brain damage. It cannot be assumed that brain damage will have the same effect in an adult, a school-age child, and an infant. Since the nature of intelligence varies at different age levels, the pattern of impairment may vary as a function of the age at which the injury is sustained. The behavioral effects will also depend upon the amount of learning and intellectual development that has occurred prior to the injury. Research on preschool children, for example, indicates that at this age level the brain-injured tend to be deficient in *all* intellectual functions (Graham, Ernhart, et al., 1963). Unlike the pattern found at older ages, impairment among brain-injured preschoolers was just as great in vocabulary as in other cognitive and perceptual functions. Similarly, other studies of young children with a history of prenatal or birth trauma have found an average reduction in IQ on the Stanford-Binet and other standardized intelligence tests. Such broad intellectual impairment may occur because the brain damage itself is diffuse or because a critical deficiency in linguistic development or attention control may seriously hinder the acquisition of other abilities. It is also interesting to note that studies with brain-injured preschool children have failed to find the emotional symptoms of the classic Strauss pattern (Graham et al., 1962; Graham, Ernhart, et al., 1963).

Chronicity has also been found to affect test performance. Available data suggest that the relationships found by Reitan and others may hold for acute but not for chronic cases, that is, for recent rather than for long-standing lesions. The amount of time that has elapsed since the injury may be related not only to progressive physiological changes but also to the extent of behavioral recovery through learning or compensatory readjustments.

Finally, it should be noted that in some cases intellectual impairment may be an *indirect result* of brain damage. Throughout the individual's development, organic and experiential factors interact. Some of the personality disorders included in the classic picture of brain-injured children, for example, may be an indirect effect of the frustrations and interpersonal difficulties experienced by the child with an organically caused intellectual deficiency. Whether or not these personality disorders develop may thus depend on the degree of understanding and the attitudes exhibited by parents, teachers, and other significant persons in the child's environment.

Another example of indirect effects of organic impairment is provided by the intellectual retardation often found among children with cerebral palsy (see, e.g., Sarason & Gladwin, 1959, Ch. 7). In some of these cases, the lesion extends to the cortical level. Both motor and intellectual disorders in these cases result directly from organic damage. In other cases, however, the lesion may be limited to subcortical levels, directly causing only the motor handicaps. If these motor handicaps are severe enough, they may seriously interfere with the development of speech and writing, as well as locomotion and other gross motor activities. In these cases, intellectual retardation is likely to result from educational and social handicaps. Through special educational procedures that bypass the motor handicaps, however, these children can reach a normal or even superior intellectual level, as evidenced by the impressive attainment of some cerebral-palsied individuals.

It is abundantly evident that brain damage covers a wide variety of organic disorders, with correspondingly diverse behavioral manifestations. The test performance of brain-injured persons can be expected to vary with the source, extent, and locus of the cerebral damage; the age at which the damage occurred; the age when the individual's behavior is being assessed; and the duration of the pathological condition. To expect behavioral homogeneity among the brain-injured would thus be highly unrealistic.

From another angle, the same intellectual or other behavioral disorder—

and the same diagnostic sign in test performance—may result from organic factors in one person and from experiential factors in another. These experiential factors, moreover, may be unrelated to the organic damage in one case and an indirect result of it in another. It follows that to interpret any specific diagnostic sign in test performance requires additional information about the individual's experiential background and personal history.

NEUROPSYCHOLOGICAL BATTERIES. Because of the wide diversity of organic brain dysfunctions, with their accompanying behavioral deficits, it follows that no one test of organicity is adequate for screening for brain damage; and single tests are even less suited for differential diagnosis. Clinicians frequently use a combination of available tests assessing different skills and deficits. This procedure has the advantage of providing combinations of tests that are tailored to individual cases. But it also has several limitations. There is likely to be some unnecessary duplication of functions among tests, while some critical deficits may be overlooked. The advance selection of tests to fit the individual case puts a heavy burden on the clinician's expertise and judgment. Moreover, independently developed tests are not likely to be comparable with regard to normative samples and score scales. Empirical data on the interrelations of different tests are also likely to be meager. Consequently, it is difficult to interpret results in terms of score patterns.

For these reasons, systematic efforts have been made to assemble comprehensive standardized batteries that provide measures of all significant neuropsychological skills. Such a battery can serve several functions. It can detect brain damage with a high degree of success. It can also identify and localize the impaired brain areas. It can differentiate among particular syndromes associated with cerebral pathology. And it can help in planning rehabilitation training by revealing specific behavioral deficits and defining the extent and location of brain damage. Two major examples of comprehensive neuropsychological batteries are the Halstead-Reitan Neuropsychological Battery and the Luria-Nebraska Neuropsychological Battery. While sharing a common purpose, these two batteries differ in several important ways.

The Halstead-Reitan has been adopted widely for clinical use and has undergone extensive research and development for over a quarter century (C. J. Golden, 1979, Ch. 9; Heaton et al., 1978; Hevern, 1980; Reitan & Davison, 1974). Developed by Reitan from the earlier work of Halstead (1947), it covers a broad scope of functions. Its content is somewhat flexible: individual clinicians and investigators include a varying number and selection of tests. Most users employ a set of 11 tests, which includes a variety of sensorimotor and perceptual tests and an aphasia test covering several sense modalities and response modes. Among the more complex tests in the set are the Category Test and the Trail Making Test. The Category Test requires the examinee to deduce general principles from the information presented on series of slides. In the Trail Making Test, the first task is to draw lines connecting numbered circles in proper numerical order. For the second task, the circles contain letters or numbers, and the task is to go from 1 to A to 2 to B and so on, alternating numbers with letters. The usual battery also includes the Wechsler Adult Intelligence Scale (Ch. 9) and the Minnesota Multiphasic Personality Inventory (MMPI), a self-report inventory for assessing emotional disorders (Ch. 17).

The more recently developed Luria-Nebraska battery differs from the Halsted-Reitan in several ways. It requires less time to administer—2½ hours as against 6 or more hours. It is more highly standardized in content, materials, administration, and scoring. It provides fuller coverage of possible neurological deficits. And it permits more specific identification of behavior deficits and more precise localization of the corresponding brain damage. The distinctive feature of this battery stems from its use of individual items rather than tests as its units. Luria's approach, incorporated in this battery, was to select items for their qualitative importance in diagnosis (Christensen, 1975, 1980; C. J. Golden, 1978, 1979, 1981a, 1981b; Golden, Hammeke, & Purisch, 1980; Luria, 1973).

In its present form, the Luria-Nebraska battery comprises 269 items. Each item represents a specific aspect of a relevant skill and differs from other items along such dimensions as mode of stimulus input, response mode, complexity, and difficulty level. Depending upon the skills they assess, items are scored for such variables as accuracy, speed, quality, or number of responses. The raw score on each item is converted to a scaled score by reference to the normative data. A scaled score of 0 covers the raw score range in which a normal respondent is more likely to score than is a brain-injured respondent; a score of 1 covers the range in which there is equal probability that a normal and a brain-injured respondent will fall; and a score of 2 represents the range in which there is greater likelihood that the brain-injured will score.

Primary summary scores in the following scales are found by adding the item scores within each skill area:

1. Motor functions
2. Rhythm
3. Tactile functions
4. Visual functions
5. Receptive speech
6. Expressive speech
7. Writing
8. Reading
9. Arithmetic
10. Memory
11. Intellectual processes

The intellectual processes scale covers a wide range of tasks requiring reasoning and problem-solving skills and includes items similar to those on several of the WAIS subtests, among others. In addition, three other sum-

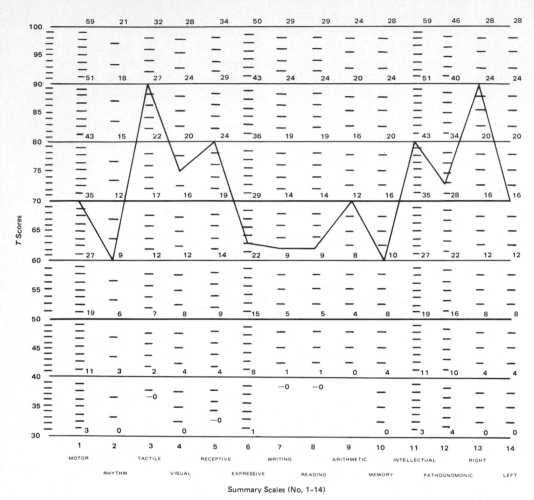

FIG. 87. Profile on Luria-Nebraska Psychoneurological Battery. In combination with qualitative data, this profile suggested damage in right parietal area including the sensory strip in the postcentral gyrus. Diagnosis was later confirmed by neurological examination (Computerized Axial Tomography).

(From Golden, C. J. *Clinical Interpretation of Objective Psychological Tests,* p. 211. Copyright © 1979 by Grune & Stratton. Reproduced by permission.)

mary scores are computed: a right-hemisphere score, a left-hemisphere score, and a pathognomic score based on 31 items found to be especially sensitive to brain damage. The 14 summary scores are plotted on a profile chart, from which corresponding T scores[2] can be read directly (Fig. 87). The 14 T scores can be averaged to give a total score as a quick summary of the individual's level of performance on the entire battery.

---

[2] Standard scores with $M = 50$, $SD = 10$ (see Ch. 4).

localizing

Available validation data on the Luria-Nebraska battery indicate a high level of success in screening for brain damage, as well as promising results in localizing the damaged areas. In using this battery, the clinician combines quantitative scores with qualitative results. Many "rules" have been worked out for interpreting score patterns. Analysis of performance on individual items is especially important for differential diagnosis. A limitation of the Luria-Nebraska battery stems from the recency of completion of the present standardized version. As a result, the amount of research—especially that pertaining to cross-validation of new, empirically derived diagnostic scales—is meager. In view of what has been accomplished thus far, however, there is reason for optimism.

Two further points should be noted. First, some neuropsychologists maintain that the Luria technique is essentially clinical and qualitative, and any attempt to standardize and quantify its observations is inappropriate. Thus, there is still controversy regarding the basic approach represented by the Luria-Nebraska battery, as well as skepticism regarding the preliminary findings (see, e.g., Adams, 1980a, 1980b; C. J. Golden, 1980). Current, large-scale demands for neuropsychological diagnosis, however, preclude the full-scale application of qualitative procedures. Although designed for use by a properly trained neuropsychologist, the Luria-Nebraska battery permits such a specialist to function more efficiently and to extend his or her services more widely. Standardization and quantification can also be defended on purely scientific grounds.

A second relevant point pertains to recent developments in the direct assessment of neurological impairment through such techniques as electroencephalography, evoked potentials, and computerized axial tomography. Although available procedures have been vastly improved, no diagnostic technique is 100% dependable. In most cases, therefore, clinical neuropsychologists utilize corroborative information from several sources. And carefully standardized behavioral measures serve an important function in such multiple approaches to assessment.

IDENTIFYING SPECIFIC LEARNING DISABILITIES

THE PROBLEM. The 1970s ushered in a wave of crash programs for the diagnosis and remediation of learning disabilities. Educators were becoming increasingly aware of the high frequency of this type of handicap among schoolchildren. In one of the first legislative efforts to define this condition, learning disabilities were described as

. . . a disorder in one or more of the basic psychological processes involved in understanding or in using language, spoken or written, which disorder may manifest itself in imperfect ability to listen, think, speak, read, write, spell, or do mathematical calculations. Such disorders include such conditions as perceptual handicaps, brain injury, minimal brain dysfunction, dyslexia, and developmental aphasia. Such term does not include children who have learning problems which are primarily the result of visual, hearing, or motor handicaps, or mental retardation, or emotional disturbance, or environmental disadvantage.[3]

It follows from this definition that the designation of learning disability should not be employed until several other conditions have been eliminated as possible causes of the child's educational or psychological difficulties. The varied terminology applied to these cases reflects both a changing approach over time and a convergence of medical, educational, and psychological orientations. What are now characterized as learning disabilities were until recently regarded as indices of brain injury or, at least, of minimal brain dysfunction. The current view is that neurological pathology *may* underlie learning disabilities. Its presence cannot be assumed in all cases, but there is evidence of its involvement in at least a sizable proportion of cases (C. J. Golden, 1978; Rourke, 1975). Learning disability specialists often insist that they have no interest in etiology but want only to pinpoint the specific pattern of behavioral disabilities in each case in order to plan an appropriate program of remedial instruction. The teacher, for example, needs to know the precise locus and limits of a child's perceptual disabilities so that he or she may "teach to strength" by utilizing the child's strongest channel, or sense modality, at the outset.

Neverthelesss, more knowledge about the underlying causes of learning disabilities should contribute to the accuracy of diagnosis and enhance the effectiveness of the treatment program in individual cases. Partly for this reason, available procedures for both diagnosis and remediation of learning disabilities need to remain flexible and responsive to new advances. It should also be recognized that there are still wide individual differences in theoretical orientation among specialists on learning disabilities. These differences are reflected in both testing instruments and remedial programs.

Typically, children with learning disabilities show normal or above-normal intelligence, in combination with pronounced difficulties in learning one or more basic educational skills (most often, reading). In addition, they manifest various combinations of associated behavioral symptoms. Chief among such symptoms are perceptual disorders in one or more sense modalities, as well as poor integration of input from different modalities and disruption of sensorimotor coordination. These perceptual disorders are often directly related to their reading difficulty and other learning problems. Deficiencies in memory, attention control, and conceptual skills are common.

Many disturbances of language development may occur. Aphasia originally referred to a loss in the ability to understand language (receptive aphasia) or to use language meaningfully (expressive aphasia) following a brain injury. In the case of a young child, however, these abilities may not

[3] Cited by Swets and Elliott (1974, pp. 1–2), from Public Law 91–230 (89 Stat. 177), Section 602–15, April 13, 1970.

have been acquired in the first place—hence the disorder is designated as "developmental aphasia." Other typical symptoms include various forms and degrees of motor incoordination (affecting gross or fine motor control or both); temporal and spatial disorientation; difficulty in organizing activities and following a plan; and undirected, impulsive hyperactivity. Aggression and other emotional and interpersonal problems may also develop, often as a direct result of the academic failures and frustrations engendered by the child's learning disabilities. In evaluating the child's behavior, it should also be borne in mind that many specific difficulties that are normal at an early age (e.g., in a 3-year-old) represent a dysfunction if they persist to an older age. A developmental frame of reference is therefore needed, with qualitative if not quantitative norms.

ASSESSMENT TECHNIQUES. Regardless of theoretical orientation, there is general agreement that the identification of learning disabilities requires a wide assortment of tests and supplementary observational procedures. This follows from at least three features of the diagnostic problem: (1) the variety of behavioral disorders associated with this condition; (2) individual differences in the particular combination of symptoms; and (3) the need for highly specific information regarding the nature and extent of the disabilities in each case.

Usually, the assessment of children with learning disabilities is a cooperative effort by a professional team. The classroom teacher can administer group tests and employ other screening or wide-band instruments. Examples of screening techniques include Slingerland's Screening Test for Identifying Children with Specific Language Disability, an eight-test group battery yielding 21 scores; and Myklebust's Pupil Rating Scale, a behavioral rating scale based on day-by-day classroom observations. Wide-range achievement tests can also be administered by teachers, either individually (e.g., Peabody Individual Achievement Test) or to groups (e.g., Jastak's Wide Range Achievement Test).

Regular achievement batteries may also serve in this connection, particularly those designed for primary and preschool levels and permitting criterion-referenced analyses of specific strengths and weaknesses. Several instruments cited in Chapter 14 are appropriate for this purpose, including the primary levels of the Stanford Achievement Test, the Stanford Early School Achievement Test (SESAT), the Metropolitan Readiness Tests, and CIRCUS. An examination of all such instruments discloses many subtests and item types that closely resemble those found in tests specially designed for identifying learning disabilities. For older children, the various diagnostic tests in reading and arithmetic provide highly relevant information (see Ch. 14 and Appendix E).

The administration and interpretation of individual intelligence tests require the services of a psychologist. Such tests as the Stanford-Binet, WISC,

WPPSI, and McCarthy Scales of Children's Abilities not only provide a global index such as an IQ to help differentiate between mental retardation and special learning disabilities, but they also yield much qualitative information regarding specific deficiencies (Kaufman, 1979; Kaufman & Kaufman, 1977; Sattler, 1982). For example, these tests can reveal possible deficiencies in the perception and recall of visual patterns, motor difficulties in copying forms, limitations of short-term memory, inability to handle abstract concepts, and many types of language disorders.

The intensive study of each individual case in order to map out the specific pattern of learning disabilities is generally the responsibility of either an educational specialist on learning disabilities or a psychologist. The batteries assembled for this purpose usually include some test of aphasia. Other tests covering the many aspects of the understanding and use of written and spoken language are of particular importance. Tests designed to detect disturbances of perception and short-term memory, such as the Bender-Gestalt and the Benton Visual Retention Test, are highly appropriate, as are tests of auditory discrimination. Motor functions also need to be covered.

In addition to these standard instruments, a number of new tests have been prepared specially for children with learning disabilities (see Appendix E).[4] All these tests should be regarded, not as psychometric instruments, but as observational aids for the clinical psychologist and learning disabilities specialist. Most provide no norms. When normative data are available, they are usually derived from small and narrowly limited samples. Moreover, such norms serve principally as reference points for defining "normal" (i.e., nonpathological) responses rather than for the quantitative evaluation of performance. Although not explicitly labeled as such, most of these tests are criterion-referenced insofar as they provide a description of the child's deficiencies in highly specific terms. Primary focus is on whether the child has mastered the skills displayed by normal children of his or her age.

One of the most widely known tests in this area, on which a large amount of research has already been conducted, is the Illinois Test of Psycholinguistic Abilities (ITPA). This is an individual test for children between the ages of 2 and 10 years. In its design, the ITPA follows the three-dimensional model shown below, which is a condensed adaptation of C. E. Osgood's theoretical model of the communication process (Kirk & Kirk, 1971):

Channels: auditory-vocal

visual-motor

---

[4] In the *Mental Measurements Yearbook*, such tests are usually listed under "Sensory and Motor Tests" and "Speech and Hearing Tests." Many can be found in the catalogs of major test publishers, especially Consulting Psychologists Press and Western Psychological Services, which include also some tests published by others.

Processes: receptive (understanding words and pictures)

organizing (association of past and present inputs and eduction of relations)

expressive (expressing ideas in words or gestures)

Levels: representational (utilizing meaning of linguistic symbols)

automatic (utilizing habitual integrated pattern—e.g., speed of perception, rote learning, memory span)

The abilities covered by the ITPA are located at the intersections of the three dimensions. For example, in the Manual Expression Test (visual-motor channel, expressive process, representational level), the child performs manual gestures to "show what we do with" each pictured object, such as pencil sharpener, telephone, and clarinet. In the Grammatic Closure Test (auditory-vocal channel, organizing process, automatic level), the task is to complete oral statements such as "Here is a child. Here are three ———," while shown the appropriate pictures. The entire battery consists of 10 regular subtests, plus two optional subtests.

Both the pictorial and verbal items of the ITPA appear to be heavily loaded with culturally restricted content. The normative samples were drawn largely from middle-class populations, in five midwestern cities. For these reasons, the applicability of the ITPA to children from lower socio-economic levels and from minority groups needs to be more fully ascertained. The test authors recommend the use of supplementary local norms.

A more recently developed battery in the same area is the Porch Index of Communicative Ability in Children (PICAC). This instrument is based on a three-part communication model which includes (1) information input through visual, auditory, and tactile modalities; (2) integration, covering various information-processing steps; and (3) output through verbal, graphic, and gestural modalities. Each subtest employs the same 10 common objects, such as key, spoon, and toothbrush. These objects are presented in several forms, including miniature models, outline drawings, oral names, written names, and statements of function (e.g., the one used for cleaning teeth). The child is asked to perform many different tasks in relation to these objects. Geometric figures are also used in a copying test. Responses are scored on a 16-category rating scale which takes into account five response characteristics: accuracy, responsiveness (ease of eliciting appropriate response), completeness in carrying out task, promptness in accomplishing response, and efficiency (facility in carrying out response). There is a Basic Battery for children who are functioning educationally at the kindergarten level or below, and an Advanced Battery for those in Grades 1 to 6.

The PICAC manual (Porch, 1979) gives percentile norms by age and grade for total battery performance, as well as for each input and output modality and each subtest. A modality score profile can be plotted, showing the child's scores in relation to the means and SDs of his or her age group. Several other types of performance evaluation are also described, including analyses of subtest and item scores. The standardization sample consisted of 614 normal schoolchildren drawn from private and parochial schools in three states. The author refers to studies in progress with various ethnic minorities, although preliminary analyses on small groups in the stardardization sample showed no significant relation of performance to ethnic group. It is also relevant to note that the items in this test do not appear to be culturally restricted.

For each of the two batteries, reliability was investigated with a sample of 50 children (including 10 mental retardates). Analyses of scorer reliability, employing the test author and two clinicians who had completed a 40-hour training program with the PICAC, indicated close agreement among scorers. Internal consistency reliabilities for subtests were in the .90s. Retest reliabilities obtained within one week were again in the .90s, for both subtest and modality scores. There is no discussion of validity in the manual, but the author refers to a three-year development period during which numerous revisions were made in the battery, presumably on the basis of clinical tryouts. The construction of this battery was also guided by results obtained with a closely similar adult form (see Appendix E), which had been in use for several years. Clearly, more research is needed on the PICAC itself, both to evaluate the battery and to enrich its interpretive background.

A different approach is illustrated by a newly published instrument, the Assessment of Basic Competencies (ABC). Focusing directly on "enabling skills for school learning," the author identified three major classes of relevant cognitive skills: information processing, language, and mathematical reasoning. Eleven tests are grouped into these three classes. Each child is tested only with items at his or her own performance level, which is located by a procedure similar to that followed with the Stanford-Binet. The total scale spans ages 3 to 15 (preschool to Grade 9). For normative evaluation, a comparable developmental score is obtained on each of the 11 tests. Criterion-referenced or diagnostic interpretation is based on performance on item clusters. These skill clusters are accompanied by suggestions regarding available instructional materials and programs for developing appropriate skills. In addition to the diagnostic battery, the ABC series includes two screening tests (for preschool and school levels) to identify children for further testing with all or part of the diagnostic battery.

The procedures employed in constructing this battery were of high technical quality. Items were selected and scaled through latent trait theory techniques (see Ch. 8). Normative data were carefully assembled in the effort to obtain a representative national sample. Reliability and validity appear promising. Because of the recency of this battery, its effectiveness in practice remains to be demonstrated.

Other batteries that provide still different emphases and combinations of functions are the Frostig·Developmental Test of Visual Perception and Ayres' Southern California Sensory Integration Tests. The former comprises five tests of visuomotor coordination, visual perception, and spatial relations; the latter is a 17-test battery covering sensorimotor and perceptual tasks, with considerable involvement of both fine and gross motor coordination. Both batteries form part of combined testing and training programs developed by the authors and distributed by the test publishers.

ASSESSMENT TECHNIQUES IN BEHAVIOR THERAPY PROGRAMS

NATURE OF BEHAVIOR MODIFICATION. The various techniques subsumed under the general concept of behavior modification represent a direct utilization of major learning principles in the practical management of behavior change. Basically, these techniques involve the application of conditioning principles to the acquisition and strengthening of wanted behavior, such as self-assertion or effective interpersonal relations, and the elimination of unwanted behavior, such as stage fright, uncontrollable temper, or excessive drinking. Behavior modification techniques are being introduced into such diverse settings as schoolrooms, factories, hospitals, and correctional institutions. They have yielded promising results in research on such varied problems as employee absenteeism, energy conservation, littering in public places, and the control of aggression. Thus far, however, their major application has been in clinical psychology, where this approach is generally designated as behavior therapy.

The specific procedures of behavior therapy utilize many types of learning, including both classical and operant conditioning, observational and imitative learning, roleplaying, rehearsal, and verbal feedback. Such conditioning concepts as stimulus generalization, extinction, counterconditioning, and contingent reinforcement are commonly encountered in the behavior therapy literature. Stimuli may be presented in vivo (e.g., a real dog in the room, a stranger with whom the client tries to converse) or through imagery (e.g., imagine yourself handling a live snake; imagine yourself studying the night before an important exam). Behavior therapy has gradually broadened to include an ever-widening repertoire of intervention techniques, and there is increasing evidence of a merging of cognitive and behavioral approaches (Bandura, 1969; Goldfried & Davison, 1976; Lazarus, 1976; Mahoney, 1974, 1977).

A distinctive feature of behavior therapy programs is their detailed specification of objectives. Such specifications should include a precise description of the desired target behavior. For example, a target behavior for a withdrawn schizophrenic might be that he converse with his associates and respond to them in other appropriate ways. In addition, more immediate subgoals are set up as a sequence of graded steps, beginning with the most readily attainable behavior, such as "glances at person speaking to him," "nods," or "utters one word." Behavior therapy has been successfully employed at all age levels and with persons of diverse educational and cultural backgrounds. It has been used with psychotics, juvenile delinquents, and mental retardates, as well as with highly sophisticated adult clients.

ASSESSMENT TECHNIQUES. The principal functions to be served by assessment procedures in behavior modification programs can be subsumed under three headings. First, assessment techniques help in *defining the individual's problem* through a functional analysis of relevant behavior (Bijou & Peterson, 1971; Kanfer & Saslow, 1969). Essentially, such an analysis involves a full specification of the treatment objective, such as the reduction of anxiety when speaking in public, overcoming a fear of snakes, or acquiring specific social competencies. This process includes a description of the stimuli that elicit the target behavior, the situations in which such behavior occurs, and the nature, magnitude, and frequencies of particular responses. It is also important to investigate the conditions that tend to maintain unwanted behavior, i.e., to ascertain what are the usual consequences of the target behavior in the individual's present environment. It should be noted that the targets for behavior modification may include not only overt behavior but also cognitions and feelings.

A second way in which assessment procedures can contribute to behavior therapy is in the *selection of appropriate treatments*. In choosing among the wide variety of available treatments, the therapist can be guided by knowledge about the problem, the characteristics of the individual client, and the present environment in which the client must operate. Although this function of assessment has received little attention, its importance is being recognized by leading exponents of behavior therapy (Ciminero, Calhoun, & Adams, 1977). A related question concerns the choice of effective reinforcing stimuli for use in the learning process. Such common reinforcers as social approval, attention from associates, and candy or similar short-term rewards may be adequate in some situations. Nevertheless, a systematic survey of the relative value of available reinforcers in individual cases will usually enhance the probability of successful retraining.

Third, there is need for *assessing the behavior change* that results from treatment. Such assessment should include techniques for monitoring change in the course of the program, so as to permit evaluation of treatment effectiveness and the introduction of procedural alterations at any treatment stage. It should also include terminal measures to establish the individual's attainment of satisfactory status, and it should include follow-up observations to ensure maintenance of satisfactory status.

In considering available assessment procedures, we should note, first, that the same procedure can often provide information relevant to all three functions. Second, the choice of procedures depends on the nature of the problem, the characteristics of the client, and the facilities available at the particular clinic. Third, a combination of several assessment procedures is desirable in many cases.

Available assessment procedures can themselves be classified under three major types: self-report by the client, direct observation of behavior, and physiological measures.[5] Although few centers can afford the facilities required for *physiological measures,* these measures provide supplementary objective data in the assessment of certain conditions, such as anxiety and sexual arousal. Examples include cardiovascular (EKG, blood pressure), gastric (peristaltic contractions, stomach acidity), sexual (penis circumference, vaginal blood volume), and cerebral (EEG, evoked electrical responses) measures.

Direct observation of target behavior can be conducted in naturalistic situations (home, school, playground, residential institution) by parents, teachers, institutional personnel, or special observers. Observational aids such as checklists, rating scales, and daily schedules may be employed. Such observations are subject to several weaknesses. For example, the observer's presence may influence the client's behavior, the observer's own viewpoint may bias his or her perception of the behavior, and the observation period may miss critical behaviors. For these reasons, analogue situations in the clinic or laboratory are often employed. These situations may range from enactment of behavior toward a significant person (e.g., parent, spouse) or object (e.g., dog, snake), to roleplaying with staff members or other clients, responding to relevant situations portrayed on audiotape or videotape, or responding to written descriptions of critical situations (McReynolds, 1978, Chs. 6, 8).

Self-report by the client comprises a diversity of techniques. They include clinical interviews by the therapist, self-monitoring records of target behavior kept by the client, and a variety of written checklists and inventories. Some adaptations of early self-report personality inventories have been used in the preliminary screening and identification of target behaviors.[6] A number of new instruments have been prepared for use in specific research projects or treatment programs; although not themselves published, they are usually fully described and reproduced in journal articles or books (Ciminero et al., 1977, Ch. 6). Several are fear-behavior surveys, which list items frequently found to evoke anxiety and ask the respondent to indicate the degree of disturbance aroused by each. An example is the

---

[5] Comprehensive surveys and critical evaluations of available behavioral assessment procedures can be found in Ciminero et al. (1977) and in Nay (1979). Two recently established journals devoted to this topic are *Behavioral Assessment* and the *Journal of Behavioral Assessment.* Cautela (1977) has assembled a manual comprising 36 self-report forms and questionnaires developed by him and his co-workers for use in behavior therapy programs.

[6] See, e.g., Wolpe (1973, Appendix) for Bernreuter Self-Sufficiency Scale and revision of Willoughby Personality Schedule.

Fear Survey Schedule (Wolpe, 1973; Wolpe & Lang, 1964), one of whose forms has actually been published (see Appendix E). It comprises 108 items, such as the noise of vacuum cleaners, open wounds, flying insects, and taking written tests. For each item, the individual indicates how much he or she is disturbed by it, by marking one of five responses from "not at all" to "very much." A 40-item fear survey schedule, which yields a profile of scores in five fear categories identified through factor analysis, is described by Tasto, Hickson, and Rubin (1971).

Another area of interest in surveys of target behaviors is that of self-assertiveness. For example, the Conflict Resolution Inventory (McFall & Lillesand, 1971; McFall & Twentyman, 1973) contains 35 items describing situations in which the individual is asked to do something unreasonable. A typical item reads:

You are in the thick of studying for exams when a person whom you know only slightly comes into your room and says, "I'm tired of studying. Mind if I come in and take a break for a while?"

For each item, respondents indicate whether or not they would be likely to refuse the request and how comfortable they would feel about refusing or acquiescing. This technique can be used not only in the initial assessment but also in monitoring the course of training. The goal of assertiveness training is the appropriate expression of feeling in ways that protect the individual's rights without humiliating or demeaning other persons.

A broader sampling of self-assertive behaviors is covered by the College Self-Expression Scale (Galassi, Delo, Galassi, & Bastien, 1974; Galassi & Galassi, 1974). Items for this instrument were designed to assess a variety of manifestations of positive assertiveness, negative assertiveness, and self-denial. Positive assertiveness includes expressions of agreement, admiration, love, and affection. Negative assertiveness refers to justified feelings of anger, annoyance, disagreement, and dissatisfaction. Self-denial is illustrated by such behaviors as overapologizing and exaggerated concern for the feelings of others. The stimulus situations presented in the College Self-Expression Scale cover interpersonal relations with strangers, authority figures, business associates, family, and peers of the same or opposite sex, as well as some nonspecific situations. Respondents indicate on a scale of 0–4 the frequency with which they engage in each of the behaviors described.

Some instruments have been designed to aid in choosing available reinforcers for use in behavior therapy programs. Among them are the Reinforcement Survey Schedule (Cautela & Kastenbaum, 1967) and the Mediator-Reinforcer Incomplete Blank (Tharp & Wetzel, 1969). The latter was constructed for use in a demonstration project on behavior modification in children. It consists of 34 incomplete sentences such as "The thing I like to do most is ———"; "I will do almost anything to get ———." In an effort to assemble a representative sample of possible reinforcing stimuli, Mac-Phillamy and Lewinsohn (1974, 1976) asked college students to describe "events, experiences, or activities which you find pleasant, rewarding, and fun." From the replies, they prepared the Pleasant Events Schedule, a list of 320 items for each of which the respondent indicates how often the event occurred in the past month and how enjoyable or pleasant it was. For events not recently experienced, the individual indicates how enjoyable it would have been if it had occurred. Lewinsohn (1975; Lewinsohn & Graf, 1973) used this schedule in a continuing research program on depression. It is particularly relevant to investigating the behavioral theory that depression is associated with inadequate or insufficient positive reinforcement of one's behavior.

EVALUATION OF BEHAVIORAL ASSESSMENT. Because of the rapid growth of behavior therapy, the development of behavioral assessment techniques to meet its needs lagged far behind. Surveys of clinical psychologists who practiced behavior therapy revealed the use of a variety of makeshift procedures and widespread dissatisfaction with available techniques (Kanfer, 1972; Wade, Baker, & Hartmann, 1979). Another circumstance that retarded progress in the development of assessment techniques was an apparent conflict between traditional trait theory and the social learning theory that underlies behavior therapy. In their approach to personality problems, behavior therapists differ from traditional clinical psychologists in several respects (Ciminero et al., 1977; Goldfried & Kent, 1972; Hartmann, Roper, & Bradford, 1979; Nay, 1979). The early view, which still survives among some clinical psychologists, regarded behavior as a function of underlying, stable traits. Accordingly, the purpose of testing was to assess these traits and to provide a diagnostic label for the individual. In contrast, the behavior therapists' view, which is more nearly in line with the prevalent psychometric view, is that behavior is a function of the individual's interaction with his or her particular environment, and that testing should sample the specific behavior of interest. The purpose of such behavior sampling is to aid in the planning and evaluation of treatment.

It has been said that behavioral assessment came of age in the 1970s. Leading specialists in behavior therapy have been arguing convincingly that behavioral assessment must meet traditional psychometric standards with regard to uniformity of materials and procedures, normative data, reliability, and validity (Goldfried & Linehan, 1977; Hartmann et al., 1979). While behavior therapy has stimulated an extensive amount of research, the lack of standardization of materials and procedures employed in different laboratories and clinics has made it difficult to compare results across studies. Norms are needed despite the fact that behavior therapy focuses on changes within the individual. Norms help in ascertaining who actually needs therapy and in setting realistic treatment goals. They also provide a uniform, objective score scale for assessing the outcome of therapy and for comparing the research findings of different investigators. The reliability of assessment techniques across observers and across occasions must also be considered. Any single observation, however obtained, contains an error of measurement; ignoring this error will not make it go away.

The content validity of behavioral assessments can be substantially improved by following the established procedures for the representative sampling of the behavior domain of interest. The construct validity of such assessment techniques can be explored in various ways. Of special interest is an investigation of the extent to which behavioral findings about an individual can be generalized across observational methods (e.g., self-reports, observer reports in naturalistic settings, analogue techniques) and across situations (e.g., clinic, home, office, school). "A fear of dogs" and "weak self-assertiveness" are constructs. The boundaries of such constructs need to be empirically delimited in order to identify the client's problem, to plan and monitor a treatment program, and to evaluate the outcomes of treatment.

CLINICAL JUDGMENT

THE NATURE OF CLINICAL ASSESSMENT. The term "clinical" is conventionally employed to refer to any methodology involving the intensive study of individual cases. Thus, clinical procedures are applied, not only by psychologists working in clinics, but also by those who function in counseling centers, schools, and industry (e.g., in the assessment of personnel for high-level jobs). A distinguishing feature of clinical assessments is their reliance on *judgment* in at least some aspects of the process. In this respect, the clinical method has been contrasted with the administration of objective, standardized tests and the use of statistical, or actuarial procedures for combining data through regression equations, multiple cutoffs, and other "mechanical formulas" (Ch. 7).

What the clinician does in assessing a client may be regarded as a special case of person cognition, or interpersonal perception—the process through which anyone comes to know and understand another person (Bakan, 1956; Gage & Cronbach, 1955; Sarbin, Taft, & Bailey, 1960). In this process, the observer often relies upon *assumed similarity* to oneself. Thus, we can utilize our own experience in interpreting the behavior of another. Although we cannot directly observe another's aches and pains or feelings of joy and sadness, we can identify them through facial expressions, gestures, verbal reports, and other overt cues that we have learned to associate with our own feelings. Assumed similarity between a newcomer and familiar others, such as one's relatives, friends, or former clients, is an extension of this mechanism. When this approach is followed in trying to understand someone quite unlike oneself—or unlike one's earlier acquaintances—it is likely to prove misleading. Errors may thus arise when clinicians make diagnostic or prognostic inferences about a client whose cultural background, education, or socioeconomic level differs markedly from their own (Wainwright, 1958).

THE CLINICIAN'S DATA-GATHERING FUNCTION. The diagnostic role of the clinician can be described in terms of data gathering and data synthesis. We shall begin by considering what the clinician can contribute to the process of data gathering. First, by establishing and maintaining rapport, the clinician may elicit from the client pertinent facts about his or her life history not readily accessible in other ways. Such life-history data provide a particularly sound basis for understanding an individual and predicting subsequent behavior (Dailey, 1960). The life history has been aptly described as "an unbiased population of events which is as convincing an operational definition of a person as one can hope for" (Dailey, 1960, p. 21). It might be added that the more data one has from the life history, the less filling-in needs to be done in the interpretive and synthesizing process.

In the search for facts, the clinician is guided partly by the client's own responses, which provide clues for further exploration. Particular responses, when considered in the light of personality theory, relevant research findings, and professional experience, lead to the formulation of tentative hypotheses. These hypotheses are then tested by gathering or examining additional pertinent data. As a result, they may be strengthened, modified, or discarded. Such interlocking of hypothesis formation and hypothesis testing represents both an advantage and a potential hazard of clinical assessment. On the one hand, it permits more flexibility of search and more effective utilization of cues than would be possible with a test, questionnaire, or other standardized procedure. On the other hand, if clinicians are unduly influenced by their early hypotheses, they may look only for data that support those hypotheses. By the type of questions they ask and the way they formulate them or by subtle expressions of agreement or disagreement, they may influence what the client reports. Sarbin and his associates (1960) called this process "soliciting" as contrasted to "probing." Such biased data-gathering techniques probably account for the remarkably uniform etiologies found among the clients of some psychoanalysts.

A third way in which the clinician contributes to the fact-finding process is by serving as a stimulus in an interpersonal situation. In this regard, the clinical interview functions as a situational test or simulation. It provides a sample of the client's interpersonal behavior, observed under more-or-less controlled conditions.

THE CLINICIAN'S DATA-SYNTHESIS FUNCTION. Much has been written about the data-processing, synthesizing, or interpretive role of the clinician. Some have proposed a special process of "clinical intuition" that is qualitatively different from other forms of inference. Belief in such a process arises partly from the fact that clinicians are often unable to report the cues they employ in reaching a conclusion (Sarbin et al., 1960, Ch. 8). The mystery disappears, however, when we realize that many of our perceptions utilize cues that are inaccessible to self-examination. A classical example is visual depth perception. We regularly perceive the world in three dimensions without being able to specify the cues we employ in the process. Similarly, after exposure to a test protocol, a set of test scores, a case history, or a face-to-face interaction with a client, the clinician may assert that the patient is creative, or a likely suicide, or a poor psychotherapy risk, even though the clinician cannot verbalize the facts he or she used in reaching such a conclusion. Being unaware of the cues that mediated the inference, the clinician may also be unaware of the probabilistic nature of the inference and may feel more confidence in it than is justified.

Research on the process of clinical judgment has thrown considerable light on the relation between the data input (test scores, specific responses, score patterns, case history items, etc.) and the clinician's output (judgment, diagnosis, prediction). Correlation and regression analyses can indicate the relative contribution of different inputs to the final judgment; and they can show whether the contribution is linear (additive) or is best represented by some nonlinear combination, as in the use of pattern or configural analysis, or moderator variables (Hammond, Hursch, & Todd, 1964; J. S. Wiggins, 1973, Ch. 4; Wiggins & Hoffman, 1968). The results show that a linear regression equation (simple additive model) can closely reproduce the clinicians' output in most cases. When a more complex model fits the data better, the differences are so slight as to be negligible (Dawes & Corrigan, 1974; Goldberg, 1968b). Clinicians' own reports of the relative weights they assign to different inputs and the ways in which they combine data may differ sharply from their actual use of the available information. Other research has illuminated some of the possible sources of error in clinical judgment, such as the influence of cultural stereotypes (Chapman and Chapman, 1967; Golding & Rorer, 1972) and reliance on fallacious prediction principles (Kahneman & Tversky, 1973). Examples of the latter include failure to consider base rates or regression effects and assumption that more highly intercorrelated predictors yield higher validity.

COMPARATIVE STUDIES OF CLINICAL AND STATISTICAL PREDICTIONS. Given the same set of facts, such as test scores or life-history data, will clinical judgment provide more accurate predictions of subsequent behavior than would be obtained by the routine application of a regression equation or other empirically derived formula? The question has practical as well as theoretical importance because, once a regression equation or other statistical strategy has been developed, it can be applied by a clerk or a computer, thus freeing the clinician for therapy, research, and other functions. In a classic book entitled *Clinical Versus Statistical Prediction,* Meehl (1954) discussed the process of clinical judgment and surveyed some 20 investigations comparing the two types of prediction. The criteria predicted in these studies included principally success in some kind of schooling or training (college, Air Force pilot training, etc.), response to therapy on the part of psychotic or neurotic patients, and criminal recidivism or institutional adjustment of reformatory inmates. Predictions were made by clinical psychologists, counselors, psychiatrists, and other professional persons with varying amounts of experience in the use of clinical procedures. Focusing only on the process of combining data, rather than on differences in the kind of data obtained, Meehl showed that, with only one questionable exception, the routine application of statistical procedures yielded at least as many correct predictions as did clinical analysis, and frequently more.

The publication of Meehl's book stimulated a lively controversy that is still active. It was also followed by further research using better controlled procedures and more clinically relevant criteria (see Sawyer, 1966; J. S. Wiggins, 1973, Ch. 5). A later review of available research led Meehl (1965) to reaffirm his earlier conclusion. Of some 50 studies examined up to that time, about two thirds favored statistical prediction and the remaining third showed no significant difference.[7] In a particularly well-designed study, Goldberg (1965) compared clinician's predictions from the score profile on the Minnesota Multiphasic Personality Inventory (see Ch. 17) with predictions made from a series of statistical formulas. Comparisons of validity coefficients showed that the statistical formulas clearly outperformed the clinicians. The highest validity coefficient in the study was obtained with an empirically derived, linear combination of scores. Another interesting finding, known as "bootstrapping," is that an actuarial model of a clinician's own behavior will usually yield more valid predictions than does the clinician (Dawes & Corrigan, 1974; Goldberg, 1970). Reflecting principally the regularities in the clinician's behavior, the model reduces the influence of random procedural errors.

It is important to bear in mind that all these studies dealt only with methods of synthesizing data, when clinical and statistical procedures are applied *to the same data.* A major contribution of the clinical method, however, is the obtaining of data in areas in which satisfactory tests are unavailable. Systematic interviewing, case histories, and direct observation of behavior are still the principal sources of information on many aspects of personality. None of the studies on clinical versus statistical prediction reflect on the clinician's data-gathering function.

In the second place, the clinical method is better suited than the statistical method to the processing of rare and idiosyncratic events whose frequency is too low to permit the development of statistical strategies. Al-

---

[7] One study, which seemed to favor the clinical method, was later shown not to support this conclusion because of methodological complications (Goldberg, 1968a; see also J. S. Wiggins, 1973, p. 184).

though any one such event occurs infrequently, it may significantly affect outcome in an individual case. Moreover, *different* "rare events" will be encountered often enough to have a substantial effect upon the decisions reached in large numbers of cases. It should be added that even if individual events occur frequently, particular combinations of these events may not be observed often enough to meet the requirements of actuarial prediction.

Furthermore, whatever the theoretical possibilities, there remains a vast multitude of clinical decisions for which no statistical formulas have yet been developed. As Meehl (1957, p. 273) expressed it, "Mostly we will use our heads, because there just aren't any formulas . . ." In this connection, it is important to differentiate between statistical or actuarial procedures, on the one hand, and automated clinical interpretations, on the other. The latter are computerized reports which have been developed for certain tests, such as the DAT (Ch. 13) and the MMPI (Ch. 17). They are not actuarial predictions in the sense of being derived statistically from empirical rela- tions. Rather, they represent essentially clinicians' interpretations of test data, which are sufficiently standardized to be coded and programmed for computer retrieval. The programs are developed by skilled clinicians, who may draw upon some statistical data from published sources along with personality theory and clinical experience. An account of various ways in which computers may be used in the clinical process is provided by Klein- muntz (1975).

In summary, the most effective procedure in our present state of knowl- edge combines clinical and statistical approaches. The clinician should uti- lize all the objective test data, norms, regression equations, and other ac- tuarial strategies applicable to the particular situation, while supplementing this information with facts and inferences attainable only through clinical methods. The validity of clinical predictions against actual outcomes should be systematically investigated whenever feasible. More data are also needed on the consistency of predictions about the same persons made by different clinicians and by the same clinicians at different times. Insofar as possible, the process and cues on which clinical predictions are based should be made explicit in clinical records. Such a practice would not only facilitate research and training, but would also serve to encourage reliance on sound data and defensible interpretations. Finally, the "clinician as instrument" is an important concept in this connection. Undoubtedly, the objectivity and skill with which data are gathered and interpreted—and the resulting ac- curacy of predictions—vary widely with the abilities, personality, profes- sional training, and experience of individual clinicians.

THE CLINICAL REPORT: A FINAL SYNTHESIS. In Chapter 3, we examined some of the broad issues involved in the communication of test results, with particular reference to ethical and social implications. For the clinical psy- chologist, such communication usually includes the preparation of a written test report or case report, which may or may not be followed by discussion or consultation with examinee, parents, teachers, or other professionals. Even in those situations that do not require a written report, it is well to prepare such a report as a record for future reference. The preparation of a report also helps to organize and clarify the clinician's own thinking about the case and to sharpen his or her interpretations. Report writing represents the final stage in the clinician's synthesizing function. In its content, the report should draw upon all the data sources (test and nontest) available to the clinician.

Several books provide guidelines for clinical report writing.[8] Without duplicating the many lists of suggestions that can be found in available sources, we shall focus briefly on some of the major points. First, there is no one standard form or outline for all clinical reports. Both content and style should and do vary with the purpose of the case study, the context in which it is conducted, the recipients to whom the report is addressed, and the theoretical orientation and professional background of the clinician. It is especially important to adapt the report to the needs, interests, and background of those who will receive it.

The content of the report should follow directly from the purpose of the testing or case study, as specified in the reasons for referral or consultation. From the mass of data the clinician has gathered by both formal and informal methods, he or she should select whatever is relevant to answering the questions raised at the outset. The current trend, moreover, is to make reports action-oriented, i.e., directed toward recommendations or decisions regarding instructional programs, therapy, occupational choice, or other appropriate actions. Diagnosis, etiology, personality description, and understanding of personality dynamics tend to be deemphasized. It should also be recognized, however, that enhancing self-understanding may be an important goal of some case studies and is an integral part of certain types of psychotherapy.

The report should concentrate on each individual's differentiating characteristics—the high and low points—rather than on traits in which the individual's standing is close to the average. A test of the effectiveness of a report is to see whether it is unique to the individual or whether it applies equally well to other persons of the same age, sex, education, socioeconomic level, or other demographic variables. It is a relatively easy task to prepare a pseudo-report from general, stereotyped statements that apply to most people. A considerable body of research has demonstrated that such reports are readily accepted as "remarkably accurate" self-descriptions by a large

---

[8] Sattler (1982, Ch. 24) gives a comprehensive view of problems and pitfalls, with many practical suggestions, and summarizes pertinent research on report writing. Other sources, with illustrative case reports, include Klopfer (1960) and Tallent (1977). Report writing pertaining to specific intelligence tests can be found in Glasser and Zimmerman (1967, Ch. 2) for the WISC; Zimmerman, Woo-Sam, and Glasser (1973, Ch. 15) for the WAIS; and Sattler (1982, Ch. 24) for Stanford-Binet, WISC, and WPPSI.

majority of persons (Snyder & Larson, 1972; Stagner, 1958). This pseudo-validation has been called the "Barnum effect," after Phineas T. Barnum, the famous showman who is credited with the remark that there is a fool born every minute. Reliance on such generally applicable personality descriptions is a favorite device of fortune tellers and other charlatans.

The primary focus of the report should be on interpretations and conclusions, although test records and other detailed data may be separately appended. Specific data, such as individual responses and subtest scores, should ordinarily be cited only to illustrate or clarify a point. The report should be a carefully organized and integrated account. If the data contain inconsistencies of sufficient importance to be included, the clinician should call attention to the inconsistency and if possible suggest reasons for it. In any descriptive statements about the individual's performance, the frame of reference should be made clear. Is the statement based on a criterion-referenced or a norm-referenced evaluation? If the latter, with what norms is the individual being compared? If the comparison is intraindividual, it should be clearly reported as such. For example, one should not write: "Her numerical aptitude is superior," but "Her numerical aptitude is clearly above the level of her other aptitudes." The clinician's statements should also be so expressed as to reflect his or her level of certainty for each fact or inference presented.

Many suggestions can be offered regarding writing style.[9] As in all scientific writing, the goal of the clinical report is to communicate, not to obfuscate. Simple, direct writing is not easy to produce. It calls for careful planning, revision, and editing; and it can be improved with practice. Avoid the use of technical terms, except when they truly serve to facilitate communication. Do not try to instruct the reader or to impress him with your competence and erudition—that is not the purpose of a clinical report. Write from the reader's point of view. Keep an image of the reader before you as you write. It will keep you from going too far astray.

[9] Books on the preparation of clinical reports usually contain helpful hints for good writing, as well as references to standard manuals of style. Special attention is here called to two rather diverse sources: *The Publication Manual of the American Psychological Association* (1974) and *The Elements of Style* by Strunk and White (1979), an entertaining little book which should make writing less painful for both writer and reader.

PART FIVE

Personality Tests

Chapter 17

Self-report Inventories

ALTHOUGH the term "personality" is sometimes employed in a broader sense, in conventional psychometric terminology "personality tests" are instruments for the measurement of emotional, motivational, interpersonal, and attitudinal characteristics, as distinguished from abilities. In the next four chapters, the major varieties of personality tests will be examined. This chapter will deal with personality inventories. Chapter 18 will consider available techniques for the measurement of interests, values, and personal styles. The instruments to be covered in both of these chapters are predominantly paper-and-pencil, self-report questionnaires suitable for group administration. The use of projective techniques for the assessment of personality characteristics will be discussed in Chapter 19. In Chapter 20, we shall survey a number of miscellaneous approaches to the assessment of personality, several of which are still in an experimental stage.

The number of available personality tests runs into several hundred. Especially numerous are the personality inventories and the projective techniques. In this book, we shall be concerned primarily with the types of approaches that have been explored in the assessment of personality. A few of the most widely known tests of each type will be briefly described for illustrative purposes. Many books have been written exclusively about personality assessment through tests as well as through other techniques. For more detailed treatment of the topic, the reader is referred to these specialized books (e.g., Lanyon & Goodstein, 1982; McReynolds, 1968, 1971, 1975, 1978, 1981; Mischel, 1968; I. G. Sarason, 1972; J. S. Wiggins, 1973).

In the development of personality inventories, several approaches have been followed in formulating, assembling, selecting, and grouping items. Among the major procedures in current use are those based on content validation, empirical criterion keying, factor analysis, and personality theory. Each of these approaches will be discussed and illustrated in the following sections. It should be noted, however, that they are not alternative or mutually exclusive techniques. Theoretically, all can be combined in the development of a single personality inventory. In actual practice, several inventories have utilized two or more of these procedures.

Although some personality tests are used as group screening instruments, the majority find their principal application in clinical and counseling contexts. For this reason, the next four chapters represent largely a continuation of the discussion of clinical testing begun in Chapter 16. In their present state of development, most personality tests should be regarded either as aids in clinical assessment or as research instruments.

CONTENT VALIDATION

The prototype of self-report personality inventories was the Woodworth Personal Data Sheet, developed for use during World War I. This inventory was essentially an attempt to standardize a psychiatric interview and to adapt the procedure for mass testing. Accordingly, Woodworth gathered information regarding common neurotic and preneurotic symptoms from the psychiatric literature as well as through conferences with psychiatrists. It was in reference to these symptoms that the inventory questions were originally formulated. The questions dealt with such deviant behaviors as abnormal fears or phobias, obsessions and compulsions, nightmares and other sleep disturbances, excessive fatigue and other psychosomatic symptoms, feelings of unreality, and motor disturbances such as tics and tremors. In the final selection of items, Woodworth applied certain empirical statistical checks, to be discussed in the next section. Nevertheless, it is apparent that the primary emphasis in the construction and use of this inventory was placed on content validity, as indicated in the sources from which items were drawn as well as in the common recognition of certain kinds of behavior as maladaptive.

One of the clearest examples of content validation in a current personality inventory is provided by the Mooney Problem Check List. Designed chiefly to identify problems for group discussion or for individual counseling, this checklist drew its items from written statements of problems submitted by about 4,000 high school students, as well as from case records, counseling interviews, and similar sources. The checklist is available in junior high school, high school, college, and adult forms. The problem areas covered vary somewhat from level to level. In the high school and college forms, they include health and physical development; finances, living conditions, and employment; social and recreational activities; social-psychological relations; personal-psychological relations; courtship, sex, and marriage; home and family; morals and religion; adjustment to school work; the future—vocational and educational; and curriculum and teaching procedure.

Although the number of items checked in each area can be recorded, the Mooney Problem Check List does not yield trait scores or measures of degree of adjustment. Emphasis is on individual items as self-perceived and self-reported problems or sources of difficulty. While no psychometric evaluation of this instrument has been undertaken, evidence has accumulated indicating its effectiveness. Published research shows that, on the average, students check from 20 to 30 problems; these results suggest that the checklist provides good coverage of problems that students are willing to report. Some data on concurrent validity are available from comparisons of contrasted groups whose reported problem frequencies in relevant areas differ in the expected direction.

Another checklist of needs and problems, suitable for Grades 7 to 12, is the STS Youth Inventory. The 167 items comprising this checklist are grouped under the following rubrics: My School, After High School, About Myself, Getting Along with Others, and Things in General. An ingenious device incorporated into this inventory is the use of response boxes of different sizes to enable the respondent to suggest the magnitude of each problem, as illustrated in Figure 88. In each of the five areas, the manual provides percentile equivalents for the weighted total of problems checked, from which an individual student profile can be plotted. A more useful analysis with this type of checklist, however, focuses on individual items. For this purpose, the manual reports the percentage of respondents in a national sample, by sex and grade, who marked each response alternative for each item. A similar problem checklist, the STS Junior Inventory, is available for Grades 4 to 8.

It should be noted that with all these inventories some efforts have been

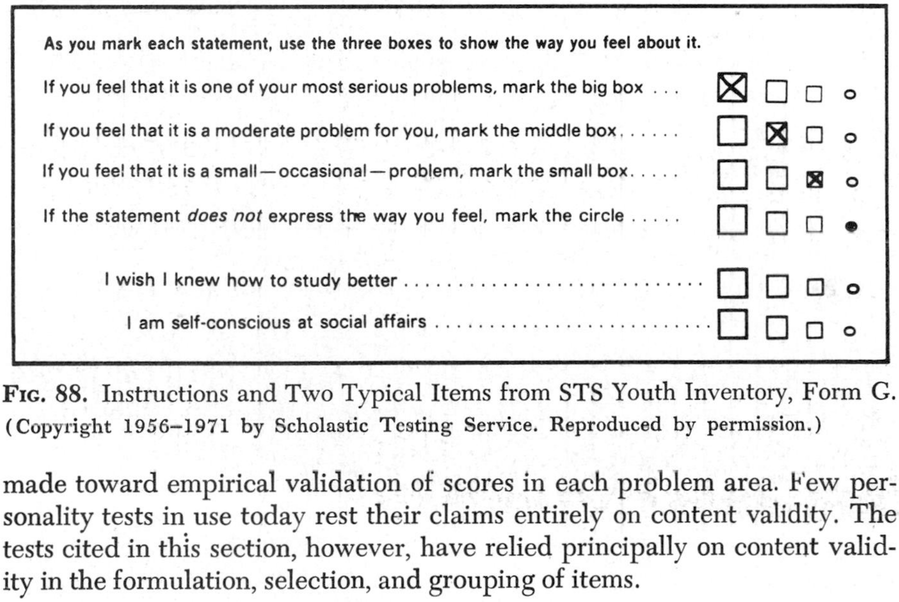

As you mark each statement, use the three boxes to show the way you feel about it.

If you feel that it is one of your most serious problems, mark the big box . . .

If you feel that it is a moderate problem for you, mark the middle box. . . . . .

If you feel that it is a small—occasional—problem, mark the small box. . . . .

If the statement *does not* express the way you feel, mark the circle . . . . .

I wish I knew how to study better . . . .

I am self-conscious at social affairs . . . .

Fig. 88. Instructions and Two Typical Items from STS Youth Inventory, Form G. (Copyright 1956–1971 by Scholastic Testing Service. Reproduced by permission.)

made toward empirical validation of scores in each problem area. Few personality tests in use today rest their claims entirely on content validity. The tests cited in this section, however, have relied principally on content validity in the formulation, selection, and grouping of items.

EMPIRICAL CRITERION KEYING

basic approach. Empirical criterion keying refers to the development of a scoring key in terms of some external criterion. This procedure involves the selection of items to be retained and the assignment of scoring weights to each response. In the construction of the previously cited Woodworth Per-

sonal Data Sheet, some of the statistical checks applied in the final selection
of items pointed the way for criterion keying. Thus, no item was retained in
this inventory if 25% or more of a normal sample answered it in the unfavorable direction. The rationale underlying this procedure was that a behavior
characteristic that occurs with such frequency in an essentially normal sample cannot be indicative of abnormality. The method of contrasted groups
was likewise employed in the selection of items. Only symptoms reported at
least twice as often in a previously diagnosed psychoneurotic group than in
a normal group were retained.

Despite some use of such empirical checks, however, content validation
rests essentially on a literal or veridical interpretation of questionnaire
items. The response to each question is regarded as an index of the actual
presence or absence of the specific problem, belief, or behavior described
by the question. In empirical criterion keying, on the other hand, the responses are treated as diagnostic or symptomatic of the criterion behavior
with which they were found to be associated. In an early description of this
approach, Meehl (1945) wrote:

. . . the verbal type of personality inventory is *not* most fruitfully seen as a
"self-rating" or self-description whose value requires the assumption of accuracy
on the part of the testee in his observations of self. Rather is the response to a
test item taken as an intrinsically interesting segment of verbal behavior, knowledge regarding which may be of more value than any knowledge of the "factual"
material about which the item superficially purports to inquire. Thus if a hypo-
chondriac says that he had "many headaches" the fact of interest is that he *says
this.* (p. 9)

A self-report inventory is indubitably a series of standardized verbal stimuli.
When criterion-keying procedures have been followed, the responses
elicited by these stimuli are scored in terms of their empirically established
behavior correlates. They are thus treated like any other psychological test
responses. That questionnaire responses may correspond to the person's
perception of reality does not alter this situation. It merely provides one
hypothesis to account for the empirically established validity of certain
items.

THE MINNESOTA MULTIPHASIC PERSONALITY INVENTORY. The outstanding
example of criterion keying in personality test construction is the Minnesota Multiphasic Personality Inventory (MMPI). Not only is the MMPI the
most widely used personality inventory, but it has also stimulated a flood of
research. To date, over 5,000 references have been published about this
test. A considerable portion of this research is concerned with factorial
analyses of the MMPI scales and with the operation of response styles in its
scores, topics to be discussed in later sections of this chapter.

The MMPI consists of 550 affirmative statements, to which the examinee
gives the responses "True," "False," or "Cannot say." In the individual form

of the test, the statements are printed on separate cards, which the respondent sorts into the three categories. Later, a group form was prepared, in
which the statements are printed in a test booklet and the responses are recorded on an answer sheet. Both forms were designed for adults from about
16 years of age upward, although they have also been employed successfully
with somewhat younger adolescents (Hathaway & Monachesi, 1963). Although the card form may be preferable when testing disturbed patients or
persons of low educational or intellectual level, the booklet form is now used
for most purposes. The MMPI items range widely in content, covering such
areas as health, psychosomatic symptoms, neurological disorders, and motor
disturbances; sexual, religious, political, and social attitudes; educational,
occupational, family, and marital questions; and many well-known neurotic
or psychotic behavior manifestations, such as obsessive and compulsive
states, delusions, hallucinations, ideas of reference, phobias, and sadistic
and masochistic trends. A few illustrative items are shown below:[1]

I do not tire quickly.

Most people will use somewhat unfair means to gain profit or an advantage
rather than to lose it.

I am worried about sex matters.

When I get bored I like to stir up some excitement.

I believe I am being plotted against.

In its regular administration, the MMPI provides scores on ten "clinical
scales" listed below:

1. Hs:	Hypochondriasis	
2. D:	Depression	
3. Hy:	Hysteria	
4. Pd:	Psychopathic deviate	
5. Mf:	Masculinity–femininity	

6. Pa:	Paranoia	
7. Pt:	Psychasthenia	
8. Sc:	Schizophrenia	
9. Ma:	Hypomania	
0. Si:	Social introversion	

Eight of these scales consist of items that differentiated between a specified
clinical group and a normal control group of approximately 700 persons.
The latter were all visitors at the University of Minnesota hospitals and represented a fairly adequate cross section of the Minnesota population of both
sexes between the ages of 16 and 55. The clinical groups varied in size, but
most contained about 50 cases. These scales were thus developed empirically by criterion keying of items, the criterion being traditional psychiatric
diagnosis. Items for the Masculinity–femininity scale were selected in terms
of frequency of responses by men and women. High scores on this scale in-

[1] Reproduced by permission. Copyright 1970 by the University of Minnesota. Published by The Psychological Corporation, New York, N.Y. All rights reserved.

dicate a predominance of interests typical of the opposite sex. The Social introversion scale, added later, was derived from the responses of two contrasted groups of college students selected on the basis of extreme scores on a test of introversion–extraversion. This scale was also found to be significantly related to the number of extracurricular activities in which high school or college students participated.

A special feature of the MMPI is its utilization of three so-called validity scales. These scales are not concerned with validity in the technical sense. In effect, they represent checks on carelessness, misunderstanding, malingering, and the operation of special response sets and test-taking attitudes. The validating scores include:

> *Lie Score* (L): based on a group of items that make the examinee appear in a favorable light, but are unlikely to be truthfully answered in the favorable direction. (E.g., I do not like everyone I know.)

> *Validity Score* (F): determined from a set of items very infrequently answered in the scored direction by the standardization group. Although representing undesirable behavior, these items do not cohere in any pattern of abnormality. Hence, it is unlikely that any one person will actually show all or most of these symptoms. A high F score may indicate scoring errors, carelessness in responding, gross eccentricity, or deliberate malingering.

> *Correction Score* (K): utilizing still another combination of specially chosen items, this score provides a measure of test-taking attitude, related to both L and F, but believed to be more subtle. A high K score may indicate defensiveness or an attempt to "fake good." A low K score may represent excessive frankness and self-criticism or a deliberate attempt to "fake bad."

The first two scores (L, F) are ordinarily used for an overall evaluation of the test record. If either of these exceeds a specified value, the record is considered invalid. The K score, on the other hand, was designed to function as a suppressor variable. It is employed to compute a correction factor which is added to the scores on some of the clinical scales in order to obtain adjusted totals. Because this use of the K score is questionable, however, scores on the affected scales are often reported with and without this correction. An unusually high K score would in itself make the record suspect and call for further scrutiny.

Since the publication of the MMPI in its initial form, about 300 new scales have been developed, most of them by independent investigators who had not participated in the construction of the original test (Dahlstrom, Welsh, & Dahlstrom, 1975). These scales vary widely in the nature and breadth of the criteria against which items were evaluated. Several scales were developed within normal populations to assess personality traits unrelated to pathology. Some scales have subsequently been applied to the test records of the original MMPI normal standardization sample, thus providing normative data comparable to those of the initial clinical scales. Examples of the new scales include Ego Strength (ES), Dependency (Dy),

Dominance (Do), Prejudice (Pr), and Social Status (St). Other scales have been developed for highly specific purposes and are more limited in their applicability. Still another grouping of MMPI items is represented by the *content scales* developed by J. S. Wiggins (1966b). In the construction of these scales, item clusters based on a subjective classification of content were revised and refined through factor-analytic and internal-consistency procedures. The resulting 13 scales have proved promising in diagnosis and may serve as a useful supplement in the interpretation of the original clinical scales.

In its regular administration, the MMPI now yields 13 scores, including the 9 original clinical scales, the Si scale, and the 3 validating scales. Norms on the original control sample of approximately 700 persons are reported in the form of standard scores wtih a mean of 50 and an *SD* of 10 (*T* scores). These standard scores are used in plotting profiles, as illustrated in Figure 89. Any score of 70 or higher—falling 2 *SD*s or more above the mean—is generally taken as the cutoff point for the identification of pathological deviations. It should be noted, however, that the clinical significance of the same score may differ from one scale to another. A score of 75 on the Hypochondriasis and on the Schizophrenia scales, for example, may not indicate the same severity of abnormality.

There is considerable evidence to suggest that, in general, the greater the number and magnitude of deviant scores on the MMPI, the more likely it is that the individual is severely disturbed. For screening purposes, however, shorter and simpler instruments are available. It is clear that the principal applications of the MMPI are to be found in differential diagnosis. In using the inventory for this purpose, the procedure is much more complex than the labels originally assigned to the scales might suggest. The test manual and related publications now caution against literal interpretation of the clinical scales. For example, we cannot assume that a high score on the Schizophrenia scale indicates the presence of schizophrenia. Other psychotic groups show high elevation on this scale, and schizophrenics often score high on other scales. Moreover, such a score may occur in a normal person. It is partly to prevent possible misinterpretations of scores on single scales that the code numbers 0 to 9 have been substituted for the scale names in later publications on the MMPI.

The original MMPI scales were designed to differentiate between normals and certain traditional diagnostic categories. In subsequent usage, however, the scales have been treated more and more as linear measures of personality traits. These traits have been identified in terms of the salient characteristics of the populations investigated. For example, an elevated score on Scale 6 (originally labeled "Paranoia") may suggest a high degree of resentfulness and suspiciousness. A further complication is that the scales are usually multidimensional. This follows from the fact that the diagnostic groups employed in selecting items generally differed from the normal controls in more than one trait. And some of the same traits may occur in more

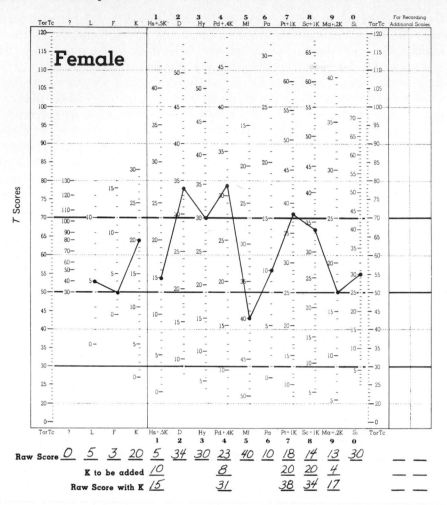

Fig. 89. MMPI Profile of a 28-Year-Old Woman. Raw scores on each scale are plotted in column above scale name.

(Data by courtesy of David R. Chabot. Profile chart copyright © 1948, renewed 1976 by The Psychological Corporation, New York, N.Y. Reproduced by permission. All rights reserved.)

than one scale, as indicated in part by the presence of common items. It is these two facts—multidimensionality and overlap of MMPI scales—that account for some of the advantages of pattern analysis over the interpretation of single scales. Comparing an individual's scores on two or more scales often helps to identify the trait associated with a particular pattern of scores.

To expedite the interpretation of score patterns, systems of numerical profile coding have been developed. In such codes, the sequence and arrangement of scale numbers show at a glance which are the high and low points in the individual's profile. As an aid in the diagnostic interpretation of MMPI profiles, Hathaway and Meehl (1951) prepared *An Atlas for the Clinical Use of the MMPI*. This *Atlas* provides coded profiles and short case histories of 968 patients, arranged according to similarity of profile pattern. A similar codebook utilizing data from over 4,000 college students examined in a college counseling center was prepared for use by counselors (Drake & Oetting, 1959). Still another atlas was prepared for use with high-school-age populations (Hathaway & Monachesi, 1961, 1963). More recent codebooks have endeavored to simplify and systematize the interpretation of a small number of major profiles, in order to permit actuarial description in "cookbook fashion" (e.g., Marks, Seeman, & Haller, 1974). Validation of the MMPI has thus proceeded by the accumulation of empirical data about persons who show each profile pattern or code. By such a process, the construct validity of each MMPI code is gradually built up. The MMPI *Handbook,* compiled by Dahlstrom, Welsh, and Dahlstrom (1972), contains a comprehensive survey of available interpretive data on major profile patterns. A much briefer, simpler introduction to MMPI profile interpretation can be found in Graham (1977).

A further step in the evolution of MMPI score interpretation is the development of several computerized systems for completely automated profile interpretations. Descriptions and critical evaluations of some of these systems can be found in the *Eighth Mental Measurements Yearbook* (Nos. 617–624). Available services vary widely in several parameters. Some are designed chiefly for screening purposes and are largely descriptive summaries; others provide highly interpretive statements. Some rely on standard published interpretive guidelines; others utilize special keys and extensive research conducted in the development of the system itself. One service provides different levels of reports to suit the needs and qualifications of different recipients. Like all test results, the MMPI computer reports need to be considered in the context of other information about the individual. Recognizing the danger of potential misuses, the American Psychological Association (1966, p. 1141) adopted a set of guidelines for computer-based test-interpretation services. The APA test *Standards* (1974, B6 & J4) also set forth as an essential requirement the reporting of the rationale and evidence on which such interpretive systems are based.

Although the misleading psychiatric labels have been dropped in the coded profiles, it should be noted that MMPI items are still grouped into scales on the basis of such obsolescent categories. Factorial analyses based on intercorrelations of items and of scales indicate that items would be differently grouped on the basis of their empirically established interrelations. Furthermore, high intercorrelations among the basic MMPI clinical scales make their value in differential diagnosis questionable. For differential diagnosis, it would have been better to select items by comparing the responses of each clinical group, not with those of normals, but with those of other clinical groups. On the other hand, an extensive body of normative data and clinical experience pertaining to the old scales has accumulated over the years (Dahlstrom et al., 1972; Dahlstrom & Dahlstrom, 1979). In order not to lose this store of information, later efforts have been directed toward the reinterpretation of the old scales in terms of empirically derived profile codes.

A closely related limitation of the MMPI stems from inadequate reliabilities of some of the scales. The effectiveness of any profile analysis is weakened by chance errors in the scores on which it is based. If individual scale scores are unreliable and highly intercorrelated, many of the interscore differences that determine the profile code may have resulted from chance. Retest reliabilities on normal and abnormal adult samples reported in the manual range from the .50s to the low .90s. Other studies, on both normal groups and psychiatric patients, have found even wider variation among scales in retest as well as split-half reliabilities. Some of the split-half reliabilities were especially low, a finding that is not surprising in view of the heterogeneity of item content of some of the scales (Dahlstrom et al, 1972, 1975), It should also be noted that certain scales (notably Scale 2—Depression) assess behavior that is so variable over time as to render retest reliability inappropriate.

Still another limitation of the MMPI pertains to the size and representativeness of the normative sample. The standard scores from which all profile codes are derived are expressed in terms of the performance of the control group of approximately 700 Minneapolis adults tested in the original standardization. Such a normative sample appears quite inadequate when compared, for example, with the nationwide standardization samples employed with many of the ability tests discussed in earlier parts of this book. In effect, the original standardization sample should be regarded as a nonnormative fixed reference group, in terms of which the score scale is defined. The much more extensive data subsequently collected with reference to profile codes can then provide all normative interpretation.

Even more than ability tests, personality tests can be expected to show large subcultural as well as cultural differences. As would be anticipated, studies conducted in other countries reveal significant elevation on certain scales when profiles are based on the original Minnesota norms (Butcher & Pancheri, 1976; Dahlstrom & Dahlstrom, 1979). Similar differences have been found among subcultures in the United States. Any explanation of such cultural and subcultural differences requires specific knowledge of cultural conditions and other circumstances prevailing within each group. As shown in Chapter 12, cultural differentials may operate at many different levels. Group differences in MMPI scores could, for example, reflect nothing more than differences in interpretation of individual items or of instructions. High elevation in some groups could result from strong traditions of self-depreciation and modesty. Cultural differences in the type of behavior considered socially desirable may likewise influence scores. In still other groups, high scores may indicate the prevalence of genuine emotional problems arising from child-rearing practices, conflicts of social roles, minority group frustrations, and other broad cultural differences. In any event, an individual's MMPI profile should be interpreted in the light of information about such demographic variables as age, sex, education, socioeconomic status, ethnic group, and geographic milieu. Some normative data have now been accumulated with reference to these variables (Dahlstrom et al., 1972, 1975; Lanyon, 1968).

In summary, the MMPI is essentially a clinical instrument whose proper interpretation calls for considerable psychological sophistication. If the simplified actuarial interpretations and computer analyses are perceived as diagnostic aids for the overworked clinician, they can serve a useful purpose. There is danger, however, that the trend toward automation may encourage interpretation of MMPI profiles by inadequately trained users.

CALIFORNIA PSYCHOLOGICAL INVENTORY. Besides stimulating a proliferation of scoring scales, the MMPI has served as a basis for the development of other widely used inventories. An outstanding example is the California Psychological Inventory (CPI). While drawing about half of its items from the MMPI, the CPI was developed specifically for use with normal populations from age 13 up. Consisting of 480 items to be answered "True" or "False," the CPI yields scores in 18 scales. Three are "validity" scales designed to assess test-taking attitudes. These scales are designated as: Sense of well-being (Wb), based on responses by normals asked to "fake bad"; Good impression (Gi), based on responses by normals asked to "fake good"; and Communality (Cm), based on a frequency count of highly popular responses. The remaining 15 scales provide scores in such personality dimensions as Dominance, Sociability, Self-acceptance, Responsibility, Socialization, Self-control, Achievement-via-conformance, Achievement-via-independence, and Femininity.

For 11 of these 15 scales, items were selected on the basis of contrasted group responses, against such criteria as course grades, social class membership, participation in extracurricular activities, and ratings. The ratings were obtained through peer nominations, found to be an effective assessment technique for many interpersonal traits. For the remaining 4 scales, items were originally grouped subjectively and then checked for internal consistency. Cross-validation of all scales on sizable samples has yielded significant group differences, although the overlapping of contrasted criterion groups in considerable and criterion correlations are often low.

As in the MMPI, all scores are reported in terms of a standard score scale with a mean of 50 and an *SD* of 10; this scale was derived from a normative sample of 6,000 males and 7,000 females, widely distributed in age, socioeconomic level, and geographic area. In addition, means and *SD*s of scores on each scale are given for many special groups. Retest as well as internal consistency reliability coefficients of the individual scales compare favorably with those found for other personality inventories (Megargee, 1972). Intercorrelations among scales are relatively high. All but four scales, for example, correlate at least .50 with one or more other scales, indicating considerable redundancy among the 18 scores.

On the whole, however, the CPI is one of the best personality inventories currently available. Its technical development is of a high order and it has been subjected to extensive research and continuous improvement (see Megargee, 1972). In contrast to the clinical interpretation of coded profiles employed with the MMPI, research with the CPI has provided a number of regression equations for the optimal weighting of scales to predict such criteria as delinquency, parole outcome, high school and college grades, and the probability of high school dropout. Cross-cultural studies with individual scales, such as Socialization and Femininity, have also yielded promising validity data against local criteria within different cultures. Extensive research with occupational groups has yielded regression equations and corresponding "derivative profiles" for predicting performance in many fields of work. Computerized profile interpretations are also available. In addition to the basic scales, several additional scales have been developed by various methods.

PERSONALITY INVENTORY FOR CHILDREN. Although not utilizing MMPI items or data, the Personality Inventory for Children (PIC) was constructed with the same general methodology as the MMPI and the CPI (Wirt & Lachar, 1981). It was developed through some 20 years of research by a group of investigators at the University of Minnesota, who had been thoroughly exposed to the rationale and the clinical use of the MMPI. The PIC is designed primarily for children and adolescents between the ages of 6 and 16, but it can also be employed with children from 3 to 5. A major difference between the PIC and the MMPI pertains to the way the information is obtained: the 600 true-false questionnaire items are answered, not by the child, but by a knowledgeable adult, usually the mother. This procedure is consistent with the common practice in child clinics of interviewing the mother as the principal source of information about the child's present problem and case history. This inventory, in effect provides a systematic way of gathering such information and of interpreting it in terms of normative and diagnostic data.

It is noteworthy that the PIC is not a self-report inventory but an inventory of observed behavior. As such, it is consonant with the behavioral assessment orientation to clinical psychology described in Chapter 16. This implication is not discussed in the test manual or the accompanying interpretive guide. The authors, however, do call attention to certain limitations of parental reporting. As they point out, the responses may reflect in part the motivation, attitudes, and personal or cultural standards of the parent. There has been some investigation of consistencies among different observers. Moreover, as in the MMPI, the "validity scales" can help in identifying such special response tendencies.

The PIC comprises 16 scales that are regularly reported on the profile sheets. These include three "validity scales": the L scale, including items that make the child appear in an unrealistically favorable light; the F scale, consisting of rarely endorsed items; and the Defensiveness scale, designed to assess parental defensiveness about the child's behavior. The fourth scale, Adjustment, is a screening scale used to identify children in need of psychological evaluation. The remaining 12 scales are clinical scales designed to assess the child's cognitive development and academic achievement, several well-established types of emotional and interpersonal problems (e.g., Depression, Anxiety, Withdrawal, Hyperactivity), and the psychological climate of the family. Raw scores on each of the 16 scales are plotted on profiles modeled after the MMPI profiles, from which T scores can be read. Like the MMPI, the PIC has a set of supplementary scales, not regularly included on the profile but available to clarify diagnosis in individual cases.

Some PIC scales were developed by empirical comparison of response frequencies in criterion and control groups; through an iterative procedure, items were added in stages until optimum scale validity was reached. Other scales followed essentially content validation procedures, whereby items were initially chosen on the basis of judges' nominations or ratings for scale relevance. Even in these cases, however, assessment of internal consistency of item responses within scales and factor analyses of items contributed toward the construct validation of the scales. Of the clinical scales, slightly less than half were empirically constructed; among the supplementary scales, empirical scales predominate, the ratio of empirical to content scales being approximately 2:1. The manual reports preliminary data on test-retest reliability and on degree of agreement between mothers and fathers in inventory responses. It also gives mean profiles of various diagnostic groups as guidelines in profile interpretation.

A more extensive interpretive guide is provided by a subsequent monograph (Lachar & Gdowski, 1979), which is based on a systematic, comprehensive validation study. This research was conducted with 431 inpatients and outpatients at an urban child-guidance facility in Michigan. The sample included 52% whites and 42% blacks and was predominantly of low socioeconomic status in terms of parental education and occupation. Detailed criterion data were obtained through three specially constructed forms, completed by parents, teachers and other school personnel, and psychiatric residents. The analysis yielded two major types of information: (1) relation of each scale with criteria; and (2) T-score range indicative of criterion presence or absence. It was thus possible to establish cutoff scores empirically on each scale to correspond to different diagnostic interpretations. The generalizability of particular scale interpretations across age, sex, and race was also investigated. The end product of these analyses is a set of

37 empirically formulated descriptive paragraphs, or interpretive hypotheses. Each paragraph relates to a critical score range on one of the 16 scales. The number of critical score ranges (and their corresponding interpretive paragraphs) varies from one to four for the individual scales. A computerized test report, based on these findings, is also available from the test publisher. Although much remains to be done and plans are evidently under way for continuing research, what has been accomplished in the short period since the publication of the PIC is impressive in extent and quality, and the results are promising.

MILLON CLINICAL MULTIAXIAL INVENTORY. Still another type of familial relationship to the ancestral MMPI is exemplified by the Millon Clinical Multiaxial Inventory (MCMI). Although following the MMPI tradition in several ways and designed for the same purposes, the MCMI introduces significant methodological innovations (Butcher & Owen, 1978; Millon, 1977). In fact, its development was deliberately undertaken to meet the criticisms of the older instrument and to utilize intervening advances in psychopathology and test construction.

The MCMI form contains 175 brief, self-descriptive statements to be marked true or false by the respondent. Suitable for either individual or group administration, it was designed for clinical patients over 17 years of age and with a reading level at or above the eighth grade. The inventory is computer-scored; automated interpretive reports are also available. The score profile includes 20 clinical scales, each based on 16 to 47 overlapping items. These scales fall into three major categories, as follows:

Basic Personality Styles: Asocial, Avoidant, Submissive-Dependent, Gregarious-Histrionic, Narcissistic, Aggressive-Antisocial, Conforming-Compulsive, Negativistic-Unstable.

Pathological Personality Syndromes: Schizoid-Schizophrenic, Cycloid-Cyclophrenic, Paranoid-Paraphrenic.

Symptom Disorders: Anxiety, Hysterical, Hypomanic, Neurotic Depression, Alcoholic Misuse, Drug Misuse, Psychotic Thinking, Psychotic Depression, Psychotic Delusions.

There are also correction scores to detect faking, random responding, and other test-taking biases

The clinical scales were designed to fit syndromes or constructs derived from personality theory. Separate scales were constructed for relatively enduring personality characteristics and for acute clinical states. The scales also distinguish between different levels of severity within parallel personality patterns. To sharpen differential diagnosis, the reference group employed for item analysis was a representative but undifferentiated psychiatric sample, rather than a normal sample. Instead of normalized standard scores, actuarial base-rate data were employed in calculating scale scores.

This procedure has advantages in setting optimal cutoff scores for differential diagnosis. Insofar as base rates may vary in different populations and clinical settings, however, their generalizability requires further empirical checking, and atypical experiential backgrounds should be considered in interpreting individual profiles.

Item development followed the multiple approach characteristic of recent practice in the construction and validation of personality inventories. In this regard, the MCMI cuts across the methodology described in later sections of this chapter. The procedure included a sequence of three major steps: (1) theoretical-substantive (i.e., writing and selecting items to fit clinically relevant constructs), (2) internal-structural (e.g., item-scale correlations, endorsement frequencies), and (3) external-criterion (e.g., differentiation of diagnostic groups from reference group, cross-validation on new samples).

A sizable array of data on the reliability and validity of the MCMI has been accumulated in the process of its development and subsequent empirical evaluation. Because of the recency of its publication, however, it is too early to assess its eventual effectiveness as a clinical instrument. The manual calls attention to additional needed research in cross-validation and cross-generalization, among other studies.

FACTOR ANALYSIS IN TEST DEVELOPMENT

THE GUILFORD INVENTORIES. In the effort to arrive at a systematic classification of personality traits, a number of psychologists have turned to factor analysis. A series of early studies by Guilford and his co-workers represents one of the pioneer ventures in this direction (see Guilford, 1959, Ch. 16; Guilford & Zimmerman, 1956). Rather than correlating total scores on existing inventories, these investigators computed the intercorrelations among individual items from many personality inventories. As a byproduct of this research, three personality inventories were developed and eventually combined into the Guilford-Zimmerman Temperament Survey. This inventory yields separate scores for the following traits, each score based on 30 different items:

G—*General activity:* tendency toward quick and vigorous activity.

R—*Restraint:* serious-mindedness and self-control as contrasted with an impulsive, carefree disposition.

A—*Ascendance:* tendency to take the initiative in social situations as contrasted with the tendency to remain in the background.

S—*Sociability:* interest in and enjoyment of social contacts and activities in contrast to shyness or seclusiveness; a need for other people as opposed to an indifference toward them.

E—*Emotional stability:* tendency to remain optimistic, cheerful, and even-tempered independent of external influences.

O—*Objectivity:* lack of hypersensitivity and self-centeredness; tendency to view situations realistically and dispassionately.

F—*Friendliness:* tendency to be friendly and compliant with desires of others as opposed to a tendency to be defensive, hostile, or belligerent.

T—*Thoughtfulness:* tendency to be introspective, reflective, observant, and analytical.

P—*Personal relations:* cooperativeness, tolerance, and acceptance of things and people as they are as opposed to critical faultfinding and demanding that others live up to personal standards.

M—*Masculinity:* masculinity of interests and emotional reactions as contrasted with feminine interests and reactions.

The items in the Guilford-Zimmerman Temperament Survey are expressed in the form of affirmative statements, rather than questions. Most concern the examinee directly. A few represent generalizations about other persons. Three examples are given below:

You start work on a new project with a great deal of enthusiasm .... YES ? NO

You are often in low spirits .... YES ? NO

Most people use politeness to cover up what is really "cutthroat" competition .... YES ? NO

The affirmative item form was chosen in the effort to reduce the resistance that a series of direct questions is likely to arouse. In addition, three verification keys are provided to detect falsification and carelessness of response.

Percentile and standard score norms were derived chiefly from college samples. Attention is called to the desirability of interpreting not only single-trait scores but also total profiles. For example, a high score in Emotional Stability is favorable if coupled with a high General Activity score, but may be unfavorable if it occurs in combination with a low General Activity score. In the latter case, the individual may be sluggish, phlegmatic, or lazy. Split-half reliabilities of separate factor scores range from .75 to .85. Higher reliabilities would of course be desirable for the differential interpretation of individual profiles. Similarly, although an effort was made to obtain independent, uncorrelated trait categories, some of the intercorrelations among the 10 traits are still appreciable. Originally presented only on the basis of its factorial validity, the inventory has subsequently been employed in scattered studies of empirical validity, with varied results.

COMREY PERSONALITY SCALES. A more recent example of a multitrait personality inventory constructed principally through factor analysis is provided by the Comrey Personality Scales. This inventory yields scores in eight personality scales, designated as follows:

T—Trust vs. Defensiveness	S—Emotional Stability vs. Neuroticism
O—Orderliness vs. Lack of Compulsion	E—Extraversion vs. Introversion
C—Social Conformity vs. Rebelliousness	M—Masculinity vs. Femininity
A—Activity vs. Lack of Energy	P—Empathy vs. Egocentrism

The inventory also includes a Validity Check scale to detect random or inappropriate marking, and a Response Bias scale to assess the tendency to respond in a socially desirable direction.

A special feature of the Comrey inventory is the use of a 7-point scale for recording item responses, which ranges from "always" to "never" or from "definitely" to "definitely not," depending upon the nature of the item. Test construction procedures followed in the selection and grouping of items were of high quality. Split-half reliabilities of scale scores are in the high .80s and .90s. Normative data are limited by the size and restricted nature of the standardization samples; users are encouraged to develop local norms. Validation research against external criteria has yielded some promising results and is still being actively pursued. Studies in several countries suggest considerable cross-cultural stability in the trait categories measured by the Comrey scales.

THE CATTELL INVENTORIES. A somewhat different application of factorial methods to the construction of personality inventories is to be found in the work of R. B. Cattell (1979). In the effort to arrive at a comprehensive description of personality, Cattell began by assembling all personality trait names occurring either in the dictionary (as compiled by Allport and Odbert, 1936) or in the psychiatric and psychological literature. This list was first reduced to 171 trait names by combining obvious synonyms. The 171-trait list was then employed in obtaining associates' ratings of a heterogenous group of 100 adults. Intercorrelations and factor analyses of these ratings were followed by further ratings of 208 men on a shortened list. Factorial analyses of the latter ratings led to the identification of what Cattell described as "the primary source traits of personality," a designation that seems to imply more universality and stability of results than appear justified by the antecedent research. It is characteristic of Cattell's approach that he regards factor analysis, not as a data-reduction technique, but as a method for discovering underlying, causal traits.

Factors identified through the correlation of ratings, however, may reflect in part the influence of social stereotypes and other constant errors of judgment, rather than the subjects' trait organization. In fact, other investigators have found the same factors when analyzing ratings given to complete strangers as when analyzing ratings assigned to persons whom the raters knew well (Passini & Norman, 1966). Essentially the same factors were again obtained when college students were asked to rate the similarity in meaning between all possible pairs of words describing bipolar trait scales (D'Andrade, 1965). Apparently factor analysis of ratings may reveal more about the raters than about the ratees.

Cattell maintains that his identification of primary personality traits is corroborated by the findings of other studies by himself and other investigators, using not only ratings but also such techniques as questionnaires and objective tests. Some of the alleged similarities in trait descriptions, however, appear forced and not too convincing (Becker, 1960). It should be recalled that an element of subjectivity is likely to enter into the identification of factors, since the process depends on an examination of those measures or items having the highest loadings on each factor (see Ch. 13). Hence, the cross-identification of factors from separate investigations using different measures is difficult. Despite the extensive research conducted by Cattell and his associates for more than three decades, the proposed traits must be regarded as tentative.

On the basis of their factorial research, Cattell and his co-workers have constructed a number of personality inventories, of which the best known is the Sixteen Personality Factor Questionnaire (16 PF) (Cattell, Eber, & Tatsuoka, 1970; Karson & O'Dell, 1976). Designed for ages 16 and over, this inventory yields 16 scores in such traits as reserved vs. outgoing, humble vs. assertive, shy vs. venturesome, and trusting vs. suspicious. A "motivational distortion" or verification key is also provided for some of the forms. A computerized, narrative reporting service is available.

Owing to the shortness of the scales, reliabilities of factor scores for any single form of the 16 PF are generally low. Even when two forms are combined, parallel-form reliabilities center in the .50s and retests after a week or less often fall below .80. There is also some question about the factorial homogeneity of items within each scale, as well as the factorial independence of scales (Levonian, 1961). Available information on normative samples and other aspects of test construction is inadequate. Empirical validation data include average profiles for more than 50 occupational groups and about the same number of psychiatric syndromes. "Specification equations" are provided for a number of occupations, in the form of multiple regression equations for predicting an individual's criterion performance from scores on the 16 PF.

Similar inventories have been developed for ages 12 to 18 (High School Personality Questionnaire), 8 to 12 (Children's Personality Questionnaire), and 6 to 8 (Early School Personality Questionnaire). Separate inventories have also been published within more limited areas, including anxiety, depression, introversion-extraversion, and neuroticism. These areas correspond to certain second-order factors identified among correlated first-order factors. Another addition to the series is the Clinical Analysis Questionnaire, a 28-scale inventory which includes: a shortened version of the 16 PF "in clinical dress," with fewer items per factor, reworded to fit clinical contexts; and 12 pathological scales identified through factor analysis of items from the MMPI and other clinical scales (Cattell et al., 1970, Ch. 14; Krug, 1980). Other adaptations of the 16 PF in special dress have been prepared for assessment purposes in such contexts as career development, marriage counseling, and the evaluation of business executives. All of these inventories are experimental instruments requiring further development, standardization, and validation.

Factor analysis provides a technique for grouping personality inventory items into relatively homogeneous and independent clusters. Such a grouping should facilitate the investigation of validity against empirical criteria and should contribute toward construct definition. It should also permit a more effective combination of scores for the prediction of specific criteria. Homogeneity and factorial purity are desirable goals in test construction. But they are not substitutes for empirical validation.

PERSONALITY THEORY IN TEST DEVELOPMENT

Personality theories have usually originated in clinical settings. The amount of experimental verification to which they have subsequently been subjected varies tremendously from one theoretical system to another. Regardless of the extent of such objective verification, a number of personality tests have been constructed within the framework of one or another personality theory. Clinically formulated hypotheses have been especially prominent in the development of projective techniques, to be considered in Chapter 19. While this approach to test construction has been followed less often for self-report inventories, a few outstanding examples are available.

EDWARDS PERSONAL PREFERENCE SCHEDULE. Among the personality theories that have stimulated test development, one of the most prolific has been the manifest need system proposed by Murray and his associates at the Harvard Psychological Clinic (Murray et al., 1938). One of the first inventories designed to assess the strength of such needs was the Edwards Personal Preference Schedule (EPPS). Beginning with 15 needs drawn from Murray's list, Edwards prepared sets of items whose content appeared to fit each of these needs. The complete list of needs, together with the normal percentile chart employed in plotting EPPS scores, can be found in Figure 90. Examples include the need for Achievement (to do one's best and accomplish something difficult), Deference (to conform to what is expected of one), Exhibition (to be the center of attention), Intraception (to

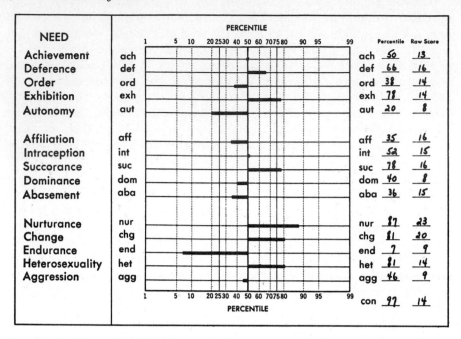

FIG. 90. Profile on the Edwards Personal Preference Schedule, together with List of Needs.

analyze the motives and feelings of oneself and others), Dominance (to influence others and to be regarded as a leader), and Nurturance (to help others in trouble).

The inventory consists of 210 pairs of statements in which items from each of the 15 scales are paired with items from the other 14.[2] Within each pair, the examinee must choose one statement as more characteristic of himself. Two pairs, used as demonstration items, are given below:[3]

A. I like to talk about myself to others.
B. I like to work toward some goal that I have set for myself.

A. I feel depressed when I fail at something.
B. I feel nervous when giving a talk before a group.

The EPPS introduced certain internal checks. To provide an index of respondent consistency, 15 pairs of statements are repeated in identical form. In Figure 90, the last entry (labeled *con* for *consistency*) shows that this

[2] This item form, which represents an important feature of the EPPS, will be discussed further in the next section, as an example of the forced-choice technique.

[3] Reproduced by permission. Copyright © 1959, The Psychological Corporation, New York, N.Y. All rights reserved.

respondent made the identical choice in 14 of the 15 pairs, which put him at the 97th percentile of the normative sample in response consistency. Another check yields a profile stability score, which is the correlation between the individual's odd and even scores in the 15 scales.

The 15 need scores on the EPPS can be evaluated in terms of both percentile and *T*-score norms for college men and college women. These norms were based on 760 men and 749 women tested in 29 colleges scattered over the country. Additional percentile norms are provided from a general adult sample, including 4,031 men and 4,932 women. Drawn from urban and rural areas in 48 states, these respondents constituted a consumer-purchase panel used for market surveys. The need for specific group norms on personality tests is highlighted by the large and significant mean differences found between this consumer panel and the college sample.

It is important to bear in mind that the EPPS employs *ipsative* scores— that is, the strength of each need is expressed, not in absolute terms, but in relation to the strength of the individual's other needs. The frame of reference in ipsative scoring is the individual rather than the normative sample. Because the individual responds by expressing a preference for one item against another, the resulting score is ipsative. Under these conditions, two individuals with identical scores on the EPPS may differ markedly in the absolute strength of their needs. Because of their ipsative nature, the conversion of EPPS scores to normative percentiles may be questioned. The combination of normative and ipsative frames of reference makes interpretation of these scores somewhat confusing and less meaningful than would be the case with a consistently ipsative *or* consistently normative approach.

Retest reliabilities of the 15 scales reported in the manual range from .74 to .88; split-half reliabilities range from .60 to .87. However, both sets of values may be somewhat inflated: the first, through recall of responses over the short interval employed (one week); the second, because of the repetition of identical statements three or four times in different pairs within each scale.

Although the validity data reported in the EPPS manual are meager, a large number of independent validation studies have been published. The results of these studies, however, are often difficult to interpret because most of them failed to take into account the ipsative nature of the scores. With ipsative scores, the mean intercorrelation of individual scales tends to be negative and the mean correlation of all the scales with any outside variable will approach zero (Hicks, 1970). Owing to these artificial constraints, ipsative scores cannot be properly analyzed by the usual correlational procedures. It is not surprising, therefore, that the published validation studies have yielded conflicting and inconclusive results. Although the EPPS introduced several noteworthy features, it is in need of: (a) revision to eliminate certain technical weaknesses, particularly with regard to item form and score interpretation; and (b) properly conducted validation studies utilizing techniques of score pattern analysis appropriate to ipsative scores.

PERSONALITY RESEARCH FORM AND JACKSON PERSONALITY INVENTORY. The Personality Research Form (PRF) reflects many technical advances in test construction, including some item-selection procedures that would have been virtually impossible before the availability of high-speed computers. The PRF exemplifies Jackson's fundamental approach to personality test development, which begins with explicit, detailed descriptions of the constructs to be measured. These descriptions form the basis for item writing as well as for defining the traits to be rated by judges in validation studies (Jackson, 1967c, 1970).

The PRF is available in two parallel short forms yielding 14 trait scores, and in two parallel longer forms yielding the same 14 scores plus 6 additional trait scores. There are also two validity scales: an Infrequency Scale in both forms and an additional Desirability Scale in the long form. Designed as an index of carelessness, failure to understand directions, and other nonpurposeful responding, the Infrequency Scale is based on the number of highly unlikely responses chosen by the examinee. Examples of items in this scale include: "I try to get at least some sleep every night" and "I make all my own clothes and shoes." A Desirability Scale is included in the long form, although desirability bias was substantially reduced in advance by the procedures employed in item development and selection. The manual correctly observes that unusually high or low scores on the Desirability Scale may indicate not only atypical test-taking attitudes (e.g., deliberate attempt to create a favorable impression vs. malingering) but also important personality characteristics in their own right (e.g., high self-regard or high degree of conventional socialization vs. low self-regard).

Like several other personality instruments, the PRF took Murray's personality theory as its starting point. Drawing upon the extensive research and theoretical literature that had accumulated during three decades, Jackson formulated behaviorally oriented and mutually exclusive definitions of 20 personality constructs or traits. Of these, 12 have the same names as those covered in the EPPS. The additional traits are designated as: Harm Avoidance, Impulsivity, Play, Social Recognition, Understanding, Cognitive Structure, Defendence, and Sentience. For each of the 20 personality scales, the manual provides a description of high scorers and a set of defining trait adjectives. Two illustrative scale definitions are shown in Table 31.

Through carefully controlled procedures, a pool of more than 100 items was generated for each scale. Twenty items were then selected for each scale on the basis of high biserial correlation with total scale score and low correlation with scores on other trait scales and on the Desirability Scale. Items yielding extreme endorsement proportions were also eliminated. Through a specially developed computer program, items were assigned to the two parallel forms in terms of biserial correlation with their own scale, as well as endorsement frequency.

Normalized standard scores (T scores) are provided from a sample of

TABLE 31

Examples of Scale Definitions from Personality Research Form

(From Jackson, 1967c, pp. 6–7; copyright © 1967 by Research Psychologists Press, Inc. Reproduced by permission.)

Scale	Description of High Scorer	Defining Trait Adjectives
Cognitive Structure	Does not like ambiguity or uncertainty in information; wants all questions answered completely; desires to make decisions based upon definite knowledge, rather than upon guesses or probabilities.	precise, exacting, definite, seeks certainty, meticulous, perfectionistic, clarifying, explicit, accurate, rigorous, literal, avoids ambiguity, defining, rigid, needs structure.
Sentience	Notices smells, sounds, sights, tastes, and the way things feel; remembers these sensations and believes that they are an important part of life; is sensitive to many forms of experience; may maintain an essentially hedonistic or aesthetic view of life.	aesthetic, enjoys physical sensations, observant, carthy, aware, notices environment, feeling, sensitive, sensuous, open to experience, perceptive, responsive, noticing, discriminating, alive to impressions.

about 1,000 male and 1,000 female students from over 30 North American colleges and universities. Although the manual reports that an attempt was made to balance the number of students from different types of colleges and different geographic regions, no data on demographic characteristics of the standardization sample are given. The manual does warn that the norms may be inapplicable to noncollege populations. Various odd-even, Kuder-Richardson, and retest reliability coefficients are reported. In general, the 14 scales in the short forms yielded reliabilities that cluster around .80; reliabilities of the additional six scales in the long form run somewhat lower, dipping as far as the .50s. The manual recommends administration of both parallel forms of each scale if time permits.

The construct validity of the PRF depends to a large extent on the procedures followed in the development and selection of items for each scale. Subsequent factorial analyses corroborated the grouping of items into the 20 scales. Correlations with comparable scales in the California Psychological Inventory and the Guilford-Zimmerman Temperament Survey provided additional support for the identification of the traits. Studies by other investigators, however, indicate that the Murray needs, as measured by such instruments as the PRF, EPPS, TAT (Ch. 19), and ACL (Ch. 20), cannot be assumed to be equivalent (Fiske, 1973, 1976; Megargee & Parker, 1968, Rezmovic & Rezmovic, 1980). Data on the empirical validity of the PRF against pooled peer ratings and self-ratings, though still meager, have yielded promising results. The PRF is an excellent research instrument; but more information is needed to determine its effectiveness in practical situations.

The Jackson Personality Inventory, developed more recently through essentially the same procedures as the PRF, has a more practical orientation (Jackson, 1977, 1978). The trait scales were chosen partly because of their relevance to the prediction of behavior in a variety of contexts. Among the traits covered by the 16 scales are anxiety, conformity, responsibility, social adroitness, and tolerance. Validity data were gathered not only through correlations with peer ratings and self-ratings but also through studies of particular groups for whom relevant behavioral data in real-life contexts were available.

In this overview of self-report inventories, the reader has probably noticed an increasing tendency to combine different approaches. This is particularly true of the PRF, which employed all strategies except the empirical criterion keying of items. There is also some evidence suggesting that personality inventory scales constructed by any of the four major methods outlined in this chapter may be equally effective (Goldberg, 1972). The current trend is to utilize multiple approaches, treating them as different steps in a sequential test-construction strategy (Jackson, 1970, 1973).

TEST-TAKING ATTITUDES AND RESPONSE BIASES

FAKING AND SOCIAL DESIRABILITY. Self-report inventories are especially subject to malingering or faking. Despite introductory statements to the contrary, most items on such inventories have one answer that is recognizable as socially more desirable or acceptable than the others. On such tests, the respondent may be motivated to "fake good," or choose answers that create a favorable impression, as when applying for a job or seeking admission to an educational institution. Under other circumstances, the respondent may be motivated to "fake bad," thus making himself appear more psychologically disturbed than he is. This may occur, for example, in the testing of persons on trial for a criminal offense.

Evidence of the success with which examinees can dissemble on personality inventories is plentiful (see, e.g., Jacobs & Barron, 1968; Radcliffe, 1966; Stricker, 1969; J. S. Wiggins, 1966a). A common classroom demonstration consists in asking different groups to assume specified roles. For example, one section of the class is directed to answer each question as it would be answered by a happy and well-adjusted college student; another section is told to respond in the manner of a severely maladjusted person;

and in the last section, respondents are instructed to answer the items truthfully with reference to their own behavior. Or the same persons may take the test twice, first with instructions to simulate in a specified way and later under ordinary conditions. The results of such studies clearly demonstrate the facility with which the desired impression can be deliberately created on such inventories.

It is interesting to note that specific simulation for a particular vocational objective can also be successfully carried out. Thus, in one study (Wesman, 1952), the responses of the same group of students were compared on two administrations of a personality inventory taken a week apart. On the first testing, the students were instructed to pretend they were applying for the position of salesperson in a large industrial organization and to answer in a manner designed to increase their chances of employment. On the second testing, the same instructions were given, but the position of librarian was substituted for that of salesperson. When the responses were scored for the trait of self-confidence, a conspicuous difference was found in the distributions of scores on the two occasions, the simulated-salesperson scores being much higher than the corresponding librarian scores. That job applicants do in fact fake personality test responses was demonstrated in another study (R. F. Green, 1951), in which the scores obtained by a group of applicants were compared with the scores of a comparable group of jobholders who were tested for research purposes only. Under these contrasting motivating conditions, the scores of the two groups differed in the expected direction.

The tendency to choose socially desirable responses on a self-report inventory need not indicate deliberate deception on the part of the respondent. A. L. Edwards (1975), who first investigated the social desirability (SD) variable, conceptualized it primarily as a façade effect or tendency to "put up a good front," of which the respondent is largely unaware. This tendency may indicate lack of insight into one's own characteristics, self-deception, or an unwillingness to face up to one's limitations. Other investigators (Crowne & Marlow, 1964; N. Frederiksen, 1965) have presented evidence to suggest that the strength of the social desirability response set is related to the individual's more general need for self-protection, avoidance of criticism, social conformity, and social approval. On the other hand, the individual who chooses unfavorable items in a self-description may be motivated by a need for attention, sympathy, or help in meeting personal problems. Persons seeking psychotherapy, for example, are likely to make themselves appear more maladjusted on a personality inventory than they actually are.

It cannot be assumed that basic research is free from the effects of response sets. In a provocative survey of studies on attitude change, for example, Silverman and Shulman (1970) described a number of such response sets. The results of these investigations may be influenced by such conditions as the subject's perception of what the experimenter expects, the desire to protect one's own image, and the wish to please or to frustrate the experimenter. Unsuspected differences in these response sets may account in part for failures to replicate results when the experiments are repeated.

In order to investigate the contribution of the social desirability variable to personality test responses, Edwards (1957) developed a special social desirability scale. Beginning with 150 heterogeneous MMPI items taken from the three validating keys and the Taylor Manifest Anxiety Scale, Edwards selected 79 items that yielded complete agreement among 10 judges with regard to the socially desirable response. Through item analyses against total scores on this preliminary scale, he shortened the list to 39 items. The SD scale correlated .81 with the K scale of the MMPI, partly because of common items between the two scales. Individual scores on this scale can be correlated with scores on any personality test as a check on the degree to which the social desirability variable has been ruled out of test responses. Whatever the cause of the relation, Edwards argued that insofar as social desirability is correlated with test scores, the effectiveness of the test in discriminating individual differences in specific, content-related traits is reduced.

Several procedures have been followed in the effort to meet the problem of faking and related response sets in personality inventories. The construction of relatively "subtle" or socially neutral items may reduce the operation of these factors in some inventories.[4] In a number of situations, the test instructions and the establishment of rapport may motivate examinees to respond frankly, if they can be convinced that it is to their own advantage to do so. This approach would be ineffective in certain situations, however; and it would not have much effect on social desirability response sets of which the individual is unaware. Other attempted solutions include verification keys that detect faking or response sets, such as the F scale of the MMPI, and correction terms, such as those provided by the K scale of the MMPI. Still another procedure, directed not to the detection but to the prevention of dissimulation, is the use of forced-choice items.

FORCED-CHOICE TECHNIQUE. Essentially, the forced-choice technique requires the respondent to choose between two descriptive terms or phrases that appear equally acceptable but differ in validity. The paired phrases may both be desirable or both undesirable. The two demonstration items from the EPPS, reproduced earlier in this chapter, illustrate this item form. Forced-choice items may also contain three, four, or five terms, as illustrated by the sample item from the Gordon Personal Inventory reproduced in Figure 91. In such cases, respondents must indicate which phrase is most characteristic and which is least characteristic of themselves. Still another vari-

4 See, e.g., the development by Block (1965, Ch. 7) of an Ego-Resiliency (Subtle) scale for the MMPI. Jackson (1971), however, has argued that so-called subtle items may be merely items of low validity for the dimension under consideration.

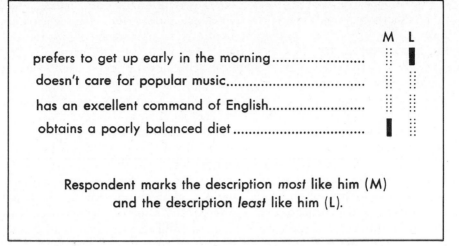

	M	L
prefers to get up early in the morning		■
doesn't care for popular music		
has an excellent command of English		
obtains a poorly balanced diet	■	

**Respondent marks the description *most* like him (M)
and the description *least* like him (L).**

FIG. 91. Sample Forced-Choice Item from Gordon Personal Inventory.
(Copyright © 1951, 1978 by Harcourt Brace Jovanovich, Inc. Reproduced by permission.)

ant requires a choice between two contrasting responses within the same trait, scored for a single scale. Although rarely employed in personality inventories, this item form has the advantage of yielding normative rather than ipsative scores and hence imposing no artificial constraints on the interrelationships among different scales. An example is provided by the Myers-Briggs Type Indicator (Appendix E).

Use of the forced-choice technique to control social desirability requires two types of information regarding each response alternative, viz., its social desirability or "preference index" and its validity or "discriminative index." The latter may be determined on the basis of any specific criterion the inventory is designed to predict, such as academic achievement or success on a particular kind of job; or it may be based on the factor loading of items or their theoretical relevance to different traits. Social desirability can be found by having the items rated for this variable by a representative group, or by ascertaining the frequency with which the item is endorsed in self-descriptions. In a series of studies on many different groups, A. L. Edwards (1957) showed that frequency of choice and judged social desirability correlate between .80 and .90. In other words, the *average* self-description of a population agrees closely with its average description of a desirable personality. Moreover, the rated SD of items remains remarkably stable in groups differing in sex, age, education, socioeconomic level, or nationality. Consistent results were also obtained when the judgments of hospitalized psychiatric patients were compared with those of normal groups.

In order to rule out the operation of the SD variable in the EPPS, Edwards relied exclusively on the forced-choice type of item. Independent research with this test since its publication, however, indicates that the influence of SD may have been reduced but was certainly not eliminated. When EPPS items were presented in a free-choice format, the scores correlated quite highly with the scores obtained with the regular forced-choice form of the test (Lanyon, 1966). The median correlation was .73, several of the correlations approaching the test-retest reliability of the scales. There is evidence that the context in which an item is encountered affects its perceived social desirability. Thus, the SD of an item rated separately may change when that item is paired with another item in a forced-choice format. Not only were significant differences in SD found between the paired items in the EPPS, but the redetermined SD values also yielded substantial correlations with the frequency of item endorsement (Corah et al., 1958). These correlations sometimes approached the correlations found between SD ratings and frequency of endorsement of items presented singly and marked "True" or "False" (A. L. Edwards, 1957, 1966). There is also evidence that forced-choice tests are no more valid than single-stimulus tests (Jackson, Neill, & Bevan, 1973).

It has been shown, furthermore, that EPPS responses *can* be deliberately faked to create the desired impressions, especially for specific purposes (Borislow, 1958; Dicken, 1959). It cannot be assumed that judged SD is constant for all purposes, even though the judgments of general social desirability obtained from different populations may agree. The relative desirability of the same items for salespersons or for physicians, for example, may differ from their desirability when judged in terms of general cultural norms. Thus, a forced-choice test whose items were equated in general social desirability could still be faked when taken by job applicants, candidates for admission to professional schools, and other specifically oriented groups. From another angle, it has been found that when items are paired on the basis of average *group* judgments of general social desirability, they may be far from equated for *individuals* (N. Wiggins, 1966).

In conclusion, it appears that the forced-choice technique has not proved as effective as had been anticipated in controlling faking or social desirability response sets. At the same time, the forced-choice item format, particularly when it yields ipsative scores, introduces other technical difficulties and eliminates information about absolute strength of individual characteristics that may be of prime importance in some testing situations.

RESPONSE SETS AND RESPONSE STYLES. The tendency to choose socially desirable response alternatives is only one of several response sets that have been identified in test responses (Jackson, 1973). Although the voluminous literature on the operation of response sets in personality inventories dates largely from midcentury, the influence of response sets in both ability and personality tests was observed by earlier investigators (see Block, 1965, Ch. 2). One of the response sets that attracted early attention was *acquiescence*, or the tendency to answer "True" or "Yes." Acquiescence is conceptualized as a continuous variable; at one end of the scale are the consistent "Yeasay-ers" and at the other end the consistent "Naysayers" (Couch & Keniston, 1960). The implications of this response set for the construction of person-ality inventories is that the number of items in which a "Yes" or "True" re-sponse is keyed positively in any trait scale should equal the number of items in which a "No" or "False" response is keyed positively. This balance can be achieved by the proper selection or rewording of items, as was done in the PRF.

A third response set that has been widely investigated is *deviation,* or the tendency to give unusual or uncommon responses. Berg (1967), who pro-posed this deviation hypothesis, has argued strongly for the content-free na-ture of this response set. Accordingly, he demonstrated its operation with nonverbal content in a specially developed test requiring an expression of preference for geometric figures.

Research on response sets such as social desirability, acquiescence, and deviation has passed through two principal stages. When first identified, re-sponse sets were regarded as a source of irrelevant or error variance to be eliminated from test scores. Efforts were therefore made to rule out their in-fluence through the reformulation of items, the development of special keys, or the application of correction terms. Later, these response sets came to be regarded as indicators of broad and durable personality characteristics that were worth measuring in their own right (Jackson & Messick, 1958, 1962; J. S. Wiggins, 1962). At this stage, they were commonly described as *re-sponse styles.*[5] We have already noted the association of the social desir-ability response set with certain general behavior tendencies to seek social approval. Evidence has likewise been gathered to suggest pervasive per-sonality differences between Yeasayers and Naysayers (Couch & Keniston, 1960) and between those who choose common responses and those who choose deviant responses (Berg, 1967).

Now we have come full circle. Personality inventory responses are again regarded to have broad diagnostic significance, but in terms of their stylistic properties rather than in terms of specific item content. At the same time the elaborate edifice that has been built around response styles shows signs of crumbling. The empirical data adduced in support of a response-style in-terpretation of scores on such inventories as the MMPI has been challenged from many directions (Block, 1965; Heilbrun, 1964; Rorer, 1965). Factorial analyses of the MMPI scales by several investigators have generally yielded two major factors that account for nearly all the common variance among the scales. The exponents of response sets and response styles have inter-preted these two factors as social desirability and acquiescence, although differing in the relative importance they attribute to each. In a sophisticated statistical analysis of MMPI scales and items, Block (1965) presented strong evidence supporting a content-oriented interpretation of these two factors

---

[5] This distinction between response sets and response styles is not universal, however. Some writers use the two terms in a different sense (e.g., Rorer, 1965).

and indicating that the contribution of response styles to the variance of MMPI scores is negligible. He also ,demonstrated that the evidence advanced earlier in support of stylistic interpretations of these factors reflected methodological artifacts.

The controversy over response sets and content-versus-style in personality assessment is far from settled.[6] Nevertheless, it may prove to be a tempest in a teapot. Like many scientific controversies, it has stimulated extensive research and has produced several hundred publications. And like many scientific controversies, its net effect will probably be to sharpen our understanding of methodological problems and thereby improve both the construction of personality inventories and the research conducted with them in the future. It is likely that some stylistic scales may ultimately prove to be valid predictors of important personality traits; but it is unlikely that stylistic scales will generally replace content-related scales in personality inventories.

TRAITS, STATES, AND SITUATIONS

INTERACTIONS OF PERSONS AND SITUATIONS. A long-standing controversy regarding the generalizability of personality traits versus the situational specificity of behavior reached a peak in the late 1960s and the 1970s. Several developments in the 1960s focused attention on narrowly defined "behaviors of interest" and away from broadly defined traits. In the cognitive domain, this focus is illustrated by individualized instructional programs and criterion-referenced testing (Chs. 4, 14) and by the diagnosis and treatment of learning disabilities (Ch. 16). In the noncognitive or personality domain, the strongest impetus toward behavioral specificity in testing came from social learning theory and the general orientation characterizing behavior modification and behavior therapy, described in Chapter 16 (Bandura, 1969; Bandura & Walters, 1963; Goldfried & Kent, 1972; Mischel, 1968, 1969, 1973). Criticism was directed especially toward the early view of traits as fixed, unchanging, underlying causal entities. This kind of criticism had been anticipated in the earlier research and writing of several psychologists, with regard to all traits—cognitive as well as noncognitive (see Ch. 13). Few psychologists today would argue for this extreme view of traits. In commenting on the scarcity of this type of "trait theorist," Jackson and Paunonen (1980, p. 523) write, "Like witches of 300 years ago, there is confidence about their existence, and even possibly their sinister properties, although one is hard pressed to find one in the flesh or even meet someone who has."

Situational specificity in particular, however, is much more characteristic of personality traits than it is of abilities. For example, a person might be

---

[6] See Bentler, Jackson, and Messick (1971, 1972), Block (1967, 1971b, 1972), Jackson (1967a, 1967b), Jackson and Paunonen (1980), and Samelson (1972).

quite sociable and outgoing at the office, but shy and reserved at social gatherings. Or a student who cheats on examinations might be scrupulously honest in money matters. An extensive body of empirical evidence was assembled by Mischel (1968) and D. Peterson (1968) showing that individuals do exhibit considerable situational specificity in many nonintellective dimensions, such as aggression, social conformity, dependency, rigidity, honesty, and attitudes toward authority. Part of the explanation for the higher cross-situational consistency of cognitive than of noncognitive functions may be found in the greater standardization of the individual's reactional biography in the intellectual than in the personality domain (Anastasi, 1948; 1958, Ch. 11; 1970). The formal school curriculum, for example, contributes to the development of broadly applicable cognitive skills in the verbal and numerical areas. Personality development, on the other hand, occurs under far less uniform conditions. In the personality domain, moreover, the same response may lead to social consequences that are positively reinforcing in one situation and negatively reinforcing in another. The individual may thus learn to respond in quite different ways in different contexts. Such dissimilarities in experiential history, across individuals as well as across situations, also lead to greater ambiguity in personality test items than is found in cognitive test items. Thus, the same response to a given question on a personality inventory may have a different significance from one person to another.

With regard to testing methodology, the impact of situational specificity was most clearly evident among investigators who identified with social learning theory (Endler & Hunt, 1966, 1968, 1969; Goldfried & D'Zurilla, 1969; Kjerulff & Wiggins, 1976; Tucker, 1966). Special instruments were developed to assess the behavior of individuals in different types of situations. Analysis of the results showed the extent to which behavior variance depended upon persons, situations, and the interaction between the two. In this context, the concept of interaction refers simply to the fact that the effect of different situations may itself vary for different persons.

This approach to behavioral assessment is illustrated by an investigation of the way graduate students cope with stressful situations (Kjerulff & Wiggins, 1976). Through a series of systematic procedural steps, the investigators assembled brief verbal descriptions of 26 stressful situations encountered by graduate students, with special reference to situations that might adversely influence their remaining in graduate school. Respondents rated each situation on a set of 7-point scales to indicate how they would feel if they were in each of the situations. Some of the rating scales concerned the degree to which the student would feel angry with others, angry with himself or herself, and responsible for the situation. Other scales involved the degree to which the student would feel anxious, rejected, depressed, and discouraged. There were also questions designed to assess the individual's professional self-concept.

The basic data in this study involved three different modes: persons, situations, and types of response. Using multimode factor analysis (Tucker, 1966), the investigators were able to identify major factors in situations (e.g., academic failure, interpersonal problems), in responses (e.g., anger at self versus others, general anxiety), and in persons. The person mode sorted students into two types: those who desire professional respect, rate themselves high in competence, and plan to be doing research of major importance versus those tending to rate themselves at the opposite pole in these characteristics. In addition, multimode factor analysis provides a core matrix which integrates the three modes and permits their joint interpretation. For example, students who rate themselves as less competent professionally tend to feel anger at themselves for academic failure and anger at others for interpersonal problems; they are extremely anxious when facing academic problems, but not at all anxious in stressful situations for which there is no clear source of blame, such as losing subjects in an experiment.

McReynolds (1979) has proposed the term "interactional assessment" to refer to the joint assessment of the person and the environment in which he or she must function. Attention focuses on how the particular individual will respond within specific situations. Although the general interactional model has been recognized for some time, McReynolds points out that little progress has been made toward the development of appropriate assessment procedures. To meet this need, he outlines six possible approaches that have been or can be followed in interactional assessment. These range from systematic assessment of the person combined with informal observation of relevant environments (as in visiting the foster home to which a child may be assigned) to direct behavioral samples of persons-in-situations and simulated behavioral samples of persons-in-situations (as in roleplaying).

Both the theoretical discussions and the research on person-by-situation interaction have undoubtedly enriched our understanding of the many conditions that determine individual behavior, and they have contributed to the development of sophisticated research designs. Concurrently, there has been a growing consensus among the adherents of contrasting views. This rapprochement was especially evident in a number of well-balanced and thoughtful discussions of the problem published in the late 1970s.[7] Several noteworthy points emerged from these discussions. Behavior exhibits considerable temporal stability when measured reliably, that is, by summing repeated observations and thereby reducing the error of measurement. When random samples of persons and situations are studied, individual differences contribute more to total behavior variance than do situational differences. Interaction between persons and situations contributes as much as do individual differences, or slightly more. To identify broad personality

[7] See especially Mischel (1977, 1979), Bem and Allen (1974), Bem and Funder (1978), Bowers (1973), Endler and Magnusson (1976), Epstein 1979, 1980), Hogan, DeSoto, and Solano (1977).

traits, we need to measure the individual across many situations and aggregate the results (Epstein, 1980).

From another angle, the degree of behavioral specificity across situations itself varies from person to person. In this connection, Mischel (1979) refers to individual differences in discriminativeness of social behavior. Persons differ in the extent to which they alter their behavior to meet the demands of each situation. In this respect, moderate inconsistency indicates effective and adaptive flexibility, while excessive consistency indicates maladaptive rigidity. Moreover, the particular situations across which behavior is consistent may vary among persons. This intersituational consistency is influenced by the way in which individuals perceive and categorize situations. And such grouping of situations, in turn, depends on the individual's goals and on his or her prior experience with similar situations.[8]

Situations also differ in the behavioral constraints they impose. Thus, we could predict with a high level of confidence that readers will remain silent in a library and that motorists will stop at a red light. Similarly, persons—whatever their trait structure—are likely to swim at the beach and to read in the library. Nevertheless, certain individuals may spend their time reading while at the beach. and others may spend all too much time daydreaming about swimming while in the library.

Still another approach to the problem of trait consistency and behavioral diversity is provided by the motivational theory formulated by J. W. Atkinson (1981) and tested through computer simulation. Representing behavior as a stream of activity rather than a series of discrete incidents, Atkinson and his co-workers were able to reconcile enduring individual differences in personality traits (such as achievement drive) with changing behavior over short time periods, even when the immediate environment remains constant. Essentially, the explanation can be found in the changing motivational state of the organism, which reflects the waxing and waning of the relative strengths of different behavior tendencies. When a particular tendency becomes dominant among simultaneously aroused competing tendencies, it is expressed in appropriate behavior. This expression of a tendency in activity reduces the strength of that tendency, whereupon another tendency rises to a dominant position and leads to other behavior.

TRAITS AND STATES. Another way to conceptualize the behavior domain assessed by personality tests involves a differentiation between traits and states. This differentiation is most clearly exemplified in the State-Trait Anxiety Inventory (STAI) developed by Spielberger and his co-workers (Spielberger, Gorsuch, & Lushene, 1970; Spielberger, Vagg, Barker, Donham, & Westberry, 1980). In the construction of this instrument, state anx-

[8] This conception of behavioral consistencies derives from the early idiographic approach to personality assessment formulated by Allport (1937) and G. A. Kelly (1963), among others.

iety (A-State) was defined as a transitory emotional condition characterized by subjective feelings of tension and apprehension. Such states vary in
intensity and fluctuate over time. A-State is measured by 20 short descriptive
statements which the individual answers in reference to how he or she feels
at the moment (e.g., I feel calm; I am jittery). The answers are recorded
by indicating the intensity of the feeling (not at all, somewhat, moderately
so, very much so).

Trait anxiety (A-Trait) refers to relatively stable anxiety-proneness, that
is, the individual's tendency to respond to situations perceived as threatening with elevated A-State intensity. Respondents are instructed to indicate
how they *generally* feel by marking the frequency with which each of the
20 statements applies to them (almost never, sometimes, often, almost always). Examples of the statements are "I am inclined to take things hard,"
"I am a steady person." Only three identical items appear in the two forms
of the inventory.

Conceptually, A-Trait is identified with a set of constructs described as
"acquired behavioral dispositions" (D. T. Campbell, 1963). These constructs
"involve residues of past experience and predispose an individual *both* to
view the world in a particular way and to manifest 'object consistent' response tendencies" (Spielberger et al., 1970, p. 3). Individuals high in
A-Trait tend to exhibit A-State elevations more often than do individuals
low in A-Trait, because they react to a wider range of situations as threatening or dangerous. They are especially responsive to interpersonal situations
posing some threat to their self-esteem, such as performance evaluation or
the experience of failure. Whether or not A-State increases in a given situation, however, depends upon the extent to which the individual perceives
the situation as threatening or dangerous on the basis of his or her past
experience.

The development of STAI illustrates several special points of test construction. Internal consistency reliability was about equally high (in the
.80s and .90s) for A-Trait and A-State forms. Retest reliability was in the
high .70s for A-Trait but much lower, as would be expected, for A-State. Retests over long intervals (2 or 104 days) yielded A-State correlations ranging from .27 to .54. Retests within one hour, following the introduction of
experimental conditions designed to raise or lower stress levels, yielded still
lower correlations. What such low correlations indicate is an interaction between persons and situational stress. Although the group means reflected
the anticipated differences in A-State following experimental manipulations,
the effects varied sufficiently among individuals to result in low test-retest
correlations.

The construct validity of both A-State and A-Trait forms was demonstrated in various ways, including original item selection, evaluation of
items and total scores in the final inventories, and subsequent research by
the authors and by independent investigators. In successive revisions, items
were selected on the basis of item-retest correlations and item correlations

with external criteria. For the A-Trait, items and total scores yielded high correlations with other self-report anxiety inventories, and they also yielded a pattern of correlations with other personality tests that was generally consistent with expectation.

For the A-State form, both items and total scores were evaluated principally against experimental variables designed to raise or lower anxiety states, such as taking a final course examination or a difficult intelligence test, seeing a film depicting accidents in a woodworking shop, or undergoing a 10-minute period of relaxation training. Simulation was also employed by asking students to respond according to how they believed they would feel "just prior to the final examination in an important course" (Spielberger et al., 1970, p. 10). Validity data for both forms were also obtained by the method of contrasted groups. Mean scores on A-Trait and A-State were found for neuropsychiatric patients in various diagnostic groups, nonpsyciatric medical and surgical patients, and students seen in a college counseling center for emotional and other types of problems.

Another noteworthy finding, with methodological implications for personality test construction, pertains to item-intensity specificity. When responses were checked after experimental manipulations of stress, individual items differed in the anxiety level at which they were most effective. For instance, "I feel rested" was quite sensitive to variation in A-State at the lower intensity levels but not at the higher levels. The reverse was true of the item "I feel overexcited and rattled," which discriminated more effectively at the higher levels. This distinction was also supported by factor analyses of item responses on both A-State and A-Trait forms (Spielberger et al., 1980).

The state-trait differentiation was applied by Spielberger and his associates (1980) in two other, recently developed inventories, the State-Trait Anger Scale (STAS) and the State-Trait Personality Inventory (STPI). Like the previously described State-Trait Anxiety Inventory, the STAS includes two subscales, for assessing state and trait anger. The STPI comprises six subscales, yielding state and trait measures for each of three variables, namely, anger, anxiety, and curiosity.

Mention should be made of still another way of categorizing noncognitive behavior in the development of personality inventories. This is illustrated by several *test anxiety inventories* (I. G. Sarason, 1980), a recent example of which was also developed by Spielberger (1980; Spielberger, Gonzalez, Taylor, Algaze, & Anton, 1978). Labeled the Test Anxiety Inventory (TAI), this instrument is essentially a trait scale restricted to a specified class of situations, those centering on tests and examinations. Persons high in test anxiety tend to perceive evaluative situations as personally threatening. The TAI follows the same general pattern as the A-Trait scale. There are 20 statements describing reactions before, during, or after tests or examinations. Respondents are asked to indicate how they *generally* feel by marking how frequently they experience each reaction (almost never, sometimes, often, almost always). Typical examples include "I freeze up on important exams; while taking examinations, I have an uneasy, upset feeling." The general instructions may be modified to define the anxiety-provoking situations even more specifically, by asking students to respond, for example, with reference to mathematics tests or essay tests.

The TAI yields a total score on anxiety proneness in test situations, as well as subscores on two major components identified through factor analysis, namely, worry and emotionality. In this context, worry is defined as "cognitive concerns about the consequences of failure" and emotionality as "reactions of the autonomic nervous system that are evoked by evaluative stress" (Spielberger, 1980, p. 1). Test construction and evaluation procedures were closely similar to those followed for the STAI. Normative data provided for all the anxiety scales described in this section compare favorably with those generally available for personality inventories, although no attempt was made to approximate a nationally representative standardization sample. The TAI has proved useful in assessing the effectiveness of programs for the treatment of test anxiety.

CURRENT STATUS OF PERSONALITY INVENTORIES

The construction and use of personality inventories are beset with special difficulties over and above the common problems encountered in all psychological testing. The question of faking and malingering is far more acute in personality measurement than in aptitude testing. The behavior measured by personality tests is also more changeable over time than that measured by tests of ability. The latter fact complicates the determination of test reliability, since random temporal fluctuations in test performance are likely to become confused with broad, systematic behavioral changes. Even over relatively short intervals, it cannot be assumed that variations in test response are restricted to the test itself and do not characterize the area of nontest behavior under consideration. A related problem is the greater situational specificity of responses in the noncognitive than in the cognitive domain.

The late 1970s and early 1980s witnessed a resurgence of research and development that faced up to the complexities of personality assessment and sought innovative solutions to these long-standing problems. The period was characterized by significant theoretical and methodological advances. The earlier critiques of personality measurement undoubtedly had a salutary effect and in part stimulated the subsequent developments in this area of psychometrics. We must, however, guard against the danger that, in the zeal to eradicate fallacious thinking, sound and useful concepts may also be lost. The occasional proposal that diagnostic personality testing and trait concepts be completely discarded, for example, indicates an unnecessarily narrow definition of both terms. Diagnosis need not imply the labeling of persons, the use of traditional psychiatric categories, or the application of the medical, "disease" model. Diagnostic testing should be used as an aid in describing and understanding the individual, identifying his or her problems, and reaching appropriate action decisions. Similarly, traits refer to the categories into which behavior must necessarily be classified if we are to deal with it at all—in science or in any other context. The optimum category breadth will vary with the specific purpose of assessment. The hierarchical trait models presented in Chapter 13 can be employed equally well in the description of noncognitive behavior. Under certain circumstances, relatively broad traits will serve best; under other circumstances, very narrow, specifically defined behaviors will need to be assessed.

CHAPTER 18

Measures of Interests, Values, and Personal Orientations

T HE STRENGTH and direction of the individual's interests, attitudes, motives, and values represent an important aspect of personality. These characteristics materially affect educational and occupational adjustment, interpersonal relations, the enjoyment one derives from recreational pursuits, and other major phases of daily living. Although certain tests are specifically directed toward the measurement of one or another of these variables, the available instruments cannot be 'rigidly classified according to such discrete categories as interests, attitudes, and values, Overlapping is the rule. Thus, a questionnaire designed to assess the relative strength of different values, such as the practical, aesthetic, or intellectual, may have much in common with interest inventories. Similarly, such a questionnaire might be said to gauge the individual's attitudes toward pure science, art for art's sake, practical applications, and the like.

The study of *interests* has probably received its strongest impetus from educational and career counseling. To a slightly lesser extent, the development of tests in this area was also stimulated by occupational selection and classification. From the viewpoint of both the worker and the employer, a consideration of the individual's interests is of practical significance. Achievement is a resultant of aptitude and interest. Although these two variables are positively correlated, a high level in one does not necessarily imply a superior status in the other. A person may have sufficient aptitude for success in a certain type of activity—educational, occupational, or recreational—without the corresponding interest. Or the individual may be interested in work for which he or she lacks the prerequisite aptitudes. A measure of both types of variables thus permits a more effective prediction of performance than would be possible from either alone.

The assessment of *opinions and attitudes* originated largely as a problem in social psychology. Attitudes toward different groups have obvious implications for intergroup relations. Similarly, the gauging and prediction of public opinion regarding a wide variety of issues, institutions, or practices are of deep concern to the social psychologist, as well as to the practical worker in business, politics, and other applied fields. The measurement of opinions and attitudes has also made rapid strides in the areas of consumer research and employee relations.

Still other types of self-report inventories are being developed to assess certain broad *personal orientations* that cut across different facets of personality. The construction and use of such inventories represent relatively recent applications of psychometric techniques. Most of the instruments are still in a research stage, and few are available from commercial publishers. The behavioral effects of these personal orientations, however, can be far-reaching, and they are receiving increasing attention. In this chapter, we shall consider self-report inventories that approach personal orientations from three quite different angles, namely, internal versus external locus of control, sex roles and androgyny, and health-related behaviors.

All instruments surveyed in this chapter are self-report inventories. It should be noted, however, that in this area, as in the measurement of all personality constructs, other procedures are being continually explored. Examples of these other procedures will be discussed in Chapters 19 and 20.

INTEREST INVENTORIES

The large majority of interest inventories were designed to assess the individual's interests in different fields of work. Some also provide an analysis of interests in educational curricula or fields of study, which in turn are usually related to career decisions. The more recently developed or revised interest inventories reflect certain major changes in career counseling. One of these changes pertains to the increasing emphasis on *self-exploration*. More and more instruments provide opportunities for the individual to study the detailed test results and relate them to occupational information and other data about personal qualifications and experience. Training in career decision-making has itself received increasing attention, as was indicated in Chapter 15. The occupational interest inventories to be discussed in this chapter should be considered against the background provided in the section on career counseling in Chapter 15.

A second and related change concerns the goal of interest measurement. Today, there is more and more emphasis on *expanding the career options* open to the individual. Thus, the interest inventory, as well as the more comprehensive career orientation programs cited in Chapter 15, are being used to acquaint the individual with suitable occupations that he or she might not otherwise have considered.

The third significant change is itself associated with this expansion of career options. It relates to a concern about the *sex fairness* of interest inventories. In general, interest inventories compare an individual's expressed interests with those typical of persons engaged in different occupations. This is done either in the scoring of individual item responses, or in the interpretation of scores in broad interest areas, or both. While this approach certainly represents an objective, empirical procedure for evaluating one's interests, it tends to perpetuate existing group differences among occupations. If there are large discrepancies in the proportion of men and women in some occupations, such as engineering or nursing, these differences would tend, in one way or another, to influence the interpretation of results obtained by males and females on interest inventories. For this reason, considerable discussion and intensive research efforts have been devoted to ways of reducing possible sex bias in interest inventories (Prediger & Johnson, 1979; Tittle & Zytowski, 1978). A set of guidelines for the assessment of sex bias and sex fairness in career interest inventories has also been prepared and widely distributed.[1] Nearly every newly developed or revised inventory shows the influence of these guidelines.

STRONG-CAMPBELL INTEREST INVENTORY (SCII). The SCII represents the 1974 revision of the Strong Vocational Interest Blank (SVIB), which has a long history. The general approach followed in its construction was first formulated by E. K. Strong, Jr., while attending a 1919–1920 graduate seminar on interest measurement at the Carnegie Institute of Technology (D. P. Campbell, 1971, Ch. 11; Fryer, 1931, Ch. 3). The SVIB introduced two principal procedures in the measurement of occupational interests. First, the items dealt with the respondent's liking or dislike for a wide variety of specific activities, objects, or types of persons that he or she commonly encountered in daily living. Second, the responses were empirically keyed for different occupations. These interest inventories were thus among the first tests to employ criterion keying of items, subsequently followed in the development of such personality inventories as the MMPI and CPI (Ch. 17). It was found that persons engaged in different occupations were characterized by common interests that differentiated them from persons in other occupations. These differences in interests extended not only to matters pertaining directly to job activities, but also to school subjects, hobbies, sports, types of plays or books the individual enjoyed, social relations, and many other facets of everyday life. It thus proved feasible to prepare an inventory that explored an individual's interests in familiar things and thereby to determine how closely her or his interests resembled those of persons successfully engaged in particular occupations.

The SCII incorporated more extensive innovations than did any earlier revision. The principal changes include the merging of the earlier men's and women's forms into a single test booklet and the introduction of a theoretical framework to guide the organization and interpretation of scores. The inventory consists of 325 items grouped into seven parts. In the first five parts, the examinee records her or his preferences by marking L, I, or D to indicate "Like," "Indifferent," or "Dislike." Items in these five parts

---

[1] Prepared as part of a study conducted by the National Institute of Education. A copy is reproduced in Tittle and Zytowski (1978, pp. 151–153).

fall into the following categories: occupations, school subjects, activities (e.g., making a speech, repairing a clock, raising money for charity), amusements, and day-to-day contact with various types of people (e.g., very old people, military officers, people who live dangerously). The remaining two parts require the respondent to express a preference between paired items (e.g., dealing with things vs. dealing with people) and marking a set of self-descriptive statements "Yes," "No," or "?."

The SCII can be scored only by computer, through several designated scoring agencies. Figures 92, 93, and 94 show sections of the two-page profile booklet on which the different types of scores are reported. For illustrative purposes, scores have been inserted from the profile of a 27-year-old female psychologist who is involved primarily in research and technical writing.[2] Figure 92 covers scores on the broadest scales, dealing with six General Occupational Themes, such as Realistic, Artistic, and Social. These themes are derived from the classification of interests developed by Holland (1973) and supported by extensive research both by Holland and by other independent investigators. Each theme characterizes not only a type of person but also the type of working environment that such a person would find most congenial. Scores on all parts of the inventory are expressed as standard scores ($M = 50$, $SD = 10$). For the General Occupational Themes, the

General Occupational Themes				Administrative Indexes			
Theme	Std Score	Result		(for the use of the counselor)			
R-Theme	51	This is a MODERATELY HIGH	Score.	TOTAL RESPONSES	325		
I-Theme	63	This is a HIGH	Score.	INFREQUENT RESPONSES	4		
					Response %		
A-Theme	63	This is a HIGH	Score.		LP	IP	DP
				OCCUPATIONS	34	11	54
S-Theme	26	This is a VERY LOW	Score.	SCHOOL SUBJECTS	42	11	47
				ACTIVITIES	35	6	59
E-Theme	35	This is a VERY LOW	Score	AMUSEMENTS	67	10	23
				TYPES OF PEOPLE	42	12	46
C-Theme	41	This is a MODERATELY LOW	Score.	PREFERENCES	40	47	13
				CHARACTERISTICS	86	7	7
				Special Scales: AOR: 60 IE: 53			

FIG. 92. Portions of SCII Profile, Showing Scores on Six General Occupational Theme Scales (Realistic, Investigative, Artistic, Social, Enterprising, Coventional), Administrative Indexes (used to detect carelessness and test-taking response sets), and Special Scales (Academic Orientation and Introversion-Extroversion).

(Form reprinted with permission of the publisher from *Manual for the Strong-Campbell Interest Inventory*, Form T325 of the STRONG VOCATIONAL INTEREST BLANK, by David P. Campbell [Stanford University Press, 1974], p. 18. Scores in Fig. 92, 93, and 94 by courtesy of Center for Interest Measurement and Research, University of Minnesota.)

[2] Data by courtesy of Center for Interest Measurement and Research, University of Minnesota.

normative group is the general reference sample consisting of 300 men and 300 women representative of all occupations covered by the inventory.[3] Numerical scores are reported with reference to the whole sample; interpretive phrases (e.g., high, moderately low) are based on the distribution of the same-sex subgroup.

The Administrative Indexes in Figure 92 are designed to detect carelessness and test-taking response sets. The two Special Scales are empirical scales developed against nonoccupational criteria. The Academic Orientation (AOR) scale was originally constructed by comparing item-response percentages of college students obtaining high grades with those of students obtaining low grades. It predicts chiefly the tendency to continue one's education through high school, college, and graduate school. The Introversion-Extroversion (IE) scale was developed from the responses of students identified as introverts and as extroverts on the MMPI. Scores reflect the person's interest in working alone or with people. Both scales have yielded large mean differences in the expected direction among groups engaged in different occupations.

Figure 93 shows the 23 Basic Interest Scales, classified under the six General Occupational Themes. These scales consist of clusters of substantially intercorrelated items. The Basic Interest Scales are more homogeneous in content than the Occupational Scales and can therefore help in understanding why an individual scores high on a particular Occupational Scale. The standard scores are again expressed in terms of the general reference sample; and the profile is plotted with reference to both sex subsamples. For each scale, the open and shaded bars show the performance of the female and male subsamples, respectively.

The Occupational Scales, which constituted the main body of the SVIB since its inception, are illustrated in Figure 94. In the continuing research program on this inventory, new scales are constantly added and old scales updated with fresh criterion samples. The 1974 form provides 124 Occupational Scales, including 67 derived from male samples and 57 from female samples. Although the goal is to have male and female criterion samples for each occupation, by 1974 it had not proved feasible to gather data on both men and women for all the occupations on the form. Most of the samples had been tested in the 1960s; a few were tested in the 1970s and a few before 1960. Even today, it is still difficult to obtain a sufficiently large sample of men in some occupations or of women in others.

Regardless of sex of respondent, each inventory is scored for all Occupational Scales and standard scores are reported in terms of both male and female criterion groups for each occupation, when available. The profile, however, is plotted only against the same-sex norms. Occupational Scale scores show degree of similarity of the individual's responses to those of the cri-

---

[3] For the detailed procedures followed to ensure representativeness, see D. P. Campbell (1971, Ch. 2; 1977).

Basic Interest Scales

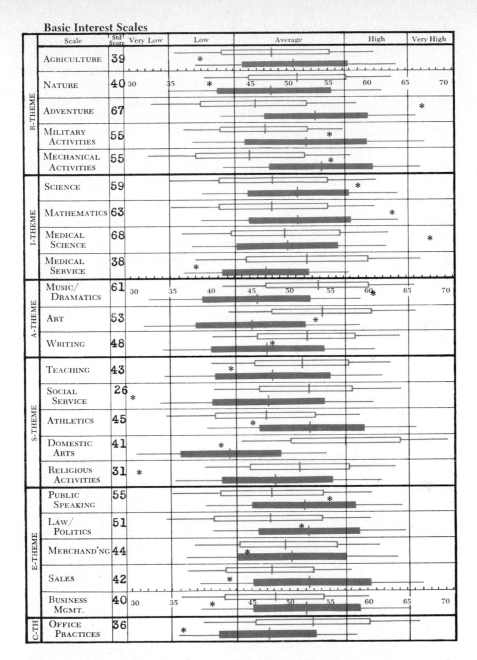

FIG. 93. Portion of SCII Profile, Showing Scores on 23 Basic Interest Scales, Classified According to General Occupational Themes. Shaded bars refer to responses of 300 men and open bars to responses of 300 women in General Reference Group; thick central portion covers range of middle 50%, thin portion range of middle 80%.

(Form reprinted with permission of the publisher from *Manual for the Strong-Campbell Interest Inventory*, Form T325 of the STRONG VOCATIONAL INTEREST BLANK, by David P. Campbell [Stanford University Press, 1974], p. 18.)

terion group for each occupation listed. Unlike the two broader types of scores, Occupational standard scores are derived from the appropriate occupational criterion groups, not from the general reference samples.

Reference to Figure 94 shows code letters preceding each occupational title. These letters indicate from one to three General Occupational Themes that predominate in that occupation. For example, the interests of psychologists are associated with Investigative (i.e., intellectual, scientific), Artistic, and Social themes. This classification was based principally on the mean scores on the General Occupational Theme scales obtained by each occupa-

Occupational Scales										
Code	Scale	Sex Norm	Std Score	Very Dissimilar	Dissimilar	Ave	Similar	Very Similar	Code	Sc
RC FARMER		m	7						AE INT. DE	
RC INSTRUM. ASSEMBL.		f	16	*					AE ADVERT	
RCE VOC. AGRIC. TCHR.		m	-10						A LANGUA	
REC DIETITIAN		m	30						A LIBRARI	
RES POLICE OFFICER		m	25						A LIBRARI	
RSE HWY. PATROL OFF.		m	15						A REPORT	
RE ARMY OFFICER		f	47				*		A REPORT	
RS PHYS. ED. TEACHER		f	35			*			AS ENGLIS	
R SKILLED CRAFTS		m	22						AS ENGLIS	
RI FORESTER		m	19						SI NURSE,	
IS SPEECH PATHOL.		f	58					*	ERC PURCHA	
IS SPEECH PATHOL.		m	59						ESR CHIROPR	
IAS PSYCHOLOGIST		f	61					*	CE ACCOUNT	
IAS PSYCHOLOGIST		m	48	15	25	45	55		CE BANKER	
IA LANGUAGE INTERPR.		f	51				*		CE BANKER	
ARI ARCHITECT		m	49						CE CREDIT	
A ADVERTISING EXEC.		f	49				*		CE DEPT. ST	
A ARTIST		f	48				*		CE BUSINESS	
A ARTIST		m	46						CES BUSINESS	
A ART TEACHER		f	27			*			CSE EXEC. HO	
A PHOTOGRAPHER		m	51						C ACCOUNT	
A MUSICIAN		f	51				*		C SECRETAR	
A MUSICIAN		m	51						CR DENTAL	
A ENTERTAINER		f	52				*		CRI NURSE, L	
AE INT. DECORATOR		f	34			*			CRE BEAUTIC	

FIG. 94. Fragments from SCII Profile, Showing Scores on Some of the 124 Occupational Scales. Standard scores on original male and female Occupational Scales are reported for all examinees, but profiles (asterisks) are plotted against like-sex group only. Letters preceding scale titles refer to General Occupational Themes empirically related to each Occupational Scale.

(Form reprinted with permission of the publisher from *Manual for the Strong-Campbell Interest Inventory*, Form T325 of the STRONG VOCATIONAL INTEREST BLANK, by David P. Campbell [Stanford University Press, 1974], p. 18.)

tional criterion sample, and on the correlations of the Occupational Scales with each of the Theme Scales.

Items for each Occupational Scale were selected and weighted on the basis of *differences* in item-response percentages between the occupational criterion sample and the reference sample. In the Farmer Scale, for example, a +1 weight indicates that the response occurs more frequently, and a −1 that it occurs less frequently, among farmers than among men-in-general. Responses that fail to differentiate farmers from men-in-general do not appear in the Farmer Scale, regardless of how frequently they were chosen by farmers. An individual's total raw score on each Occupational Scale is simply the algebraic sum of his or her plus and minus weights. The raw scores are converted to standard scores in terms of the distribution of scores in each occupational criterion group. These criterion groups, usually containing from 100 to 500 cases, included persons between the ages of 25 and 55, employed in the given occupation for at least three years, who reported satisfaction with their work and met certain minimum standards of successful achievement.

The SVIB-SCII has been subjected to a continuing research program that has yielded extensive data about its reliability and validity (D. P. Campbell, 1971, 1977). Median retest reliabilities over a 30-day period for General Occupational Themes, Basic Interest Scales, and Occupational Scales are all in the high .80s. Long-term stability of the Occupational Scales for periods ranging from 1 year to over 20 years is also high, the correlations falling mostly in the .60s and .70s. A recent three-year retest yielded a median reliability of .85 for these scales (D. P. Campbell, 1977, pp. 58–59). Another type of analysis concerns the stability of mean occupational profiles over time (D. P. Campbell, 1971, Ch. 9). For this purpose, the SVIB was administered to different samples of men holding the same jobs in the same organizations on two occasions separated by an interval of 30 years or more. This procedure was followed with four occupational groups: ministers, bankers, school superintendents, and corporation presidents. In general, the mean occupational profiles obtained over this interval were remarkably similar, suggesting that the scales developed on the original criterion groups were still applicable. Similar results have been obtained with the Basic Interest Scales administered to different samples from the same occupation over a 30-year span.

Concurrent validity is indicated by the degree of differentiation among different occupational samples, and between occupational samples and reference samples. Predictive validity has been checked in several samples over long intervals. The evidence indicates substantial correspondence between the initial occupational profile and the occupation eventually pursued. A specific example is provided by a 40-year follow-up of a sample of psychologists, whose professional careers revealed some suggestive relations between the flatness versus distinctness of their original profile and such occurrences as frequency of job changes and shifting from teaching or re-

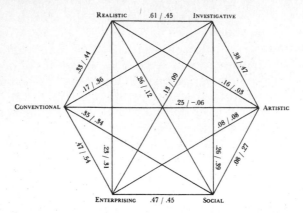

FIG. 95. Holland's Hexagonal Model of General Occupational Themes. For each pair of themes, first correlation is based on female sample, second correlation on male sample.

(Reprinted with permission of the publisher from *Manual for the Strong-Campbell Interest Inventory*, Form T325 of the STRONG VOCATIONAL INTEREST BLANK, by David P. Campbell [Stanford University Press, 1974], p. 34.)

search to administrative or applied work (Vinitsky, 1973). Another investigation found strikingly high cross-cultural profile similarities among samples of psychologists tested in nine Western nations (Lonner & Adams, 1972).

With regard to construct validity, the relations of the Occupational Scales to the General Occupational Themes, as well as the interrelations of the themes among themselves, are of special relevance. Figure 95 shows the six themes at the corners of the hexagonal model developed by Holland (1966, 1973). It will be noted that the highest correlations, in both female and male samples, were obtained between theme scales occupying adjacent positions along the perimeter of the hexagon. The lowest correlations were found between scales at opposite ends of diagonals. Among women, for example, the Realistic Scale correlates .61 with the Investigative Scale, but only .16 with the Artistic and .26 with the Social Scale. Similarly, if the Occupational Scales are plotted on the hexagon, most of them follow the expected order along the perimeter. For example, Farmer, coded RC, falls between Realistic and Conventional; Psychologist, coded IAS, falls along the Investigative, Artistic, Social continuum. Usually, occupations that score high on one theme score low on its direct opposite (e.g., Artistic and Conventional). When an Occupational Scale shows substantial correlations with themes at opposite points of the hexagon, it often includes heterogeneous subgroups with recognizably different occupational functions.

JACKSON VOCATIONAL INTEREST SURVEY (JVIS). The JVIS was chosen as the second example of interest inventories, first, because it illustrates sophisticated test construction procedures and, second, because in several respects its approach is the opposite from that of the SVIB-SCII. The Strong inventory is the oldest in current use and has a long history of research and development; the Jackson inventory is one of 'the newest. The Strong focuses on specific occupations, both in item selection and normative interpretations; the Jackson utilizes broad interest areas in both item development and scoring system. The Strong represents an extreme example of empirical criterion keying and criterion-related validation; the Jackson exemplifies construct validation at every stage in its development. In the Strong, the large majority of items are independently marked L, I, or D by the respondent; in the Jackson, all items are of the forced-choice type.

In its construction, the JVIS reflects the current, more strongly theory-based approach to test construction, as well as methodological advances made possible by the advent of high-speed computers (Jackson, 1977). As in the development of the Personality Research Form and the Jackson Personality Inventory described in Chapter 17, the first step in the development of the JVIS was to define the constructs or dimensions to be measured. These dimensions were of two types, one defined in terms of work roles, the other in terms of work styles. *Work roles* pertain to what a person does on the job. Some of these roles are closely associated with a particular occupation or type of occupation, such as engineering, law, or elementary education. Others, such as human-relations management and professional advising, cut across many occupations. *Work styles* refer, not to job-related activities, but to a working environment in which a certain kind of behavior is expected. Examples of work styles include planfulness, independence, and dominant leadership.

The choice of particular dimensions to be measured was guided by published research on the psychology of work and on factor-analytic and rational classifications of vocational interest items. The definitions of the chosen dimensions and the descriptions of their most relevant job manifestations were refined by reference to the data available in the *Dictionary of Occupational Titles*. Items were prepared to fit these detailed specifications for each of the work roles and work styles.

Development of the final forms followed several steps, including successive tryouts and statistical analyses of items. With an initial pool of over 3,000 items, the procedure included factor analyses of subsets of the items prepared for each scale. Because each item was originally presented singly for a like-dislike response, the results yielded a large general factor reflecting a response bias. Individuals differed substantially in the total number of items to which they responded "Like" or "Dislike." At this stage, the response bias was removed statistically before proceeding with further item analyses. Subsequent empirical analyses involved the computation of internal consistency measures and the selection of items showing high correlations with total factor scores on their own scale and low correlations with other scales. Items were then assembled for the forced-choice format through a computer program that paired items representing different work roles or work styles, while showing similar endorsement frequencies when they had been presented singly.

The final form of the JVIS contains 34 scales, covering 26 work roles and 8 work styles. The inventory was designed to be equally applicable to both sexes. An equal number of men and women was employed in item selection and scale construction. Standard score norms on each scale were computed from combined and equally weighted male and female normative samples. Separate percentile norms in terms of male and female subgroups are also available as supplementary data. Norms were derived from large samples of college and high school students in the United States and Canada, chosen so as to encompass a wide range of geographic and community characteristics.

A high score on any of the 34 JVIS scales indicates interest in the things people do in a particular field of work, as well as in the way people in that work context are expected to act. In interpreting a score profile, the first step is to examine the high and low scale scores, in order to obtain a general picture of the individual's broad areas of interest. The JVIS can be hand-scored quickly and conveniently for the 34 scales, and the raw scores can be transferred directly to the profile chart, on which they are converted to standard scores with a mean of 30 and an *SD* of 10. Computer scoring, however, provides several additional score analyses in a short, two-page report. There is also an extended, computerized narrative report, giving individualized descriptive and interpretive material as well as other information to aid in career exploration.

Some of the available score analyses involve evaluations of the profile as a whole, in which the respondent's profile is compared with modal profiles obtained by college students enrolled in different academic programs and by persons engaged in different occupations. The mean scores of the college students on each scale were obtained directly by testing male and female entering freshmen admitted to various colleges of the Pennsylvania State University. Although these means are available in the manual for inspectional comparisons, the computer reports provide an index of profile similarity between the respondent's profile and the profile of each group. This index is also given for degree of similarity with the profiles of each of 32 occupational clusters.

The derivation of the occupational cluster profiles was more indirect and considerably more complex than the procedure followed for the college profiles. A look at the major steps will provide a general idea of the methodology.[4] First, a reference group was employed to establish correspondences between JVIS and SVIB basic interest scales. This group, consisting of 538 male freshmen at Pennsylvania State University, took both interest inven-

---

[4] For a full description of procedure, see Jackson (1977, Ch. 4) and Jackson and Williams (1975). A revised manual is in preparation, with anticipated publication date in 1982.

tories. From these data, a combined table of intercorrelations was prepared for both sets of scores. These intercorrelations were used in a specially developed statistical analysis to work out regression weights for predicting JVIS scores from SVIB scores. These weights were then applied to the published SVIB means for 189 male occupational groups and 89 female occupational groups. Finally, the predicted mean occupational profiles on the JVIS were further analyzed for profile similarity. This analysis led to the identification of 32 occupational clusters, each with its characteristic modal profile. In the development of these occupational clusters, male and female occupational groups were combined.

Still another interpretive analysis is based on General Occupational Themes. Modeled after Holland' six themes (used in the SVIB), this analysis was based on a new factor analysis of JVIS data, which yielded 10 themes: Expressive, Logical, Inquiring, Practical, Assertive, Socialized, Helping, Conventional, Enterprising, and Communicative. The larger number of factors, or themes, found with the JVIS is attributed to the larger number of basic interest scales and to the greater scale independence which resulted from the method of scale construction. In the computerized score reports, the individual's standing in each of the 10 themes is given in terms of percentile norms from male and female standardization groups.

Reliability of the JVIS has been investigated from several standpoints. A reliability is computed for each individual, giving an index of profile consistency. This is found by computing the individual's odd and even scores within each scale, correlating them across the 34 scales, and applying the Spearman-Brown correction. This index is provided in all computer-scored reports. When examined in a sample of high school students, these individual indices of profile consistency clustered closely around .80. Internal consistency coefficients for each of the 34 scales, computed in the usual way on a large high school sample, ranged from .70 to .91. Test-retest reliability was investigated with college and medical school groups over intervals of one or two weeks. Median coefficients were in the .80s. Stability of the total profile over a two-week interval was investigated by correlating each individual's scores on the 34 scales on the two occasions. For 54 university students, the median correlation was .87, with a range from .59 to .96. For the same group, the correlation between General Occupational Theme scores on the two occasions averaged .94.

Data for the *construct validity* of the JVIS derive largely from the test construction procedures, including item analysis, scale intercorrelations, and factor analyses. In addition, the mean scores obtained by college students in different academic programs, as well as the predicted means of particular occupational groups, provide data pertaining to *criterion-related validation*. As research with this inventory continues, additional empirical data on educational and occupational groups should become available. Such data are needed for both validation and interpretive purposes.

OTHER OCCUPATIONAL INTEREST INVENTORIES. It will be recalled that each of the comprehensive programs for career exploration described in Chapter 15 includes some measure of occupational interests, which is used in combination with multiple-aptitude test scores and job information. Interest data are included in the Career Planning Questionnaire employed with the Differential Aptitude Tests. The United States Employment Service *Guide for Occupational Exploration* groups occupations by major interest areas as well as by ability patterns; the USES Interest Inventory and the shorter USES Interest Check List are designed to assist individuals in exploring their occupational interests for this purpose. Interest tests are also incorporated in Planning Career Goals, a system for career exploration that originated in the longitudinal studies of Project TALENT.

Some interest inventories are noteworthy because they were designed for special groups or because they illustrate special features in test construction or administration. The Career Assessment Inventory (Johansson, 1976; Johansson, C. B. & Johansson, J. C., 1978) is patterned closely after the SVIB-SCII. In contrast to those instruments, however, it was designed specifically for persons seeking a career that does *not* require a four-year college degree or advanced professional training. It concentrates on skilled trades, clerical and technical work, and semiprofessional occupations. Examples of the 89 currently available occupational scales are auto mechanic, dental hygienist, cafeteria worker, keypunch operator, and registered nurse. Test construction procedures are of high quality, and the psychometric properties of the instrument are impressive, especially in view of its recency.

The Kuder interest inventories have been in use almost as long as the Strong series. The earliest was the Kuder Preference Record—Vocational, whose approach to the measurement of interest differed from the Strong in two major ways. First, Kuder used forced-choice triad items, in which the respondents indicated which of the three activities they would like most and which least. Second, scores were obtained, not for specific occupations, but for 10 broad interest areas. Items for each scale were formulated and tentatively grouped on the basis of content validity; final item selection was based on internal consistency and low correlations with other scales. The Kuder General Interest Survey was developed later as a revision and downward extension of the Kuder Preference Record—Vocational. Designed for Grades 6 to 12, this form uses simpler language and easier vocabulary, requiring only a sixth-grade reading level.

Still another version, the Kuder Occupational Interest Survey, has been developed through criterion keying procedures similar to those followed with the SVIB (Kuder, 1966, 1970, 1979). Unlike the SVIB and an earlier Kuder occupational form, however, this form does not employ a general reference group. Instead, the individual's score on each occupational scale is expressed as a correlation between his or her interest pattern and the interest pattern of the particular occupational group.[5] This interest survey cannot be hand-scored; answer sheets are returned to the publisher for computer scoring. Scores are currently available for 127 specific occupational groups and 48 college majors. Thus far, some scales have been developed only on men, some only on women, and some on both. Scores on all scales, however, are reported for both male and female respondents. The occupations covered by this inventory vary widely in level, ranging from beautician and truck driver to chemist and lawyer. The elimination of a reference group permits this broad coverage within a single instrument.

Through intensive statistical analysis of the scores of 3,000 persons (100 in each of 30 core groups representative of the occupations and college-major fields covered by the inventory), Kuder demonstrated that better differentiation between occupational groups can be achieved with the scoring system employed in this survey than with the occupational scales derived through the use of a general reference group. The same 30 scales have been employed in extensive analyses of retest reliability, intercorrelation of scores on different scales, and other technical aspects of the inventory. In all these analyses, the Occupational Interest Survey appears to be highly satisfactory. Research on other occupational scales is continuing, especially in nontraditional occupations for men and women.

Another approach to the assessment of occupational interests is illustrated by the Self-Directed Search (SDS). This instrument was developed by Holland, whose hexagonal model of general occupational themes has attracted wide attention and was incorporated in the SCII (Holland, 1973, 1979; Holland & Gottfredson, 1976). As its title implies, the SDS was designed as a self-administered, self-scored, and self-interpreted vocational counseling instrument. Although organized around interests, the procedure also calls for self-ratings of abilities and reported competencies. The individual fills out the Self-Assessment Booklet, scores the responses, and calculates six summary scores corresponding to the themes of the Holland model (Realistic, Investigative, Artistic, Social, Enterprising, Conventional). The three highest summary scores are used to find a three-letter code.[6] An accompanying booklet, the Occupations Finder, is employed to locate, among 500 occupations, those whose codes resemble the respondent's summary code. These occupations were chosen so as to represent more than 99% of all workers; with a conversion code, the user can also explore all occupations in the *Dictionary of Occupational Titles*. Additional instructions, procedures, and

[5] The correlation employed is the lambda coefficient developed by Clemans (1958). This is essentially a point-biserial correlation adjusted for differences in homogeneity of different criterion groups. The dichotomous variable consists of the marked versus unmarked responses on the individual's answer sheet; the continuous variable is the proportion of persons in the criterion group marking each response.

[6] Although the SDS is designed to be self-scoring, the manual recommends some supervision and checking of scores, since an error rate of 3%–4% was found with the 1977 form.

sources of information are provided to facilitate the individual's career decisions.

The SDS has already been widely used in a variety of settings and has generated considerable research, both by the author and by independent investigators. In the few years since its publication, it has undergone repeated revisions to simplify procedure and reduce sex bias in career decisions. Its chief practical appeal stems from its brevity and simplicity, its do-it-yourself feature, and its role in expanding the individual's career options. With regard to the psychometric properties of the SDS, indices of reliability are generally satisfactory for the summary scores. Construct validation of the basic six themes relies principally on the earlier research that led to the formulation of these themes. Specific hypothesis have thus far received mixed support, and Holland (1979) recognizes that much research is still needed regarding the implementation of the model. Validity data reported for the SDS itself are meager. There is still controversy among psychometricians and counselors about the underlying theory and the scoring and interpretive procedures of the SDS. The rapid rate at which research on this instrument is accumulating should help to resolve some of these debatable questions.

From a different perspective, Holland's general approach to the assessment of vocational interests is in line with certain developments in the psychology of career decisions. Super (1953, 1957) has repeatedly maintained that vocational choice is the implementation of a self-concept. There is a growing accumulation of research literature dealing with personality differences among occupational groups (see, e.g., Anastasi, 1979, pp. 426–430; Osipov, 1973, Ch. 6; Pietrofesa & Splete, 1975, Ch. 4; Super & Bohn, 1970, Ch. 5). Occupational choice often reflects the individual's basic emotional needs. And occupational adjustment is a major component of general life adjustment. The assessment of vocational interests—and more specifically the identification of those occupational groups whose interests and attitudes the individual shares most closely—thus becomes a focal point in the understanding of different personalities.

Holland (1966, 1973) aligns himself clearly with those who regard occupational preferences as the choice of a way of life—a choice that reflects the individual's self-concept and major personality characteristics. Each of Holland's occupational themes corresponds to a "type" or cluster of personal attributes. A given individual may be described in terms of one or more predominant types. The occupational themes also correspond to model environments in terms of which different occupational environments may be characterized. These environments comprise not only physical features and work demands but also the kinds of persons with whom the individual works (co-workers, supervisors, customers, clients, students). According to Holland, individuals seek environments that are congruent with their personality types; and such congruence enhances work satisfaction, job stability, and achievement.

ASSESSMENT OF VALUES AND RELATED VARIABLES

Since the 1960s, there has been a resurgence of interest in the assessment of values and evaluative orientations (see, e.g., Hogan, 1973; Holtzman, 1975a). The instruments designed for this purpose vary widely in methodology, content, and specific objectives. They have much in common with measures of interests and attitudes. Some also overlap tests of other personality variables, discussed in earlier and later chapters. To illustrate the scope and variety of such instruments, three examples have been chosen.

STUDY OF VALUES. A widely used and viable early instrument in this category is the Study of Values, prepared by Allport, Vernon, and Lindzey. Originally suggested by Spranger's *Types of Men* (1928), this inventory was designed to measure the relative strength of six basic interests, motives, or evaluative attitudes, as described below:

Theoretical: Characterized by a dominant interest in the discovery of truth and by an empirical, critical, rational, "intellectual" approach.

Economic: Emphasizing useful and practical values; conforming closely to the prevailing stereotype of the "average American businessman."

Aesthetic: Placing the highest value on form and harmony; judging and enjoying each unique experience from the standpoint of its grace, symmetry, or fitness.

Social: Originally defined as love of people, this category was more narrowly limited in later revisions of the test to cover only altruism and philanthropy.

Political: Primarily interested in personal power, influence, and renown; not necessarily limited to the field of politics.

Religious: Mystical, concerned with the unity of all experience, and seeking to comprehend the cosmos as a whole.

The overlap of these types with both Holland's occupational themes and Kuder's interest areas is quite evident.

Items for the Study of Values were first formulated on the basis of the theoretical framework provided by Spranger. The criterion for the final item selection was internal consistency within each of the six areas. The items are arranged in random order in the test booklet, wtih no clue regarding the categories according to which they will be scored. Each item requires the preferential rating of either two or four alternatives falling in different value categories. Two sample items are reproduced in Figure 96.

Total raw scores on each of the six values are plotted in a profile. Although normative data are provided for comparative purposes, the authors clearly recognize the ipsative nature of these scores and do not recommend

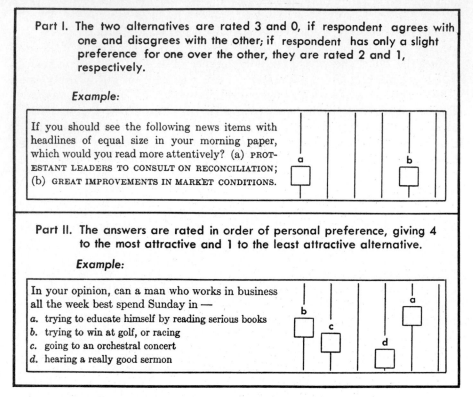

Part I. The two alternatives are rated 3 and 0, if respondent agrees with one and disagrees with the other; if respondent has only a slight preference for one over the other, they are rated 2 and 1, respectively.

Example:

If you should see the following news items with headlines of equal size in your morning paper, which would you read more attentively? (a) PROTESTANT LEADERS TO CONSULT ON RECONCILIATION; (b) GREAT IMPROVEMENTS IN MARKET CONDITIONS.

Part II. The answers are rated in order of personal preference, giving 4 to the most attractive and 1 to the least attractive alternative.

Example:

In your opinion, can a man who works in business all the week best spend Sunday in —
a. trying to educate himself by reading serious books
b. trying to win at golf, or racing
c. going to an orchestral concert
d. hearing a really good sermon

FIG. 96. Sample Items from Allport-Vernon-Lindzey Study of Values.

(Copyright © 1960 by Gordon W. Allport, Philip E. Vernon, and Gardner Lindzey. Reproduced by permission of Houghton Mifflin Company.)

the use of percentiles or other normative types of scores. Mean scores in each value are given for each sex within high school and college populations, as well as for different types of colleges and for several occupational groups. The split-half reliabilities of the six scores range from .84 to .95. Retests after one or two months yielded reliabilities between .77 and .93 for the six scales.

Validity has been checked partly by the method of contrasted groups. Profiles of various educational and occupational samples exhibit significant differences in the expected directions. For example, medical students obtained their highest scores in the theoretical area, theological students in the religious area. Some relationship has been demonstrated between value profiles and academic achievement, especially when relative achievement in different fields is considered. Data are also available on the correlation of value scores with self-ratings and associates' ratings. Other overt behavioral indices of attitudes with which scores on the Study of Values have been compared include newspaper reading, descriptions of one's "ideal person," club membership, church attendance, and the like. Significant relationships in the expected directions have likewise been reported with a number of other tests, such as SVIB and Thurstone attitude scales. Finally, some studies have shown significant changes in score following specific types of experience, such as a period of study under different styles of education.

WORK VALUES INVENTORY. A more specifically focused objective guided the development of the Work Values Inventory by Super. Designed for use in academic or vocational guidance of high school and college students, as well as in personnel selection, this self-report inventory explores the sources of satisfaction the individual seeks in his or her work. The respondent rates each of 45 work values on a 5-point scale to indicate how important it is for him or her (e.g., help others, can get a raise, make your own decisions).

The Work Values Inventory yields 15 scores, such as creativity, intellectual stimulation, associates, economic return, security, prestige, and altruism. Percentile norms by grade and sex are reported for a representative national sample of over 10,000 students in Grades 7 to 12. Occupational norms are being accumulated. Although there are only three items for each of the 15 values, an exploratory study with a high school sample yielded a median retest reliability of .83 for the scale scores over a two-week interval. Published in 1970, this inventory represents the culmination of some 20 years of research. Hence, the available validation data were gathered largely with earlier forms. Some suggestive findings on construct and concurrent validity are cited in the manual. Further research with the current form will provide a better basis for evaluating its effectiveness.

MORAL JUDGMENT SCALE. Although not providing any published or standardized instruments, the approach proposed by Kohlberg (1969, 1974) for assessing moral development has aroused interest among research workers. Following a Piagetian orientation, Kohlberg describes six stages of moral development, ranging from a premoral level, through a morality of conventional conformity, to the formulation of self-accepted moral principles. Kohlberg offers a cognitive model of moral development, based on the premise that individuals prefer the highest stage they can comprehend. The Moral Judgment Scale utilizes nine hypothetical dilemmas, presented one at a time. A typical example involves a man whose wife is dying of cancer but might be saved by a new drug for which an exorbitant price is demanded. Unable to raise the money, the husband steals the drug. The respondent judges the behavior described and states reasons for his or her judgment. In typical Piagetian *"méthode clinique,"* the interviewer elicits fuller explanations through probing questions.

Kohlberg recommends that his Moral Judgment Scale be used primarily to enhance the individual's own self-understanding and to stimulate development in the direction she or he is already moving. As a research instrument, however, the scale has psychometric weaknesses that limit the generalizability of its findings (Kurtines & Greif, 1974). Both administration and scoring need to be more highly standardized to ensure comparability of results from different investigations. No data are given on short-term stability of the individual's stage of moral judgment as assessed by the scale. Nor is there evidence of internal consistency among responses to the different dilemmas. Yet these responses are combined to yield an overall index of the maturity of moral judgment reached by the individual. Like Piaget, Kohlberg argues for an invariant sequence, or ordinality, of his stages. Thus, the attainment of a higher stage should depend on the attainment of each of the preceding stages. The evidence for such invariance, however, is meager and often questionable. In summary, while the Kohlberg scale has heuristic value in stimulating discussion in a training program, it does not appear to be an effective research instrument in its present form.

OPINION SURVEYS AND ATTITUDE SCALES

NATURE OF INSTRUMENTS. An attitude is often defined as a tendency to react favorably or unfavorably toward a designated class of stimuli, such as a national or ethnic group, a custom, or an institution. It is evident that, when so defined, attitudes cannot be directly observed, but must be inferred from overt behavior, both verbal and nonverbal. In more objective terms, the concept of attitude may be said to connote *response consistency* with regard to certain categories of stimuli. In actual practice, the term "attitude" has been most frequently associated with social stimuli and with emotionally toned responses.

Opinion is sometimes differentiated from attitude, but the proposed distinctions are neither consistent nor logically defensible. More often the two terms are used interchangeably, and they will be so employed in this discussion. With regard to assessment methodology, however, opinion surveys are traditionally distinguished from attitude scales. *Opinion surveys* are characteristically concerned with replies to specific questions, which need not be related. The answers to such questions are kept separate rather than being combined into a total score. An employee opinion survey, for example, might include questions about work schedules, rate of pay, fringe benefits, company cafeteria, and relation to supervisors; each of these items is included because of its intrinsic relevance to the improvement of employee relations. The replies to each question are separately tabulated in the effort to identify sources of employee satisfaction and dissatisfaction.

Attitude scales, on the other hand, typically yield a total score indicating the direction and intensity of the individual's attitude toward a company, group of people, policy, or other stimulus category. In the construction of an attitude scale, the different questions are designed to measure a single attitude or unidimensional variable, and some objective procedures are usually followed in the effort to approach this goal. An employee attitude scale, for example, yields a single score showing the individual's degree of job satisfaction or overall attitude toward the company.

MAJOR TYPES OF ATTITUDE SCALES. In all attitude scales, respondents indicate their agreement or disagreement with a series of statements about the object of the attitude. Special procedures have been devised in the effort to achieve unidimensionality or homogeneity of items, equality of distances between scale units, and comparability of scores from scale to scale. The technical problems involved in constructing attitude scales have received extensive attention, and the methodology has made notable theoretical and statistical advances. It is beyond the scope of this text to discuss specialized scaling techniques, which now constitute a growing area of statistical method.[7] Nevertheless, we can briefly examine three major approaches to attitude scale construction that are commonly encountered in the psychological testing literature. These approaches are represented by the Thurstone, Guttman, and Likert types of scales.

Thurstone's adaptation of psychophysical methods to the quantification of judgment data represented an important milestone in attitude scale construction (Thurstone, 1959; Thurstone & Chave, 1929). By these procedures, Thurstone and his co-workers prepared about 20 scales for measuring attitudes toward war, capital punishment, the church, patriotism, censorship, and many other institutions, practices, issues, and national or ethnic groups. The development of a *Thurstone-type scale* begins with the assembling of many statements expressing a wide range of attitude toward the object under consideration. A large number of judges are asked individually to sort the statements into piles (usually 11) for degree of favorableness. The judges do not indicate their own attitudes, but only classify the statements. The median position assigned to each statement by the judges is the scale value of that statement. The variability of the judgments is taken as an index of its ambiguity, insofar as different judges assign the statement to different categories. Items are chosen so as to exhibit minimum variability and a wide spread of scale values, approximating equal spacing across the 11-point range. In the final attitude scale, the statements are presented in random order, with no indication of their scale values. The respondent's score is the median scale value of all the statements she or he endorses.

The *Guttman-type scale* was originally developed as a technique for determining whether a set of attitude statements is unidimensional (Guttman, 1944, 1947). In Guttman's sense, a perfect scale exists if a respondent who agrees with a certain statement of a particular attitude also agrees with milder statements of that attitude. In other words, such attitude scale items can be ordered along a continuum of intensity or difficulty of accept-

---

[7] Gulliksen (1974, pp. 254–255) gives a quick overview of some important developments in this area. See also Fishbein (1967), Shaw and Wright (1967, Chs. 2 and 11), Summers (1970), J. D. Carroll (1980), and Zimbardo and Ebbesen (1970).

ance. Each person's position on the scale would thus completely determine his or her responses. If we know the most extreme statement an individual will accept, we should be able to reproduce all his or her responses. In actual practice, such reproducibility cannot be fully attained, because of errors of measurement in each response; it can only be approximated within certain limits. The essential procedure in the development of a Guttman scale is to identify a set of items that fall into an ordered sequence in terms of their endorsement by respondents. Items that do not fit this requirement are discarded. A person's score on a Guttman scale is found by examining the pattern of items that he or she endorses. It may be recalled that the same concept of ordinality, or uniform progression of performance, underlies the Piagetian scales discussed in Chapters 4 and 10.

Because the construction of a Thurstone scale requires rather elaborate procedures, and the conditions of a Guttman scale are difficult to meet in practice, Likert (1932) developed a type of scale that is easier to construct while yielding equally satisfactory reliability. The *Likert-type scale* begins with a series of statements, each of which expresses an attitude that is either clearly favorable or clearly unfavorable. Items are selected on the basis of the responses of persons to whom they are administered in the process of test construction. The principal basis for item selection is internal consistency, although external criteria are also employed when available. Likert scales call for a graded response to each statement. The response is usually expressed in terms of the following five categories: strongly agree (SA), agree (A), undecided (U), disagree (D), and strongly disagree (SD). To score the scale, the response options are credited 5, 4, 3, 2, or 1 from the favorable to the unfavorable end. For example, "strongly agree" with a favorable statement would receive a score of 5, as would "strongly disagree" with an unfavorable statement. The sum of the item credits represents the individual's total score, which must be interpreted in terms of empirically established norms.

An example of a modified Likert-type scale is the Minnesota Teacher Attitude Inventory. Each statement on this inventory is to be marked in the usual way as SA, A, U, D, or SD. The numerical weights assigned to these response options, however, were based on criterion keying, rather than on the standard 1-to-5 scale. Designed to assess pupil–teacher relations, this inventory was developed by administering over 700 items to 100 teachers nominated by their principals as superior in pupil–teacher relations and 100 nominated as inferior. Cross-validation of the resulting 150-item inventory in different groups yielded concurrent validity coefficients of .46 to .60 with a composite criterion derived from principal's estimate, pupils' ratings, and evaluations by an expert observer. Subsequent longitudinal studies by the test author found predictive validities in the .50s against the same criterion (Leeds, 1969, 1972).

Most attitude scales have been developed for use in particular research projects. Some were designed for the investigation of employee attitudes and morale. Others have been used to assess the outcome of educational and training programs. Attitude scales may contribute to the evaluation of different instructional procedures designed to modify 'particuluar attitudes. Or they may be employed in measuring the changes in student attitudes toward literature, art, different ethnic and cultural groups, or social and economic problems following a given educational program. One of the most extensive applications of attitude measurement is to be found in research in social psychology. Practically every textbook on social psychology contains sections on attitudes and their measurement. Among the many problems investigated through attitude measurement may be mentioned group differences in attitudes, the role of attitudes in intergroup relations, background factors associated with the development of attitudes, the interrelation of attitudes (including factor analyses), trends and temporal shifts in attitudes, and the experimental alteration of attitudes through interpolated experiences. Few attitude scales have been published, although most are fully described in the research literature. An extensive collection of attitude scales constructed for a variety of purposes was assembled in a book by Shaw and Wright (1967). Information about more recently developed measures of certain attitudes and values, such as alienation and anomie, self-esteem, and locus of control, can be found in *Measures of Social Psychological Attitudes* by Robinson and Shaver (1973).

LOCUS OF CONTROL

The construct described as "locus of control" first came into prominence with the publication of a monograph by Rotter (1966). In this publication, Rotter presented the scale he had developed to assess the individual's generalized expectancies for internal versus external control of reinforcement (I-E Scale). This instrument was constructed within the context of social-learning theory. In explaining its use, Rotter wrote, "The effect of reinforcement following some behavior . . . is not a simple stamping-in process but depends upon whether or not the person perceives a causal relationship between his own behavior and the reward" (1966, p. 1). Internal control refers to the perception of an event as contingent upon one's own behavior or one's relatively permanent characteristics. External control, on the other hand, indicates that a positive or negative reinforcement following some action of the individual is perceived as not being entirely contingent upon his or her own action but the result of chance, fate, or luck; or it may be perceived as under the control of powerful others and unpredictable because of the complexity of forces surroundng the individual.

The I-E scale is a forced-choice self-report inventory. Two illustrative items are given in Table 32. The complete list of items, together with standard instructions for administering them, can be found in Rotter's monograph (1966). Considerable information is available regarding the I-E scale. Split-

TABLE 32

Illustrative Items from Internal-External (I-E) Scale

(From Rotter, 1966, p. 11. Copyright 1966 by the American Psychological Association. Reprinted by permission.)

(a) In the long run, people get the respect they deserve in this world.

(b) Unfortunately, an individual's worth often passes unrecognized no matter how hard he tries.

(a) Becoming a success is a matter of hard work; luck has little or nothing to do with it.

(b) Getting a good job depends mainly on being in the right place at the right time.

Instructions state: "This is a questionnaire to find out the way in which certain important events in our society affect different people. . . . Please select the one statement of each pair (*and only one*) which you more strongly *believe* to be the case as far as you're concerned."

half and Kuder-Richardson reliabilities of total scores cluster around .70. Retest reliabilities after intervals of one to two months are at the same level but vary somewhat with the length of the interval, conditions of administration, and nature of the group. Correlations with social desirability scores and interest tests are low. The original publication gives preliminary percentile norms on several hundred male and female students from a single university, together with means and SDs of some dozen other samples comprising mostly college groups. Data on many other groups have subsequently accumulated from independent research projects. A substantial body of data on construct validity is also available. Factorial analyses indicate that a single general factor can account for most of the response variance. Other factor analyses, however, suggest that the construct may be subdivided into several distinguishable factors, as illustrated by a belief in a difficult world, an unjust world, an unpredictable world, and a politically unresponsive world (Collins, 1974). Several later studies likewise found a multifactorial structure in measures of locus of control (Garza & Widlak, 1977; Kendall, Finch, Little, Chirico, & Ollendick, 1978; Zuckerman & Gerbasi (1977).

Comparable scales have been developed for use with school-age and preschool children (see, e.g., Herzberger, Linney, Seidman, & Rappaport, 1979; Mischel, Zeiss, & Zeiss, 1974; Nowicki & Duke, 1974, 1979; Stephens & Delys, 1973). Reproductions of available scales, with normative data, can be found in two books by Lefcourt (1976) and Phares (1976), which also summarize much of the research on locus of control. Research on this personality construct continues with undiminished vigor (Jackson & Paunonen,

1980, pp. 535–537). Locus of control is being investigated in relation to such performance variables as learning, creative thinking, and achievement drive, and such demographic variables as sex, socioeconomic level, and ethnic identification. A study on schoolchildren reported a significant positive relation between external locus of control and depression, and a significant negative relation between both variables and academic achievement (Tesiny, Lefkowitz, & Gordon, 1980). A longitudinal investigation of a representative national sample of nearly 3,000 adult men found that locus of control is significantly related to indices of occupational success (Andrisana & Nestel, 1976). In the same investigation, there was also evidence that success in the world of work itself enhances the expectancy of internal control. It is clear that the available instruments for assessing locus of control are playing a significant part in ongoing personality research.

SEX ROLES AND ANDROGYNY

ANTECEDENTS. In the extensive psychological research on sex differences, several investigators have used self-report inventories designed to assess the respondents' sex-role concepts, personal preferences for traditional male or female activities, or their own sex-role identification. The pioneer instrument for measuring the psychological construct designated as masculinity-femininity (M-F) was developed by Terman and Miles (1936).[8] Although some of the subtests in this instrument were of the self-report type, other paper-and-pencil procedures were also included. Essentially, items were selected empirically in terms of the relative frequency of each response given by males and by females in the American culture of the time. The resulting inventory, labeled "Attitude-Interest Analysis," included seven subtests: Word Association, Inkblot Association, Information, Emotional and Ethical Attitudes, Interests, Personalities and Opinions, and Introvertive Response.

The next two decades saw the development of several second-generation M-F scales. The most widely used examples are the M-F scales included in the Strong Vocational Interest Blank, the MMPI, the California Psychological Inventory, and the Guilford-Zimmerman Temperament Survey. Although all followed the basic Terman-Miles model of empirical item selection and criterion keying, details of construction in each case produced differences in emphasis and content coverage. Nor did the scales correlate very highly with each other, most correlations falling in the .40s and .50s.

One feature they all shared, however, is that they were shorter than the Terman-Miles and yielded a single global score. Although Terman and Miles also worked principally with their total score, it was possible to obtain scores on the separate subtests. And the authors themselves reported some provocative results from subtest score analyses. Groups with the same

[8] For an excellent survey of early M-F instruments, together with their methodological and interpretive problems, see Constantinople (1973)

total score could achieve that score through different patterns of subtest scores. For example, among the most "masculine" groups in terms of total M-F index were high school boys and engineers. Both obtained identical mean total scores, but the high masculinity of the high school boys resulted largely from their Interests and Information subscores, while that of the engineers was due primarily to their scores on Ethical and Emotional Attitudes. On the latter subtest, the high school boys were actually more feminine than the general male population. Similarly, women artists averaged significantly more feminine than the women's norms in Interests, but more masculine in the Information subtest. Factor analyses of both the original Terman-Miles (Ford & Tyler, 1952) and other instruments identified several relatively independent item clusters, but these clusters were rarely used in scoring or interpretation.

Another limitation of both first- and second-generation M-F scales arises from their bipolarity. All were constructed on the assumption that masculinity and femininity represent opposite poles of a single, bipolar scale. Yet even in the original results reported by Terman and Miles, there was evidence that masculinity and femininity might be two variables whose intercorrelation fell far short of the implied -1.00. For instance, at higher educational levels, the sex differentiation in M-F scores tended to become less sharp, both men and women giving more responses characteristic of the other sex. These early results are suggestive of androgyny, although the term did not come into use in this context until many years later.

CURRENT DEVELOPMENTS. Against this background, we can examine the third-generation M-F instruments, appearing in the 1970s and still in the process of evolving. Among the best-known examples are the Bem Sex-Role Inventory (Bem, 1974, 1977, 1981) and the Personal Attributes Questionnaire developed by Spence and Helmreich (1978). A children's form of the latter has also been constructed (Hall & Halberstadt, 1980). These third-generation instruments have made significant strides toward eliminating certain limitations of the earlier instruments. First, the items are selected in terms of judges' ratings of their relative desirability for males or females and the degree to which they characterize each sex in our society. This procedure helps in sharpening the scale definition, clarifying content coverage, and reducing chance variance in scores. Second, masculinity and femininity are treated as independent (and probably orthogonal) variables; and persons high on both are classified as androgynous. Third, some efforts are being made to recognize multidimensionality through the empirical identification of item clusters and the consideration of situational influences.

As the term "androgyny" is currently used in personality research, it characterizes the individual who manifests the favorable traits ascribed to *both* sexes, as in combining assertiveness and competence with compassion, warmth, and emotional expressiveness. Thus, the androgynous person should be more flexible and more capable of adapting to varying situational demands than is the traditionally sex-typed person. It has been hypothesized that androgyny should be associated with effective interpersonal behavior and with psychological well-being. Research findings on this relationship, however, are mixed (Hall & Halberstadt, 1980; Jackson & Paunonen, 1980; Kelly & Worell, 1977; Worell, 1978). The relationship is probably complex and is influenced by the sociocultural context and the criterion employed in assessing effectiveness or well-being. With regard to available instruments for measuring masculinity-femininity, all are still in a formative stage. Both the underlying personality theory and the test construction procedures are in the process of development. Some serious unsolved methodological problems remain (Jackson & Paunonen, 1980; Kelly & Worell, 1977; Worell, 1978). More information is needed, for example, on the factorial composition of the construct measured by different instruments and on the adequacy with which the social desirability response tendency has been controlled.

HEALTH-RELATED INVENTORIES

In the rapidly growing field of health psychology (APA, 1976; Anastasi, 1979, Ch. 18; Haynes, Taylor, & Sackett, 1979; Stone, Cohen, Adler, et al., 1979), which bridges the gap between psychology and medicine, the diverse contributions of psychologists have included the development of new types of behavioral measurement instruments. These instruments are designed to provide systematic and standardized behavioral information about individuals that can be useful in general medical practice. In their development, some of these instruments have employed psychometric procedures of high technical quality. To illustrate the range of functions served, we shall consider three types of health-related inventories whose purposes vary widely.

JENKINS ACTIVITY SURVEY. Several standardized personality inventories, as well as life-history data, have been used in research on the personality patterns associated with susceptibility to certain diseases, such as cancer, tuberculosis, and coronary disorders, and with recovery from such conditions. More recently, special instruments have been developed for particular diseases. One of the best-known examples concerns the association of Type-A personality with proneness to coronary heart disease. This association was identified and intensively investigated by two cardiologists, Friedman and Rosenman (1969), through laboratory, clinical, and epidemiological studies. In their major research, these cardiologists used a structured interview, covering not only the verbal content but also the individual's behavior during the interview. The validation of the Type-A construct was based on both cross-sectional and longitudinal studies of a large sample of employed, middle-aged men (Rosenman, 1978; Rosenman, Friedman, Straus, Jenkins, Zyzanski, & Wurm, 1975).

Several other procedures were investigated to approximate the intensive clinical interview, including a battery of performance tests and a short rating scale. The Jenkins Activity Survey (JAS), a 52-item self-report inventory, was developed for the same purpose by Jenkins, Zyzanski, and Rosenman (1979). As defined in this inventory, Type-A behavior is characterized by extreme competitiveness, striving for achievement, aggressiveness, impatience, haste, restlessness, and feelings of being challenged by responsibility and under pressure of time (Jenkins et al., 1979, p. 3). In contrast, Type-B persons, although they may also be interested in progress and achievement, are characterized by a relaxed, unhurried, mellow style. In its present form, the JAS yields a total Type-A score, as well as scores for three components identified through factor analysis, namely, a Speed and Impatience factor, a Job Involvement factor, and a Hard-Driving and Competitive factor.

Validity of this inventory was investigated against results obtained with the structured interview and, more directly, through both retrospective and predictive studies of the occurrence of coronary heart disease. The JAS was standardized on a sample of approximately 2,500 men aged 48 to 64, holding middle- to upper-level jobs in 10 large corporations in California. Means and SDs of many subsequently tested groups are also provided, as a way of adjusting the interpretation of individual scores for occupational, educational, geographic, and cultural differences. Although item content is appropriate for both sexes, relatively few female groups were tested. There are still unanswered questions about the meaning of the construct. For instance, there is some evidence that coronory proneness may be related, not so much to achievement drive and upward mobility, as to the frustration and anger of motivated strivers whose achievement lags behind their ambition (Hinkle, Whitney, & Lehman, 1968; Spielberger, Crane, & Rosenman, 1982).

MILLON BEHAVIORAL HEALTH INVENTORY. The medical practitioner often needs information about the patient's characteristic coping styles, attitudes toward illness and treatment, and other personality tendencies that may substantially affect the individual's reaction to treatment and the course of the illness. Personality inventories designed for use with psychiatric patients are usually inappropriate for a nonpsychiatric medical population. The Millon Behavioral Health Inventory (MBHI) represents an attempt to combine in a single instrument a set of variables judged to be particularly relevant to assessment and decision making in general medical settings (Millon, Green, & Meagher, 1979a, 1979b).

Consisting of 150 self-descriptive statements to be marked true or false by the respondent, the MBHI yields scores on 20 scales. The largest number of scales pertain to basic personality styles that are likely to influence the patient's relation to health-care personnel. These personality styles are designated as introversive, inhibited, cooperative, sociable, confident, forceful, respectful, and sensitive. Another set of scales was designed to identify long-standing attitudes or recent stresses that may interfere with treatment and recovery. Examples include chronic tension, recent upsetting experiences, habitual pessimism, bleak outlook, and social alienation. The third set of scales assesses the individual's similarity to patients with psychosomatic complications (e.g., allergies, gastrointestinal susceptibility) and to those showing poor response to either illness or treatment interventions. The scales in the third set were empirically derived by selecting those items in the final inventory that differentiated between patients who exhibited the specified behavior and those with the same physical illness who did not. These empirical scales were cross-validated one or more times.

The construction and validation of the entire inventory followed three major steps: (1) preparation of a theoretically based item pool; (2) item analysis for internal consistency within scales; and (3) criterion-related validation of scale scores. Thus far, criterion-related validation of the final inventory has employed chiefly correlations with other diagnostic inventories; and the correlational pattern generally fits theoretical expectation. Norms were derived from both patient and nonpatient samples, chosen so as to range across socioeconomic levels and ethnic groups. Hand scoring, while possible, is complicated and time-consuming. Machine scoring is available, with a printed profile report and an automated interpretive report if desired. The inventory has already been widely used in several medical settings, such as pain clinics, cancer centers, renal dialysis programs, and health maintenance organizations. Plans for ongoing and future research include assessment of the entire inventory through criterion-related validation and studies of the generalizability of validity and norms with diverse populations.

HEALTH STATUS MEASURES. Still another application of psychometric techniques to medical problems is illustrated by the development of health status measures. An example of such a measure is provided by the Sickness Impact Profile (SIP). Developed by an interdisciplinary team, this instrument exemplifies an effective cooperative enterprise of high technical quality (Bergner, Bobbitt, et al., 1981; Bergner & Gilson, 1981). The SIP yields scores in 12 categories: sleep and rest, eating, work, home management, recreation and pastimes, ambulation, mobility, body care and movement, social interaction, alertness behavior (e.g., confusion and disorientation, decision making, learning new things), emotional behavior, and communication. Items within each category cover the full range from normal behavior to extreme dysfunction. The form can be filled out by the respondent or by an interviewer. In either case, the patient is asked to indicate which statements describe his or her performance or state of health *on that day.*

Equal-interval scaling was employed in item selection. As in the Thurstone-type scales, judges rated items on an 11-point scale for degree of dysfunction. Ratings for total patient protocols correlated highly with the total health status score computed from item responses. Various techniques were employed to assess test-retest reliability across forms, occasions, and interviewers, as well as internal consistency of response patterns. Validity for each scale was investigated against assessments of status by the patient, by the clinician, and by another instrument. The resulting correlations were analyzed in a complete multitrait-multimethod matrix. Norms were established on a stratified random sample of the members of a health plan. Profiles of patients with particular illnesses, such as arthritis or hyperthyroid condition, closely approximated the mean profile for that illness. More than eight years of research, development, and field trials went into the construction of the SIP. Its production is a noteworthy example of the use of sophisticated psychometric methodology in the burgeoning field of health psychology.

A comprehensive approach to the measurement of health is provided by a long-term research project conducted by R. M. Kaplan and his associates (R. M. Kapan, 1980; Kaplan, Bush, & Berry, 1976). The Index of Well-Being designed in this project also utilizes the respondent's report of his or her actual performance at the time. The data include the person's function level, assessed along three scales: mobility, physical activity, and social activity. The items were developed after an exhaustive survey of all the ways that disease or injury can affect one's behavior and role performance. In addition, the index takes into account the presence of specific symptoms and problems, both overt (e.g., vomiting, paralyzed limb), and subjective (e.g., pain, dizziness). In the development of the index, the various combinations of function levels and symptom/problem categories were evaluated on an equal-interval scale of well-being through judgments obtained in systematic community surveys. The resulting scale values proved to be relatively independent of socioeconomic, ethnic, and other demographic variables of the judges. The scale ranges from complete freedom from dysfunctions that interfere with normal life activities, at one end, to death, at the other. The resulting Index of Well-Being has been subjected to extensive research that demonstrates its content and construct validity. It has proved useful in planning therapy and rehabilitation programs and in evaluating the individual's response to therapy.

A further index is the Well-Life Expectancy, which adds a temporal dimension to the Index of Well-Being. The time unit employed for this purpose is a "well year." For example, a disease that reduces one's quality of life by one-fourth will take away .25 of a well year over the course of a year. A treatment that improves the quality of life by one-tenth for each person will produce one well year if this effect occurs for 10 persons over one year. With this index, the usual life expectancy can be adjusted for the quality of life the individual is able to enjoy as a result of his or her health status.

Such an index provides a comprehensive social indicator for health, which is applicable on a national or a community basis. It can be used in comparing the relative effectiveness of different preventive or treatment programs. It can also contribute to public-health policy decisions by directing attention to the health-related quality of life, in addition to the traditional focus on increasing life expectancy as such.

CHAPTER 19

Projective Techniques

THE AVAILABLE supply of projective techniques is large and diversified. In this chapter, we shall consider the major varieties of such techniques, together with some well-known examples. Except for special points peculiar to particular techniques, no critical evaluation of individual instruments will be undertaken. Instead, a summary evaluation of projective techniques will be given in a separate section, with emphasis on common methodological problems. Projective techniques present a curious discrepancy between research and practice. When evaluated as psychometric instruments, the large majority make a poor showing. Yet their popularity in clinical use continues unabated (Klopfer & Taulbee, 1976; Wade & Baker, 1977). The nature and implications of this inconsistency will be examined in the last section.

The literature on projective techniques is vast, running to over 4,000 references on a single instrument. For a broader coverage of available projective techniques, the reader is referred to the survey by Klopfer and Taulbee (1976). The *Mental Measurements Yearbooks* contain a separate section on projective techniques, in which multiple reviews are given for some of the more popular instruments.

NATURE OF PROJECTIVE TECHNIQUES

A major distinguishing feature of projective techniques is to be found in their assignment of a relatively *unstructured* task, i.e., a task that permits an almost unlimited variety of possible responses. In order to allow free play to the individual's fantasy, only brief, general instructions are provided. For the same reason, the test stimuli are usually vague or ambiguous. The underlying hypothesis is that the way in which the individual perceives and interprets the test material, or "structures" the situation, will reflect fundamental aspects of her or his psychological functioning. In other words, it is expected that the test materials will serve as a sort of screen on which respondents "project" their characteristic thought processes, needs, anxieties, and conflicts.

Typically, projective instruments also represent *disguised* testing procedures, insofar as examinees are rarely aware of the type of psychological interpretation that will be made of their responses. Projective techniques are likewise characterized by a *global* approach to the appraisal of personality. Attention is focused on a composite picture of the whole personality, rather than on the measurement of separate traits. Finally, projective techniques are usually regarded by their exponents as especially effective in revealing *covert, latent,* or *unconscious* aspects of personality. Moreover, the more unstructured the test, it is argued, the more sensitive it is to such covert material. This follows from the assumption that the more unstructured or ambiguous the stimuli, the less likely they are to evoke defensive reactions on the part of the respondent.

Projective methods originated within a clinical setting and have remained predominantly a tool for the clinician. Some have evolved from therapeutic procedures (such as art therapy) employed with psychiatric patients. In their theoretical framework, most projective techniques reflect the influence of psychoanalytic concepts. There have also been scattered attempts to lay a foundation for projective techniques in stimulus-response theory and in perceptual theories of personality (see Lindzey, 1977). It should be noted, of course, that the specific techniques need not be evaluated in the light of their particular theoretical slants or historical origins. A procedure may prove to be practically useful or empirically valid for reasons other than those initially cited to justify its introduction.

In line with their typically global approach, projective techniques have been concerned not only with emotional, motivational, and interpersonal characteristics but also with certain intellectual aspects of behavior. Examples of the latter include general intellectual level, originality, and problem-solving styles. It might be added that any psychological test, regardless of the purpose for which it was designed, may serve as a projective instrument. Intelligence tests, for example, have been employed in this fashion by some clinicians (Fromm, Hartman, & Marschak, 1957).

INKBLOT TECHNIQUES

THE RORSCHACH. One of the most popular projective techniques is that employing the Rorschach inkblots. Developed by the Swiss psychiatrist Hermann Rorschach (1942), this technique was first described in 1921. Although standardized series of inkblots had previously been utilized by psychologists in studies of imagination and other functions, Rorschach was the first to apply inkblots to the diagnostic investigation of the personality as a whole. In the development of this technique, Rorschach experimented with a large number of inkblots, which he administered to different psychiatric groups. As a result of such clinical observations, those response characteristics that differentiated between the various psychiatric syndromes were gradually incorporated into the scoring system. The scoring procedures were further sharpened by supplementary testing of mental retardates, normals, artists, scholars, and other persons of known characteristics.

Rorschach's methodology thus represented an early, informal, and relatively subjective application of criterion keying.

The Rorschach utilizes 10 cards, on each of which is printed a bilaterally symmetrical inkblot similar to that illustrated in Figure 97. Five of the blots are executed in shades of gray and black only; two contain additional touches of bright red; and the remaining three combine several pastel shades. As the examinee is shown each inkblot, he or she is asked to tell what the blot could represent. Besides keeping a verbatim record of the responses to each card, the examiner notes time of responses, position or positions in which cards are held, spontaneous remarks, emotional expressions, and other incidental behavior of the examinee during the test session. Following the presentation of all 10 cards, the examiner questions the individual systematically regarding the parts and aspects of each blot to which the associations were given. During this inquiry, the respondents also have an opportunity to clarify and elaborate their earlier responses.

While several systems for scoring and interpreting the Rorschach have been developed, the most common scoring categories include location, determinants, and content. *Location* refers to the part of the blot with which the examinee associates each response. Does he or she use the whole blot, a common detail, an unusual detail, white space, or some combination of these areas? The *determinants* of the response include form, color, shading, and "movement." Although there is of course no movement in the blot itself, the respondent's perception of the blot as a representation of a moving object is scored in this category. Further differentiations are made within these categories. For example, human movement, animal movement, and abstract or inanimate movement are separately scored. Similarly, shading

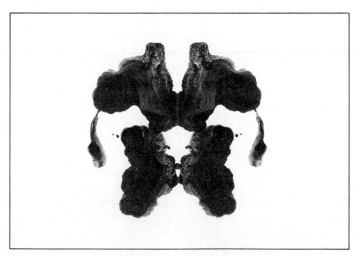

FIG. 97. An Inkblot of the Type Employed in the Rorschach Technique.

may be perceived as representing depth, texture, hazy forms such as clouds, or achromatic reproductions of colors as in a photograph.

The treatment of *content* varies from one scoring system to another, although certain major categories are regularly employed. Chief among these are human figures, human details (or parts of human figures), animal figures, animal details, and anatomical diagrams. Other broad scoring categories include inanimate objects, plants, maps, clouds, blood, X-rays, sexual objects, and symbols. A *popularity* score is often found on the basis of the relative frequency of different responses among people in general. For each of the 10 cards, certain responses, if given by the examinee, are scored as popular because of their common occurrence.

Further analysis of Rorschach responses is based on the relative number of responses falling into the various categories, as well as on certain ratios and interrelations among different categories. Examples of the sort of qualitative interpretations that have commonly been utilized with Rorschach responses include the association of "whole" responses with conceptual thinking, of "color" responses with emotionality, and "human movement" responses with imagination and fantasy life. In the usual application of the Rorschach, major emphasis is placed on the final "global" description of the individual, in which the clinician integrates the results from different parts of the protocol and takes into account the interrelations of different scores and indices. In actual practice, information derived from outside sources, such as other tests, interviews, and case history records, is also utilized in preparing these global descriptions.

Although the Rorschach is considered to be applicable from the preschool to the adult level, its normative data were originally derived in large part from adult groups. This limitation also characterizes the general fund of clinical experience accumulated through the use of the Rorschach and employed in the qualitative interpretation of protocols. In the effort to extend the empirical framework for Rorschach interpretation to other age groups, Ames and her co-workers at the Gesell Institute of Child Development at Yale collected and published Rorschach norms on children between the ages of 2 and 10 years, on adolescents between the ages of 10 and 16, and on older persons from the age of 70 up (Ames, Metraux, Rodell, & Walker, 1973, 1974; Ames, Metraux, & Walker, 1971). A comprehensive and integrated summary of published normative data for children and adolescents was prepared by Levitt and Truumaa (1972). Combining data from 15 studies, the authors provide means of various quantitative Rorschach indices by intellectual level and by age up to 16 years.

Some of the underlying assumptions of traditional Rorschach scoring have been called into question by a growing body of research findings. Comparative studies with standard and achromatic series of Rorschach cards, for example, demonstrated that color itself has no effect on most of the response characteristics customarily attributed to it (Baughman, 1958). There is also evidence that verbal aptitude influences several Rorschach scores commonly interpreted as indicators of personality traits (Lotsof, 1953; Sachman, 1952). In one study (Sachman, 1952), an analysis of the verbal complexity of individual Rorschach responses given by 100 persons revealed that "movement" responses tended to be longer and linguistically more complex than "form" responses. It was also found that verbal complexity of Rorschach responses was highly correlated with the respondents' scores on a verbal aptitude test, as well as with age and educational level.

A major complicating factor in the interpretation of Rorschach scores is the total number of responses—known as response productivity, or R (Fiske & Baughman, 1953). Because of large individual differences in R, the practice of considering the absolute number of responses in various categories is obviously misleading. If two individuals or groups differ in R, they are also likely to differ in the same direction in the number of responses falling in specific categories. Thus, the differences found in certain categories may be only an artifact resulting from the variation in total number of responses. Nor is the use of percentages a completely satisfactory solution. For example, a protocol containing many responses is likely to include a smaller *proportion* of "whole" responses, since the number of "whole" responses that can reasonably be perceived in the blots is quite limited, while associations to isolated details of the blots may continue indefinitely.

To these intrinsic characteristics of the Rorschach scores may be added the empirical fact that response productivity appears to be closely related to age, intellectual level, and amount of education. Even more disturbing is the finding that R varies significantly from one examiner to another. All of these results suggest that R, which may itself be a major determinant of many of the common Rorschach scores, is influenced by factors quite extraneous to the basic personality variables allegedly measured by the Rorschach. Findings such as these strike at the very foundation on which the entire elaborate superstructure of Rorschach scoring is supported.

Within the mass of negative and inconclusive research findings about the Rorschach, a few encouraging trends can be noted. A handbook by Goldfried, Stricker, and Weiner (1971) presents a systematic survey of available data on norms, reliability, and validity for a number of specific applications of the Rorschach technique in both research and clinical practice. Examples of these applications include proposed sets of scoring signs for developmental level, hostility, anxiety, and brain dysfunction. Each application is accompanied by a thorough and well-balanced evaluation of its strengths and weaknesses. The authors conclude that, while several of the Rorschach indices surveyed have demonstrated enough validity to justify their use in research, their suitability for clinical use has not been sufficiently established. They offer methodological suggestions for the kinds of research needed to provide adequate evaluation of each technique. They also conclude that the Rorschach appears most promising when used as a direct measure of cognitive style and perceptual organization, or as a structured interview in the hands of a skilled clinician. Results are least encouraging when the Rorschach is used to elicit fantasy production for psychoanalytic and other symbolic interpretations.

The most ambitious effort to put the Rorschach on a psychometrically sound basis was undertaken by Exner (1974, 1978; Wiener-Levy & Exner, 1981). First, Exner (1974) developed a comprehensive Rorschach system which integrated elements culled from the diverse scoring systems followed by different clinicians and researchers. For this comprehensive system, he provides standardized administrative, scoring, and interpretive procedures. The emphasis is on structural rather than content variables, and on the utilization of ratios, indices, and combinations of variables, rather than single scores. Using this uniform system, Exner (1978) and his associates have already collected a considerable body of psychometric data, including adult and child norms on many Rorschach variables, obtained from both patient and nonpatient samples. Studies of retest reliability over several time intervals indicated considerable temporal stability for most of the scored variables. Results are also reported from a number of experiments that contribute to the construct validation of Rorschach variables. The interpretations are not linked to any one personality theory but are predominantly data-based. A major contribution of Exner's work is the provision of a uniform Rorschach system that permits comparability among the research findings of different investigators. The availability of this system, together with the research completed thus far, has injected new life into the Rorschach as a potential psychometric instrument.

An alternative approach to the Rorschach, more strongly clinical in its orientation, is described by Aronow and Reznikoff (1976). This approach treats the Rorschach essentially as a semistandardized clinical interview. It focuses on the interpretation of content, rather than on structural scoring systems based on the perceptual determinants of responses. Nevertheless, available content scales and scoring systems are not considered sufficiently dependable as psychometric instruments for use in individual diagnosis. Rather, the authors recommend a strictly clinical application of the Rorschach as a means of enhancing the idiographic understanding of the individual case—and they observe that this is, in fact, how most clinicians use the Rorschach. The interpretations rely principally on the content of the responses, supplemented by verbal and nonverbal behavior. On the basis of available research and clinical experience, the authors prepared a set of guidelines for more effective and dependable idiographic interpretations. For example, responses that depart from the commonplace and those less closely bound to the stimulus properties of particular blots are more likely to be significant in the individual case. Similarly, the authors caution against rigid systems of symbol interpretation and offer instead procedures for investigating the meaning of responses within the individual's own experiential history.

A special clinical application of the Rorschach is illustrated by the consensus Rorschach (Aronow & Reznikoff, 1976, Ch. 13; Blanchard, 1968; Cutter & Farberow, 1970). In this adaptation, the inkblots are presented for joint interpretation by married couples or other family members, co-workers, juvenile gang members, or other natural groups. Through discussion and negotiation, the participants must reach agreement on a single, common set of responses. The technique has been used as a basis for exploring interpersonal behavior.

THE HOLTZMAN INKBLOT TECHNIQUE. Unlike most projective devices, the Holtzman Inkblot Technique (HIT) represents a genuine attempt to meet the technical standards of psychometric instruments in its original development (Holtzman, 1968, 1975b; Holtzman, Thorpe, Swartz, & Herron, 1961). Modeled after the Rorschach, the Holtzman test was so designed as to eliminate the principal technical deficiencies of the earlier instrument. The changes in stimulus materials and procedure are sufficiently extensive, however, to require that the Holtzman be regarded as a new test and evaluated without reference to either the theoretical or the empirical characteristics of the Rorschach. The Holtzman technique provides two parallel series of 45 cards each. Only one response per card is obtained. Both achromatic and colored cards are included; a few inkblots are markedly asymmetric. The blots were selected from a large preliminary pool on the basis of three empirical criteria: (1) discrimination between a group of college student volunteers and a group of hospitalized psychotics; (2) "pulling power" of the blot in eliciting responses scorable on such traditional Rorschach variables as location, color, shading, and movement; and (3) scorer reliability.

Administration and scoring of the HIT are well standardized and clearly described. Scores are obtained in 22 response variables, including most of the Rorschach form variables and such additional variables as pathognomic verbalization, anxiety, and hostility. For each variable, percentile scores are reported for several normal samples ranging from 5-year-olds to adults, and for a number of deviant groups, such as schizophrenics, mental retardates, emotionally disturbed children, juvenile delinquents, and alcoholics (Hill, 1972). Although these norms were derived from nearly 2,000 persons, the number of cases in most of the groups is small.

Scorer reliability appears to be highly satisfactory. Both split-half and alternate-form reliability have been extensively investigated, with generally encouraging results. A group form of the test, using slides, yields scores on most variables that are closely similar to those obtained through individual administration (Holtzman, Moseley, Reinehr, & Abbott, 1963). A short, 30-item version of the group form also gives similar results (Herron, 1963). Computer scoring is available for the group form (D. R. Gorham, 1967).

It is apparent that the HIT has many psychometric advantages over the Rorschach. The availability of parallel forms permits not only the measurement of retest reliability but also follow-up studies with alternate forms.

The restriction of responses to one per card holds response productivity (R) constant for each examinee, thus avoiding many of the pitfalls of Rorschach scoring. It should be noted, however, that response length (number of words) is still uncontrolled and, as in the Rorschach, has proved to be significantly related to several HIT scores, notably the frequency of movement responses (Megargee, 1966).

Considerable validity data on the HIT have been accumulated (Gamble, 1972; Holtzman, 1968, 1975b; Swartz, 1973). The validation research has followed a variety of approaches, including the study of developmental trends, cross-cultural comparisons, correlation with other tests and with behavioral indicators of personality characteristics, and contrasted group comparisons with both normal and pathological subjects. Available results are promising; but more data are needed to establish the diagnostic significance of the various scores and the construct validity of the personality variables assessed by this technique. A handbook prepared by Hill (1972) is directed particularly to the clinical use of the HIT. Integrating research findings on the HIT with the accumulated Rorschach literature and clinical experience, Hill provides a guide for interpreting HIT protocols on two levels. The first level is concerned with the 22 quantitatively scored variables and their interrelations. The second represents a deeper interpretive level in terms of broader and more highly integrated personality variables. Three major descriptive categories are employed: cognitive functioning (intellectual level and thought disturbances), affective functioning (e.g., levels of maturity, forms of anxiety, defense mechanisms), and self-concept (including several forms of sexual identity). The handbook also provides five detailed case studies.

THEMATIC APPERCEPTION TEST AND
RELATED INSTRUMENTS

THEMATIC APPERCEPTION TEST. In contrast to inkblot techniques, the Thematic Apperception Test (TAT) presents more highly structured stimuli and requires more complex and meaningfully organized verbal responses. Interpretation of responses by the examiner is usually based on content analysis of a rather qualitative nature. First developed by Murray and his staff at the Harvard Psychological Clinic (Murray et al., 1938), the TAT has not only been widely used in clinical practice and research, but it has also served as a model for the development of many other instruments (J. W. Atkinson, 1958; Harrison, 1965; Henry, 1956, Klopfer & Taulbee, 1976, pp. 554–558; Varble, 1971).

The TAT materials consist of 19 cards containing vague pictures in black and white and one blank card. The examinee is asked to make up a story to fit each picture, telling what led up to the event shown in the picture, describing what is happening at the moment and what the characters are feeling and thinking, and giving the outcome. In the case of the blank card, the respondent is instructed to imagine some picture on the card, describe it, and then tell a story about it. The original procedure outlined by Murray in the test manual requires two one-hour sessions, 10 cards being employed during each session. The cards reserved for the second session were deliberately chosen to be more unusual, dramatic, and bizarre, and the accompanying instructions urge respondents to give free play to their imagination. Four overlapping sets of 20 cards are available—for boys, girls, males over 14, and females over 14. Most clinicians use abridged sets of specially selected cards, seldom giving more than 10 cards to a single respondent. A card from the second set of the adult women's series is shown in Figure 98.

In interpreting TAT stories, the examiner first determines who is the "hero," the character of either sex with whom the respondent has presumably identified herself or himself. The content of the stories is then analyzed principally in reference to Murray's list of "needs" and "press." Several of the proposed needs were described in Chapter 17, in connection with the Edwards Personal Preference Schedule and the Personality Research Form. Examples include achievement, affiliation, and aggression. Press refers to environmental forces that may facilitate or interfere with the satisfaction of needs. Being attacked or criticized by another person, receiving affection, being comforted, and exposure to physical danger as in a shipwreck are illustrations of press. In assessing the importance or strength of a particular need or press for the individual, special attention is given to the intensity,

FIG. 98. One of the Pictures Used in the Thematic Apperception Test.

duration, and frequency of its occurrence in different stories, as well as to the uniqueness of its association with a given picture. The assumption is made that unusual material, which departs from the common responses to each picture, is more likely to have significance for the individual.

A fair amount of normative information has been published regarding the most frequent response characteristics for each card, including the way each card is perceived, the themes developed, the roles ascribed to the characters, emotional tones expressed, speed of responses, length of stories, and the like (J. W. Atkinson, 1958; Henry, 1956; Murstein, 1972). Although these normative data provide a general framework for interpreting individual responses, most clinicians rely heavily on "subjective norms" built up through their own experience with the test. A number of quantitative scoring schemes and rating scales have been developed that yield good scorer reliability. Since their application is rather time-consuming, however, such scoring procedures are seldom used in clinical practice. Although typically given as an individual oral test in the clinical situation, the TAT may also be administered in writing and as a group test. There is some evidence suggesting that under the latter conditions, productivity of meaningful material may be facilitated.

The TAT has been used extensively in personality research. Several investigations have been concerned with the assumptions that underlie TAT interpretations, such as self-identification with the hero and personal significance of uncommon responses (Lindzey, 1959). Although they cannot establish criterion-related validity of the TAT for specific uses, such studies contribute to the construct validation of TAT interpretations. A basic assumption that TAT shares with other projective techniques is that present motivational and emotional condition of the subject affects his or her responses to an unstructured test situation. A considerably body of experimental data is available to show that such conditions as hunger, sleep deprivation, social frustration, and the experience of failure in a preceding test situation significantly affect TAT responses (J. W. Atkinson, 1958). While supporting the projective hypothesis, the sensitivity of the TAT to such temporary conditions may complicate the detection of more enduring personality traits. Interpretation of the constructs assessed by the TAT must also take into account the finding that measures of the same needs through such instruments as the TAT, EPPS, and Adjective Check List have shown little correspondence of results (Megargee & Parker, 1968). It is possible that these different techniques assess different aspects of the common needs. In any event, such discrepancies limit the generalizability of scores. The question of internal consistency of TAT responses has also received attention (Entwistle, 1972; J. W. Atkinson, 1981; Atkinson & Birch, 1978, pp. 368–378). And some control should be applied for length of stories, or productivity—a problem that the TAT shares with the Rorschach (Veroff, Atkinson, Feld, & Gurin, 1974).

ADAPTATIONS OF THE TAT AND RELATED TESTS. Many adaptations of the TAT have been developed for special purposes. These exhibit varying degrees of resemblance to the original. Where to draw the line between modified versions of the TAT and new tests based on the same general approach as the TAT is arbitrary. Several versions of the TAT have been prepared for use in attitude surveys; examples include sets for assessing attitudes toward labor problems, minority groups, school, and authority (D.T. Campbell, 1960; Harrison, 1965). Other adaptations have been developed for use in career counseling, executive appraisal, and a wide variety of research projects. Forms have been constructed for special populations, including preschool children, elementary-school children, adolescents, crippled children, and various national and ethnic groups (Harrison, 1965).

Some TAT adaptations have focused on the intensive measurement of a single need or drive, such as sex or aggression. Of special interest is the extensive research on the achievement need (n-Ach) conducted over some thirty years by McClelland, J. W. Atkinson, and their associates (J. W. Atkinson, 1958; Atkinson & Feather, 1966; Atkinson & Raynor, 1974; McClelland, Atkinson, Clark, & Lowell, 1976). To measure n-Ach, four pictures were employed, two of which were taken from the TAT. The cards portray men working at a machine, a boy at a desk with a book, a father and son picture, and a boy who is apparently daydreaming. Detailed scoring schemes have been developed for scoring the resulting stories with regard to expressions of n-Ach. This technique has been utilized in an extensive program of research on achievement motivation. The problems investigated range from basic motivation theory (Atkinson & Feather, 1966) to the social origins and consequences of n-Ach and its role in the rise and fall of societies (McClelland, 1976). Still another special set of cards (six in a male form and six in a female form) was developed for use in a national survey of three needs: achievement, affiliation, and power (Veroff et al., 1974). For this purpose, the instructions to respondents were more highly standardized; and responses were given orally and recorded by the interviewers.

Although the original TAT is said to be applicable to children as young as 4 years of age, the Children's Apperception Test (CAT) was specially designed for use between the ages of 3 and 10 years (Bellak, 1975). The CAT cards substitute animals for people on the assumption that young children project more readily to pictures of animals than to pictures of humans. The various animals in the pictures are portrayed in typically human situations, in the characteristic anthropomorphic fashion of comic strips and children's books. The pictures are designed to evoke fantasies relating to problems of feeding and other oral activity, sibling rivalry, parent–child relations, aggression, toilet training, and other childhood experiences. Contrary to the author's assumption, several studies with children from the first grade up found either no difference or, more often, greater productivity of clinically significant material with human than with animal pictures (Murstein, 1963). In response to these research findings, the authors of the CAT prepared a human modification of the test (CAT-H) for use with older children, especially those with a mental age beyond 10 years (Bellak & Hurvich, 1966). The authors maintain that either the human or the animal form may be more effective depending on the age and personality characteristics of the child.

Similar thematic apperception tests have been developed for the aged, including the Gerontological Apperception Test (Wolk & Wolk, 1971) and the Senior Apperception Technique (Bellak, 1975; Bellak & Bellak, 1973). Both employ sets of cards featuring one or more elderly persons and illustrating problems of concern to the aged, such as loneliness, family difficulties, dependence, and helplessness. Both instruments have been criticized because of premature publication and the use of pictures that tend to perpetuate adverse stereotypes of aging (J. P. Schaie, 1978; K. W. Schaie, 1978).

OTHER PROJECTIVE TECHNIQUES

VERBAL TECHNIQUES. Although all projective instruments discussed thus far require verbal responses, certain projective techniques are wholly verbal, utilizing only words in both stimulus materials and responses. Some of these verbal techniques can be administered in either oral or written form; but all are suitable for written group administration. When so administered, of course, they presuppose a minimum reading level and thorough familiarity with the language in which the test was developed. These requirements thus preclude the use of such techniques with young children, illiterates, or foreign-speaking persons.

A technique that antedated the flood of projective tests by more than half a century is the *word association test*. Originally known as the "free association test," this technique was first systematically described by Galton (1879). Wundt and J. McK. Cattell subsequently introduced it into the psychological laboratory, where it was adapted to many uses. The procedure involves simply the presentation of a series of disconnected words, to each of which the individual is told to respond by giving the first word that comes to mind. The early experimental psychologists, as well as the first mental testers, saw in such association tests a tool for the exploration of thinking processes.

The clinical application of word association methods was stimulated largely by the psychoanalytic movement, although other psychiatrists, such as Kraepelin, had previously investigated such techniques. Among the psychoanalysts, Jung's contribution to the systematic development of the word association test is most conspicuous. Jung (1910) selected stimulus words to represent common "emotional complexes" and analyzed the responses with reference to reaction time, content, and physical expressions of emotional tension. Over thirty years later, a word association technique was developed at the Menninger Clinic by Rapaport and his associates (1968—1st ed., 1946). In its general orientation, this adaptation reveals its kinship to the earlier Jung test. The 60-word list contains a preponderance of words selected for their psychoanalytic significance, many of them being associated with psychosexual conflicts. According to its authors, the test had a dual aim: to aid in detecting impairment of thought processes and to suggest areas of significant internal conflicts. Results are analyzed with reference to such characteristics as proportion of common or popular responses, reaction time, associative disturbances, and impaired reproduction on retest.

Mention may also be made of the use of the word association technique as a "lie detector." This application was likewise initiated by Jung and was subsequently subjected to extensive research—both in the laboratory and in practical situations (Burtt, 1931; Lindsley, 1955). The rationale offered to justify the employment of word association in the detection of lying or guilt is similar to that which underlies its utilization in uncovering areas of emotional conflict. Content analysis, reaction time, and response disturbances have all been explored as indices of lying or guilt. Frequently, physiological measures of emotional excitement are obtained concurrently with the verbal responses. The word lists chosen for lie detection purposes are usually custom-made to cover distinctive features of the particular crime or other situation under investigation. Whether word association has any practical value as a lie detector is still a moot point. Its effectiveness certainly varies widely with the specific circumstances under which it is used.

A different approach to the word association test is illustrated by the early work of Kent and Rosanoff (1910). Designed principally as a psychiatric screening instrument, the Kent-Rosanoff Free Association Test utilized completely objective scoring and statistical norms. The stimulus words consisted of 100 common, neutral words, chosen because they tend to evoke the same associations from people in general. For example, to the word *table,* most people respond "chair"; to *dark,* they say "light." A set of frequency tables was prepared—one for each stimulus word—showing the number of times each response was given in a standardization sample of 1,000 normal adults.

In scoring the Kent-Rosanoff test, the median frequency value of the responses the examinee gives to the 100 stimulus words is employed as an "index of commonality." Any responses not found in the normative tables are designed as "individual." Comparisons of psychotics with normals suggested that psychotics give more individual responses and obtain a lower index of commonality than normals. The diagnostic use of the test declined, however, with the gradual realization that response frequency also varies widely with age, socioeconomic and educational level, regional and cultural background, creativity, and other factors. Hence, proper interpretation of scores requires norms on many subgroups, as well as supplementary information about the examinee. The Kent-Rosanoff test has nevertheless retained its position as a standard laboratory technique. Additional norms have been gathered in several countries, and the technique has been extensively employed in research on verbal behavior and personality (Jenkins & Russell, 1960; Palermo & Jenkins, 1963; Postman & Keppel, 1970; Van der Made-Van Bekkum, 1971).

Another verbal projective technique, *sentence completion,* has been widely employed in both research and clinical practice. Generally, the opening words, or sentence stems, permit an almost unlimited variety of possible completions. Examples might be: My ambition . . . ; Women . . . ; What worries me . . . ; My mother. . . . The sentence stems are frequently formulated so as to elicit responses relevant to the personality domain under investigation. This flexibility of the sentence completion technique represents one of its advantages for clinical and research purposes. Nevertheless, some standardized forms have been published for more general application.

An example is the Rotter Incomplete Sentences Blank, consisting of 40 sentence stems. The directions to the examinee read: "Complete these sentences to express *your real feelings.* Try to do every one. Be sure to make a complete sentence." Each completion is rated on a 7-point scale according to the degree of adjustment or maladjustment indicated. Illustrative completions corresponding to each rating are given in the manual. With the aid of these specimen responses, fairly objective scoring is possible. The sum of the individual ratings provides a total adjustment score that can be used for screening purpes. The response content can also be examined clinically for more specific diagnostic clues.

A more specialized application of the sentence completion technique is provided by the Washington University Sentence Completion Test (WUSCT), based on Loevinger's broadly defined construct of ego development. Closely reflecting the author's theoretical framework, the WUSCT classifies the responses with reference to a seven-stage scale of ego development, or I-level, as follows: presocial and symbiotic, impulsive, self-protective, conformist, conscientious, autonomous, and integrated. Each response is assigned to a single I-level, and a composite score on the entire test is computed from these values. Although most of the research has been done with adult women, forms are also available for use with men and with younger persons of either sex. The two-volume report on the development of the WUSCT contains detailed instructions for scoring and interpretation, as well as an effective set of self-training exercises for scorers (Loevinger, Wessler, & Redmore, 1970).

PICTORIAL TECHNIQUES. Projective techniques employ pictorial material in a variety of ways. The use of pictures to stimulate the free play of fantasy and to evoke elaborate verbal responses, as in the TAT, has already been considered. In contrast, the Rosenzweig Picture-Frustration Study (P-F Study), described in this section, is more circumscribed in coverage and calls for simpler responses. This instrument is available in separate forms for adults, aged 18 and over (Rosenzweig, 1950, 1978a, 1978d); for adolescents, aged 12 to 18 (Rosenzweig, 1970, 1976b); and for children, aged 4 to 13 (Rosenzweig, 1960, 1977). Derived from the author's theory of frustration and aggression, the P-F Study presents a series of cartoons in which one person frustrates another or calls attention to a frustrating condition. Two of these cartoons, taken from the children's form, are shown in Figure 99. In the blank space provided, the respondent writes what the frustrated person would reply.

Responses on the P-F Study are classified with reference to type and direction of aggression. Types of aggression include: obstacle-dominance, emphasizing the frustrating object; ego-defense, focusing attention on the protection of the frustrated person; and need-persistence, concentrating on the constructive solution of the frustrating problem. Direction of aggression is scored as: extraggressive, or turned outward onto the environment; intraggressive, or turned inward upon oneself; and imaggressive, or turned off in an attempt to gloss over or evade the situation. In scoring the test, the percentage of responses falling into each of these categories is compared with the corresponding normative percentages. A group conformity rating (GCR), showing the individual's tendency to give responses that agree with the modal responses of the standardization sample, may also be obtained.

Being more limited in coverage, more highly structured, and relatively objective in its scoring procedures, the P-F Study lends itself better to statistical analysis than do most other projective techniques. Systematic efforts

FIG. 99. Typical Items from the Rosenzweig Picture-Frustration Study, Children's Form.

(Copyright © 1976 by Saul Rosenzweig. Reproduced by permission.)

have been made from the outset to gather norms and to check its reliability and validity. Over some forty years, considerable research has been conducted with the P-F Study, by both the test author and other investigators. Much of this research literature, dealing with such topics as reliability, criterion-related and construct validity, clinical diagnosis, sex differences, and cultural differences, has been brought together in several recent publications by Rosenzweig (1976a, 1978b, 1978c; Rosenzweig & Adelman, 1977).

EXPRESSIVE TECHNIQUES. A large and amorphous category of projective techniques comprises many forms of relatively free self-expression. It is characteristic of all these techniques that they have been employed as therapeutic as well as diagnostic procedures. Through the opportunities for self-expression that these activities afford, it is believed that the individual not only reveals his or her emotional difficulties but also relieves them. The techniques most frequently employed in this category are drawing and dramatic use of toys.

Although almost every art medium, technique, and type of subject matter had been investigated in the search for significant diagnostic clues, special attention has centered on *drawings of the human figure*. A well-known example is provided by the Machover Draw-a-Person Test (D-A-P). In this test, the examinee is provided with paper and pencil and is told simply to "draw a person." Upon completion of the first drawing, he or she is asked to draw a person of the opposite sex from that of the first figure. While the individual draws, the examiner notes his or her comments, the sequence in which different parts are drawn, and other procedural details. The drawing may be followed by an inquiry, in which the examinee is asked to make up a story about each person drawn, "as if he were a character in a play or novel." A series of questions is also employed during the inquiry to elicit specific information about age, schooling, occupation, family, and other facts associated with the characters portrayed.

Scoring of the Draw-a-Person Test is essentially qualitative, involving the preparation of a composite personality description from an analysis of many features of the drawings. Among the factors considered in this connection are the absolute and relative size of the male and female figures, their position on the page, quality of lines, sequence of parts drawn, stance, front or profile view, position of arms, depiction of clothing, and background and grounding effects. Special interpretations are given for the omission of different bodily parts, disproportions, shading, amount and distribution of details, erasures, symmetry, and other stylistic features. There is also detailed discussion of the significance of each major body part, such as head, individual facial features, hair, neck, shoulders, breast, trunk, hips, and extremities.

The interpretive guide for the Draw-a-Person Test abounds in sweeping generalizations, such as "Disproportionately large heads will often be given by individuals suffering from organic brain disease," or "The sex given the proportionately larger head is the sex that is accorded more intellectual and social authority." But no evidence is provided in support of these statements. Reference is made to a file of "thousands of drawings" examined in clinical contexts, and a few selected cases are cited for illustrative purposes. No systematic presentation of data, however, accompanies the original published report of the test (Machover, 1949). Validation studies by other investigators have yielded conflicting results, the better controlled studies lending no support to the diagnostic interpretations proposed by Machover (Klopfer & Taulbee, 1976, pp. 558–561). It would seem that the D-A-P can serve best, not as a psychometric instrument, but as part of a clinical interview, in which the drawings are interpreted in the context of other information about the individual.

Toy tests, involving such objects as puppets, dolls, and miniatures, have been widely utilized in projective testing. Originating in play therapy with children, these materials have subsequently been adapted for the diagnostic testing of both adults and children. The objects are usually selected because of their expected associative value. Among the articles most frequently employed for these purposes, for example, are dolls representing adults and children of both sexes, furniture, bathroom and kitchen fixtures, and other household furnishings. Play with such articles is expected to reveal the child's attitudes toward her or his own family, as well as sibling rivalries, fears, aggressions, conflicts, and the like. The examiner notes what items the child chooses and what he or she does with them, as well as the child's verbalizations, emotional expressions, and other overt behavior.

With children, these techniques often take the form of free play with the collection of toys that the examiner simply makes available. With adults, the materials are presented with general instructions to carry out some task of a highly unstructured nature. These instructions may, of course, also be employed with children. Frequently, the task has certain dramatic features, as in the arrangement of figures on a miniature stage set. Several investigators have used play techniques in studying prejudice and other intergroup attitudes (D. T. Campbell, 1950).

EVALUATION OF PROJECTIVE TECHNIQUES

It is evident that projective techniques differ widely among themselves. Some appear more promising than others because of more favorable empirical findings, sounder theoretical orientation, or both. Regarding some techniques, such as the Rorschach, voluminous data have been gathered, although their interpretation is often uncertain. About others little is known, either because of their recent origin, or because objective verification is hindered by the intrinsic nature of the instruments or by the attitudes of their exponents.

To evaluate each instrument individually and to attempt to summarize the extensive pertinent literature would require a separate volume. Within this chapter, critical comments have been interjected only in the cases of instruments that presented unique features—whether of a favorable or an unfavorable nature. There are certain points, however, that apply to a greater or lesser extent to the bulk of projective techniques. These points can be conveniently considered in summary form.

RAPPORT AND APPLICABILITY. Most projective techniques represent an effective means for "breaking the ice" during the initial contacts between examiner and examinee. The task is usually intrinsically interesting and often entertaining. It tends to divert the individual's attention away from himself or herself and thus reduces embarrassment and defensiveness. And it offers little or no threat to the respondent's prestige, since any response one gives is "right."

Certain projective techniques may be especially useful with young children, illiterates, and persons with language handicaps or speech defects. Nonverbal media would be readily applicable to all these groups. And oral responses to pictorial and other nonlanguage stimuli could be secured from the first two. With all these verbally limited groups, projective techniques may help the examinee to communicate with the examiner. These techniques may also aid individuals in clarifying for themselves some of their own behavior that they had not previously verbalized.

FAKING. In general, projective instruments are less susceptible to faking than are self-report inventories. The purpose of projective techniques is usually disguised. Even if an individual has some psychological sophistication and is familiar with the general nature of a particular instrument, such as the Rorschach or TAT, it is still unlikely that he or she can predict the intricate ways in which the responses will be scored and interpreted. Moreover, the examinee soon becomes absorbed in the task and hence is less likely to resort to the customary disguises and restraints of interpersonal communication.

On the other hand, it cannot be assumed that projective tests are completely immune to faking. Several experiments with the Rorschach, TAT, and other projective instruments have shown that significant differences do occur when examinees are instructed to alter their responses so as to create favorable or unfavorable impressions, or when they are given statements suggesting that certain types of responses are more desirable (Masling, 1960). In a particularly well-controlled study, Davids and Pildner (1958) administered a battery of self-report and projective tests to two groups of college students, one of which took the tests as genuine job applicants, the other as participants in a research project. Under these conditions, the job applicants obtained significantly better-adjusted scores than did the research participants on the self-report but *not* on the projective tests. Certain types of projective test items, however, were found to be susceptible to faking. For example, sentence completion stems expressed in the first person yielded significantly more favorable responses than did those expressed in the third person.

EXAMINER AND SITUATIONAL VARIABLES. It is obvious that most projective techniques are inadequately standardized with respect to both administration and scoring. Yet there is evidence that even subtle differences in the phrasing of verbal instructions and in examiner–examinee relationships can appreciably alter performance on these tests (Baughman, 1951; Hamilton & Robertson, 1966; Herron, 1964; Klinger, 1966; Klopfer & Taulbee, 1976; Masling, 1960). Even when employing identical instructions, some examiners may be more encouraging or reassuring, others more threatening, owing to their general manner and appearance. Such differences may affect response productivity, defensiveness, stereotypy, imaginativeness, and other basic performance characteristics. In the light of these findings, problems of administration and testing conditions assume even greater importance than in other psychological tests.

Equally serious is the lack of objectivity in scoring. Even when objective scoring systems have been developed, the final steps in the evaluation and integration of the raw data usually depend on the skill and clinical experience of the examiner. Such a situation has several implications. In the first place, it reduces the number of examiners who are properly qualified to employ the technique and thus limits the range of its effective application. It also means that the results obtained by different examiners may not be comparable, a fact that complicates research with the instrument. But perhaps the most disturbing implication is that the interpretation of scores is often as projective for the examiner as the test stimuli are for the examinee. In other words, the final interpretation of projective test responses may reveal more about the theoretical orientation, favorite hypotheses, and personality idiosyncrasies of the examiner than it does about the examinee's personality dynamics.

NORMS. Another conspicuous deficiency common to many projective instruments pertains to normative data. Such data may be completely lacking, grossly inadequate, or based on vaguely described populations. In the absence of adequate objective norms, the clinician falls back on his or her "general clinical experience" to interpret projective test performance. But such a frame of reference is subject to all the distortions of memory that are themselves reflections of theoretical bias, preconceptions, and other idiosyncrasies of the clinician. Moreover, any one clinician's contacts may have been limited largely to persons who are atypical in education, socioeconomic level, sex ratio, age distribution, or other relevant characteristics. In at least one respect, the clinician's experience is almost certain to produce a misleading picture, since he or she deals predominantly with disturbed or pathological cases. The clinician may thus lack sufficient firsthand familiarity with the characteristic reactions of normal people. The Rorschach norms gathered by Ames and her associates—and more recently by Exner—represent efforts to correct some of the more obvious lacks in this regard.

Interpretation of projective test performance often involves subgroup norms, of either a subjective or an objective nature. Thus, the clinician may have a general subjective picture of what constitutes a "typical" schizophrenic or psychoneurotic performance on a particular test. Or the published data may provide qualitative or quantitative norms that delineate the characteristic performance of different diagnostic groups. In either case, the subgroup norms may lead to faulty interpretations unless the subgroups were equated in other respects. For example, if the schizophrenics and normals on whom the norms were derived differed also in educational level, the observed disparities between schizophrenic and normal performance may have resulted from educational inequality rather than from schizophrenia. Similar systematic or constant errors may operate in the comparison of various psychiatric syndromes. For example, schizophrenics as a group tend to be younger than manic-depressives; anxiety neurotics are likely to come from higher educational and socioeconomic levels than hysterics.

RELIABILITY. In view of the relatively unstandardized scoring procedures and the inadequacies of normative data, *scorer reliability* becomes an important consideration in projective testing. For projective techniques, a proper measure of scorer reliability should include not only the more objective preliminary scoring but also the final integrative and interpretive stages. It is not enough, for example, to demonstrate that examiners who have mastered the same system of Rorschach scoring agree closely in their tallying of such characteristics as whole, unusual detail, or color responses. On a projective test like the Rorschach, these raw quantitative measures cannot be interperted directly from a table of norms, as in the usual type of psychological test. Interpretive scorer reliability is concerned with the extent to which different examiners attribute the same personality characteristics to the examinee on the basis of their interpretations of the identical record. Few adequate studies of this type of scorer reliability have been conducted with projective tests. Some investigations have revealed marked divergencies in the interpretations given by reasonably well-qualified test users. A fundamental ambiguity in such results stems from the unknown contribution of the interpreter's skill. Neither high nor low scorer reliability can be directly generalized to other scorers differing appreciably from those utilized in the particular investigation.

Attempts to measure other types of test reliability have fared equally poorly in the field of projective testing. Coefficients of *internal consistency*, when computed, have usually been low. In such tests as the Rorschach, TAT, and Rosenzweig P-F Study, it has been argued that different cards or items are not comparable and hence should not be used in finding split-half reliabilities. In fact, individual items in such instruments were designed to measure different variables. Moreover, the trend of responses over successive items is often considered significant in interpreting responses. J. W. Atkinson (1981; Atkinson & Birch, 1978, pp. 370–374) has demonstrated through computer simulation that, with a TAT-type procedure, it is possible to obtain high construct validity of total scores (e.g., .90) when internal consistency is very low (e.g., .07). He observes that the individual does not respond to each successive card independently, but responds through a continuous stream of activity that reflects the rise and fall in relative strength of different behavior tendencies. The expression of a tendency in activity reduces its strength. The proportion of time the examinee spends describing, for example, achievement-motivated activities in response to different cards is a function of the cumulative effect of responding to successive cards and the differential incentives for achievement or other competing motives in the individual cards. In view of the various arguments against the applicability of internal consistency measures of reliability to projective tests, one solution is to construct *parallel forms* that are, in fact, comparable, as was done in the Holtzman Inkblot Technique.

Retest reliability also presents special problems. With long intervals, genuine personality changes may occur which the test should detect. With short intervals, a retest may show no more than recall of original responses. When investigators instructed examinees to write different TAT stories on a retest, in order to determine whether the same themes would recur, most of the scored variables yielded insignificant retest correlations (Lindzey & Herman, 1955). It is also relevant to note that many scores derived from projective techniques are based on very inadequate response samples. In the case of the Rorschach, for instance, the number of responses within a given individual's protocol that fall into such categories as animal movement, human movement, shading, color, unusual detail, and the like may be so few as to yield extremely unreliable indices. Large chance variations are to be expected under such circumstances. Ratios and percentages computed with such unreliable measures are even more unstable than the individual measures themselves (Cronbach, 1949, pp. 411–412).

VALIDITY. For any test, the most fundamental question is that of validity. Many validation studies of projective tests have been concerned with concurrent criterion-related validity. Most of these have compared the performance of contrasted groups, such as occupational or diagnostic groups. As was pointed out in connection with norms, however, these groups often differ in other respects, such as age or education. Other investigations of concurrent validity have used essentially a matching technique, in which personality descriptions derived from test records are compared with descriptions or data about the same persons taken from case histories, psychiatric interviews, or long-range behavioral records. A few studies have investigated predictive validity against such criteria as success in specialized types of training, job performance, or response to psychotherapy. There has been an increasing trend to investigate the construct validity of projective instruments by testing specific hypotheses that underlie the use and interpretation of each test.

The large majority of published validation studies on projective techniques are inconclusive because of procedural deficiencies in either experimental controls or statistical analysis, or both. This is especially true of studies concerned with the Rorschach. Some methodological deficiencies may have the effect of producing *spurious evidence of validity* where none exists. An example is the contamination of either criterion or test data. Thus, the criterion judges may have had some knowledge of the examinees' test performance. Similarly, the examiner may have obtained cues about the examinee's characteristics from conversation with her or him in the course of test administration, or from case history material and other nontest sources. The customary control for the latter type of contamination in validation studies is to utilize blind analysis, in which the test record is interpreted by a scorer who has had no contact with the examinee and who has no information about her or him other than that contained in the test protocol. Clinicians have argued, however, that blind analysis is an unnatural way to interpret projective test responses and does not correspond to the way these instruments are used in clinical practice.

Another common source of spurious validity data is failure to cross-validate (Kinslinger, 1966). Because of the large number of potential diagnostic signs or scorable elements that can be derived from most projective tests, it is very easy by chance alone to find a set of such signs that differentiate significantly between criterion groups. The validity of such a scoring key, however, will collapse to zero when applied to new samples.

A more subtle form of error is illustrated by stereotype accuracy. Certain descriptive statements, such as might occur in a Rorschach protocol, may apply widely to persons in general, or to young men, or to hospitalized patients, or to whatever category of persons is sampled by the particular investigation.[1] Agreement between criterion and test data with regard to such statements would therefore yield a spurious impression of validity. Some check on this error is needed, such as a measure of the agreement between the test evaluation of one examinee and the criterion evaluation of another

[1] The use of such generally applicable statements will be recognized as an example of the "Barnum effect" described in Chapter 16.

examinee in the same category. This measure would indicate the amount of spurious agreement resulting from stereotype accuracy under the conditions of the particular investigation (see, e.g., Silverman, 1959).

Still another common source of error, arising from reliance on clinical experience in the validation of diagnostic signs, is what Chapman (1967) labeled "illusory validation." This phenomenon may account in part for the continued clinical use of instruments and systems of diagnostic signs for which empirical validity findings are predominantly negative. In a series of experiments to test this phenomenon, Chapman and Chapman (1967) presented college students with a set of human figure drawings similar to those obtained in the Machover Draw-a-Person Test (D-A-P). Each drawing was accompanied by brief descriptions of two symptoms supposedly manifested by the person who made the drawing. For example, one pair included: (1) is suspicious of other people; (2) is worried about how manly he is. The students had no previous familiarity with the D-A-P or its rationale. The symptoms chosen were those most often linked with certain drawing characteristics by a group of clinicians previously surveyed in a mail questionnaire, and were thus part of the clinical lore associated with the use of the D-A-P. In the experiment itself, however, the symptoms were distributed at random among the drawings, and different participants received different combinations of drawings and symptoms. Thus, the participants' learning experience did *not* support the traditional, stereotyped associations of symptoms and drawing characteristics.

Following the learning session, participants were given a list of symptoms and asked to describe under each the drawing characteristics they had observed to be associated with it. The results showed that participants responded in terms of preestablished popular stereotypes, even though these associations were not supported by the data presented during their learning experience. For example, they listed atypical eyes as being associated with suspiciousness; large head with worry about intelligence; and broad shoulders with concern about manliness. Not only were the interpretations unrelated to the empirical associations which the participants had "studied," but in other experiments these stereotyped cultural associations also proved to be resistant to change under intensive training conditions designed to establish counter associations. In other words, persons retained their a priori expectations even when exposed to contradictory observations.

Illustory correlation is a special example of the mechanism that underlies the survival of superstitions. We tend to notice and recall whatever fits our expectations; and we tend to ignore and forget whatever is contrary to our expectations. This mechanism may actually interfere with the discovery and use of valid diagnostic signs in the course of clinical observation by clinicians who are strongly identified with a particular diagnostic system. The original research of Chapman and Chapman with the D-A-P has been corroborated by similar studies with the Rorschach (Chapman & Chapman,

1969; Golding & Rorer, 1972) and with the Incomplete Sentences Blank (Starr & Katkin, 1969).

It should be noted, on the other hand, that certain inadequacies of experimental design may have the opposite effect of *underestimating the validity* of a diagnostic instrument. It is widely recognized, for example, that traditional psychiatric categories, such as schizophrenia, manic-depressive psychosis, and hysteria, represent crude and unrealistic classifications of the personality disorders actually manifested by patients. Hence, if such diagnostic categories are used as the sole criterion for checking the validity of a personality test, negative results are inconclusive. Similarly, failure to predict occupational criteria may reflect no more than the examiner's ignorance of the traits required for the jobs under consideration. When such criteria are employed, it is possible that the projective test is a valid measure of the personality traits it is designed to measure, but that these traits are irrelevant to success in the chosen criterion situations.

Those who stress the importance of configural scoring, response patterns, and trait interrelationships in personality assessment have also objected to attempts to validate isolated scores or diagnostic signs derived from projective techniques. That insignificant correlations may result from failure to allow for complex patterns of relationship among personality variables can be illustrated by studies of aggression indicators in TAT stories. In interpreting the results of such investigations, it has been repeatedly pointed out that the hypothesized relation between aggression in fantasy, as revealed in the TAT, and aggression in overt behavior is not a simple one. Depending on other concomitant personality characteristics, high aggression in fantasy may be associated with either high or low overt aggression. There is some evidence suggesting that, if strong aggressive tendencies are accompanied by high anxiety or fear of punishment, expressions of aggression will tend to be high in fantasy and low in overt behavior; when anxiety and fear of punishment are low, high fantasy aggression is associated with high overt aggression (Harrison, 1965; Mussen & Naylor, 1954; Pittluck, 1950).

Lack of significant correlation between expressions of aggression in TAT stories and in overt behavior in a random sample of cases is thus consistent with expectation, since the relation may be positive in some individuals and negative in others. Obviously, however, such a lack of correlation is also consistent with the hypothesis that the test has no validity at all in detecting aggressive tendencies. What is needed, of course, is more studies using complex experimental designs that permit an analysis of the conditions under which each assumption is applicable.

Not many research projects have been so designed as to avoid all the major pitfalls of projective test validation. A few used sophisticated experimental designs and are worth examining for their methodological contributions (M. Golden, 1964; Henry & Farley, 1959; Little & Shneidman, 1959; Silverman, 1959). While differing in the type of persons examined and in the specific problems they set out to investigate, these studies point to a common conclusion: when experienced clinicians are given an opportunity to examine and interpret in their own way examinees' protocols from such projective tests as the Rorschach and TAT, their evaluations of the examinees' personalities tend to match independent case history evaluations significantly better than chance. Insofar as can be ascertained, however, the obtained relations are low. Moreover, the relationship appears to be a function of the particular clinician and examinee, a number of individual matches being no better than chance. There is also little agreement among evaluations based on different projective techniques, or among different clinicians using the same technique.

THE PROJECTIVE HYPOTHESIS. It is a fundamental assumption of all projective techniques that the individual's responses to the ambiguous stimuli presented to her or him reflect significant and relatively enduring personality attributes. Yet there is a large and growing body of research data indicating that many other factors affect the individual's projective test responses. To the extent that retest reliability has been measured, marked temporal shifts have frequently been observed, indicating the operation of considerable chance error. More direct evidence regarding the susceptibility of projective test responses to temporary states is provided by several experimental studies demonstrating the effect of such factors as hunger, sleep deprivation, drugs, anxiety, and frustration on such responses.

The response variability associated with even slight changes in stimulus characteristics, furthermore, suggests that the responses are stimulus-specific and hence of questionable generalizability. Significant response differences have likewise been found in relation to instructional sets, examiner characteristics, and the examinee's perception of the testing situation. Ability factors—and particularly verbal ability—clearly affect scores on most projective tests. In the light of all these findings, projective test responses can be meaningfully interpreted only when the examiner has extensive information about the circumstances under which they were obtained and the aptitudes and experiential background of the examinee.

From another angle, the advantages of using unstructured or ambiguous stimuli have been questioned (Epstein, 1966). Such stimuli are ambiguous for the examiner as well as for the examinee; thus, they tend to increase the ambiguity of the examiner's interpretations of the examinee's responses. With structured stimuli, on the other hand, it is possible to select stimuli relevant to the personality characteristics to be assessed and to vary the nature of the stimuli in a systematic and balanced manner so as to explore fully a given personality dimension. Such a procedure makes for clearer interpretation of test performance than is possible with the shotgun approach of unstructured stimuli. There is also evidence against the common assumption that the less structured the stimuli, the more likely they are to elicit projection and to tap "deep" layers of personality (Murstein, 1963; Klopfer & Taulbee, 1976). Actually, the relation between ambiguity and projection appears to be nonlinear, with an intermediate degree of ambiguity representing an optimum for purposes of projection.

The assumption that fantasy, as elicited by such projective techniques as the TAT, reveals covert motivational dispositions has also been called into question. One survey of the experimental literature on the projective assessment of achievement need indicated that the data were more nearly consistent with alternative explanations involving perceptual and cognitive factors (Klinger, 1966). Similarly, in a 20-year longitudinal study of TAT fantasy and relevant overt behavior, adolescent activities predicted adult TAT imagery much better than adolescent TAT imagery predicted adult activities (McClelland, 1966; Skolnick, 1966). For example, individuals who had shown upward social mobility obtained higher scores on achievement needs as adults; but those who obtained higher achievement need scores in adolescence were not among the ones who subsequently showed upward social mobility.

Findings such as these reverse the relationship implied by the traditional rationale of projective techniques. They can be explained if we regard TAT responses, not as direct projective expressions of motives, but as samples of the individual's thoughts, which may in turn have been influenced by her or his previous actions. Individuals who have achieved more and those who were more often exposed to achievement-oriented models in their developmental history tend to perceive more achievement themes in unstructured pictures.

In summary, many types of research have tended to cast doubt on the projective hypothesis. There is ample evidence that alternative explanations may account as well or better for the individual's responses to unstructured test simuli.

PROJECTIVE TECHNIQUES AS PSYCHOMETRIC INSTRUMENTS. Besides their questionable theoretical rationale, projective techniques are clearly found wanting when evaluated in accordance with test standards. This is evident from the data summarized in the preceding sections with regard to standardization of administration and scoring procedures, adequacy of norms, reliability, and validity. The accumulation of published studies that have *failed* to demonstrate any validity for such projective techniques as the Rorschach and the D-A-P is truly impressive. Yet after five decades of negative results, the status of projective techniques remains substantially unchanged (Wade & Baker, 1977). In the words of one reviewer, "There are still enthusiastic clinicians and doubting statisticians" (Adcock, 1965).

This apparent contradiction can perhaps be understood if we recognize that, with a few exceptions, projective techniques are not truly tests. Among the notable exceptions are the Holtzman Inkblot Technique, the recent work of Exner and a few others with standardized Rorschach techniques, some adaptations of the TAT, and the Rosenzweig P-F Study. Even in the case of these instruments, however, there is need for much more validity data to specify the nature of the constructs measured by their scores, as well as for more normative data on clearly defined populations. Thus, while coming closer to meeting test standards than have other projective techniques, even these instruments are not ready for routine operational use.

A few other examples of quasi-tests could undoubtedly be found among the many remaining projective techniques that were not discussed in this chapter. Such exceptions, however, only serve to demonstrate that unstructured stimuli may be used in constructing psychometric instruments. The fact remains, nevertheless, that they have not been so used in the vast majority of projective techniques, particularly in the more popular and firmly entrenched techniques.

PROJECTIVE TECHNIQUES AS CLINICAL TOOLS. Rather than being regarded and evaluated as psychometric instruments, or *tests* in the strict sense of the term, projective techniques are coming more and more to be regarded as clinical tools. Thus, they may serve as supplementary qualitative interviewing aids in the hands of a skilled clinician.[2] Their value as clinical tools is proportional to the skill of the clinician and hence cannot be assessed independently of the individual clinician using them. Attempts to evaluate them in terms of the usual psychometric procedures would thus be inappropriate. But by the same token, the use of elaborate scoring systems that yield quantitative scores is not only wasteful but also misleading. Such scoring procedures lend the scores an illusory semblance of objectivity and may create the unwarranted impression that the given technique can be treated as a test. The special value that projective techniques may have is more likely to emerge when they are interpreted by qualitative, clinical procedures than when they are quantitatively scored and interpreted as psychometric instruments.

Borrowing a concept from informaion theory, Cronbach and Gleser (1965) characterized interviewing and projective techniques as "wideband" procedures. Bandwidth, or breadth of coverage, is achieved at the cost of lowered fidelity or dependability of information. Objective psychometric tests characteristically yield a narrow band of information at a high level of dependability. In contrast, projective and interviewing techniques provide a much wider range of information of lower dependability. Moreover, the kinds of data furnished by any one projective technique may vary from individual to individual. One person's TAT responses, for example,

---

[2] A provoactive account by L. J. Kaplan (1975) provides examples of the use of both projective and standardized instruments in nonstandard ways in the clinical examination of otherwise untestable children.

may tell us a good deal about her or his aggression and little or nothing about creativity or achievement need; another person's record may permit a thorough assessment of the degree of creativity and of the strength of achievement need, while revealing little about her or his aggression. Such a lack of uniformity in the kinds of information provided in individual cases helps to explain the low validities found when projective test responses are analyzed for any single trait across a group of persons.

It is interesting to note that a similar unevenness characterizes clinicians' interpretations of individual records. Thus, in an early study of the validity of the TAT, Henry and Farley (1959, p. 22) concluded:

> There is no single correct way of employing the TAT interpretation. There was little item agreement between judges, but each judge made enough "correct" decisions to yield a highly significant agreement figure. Judges may arrive at essentially the same interpretive implications of the test report, by quite different routes; or judges may differ individually in their ability to utilize TAT predictions in different areas . . . or for different subjects.

The nature of clinical judgment through which projective and interviewing data may be utilized in reaching decisions about individual cases is receiving increasing attention from psychologists (see Ch. 16). In this process, the very constructs or categories in terms of which the data are organized are built up inductively through an examination of the particular combination of data available in the individual case. The special function of the clinician is to make predictions from unique or rare combinations of events about which it is impracticable to prepare any statistical table or equation. By creating new constructs to fit the individual case, the clinician can predict from combinations of events that he or she has never encountered before in any other case. In making these predictions, the clinician can also take into account the varied significance of similar events for different individuals. Such clinical predictions are helpful, provided they are not accepted as final but are constantly tested against information elicited through subsequent inquiry, test responses, reaction to therapy, or other behavior on the part of the client. It follows from the nature of interviewing and projective techniques that decisions should not be based on any single datum or score obtained from such sources. These techniques serve best in sequential decisions, by suggesting leads for further exploration or hypotheses about the individual for subsequent verification.

CHAPTER 20

Other Assessment Techniques

T HE SELF-REPORT inventories and projective techniques surveyed
in the preceding chapters represent the best-known and most widely
used instruments for personality appraisal. Neverthelesss, there still
remains a rich supply of other devices that are being explored for this purpose. Out of this diversity of approaches may come techniques that will
eventually stimulate progress in new directions. The procedures to be considered in this chapter are principally research techniques, although some
may also serve as supplementary clinical aids in the hands of a skilled clinician. A wide variety of approaches is represented by the specific assessment
techniques cited. Three major categories include "objective" performance
tests utilizing perceptual, cognitive, or evaluative tasks; several kinds of
situational tests; and techniques designed to assess self-concepts and personal constructs. To add further perspective to this survey of personality
tests, brief mention will be made of the role of direct behavioral observations and ratings in personality assessment; the analysis of life-history data
for predictive purposes; and the assessment of environments.

"OBJECTIVE" PERFORMANCE TESTS

A large and heterogeneous category of personality tests comprises relatively simple and objective procedures, which usually require perceptual,
cognitive, or evaluative responses. The examinee is given a task that bears
little resemblance to the criterion behavior under investigation. For this
reason, these techniques are sometimes described as "indirect" tests.

Although varying widely in content and specific techniques, these tests
have several distinguishing features. First, examinees are *task-oriented*,
rather than being report-oriented as in personality questionnaires. They are
given an objective task to perform, rather than being asked to describe their
habitual behavior. Second, the purpose of these tests is *disguised*, the examinees not realizing which aspects of their performance are to be scored.
Third, the tasks set for the examinees are *structured*. In this feature lies
their principal difference from the tasks utilized in projective techniques.
To be sure, structuring is a matter of degree. As a group, however, the tests
now under consideration are more highly structured than are typical projective devices. A fourth and related feature pertains to the apparent exist-

ence of a *"right solution"* for each task or problem—at least from the examinee's viewpoint. Many of the tests are perceived as aptitude measures, in which the examinee endeavors to give "correct" answers. Thus, the individual's approach to the test is quite unlike that encouraged by projective tests, in which "anything goes."

Several tests in the present category were developed in the course of long-term research projects. The most extensive collection has been assembled by Cattell and Schuerger (1978), as one approach to Cattell's comprehensive factor-analytic identification of personality traits (see Ch. 17). These tests are quite varied, ranging from physiological measures to tests of musical preference and the appreciation of humor.

Some objective personality tests have been constructed as measures of cognitive styles, as illustrated by the research of Witkin (1978) and his associates. Cognitive styles refer essentially to one's preferred and typical modes of perceiving, remembering, thinking, and problem solving (Messick, 1970; Messick & associates, 1976). They are regarded as broad stylistic behavioral characteristics that cut across abilities and personality and are manifested in many activities and media. An extensive research literature has accumulated on various cognitive styles (Goldstein & Blackman, 1977, 1978; Kogan, 1976; Messer, 1976).

PERCEPTUAL FUNCTIONS. One of the principal sources of the simple, objective personality tests under consideration is to be found in the area of perceptual functions. A large body of experimental literature has demonstrated significant relationships between the individual's attitudinal, motivational, or emotional characteristics and his or her performance on perceptual or cognitive tasks. It should also be recognized that a number of projective techniques—notably the Rorschach—are essentially perceptual tests.

Of the factors identified in early factorial analyses of perception, one that has proved particularly fruitful in personality research is flexibility of closure (Pemberton, 1952; Thurstone, 1944). A common type of test for this factor requires the identification of a figure amid distracting and confusing details. Two items from a test with a high loading in this factor (Gottschaldt Figures) are shown in Figure 100. Several studies have reported suggestive data indicating possible relationships between this perceptual factor and personality traits. In one early investigation (Pemberton, 1952), for example, persons who excelled in flexibility of closure had high self-ratings on such traits as socially retiring, independent of the opinions of others, analytical, interested in theoretical and scientific problems, and disliking rigid systematization and routine.

Over the intervening years, several investigators have employed adaptations of the Gottschaldt Figures in research on both cognitive and noncognitive behavior. Approaching the problem from a different angle, Witkin and his associates (Witkin, Lewis, Hertzman, Machover, Meissner, & Wap-

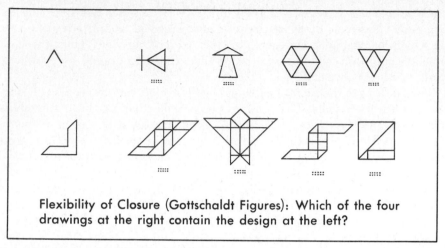

Flexibility of Closure (Gottschaldt Figures): Which of the four drawings at the right contain the design at the left?

FIG. 100. Items Illustrating Perceptual Tasks Employed in Personality Assessment. (From Thurstone, 1950, p. 7.)

ner, 1954) identified the ability to resist the disruptive influence of conflicting contextual cues as an important variable in a long-term study of perceptual spatial orientation. Through various tests utilizing a rod and frame that could be independently moved, a tilting chair, and a tilting room, these investigators were able to show that individuals differ widely in their "field dependence," or the extent to which their perception of the upright is influenced by the surrounding visual field.

A substantial body of data was amassed to indicate that field dependence is a relatively stable, consistent trait, having a certain amount of generality. Thus, both odd-even and retest reliabilities were high, and most of the intercorrelations among the different spatial orientation tests were significant.

Of even more interest are the significant correlations between these orientation tests and the Embedded Figures Test (similar to the Gottschaldt Figures illustrated in Figure 100), which may be regarded as measuring field dependence in a purely visual, paper-and-pencil situation. As more research accumulated, field dependence came to be regarded as the perceptual component of a broader personality dimension, designated as global versus articulated cognitive style, or psychological differentiation (Witkin, Dyk, Faterson, Goodenough, & Karp, 1962). There is evidence that this cognitive style exhibits considerable stability through childhood and early adulthood and is related to a number of personality variables, such as leadership (Weissenberg & Gruenfeld, 1966) and social conformity (Witkin et al., 1974).

The scope and diversity of research on field dependence is truly impressive, ranging from interpersonal relations (Witkin & Goodenough, 1977) to learning and memory (D. R. Goodenough, 1976), mathematics achievement (Vaidya & Chansky, 1980), and cross-cultural differences (Berry, 1976). An example of the suggestive relationships that emerge from surveys of many studies is the finding that field-independent persons tend to follow active, "participant" approaches to learning, while field-dependent persons more often use "spectator" approaches. In interpersonal situations, on the other hand, the field-dependent tend to have certain advantages in getting along with others. They tend to be more attentive to social cues, more responsive to other persons' behavior, and more emotionally open than are the field-independent persons. It appears that neither end of the field-dependent-independent continuum is necessarily or uniformly favorable or unfavorable; rather, the value of deviations in either direction depends on the demands of particular situations.

Much of this research has used the Embedded Figures Test, which is relatively easy to administer. Published forms of this test are now available for the adult, child, and preschool levels, as well as for group administra-

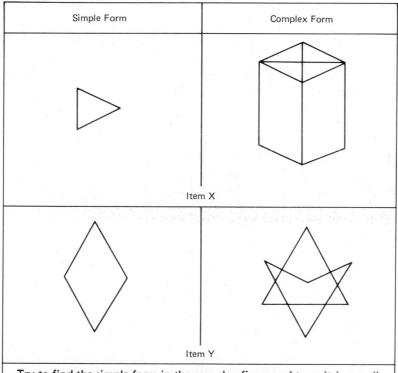

Simple Form	Complex Form

Item X

Item Y

Try to find the simple form in the complex figure and trace it *in pencil* directly over the lines of the complex figure. It is the SAME SIZE, in the SAME PROPORTIONS, and FACES IN THE SAME DIRECTION within the complex figure as when it appeared alone.

FIG. 101. Demonstration Items from Group Embedded Figures Test.

Following warm-up fore-exercises, the child is asked to trace with his or her finger the *same triangle* in each successive picture. The triangle is always the same size and in the same position as in the simple form.

FIG. 102. Typical Item from Preschool Embedded Figures Test.
(Copyright © 1972 by Consulting Psychologists Press. Reproduced by permission.)

tion. Two demonstration items from the Group Embedded Figures Test are shown in Figure 101. A typical item from the Preschool Embedded Figures Test is reproduced in Figure 102. In both the children's and the preschool forms, the complex figures are recognizable, familiar objects, and the tests are administered individually. The original—and more commonly used— adult form is also individually administered.

Much research remains to be done to clear up inconsistencies found with regard to several hypotheses pertaining to the relationships between field independence or differentiation and a wide diversity of behavioral variables. Another obstacle to generalization is presented by lack of uniformity among studies with regard to both participant characteristics and methodology. But the research seems to be continuing with undiminished vigor, and data should be forthcoming to meet these difficulties. Moreover, there is evidence cutting across different cognitive styles to suggest the operation of a broad personality construct that could be described as a differentiated cognitive style (Goldstein & Blackman, 1978).

AESTHETIC PREFERENCES. Another approach utilizes aesthetic preferences as a means of assessing personality styles. This technique is illustrated by the Barron-Welsh Art Scale, in which the examinee simply records whether he or she likes or dislikes each of 86 black-and-white figures. Two examples are reproduced in Figure 103. The items in this scale were originally selected from a pool of 400 figures because they differentiated between the responses of contrasted criterion groups of artists and nonartists. Subsequent research suggested, however, that performance on the scale may be related to creativity not only in art but also in other fields (Barron, 1965; Welsh, 1975b).

FIG. 103. Typical Figures from the Barron-Welsh Art Scale. For each figure, the respondent merely records "Like" or "Don't Like."
(Copyright © 1949, 1977 by George S. Welsh. Reproduced by permission.)

There are also considerable data on the relation of the Barron-Welsh scale to personality variables. For example, low scorers on this scale tended more often to yield to social pressure, while high scorers tended more often to form independent judgments. In self-descriptions, high scorers more often chose such terms as adventurous, argumentative, dominant, impulsive, shrewd, and unconventional, while low scorers more often chose the adjectives conservative, conventional, industrious, persevering, and thorough, among others. This test has been used extensively in research and has shown some promise as an indicator of fairly broad personality variables.

HUMOR. Reactions to humor have likewise been explored as possible indicators of personality variables. The IPAT Humor Test of Personality (Cattell & Luborsky, 1947; Luborsky & Cattell, 1947), available in two forms, provides jokes and cartoons to be evaluated. Form A consists of 104 pairs of jokes, in each of which the respondent chooses the joke he or she considers funnier. A sample item is shown below:

(*a*) Epitaph to a waiter: (*b*) One prehistoric man to another:
    By and by   "Now that we've learned to communi-
    God caught his eye.   cate with each other—shut up!"

In Form B, 130 jokes or cartoons are individually rated as funny or dull. Although Form A controls the response set to check many or few jokes as funny, Form B provides additional information about the individual's general tendency to regard jokes as funny. For scoring purposes, the items on the Humor test were grouped into clusters on the basis of factor analysis. A separate score is reported for each of 13 personality factors. The rating of jokes has also been used in research on the assessment of attitudes toward contrasting orientations, viewpoints, and social groups (La Fave, Haddad, & Marshall, 1974).

EVALUATION OF PROVERBS. Still another technique utilizes reactions to proverbs or aphorisms. In the Famous Sayings test (Bass, 1958), the examinee responds to each of 130 statements by indicating whether he agrees, disagrees, or is uncertain. Scales identified as Hostility, Fear of Failure, and Conventional Mores were derived through factor analysis. A Social Acquiescence score is also found on the basis of the respondent's general acceptance or rejection of items. Apart from the factorial analyses and a few significant correlations with certain personality inventory scores, validity data for this test were based largely on significant differences between various occupational, regional, educational, and clinical groups (Bass, 1957; Eisenman & Platt; Walsh, 1966).

SITUATIONAL TESTS

Although the term "situational test" was popularized during and following World War II, tests fitting this description had been developed prior to that time. Essentially, a situational test is one that places the examinee in a situation closely resembling or simulating a "real-life" criterion situation. Such tests thus show certain basic similarities to the job-sample technique employed in constructing occupational achievement tests, such as the in-basket test described in Chapter 15. In the present tests, however, the criterion behavior that is sampled is more varied and complex. Moreover, performance is evaluated primarily in terms of emotional, social, attitudinal, and other personality variables, rather than in terms of abilities and knowledge.

TESTS OF THE CHARACTER EDUCATION INQUIRY. Among the earliest situational tests—although they were not so labeled at the time—were those constructed by Hartshorne, May, and their associates (1928, 1929, 1930) for the Character Education Inquiry (CEI). These tests were designed principally as research instruments for use in an extensive project on the nature and development of character in children. Nevertheless, the techniques can be adapted to other testing purposes, and a number have been so utilized.

In general, the CEI techniques made use of familiar, natural situations within the schoolchild's daily routine. The tests were administered in the form of regular classroom examinations, as part of the pupil's homework, in the course of athletic contests, or as party games. Moreover, the children were not aware that they were being tested, except insofar as ordinary school examinations might be involved in the procedure. At the same time, all of the Hartshorne-May tests represented carefully standardized instruments which yielded objective, quantitative scores.

The CEI tests were designed to measure such behavior characteristics as honesty, self-control, and altruism. The largest number were concerned with honesty. One group of tests developed for this purpose utilized a duplicating technique. Common tests such as vocabulary, sentence completion, or arithmetic reasoning were administered in the classroom. The test papers were then collected and a duplicate of each child's responses was made. At a subsequent session, the original, unmarked test papers were returned, and each child scored his or her own paper from a key. Comparison with the duplicate record revealed any changes the individual had made in scoring the paper. Another technique was based on improbable achievement. In the Circles Puzzle, for example, the child was instructed to make a mark in each of 10 small, irregularly arranged circles, while keeping the eyes shut. Control tests under conditions that precluded peeking indicated that a score of more than 13 correctly placed marks in a total of three trials was highly improbable. A score above 13 was therefore recorded as evidence of peeking.

Self-control was assessed in part by the length of time the child persisted in a given task, such as solving a difficult puzzle or reading the ending of a story in which the words were run together. In the latter test, the examiner read aloud the beginning of an exciting story. The children were then given pages containing the rest of the story printed in a form that made reading difficult. As the end of the story was approached, moreover, the difficulty of deciphering the words increased further, as shown in the three successive samples given below (Hartshorne, May, & Maller, 1929):

CHARLESLIFTEDLUCILLETOHISBACK"PUTYOURARMSTIGHT AROUNDMYNECKANDHOLDON"

NoWhoWTogETBaCkONthETREStle.HoWTOBRingTHaTTerrIFIED BURDeNOFAChILDuPtOSafeTY

fiN ALly tAP-tAPC AME ARHYTH Month eBriD GeruNNing fee Tfee Tcom INGtow ArdT Hem

Most of the CEI tests proved to have good discriminative power, yielding a wide range of individual differences in scores. Reliability also appeared to be fairly satisfactory. The children's responses, however, showed considerable situational specificity. The intercorrelations of different tests within each category (e.g., honesty tests or persistence tests) proved to be very low. This specificity is understandable when we consider the operations of the child's interests, values, and motives in different situations. For example, the child who is motivated to excel in school work is not necessarily concerned about achievement in athletic contests or party games. These motivational differences would in turn be reflected in the child's behavior on honesty tests administered in these different contexts. The influence of individual teachers was also apparent in the results; children who cheated in one teacher's room would not do so in another teacher's room. Both in their findings and in their interpretations, the CEI investigators anticipated the subsequent emphasis on situational specificity by four decades. A recent reanalysis of the CEI data, by sophistcated statistical techniques, suggests that a more appropriate model includes both a general factor of honesty and a situational component (Burton, 1963).

SITUATIONAL TESTS IN ASSESSMENT CENTERS. Situational tests constituted a major part of the assessment-center program introduced by the United States Office of Strategic Services (OSS) during World War II. The assessment-center technique involves essentially a "living-in" period of several days, during which candidates are observed and examined in a wide variety of ways. It represented the principal procedure in the selection of military personnel for critical overseas assignments (Murray & MacKinnon, 1946; OSS Assessment Staff, 1948). Similar procedures were subsequently incorporated in the newly established Institute for Personality Assessment and Research at the University of California, as well as in a number of large-scale assessment projects for both military and civilian personnel.[1] Still later, the assessment-center technique, together with some situational tests, was adopted by large industrial corporations for the evaluation of high-level executives. These applications were cited in Chapter 15.

One type of test developed by the OSS was the *situational stress* test, designed to sample the individual's behavior under stressful, frustrating, or emotionally disruptive conditions. For example, the examinee was assigned a task to perform with two "helpers" who were obstructive and uncooperative. Another type of situational test employed a *leaderless group* as a device for appraising such characteristics as teamwork, resourcefulness, initiative, and leadership. In such tests, the assigned task requires the cooperative efforts of a group of examinees, none of whom is designated as leader or given specific responsibilities. Examples from the OSS program include the Brook Situation, involving the transfer of personnel and equipment across a brook

[1] An account of these milestone assessment studies, beginning with the OSS program. can be found in Wiggins (1973, Ch. 11).

with maximum speed and safety; and the Wall Situation, in which men and materials had to be conveyed over a double wall separated by an imaginary canyon.

A promising variant of this technique is the Leaderless Group Discussion (LGD). Requiring a minimum of equipment and time, this technique has been used widely in the selection of such groups as military officers, civil service supervisors and administrators, industrial executives and management trainees, sales trainees, teachers, and social workers (Bass, 1954). Essentially, the group is assigned a topic for discussion during a specified period. Examiners observe and rate each person's performance but do not participate in the discussion. Although often used under informal and unstandardized conditions, the LGD has been subjected to considerable research. Rater reliability has been found to be reasonably high for both LGD and other situational tests based on group decision-making through discussion (Greenwood & McNamara, 1967). Rating accuracy can also be improved through training programs that emphasize the observation and recording of specific behavior and that alert raters to common errors of observation and judgment (Thornton & Zorich, 1980).

Validity studies suggest that LGD techniques are among the most effective applications of situational tests. Many significant and sizable correlations have been found between ratings from LGD performance and follow-up or concurrent ratings obtained in military, industrial, and social settings (Bass, 1954; Guilford, 1959). Some of these correlations are as high as .60. It is also interesting to note that leadership ratings based on a one-hour LGD correlated over .60 with leadership assessment from three days of situational testing in the OSS program (OSS Assessment Staff, 1948). A similar correlation between LGD and an entire battery of situational tests was found by Vernon (1950) in a British study.

Neither LGD nor other, more elaborate situational tests, however, have proved valid as devices for assessing broad personality traits. All such tests appear to be most effective when they approximate actual worksamples of the criterion behavior they are designed to predict. The LGD tests in particular have some validity in predicting performance in jobs requiring a certain amount of verbal communication, verbal problem-solving, and acceptance by peers. Another factor that seems to increase the predictive validity of situational tests is job familiarity on the part of the raters. Such a finding again suggests that situational tests work best when the examinee's performance is interpreted as a worksample rather than in terms of underlying personality variables.

ROLEPLAYING OR IMPROVISATION. Some situational tests employ roleplaying to elicit the behavior of interest. Although roleplaying was one of the techniques used in the OSS assessment program, it has earlier origins and wider applications. A comprehensive survey of the history, rationale, and varieties of the roleplaying or improvisation technique can be found in McReynolds and DeVoge (1978). In this technique, the individual is explicitly instructed to play a part, either overtly (with or without other persons) or by reporting verbally what he or she would do or say. The situation may be presented realistically, as on a stage, or through audiotape, videotape, or printed description. The previously cited leaderless group discussion, as well as certain other situational tests, may be regarded as variants or elaborations of roleplaying.

In the 1970s, the improvisation technique underwent significant technological advances and enjoyed heightened popularity. A major current application is in the occupational assessment of personnel, especially when interpersonal behavior is important in the job functions. This application is illustrated by several assessment-center activities cited in Chapter 15. A special example pertains to the evaluation of counselor effectiveness. In this situation, the counselor is observed and rated while conducting a counseling session with a "coached client," i.e., a member of the assessment staff in the role of a client who presents a preselected and standardized problem (Kelz, 1966).

Other growing applications can be found in the selection of recruits for police work and in the evaluation of physicians' skills in communicating with patients. An example of the former involves a loitering situation (Mills, 1976). The problem pertains to complaints about a juvenile gang bothering people in a certain neighborhood and stealing small items. The scene begins with two police recruits—one in the role of police officer, the other in the role of the gang leader—meeting to discuss the problem. In the course of the discussion, a store owner (played by a staff member) interrupts and demands that the police officer make the gang leave. Improvisation continues from that point on. In the medical application (Levine & McGuire, 1968), the candidate may conduct a diagnostic interview with a member of the assessment staff in the role of patient; or the candidate, having received a description of the medical problem of the simulated patient, is asked to explain the treatment plan to the patient.

In clinical psychology, roleplaying has undergone its most extensive and systematic development. Although employed over several decades by psychotherapists representing several different theoretical orientations, it has recently come into special prominence in behavior modification programs. It lends itself particularly well to the evaluation of self-assertiveness, social skills, and the expression of anger. The realism of roleplaying as perceived by participants is evidenced by the finding that the roleplaying of anger-arousing situations is accompanied by such physiological changes as rise in blood pressure and increase in galvanic skin response (Novaco, 1975). Roleplaying is also being applied effectively in family therapy and in the counseling of married couples.

SELF-CONCEPTS AND PERSONAL CONSTRUCTS

PHENOMENOLOGICAL INFLUENCE. A number of current approaches to personality assessment concentrate on the way individuals view themselves and others. Such techniques reflect the influence of phenomenological psychology, which focuses on how events are *perceived* by the individual (G. A. Kelly, 1955, 1963, 1970; Snygg & Combs, 1959). The individual's self-description thus becomes of primary importance in its own right, rather than being regarded as a second-best substitute for other behavioral observations. Interest also centers on the extent of self-acceptance shown by the individual.

It might be argued that self-concept tests do not differ essentially from the self-report inventories discussed in Chapter 17. True, but it would be more accurate to say that self-report inventories are actually measures of self-concept. The interpretation of personality inventory responses in terms of self-conceptualization forms the basis of a provocative hypothesis formulated by Loevinger (1966a, 1966b; Loevinger & Ossorio, 1958; Loevinger, Wessler, & Redmore, 1970). Bringing together many disparate findings from her own research and that of others, Loevinger proposed a personality trait which she defined as the capacity to conceptualize oneself, or to "assume distance" from oneself and one's impulses. According to Loevinger, it is the manifestations of this trait in personality inventories that have been described in such terms as façade, test-taking defensiveness, response set, social desirability, acquiescence, and personal style. In common with a number of other psychologists, Loevinger regards such test-taking attitudes, not as instrumental errors to be ruled out, but as the major source of valid variance in personality inventories.

On the basis of data from many sources, Loevinger suggested that ability to form a self-concept increases with age, intelligence, education, and socioeconomic level. At the lowest point, illustrated by the infant, the individual is incapable of self-conceptualization. As the ability develops, the child gradually forms a stereotyped, conventional, and socially acceptable concept of himself or herself. This stage Loevinger considers typical of adolescence. With increasing maturity, the individual progresses beyond such a stereotyped concept to a differentiated and realistic self-concept. At this point, individuals are fully aware of their idiosyncrasies and accept themselves for what they are. It is this trait of self-conceptualization, later designated as ego development or I-level, that Loevinger and her associates undertook to measure in the Washington University Sentence Completion Test, described in Chapter 19.

According to Loevinger, many (if not most) persons fail to reach the final stage of differentiated self-concept. Insofar as personality inventory responses are evaluated in terms of normative data, individuals whose self-concepts are at the stereotyped conventional stage receive higher or "better-adjusted" scores. In the course of psychotherapy, some persons may advance beyond this stage to the individualized self-concept and hence may show a decline in scores on adjustment inventories (Loevinger & Ossorio, 1958). Such a hypothesis could account for the apparent failures of personality inventories when used in a clinical setting. The finding by some investigators (Sanford, 1956) that, when evaluated in terms of personality inventory norms, college seniors appear to have poorer emotional adjustment than college freshmen may have a similar explanation. Essentially, Loevinger argues that the capacity for self-conceptualization is an important personality trait and that the relation of this trait to personality inventory scores is not linear but curvilinear.

The procedures to be considered in this section all have as their primary focus individuals' perceptions of themselves and others. Another common feature of these procedures is their applicability to intensive investigation of the individual case. For this reason, they are of special interest to the clinical psychologist. Many of them, in fact, have originated within a clinical setting.

THE ADJECTIVE CHECK LIST. Several techniques have been specially developed for assessing self-concepts (Strong & Feder, 1961). A widely applicable instrument that is commercially available is the Adjective Check List (ACL). Originally constructed for use in the research program of the Institute for Personality Assessment and Research (IPAR), this instrument provides a list of 300 adjectives arranged alphabetically from "absentminded" to "zany" (Gough, 1960; Gough & Heilbrun, 1980b). Respondents mark all the adjectives they consider descriptive of themselves.

In its current form, the ACL can be scored for 37 scales. Four are response set scales,[2] including the total number of adjectives marked, the number of these that are favorable, the number unfavorable, and a communality score based on a set of frequently endorsed and a set of infrequently endorsed adjectives. The total number of items marked is not only used to adjust the scores on the other scales but is also of interest in its own right. Persons marking many adjectives tend to be described as vivacious, enthusiastic, and self-seeking; those marking few adjectives, as quiet, reserved, and conventional. Similarly, an extremely low score on the communality scale may indicate either erratic and careless responding or a deliberate attempt to falsify responses. Above such a designated cutoff point, however, individual differences on this scale can also be interpreted in terms of empirically established diagnostic implications.

A major cluster of scales was originally prepared on a rational or content basis, by assigning adjectives to each of the 15 Murray needs covered by the EPPS (Ch. 17). Examples are the need for Achievement, Dominance, Affiliation, Order, and Autonomy. The ACL is thus one more instrument re-

[2] Described in the manual as "modus operandi scales."

flecting the influence of Murray's classification of personality needs. A set of nine "topical scales" was developed principally through empirical criterion keying of items to measure various traits considered important in interpersonal behavior. Among them are Self-Control, Self-Confidence, and Personal Adjustment. The two remaining clusters of scales were designed to fit specialized personality theories. A set of five Transactional Analysis scales was developed by assigning items to personality components defined on the basis of a theory of personality and psychopathology proposed by Berne (1961, 1966). A set of four Origence-Intellectence scales was constructed through empirical selection of items against criteria derived from Welsh's (1975b) theory of creativity and intelligence. For all 37 scales, a major source of empirical validation data, employed at some stage in the development of each scale, was the direct observation of participants in assessment center programs at IPAR. Derived from extensive behavioral observations by multiple staff members, the resulting trait ratings provided criterion data with a high degree of interjudge agreement. On the basis of these IPAR assessments as well as other supplementary research, the manual provides personality descriptions of persons scoring high and low on each scale.

As a research instrument, the ACL has been applied to a staggering variety of problems, drawn from such areas as psychopathology, occupational choice, creativity, political and economic behavior, and even patients' reactions to orthodontia and to contact lenses. It has also been employed in rating historical personages from their biographies and published works (Welsh, 1975a) and in characterizing inanimate objects, such as cities or automobiles. Its use has so far been reported in some 700 publications.[3]

Q SORT. Another special technique suitable for investigating self-concepts is the Q sort originally developed by Stephenson (1953). In this technique, the individual is given a set of cards containing statements or trait names to be sorted into piles ranging from "most characteristic" to "least characteristic" of himself or herself. The items may come from a standard list, but more often are designed to fit the individual case. To ensure uniform distribution of ratings, a "forced-normal" distribution is used, the respondent being instructed to place a specified number of cards in each pile. Such a distribution can be prepared for any size of item sample by reference to a normal curve table. It should be noted that, like the forced-choice technique discussed in Chapter 17, the Q sort yields ipsative rather than normative data. In other words, respondents tell us which they consider their strong and which their weak traits, but not how strong they believe themselves to be in comparison with other persons or with some outside norm.

Q sorts have been employed to study a variety of psychological problems (Bem & Funder, 1978; Block, 1971a, 1978; S. R. Brown, 1968; Mowrer, 1953;

[3] A complete ACL bibliography is available from the test publisher (Gough & Heilbrun, 1980a). For a review of the general ACL technique, see Masterson (1975).

Rogers & Dymond, 1954). In intensive investigations of individual personality, the respondent is often asked to re-sort the same set of items within different frames of reference. For example, the items may be sorted as they apply to oneself and to other persons, such as one's father, mother, husband, or wife. Or they may be sorted as they apply to oneself in different settings, such as job, home, or social situations. Q sorts can likewise be obtained for individuals as they believe they actually are (real self), as they believe others see them (social self), and as they would like to be (ideal self). To observe change, Q sorts may be obtained successively at different stages during psychotherapy, a procedure that has been followed especially by client-centered therapists. With therapy, the self-concept tends to become more favorable and to resemble more closely the individual's ideal-self concept[4] (Rogers & Dymond, 1954, Ch. 4).

THE SEMANTIC DIFFERENTIAL. This technique was first developed by Osgood and his associates (Osgood, Suci, & Tannenbaum, 1957) as a tool for research on the psychology of meaning, although its possibilities for personality assessment were soon recognized. The Semantic Differential represents a standardized and quantified procedure for measuring the connotations of any given concept for the individual. Each concept is rated on a 7-point graphic scale as being more closely related to one or the other of a

FATHER

Good	Bad
Clean	Dirty
Cruel	Kind
Slow	Fast
Valuable	Worthless
Tense	Relaxed
Strong	Weak
Large	Small

FIG. 104. Illustration of the Semantic Differential Technique. In rating the concept "Father," respondent places a check mark on the appropriate segment of each scale. Usually a much larger number of scales is employed.

4 All these procedures can, of course, be followed also with the previously described Adjective Check List or with any other techniques for assessing self-concepts.

pair of opposites, as illustrated in Figure 104. For every concept, a series of these bipolar adjectival scales is employed; usually 15 or more scales are included. Intercorrelations and factorial analyses of the original set of 50 scales developed by Osgood revealed three major factors: *Evaluative,* with high loadings in such scales as good-bad, valuable-worthless, and clean-dirty; *Potency,* found in such scales as strong-weak, large-small, and heavy-light; and *Activity,* identified in such scales as active-passive, fast-slow, and sharp-dull. The evaluative factor is the most conspicuous, accounting for the largest percentage of total variance.

Responses on the Semantic Differential can be analyzed in several ways. For quantitative treatment, the ratings on each scale can be assigned numerical values from 1 to 7, or from -3 to $+3$. The overall similarity of any two concepts for an individual or a group can then be measured in terms of their positions on all scales. The connotations of all concepts rated by a single individual can be investigated by computing the "score" of each concept in the three principal factors described above. Thus, on a scale extending from -3 to $+3$, a given individual's concept of "My Brother" may rate -2 in the evaluative factor, 0.1 in potency, and 2.7 in activity.

The concepts to be rated can be chosen to fit whatever problem is being investigated. Respondents can, for example, be asked to rate themselves, members of their family, friends, employers, teachers, or public figures; members of different ethnic or cultural groups; persons engaged in different occupations; activities, such as studying or outdoor sports; abstract ideas, such as confusion, hatred, sickness, peace, or love; product names or brand names; and radio or television programs. The Semantic Differential has been applied in many different contexts, in research on such varied problems as clinical diagnosis and therapy, vocational choices, cultural differences, and consumers' reactions to products and brand names (Snider & Osgood, 1969). The bibliography on the Semantic Differential includes over 1,500 references.

ROLE CONSTRUCT REPERTORY TEST. A technique devised specifically as an aid in clinical practice is the Role Construct Repertory Test (Rep Test) developed by G. A. Kelly (1955, 1963, 1970). The development of the Rep Test is intimately related to Kelly's personality theory. A basic proposition in this theory is that the concepts or constructs an individual uses to perceive objects or events influence his or her behavior. In the course of psychotherapy, it is frequently necessary to build new constructs and to discard some old constructs before progress can be made.

The Rep Test is designed to help the clinician identify some of the client's important constructs about people. Although the test can be administered in many ways, including both group and individual versions, one of its simpler variants will serve to illustrate its essential characteristics.[5] In this variant,

[5] For descriptions of other procedural variants, see Bannister and Mair (1968).

the examinee is first given a Role Title List and asked to name a person in his or her experience who fits each role title. Typical roles might include: your father, your wife or present girlfriend, a teacher you liked, a person with whom you have been closely associated recently who appears to dislike you. The examiner next selects three of the persons named and asks, "In what *important way* are two of them alike but diffeernt from the third?" This procedure is repeated with many other sets of three names, in which some of the names recur in different combinations.

The Rep Test yields a wealth of qualitative data. A simplified factor-analytic procedure was also developed for quantitative identification of constructs that are important for each individual. Other investigators have identified major dimensions of role constructs through analyses of group data (Messick & Kogan, 1966). When individuals were scored on these dimensions, the scores were found to correlate significantly with certain cognitive and personality variables. In another study, retests over a two-week interval with both identical and different instructions revealed a high level of stability in the constructs employed by individuals (Fjeld & Landfield, 1961).

The Rep Test, in its various modifications, has been used in considerable research on various problems relating to personality theory. Among the indices derived from the respondent's classifications of familiar persons is one designated as *cognitive complexity*. This index is based on the number of different constructs employed by an individual and is regarded as a measure of cognitive style. A higher degree of cognitive complexity means that the individual employs more dimensions, and hence a more differentiated cognitive system, in organizing or representing the environment (Bieri, 1971; Bieri, Atkins, Briar, Leaman, Miller, & Tripodi, 1966; McReynolds & Blackman, 1978a, pp. 483–487; 1978b). Psychometric data on the Rep Test as a measure of cognitive complexity are reported by Menasco and Curry (1978), with special reference to reliability and construct validation.

OBSERVER REPORTS

The tests considered thus far give ample evidence of the variety of approaches that have been followed in the assessment of personality. Yet the best that can be said about most of them is that they are promising experimental instruments, suitable for research purposes, or useful adjuncts in the hands of the skilled clinician. It is apparent that for the assessment of personality variables today one cannot rely entirely on standardized tests. Other sources of information are needed to follow up or supplement the leads provided by test scores, to assess traits for which no adequate tests are available, and to obtain criterion data for developing and validating personality tests.

It is important to recognize that, especially in the domain of personality, tests cannot do the whole assessment job. Direct observations of behavior play an essential part in personality appraisal, whether in the clinic, counseling center, classroom, personnel office, or any other context calling for individual evaluations. To place such behavioral observations in the proper perspective, we must remember that all tests are themselves evaluations of small samples of behavior. To be sure, these behavior samples are obtained and evaluated under standardized conditions. But against the obvious advantages of such standardized procedures, we must balance the advantages of a much more extensive sampling of behavior available through observational techniques in natural settings. To take an extreme example, if we had a detailed biography of a person extending from birth to age 30, we could probably predict his or her subsequent behavior more accurately than could be done with any test or battery of tests. Such a record of all the minutiae and circumstances of a person's life would be hard to come by; but if we had it, we could make predictions from a 30-year behavior sample rather than from the one- or two-hour samples provided by tests.

In all the techniques to be considered in this section, what the individual does in natural contexts over relatively long periods of time is transmitted through the medium of one or more observers. Much can be done to improve the accuracy and communicability of such observations.

NATURALISTIC OBSERVATION. Techniques for the direct observation of spontaneous behavior in natural settings have been employed most widely by child psychologists, particularly with preschool children. Although such procedures can be followed with persons of any age, the younger the individual the less likely is it that the behavior of interest will be affected by the presence of the observer or that the individual has developed the social façades that complicate the interpretation of behavior. These observational techniques have also proved useful in the classroom, especially if the observer is the teacher or someone else who fits readily into the normal school setting. A major application of such assessment techniques is to be found in behavior modification programs conducted in schools, homes, child-care centers, clinics, hospitals, or any other context (Kent & Foster, 1977). Several ingenious applications of naturalistic observation have also been devised for research in social psychology (Webb, Campbell, Schwartz, Sechrest & Grove, 1981).

Naturalistic observation covers a wide variety of procedures (Jones, Reid, & Patterson, 1975; J. S. Wiggins, 1973, pp. 295–327). They range from comprehensive, long-term techniques, as illustrated by the diary method, to more narrowly circumscribed, shorter, and more highly controlled observations, as illustrated by time sampling. The latter comprises a representative distribution of short observation periods. Depending on the nature and purpose of the observations, such periods may vary in length from less than a minute to several hours; periods of five minutes or less are the most common. The observations may be concentrated in one day or spaced over several months. They may cover all behavior occurring during the specified period; but more often they are limited to a particular kind of behavior, such as language, locomotion, interpersonal behavior, or aggression. Checklists of what to look for are a useful observational aid. Other procedural aids include observational schedules, record forms, coding systems, and mechanical recording devices. When practicable, automatic recordings can be made on tape, film, or videotape. The use of radio telemetry is also being explored for this purpose (Miklich, 1975). The late 1970s witnessed a dramatic increase in research on naturalistic-observation techniques, with special reference to their psychometric evaluation (Kent & Foster, 1977).

It might be noted that naturalistic observations have much in common with the previously discussed situational tests. They differ principally in two respects: in naturalistic observations, no control is exerted over the stimulus situation, and—at least in most observational methods—a more extensive behavior sample is observed.

THE INTERVIEW. Mention should also be made of the time-honored source of information provided by interviewing techniques. Interviewing serves many purposes in clinical psychology, counseling, personnel psychology, and education. Discussions of the methods, applications, and effectiveness of interviewing, and of research on the interviewing process can be found in several sources.[6] In form, interviews may vary from the highly structured (representing little more than an orally administered questionnaire), through patterned or guided interviews covering certain predetermined areas, to nondirective and depth interviews in which the interviewer merely sets the stage and encourages the interviewee to talk as freely as possible.

Interviews provide chiefly two kinds of information. First, they afford an opportunity for direct observation of a rather limited sample of behavior manifested during the interview situation itself. For example, the individual's speech, language usage, poise, and manner in meeting a stranger can be noted. A much more important function of interviewing, however, is to elicit life-history data. What the individual has done in the past is a good indicator of what he or she may do in the future, especially when interpreted in the light of concomitant circumstances and of the person's own comments regarding his or her actions. The interview should concern itself not only with what has happened to the individual but also with his or her perceptions of these events and current evaluations of them.

On the interviewer's part, the interview requires skill in data gathering and in data interpreting. An interview may lead to wrong decisions

6 See, e.g., Arvey (1979), Bernstein, Bernstein, and Dana (1974), Bingham, Moore, and Gustad (1959), Dunnette and Borman (1979), Fear (1973), Grant and Bray (1969), Kahn and Cannell (1957), Matarazzo and Wiens (1972), Meyer, Liddell, and Lyons (1977), and Ulrich and Trumbo (1965).

because important data were not elicited or because given data were inadequately or incorrectly interpreted. An important qualification of the successful interviewer is sensitivity in identifying clues in the interviewee's behavior or in facts he or she reports. Such clues then lead to further probing for other facts that may either support or contradict the original hypothesis.

RATINGS. Although ratings may be obtained in many contexts and for diverse purposes, the present section is concerned with the use of ratings as an evaluation of the individual by the rater on the basis of cumulative, uncontrolled observations of daily life. Such ratings differ from naturalistic observations in that the data are accumulated casually and informally; they also involve interpretation and judgment, rather than simple recording of observations. In contrast to both naturalistic observation and interviews, however, they typically cover a longer observation period and the information is obtained under more realistic conditions. Ratings are used extensively in assessing individuals in educational and industrial settings, in obtaining criterion data for test validation, and for many research purposes. The 1970s and 1980s saw a significant upsurge of research on rating techniques, with emphasis on comprehensive, systematic investigations and sufficient standardization of definitions and procedures to facilitate comparison of findings across studies (Landy & Farr, 1980; Saal, Downey, & Lahey, 1980).

Much can be done to improve the accuracy of ratings. A common difficulty arises from ambiguity in either trait names, scale units, or both. To meet this problem, each trait should be defined in specific terms, and the ratings should be expressed in a form that will be uniformly interpreted by all raters. Rather than using numbers or general descriptive adjectives that convey different meanings to different raters, degrees of a trait may be more clearly identified in terms of critical incidents or graded behavior samples. Smith and Kendall (1963) developed a refinement of such behaviorally anchored rating scales whereby both the qualities to be rated and the behavior samples are empirically formulated and scaled by groups of judges drawn from the same populations as the raters who will eventually use the scales. Although this method has proved effective in the development of rating scales for assessing performance in a variety of business and professional groups, scale format seems less important than is the use of carefully formulated behavioral anchors (Dickinson & Zellinger, 1980). There is also evidence that the relative accuracy of different scale formats may vary with the nature of the job or the performance function to be rated (Borman, 1979).

One of the conditions that affects the validity of ratings is the extent of the rater's *relevant contact* with the person to be rated (Freeberg, 1969; Landy & Farr, 1980). It is not enough to have known the person for a long time. The rater should have had an opportunity to observe him or her in situations in which the behavior in question could be manifested. For example, if an employee has never had an opportunity to make decisions on the job, her or his ability to do so cannot be evaluated by the supervisor. In many rating situations, it is desirable to include a space to be checked in lieu of a rating if the rater has had no opportunity to observe the particular trait in a given individual.

Ratings are subject to a number of constant errors. A well-known example is the *halo effect*. This is a tendency on the part of raters to be unduly influenced by a single favorable or unfavorable trait, which colors their judgment of the individual's other traits. One way to reduce halo effect is to define traits in terms of concrete behavior. Various other procedures have been found to lower the halo effect, but only by small amounts. No method has been devised that effectively eliminates it, and research on alternative solutions still goes on (King, Hunter, & Schmidt, 1980; Landy, Vance, Barnes-Farrell, & Steele, 1980).

Another constant error is the *error of central tendency*, or the tendency to place persons in the middle of the scale and to avoid extreme positions. Still another is the *leniency error*, referring to the reluctance of many raters to assign unfavorable ratings. The former causes a bunching of ratings in the center of the scale, the latter at the upper end. Both errors reduce the effective width of the scale and make ratings less discriminative. One way to eliminate these errors is to employ ranking or other *order-of-merit procedures*. All these procedures force discrimination among individuals and hence maximize the information yielded by the ratings. They also share the common feature of providing only relative evaluations within a group, rather than absolute evaluations against a constant, external standard. In simple ranking, someone in each group must be first and someone must be last, regardless of the quality of the group as a whole. This is also true of such techniques as paired comparisons, in which each individual is compared in turn with every other, and of forced distributions, in which the number of persons to be classified in each category is specified. All these techniques are applicable when comparisons are made within a single group; but they do not permit direct comparisons across groups evaluated by different raters.

The rating process can usually be improved by training the raters. Research in various settings has demonstrated the effectiveness of training in increasing reliability and validity of ratings and in reducing common judgment errors (Bernardin & Pence, 1980; Borman, 1979; Ivancevich, 1979; Landy & Farr, 1980). It should be noted, however, that many different types of training have been included in rater training programs, and their effects vary in kind, amount, and duration. Training may involve familiarization with the use of a particular rating format, strengthening rater knowledge of job requirements, analysis of common rating errors and ways of minimizing their influence, or improvement of observational skills. Any one or some combination of these and other types of training would be most appropriate for particular rating contexts. In most situations, however, enhancing the raters' observational skills is likely to yield favorable results.

NOMINATING TECHNIQUE. A rating procedure that is especially useful in obtaining peer assessments is the nominating technique. Originally developed in sociometry (Moreno, 1953) for investigating group structure, this technique may be used within any group of persons who have been together long enough to be acquainted with one another, as in a class, factory, institution, club, or military unit. Each individual is asked to choose one or more group members with whom he or she would like to study, work, eat lunch, play, or carry out any other designated function. Respondents may be asked to nominate as many group members as they wish, or a specified number (such as first, second, and third choice), or only one person for each function.

When used for individual assessment, the nominations received by any one person can serve to identify potential leaders (who receive many choices) as well as isolates (who are rarely or ever mentioned). In addition, several indices can be computed for a more precise assessment of each individual. The simplest is a count of the number of times an individual was nominated for a specific function, which can be treated as her or his peer rating. The nominating technique can be employed with reference to any behavior of interest. For example, the respondents may be asked to name the person who has the most original ideas, who can be counted on to get the job done, or who is the best sport. They may be asked to designate not only the person who is most like the given description but also the one who is least like it. In that case, positive nominations would be weighted +1 and negative nominations −1 in totaling each person's score. It should be added that peer assessments can also be obtained through other procedures, such as ranking or rating; but the nominating technique seems to have proved most successful and has been used most often (Kane & Lawler, 1978 —see also Brief, 1980; Kane & Lawler, 1980).

A variant of the nominating technique that is especially applicable in obtaining children's ratings of each other is the "Guess Who" technique, first used in the Character Education Inquiry together with the previously discussed situational tests. In this technique, the children are given a number of brief "word pictures" and are instructed to write under each the name of every classmate who might fit the description. Examples include (Hartshorne, May, & Maller, 1929, p. 88):

This is a jolly good fellow—friends with everyone, no matter who they are.

This one is always picking on others and annoying them.

Using the same approach with more sophisticated psychometric procedures, Wiggins and Winder (J. S. Wiggins, 1973, pp. 358–363; Wiggins &

Winder, 1961a, 1961b) developed the Peer Nomination Inventory for assessing the social adjustment of preadolescent boys. The items or descriptive statements for which individuals are nominated were themselves empirically developed from recorded interviews with some 250 8- to 12-year-old boys. The end product was a list of 64 peer-rating items, such as "He's absent from school a lot" or "He's always losing things." The inventory yields scores in five variables: aggression, dependency, withdrawal, depression, and likability.

Still another variant was developed for use with preschool children (Asher, Singleton, Tinsley, & Hymel, 1979). The materials consisted of individual photographs of each child in the group. In one part of the study, the usual sociometric procedure was followed, each child being asked to point to the pictures of three classmates he or she liked to play with and three he or she did not like to play with. In another part, children were asked to rate pictures of *each* classmate according to how much they liked to play with that child, by assigning the picture to one of three faces: a happy face, a neutral face, or a sad face. Individual mean ratings obtained by the latter procedure yielded a much higher retest reliability over a four-week interval than did those obtained by the usual sociometric procedure.

However obtained, peer assessments have generally proved to be one of the most dependable of rating techniques in such diverse groups as military personnel, industrial supervisors, Peace Corps volunteers, and college students (Kane & Lawler, 1978; Reynolds, 1966; J. S. Wiggins, 1973, pp. 356–357). When checked against a variety of practical criteria dependent on interpersonal relations, such ratings have been found to have good predictive validity. These findings are understandable when we consider some of the features of peer ratings. First, the number of raters is large, including all group members. Second, an individual's peers are often in a particularly favorable position to observe his or her typical behavior. They may thus be better judges of certain interpersonal traits than teachers, supervisors, and other outside observers. Third, and probably most important, is the fact that the opinions of group members—right or wrong—influence their actions and hence partly determine the nature of the individual's subsequent interactions with the group. Other comparable groups may be expected to react toward the individual in a similar fashion. Sociometric ratings may thus be said to have content validity in the same sense as worksamples.

CHECKLISTS AND Q SORTS. Any self-report instrument, such as the personality and interest inventories discussed in Chapters 17 and 18, may also be employed by an observer in describing another person. Instruments designed to assess self-concept are especially well suited to this purpose. The Adjective Check List (ACL) has been used extensively to obtain observers' evaluations in the IPAR research program (Gough & Heilbrun, 1980). Trained psychologists who have observed the subject closely over a two- or three-day assessment period record their evaluations by checking the appropriate adjectives on the list.

The Q sort has also been widely used for observer evaluations. Block (1978) describes the California Q-Sort Deck, which was specially developed to provide a standard language for comprehensive personality evaluations by professionally trained observers. The materials consist of 100 statements to be sorted into a 9-point forced distribution. The statements are sorted with regard to their "salience" for the individual—that is, their importance in specifying the unique and essential characteristics of the individual. Thus, the ipsative frame of reference typical of Q sorts is retained; the individual is not compared with outside normative standards.

The availability of such a uniform set of Q-sort items facilitates communication and assures comparability of data from different observers. The standard Q sort can also be used for a number of other research or clinical purposes. With it, evaluations can be recorded not only from personal observations but also from case histories, interviews, or projective tests. In validation research on projective techniques, for example, Q sorts have been used to obtain both criterion and test evaluations from different observers. Since the two sets of evaluations are expressed in the same terms, direct comparisons between them can be made. Another application involves the use of this technique in individual assessments. In this connection, Block (1978) provides examples of three "defining Q sorts," representing a consensus evaluation of an optimally normal individual and two psychiatric syndromes, against which a given individual's Q sort can be compared. Similar defining Q sorts may be developed for any desired category of persons. Block (1971a) has also used the Q sort in a global, developmental study of personality data from the files of two major longitudinal studies, the Oakland Growth Study and the California Guidance Study, both conducted in the San Francisco Bay Area. The age range covered by the data extends from adolescence to the mid-30s.

BIOGRAPHICAL INVENTORIES

Both in the discussion of interviewing techniques earlier in this chapter and in the discussion of the clinician's data-gathering function in Chapter 16, reference was made to the importance of life-history data. Carefully designed biographical inventories represent an attempt to obtain some of the same types of information under uniform conditions and in situations where it would not be feasible to conduct individual interviews. In some cases, moreover, the biographical inventory may be used as a preliminary instrument to facilitate and expedite the interview.

Like the personality inventories surveyed in Chapters 17 and 18, the biographical inventory is a self-report instrument. But most of its questions generally pertain to relatively objective and readily verifiable facts. The application forms filled out by prospective employees or by students seeking admission to an educational institution are examples of biographical inventories. Typical items deal with amount and nature of education, job experiences, special skills, hobbies, and recreational activities. Frequently the individual's reaction to prior experiences is sought, as when respondents are asked about the courses they liked best and least in school, or what they liked and disliked in their job experiences. Some biographical inventories also include items quite similar to those found in interest inventories.

For maximum predictive effectiveness, biographical inventory items have often been selected and weighted by criterion keying, as in the construction of such inventories as the MMPI and the SCII discussed in Chapters 17 and 18. The resulting inventory should then be cross-validated against the same criterion in a new sample. When this procedure has been followed, biographical inventories have proved to be consistently good predictors of performance in a wide diversity of contexts. Biographical inventories have been empirically developed against such varied criteria as amount of insurance sold by life insurance agents, job turnover of bank clerks, productivity of research scientists, artistic creativity of high school students, and performance of naval personnel in diver training. Such inventories have proved valid as predictors of job performance in groups ranging from unskilled workers, office clerks, and service station dealers to chemists, engineers, and high-level executives (Anastasi, 1979, pp. 79–80; Owens, 1976).

Special applications of the biographical inventory technique have been developed by the United States Office of Personnel Management (Primoff, 1980; Schmidt & Bemis, 1979). The basic approach begins with the premise that "the best predictor of future behaviors of a given kind is a measure of past behaviors of a similar nature" (Schmidt & Bemis, 1979, p. 7). The procedure was designed as a replacement for the traditional "credentialing" approach to applicant evaluation. Unlike the latter, it focuses on specific, job-relevant past achievements, rather than on the passive exposure implied by the customary education and experience records. Because it enables applicants to cite *any* job-relevant achievements—drawn from similar or dissimilar jobs or from nonoccupational settings—this procedure is especially appropriate for assessing the qualifications of women and minority groups.

In its most fully developed current form, designated as the *behavioral consistency method*, the procedure involves the following major steps. First, for each job, one must identify a small number of behavioral dimensions that differentiate between superior and marginal job performers. Parenthetically, it might be noted that this is one more application of Clark Hull's critical part activities (Ch. 15). The necessary information for this step is obtained from experienced job supervisors. The critical behavioral dimensions finally chosen (usually five to seven) are incorporated in the application form. Two samples of such dimensions are:

Analytical Reasoning Abilities: How good are you at logical reasoning? Can you distinguish essential from unessential information in problem solving? Consider especially complex and technical information. Such information may be either numerical or verbal.

Interpersonal Skills: How well can you deal with all types of people? Do you show tact and diplomacy in getting work done with and through others?

Second, the applicant reports any past achievements that are related to each of these behavioral dimensions. Applicants are encouraged to describe in detail at least two specific achievements for each dimension, giving the following information for each recorded achievement:

A. What the problem or objective was.

B. What he or she actually did and when.

C. What the outcome or result was.

D. What percentage of the credit he or she claims for the outcome.

E. The name of someone who can verify the achievement, with address and phone number if possible.

Third, in arriving at a final evaluation of the applicant's job qualifications, personnel staffing specialists rate each reported achievement for degree of relevance to the particular job. In this rating, they use as a guide a set of scaled, job-performance benchmarks, which were developed for the given job. Preliminary research with the behavioral consistency method has shown that the procedures are practicable and that the results have promising reliability and validity.

From another angle, Owens and Schoenfeldt (Owens, 1968; Owens & Schoenfeldt, 1979) present a theoretical rationale for the use of biographical inventory data to bridge the gap between psychometric and experimental approaches to psychological research. For the psychometrician, the biographical inventory can provide the antecedent information from the individual's experiential history needed for a better understanding of the correlations found among current variables, such as test scores and criterion measures. For the experimental psychologist, the biographical inventory can help to identify relatively homogeneous subgroups or types of persons, classified on the basis of their past experience. Generalizations regarding the effects of experimental variables could then be tested separately in such subgroups and, if necessary, modified.

THE ASSESSMENT OF ENVIRONMENTAL QUALITIES AND ECOLOGICAL ATTITUDES

APPROACHES TO ENVIRONMENTAL PSYCHOLOGY. Emerging as a distinct field of study in the mid-1960s, environmental psychology has exhibited a phenomenal growth in scope and activity. In view of the many ways in which the concept of environment enters into the science of psychology, it is not surprising that the terms "environmental psychology" and "ecological psychology" have been used to cover a wide diversity of topics (Craik, 1971, 1973; Moos, 1973, 1976; W. B. Walsh, 1973; Wicker, 1981). In its more restricted sense, current environmental psychology reflects the general societal concern with such problems as conservation of animal and plant life, depletion of natural resources, and pollution of air and water. Within this area, a variety of assessment techniques are being explored, ranging from a Landscape Adjective Check List for describing natural scenery (Craik, 1971) to self-report inventories on environmental attitudes.

Other aspects of environmental psychology have their roots in earlier fields of psychological research and practice. Thus, environmental psychology overlaps much of engineering psychology and systems research, which are concerned with the effects of the immediate environment on the individual's performance level and general well-bing (Moos, 1976). The relevant environmental variables pertain not only to such physical factors as lighting, temperature, air quality, noise, and equipment design and arrangement but also to interpersonal relations and organizational climate. From a somewhat different angle, Barker (1968, 1978) and his associates at the Midwest Psychological Field Station have been conducting an intensive, long-term research program on the behavioral demands and constraints exerted by particular behavioral settings, such as classrooms, churches, and basketball games.

A third source of interest in the assessment of environments stems from social learning theory and behavior modification techniques, with their emphasis on situational specificity (Mischel, 1968). In this approach, attention centers principally on the influence of the social environment in reinforcing specific behaviors. Information is sought on how and why an individual behaves differently in different situations. Such information should improve the prediction of the individual's behavior in particular settings. In this connection, the need for a taxonomy of situations has been recognized by several investigators, and some procedures have been proposed for working toword such a classification (N. Frederiksen, 1972).

Still another approach to environmental assessment is concerned with the cumulative effects of environment in shaping the individual's psychological development in both cognitive and noncognitive domains. Representing one aspect of the general heredity–environment problem, this field of investigation has engaged the efforts of psychologists for at least half a century. But in this area, too, there has been an upsurge of activity since the 1960s. It is characteristic of this approach that information about an individual's prior environment is used as an aid in interpreting her or his test performance. Moreover, as was reported in Chapter 12, the prediction of later behavior from test scores can be substantially improved if combined with knowledge about the characteristics of the environment to which the individual has been exposed during the intervening period.

OBJECTIVE INDICES OF ENVIRONMENTAL STATUS. The traditional approach to environmental assessment has relied on some global, composite index of socioeconomic level.[7] Sociologists have utilized elaborate procedures for identifying an individual's social class membership (Warner, Meeker, & Eells, 1949). Simpler and more readily applicable indices, however, have proved to be equally effective, yielding results that agree very closely with those obtained by the more laborious methods. In fact, a reasonably close approximation of socioeconomic level can be found from the occupation of the father or other principal wage earner in the family. Several rough scales have been constructed for classifying parental occupation into levels; some combine occupational information with parental educational level, as in the widely used Two-Factor Index of Social Position. First described by Hollingshead (1957), this index can be found in several sources (e.g., Bonjean et al., 1967; Hopkins & Stanley, 1981).

Other scales have attempted to give a more highly differentiated picture of home environment, including not only parental characteristics but also such data as size and nature of home; availability of such material possessions as telephones, vacuum cleaners, and refrigerators; presence of books, magazines, and newspapers in the home; and aesthetic and socio-civic involvement of the family. For these scales, data may be gathered through questionnaires, interviews, home visits, or some combination of these procedures. Examples include the American Home Scale (Appendix E), the Home Index (Appendix E; Gough, 1971a, 1971b), and the Living Room Check List (Laumann & House, 1970; see also Craik, 1971, pp. 41–45).

Objective data are also frequently employed to evaluate institutions, such as industrial organizations or colleges and universities. To what extent such university characteristics as number of books in the library, faculty-student ratio, and percentage of faculty with PhD degrees actually contribute to student achievement is a matter of controversy (Astin, 1968b; Moos, 1973). A somewhat different approach describes an environment in terms of the behavioral characteristics of the persons in it. The rationale underlying this procedure is that the dominant features of an environment depend on the typical characteristics of its members. The behavioral impact of a given setting is mediated by and reflected in the behavior of the persons who inhabit it. An example of this technique is provided by the Inventory of College Activities (Appendix E; Astin, 1968a), in which students report factual information about themselves, such as the median number of hours per week spent in different activities and the college organizations to which they belong.

[7] Surveys of available indices can be found in Bonjean, Hill, and McLemore (1967), Gerberich, Greene, and Jorgensen (1962, Ch. 4), Hopkins & Stanley (1981, pp. 454–457), and Stricker (1980).

OBSERVER ASSESSMENT OF SELECTED ENVIRONMENTAL VARIABLES. Another approach to environmental assessment utilizes direct observations of relevant variables by a teacher, home visitor, or other appropriate investigator. A major limitation of the traditional global indices stems from the fact that they classify environments along a single continuum of better-or-worse or higher-or-lower. Environments, however, differ in the particular behaviors they reinforce, and hence in their effects on specific individual characteristics (Bloom, 1964; Mischel, 1968). Thus the optimal environments for muscular development, school achievement, creativity, and social conformity may be quite dissimilar.

Investigators working with Bloom at the University of Chicago explored the possibility of constructing "subenvironment" scales for the prediction of selected behavior domains, namely, intelligence test performance and academic achievement (Bloom, 1964; R. Wolf, 1966). The focus was on what parents do in relation to the child, rather than on parental status and physical characteristics of the home. Examples of the variables assessed include the kinds of work habits expected of the child, social pressure and rewards for academic achievement, the opportunities provided for language development and the quality of the language models available to the child, and the nature and amount of assistance provided in overcoming academic difficulties. In some suggestive validation research with 60 first-grade children, the intelligence scale correlated .69 with scores on a group intelligence test, in contrast with the correlations of .20 to .40 generally found between intelligence test scores and indices of socioeconomic level. Similarly, the academic achievement scale correlated .80 with an achievement battery, in contrast with the usual correlations of the order of .50 obtained with socioeconomic level. Equally promising results were obtained in a more elaborate study with a home environment scale designed to predict performance on the SRA tests of Primary Mental Abilities in a group of Canadian schoolboys (Marjoribanks, 1972, 1974; Walberg & Marjoribanks, 1973—see also Harris & McArthur, 1974).

Mention should also be made of the environmental data included in the CIRCUS assessment program for early childhood education, described in Chapter 14. Through teacher questionnaires, information is collected regarding the *context* within which the child's test scores must be interpreted (Messick, 1973). Thus, inferences about the child's competencies from her or his test performance are moderated by knowledge regarding the opportunities the child has had at home and in school to learn the required skills. A similar application of environmental data is illustrated by the four sociocultural scales included in the SOMPA assessment program discussed in Chapter 9. Covering information on family size, family structure, socioeconomic status, and urban acculturation, these scales are used to aid in the interpretation of the child's intelligence test performance.

PERCEIVED SOCIAL CLIMATES. Some investigators have approached the assessment of environments through the reported perceptions of the persons within each milieu. According to this theoretical orientation, the most direct measure of the social climate of a particular environment is the consensus of these individual perceptions. Every institution—be it a family, school, business organization, correctional institution, or therapeutic program—provides a social environment that tends to reinforce some types of behavior and to weaken others. The social climates of institutions, through which they influence the behavior of their members, have been described in such terms as supportive, structured, flexible, controlling, artistic, intellectual, practical.

One of the scales designed within this framework is the College Characteristics Index (Stern, 1970). Other versions of this instrument have been developed for use in high school and evening colleges. A more general form, the Organizational Climate Index, was designed to be applicable to any organization regardless of setting. Paralleling these environmental instruments is the Activities Index, applicable to individuals. Together, the two types of instruments provide a basic taxonomy for characterizing both persons and situations in comparable terms.

The College Characteristics Index (CCI) and the Activities Index take as their point of departure Murray's theoretical model of individual needs and environmental press. The Activities Index covers 30 needs, similar to those sampled by the EPPS, the Personality Research Form, and the TAT. The CCI (and the other versions of this environmental index) measure a parallel set of "environmental press" or situational characteristics. In both types of instruments, 10 items are employed to sample each need (or press). Typical items from the CCI include:

There would be a capacity audience for a lecture by an outstanding philosopher or theologian.

The school has an excellent reputation for academic freedom.

Professors usually take attendance in class.

There is considerable interest in the analysis of value systems and the relativity of societies and ethics.

Data on each institution are obtained by having the CCI filled out by a sample of students. The percentages of students answering each item affirmatively or negatively are then employed in plotting the institutional profile. The index thus describes the institution as it is perceived by its students. The results for a given institution, however, are quite consistent with data obtained from other sources, such as faculty and administration. In addition to the 30 basic scores in both CCI and Activity Index, factor analyses have identified certain broader descriptive variables representing both first-order and second-order factors.

More recently, Moos (1974a, 1974b, 1975a, 1975b, 1976), at the Social

Ecology Laboratory of Stanford University, has developed a series of nine Social Climate Scales applicable in the following contexts: hospital-based and community-based psychiatric treatment programs, correctional facilities, military companies,[8] university student residences, high school classrooms, community groups, work milieus, and families. Each scale consists of 80 to 100 true-false items with which the respondent describes his or her perception of the given environment. Items were originally prepared to tap theoretically chosen environmental dimensions, such as press toward involvement, autonomy, or order; final items were empirically selected on the basis of their ability to discriminate among contexts, as well as their internal consistency within subscales.

Each environmental context is described in terms of 7 to 10 subscale scores. Several of these subscales recur in the scales for different contexts. In fact, despite the wide diversity of contexts covered by the Social Climate Scales, the subscales in each context fit into the same tripartite classification, including (1) relationship dimensions (e.g., involvement, support, peer cohesion); (2) personal development dimensions (e.g., autonomy, task orientation, competition); and (3) system maintenance and change dimensions (e.g., order and organization, clarity, innovation). It is also noteworthy that the Social Climate Scales were designed for relatively small units within complex and heterogeneous institutions—for example, a classroom rather than a whole school, a treatment program rather than a whole hospital, a university student residence rather than a whole university. In this respect, these scales should yield more readily interpretable and less ambiguous data than would be obtained from a composite assessment of an entire organization.

ENVIRONMENTAL ATTITUDES. Another type of measure that is gradually appearing on the psychometric scene concerns self-reported feelings, preferences, and attitudes about environmental matters. Some of these instruments deal specifically with problems of conservation, pollution, and environmental protection. An example is provided by a scale for assessing general ecological attitudes and information (Maloney & Ward, 1973; Maloney, Ward, & Braucht, 1975). It consists of an objectively scored, self-report inventory yielding subscale scores in (1) verbal commitment—what respondents state they are willing to do in reference to specific environmental issues; (2) actual commitment—what they actually do; (3) affect, or degree of emotionality related to each issue; and (4) knowledge about specific factual matters pertaining to ecological issues. Preliminary findings suggested a high degree of verbal commitment and affect about ecological problems, but a lower degree of actual commitment and a particularly low degree of pertinent knowledge. The latter deficit indicates a strong need for public educational programs in this area.

[8] Not yet published.

Another assessment objective is illustrated by the Environmental Response Inventory (ERI—McKechnie, 1974, 1977; Appendix E). This instrument set out to measure environmental dispositions, defined as "individual differences in the ways people think about and relate to the everyday physical environment" (McKechnie, 1974, p. 1). Among the practical applications suggested for such a measure are as an aid in recreational counseling and planning and in making decisions about a place to live. At a more theoretical level, environmental dispositions can be investigated with reference to how much they contribute to the explanation of one's behavior, over and above the contribution of traditional personality measures.

The ERI was developed by a combination of theoretical and empirical procedures. Its construction comprised a series of steps leading to successive revision and refinement of item selection and placement. The final inventory contains 184 statements sampling attitudes toward a wide array of environmental themes. Respondents indicate on a 5-point scale the extent to which they agree or disagree with each statement. The results yield a profile of scores on eight environmental dispositions identified through factor analysis, plus a validity score to detect careless responding. Examples of the environmental dispositions (with abbreviated descriptions) include *Pastoralism* (opposition to land development; preservation of natural resources); *Urbanism* (interest in cultural life and varied stimulus patterns of city; enjoyment of interpersonal richness and diversity); *Stimulus Seeking* (interest in travel and exploration of unusual places); and *Need for Privacy* (desire for physical isolation, solitude, freedom from distraction). Although split-half reliabilities appear satisfactory and some validity data are reported, this inventory is still in a preliminary, research stage, as is clearly stated in the manual.

Still another approach to the assessment of environmental attitudes is exemplified by the Leisure Activities Blank (LAB—McKechnie, 1975, 1977; Appendix E). In this inventory, respondents rate each of 120 common leisure activities on a 4-point scale for degree to which they have engaged in it in the past, and on a 3-point scale for degree to which they intend to participate in it in the future. Different scoring scales are used to analyze the two sets of responses, although some common scales occur in both sets. Examples of the scales include Mechanics, Crafts, Intellectual, Sports, Adventure, and Slow Living (i.e., low-keyed, relaxed recreational activities, such as gardening, sunbathing, window shopping). Two validity scales are also included to check on careless or random responding.

The LAB scales were developed through factor analysis of item responses. The items were originally written so as to represent easily identifiable leisure activities in the contemporary American culture. Data were obtained from a deliberately selected sample in a single, affluent California county, chosen because it represented a "population having recreation opportunities unrestricted by climate, geography, or insufficient leisure time or disposable income" (McKechnie, 1977, p. 157). Obviously, this was not intended as a normative sample. It has also been pointed out that, because of the geographical location of the sample, snowmobiling was *not* included in the list although it is popular in other regions of the country (·Feldt, 1978). The LAB has been published as a research instrument, not ready for operational use with individuals or groups. It provides a means of investigating recreational activities, not only at a descriptive level, but also in relation to more pervasive personality differences that may be associated with preferences for different types of activities. Preliminary suggestive findings on such associations are reported in the manual.

It is evident that all currently available assessment instruments in the emerging area of environmental psychology are in an exploratory stage. Some of their basic methodology is still controversial, as indicated by reviews of such instruments in the *Mental Measurements Yearbooks* (e.g., 7–93, 7–143, 8–550, 8–602, 8–681). Unresolved problems remain, and much more empirical research is needed. Nevertheless, these instruments represent innovative attempts to extend psychometric techniques into relatively unknown fields, and they hold promise of significant progress in the not too distant future.

APPENDIXES

A. *Ethical Principles of Psychologists*

B. *Uniform Guidelines on Employee Selection Procedures (1978)*

C. *A Suggested Outline for Test Evaluation*

D. *Test Publishers*

E. *Classified List of Representative Tests*

APPENDIX A

Ethical Principles of Psychologists[1,2]

PREAMBLE

Psychologists respect the dignity and worth of the individual and strive for the preservation and protection of fundamental human rights. They are committed to increasing knowledge of human behavior and of people's understanding of themselves and others and the utilization of such knowledge for the promotion of human welfare. While pursuing these objectives, they make every effort to protect the welfare of those who seek their services and of the research participants that may be the object of study. They use their skills only for purposes consistent with these values and do not knowingly permit their misuse by others. While demanding for themselves freedom of inquiry and communication, psychologists accept the responsibility this freedom requires: competence, objectivity in the application of skills, and concern for the best interests of clients, colleagues, students, research participants, and society. In the pursuit of these ideals, psychologists subscribe to principles in the following areas: 1. Responsibility, 2. Competence. 3. Moral and Legal Standards, 4. Public Statements, 5. Confidentiality, 6. Welfare of the Consumer, 7. Professional Relationships, 8. Assessment Techniques, 9. Research with Human Participants, and 10. Care and Use of Animals.

Acceptance of membership in the American Psychological Association commits the member to adherence to these principles.

Psychologists cooperate with duly constituted committees of the American Psychological Association, in particular, the Committee on Scientific and Professional Ethics and Conduct, by responding to inquiries promptly and completely. Members also respond promptly and completely to inquiries

[1] Approved by the Council of Representatives (January 1981). Published in *American Psychologist,* 1981, 36, 633–638.

[2] These Ethical Principles apply to psychologists, to students of psychology, and to others who do work of a psychological nature under the supervision of a psychologist. They are also intended for the guidance of non-members of the Association who are engaged in psychological research or practice.

from duly constituted state association ethics committees and professional standards review committees.

SPECIFIC PRINCIPLES

Principle 1. Responsibility. In providing services, psychologists maintain the highest standards of their profession. They accept responsibility for the consequences of their acts and make every effort to insure that their services are used appropriately.

a. As scientists, psychologists accept responsibility for the selection of their research topics and the methods used in investigation, analysis, and reporting. They plan their research in ways to minimize the possibility that their findings will be misleading. They provide thorough discussion of the limitations of their data, especially where their work touches on social policy or might be construed to the detriment of persons in specific age, sex, ethnic, socioeconomic or other social groups. In publishing reports of their work, they never suppress disconfirming data, and they acknowledge the existence of alternative hypotheses and explanations of their findings. Psychologists take credit only for work they have actually done.

b. Psychologists clarify in advance with all appropriate persons and agencies the expectations for sharing and utilizing research data. They avoid relationships which may limit their objectivity or create a conflict of interest. Interference with the milieu in which the data are collected is kept to a minimum.

c. Psychologists have the responsibility to attempt to prevent distortion, misuse, or suppression of psychological findings by the institution or agency of which they are employees.

d. As members of governmental or other organizational bodies, psychologists remain accountable as individuals to the highest standards of their profession.

e. As teachers, psychologists recognize their primary obligation to help others acquire knowledge and skill. They maintain high standards of scholarship by presenting psychological information objectively, fully, and accurately.

f. As practitioners, psychologists know that they bear a heavy social responsibility because their recommendations and professional actions may alter the lives of others. They are alert to personal, social, organizational, financial, or political situations and pressures that might lead to misuse of their influence.

Principle 2. Competence. The maintenance of high standards of competence is a responsibility shared by all psychologists in the interest of the public and the profession as a whole. Psychologists recognize the boundaries of their competence and the limitations of their techniques. They only provide services and only use techniques for which they are qualified by training and experience. In those areas in which recognized standards do not yet exist, psychologists take whatever precautions are necessary to protect the welfare of their clients. They maintain knowledge of current scientific and professional information related to the services they render.

a. Psychologists accurately represent their competence, education, training, and experience. They claim as evidence of educational qualifications only those degrees obtained from institutions acceptable under the Bylaws and Rules of Council of the American Psychological Association.

b. As teachers, psychologists perform their duties on the basis of careful preparation so that their instruction is accurate, current, and scholarly.

c. Psychologists recognize the need for continuing education and are open to new procedures and changes in expectations and values over time.

d. Psychologists recognize differences among people, such as those that may be associated with age, sex, socioeconomic, and ethnic backgrounds. When necessary, they obtain training, experience, or counsel to assure competent service or research relating to such persons.

e. Psychologists responsible for decisions involving individuals or policies based on test results have an understanding of psychological or educational measurement, validation problems, and test research.

f. Psychologists recognize that personal problems and conflicts may interfere with professional effectiveness. Accordingly, they refrain from undertaking any activity in which their personal problems are likely to lead to inadequate performance or harm to a client, colleague, student, or research participant. If engaged in such activity when they become aware of their personal problems, they seek competent professional assistance to determine whether they should suspend, terminate, or limit the scope of their professional and/or scientific activities.

Principle 3. Moral and Legal Standards. Psychologists' moral and ethical standards of behavior are a personal matter to the same degree as they are for any other citizen, except as these may compromise the fulfillment of their professional responsibilities, or reduce the public trust in psychology and psychologists. Regarding their own behavior, psychologists are sensitive to prevailing community standards and to the possible impact that conformity to or deviation from these standards may have upon the quality of their performance as psychologists. Psychologists are also aware of the possible impact of their public behavior upon the ability of colleagues to perform their professional duties.

a. As teachers, psychologists are aware of the fact that their personal values may affect the selection and presentation of instructional materials. When dealing with topics that may give offense, they recognize and respect the diverse attitudes that students may have toward such materials.

b. As employees or employers, psychologists do not engage in or condone practices that are inhumane or that result in illegal or unjustifiable actions. Such practices include but are not limited to those based on considerations of race, handicap, age, gender, sexual preference, religion, or national origin in hiring, promotion, or training.

c. In their professional roles, psychologists avoid any action that will violate or diminish the legal and civil rights of clients or of others who may be affected by their actions.

d. As practitioners and researchers, psychologists act in accord with Association standards and guidelines related to the practice and to the conduct of research with human beings and animals. In the ordinary course of events psychologists adhere to relevant governmental laws and institutional regulations. When federal, state, provincial, organizational, or institutional laws, regulations, or practices are in conflict with Association standards and guidelines, psychologists make known their commitment to Association standards and guidelines, and wherever possible work toward a resolution of the conflict. Both practitioners and researchers are concerned with the development of such legal and quasi-legal regulations as best serve the public interest, and they work toward changing existing regulations that are not beneficial to the public interest.

Principle 4. Public Statements. Public statements, announcements of services, advertising, and promotional activities of psychologists serve the purpose of helping the public make informed judgments and choices. Psychologists represent accurately and objectively their professional qualifications, affiliations, and functions, as well as those of the institutions or organizations with which they or the statements may be associated. In public statements providing psychological information or professional opinions or providing information about the availability of psychological products, publications, and services, psychologists base their statements on scientifically acceptable psychological findings and techniques with full recognition of the limits and uncertainties of such evidence.

a. When announcing or advertising professional services, psychologists may list the following information to describe the provider and services provided: name, highest relevant academic degree earned from a regionally accredited institution, date, type and level of certification or licensure, diplomate status, APA membership status, address, telephone number, office hours, a brief listing of the type of psychological services offered, an appropriate presentation of fee information, foreign languages spoken, and policy with regard to third-party payments. Additional relevant or important consumer information may be included if not prohibited by other sections of these Ethical Principles.

b. In announcing or advertising the availability of psychological products, publications, or services, psychologists do not present their affiliation with any organization in a manner that falsely implies sponsorship or certification by that organization. In particular and for example, psychologists do not state APA membership or fellow status in a way to suggest that such status implies specialized professional competence or qualifications. Public statements include, but are not limited to, communication by means of periodical, book, list, directory, television, radio, or motion picture. They do not contain: (i) a false, fraudulent, misleading, deceptive, or unfair statement; (ii) a misinterpretation of fact, or a statement likely to mislead or deceive because in context it makes only a partial disclosure of relevant facts; (iii) a testimonial from a patient regarding the quality of a psychologist's services or products; (iv) a statement intended or likely to create false or unjustified expectations of favorable results; (v) a statement implying unusual, unique, or one-of-a-kind abilities; (vi) a statement intended or likely to appeal to a client's fears, anxieties, or emotions concerning the possible results of a failure to obtain the offered services; (vii) a statement concerning the comparative desirability of offered service; (viii) a statement of direct solicitation of individual clients.

c. Psychologists do not compensate or give anything of value to a representative of the press, radio, television, or other communication medium in anticipation of or in return for professional publicity in a news item. A paid advertisement must be identified as such, unless it is apparent from the context that it is a paid advertisement. If communicated to the public by use of radio or television, an advertisement shall be prerecorded and approved for broadcast by the psychologist, and a recording of the actual transmission shall be retained by the psychologist.

d. Announcements of advertisements of "personal growth groups," clinics, and agencies give a clear statement of purpose and a clear description of the experiences to be provided. The education, training, and experience of the staff members are appropriately specified.

e. Psychologists associated with the development or promotion of psychological devices, books, or other products offered for commercial sale make reasonable efforts to insure that announcements and advertisements are presented in a professional, scientifically acceptable, and factually informative manner.

f. Psychologists do not participate for personal gain in commercial announcements or advertisements recommending to the public the purchase or use of proprietary or single-source products or services when that participation is based solely upon their identification as psychologists.

g. Psychologists present the science of psychology and offer their services, products, and publications fairly and accurately, avoiding misrepresentation through sensationalism, exaggeration, or superficiality. Psychologists are guided by the primary obligation to aid the public in developing informed judgments, opinions, and choices.

h. As teachers, psychologists insure that statements in catalogs and course outlines are accurate and not misleading, particularly in terms of subject matter to be covered, bases for evaluating progress, and the nature of course experiences. Announcements, brochures, or advertisements describing workshops, seminars, or other educational programs accurately describe the audience for which the program is intended as well as eligibility requirements, educational objectives, and nature of the materials to be covered. These announcements also accurately represent the education, training, and experience of the psychologists presenting the programs, and any fees involved.

i. Public announcements or advertisements soliciting research participants, in which clinical services or other professional services are offered as an inducement, make clear the nature of the services as well as the costs and other obligations to be accepted by the participants of the research.

j. A psychologist accepts the obligation to correct others who represent the psychologist's professional qualifications, or associations with products or services, in a manner incompatible with these guidelines.

k. Individual diagnostic and therapeutic services are provided only in the context of a professional psychological relationship. When personal advice is given by means of public lecture or demonstration, newspaper or magazine articles, radio or television programs, mail, or similar media, the psychologist utilizes the most current relevant data and exercises the highest level of professional judgment.

l. Products that are described or presented by means of public lectures or demonstrations, newspaper or magazine articles, radio or television programs, or similar media meet the same recognized standards as exist for use in the context of a professional relationship.

Principle 5. Confidentiality. Psychologists have a primary obligation to respect the confidentiality of information obtained from persons in the course of their work as psychologists. They reveal such information to others only with the consent of the person or the person's legal representative, except in those unusual circumstances in which not to do so would result in clear danger to the person or to others. Where appropriate, psychologists inform their clients of the legal limits of confidentiality.

a. Information obtained in clinical or consulting relationships, or evaluative data concerning children, students, employees, and others, are discussed only for professional purposes and only with persons clearly concerned with the case. Written and oral reports present only data germane to the purposes of the evaluation and every effort is made to avoid undue invasion of privacy.

b. Psychologists who present personal information obtained during the course of professional work in writings, lectures, or other public forums either obtain adequate prior consent to do so or adequately disguise all identifying information.

c. Psychologists make provisions for maintaining confidentiality in the storage and disposal of records.

d. When working with minors or other persons who are unable to give voluntary, informed consent, psychologists take special care to protect these persons' best interests.

Principle 6. Welfare of the Consumer. Psychologists respect the integrity and protect the welfare of the people and groups with whom they work. When there is a conflict of interest between a client and the psychologist's employing institution, psychologists clarify the nature and direction of their loyalties and responsibilities and keep all parties informed of their commitments. Psychologists fully inform consumers as to the purpose and nature of an evaluative, treatment, educational or training procedure, and they freely acknowledge that clients, students, or participants in research have freedom of choice with regard to participation.

a. Psychologists are continually cognizant of their own needs and of their potentially influential position vis-a-vis persons such as clients, students, and subordinates. They avoid exploiting the trust and dependency of such persons. Psychologists make every effort to avoid dual relationships which could impair their professional judgment or increase the risk of exploitation. Examples of such dual relationships include but are not limited to research with and treatment of employees, students, supervisees, close friends, or relatives. Sexual intimacies with clients are unethical.

b. When a psychologist agrees to provide services to a client at the request of a third party, the psychologist assumes the responsibility of clarifying the nature of the relationships to all parties concerned.

c. Where the demands of an organization require psychologists to violate these Ethical Principles, psychologists clarify the nature of the conflict between the demand and these principles. They inform all parties of psychologists' ethical responsibilities, and take appropriate action.

d. Psychologists make advance financial arrangements that safeguard the best interests of and are clearly understood by their clients. They neither give nor receive any remuneration for referring clients for professional services. They contribute a portion of their services to work for which they receive little or no financial return.

e. Psychologists terminate a clinical or consulting relationship when it is reasonably clear that the consumer is not benefiting from it. They offer to help the consumer locate alternative sources of assistance.

Principle 7. Professional Relationships. Psychologists act with due regard for the needs, special competencies, and obligations of their colleagues in psychology and other professions. They respect the prerogatives and obligations of the institutions or organizations with which these other colleagues are associated.

a. Psychologists understand the areas of competence of related professions. They make full use of all the professional, technical, and administrative resources that serve the best interests of consumers. The absence of formal relationships with other professional workers does not relieve psychologists of the responsibility of securing for their clients the best possible professional service nor does it relieve them of the obligation to exercise foresight, diligence, and tact in obtaining the complementary or alternative assistance needed by clients.

b. Psychologists know and take into account the traditions and practices of other professional groups with whom they work and cooperate fully with such groups. If a person is receiving similar services from another professional, psychologists do not offer their own services directly to such a person. If a psychologist is contacted by a person who is already receiving similar services from another professional, the psychologist carefully considers that professional relationship and proceeds with caution and sensitivity to the therapeutic issues as well as the client's welfare. The psychologist discusses these issues with the client so as to minimize the risk of confusion and conflict.

c. Psychologists who employ or supervise other professionals or professionals in training accept the obligation to facilitate the further professional development of these individuals. They provide appropriate working conditions, timely evaluations, constructive consultation, and experience opportunities.

d. Psychologists do not exploit their professional relationships with clients, supervisees, students, employees, or research participants sexually or otherwise. Psychologists do not condone nor engage in sexual harrassment. Sexual harrassment is defined as deliberate or repeated comments, gestures, or physical contacts of a sexual nature that are unwanted by the recipient.

e. In conducting research in institutions or organizations, psychologists secure appropriate authorization to conduct such research. They are aware of their obligation to future research workers and insure that host institutions receive adequate information about the research and proper acknowledgement of their contributions.

f. Publication credit is assigned to those who have contributed to a publication in proportion to their professional contribution. Major contributions of a professional character made by several persons to a common project are recognized by joint authorship, with the individual who made the principal contribution listed first. Minor contributions of a professional character and extensive clerical or similar nonprofessional assistance may be acknowledged in footnotes or in an introductory statement. Acknowledgement through specific citations is made for unpublished as well as published material that has directly influenced the research or writing. A psychologist who compiles and edits material of others for publication publishes the material in the name of the originating group, if appropriate, with his/her own name appearing as chairperson or editor. All contributors are to be acknowledged and named.

g. When psychologists know of an ethical violation by another psychologist, and it seems appropriate, they informally attempt to resolve the issue by bringing the behavior to the attention of the psychologist. If the misconduct is of a minor nature and/or appears to be due to lack of sensitivity, knowledge, or experience, such an informal solution is usually appropriate. Such informal corrective efforts are sensitive to any rights to confidentiality involved. If the violation does not seem amenable to an informal solution, or is of a more serious nature, psychologists bring it to the attention of the appropriate local, state, and/or national committee on professional ethics and conduct.

Principle 8. Assessment Techniques. In the development, publication, and utilization of psychological assessment techniques, psychologists make every effort to promote the welfare and best interests of the client. They guard against the misuse of assessment results. They respect the client's right to know the results, the interpretations made and the bases for their conclusions and recommendations. Psychologists make every effort to maintain the security of tests and other assessment techniques within limits of legal mandates. They strive to assure the appropriate use of assessment techniques by others.

a. In using assessment techniques, psychologists respect the right of clients to have a full explanation of the nature and purpose of the techniques in language that the client can understand, unless an explicit exception to this right has been agreed upon in advance. When the explanations are to be provided by others, the psychologist establishes procedures for insuring the adequacy of these explanations.

b. Psychologists responsible for the development and standardization of psychological tests and other assessment techniques utilize established scientific procedures and observe the relevant APA standards.

c. In reporting assessment results, psychologists indicate any reservations that exist regarding validity or reliability because of the circumstances of the assessment or the inappropriateness of the norms for the person tested. Psychologists strive to insure that the results of assessments and their interpretations are not misused by others.

d. Psychologists recognize that assessment results may become obsolete. They make every effort to avoid and prevent the misuse of obsolete measures.

e. Psychologists offering scoring and interpretation services are able to produce appropriate evidence for the validity of the programs and procedures used in arriving at interpretations. The public offering of an automated interpretation service is considered as a professional-to-professional consultation. The psychologist makes every effort to avoid misuse of assessment reports.

f. Psychologists do not encourage or promote the use of psychological assessment techniques by inappropriately trained or otherwise unqualified persons through teaching, sponsorship, or supervision.

Principle 9. Research with Human Participants. The decision to undertake research rests upon a considered judgment by the individual psychologist about how best to contribute to psychological science and human welfare. Having made the decision to conduct research, the psychologist considers alternative directions in which research energies and resources might be invested. On the basis of this consideration, the psychologist carries out the investigation with respect and concern for the dignity and welfare of the people who participate, and with cognizance of federal and state regulations and professional standards governing the conduct of research with human participants.

a. In planning a study, the investigator has the responsibility to make a careful evaluation of its ethical acceptability. To the extent that the weighing of scientific and human values suggests a compromise of any principle, the investigator incurs a correspondingly serious obligation to seek ethical advice and to observe stringent safeguards to protect the rights of human participants.

b. Considering whether a participant in a planned study will be a "subject at risk" or a "subject at minimal risk," according to recognized standards, is of primary ethical concern to the investigator.

c. The investigator always retains the responsibility for insuring ethical practice in research. The investigator is also responsible for the ethical treatment of research partcipants by collaborators, assistants, students, and employees, all of whom, however, incur similar obligations.

d. Except for minimal risk research, the investigator establishes a clear and fair agreement with the research participants, prior to their participation, that clarifies the obligations and responsibilities of each. The investigator has the obligation to honor all promises and commitments included in that agreement. The investigator informs the participant of all aspects of the research that might reasonably be expected to influence willingness to participate, and explains all other aspects of the research about which the participant inquires. Failure to make full disclosure prior to obtaining informed consent requires additional safeguards to protect the welfare and dignity of the research participant. Research with children or participants who have impairments which would limit understanding and/or communication, requires special safeguard procedures.

'e. Methodological requirements of a study may make the use of concealment or deception necessary. Before conducting such a study, the investigator has a special responsibility to: (i) determine whether the use of such techniques is justified by the study's prospective scientific, educational, or applied value; (ii) determine whether alternative procedures are available that do not utilize concealment or deception; and (iii) insure that the participants are provided with sufficient explanation as soon as possible.

f. The investigator respects the individual's freedom to decline to participate in or to withdraw from the research at any time. The obligation to protect this freedom requires careful thought and consideration when the investigator is in a position of authority or influence over the participant. Such positions of authority include but are not limited to situations when research participation is required as part of employment or when the participant is a student, client, or employee of the investigator.

g. The investigator protects the participants from physical and mental discomfort, harm, and danger that may arise from research procedures. If risks of such consequences exist, the investigator informs the participant of that fact. Research procedures likely to cause serious or lasting harm to a participant are not used unless the failure to use these procedures might expose the participant to risk of greater harm, or unless the research has great potential benefit and fully informed and voluntary consent is obtained from each participant. The participant should be informed of procedures for contacting the investigator within a reasonable time period following participation should stress, potential harm, or related questions or concerns arise.

h. After the data are collected, the investigator provides the participant with information about the nature of the study and attempts to remove any misconceptions that may have arisen. Where scientific or humane values justify delaying or withholding information, the investigator incurs a special responsibility to monitor the research and to assure that there are no damaging consequences for the participant.

i. Where research procedures result in undesirable consequences for the individual participant, the investigator has the responsibility to detect and remove or correct these consequences, including long-term effects.

j. Information obtained about the research participant during the course of an investigation is confidential unless otherwise agreed upon in advance. When the possibility exists that others may obtain access to such information, this possibility, together with the plans for protecting confidentiality, is explained to the participant as part of the procedure for obtaining informed consent.

Principle 10. Care and Use of Animals. An investigator of animal behavior strives to advance our understanding of basic behavioral principles and/or to contribute to the improvement of human health and welfare. In seeking these ends, the investigator insures the welfare of the animals and treats them humanely. Laws and regulations notwithstanding, the animal's immediate protection depends upon the scientist's own conscience.

a. The acquisition, care, use, and disposal of all animals is in compliance with current federal, state or provincial, and local laws and regulations.

b. A psychologist trained in research methods and experienced in the care of laboratory animals closely supervises all procedures involving animals and is responsible for insuring appropriate consideration of their comfort, health, and humane treatment.

c. Psychologists insure that all individuals using animals under their supervision have received explicit instruction in experimental methods and in the care, maintenance, and handling of the species being used. Responsibilities and activities of individuals participating in a research project are consistent with their respective competencies.

d. Psychologists make every effort to minimize discomfort, illness, and pain to the animals. A procedure subjecting animals to pain, stress, or privation is used only when an alternative procedure is unavailable and the goal is justified by its prospective scientific, educational, or applied value. Surgical procedures are performed under appropriate anesthesia; techniques to avoid infection and minimize pain are followed during and after surgery.

e. When it is appropriate that the animal's life be terminated, it is done rapidly and painlessly.

APPENDIX B

Uniform Guidelines on Employee Selection Procedures (1978)[1]

GENERAL PRINCIPLES

Section 1. Statement of purpose.

A. *Need for uniformity—Issuing agencies.* The Federal government's need for a uniform set of principles on the question of the use of tests and other selection procedures has long been recognized. The Equal Employment Opportunity Commission, the Civil Service Commission, the Department of Labor, and the Department of Justice jointly have adopted these uniform guidelines to meet that need, and to apply the same principles to the Federal government as are applied to other employers.

B. *Purpose of guidelines.* These guidelines incorporate a single set of principles which are designed to assist employers, labor organizations, employment agencies, and licensing and certification boards to comply with requirements of Federal law prohibiting employment practices which discriminate on grounds of race, color, religion, sex, and national origin. They are designed to provide a framework for determining the proper use of tests and other selection procedures. These guidelines do not require a user to conduct validity studies of selection procedures where no adverse impact results. However, all users are encouraged to use selection procedures which are valid, especially users operating under merit principles.

C. *Relation to prior guidelines.* These guidelines are based upon and supersede previously issued guidelines on employee selection procedures. These guidelines have been built upon court decisions, the previously issued guidelines of the agencies, and the practical experience of the agencies, as well as the standards of the psychological profession. These guidelines are intended to be consistent with existing law.

Sec. 2. Scope.

A. *Application of guidelines.* These guidelines will be applied by the Equal Employment Opportunity Commission in the enforcement of title VII of the Civil Rights Act of 1964, as amended by the Equal Employment Opportunity Act of 1972 (hereinafter "Title VII"); by the Department of Labor, and the contract compliance agencies until the transfer of authority contemplated by the President's Reorganization Plan No. 1 of 1978, in the administration and en-

[1] From *Federal Register*, Vol. 43, No. 166—Friday, August 25, 1978, pp. 38296–38309.

637

forcement of Executive Order 11246, as amended by Executive Order 11375 (hereinafter "Executive Order 11246"); by the Civil Service Commission and other Federal agencies subject to section 717 of Title VII; by the Civil Service Commission in exercising its responsibilities toward State and local governments under section 208(b)(1) of the Intergovernmental-Personnel Act; by the Department of Justice in exercising its responsibilities under Federal law; by the Office of Revenue Sharing of the Department of the Treasury under the State and Local Fiscal Assistance Act of 1972, as amended; and by any other Federal agency which adopts them.

B. *Employment decisions.* These guidelines apply to tests and other selection procedures which are used as a basis for any employment decision. Employment decisions include but are not limited to hiring, promotion, demotion, membership (for example, in a labor organization), referral, retention, and licensing and certification, to the extent that licensing and certification may be covered by Federal equal employment opportunity law. Other selection decisions, such as selection for training or transfer, may also be considered employment decisions if they lead to any of the decisions listed above.

C. *Selection procedures.* These guidelines apply to selection procedures which are used as a basis for making employment decisions. For example, the use of recruiting procedures designed to attract members of a particular race, sex, or ethnic group, which were previously denied employment opportunities or which are currently underutilized, may be necessary to bring an employer into compliance with Federal law, and is frequently an essential element of any effective affirmative action program; but recruitment practices are not considered by these guidelines to be selection procedures. Similarly, these guidelines do not pertain to the question of the lawfulness of a seniority system within the meaning of section 703(h), Executive Order 11246 or other provisions of Federal law or regulation, except to the extent that such systems utilize selection procedures to determine qualifications or abilities to perform the job. Nothing in these guidelines is intended or should be interpreted as discouraging the use of a selection procedure for the purpose of determining qualifications or for the purpose of selection on the basis of relative qualifications, if the selection procedure has been validated in accord with these guidelines for each such purpose for which it is to be used.

D. *Limitations.* These guidelines apply only to persons subject to Title VII, Executive Order 11246, or other equal employment opportunity requirements of Federal law. These guidelines do not apply to responsibilities under the Age Discrimination in Employment Act of 1967, as amended, not to discriminate on the basis of age, or under sections 501, 503, and 504 of the Rehabilitation Act of 1973, not to discriminate on the basis of handicap.

E. *Indian preference not affected.* These guidelines do not restrict any obligation imposed or right granted by Federal law to users to extend a preference in employment to Indians living on or near an Indian reservation in connection with employment opportunities on or near an Indian reservation.

Sec. 3. Discrimination defined: Relationship between use of selection procedures and discrimination.

A. *Procedure having adverse impact constitutes discrimination unless justified.* The use of any selection procedure which has an adverse impact on the hiring, promotion, or other employment or membership opportunities of members of any race, sex, or ethnic group will be considered to be discriminatory and inconsistent with these guidelines, unless the procedure has been validated in accordance with these guidelines, or the provisions of section 6 below are satisfied.

B. *Consideration of suitable alternative selection procedures.* Where two or more selection procedures are available which serve the user's legitimate interest in efficient and trustworthy workmanship, and which are substantially equally valid for a given purpose, the user should use the procedure which has been demonstrated to have the lesser adverse impact. Accordingly, whenever a validity study is called for by these guidelines, the user should include, as a part of the validity study, an investigation of suitable alternative selection procedures and suitable alternative methods of using the selection procedure which have as little adverse impact as possible, to determine the appropriateness of using or validating them in accord with these guidelines. If a user has made a reasonable effort to become aware of such alternative procedures and validity has been demonstrated in accord with these guidelines, the use of the test or other selection procedure may continue until such time as it should reasonably be reviewed for currency. Whenever the user is shown an alternative selection procedure with evidence of less adverse impact and substantial evidence of validity for the same job in similar circumstances, the user should investigate it to determine the appropriateness of using or validating it in accord with these guidelines. This subsection is not intended to preclude the combination of procedures into a significantly more valid procedure, if the use of such a combination has been shown to be in compliance wtih the guidelines.

Sec. 4. Information on impact.

A. *Records concerning impact.* Each user should maintain and have available for inspection records or other information which will disclose the impact which its tests and other selection procedures have upon employment opportunities of persons by identifiable race, sex, or ethnic group as set forth in subparagraph B below in order to determine compliance with these guidelines. Where there are large numbers of applicants and procedures are administered frequently, such information may be retained on a sample basis, provided that the sample is appropriate in terms of the applicant population and adequate in size.

B. *Applicable race, sex, and ethnic groups for recordkeeping.* The records called for by this section are to be maintained by sex, and the following races and ethnic groups: Blacks (Negroes), American Indians (including Alaskan Natives), Asians (including Pacific Islanders), Hispanic (including persons of Mexican, Puerto Rican, Cuban, Central or South American, or other Spanish origin or culture regardless of race), whites (Caucasians) other than Hispanic, and totals. The race, sex, and ethnic classifications called for by this section are consistent with the Equal Employment Opportunity Standard Form 100, Employer Information Report EEO–1 series of reports. The user should adopt safeguards to insure that the records required by this paragraph are used for appropriate purposes such as determining adverse impact, or (where required) for developing and monitoring affirmative action programs, and that such records are not used improperly. See sections 4E and 17(4), below.

C. *Evaluation of selection rates. The "bottom line."* If the information called for by sections 4A and B above shows that the total selection process for a job has an adverse impact, the individual components of the selection process should be evaluated for adverse impact. If this information shows that the total selection process does not have an adverse impact, the Federal enforcement agencies, in the exercise of their administrative and prosecutorial discretion, in usual circumstances, will not expect a user to evaluate the individual components for adverse impact, or to validate such individual components, and will not take enforcement action based upon adverse impact of any component of that process, including the separate parts of a multipart selection procedure or any separate procedure that is used as an alternative method of selection. However, in the following circumstances the Federal enforcement agencies will expect a user to evaluate the individual components for adverse impact and may, where appropriate, take enforcement action with respect to the individual components: (1) where the selection procedure is a significant factor in the continuation of patterns of assignments of incumbent employees caused by prior discriminatory employment practices, (2) where the weight of court decisions or administrative interpretations hold that a specific procedure (such as height or weight requirements or no-arrest records) is not job related in the same or similar circumstances. In unusual circumstances, other than those listed in (1) and (2) above, the Federal enforcement agencies may request a user to evaluate the individual components for adverse impact and may, where appropriate, take enforcement action with respect to the individual component.

D. *Adverse impact and the "four-fifths rule."* A selection rate for any race, sex, or ethnic group which is less than four-fifths (⅘) (or eighty percent) of the rate for the group with the highest rate will generally be regarded by the Federal enforcement agencies as evidence of adverse impact, while a greater than four-fifths rate will generally not be regarded by Federal enforcement agencies as evidence of adverse impact. Smaller differences in selection rate may nevertheless constitute adverse impact, where they are significant in both statistical and practical terms or where a user's actions have discouraged applicants disproportionately on grounds of race, sex, or ethnic group. Greater differences in selection rate may not constitute adverse impact where the differences are based on small numbers and are not statistically significant, or where special recruiting or other programs cause the pool of minority or female candidates to be atypical of the normal pool of applicants from that group. Where the user's evidence concerning the impact of a selection procedure indicates adverse impact but is based upon numbers which are too small to be reliable, evidence concerning the impact of the procedure over a longer period of time and/or evidence concerning the impact which the selection procedure had when used in the same manner in similar circumstances elsewhere may be considered in determining adverse impact. Where the user has not maintained data on adverse impact as required by the documentation section of applicable guidelines, the Federal enforcement agencies may draw an inference of adverse impact of the selection process from the failure of the user to maintain such data, if the user has an underutilization of a group in the job category, as compared to the group's representation in the relevant labor market or, in the case of jobs filled from within, the applicable work force.

E. *Consideration of user's equal employment opportunity posture.* In carrying out their obligations, the Federal enforcement agencies will consider the general posture of the user with respect to equal employment opportunity for the job or group of jobs in question. Where a user has adopted an affirmative action program, the Federal enforcement agencies will consider the provisions of that program, including the goals and timetables which the user has adopted and the progress which the user has made in carrying out that program and in meeting the goals and timetables. While such affirmative action programs may in design and execution be race, color, sex, or ethnic conscious, selection procedures under such programs should be based upon the ability or relative ability to do the work.

Sec. 5. General standards for validity studies.

A. *Acceptable types of validity studies.* For the purposes of satisfying these guidelines, users may rely upon criterion-related validity studies, content validity studies, or construct validity studies, in accordance with the standards set forth in the technical standards of these guidelines, section 14 below. New strategies for showing the validity of selection procedures will be evaluated as they become accepted by the psychological profession.

B. *Criterion-related, content, and construct validity.* Evidence of the validity of a test or other selection procedure by a criterion-related validity study should consist of empirical data demonstrating that the selection procedure is predictive of or significantly correlated with important elements of job performance. See section 14B below. Evidence of the validity of a test or other selection procedure by a content validity study should consist of data showing that the content of the selection procedure is representative of important aspects of performance on the job for which the candidates are to be evaluated. See section 14C below. Evidence of the validity of a test or other selection procedure through a construct validity study should consist of data showing that the procedure measures the degree to which candidates have identifiable characteristics which have been determined to be important in successful performance in the job for which the candidates are to be evaluated. See section 14D below.

C. *Guidelines are consistent with professional standards.* The provisions of these guidelines relating to validation of selection procedures are intended to be consistent with generally accepted professional standards for evaluating standardized tests and other selection procedures, such as those described in the Standards for Educational and Psychological Tests prepared by a joint committee of the American Psychological Association, the American Educational Research Association, and the National Council on Measurement in Education (American Psychological Association, Washington, D.C., 1974) (hereinafter "A.P.A. Standards") and standard textbooks and journals in the field of personnel selection.

D. *Need for documentation of validity.* For any selection procedure which is part of a selection process which has an adverse impact and which selection procedure has an adverse impact, each user should maintain and have available such documentation as is described in section 15 below.

E. *Accuracy and standardization.* Validity studies should be carried out under conditions which assure insofar as possible the adequacy and accuracy of the research and the report. Selection procedures should be administered and scored under standardized conditions.

F. *Caution against selection on basis of knowledges, skills, or ability learned in brief orientation period.* In general, users should avoid making employment decisions on the basis of measures of knowledges, skills, or abilities which are normally learned in a brief orientation period, and which have an adverse impact.

G. *Method of use of selection procedures.* The evidence of both the validity and utility of a selection procedure should support the method the user chooses for operational use of the procedure, if that method of use has a greater adverse impact than another method of use. Evidence which may be sufficient to support the use of a selection procedure on a pass/fail (screening) basis may be insufficient to support the use of the same procedure on a ranking basis under these guidelines. Thus, if a user decides to use a selection procedure on a ranking basis, and that method of use has a greater adverse impact than use on an appropriate pass/fail basis (see section 5H below), the user should have sufficient evidence of validity and utility to support the use on a ranking basis. See sections 3B, 14B (5) and (6), and 14C (8) and (9).

H. *Cutoff scores.* Where cutoff scores are used, they should normally be set so as to be reasonable and consistent with normal expectations of acceptable proficiency within the work force. Where applicants are ranked on the basis of properly validated selection procedures and those applicants scoring below a higher cutoff score than appropriate in light of such expectations have little or no chance of being selected for employment, the higher cutoff score may be appropriate, but the degree of adverse impact should be considered.

I. *Use of selection procedures for higher level jobs.* If job progression structures are so established that employees will probably, within a reasonable period of time and in a majority of cases, progress to a higher level, it may be considered that the applicants are being evaluated for a job or jobs at the higher level. However, where job progression is not so nearly automatic, or the time span is such that higher level jobs or employees' potential may be expected to change in significant ways, it should be considered that applicants are being evaluated for a job at or near the entry level. A "reasonable period of time" will vary for different jobs and employment situations but will seldom be more than 5 years. Use of selection procedures to evaluate applicants for a higher level job would not be appropriate:

(1) If the majority of those remaining employed do not progress to the higher level job;

(2) If there is a reason to doubt that the higher level job will continue to require essentially similar skills during the progression period; or

(3) If the selection procedures measure knowledges, skills, or abilities required for advancement which would be expected to develop principally from the training or experience on the job.

J. *Interim use of selection procedures.* Users may continue the use of a selection procedure which is not at the moment fully supported by the required evidence of validity, provided: (1) The user has available substantial evidence of validity, and (2) the user has in progress, when technically feasible, a study which is designed to produce the additional evidence required by these guidelines within a reasonable time. If such a study is not technically feasible, see section 6B. If the study does not demonstrate validity, this provision of these guidelines for interim use shall not constitute a defense in any action, nor shall it relieve the user of any obligations arising under Federal law.

K. *Review of validity studies for currency.* Whenever validity has been shown in accord with these guidelines for the use of a particular selection procedure for a job or group of jobs, additional studies need not be performed until such time as the validity study is subject to review as provided in section 3B above. There are no absolutes in the area of determining the currency of a validity study. All circumstances concerning the study, including the validation strategy used, and changes in the relevant labor market and the job should be considered in the determination of when a validity study is outdated.

Sec. 6. Use of selection procedures which have not been validated.

A. *Use of alternate selection procedures to eliminate adverse impact.* A user may choose to utilize alternative selection procedures in order to eliminate adverse impact or as part of an affirmative action program. See section 13 below. Such alternative procedures should eliminate the adverse impact in the total selection process, should be lawful, and should be as job related as possible.

B. *Where validity studies cannot or need not be performed.* There are circumstances in which a user cannot or need not utilize the validation techniques contemplated by these guidelines. In such circumstances, the user should utilize selection procedures which are as job related as possible and which will minimize or eliminate adverse impact, as set forth below.

(1) *Where informal or unscored procedures are used.* When an informal or unscored selection procedure which has an adverse impact is utilized, the user should eliminate the adverse impact, or modify the procedure to one which is a formal, scored, or quantified measure or combination of measures and then validate the procedure in accord with these guidelines, or otherwise justify continued use of the procedure in accord with Federal law.

(2) *Where formal and scored procedures are used.* When a formal and scored selection procedure is used which has an adverse impact, the validation techniques contemplated by these guidelines usually should be followed if technically feasible. Where the user cannot or need not follow the validation techniques anticipated by these guidelines, the user should modify the procedure to eliminate adverse impact or otherwise justify continued use of the procedure in accord with Federal law.

Sec. 7. Use of other validity studies.

A. *Validity studies not conducted by the user.* Users may, under certain circumstances, support the use of selection procedures by validity studies conducted by other users or conducted by test publishers or distributors and described in test manuals. While publishers of selection procedures have a professional obligation to provide evidence of validity which meets generally accepted professional standards (see section 5C above), users are cautioned that they are responsible for compliance with these guidelines. Accordingly, users seeking to obtain selection procedures from publishers and distributors should be careful to determine that, in the event the user becomes subject to the validity requirements of these guidelines, the necessary information to support validity has been determined and will be made available to the user.

B. *Use of criterion-related validity evidence from other sources.* Criterion-related validity studies conducted by one test user, or described in test manuals and the professional literature, will be considered acceptable for use by another user when the following requirements are met:

(1) *Validity evidence.* Evidence from the available studies meeting the standards of section 14B below clearly demonstrates that the selection procedure is valid;

(2) *Job similarity.* The incumbents in the user's job and the incumbents in the job or group of jobs on which the validity study was conducted perform substantially the same major work behaviors, as shown by appropriate job analyses both on the job or group of jobs on which the validity study was performed and on the job for which the selection procedure is to be used; and

(3) *Fairness evidence.* The studies include a study of test fairness for each race, sex, and ethnic group which constitutes a significant factor in the borrowing user's relevant labor market for the job or jobs in question. If the studies under consideration satisfy (1) and (2) above but do not contain an investigation of test fairness, and it is not technically feasible for the borrowing user to conduct an internal study of test fairness, the borrowing user may utilize the study until studies conducted elsewhere meeting the requirements of these guidelines show test unfairness, or until such time as it becomes technically feasible to conduct an internal study of test fairness and the results of that study can be acted upon. Users obtaining selection procedures from publishers should consider, as one factor in the decision to purchase a particular selection procedure, the availability of evidence concerning test fairness.

C. *Validity evidence from multiunit study.* If validity evidence from a study covering more than one unit within an organization satisfies the requirements of section 14B below, evidence of validity specific to each unit will not be required unless there are variables which are likely to affect validity significantly.

D. *Other significant variables.* If there are variables in the other studies which are likely to affect validity significantly, the user may not rely upon such studies, but will be expected either to conduct an internal validity study or to comply with section 6 above.

Sec. 8. Cooperative studies.

A. *Encouragement of cooperative studies.* The agencies issuing these guidelines encourage employers, labor organizations, and employment agencies to cooperate in research, development, search for lawful alternatives, and validity studies in order to achieve procedures which are consistent with these guidelines.

B. *Standards for use of cooperative studies.* If validity evidence from a cooperative study satisfies the requirements of section 14 below, evidence of validity specific to each user will not be required unless there are variables in the user's situation which are likely to affect validity significantly.

Sec. 9. No assumption of validity.

A. *Unacceptable substitutes for evidence of validity.* Under no circumstances will the general reputation of a test or other selection procedures, its author or its publisher, or casual reports of its validity be accepted in lieu of evidence of validity. Specifically ruled out are: assumptions of validity based on a procedure's name or descriptive labels; all forms of promotional literature; data bearing on the frequency of a procedure's usage; testimonial statements and credentials of sellers, users, or consultants; and other nonempirical or anecdotal accounts of selection practices or selection outcomes.

B. *Encouragement of professional supervision.* Professional supervision of selection activities is encouraged but is not a substitute for documented evidence of validity. The enforcement agencies will take into account the fact that a thorough job analysis was conducted and that careful development and use of a selection procedure in accordance with professional standards enhance the probability that the selection procedure is valid for the job.

Sec. 10. Employment agencies and employment services.

A. *Where selection procedures are devised by agency.* An employment agency, including private employment agencies and State employment agencies, which agrees to a request by an employer or labor organization to devise and utilize a selection procedure, should follow the standards in these guidelines for determining adverse impact. If adverse impact exists the agency should comply with these guidelines. An employment agency is not relieved of its obligation herein because the user did not request such validation or has requested the use of some lesser standard of validation than is provided in these guidelines. The use of an employment agency does not relieve an employer or labor organization or other user of its responsibilities under Federal law to provide equal employment opportunity or its obligations as a user under these guidelines.

B. *Where selection procedures are devised elsewhere.* Where an employment agency or service is requested to administer a selection procedure which has been devised elsewhere and to make referrals pursuant to the results, the employment agency or service should maintain and have available evidence of the impact of the selection and referral procedures which it administers. If adverse impact results, the agency or service should comply with these guidelines. If the agency or service seeks to comply with these guidelines by reliance upon validity studies or other data in the possession of the employer, it should obtain and have available such information.

Sec. 11. Disparate treatment.

The principles of disparate or unequal treatment must be distinguished from the concepts of validation. A selection procedure—even though validated against job performance in accordance with these guidelines—cannot be imposed upon members of a race, sex, or ethnic group where other employees, applicants, or members have not been subjected to that standard. Disparate treatment occurs where members of a race, sex, or ethnic group have been denied the same employment, promotion, membership, or other employment opportunities as have been available to other employees or applicants. Those employees or applicants who have been denied equal treatment, because of prior discriminatory practices or policies, must at least be afforded the same opportunities as had existed for other employees or applicants during the period of discrimination. Thus, the persons who were in the class of persons discriminated against during the period the user followed the discriminatory practices should be allowed the opportunity to qualify under less stringent selection procedures previously followed, unless the user demonstrates that the increased standards are required by business necessity. This section does not prohibit a user who has not previously followed merit standards from adopting merit standards which are in compliance with these guidelines; nor does it preclude a user who has previously used invalid or unvalidated selection procedures from developing and using procedures which are in accord with these guidelines.

Sec. 12. Retesting of applicants.

Users should provide a reasonable opportunity for retesting and reconsideration. Where examinations are administered periodically with public notice, such reasonable opportunity exists, unless persons who have previously been tested are precluded from retesting. The user may however take reasonable steps to preserve the security of its procedures.

Sec. 13. Affirmative action.

A. *Affirmative action obligations.* The use of selection procedures which have been validated pursuant to these guidelines does not relieve users of any obligations they may have to undertake affirmative action to assure equal employment opportunity. Nothing in these guidelines is intended to preclude the use of lawful selection procedures which assist in remedying the effects of prior discriminatory practices, or the achievement of affirmative action objectives.

B. *Encouragement of voluntary affirmative action programs.* These guidelines are also intended to encourage the adoption and implementation of voluntary affirmative action programs by users who have no obligation under Federal law to adopt them; but are not intended to impose any new obligations in that regard. The agencies issuing and endorsing these guidelines endorse for all private employers and reaffirm for all governmental employers the Equal Employment Opportunity Coordinating Council's "Policy Statement on Affirmative Action Programs for State and Local Government Agencies" (41 FR 38814, September 13, 1976). That policy statement is attached hereto as appendix, section 17.

TECHNICAL STANDARDS

Sec. 14. Technical standards for validity studies.

The following minimum standards, as applicable, should be met in conducting a validity study. Nothing in these guidelines is intended to preclude the development and use of other professionally acceptable techniques with respect to validation of selection procedures. Where it is not technically feasible for a user to conduct a validity study, the user has the obligation otherwise to comply with these guidelines. See sections 6 and 7 above.

A. *Validity studies should be based on review of information about the job.* Any validity study should be based upon a review of information about the job for which the selection procedure is to be used. The review should include a job analysis except as provided in section 14B(3) below with respect to criterion-related validity. Any method of job analysis may be used if it provides the information required for the specific validation strategy used.

B. *Technical standards for criterion-related validity studies.*—(1) *Technical feasibility.* Users choosing to validate a selection procedure by a criterion-related validity strategy should determine whether it is technically feasible (as defined in section 16) to conduct such a study in the particular employment context. The determination of the number of persons necessary to permit the conduct of a meaningful criterion-related study should be made by the user on the basis of all relevant information concerning the selection procedure, the potential sample, and the employment situation. Where appropriate, jobs with substantially the same major work behaviors may be grouped together for validity studies, in order to obtain an adequate sample. These guidelines do not require a user to hire or promote persons for the purpose of making it possible to conduct a criterion-related study.

(2) *Analysis of the job.* There should be a review of job information to determine measures of work behavior(s) or performance that are relevant to the job or group of jobs in question. These measures or criteria are relevant to the extent that they represent critical or important job duties, work behaviors, or work outcomes as developed from the review of job information. The possibility of bias should be considered both in selection of the criterion measures and their application. In view of the possibility of bias in subjective evaluations, supervisory rating techniques and instructions to raters should be carefully developed. All criterion measures and the methods for gathering data need to be examined for freedom from factors which would unfairly alter scores of members of any group. The relevance of criteria and their freedom from bias are of particular concern when there are significant differences in measures of job performance for different groups.

(3) *Criterion measures.* Proper safeguards should be taken to insure that scores on selection procedures do not enter into any judgments of employee adequacy that are to be used as criterion measures. Whatever criteria are used should represent important or critical work behavior(s) or work outcomes. Certain criteria may be used without a full job analysis if the user can show the importance of the criteria to the particular employment context. These criteria include but are not limited to production rate, error rate, tardiness, absenteeism, and length of service. A standardized rating of overall work performance may be used where a study of the job shows that it is an appropriate criterion. Where performance in training is used as a criterion, success in training should be properly measured and the relevance of the training should be shown either through a comparison of the content of the training program with the critical or important work behavior(s) of the job(s), or through a demonstration of the relationship between measures of performance in training and measures of job performance. Measures of relative success in training include but are not limited to instructor evaluations, performance samples, or tests. Criterion measures consisting of paper and pencil tests will be closely reviewed for job relevance.

(4) *Representativeness of the sample.* Whether the study is predictive or concurrent, the sample subjects should insofar as feasible be representative of the candidates normally available in the relevant labor market for the job or group of jobs in question, and should insofar as feasible include the races, sexes, and ethnic groups normally available in the relevant job market. In determining the representativeness of the sample in a concurrent validity study, the user should take into account the extent to which the specific knowledges or skills which are the primary focus of the test are those which employees learn on the job.

Where samples are combined or compared, attention should be given to see that such samples are comparable in terms of the actual job they perform, the length of time on the job where time on the job is likely to affect performance, and other relevant factors likely to affect validity differences; or that these factors are included in the design of the study and their effects identified.

(5) *Statistical relationships.* The degree of relationship between selection procedure scores and criterion measures should be examined and computed, using

professionally acceptable statistical procedures. Generally, a selection procedure is considered related to the criterion, for the purposes of these guidelines, when the relationship between performance on the procedure and performance on the criterion measure is statistically significant at the .05 level of significance, which means that it is sufficiently high as to have a probability of no more than one (1) in twenty (20) to have occurred by chance. Absence of a statistically significant relationship between a selection procedure and job performance should not necessarily discourage other investigations of the validity of that selection procedure.

(6) *Operational use of selection procedures.* Users should evaluate each selection procedure to assure that it is appropriate for operational use, including establishment of cutoff scores or rank ordering. Generally, if other factors remain the same, the greater the magnitude of the relationship (e.g., correlation coefficient) between performance on a selection procedure and one or more criteria of performance on the job, and the greater the importance and number of aspects of job performance covered by the criteria, the more likely it is that the procedure will be appropriate for use. Reliance upon a selection procedure which is significantly related to a criterion measure, but which is based upon a study involving a large number of subjects and has a low correlation coefficient will be subject to close review if it has a large adverse impact. Sole reliance upon a single selection instrument which is related to only one of many job duties or aspects of job performance will also be subject to close review. The appropriateness of a selection procedure is best evaluated in each particular situation and there are no minimum correlation coefficients applicable to all employment situations. In determining whether a selection procedure is appropriate for operational use the following considerations should also be taken into account: the degree of adverse impact of the procedure, the availability of other selection procedures of greater or substantially equal validity.

(7) *Overstatement of validity findings.* Users should avoid reliance upon techniques which tend to overestimate validity findings as a result of capitalization on chance unless an appropriate safeguard is taken. Reliance upon a few selection procedures or criteria of successful job performance when many selection procedures or criteria of performance have been studied, or the use of optimal statistical weights for selection procedures computed in one sample, are techniques which tend to inflate validity estimates as a result of chance. Use of a large sample is one safeguard; cross-validation is another.

(8) *Fairness.* This section generally calls for studies of unfairness where technically feasible. The concept of fairness or unfairness of selection procedures is a developing concept. In addition, fairness studies generally require substantial numbers of employees in the job or group of jobs being studied. For these reasons, the Federal enforcement agencies recognize that the obligation to conduct studies of fairness imposed by the guidelines generally will be upon users or groups of users with a large number of persons in a job class, or test developers; and that small users utilizing their own selection procedures will generally not be obligated to conduct such studies because it will be technically infeasible for them to do so.

(a) *Unfairness defined.* When members of one race, sex, or ethnic group characteristically obtain lower scores on a selection procedure than members of another group, and the differences in scores are not reflected in differences in a measure of job performance, use of the selection procedure may unfairly deny opportunities to members of the group that obtains the lower scores.

(b) *Investigation of fairness.* Where a selection procedure results in an adverse impact on a race, sex, or ethnic group identified in accordance with the classifications set forth in section 4 above and that group is a significant factor in the relevant labor market, the user generally should investigate the possible existence of unfairness for that group if it is technically feasible to do so. The greater the severity of the adverse impact on a group, the greater the need to investigate the possible existence of unfairness. Where the weight of evidence from other studies shows that the selection procedure predicts fairly for the group in question and for the same or similar jobs, such evidence may be relied on in connection with the selection procedure at issue.,

(c) *General considerations in fairness investigations.* Users conducting a study of fairness should review the A.P.A. Standards regarding investigation of possible bias in testing. An investigation of fairness of a selection procedure depends on both evidence of validity and the manner in which the selection procedure is to be used in a particular employment context. Fairness of a selection procedure cannot necessarily be specified in advance without investigating these factors. Investigation of fairness of a selection procedure in samples where the range of scores on selection procedures or criterion measures is severely restricted for any subgroup sample (as compared to other subgroup samples) may produce misleading evidence of unfairness. That factor should accordingly be taken into account in conducting such studies and before reliance is placed on the results.

(d) *When unfairness is shown.* If unfairness is demonstrated through a showing that members of a particular group perform better or poorer on the job than their scores on the selection procedure would indicate through comparison with how members of other groups perform, the user may either revise or replace the selection instrument in accordance with these guidelines, or may continue to use the selection instrument operationally with appropriate revisions in its use to assure compatibility between the probability of successful job performance and the probability of being selected.

(e) *Technical feasibility of fairness studies.* In addition to the general conditions needed for technical feasibility for the conduct of a criterion-related study (see section 16, below) an investigation of fairness requires the following:

(i) An adequate sample of persons in each group available for the study to achieve findings of statistical significance. Guidelines do not require a user to hire or promote persons on the basis of group classifications for the purpose of making it possible to conduct a study of fairness; but the user has the obligation otherwise to comply with these guidelines.

(ii) The samples for each group should be comparable in terms of the actual job they perform, length of time on the job where time on the job is likely to affect performance, and other relevant factors likely to affect validity differences; or such factors should be included in the design of the study and their effects identified.

(f) *Continued use of selection procedures when fairness studies not feasible.* If a study of fairness should otherwise be performed, but is not technically feasible, a selection procedure may be used which has otherwise met the validity standards of these guidelines, unless the technical infeasibility resulted from discriminatory employment practices which are demonstrated by facts other than past failure to conform with requirements for validation of selection procedures. However, when it becomes technically feasible for the user to perform a study of fairness and such a study is otherwise called for, the user should conduct the study of fairness.

C. *Technical standards for content validity studies.*—(1) *Appropriateness of content validity studies.* Users choosing to validate a selection procedure by a content validity strategy should determine whether it is appropriate to conduct such a study in the particular employment context. A selection procedure can be supported by a content validity strategy to the extent that it is a representative sample of the content of the job. Selection procedures which purport to measure knowledges, skills, or abilities may in certain circumstances be justified by content validity, although they may not be representative samples, if the knowledge, skill, or ability measured by the selection procedure can be operationally defined as provided in section 14C(4) below, and if that knowledge, skill, or ability is a necessary prerequisite to successful job performance.

A selection procedure based upon inferences about mental processes cannot be supported solely or primarily on the basis of content validity. Thus, a content strategy is not appropriate for demonstrating the validity of selection procedures which purport to measure traits or constructs, such as intelligence, aptitude, personality, common sense, judgment, leadership, and spatial ability. Content validity is also not an appropriate strategy when the selection procedure involves knowledges, skills, or abilities which an employee will be expected to learn on the job.

(2) *Job analysis for content validity.* There should be a job analysis which includes an analysis of the important work behavior(s) required for successful performance and their relative importance and, if the behavior results in work product(s), an analysis of the work product(s). Any job analysis should focus on the work behavior(s) and the tasks associated with them. If work behavior(s) are not observable, the job analysis should identify and analyze those aspects of the behavior(s) that can be observed and the observed work products. The work behavior(s) selected for measurement should be critical work behavior(s) and/or important work behavior(s) constituting most of the job.

(3) *Development of selection procedures.* A selection procedure designed to measure the work behavior may be developed specifically from the job and job analysis in question, or may have been previously developed by the user, or by other users or by a test publisher.

(4) *Standards for demonstrating content validity.* To demonstrate the content validity of a selection procedure, a user should show that the behavior(s) demonstrated in the selection procedure are a representative sample of the behavior(s) of the job in question or that the selection procedure provides a representative sample of the work product of the job. In the case of a selection procedure measuring a knowledge, skill, or ability, the knowledge, skill, or ability being measured should be operationally defined. In the case of a selection procedure measuring a knowledge, the knowledge being measured should be operationally defined as that body of learned information which is used in and is a necessary prerequisite for observable aspects of work behavior of the job. In the case of skills or abilities, the skill or ability being measured should be operationally defined in terms of observable aspects of work behavior of the job. For any selection procedure measuring knowledge, skill, or ability the user should show that (a) the selection procedure measures and is a representative sample of that knowledge, skill, or ability; and (b) that knowledge, skill, or ability is used in and is a neces-

sary prerequisite to performance of critical or important work behavior(s). In addition, to be content valid, a selection procedure' measuring a skill or ability should either closely approximate an observable work behavior, or its product should closely approximate an observable work product. If a test purports to sample a work behavior or to provide a sample of a work product, the manner and setting of the selection procedure and its level and complexity should closely approximate the work situation. The closer the content and the context of the selection procedure are to work samples or work behaviors, the stronger is the basis for showing content validity. As the content of the selection procedure less resembles a work behavior. or the setting and manner of the administration of the selection procedure less resemble the work situation, or the result less resembles a work product, the less likely the selection procedure is to be content valid, and the greater the need for other evidence of validity.

(5) *Reliability.* The reliability of selection procedures justified on the basis of content validity should be a matter of concern to the user. Whenever it is feasible, appropriate statistical estimates should be made of the reliability of the selection procedure.

(6) *Prior training or experience.* A requirement for or evaluation of specific prior training or experience based on content validity, including a specification of level or amount of training or experience, should be justified on the basis of the relationship between the content of the training or experience and the content of the job for which the training or experience is to be required or evaluated. The critical consideration is the resemblance between the specific behaviors, products, knowledges, skills, or abilities in the experience or training and the specific behaviors, products, knowledges, skills, or abilities required on the job, whether or not there is close resemblance between the experience or training as a whole and the job as a whole.

(7) *Content validity of training success.* Where a measure of success in a training program is used as a selection procedure and the content of a training program is justified on the basis of content validity, the use should be justified on the relationship between the content of the training program and the content of the job.

(8) *Operational use.* A selection procedure which is supported on the basis of content validity may be used for a job if it represents a critical work behavior (i.e., a behavior which is necessary for performance of the job) or work behaviors which constitute most of the important parts of the job.

(9) *Ranking based on content validity studies.* If a user can show, by a job analysis or otherwise, that a higher score on a content valid selection procedure is likely to result in better job performance, the results may be used to rank persons who score above minimum levels. Where a selection procedure supported solely or primarily by content validity is used to rank job candidates, the selection procedure should measure those aspects of performance which differentiate among levels of job performance.

D. *Technical standards for construct validity studies.*—(1) *Appropriateness of construct validity studies.* Construct validity is a more complex strategy than either criterion-related or content validity. Construct validation is a relatively new and developing procedure in the employment field, and there is at present a lack of substantial literature extending the concept to employment practices. The user should be aware that the effort to obtain sufficient empirical support for construct validity is both an extensive and arduous effort involving a series of research studies, which include criterion-related validity studies and which may include content validity studies. Users choosing to justify use of a selection procedure by this strategy should therefore take particular care to assure that the validity study meets the standards set forth below.

(2) *Job analysis for construct validity studies.* There should be a job analysis. This job analysis should show the work behavior(s) required for successful performance of the job, or the group of jobs being studied, the critical or important work behavior(s) in the job or group of jobs being studied, and an identification of the construct(s) believed to underlie successful performance of these critical or important work behaviors in the job or jobs in questions. Each construct should be named and defined, so as to distinguish it from other constructs. If a group of jobs is being studied the jobs should have in common one or more critical or important work behaviors at a comparable level of complexity.

(3) *Relationship to the job.* A selection procedure should then be identified or developed which measures the construct identified in accord with subparagraph (2) above. The user should show by empirical evidence that the selection procedure is validly related to the construct and that the construct is validly related to the performance of critical or important work behavior(s). The relationship between the construct as measured by the selection procedure and the related work behavior(s) should be supported by empirical evidence from one or more criterion-related studies involving the job or jobs in question which satisfy the provisions of section 14B above.

(4) *Use of construct validity study without new criterion-related evidence.*— (a) *Standards for use.* Until such time as professional literature provides more guidance on the use of construct validity in employment situations, the Federal agencies will accept a claim of construct validity without a criterion-related study which satisfies section 14B above only when the selection procedure has been used elsewhere in a situation in which a criterion-related study has been conducted and the use of a criterion-related validity study in this context meets the standards for transportability of criterion-related validity studies as set forth above in section 7. However, if a study pertains to a number of jobs having common critical or important work behaviors at a comparable level of complexity, and the evidence satisfies subparagraphs 14B (2) and (3) above for those jobs with criterion-related validity evidence for those jobs, the selection procedure may be used for all the jobs to which the study pertains. If construct validity is to be generalized to other jobs or groups of jobs not in the group studied, the Federal enforcement agencies will expect at a minimum additional empirical research evidence meeting the standards of subparagraphs section 14B (2) and (3) above for the additional jobs or groups of jobs.

(b) *Determination of common work behaviors.* In determining whether two or more jobs have one or more work behavior(s) in common, the user should compare the observed work behavior(s) in each of the jobs and should compare the observed work product(s) in each of the jobs. If neither the observed work behavior(s) in each of the jobs nor the observed work product(s) in each of the jobs are the same, the Federal enforcement agencies will presume that the work behavior(s) in each job are different. If the network behaviors are not observable, then evidence of similarity of work products and any other relevant research evidence will be considered in determining whether the work behavior(s) in the two jobs are the same.

DOCUMENTATION OF IMPACT AND VALIDITY EVIDENCE

Sec. 15. Documentation of impact and validity evidence.

A. *Required information.* Users of selection procedures other than those users complying with section 15A(1) below should maintain and have available for each job information on adverse impact of the selection process for that job and, where it is determined a selection process has an adverse impact, evidence of validity as set forth below.

(1) *Simplified recordkeeping for users with less than 100 employees.* In order to minimize recordkeeping burdens on employers who employ one hundred (100) or fewer employees, and other users not required to file EEO–1, et seq., reports, such users may satisfy the requirements of this section 15 if they maintain and have available records showing, for each year:

(a) The number of persons hired, promoted, and terminated for each job, by sex, and where appropriate by race and national origin;

(b) The number of applicants for hire and promotion by sex and where appropriate by race and national origin; and

(c) The selection procedures utilized (either standardized or not standardized).

These records should be maintained for each race or national origin group (see section 4 above) constituting more than two percent (2%) of the labor force in the relevant labor area. However, it is not necessary to maintain records by race and/or national origin (see section 4 above) if one race or national origin group in the relevant labor area constitutes more than ninety-eight percent (98%) of the labor force in the area. If the user has reason to believe that a selection procedure has an adverse impact, the user should maintain any available evidence of validity for that procedure (see sections 7A and 8).

(2) *Information on impact.*—(a) *Collection of information on impact.* Users of selection procedures other than those complying with section 15A(1) above should maintain and have available for each job records or other information showing whether the total selection process for that job has an adverse impact on any of the groups for which records are called for by section 4B above. Adverse impact determinations should be made at least annually for each such group which constitutes at least 2 percent of the labor force in the relevant labor area or 2 percent of the applicable workforce. Where a total selection process for a job has an adverse impact, the user should maintain and have available records or other information showing which components have an adverse impact. Where the total selection process for a job does not have an adverse impact, information need not be maintained for individual components except in circumstances set forth in subsection 15A(2)(b) below. If the determination of adverse impact is made using a procedure other than the "four-fifths rule," as defined in the first sentence of section 4D above, a justification, consistent with section 4D above, for the procedure used to determine adverse impact should be available.

(b) *When adverse impact has been eliminated in the total selection process.*

Whenever the total selection process for a particular job has had an adverse impact, as defined in section 4 above, in any year, but no longer has an adverse impact, the user should maintain and have available the information on individual components of the selection process required in the preceding paragraph for the period in which there was adverse impact. In addition, the user should continue to collect such information for at least two (2) years after the adverse impact has been eliminated.

(c) *When data insufficient to determine impact.* Where there has been an insufficient number of selections to determine whether there is an adverse impact of the total selection process for a particular job, the user should continue to collect, maintain, and have available the information on individual components of the selection process required in section 15A(2)(a) above until the information is sufficient to determine that the overall selection process does not have an adverse impact as defined in section 4 above, or until the job has changed substantially.

(3) *Documentation of validity evidence.—*(a) *Types of evidence.* Where a total selection process has an adverse impact (see section 4 above) the user should maintain and have available for each component of that process which has an adverse impact, one or more of the following types of documentation evidence:

(i) Documentation evidence showing criterion-related validity of the selection procedure (see section 15B, below).

(ii) Documentation evidence showing content validity of the selection procedure (see section 15C, below).

(iii) Documentation evidence showing construct validity of the selection procedure (see section 15D, below).

(iv) Documentation evidence from other studies showing validity of the selection procedure in the user's facility (see section 15E, below).

(v) Documentation evidence showing why a validity study cannot or need not be performed and why continued use of the procedure is consistent with Federal law.

(b) *Form of report.* This evidence should be compiled in a reasonably complete and organized manner to permit direct evaluation of the validity of the selection procedure. Previously written employer or consultant reports of validity, or reports describing validity studies completed before the issuance of these guidelines are acceptable if they are complete in regard to the documentation requirements contained in this section, or if they satisfied requirements of guidelines which were in effect when the validity study was completed. If they are not complete, the required additional documentation should be appended. If necessary information is not available the report of the validity study may still be used as documentation, but its adequacy will be evaluated in terms of compliance with the requirements of these guidelines.

(c) *Completeness.* In the event that evidence of validity is reviewed by an enforcement agency, the validation reports completed after the effective date of these guidelines are expected to contain the information set forth below. Evidence denoted by use of the word "(Essential)" is considered critical. If information denoted essential is not included, the report will be considered incomplete unless the user affirmatively demonstrates either its unavailability due to circumstances beyond the user's control or special circumstances of the user's study which make the information irrelevant. Evidence not so denoted is desirable but its absence will not be a basis for considering a report incomplete. The user should maintain and have available the information called for under the heading "Source Data" in sections 15B(11) and 15D(11). While it is a necessary part of the study, it need not be submitted with the report. All statistical results should be organized and presented in tabular or graphic form to the extent feasible.

B. *Criterion-related validity studies.* Reports of criterion-related validity for a selection procedure should include the following information:

(1) *User(s), location(s), and date(s) of study.* Dates and location(s) of the job analysis or review of job information, the date(s) and location(s) of the administration of the selection procedures and collection of criterion data, and the time between collection of data on selection procedures and criterion measures should be provided (Essential). If the study was conducted at several locations, the address of each location, including city and State, should be shown.

(2) *Problem and setting.* An explicit definition of the purpose(s) of the study and the circumstances in which the study was conducted should be provided. A description of existing selection procedures and cutoff scores, if any, should be provided.

(3) *Job analysis or review of job information.* A description of the procedure used to analyze the job or group of jobs, or to review the job information should be provided (Essential). Where a review of job information results in criteria which may be used without a full job analysis [see section 14B(3)], the basis for the selection of these criteria should be reported (Essential). Where a job analysis is required a complete description of the work behavior(s) or work outcome(s) and measures of their criticality or importance should be provided (Essential). The report should describe the basis on which the behavior(s) or outcome(s) were determined to be critical or important, such as the proportion of time spent on the respective behaviors, their level of difficulty, their frequency of performance, the consequences of error, or other appropriate factors (Essential). Where two or more jobs are grouped for a validity study, the information called for in this subsection should be provided for each of the jobs, and the justification for the grouping [see section 14B(1)] should be provided (Essential).

(4) *Job titles and codes.* It is desirable to provide the user's job title(s) for the job(s) in question and the corresponding job title(s) and code(s) from U.S. Employment Service's Dictionary of Occupational Titles.

(5) *Criterion measures.* The bases for the selection of the criterion measures should be provided, together with references to the evidence considered in making the selection of criterion measures (Essential). A full description of all criteria on which data were collected and means by which they were observed, recorded, evaluated, and quantified, should be provided (Essential). If rating techniques are used as criterion measures, the appraisal form(s) and instructions to the rater(s) should be included as part of the validation evidence, or should be explicitly described and available (Essential). All steps taken to insure that criterion measures are free from factors which would unfairly alter the scores of members of any group should be described (Essential).

(6) *Sample description.* A description of how the research sample was identified and selected should be included (Essential). The race, sex, and ethnic composition of the sample, including those groups set forth in section 4A above, should be described (Essential). This description should include the size of each subgroup (Essential). A description of how the research sample compares with the relevant labor market or work force, the method by which the relevant labor

market or work force was defined, and a discussion of the likely effects on validity of differences between the sample and the relevant labor market or work force, are also desirable. Descriptions of educational levels, length of service, and age are also desirable.

(7) *Description of selection procedures.* Any measure, combination of measures, or procedure studied should be completely and explicitly described or attached (Essential). If commercially available selection procedures are studied, they should be described by title, form, and publisher (Essential). Reports of reliability estimates and how they were established are desirable.

(8) *Techniques and results.* Methods used in analyzing data should be described (Essential). Measures of central tendency (e.g., means) and measures of dispersion (e.g., standard deviations and ranges) for all selection procedures and all criteria should be reported for each race, sex, and ethnic group which constitutes a significant factor in the relevant labor market (Essential). The magnitude and direction of all relationships between selection procedures and criterion measures investigated should be reported for each relevant race, sex, and ethnic group and for the total group (Essential). Where groups are too small to obtain reliable evidence of the magnitude of the relationship, results need not be reported separately. Statements regarding the statistical significance of results should be made (Essential). Any statistical adjustments, such as for less than perfect reliability or for restriction of score range in the selection procedure or criterion, should be described and explained; and uncorrected correlation coefficients should also be shown (Essential). Where the statistical technique categorizes continuous data, such as biserial correlation and the phi coefficient, the categories and the bases on which they were determined should be described and explained (Essential). Studies of test fairness should be included where called for by the requirements of section 14B(8) (Essential). These studies should include the rationale by which a selection procedure was determined to be fair to the group(s) in question. Where test fairness or unfairness has been demonstrated on the basis of other studies, a bibliography of the relevant studies should be included (Essential). If the bibliography includes unpublished studies, copies of these studies, or adequate abstracts or summaries, should be attached (Essential). Where revisions have been made in a selection procedure to assure compatibility between successful job performance and the probability of being selected, the studies underlying such revisions should be included (Essential). All statistical results should be organized and presented by relevant race, sex, and ethnic group (Essential).

(9) *Alternative procedures investigated.* The selection procedures investigated and available evidence of their impact should be identified (Essential). The scope, method, and findings of the investigation, and the conclusions reached in light of the findings, should be fully described (Essential).

(10) *Uses and applications.* The methods considered for use of the selection procedure (e.g., as a screening device with a cutoff score, for grouping or ranking, or combined with other procedures in a battery) and available evidence of their impact should be described (Essential). This description should include the rationale for choosing the method for operational use, and the evidence of the validity and utility of the procedure as it is to be used (Essential). The purpose for which the procedure is to be used (e.g., hiring, transfer, promotion) should be described (Essential). If weights are assigned to different parts of the selection

procedure, these weights and the validity of the weighted composite should be reported (Essential). If the selection procedure is used with a cutoff score, the user should describe the way in which normal expectations of proficiency within the work force were determined and the way in which the cutoff score was determined (Essential).

(11) *Source data.* Each user should maintain records showing all pertinent information about individual sample members and raters, where they are used, in studies involving the validation of selection procedures. These records should be made available upon request of a compliance agency. In the case of individual sample members these data should include scores on the selection procedure(s), scores on criterion measures, age, sex, race, or ethnic group status, and experience on the specific job on which the validation study was conducted, and may also include such things as education, training, and prior job experience, but should not include names and social security numbers. Records should be maintained which show the ratings given to each sample member by each rater.

(12) *Contact person.* The name, mailing address, and telephone number of the person who may be contacted for further information about the validity study should be provided (Essential).

(13) *Accuracy and completeness.* The report should describe the steps taken to assure the accuracy and completeness of the collection, analysis, and report of data and results.

C. *Content validity studies.* Reports of content validity for a selection procedure should include the following information:

(1) *User(s), location(s), and date(s) of study.* Dates and location(s) of the job analysis should be shown (Essential).

(2) *Problem and setting.* An explicit definition of the purpose(s) of the study and the circumstances in which the study was conducted should be provided. A description of existing selection procedures and cutoff scores, if any, should be provided.

(3) *Job analysis.—Content of the job.* A description of the method used to analyze the job should be provided (Essential). The work behavior(s), the associated tasks, and if the behavior results in a work product, the work products should be completely described (Essential). Measures of criticality and/or importance of the work behavior(s) and the method of determining these measures should be provided (Essential). Where the job analysis also identified the knowledges, skills, and abilities used in work behavior(s), an operational definition for each knowledge in terms of a body of learned information and for each skill and ability in terms of observable behaviors and outcomes, and the relationship between each knowledge, skill, or ability and each work behavior, as well as the method used to determine this relationship, should be provided (Essential). The work situation should be described, including the setting in which work behavior(s) are performed, and where appropriate, the manner in which knowledges, skills, or abilities are used, and the complexity and difficulty of the knowledge, skill, or ability as used in the work behavior(s).

(4) *Selection procedure and its content.* Selection procedures, including those constructed by or for the user, specific training requirements, composites of selection procedures, and any other procedure supported by content validity, should be completely and explicitly described or attached (Essential). If commercially available selection procedures are used, they should be described by title, form,

and publisher (Essential). The behaviors measured or sampled by the selection procedure should be explicitly described (Essential). Where the selection procedure purports to measure a knowledge, skill, or ability, evidence that the selection procedure measures and is a representative sample of the knowledge, skill, or ability should be provided (Essential).

(5) *Relationship between the selection procedure and the job.* The evidence demonstrating that the selection procedure is a representative work sample, a representative sample of the work behavior(s), or a representative sample of a knowledge, skill, or ability as used as a part of a work behavior and necessary for that behavior should be provided (Essential). The user should identify the work behavior(s) which each item or part of the selection procedure is intended to sample or measure (Essential). Where the selection procedure purports to sample a work behavior or to provide a sample of a work product, a comparison should be provided of the manner, setting, and the level of complexity of the selection procedure with those of the work situation (Essential). If any steps were taken to reduce adverse impact on a race, sex, or ethnic group in the content of the procedure or in its administration, these steps should be described. Establishment of time limits, if any, and how these limits are related to the speed with which duties must be performed on the job, should be explained. Measures of central tendency (e.g., means) and measures of dispersion (e.g., standard deviations) and estimates of reliability should be reported for all selection procedures if available. Such reports should be made for relevant race, sex, and ethnic subgroups, at least on a statistically reliable sample basis.

(6) *Alternative procedures investigated.* The alternative selection procedures investigated and available evidence of their impact should be identified (Essential). The scope, method, and findings of the investigation, and the conclusions reached in light of the findings, should be fully described (Essential).

(7) *Uses and applications.* The methods considered for use of the selection procedure (e.g., as a screening device with a cutoff score, for grouping or ranking, or combined with other procedures in a battery) and available evidence of their impact should be described (Essential). This description should include the rationale for choosing the method for operational use, and the evidence of the validity and utility of the procedure as it is to be used (Essential). The purpose for which the procedure is to be used (e.g., hiring, transfer, promotion) should be described (Essential). If the selection procedure is used with a cutoff score, the user should describe the way in which normal expectations of proficiency within the work force were determined and the way in which the cutoff score was determined (Essential). In addition, if the selection procedure is to be used for ranking, the user should specify the evidence showing that a higher score on the selection procedure is likely to result in better job performance.

(8) *Contact person.* The name, mailing address, and telephone number of the person who may be contacted for further information about the validity study should be provided (Essential).

(9) *Accuracy and completeness.* The report should describe the steps taken to assure the accuracy and completeness of the collection, analysis, and report of data and results.

D. *Construct validity studies.* Reports of construct validity for a selection procedure should include the following information:

(1) *User(s), location(s), and date(s) of study.* Date(s) and location(s) of

the job analysis and the gathering of other evidence called for by these guidelines should be provided (Essential).

(2) *Problem and setting.* An explicit definition of the purpose(s) of the study and the circumstances in which the study was conducted should be provided. A description of existing selection procedures and cutoff scores, if any, should be provided.

(3) *Construct definition.* A clear definition of the construct(s) which are believed to underlie successful performance of the critical or important work behavior(s) should be provided (Essential). This definition should include the levels of construct performance relevant to the job(s) for which the selection procedure is to be used (Essential). There should be a summary of the position of the construct in the psychological literature, or in the absence of such a position, a description of the way in which the definition and measurement of the construct was developed and the psychological theory underlying it (Essential). Any quantitative data which identify or define the job constructs, such as factor analyses, should be provided (Essential).

(4) *Job analysis.* A description of the method used to analyze the job should be provided (Essential). A complete description of the work behavior(s) and, to the extent appropriate, work outcomes and measures of their criticality and/or importance should be provided (Essential). The report should also describe the basis on which the behavior(s) or outcomes were determined to be important, such as their level of difficulty, their frequency of performance, the consequences of error, or other appropriate factors (Essential). Where jobs are grouped or compared for the purposes of generalizing validity evidence, the work behavior(s) and work product(s) for each of the jobs should be described, and conclusions concerning the similarity of the jobs in terms of observable work behaviors or work products should be made (Essential).

(5) *Job titles and codes.* It is desirable to provide the selection-procedure user's job title(s) for the job(s) in question and the corresponding job title(s) and code(s) from the United States Employment Service's Dictionary of Occupational Titles.

(6) *Selection procedure.* The selection procedure used as a measure of the construct should be completely and explicitly described or attached (Essential). If commercially available selection procedures are used, they should be identified by title, form, and publisher (Essential). The research evidence of the relationship between the selection procedure and the construct, such as factor structure, should be included (Essential). Measures of central tendency, variability, and reliability of the selection procedure should be provided (Essential). Whenever feasible, these measures should be provided separately for each relevant race, sex, and ethnic group.

(7) *Relationship to job performance.* The criterion-related study(ies) and other empirical evidence of the relationship between the construct measured by the selection procedure and the related work behavior(s) for the job or jobs in question should be provided (Essential). Documentation of the criterion-related study(ies) should satisfy the provision of section 15B above or section 15E(1) below, except for studies conducted prior to the effective date of these guidelines (Essential). Where a study pertains to a group of jobs, and on the basis of the study, validity is asserted for a job in the group, the observed work behaviors and the observed work products for each of the jobs should be described (Essen-

tial). Any other evidence used in determining whether the work behavior(s) in each of the jobs is the same should be fully described (Essential).

(8) *Alternative procedures investigated.* The alternative selection procedures investigated and available evidence of their impact should be identified (Essential). The scope, method, and findings of the investigation and the conclusions reached in light of the findings should be fully described (Essential).

(9) *Uses and applications.* The methods considered for use of the selection procedure (e.g., as a screening device with a cutoff score, for grouping or ranking, or combined with other procedures in a battery) and available evidence of their impact should be described (Essential). This description should include the rationale for choosing the method for operational use and the evidence of the validity and utility of the procedure as it is to be used (Essential). The purpose for which the procedure is to be used (e.g., hiring, transfer, promotion) should be described (Essential). If weights are assigned to different parts of the selection procedure, these weights and the validity of the weighted composite should be reported (Essential). If the selection procedure is used with a cutoff score, the user should describe the way in which normal expectations of proficiency within the work force were determined and the way in which the cutoff score was determined (Essential).

(10) *Accuracy and completeness.* The report should describe the steps taken to assure the accuracy and completeness of the collection, analysis, and report of data and results.

(11) *Source data.* Each user should maintain records showing all pertinent information relating to its study of construct validity.

(12) *Contact person.* The name, mailing address, and telephone number of the individual who may be contacted for further information about the validity study should be provided (Essential).

E. *Evidence of validity from other studies.* When validity of a selection procedure is supported by studies not done by the user, the evidence from the original study or studies should be compiled in a manner similar to that required in the appropriate section of this section 15 above. In addition, the following evidence should be supplied:

(1) *Evidence from criterion-related validity studies.*—a. *Job information.* A description of the important job behavior(s) of the user's job and the basis on which the behaviors were determined to be important should be provided (Essential). A full description of the basis for determining that these important work behaviors are the same as those of the job in the original study (or studies) should be provided (Essential).

b. *Relevance of criteria.* A full description of the basis on which the criteria used in the original studies are determined to be relevant for the user should be provided (Essential).

c. *Other variables.* The similarity of important applicant pool or sample characteristics reported in the original studies to those of the user should be described (Essential). A description of the comparison between the race, sex, and ethnic composition of the user's relevant labor market and the sample in the original validity studies should be provided (Essential).

d. *Use of the selection procedure.* A full description should be provided showing that the use to be made of the selection procedure is consistent with the findings of the original validity studies (Essential).

e. *Bibliography.* A bibliography of reports of validity of the selection procedure for the job or jobs in question should be provided (Essential). Where any of the studies included an investigation of test fairness, the results of this investigation should be provided (Essential). Copies of reports published in journals that are not commonly available should be described in detail or attached (Essential). Where a user is relying upon unpublished studies, a reasonable effort should be made to obtain these studies. If these unpublished studies are the sole source of validity evidence they should be described in detail or attached (Essential). If these studies are not available, the name and address of the source, an adequate abstract or summary of the validity study and data, and a contact person in the source organization should be provided (Essential).

(2) *Evidence from content validity studies.* See section 14C(3) and section 15C above.

(3) *Evidence from construct validity studies.* See sections 14D(2) and 15D above.

F. *Evidence of validity from cooperative studies.* Where a selection procedure has been validated through a cooperative study, evidence that the study satisfies the requirements of sections 7, 8, and 15E should be provided (Essential).

G. *Selection for higher level job.* If a selection procedure is used to evaluate candidates for jobs at a higher level than those for which they will initially be employed, the validity evidence should satisfy the documentation provisions of this section 15 for the higher level job or jobs, and in addition, the user should provide: (1) a description of the job progression structure, formal or informal; (2) the data showing how many employees progress to the higher level job and the length of time needed to make this progression; and (3) an identification of any anticipated changes in the higher level job. In addition, if the test measures a knowledge, skill, or ability, the user should provide evidence that the knowledge, skill, or ability is required for the higher level job and the basis for the conclusion that the knowledge, skill, or ability is not expected to develop from the training or experience on the job.

H. *Interim use of selection procedures.* If a selection procedure is being used on an interim basis because the procedure is not fully supported by the required evidence of validity, the user should maintain and have available (1) substantial evidence of validity for the procedure, and (2) a report showing the date on which the study to gather the additional evidence commenced, the estimated completion date of the study, and a description of the data to be collected (Essential).

DEFINITIONS

Sec. 16. Definitions.

The following definitions shall apply throughout these guidelines:

A. *Ability.* A present competence to perform an observable behavior or a behavior which results in an observable product.

B. *Adverse impact.* A substantially different rate of selection in hiring, promotion, or other employment decision which works to the disadvantage of members of a race, sex, or ethnic group. See section 4 of these guidelines.

C. *Compliance with these guidelines.* Use of a selection procedure is in compliance with these guidelines if such use has been validated in accord with these guidelines (as defined below), or if such use does not result in adverse impact on any race, sex, or ethnic group (see section 4, above), or in unusual circumstances, if use of the procedure is otherwise justified in accord with Federal law. See section 6B, above.

D. *Content validity*. Demonstrated by data showing that the content of a selection procedure is representative of important aspects of performance on the job. See section 5B and section 14C.

E. *Construct validity*. Demonstrated by data showing that the selection procedure measures the degree to which candidates have identifiable characteristics which have been determined to be important for successful job performance. See section 5B and section 14D.

F. *Criterion-related validity*. Demonstrated by empirical data showing that the selection procedure is predictive of or significantly correlated with important elements of work behavior. See sections 5B and 14B.

G. *Employer*. Any employer subject to the provisions of the Civil Rights Act of 1964, as amended, including State or local governments and any Federal agency subject to the provisions of section 717 of the Civil Rights Act of 1964,˜ as amended, and any Federal contractor or subcontractor or federally assisted construction contractor or subcontractor covered by Executive Order 11246, as amended.

H. *Employment agency*. Any employment agency subject to the provisions of the Civil Rights Act of 1964, as amended.

I. *Enforcement action*. For the purposes of section 4 a proceeding by a Federal enforcement agency such as a lawsuit or an administrative proceeding leading to debarment from or withholding, suspension, or termination of Federal Government contracts or the suspension or withholding of Federal Government funds; but not a finding of reasonable cause or a conciliation process or the issuance of right to sue letters under title VII or under Executive Order 11246 where such finding, conciliation, or issuance of notice of right to sue is based upon an individual complaint.

J. *Enforcement agency*. Any agency of the executive branch of the Federal Government which adopts these guidelines for purposes of the enforcement of the equal employment opportunity laws or which has responsibility for securing compliance with them.

K. *Job analysis*. A detailed statement of work behaviors and other information relevant to the job.

L. *Job description*. A general statement of job duties and responsibilities.

M. *Knowledge*. A body of information applied directly to the performance of a function.

N. *Labor organization*. Any labor organization subject to the provisions of the Civil Rights Act of 1964, as amended, and any committee subject thereto controlling apprenticeship or other training.

O. *Observable*. Able to be seen, heard, or otherwise perceivel by a person other than the person performing the action.

P. *Race, sex, or ethnic group*. Any group of persons identifiable on the grounds of race, color, religion, sex, or national origin.

Q. *Selection procedure*. Any measure, combination of measures, or procedure used as a basis for any employment decision. Selection procedures include the full range of assessment techniques from traditional paper and pencil tests, performance tests, training programs, or probationary periods and physical, educational, and work experience requirements through informal or casual interviews and unscored application forms.

R. *Selection rate.* The proportion of applicants or candidates who are hired, promoted, or otherwise selected.

S. *Should.* The term "should" as used in these guidelines is intended to connote action which is necessary to achieve compliance with the guidelines, while recognizing that there are circumstances where alternative courses of action are open to users.

T. *Skill.* A present, observable competence to perform a learned psychomotor act.

U. *Technical feasibility.* The existence of conditions permitting the conduct of meaningful criterion-related validity studies. These conditions include: (1) An adequate sample of persons available for the study to achieve findings of statistical significance; (2) having or being able to obtain a sufficient range of scores on the selection procedure and job performance measures to produce validity results which can be expected to be representative of the results if the ranges normally expected were utilized; and (3) having or being able to devise unbiased, reliable and relevant measures of job performance or other criteria of employee adequacy. See section 14B(2). With respect to investigation of possible unfairness, the same considerations are applicable to each group for which the study is made. See section 14B(8).

V. *Unfairness of selection procedure.* A condition in which members of one race, sex, or ethnic group characteristically obtain lower scores on a selection procedure than members of another group, and the differences are not reflected in differences in measures of job performance. See section 14B(7).

W. *User.* Any employer, labor organization, employment agency, or licensing or certification board, to the extent it may be covered by Federal equal employment opportunity law, which uses a selection procedure as a basis for any employment decision. Whenever an employer, labor organization, or employment agency is required by law to restrict recruitment for any occupation to those applicants who have met licensing or certification requirements, the licensing or certifying authority to the extent it may be covered by Federal equal employment opportunity law will be considered the user with respect to those licensing or certification requirements. Whenever a State employment agency or service does no more than administer or monitor a procedure as permitted by Department of Labor regulations, and does so without making referrals or taking any other action on the basis of the results, the State employment agency will not be deemed to be a user.

X. *Validated in accord with these guidelines or properly validated.* A demonstration that one or more validity study or studies meeting the standards of these guidelines has been conducted, including investigation and, where appropriate, use of suitable alternative selection procedures as contemplated by section 3B, and has produced evidence of validity sufficient to warrant use of the procedure for the intended purpose under the standards of these guidelines.

Y. *Work behavior.* An activity performed to achieve the objectives of the job. Work behaviors involve observable (physical) components and unobservable (mental) components. A work behavior consists of the performance of one or more tasks. Knowledges, skills, and abilities are not behaviors, although they may be applied in work behaviors.

Sec. 17. Policy statement on affirmative action (see section 13B).

The Equal Employment Opportunity Coordinating Council was established by act of Congress in 1972, and charged with responsibility for developing and implementing agreements and policies designed, among other things, to eliminate conflict and inconsistency among the agencies of the Federal Government responsible for administering Federal law prohibiting discrimination on grounds of race, color, sex, religion, and national origin. This statement is issued as an initial response to the requests of a number of State and local officials for clarification of the Government's policies concerning the role of affirmative action in the overall equal employment opportunity program. While the Coordinating Council's adoption of this statement expresses only the views of the signatory agencies concerning this important subject, the principles set forth below should serve as policy guidance for other Federal agencies as well.

(1) Equal employment opportunity is the law of the land. In the public sector of our society this means that all persons, regardless of race, color, religion, sex, or national origin shall have equal access to positions in the public service limited only by their ability to do the job. There is ample evidence in all sectors of our society that such equal access frequently has been denied to members of certain groups because of their sex, racial, or ethnic characteristics. The remedy for such past and present discrimination is twofold.

On the one hand, vigorous enforcement of the laws against discrimination is essential. But equally, and perhaps even more important are affirmative, voluntary efforts on the part of public employers to assure that positions in the public service are genuinely and equally accessible to qualified persons, without regard to their sex, racial, or ethnic characteristics. Without such efforts equal employment opportunity is no more than a wish. The importance of voluntary affirmative action on the part of employers is underscored by title VII of the Civil Rights Act of 1964, Executive Order 11246, and related laws and regulations—all of which emphasize voluntary action to achieve equal employment opportunity.

As with most management objectives, a systematic plan based on sound organizational analysis and problem identification is crucial to the accomplishment of affirmative action objectives. For this reason, the Council urges all State and local governments to develop and implement results-oriented affirmative action plans which deal with the problems so identified.

The following paragraphs are intended to assist State and local governments by illustrating the kinds of analyses and activities which may be appropriate for a public employer's voluntary affirmative action plan. This statement does not address remedies imposed after a finding of unlawful discrimination.

(2) Voluntary affirmative action to assure equal employment opportunity is appropriate at any stage of the employment process. The first step in the construction of any affirmative action plan should be an analysis of the employer's work force to determine whether percentages of sex, race, or ethnic groups in individual job classifications are substantially similar to the percentages of those

groups available in the relevant job market who possess the basic job-related qualifications.

When substantial disparities are found through such analyses, each element of the overall selection process should be examined to determine which elements operate to exclude persons on the basis of sex, race, or ethnic group. Such elements include, but are not limited to, recruitment, testing, ranking certification, interview, recommendations for selection, hiring, promotion, etc. The examination of each element of the selection process should at a minimum include a determination of its validity in predicting job performance.

(3) When an employer has reason to believe that its selection procedures have the exclusionary effect described in paragraph 2 above, it should initiate affirmative steps to remedy the situation. Such steps, which in design and execution may be race, color, sex, or ethnic "conscious," include, but are not limited to, the following:

(a) The establishment of a long-term goal, and short-range, interim goals and timetables for the specific job classifications, all of which should take into account the availability of basically qualified persons in the relevant job market;

(b) A recruitment program designed to attract qualified members of the group in question;

(c) A systematic effort to organize work and redesign jobs in ways that provide opportunities for persons lacking "journeyman" level knowledge or skills to enter and, with appropriate training, to progress in a career field;

(d) Revamping selection instruments or procedures which have not yet been validated in order to reduce or eliminate exclusionary effects on particular groups in particular job classifications;

(e) The initiation of measures designed to assure that members of the affected group who are qualified to perform the job are included within the pool of persons from which the selecting official makes the selection;

(f) A systematic effort to provide career advancement training, both classroom and on-the-job, to employees locked into dead end jobs; and

(g) The establishment of a system for regularly monitoring the effectiveness of the particular affirmative action program, and procedures for making timely adjustments in this program where effectiveness is not demonstrated.

(4) The goal of any affirmative action plan should be achievement of genuine equal employment opportunity for all qualified persons. Selection under such plans should be based upon the ability of the applicant(s) to do the work. Such plans should not require the selection of the unqualified, or the unneeded, nor should they require the selection of persons on the basis of race, color, sex, religion, or national origin. Moreover, while the Council believes that this statement should serve to assist State and local employers, as well as Federal agencies, it recognizes that affirmative action cannot be viewed as a standardized program which must be accomplished in the same way at all times in all places.

Accordingly, the Council has not attempted to set forth here either the minimum or maximum voluntary steps that employers may take to deal with their respective situations. Rather, the Council recognizes that under applicable authorities, State and local employers have flexibility to formulate affirmative action plans that are best suited to their particular situations. In this manner, the Council believes that affirmative action programs will best serve the goal of equal employment opportunity.

APPENDIX C

A Suggested Outline for Test Evaluation

NOTE: The following outline contains basic features applicable to nearly all tests. Additional features are undoubtedly noteworthy in the case of particular tests. A good preparation for one's own evaluation of tests should include a thorough reading of the *Standards for Educational and Psychological Tests* and a perusal of a sample of test reviews in the *Mental Measurements Yearbooks*.

A. GENERAL INFORMATION

Title of test (including edition and forms if applicable)

Author(s)

Publisher, dates of publication, including dates of manuals, norms, and supplementary materials (especially important for tests whose context or norms may become outdated)

Time required to administer

Cost (booklets, answer sheets, other test materials, available scoring services)

B. BRIEF DESCRIPTION OF PURPOSE AND NATURE OF TEST

General type of test (e.g., individual or group, performance, multiple aptitude battery, interest inventory)

Population for which designed (age range, type of person)

Nature of content (e.g., verbal, numerical, spatial, motor)

Subtests and separate scores

Item types

C. PRACTICAL EVALUATION

Qualitative features of test materials (e.g., design of test booklet, editorial quality of content, ease of using, attractiveness, durability, appropriateness for examinees)

Ease of administration

Clarity of directions

Scoring procedures

Examiner qualifications and training

Face validity and examinee rapport

D. TECHNICAL EVALUATION

1. Norms

Type (e.g., percentiles, standard scores)

Standardization sample: nature, size, representativeness, procedures followed in obtaining sample, availability of subgroup norms (e.g., age, sex, education, occupation, region)

2. Reliability

Types and procedure (e.g., retest. parallel-form, split-half, Kuder-Richardson or coefficient alpha), including size and nature of samples employed

Scorer reliability if applicable

Equivalence of forms

Long-term stability when available

3. Validity

Appropriate types of validation procedures (content, criterion-related predictive or concurrent, construct)

Specific procedures followed in assessing validity and results obtained

Size and nature of samples employed

E. REVIEWER COMMENTS

From *Mental Measurements Yearbooks* and other sources

F. SUMMARY EVALUATION

Major strengths and weaknesses of the test, cutting across all parts of the outline

Appendix D

Test Publishers

BELOW are the names and addresses of some of the larger American publishers and distributors of psychological tests. Catalogs of current tests can be obtained from these publishers on request. Each catalog lists all tests sold by that publisher, including any published by others. For names and addresses of other test publishers, see Publishers Directory in the latest *Mental Measurements Yearbook*.

American Guidance Service, Publishers' Building, Circle Pines, MN 55014.
American Testronics, P.O. Box 2270, Iowa City, IO 52244.
Bobbs-Merrill Educational Publishing, 4300 West 62nd Street, Indianapolis, IN 46206.
Bureau of Educational Research and Service, University of Iowa, Iowa City, IO 52242.
CTB/McGraw-Hill, Del Monte Research Park, Monterey, CA 93940.
Consulting Psychologists Press, Inc., 577 College Avenue, Palo Alto, CA 94306.
Educational and Industrial Testing Service, P.O. Box 7234, San Diego, CA 92107.
Educational Testing Service, Princeton, NJ 08540.
Industrial Relations Center, University of Chicago, 1225 East 60th Street, Chicago, IL 60637.
Institute for Personality and Ability Testing, 1602 Coronado Drive, Champaign, IL 61820.
Jastak Associates, Inc., 1526 Gilpin Avenue, Wilmington, DE 19806.
NCS Interpretive Scoring Systems, P.O. Box 1416, Minneapolis, MN 55440.
The Psychological Corporation (a subsidiary of Harcourt Brace Jovanovich, Inc.), 7500 Old Oak Blvd., Cleveland, OH 44130.
Psychological Test Specialists, Box 9229, Missoula, MT 59807.
Psychometric Affiliates, Box 3167, Munster, IN 46321.
Riverside Publishing Company, 8420 Bryn Mawr Avenue, Chicago, IL 60631.
Scholastic Testing Service, Inc., 480 Meyer Road, Bensenville, IL 60106.
Science Research Associates, Inc., 155 North Wacker Drive, Chicago, IL 60606.
Sheridan Psychological Services, P.O. Box 6101, Orange, CA 92667.
C. H. Stoelting Company, 1350 South Kostner Avenue, Chicago, IL 60623.
Western Psychological Services, 12031 Wilshire Boulevard, Los Angeles, CA 90025.

APPENDIX E

Classified List of Representative Tests

THIS table includes all published tests discussed in the text, except out-of-print tests cited for historical reasons only. In order to provide a more representative sample, a few additional tests not cited in the text are also listed under the appropriate categories. For fuller coverage, the reader is referred to the *Mental Measurements Yearbooks* and other sources cited in Chapter 1.

For each listed test, the table gives the volume and entry number in the *Eighth Mental Measurements Yearbook* (MMY–8) where the latest citation of that test can be found, including references to earlier reviews. When the latest edition of a test has not yet been included in the MMY, reference to an earlier edition of the test is given, together with the publication date of the revised edition in parentheses. This practice has also been followed in a few instances of substantial revisions in the manual, such as entirely new norms or extensive additions to validity data. For new tests, not yet covered in the MMY, only the publication date is given, again in parentheses. If a test is not listed in MMY–8 but is listed in *Tests in Print—II* (T–2), its entry number in T–2 is given. This source includes references to reviews in earlier MMY volumes and an updated bibliography.

For publishers not listed in Appendix D, the address is included in this table. It should be noted, however, that several of the major test publishers listed in Appendix D distribute tests in addition to those they publish. For convenience in ordering tests, the catalogs of those publishers should be consulted.

The tests are classified under the same categories employed in the text, and the corresponding chapter numbers are given for each category. All tests listed in this table are also included in the subject index.

Title	Publisher	MMY–8 or T–2 (or date)
INTELLIGENCE TESTS AND DEVELOPMENTAL SCALES		
INDIVIDUAL TESTS (CHS. 9, 10)		
AAMD Adaptive Behavior Scale, 1974 Revision	American Association on Mental Deficiency, 5201 Connecticut Avenue, N.W., Washington, DC 20015	493
Arthur Point Scale of Performance Tests:		T–2:483
Form 1	Stoelting	
Form 2	Psychological Corporation	
Bayley Scales of Infant Development	Psychological Corporation	206
The Blind Learning Aptitude Test	T. Ernest Newland, 709 South Race Street, Urbana, IL 61801	320
Bruininks-Oseretsky Test of Motor Proficiency	American Guidance Service	(1978)
Cain-Levine Social Competency Scale	Consulting Psychologists Press	512
Columbia Mental Maturity Scale	Psychological Corporation	210
Concept Assessment Kit— Conservation	Educational and Industrial Testing Service	238
Full Range Picture Vocabulary Test	Psychological Test Specialists	216
Gesell Developmental Schedules	*See* Knobloch & Pasamanick (1974) for testing procedure and discussion	T–2:497 (1974)
Hiskey-Nebraska Test of Learning Aptitude	Marshall S. Hiskey, 5640 Baldwin, Lincoln, NE 68507	217
Leiter International Performance Scale	Stoelting	T–2:505
Lincoln-Oseretsky Motor Development Scale (Sloan, 1955)	Stoelting	T–2:1895
McCarthy Scales of Children's Abilities	Psychological Corporation	219
Peabody Picture Vocabulary Test —Revised	American Guidance Service	222 (1981)
Pictorial Test of Intelligence	Riverside Publishing Company	223
Porteus Maze Test	Psychological Corporation	224
Quick Test	Psychological Test Specialists	225
Stanford-Binet Intelligence Scale, Form L-M, 1972 Norms Edition	Riverside Publishing Company	229
System of Multicultural Pluralistic Assessment (SOMPA)	Psychological Corporation	(1979)
T.M.R. School Competency Scales	Consulting Psychologists Press	(1976)
Vineland Social Maturity Scale	American Guidance Service	703 (1982)
Wechsler Adult Intelligence Scale —Revised (WAIS-R)	Psychological Corporation	230 (1981)

Title	Publisher	MMY–8 or T–2 (or date)
INTELLIGENCE TESTS AND DEVELOPMENTAL SCALES (Cont.)		
Wechsler Intelligence Scale for Children—Revised (WISC-R)	Psychological Corporation	232
Wechsler Preschool and Primary Scale of Intelligence (WPPSI)	Psychological Corporation	234

GROUP TESTS (CHS. 10, 11)

Title	Publisher	MMY–8 or T–2 (or date)
ACT Assessment: Academic Tests	American College Testing Program, P.O. Box 168, Iowa City, IO 52240	469
The BITCH Test (Black Intelligence Test of Cultural Homogeneity)	Robert L. Williams and Associates, 7201 Creveling Drive, St. Louis, MO 63130	176
Cognitive Abilities Test	Riverside Publishing Company	181 (1978)
College Board Scholastic Aptitude Test (SAT)	Educational Testing Service (for the College Entrance Examination Board)	182
Concept Mastery Test	Psychological Corporation.	T–2:359 (1973)
Culture Fair Intelligence Test	Institute of Personality and Ability Testing	184
Developing Cognitive Abilities Test	American Testronics	(1980)
Goodenough-Harris Drawing Test	Psychological Corporation	187
Graduate Record Examinations (GRE) Aptitude Test	Educational Testing Service (for the Graduate Record Examinations Board)	188 (1977)
Henmon-Nelson Tests of Mental Ability, 1973 Revision	Riverside Publishing Company	190
Kuhlmann-Anderson Tests	Scholastic Testing Service	T–2:398
Miller Analogies Test	Psychological Corporation	192
Otis-Lennon School Ability Test	Psychological Corporation	198 (1980)
Progressive Matrices (Raven)	H. K. Lewis & Co., Ltd. (U.S. distributor: Psychological Corporation)	200
School and College Ability Tests —Series III (SCAT-III)	CTB/McGraw-Hill	183 (1980)

MULTIPLE APTITUDE BATTERIES (Ch. 13)

Title	Publisher	MMY–8 or T–2 (or date)
ACT Career Planning Program (CPP): Ability Tests	American College Testing Program, P.O. Box 168, Iowa City, IO 52240	989
Armed Services Vocational Aptitude Battery (ASVAB)	U.S. Military Enlistment Processing Command. Ft. Sheridan, IL 60037	483

Title	Publisher	MMY–8 or T–2 (or date)
MULTIPLE APTITUDE BATTERIES (Ch. 13) (Cont.)		
Differential Aptitude Tests (DAT)	Psychological Corporation	485
Flanagan Aptitude Classification Tests (FACT)	Science Research Associates	T–2:1072
Planning Career Goals: Ability Measures	CTB/McGraw-Hill	1019
SRA Primary Mental Abilities, 1962 Edition	Science Research Associates	488
USES General Aptitude Test Battery (GATB)	U.S. Employment Service (distributed by U.S. Government Printing Office, Washington, DC 20402)	490
USES Nonreading Aptitude Test Battery (NATB)	U.S. Employment Service (distributed by U.S. Government Printing Office, Washington, DC 20402)	491
TESTS OF CREATIVITY AND REASONING (Ch. 13)		
Alternate Uses	Sheridan Psychological Services	235
Christensen-Guilford Fluency Tests	Sheridan Psychological Services	237
Consequences	Sheridan Psychological Services	239
Creativity Tests for Children	Sheridan Psychological Services	241
Thinking Creatively with Sounds and Words: Research Edition	Scholastic Testing Service	248
Torrance Tests of Creative Thinking	Scholastic Testing Service	249
Watson-Glaser Critical Thinking Appraisal	Psychological Corporation	822 (1980)
EDUCATIONAL TESTS (Ch. 14)		
GENERAL ACHIEVEMENT BATTERIES		
California Achievement Tests	CTB/McGraw-Hill	10 (1977)
CAP Achievement Series	American Testronics	(1980–1981)
Iowa Tests of Basic Skills: Primary Battery, 1979 Multilevel Battery, 1978	Riverside Publishing Company	19 (1978, 1979)
Iowa Tests of Educational Development	Science Research Associates	20
Metropolitan Achievement Tests	Psychological Corporation	22 (1978)
Sequential Tests of Educational Progress, Series III (STEP-III)	CTB/McGraw-Hill	28 (1980)
SRA Achievement Series: Forms 1 and 2, 1978 Edition	Science Research Associates	1 (1978)

Title	Publisher	MMY–8 or T–2 (or date)

EDUCATIONAL TESTS (Ch. 14) (Cont.)

Stanford Achievement Test	Psychological Corporation	29 (1982)
Stanford Test of Academic Skills (TASK)	Psychological Corporation	31 (1982)
Tests of Achievement and Proficiency (TAP)	Riverside Publishing Company	(1978)
Tests of General Educational Development	Testing Service of the American Council on Education, 1 Dupont Circle, Washington, DC 20036	35

TESTS OF MINIMUM COMPETENCY IN BASIC SKILLS

Adult Basic Learning Examination	Psychological Corporation	2
Basic Skills Assessment Program	CTB/McGraw-Hill	(1977)
Life Skills	Riverside Publishing Company	(1980)
Minimum Essentials Test	American Testronics	(1980)
Peabody Individual Achievement Test	American Guidance Service	24
Reading-Arithmetic Index	Science Research Associates	307, 813
USES Basic Occupational Literacy Test (BOLT)	U.S. Employment Service (distributed by U.S. Government Printing Office, Washington, DC 20402)	489
Wide Range Achievement Test, Revised Edition	Jastak Associates, Inc.	37

ACHIEVEMENT TESTS IN SEPARATE SUBJECTS

ACT Proficiency Examination Program	American College Testing Program, P.O. Box 168, Iowa City, IO 52240	470
Advanced Placement Examinations	Educational Testing Service (for the College Entrance Examination Board)	471
College Board Achievement tests	Educational Testing Service (for the College Entrance Examination Board)	472*
College-Level Examination Program (CLEP)	Educational Testing Service (for the College Entrance Examination Board)	473
Content Evaluation Series:	Riverside Publishing Company	
Language Arts Tests		T–2:91
Mathematics Test		T–2:633
Modern Algebra Test		300
Modern Geometry Test		311
Science Tests		T–2:1792

* Individual tests listed separately in MMY.

Title	Publisher	MMY–8 or T–2 (or date)
EDUCATIONAL TESTS (Ch. 14) (Cont.)		
Cooperative achievement tests in English, reading, writing skills, literature, mathematics, sciences, social studies, foreign languages, and health education	CTB/McGraw-Hill	**
High School Subject Tests	American Testronics	(1980–1981)

** Individual tests listed separately in MMY–8; series reviews of all tests in particular fields are given in MMY–7 for mathematics (465), sciences (787), and foreign languages (254).

DIAGNOSTIC AND CRITERION-REFERENCED TESTS

Title	Publisher	MMY–8 or T–2 (or date)
Achievement Improvement Monitors	American Testronics	(1980)
Diagnosis—An Instructional Aid:	Science Research Associates	
Mathematics (1979 revision)		263 (1979)
Reading		752
Diagnostic Mathematics Inventory	CTB/McGraw-Hill	264
Diagnostic Protocols	American Testronics	(1980)
Diagnostic Reading Scales	CTB/McGraw-Hill	753 (1981)
Durrell Analysis of Reading Difficulty: Revised	Psychological Corporation	T–2:1628 (1980)
Gates-MacGinitie Reading Tests	Riverside Publishing Company	726A, 727 (1978)
Individual Pupil Monitoring System:	Riverside Publishing Company	
Mathematics		274
Reading		763
Metropolitan Achievement Tests —Instructional Tests: Reading Mathematics Language	Psychological Corporation	(1978–1979)
Nelson-Denny Reading Test	Riverside Publishing Company	735
Nelson Reading Skills Test	Riverside Publishing Company	(1977)
Prescriptive Reading Inventory	CTB/McGraw-Hill	769
Skills Monitoring System: Reading	Psychological Corporation	776
Stanford Diagnostic Mathematics Test	Psychological Corporation	292
Stanford Diagnostic Reading Test	Psychological Corporation	777

Title	Publisher	MMY–8 or T–2 (or date)

EDUCATIONAL TESTS (Ch. 14) (Cont.)

SPECIALIZED PROGNOSTIC TESTS

Title	Publisher	
Elementary Modern Language Aptitude Test	Psychological Corporation	T–2:222
Modern Language Aptitude Test	Psychological Corporation	T–2:221
Orleans-Hanna Algebra Prognosis Test	Psychological Corporation	T–2:688 (1982)
Pimsleur Language Aptitude Battery	Psychological Corporation	T–2:223

TESTS FOR EARLY CHILDHOOD EDUCATION

Title	Publisher	
Analysis of Readiness Skills: Reading and Mathematics	Riverside Publishing Company	796
Boehm Test of Basic Concepts	Psychological Corporation	178
CIRCUS, Levels A–D	CTB/McGraw-Hill	7A (1979)
Cooperative Preschool Inventory —Revised Edition	CTB/McGraw-Hill	T–2:490
Let's Look at Children II	Educational Testing Service	(1980)
Metropolitan Readiness Tests	Psychological Corporation	802
Stanford Early School Achievement Test (SESAT)	Psychological Corporation	30 (1982)
Tests of Basic Experiences, Second Edition (TOBE 2)	CTB/McGraw-Hill	34 (1978)

OCCUPATIONAL TESTS (Ch. 15)

COGNITIVE SCREENING TESTS

Title	Publisher	
Personnel Tests for Industry	Psychological Corporation	T–2:433
Thurstone Test of Mental Alertness	Science Research Associates	T–2:469
Wesman Personnel Classification Test	Psychological Corporation	T–2:480
Wonderlic Personnel Test	E. F. Wonderlic & Associates, Box 7, Northfield, IL 60093	T–2:482

PSYCHOMOTOR TESTS

Title	Publisher	
Crawford Small Parts Dexterity Test	Psychological Corporation	T–2:2223
Purdue Pegboard	Science Research Associates	T–2:2234
Stromberg Dexterity Test	Psychological Corporation	T–2:2235

Title	Publisher	MMY–8 or T–2 (or date)

OCCUPATIONAL TESTS (Ch. 15) (Cont.)

MECHANICAL APTITUDE TESTS

Bennett Mechanical Comprehension Test	Psychological Corporation	T–2:2239
Revised Minnesota Paper Form Board	Psychological Corporation	T–2:2266
SRA Mechanical Aptitudes	Science Research Associates	T–2:2267

CLERICAL TESTS

General Clerical Test	Psychological Corporation	1033
Minnesota Clerical Test	Psychological Corporation	T–2:2135
Seashore-Bennett Stenographic Proficiency Test	Psychological Corporation	T–2:2148
Short Employment Tests	Psychological Corporation	1037
Short Tests of Clerical Ability	Science Research Associates	1039
SRA Clerical Aptitudes	Science Research Associates	328
SRA Typing Skills	Science Research Associates	1036
Typing Test for Business	Psychological Corporation	T–2:2164

ARTISTIC APTITUDE TESTS

Graves Design Judgment Test	Psychological Corporation	T–2:185
Horn Art Aptitude Inventory	Stoelting	T–2:186
Meier Art Tests: 1. Art Judgment 2. Aesthetic Perception	Bureau of Educational Research and Service	T–2:189

MUSICAL APTITUDE TESTS

Musical Aptitude Profile	Riverside Publishing Company	98
Seashore Measures of Musical Talents	Psychological Corporation	T–2:211
Wing Standardized Tests of Musical Intelligence	NFER-Nelson Publishing Co., Ltd., 2 Oxford Road East, Windsor, Berks, SL4 1DF, England	T–2:217

TESTS FOR CAREER COUNSELING

ACT Career Planning Program	American College Testing Program, P.O. Box 168, Iowa City, IO 52240	989
Career Development Inventory (Super et al.)	Consulting Psychologists Press	(1981–1982)
Career Maturity Inventory	CTB/McGraw-Hill	997
DAT Career Planning Program	Psychological Corporation	1001
Planning Career Goals	CTB/McGraw-Hill	1019

Title	Publisher	MMY–8 or T–2 (or date)

OCCUPATIONAL TESTS (Ch. 15) (Cont.)

TESTS IN THE PROFESSIONS

Title	Publisher	
Dental Admission Testing Program	Division of Educational Measurements, Council on Dental Education, American Dental Association, 211 East Chicago Avenue, Chicago, IL 60611	1085
Examination for Professional Practice in Psychology	American Association of State Psychology Boards, P.O. Box 4389, Montgomery, AL 36103	(1980)
Law School Admission Test (LSAT)	Educational Testing Service (for the Law School Admission Council)	1093
Minnesota Engineering Analogies Test (MEAT)	Psychological Corporation	T–2:2344
National Teacher Examination	Educational Testing Service	381
New Medical College Admission Test (New MCAT)	Association of American Medical Colleges, One Dupont Circle, N.W., Washington, DC 20036	1101
NLN tests for nursing	National League for Nursing, Inc., 10 Columbus Circle, New York, NY 10019	T–2:2382 to T–2:2387

CLINICAL TESTS IN SPECIAL AREAS (Ch. 16)

LEARNING DISABILITIES AND NEUROPSYCHOLOGICAL DYSFUNCTIONS

Title	Publisher	
Assessment of Basic Competencies	Scholastic Testing Service	(1981)
Auditory Discrimination Test, 1973 Revision	Western Psychological Services	932
Bender-Gestalt Test	American Orthopsychiatric Association, Inc., 1775 Broadway, New York, NY 10019	506
Benton Visual Retention Test, Revised Edition	Psychological Corporation	236
Examining for Aphasia (Second Edition)	Psychological Corporation	T–2:2071
Frostig Developmental Test of Visual Perception, Third Edition	Consulting Psychologists Press	882
Frostig Movement Skills Test Battery, Experimental Edition	Consulting Psychologists Press	871
Goldman-Fristoe-Woodcock Auditory Skills Test Battery	American Guidance Service	937
Goldman-Fristoe-Woodcock Test of Auditory Discrimination	American Guidance Service	938

Title	Publisher	MMY–8 or T–2 (or date)
CLINICAL TESTS IN SPECIAL AREAS (Ch. 16) (Cont.)		
Illinois Test of Psycholinguistic Abilities, Revised Edition	University of Illinois Press, Urbana, IL 61801	431
Luria-Nebraska Neuropsychological Battery	Western Psychological Services	(1980)
Memory for Designs Test (Graham & Kendall)	Psychological Test Specialists	613
Minnesota Test for Differential Diagnosis of Aphasia	University of Minnesota Press, 2037 University Avenue, S.E., Minneapolis, MN 55455	T–2:2080
Porch Index of Communicative Ability	Consulting Psychologists Press	971
Porch Index of Communicative Ability in Children	Consulting Psychologists Press	972 (1979)
Primary Visual Motor Test	Grune & Stratton, 111 Fifth Avenue, New York, NY 10003	873
The Pupil Rating Scale (Rev.): Screening for Learning Disabilities (Myklebust)	Grune & Stratton, 111 Fifth Avenue, New York, NY 10003	439 (1981)
Screening Tests for Identifying Children with Specific Language Disability, Revised Edition (Slingerland)	Educators Publishing Service, Inc., 75 Moulton Street, Cambridge, MA 02138	446
Southern California Sensory Integration Tests	Western Psychological Services	875

- -

Title	Publisher	MMY–8 or T–2 (or date)
BEHAVIORAL ASSESSMENT		
Behavior Analysis Forms for Clinical Intervention*	Research Press Company, 2612 North Mattis Avenue, Champaign, IL 61820	(1977)
College Self-Expression Scale	John P. Gallassi, Jr., School of Education, University of North Carolina, Chapel Hill, NC 27514	(1974)
Conflict Resolution Inventory	Richard M. McFall, Department of Psychology, University of Wisconsin, Madison, WI 53706	(1971)
Fear Survey Schedule	Educational and Industrial Testing Service	559
Pleasant Events Schedule	Peter M. Lewinsohn, Department of Psychology, University of Oregon, Eugene, OR 97403	(1976)

* A set of 36 forms developed by J. P. Cautela and his collaborators.

Title	Publisher	MMY–8 or T–2 (or date)

SELF-REPORT PERSONALITY INVENTORIES (Ch. 17)

Title	Publisher	MMY–8 or T–2 (or date)
California Psychological Inventory (CPI)	Consulting Psychologists Press	514
Children's Personality Questionnaire	Institute for Personality and Ability Testing	520
Clinical Analysis Questionnaire, Research Edition	Institute for Personality and Ability Testing	522
Comrey Personality Scales	Educational and Industrial Testing Service	527
Early School Personality Questionnaire	Institute for Personality and Ability Testing	540
Edwards Personal Preference Schedule (EPPS)	Psychological Corporation	542
Eysenck Personality Questionnaire	Educational and Industrial Testing Service	554
Gordon Personal Inventory	Psychological Corporation	568
Gordon Personal Profile	Psychological Corporation	569
Guilford-Zimmerman Temperament Survey	Sheridan Psychological Services	574
High School Personality Questionnaire	Institute for Personality and Ability Testing	597
IPAT Anxiety Scale	Institute for Personality and Ability Testing	582
IPAT Depression Scale	Institute for Personality and Ability Testing	583
Jackson Personality Inventory	Research Psychologists Press, Inc., P.O. Box 984, Port Huron, MI 48060	593
Millon Clinical Multiaxial Inventory	NCS Interpretive Scoring	(1977, 1983
Minnesota Multiphasic Personality Inventory (MMPI)	Psychological Corporation	616
Mooney Problem Check List	Psychological Corporation	626
Myers-Briggs Type Indicator	Consulting Psychologists Press	630
Personality Inventory for Children	Western Psychological Services	(1977)
Personality Research Form	Research Psychologists Press, Inc., P.O. Box 984, Port Huron, MI 48060	643
Psychological Screening Inventory	Research Psychologists Press, Inc., P.O. Box 984, Port Huron, MI 48060	654
Sixteen Personality Factor Questionnaire (16 PF)	Institute for Personality and Ability Testing	679
State-Trait Anxiety Inventory (STAI)	Consulting Psychologists Press	683
State-Trait Anxiety Inventory for Children (STAIC)	Consulting Psychologists Press	684

Title	Publisher	MMY–8 or T–2 (or date)
SELF-REPORT PERSONALITY INVENTORIES (Ch. 17) (Cont.)		
STS Junior Inventory	Scholastic Testing Service	T–2:1360
STS Youth Inventory	Scholastic Testing Service	T–2:1361
Test Anxiety Inventory	Consulting Psychologists Press	(1980)

MEASURES OF INTERESTS, VALUES, AND PERSONAL ORIENTATIONS (Ch. 18)

Title	Publisher	MMY–8 or T–2 (or date)
Bem Sex-Role Inventory	Consulting Psychologists Press	(1981)
California Occupational Preference System	Educational and Industrial Testing Service	992
Career Assessment Inventory	NCS Interpretive Scoring	993
The Harrington/O'Shea System for Career Decision Making	American Guidance Service	1004
Jackson Vocational Interest Survey	Research Psychologists Press, Inc., P.O. Box 984, Port Huron, MI 48060	(1977, 1982)
Jenkins Activity Survey	Psychological Corporation	(1979)
Kuder General Interest Survey	Science Research Associates	1009
Kuder Occupational Interest Survey, Revised	Science Research Associates	1010 (1979–1980)
Kuder Preference Record—Vocational	Science Research Associates	1011
Millon Behavioral Health Inventory	NCS Interpretive Scoring Systems 4401 W. 76 Street Minneapolis, MN 55435	(1979)
Minnesota Teacher Attitude Inventory	Psychological Corporation	377
Ohio Vocational Interest Survey	Psychological Corporation	1016
Personal Orientation Inventory	Educational and Industrial Testing Service	641
School Attitude Measure	American Testronics	(1980)
Self-Directed Search (SDS)	Consulting Psychologists Press	1022 (1977–1979)
Sickness Impact Profile	Marilyn Bergner or Betty S. Gilson, Department of Health Services, University of Washington, Seattle, WA 98195	(1977–1981)
Strong-Campbell Interest Inventory (SCII)	Stanford University Press, Stanford, CA 94305	1023
Study of Values	Riverside Publishing Company	686
Survey of Interpersonal Values	Science Research Associates	688
Survey of School Attitudes	Psychological Corporation	402
USES Interest Check List	U.S. Employment Service (distributed by U.S.	(1979)

Title	Publisher	MMY–8 or T–2 (or date)

MEASURES OF INTERESTS, VALUES, AND PERSONAL ORIENTATIONS (Ch. 18) (Cont.)

Title	Publisher	MMY–8 or T–2 (or date)
USES Interest Inventory	Government Printing Office, Washington, DC 20402) U.S. Employment Service (distributed by U.S. Government Printing Office, Washington, DC 20402)	(1981)
Vocational Interest, Experience, and Skill Assessment	Riverside Publishing Company	1025
Vocational Preference Inventory	Consulting Psychologists Press	1028 (1977–1979)
Work Values Inventory	Riverside Publishing Company	1030

PROJECTIVE TECHNIQUES (Ch. 19)

Title	Publisher	MMY–8 or T–2 (or date)
Children' Apperception Test	C.P.S., Inc., P.O. Box 83, Larchmont, NY 10538	T–2:1451
Gerontological Apperception Test	Human Sciences Press, 72 Fifth Avenue, New York, NY 10011	566
Holtzman Inkblot Technique	Psychological Corporation	578
Kent-Rosanoff Free Association Test	Stoelting	T–2:1480
Machover Draw-a-Person Test	Charles C Thomas, 301–327 East Lawrence Avenue, Springfield, IL 62717	606
Make A Picture Story (MAPS)	Psychological Corporation	T–2:1482
Rorschach	Grune & Stratton, Inc., 111 Fifth Avenue, New York. NY 10003 (U.S. distributor)	661
Rosenzweig Picture-Frustration Study (P-F Study)	Saul Rosenzweig, 8029 Washington Street, St. Louis, MO 63114	662
Rotter Incomplete Sentences Blank	Psychological Corporation	663
Senior Apperception Technique	C.P.S., Inc., P.O. Box 83, Larchmont, NY 10538	676
Thematic Apperception Test (TAT)	Harvard University Press, 79 Garden Street, Cambridge, MA 02138	697
Washington University Sentence Completion Test	Jossey-Bass, Inc., 615 Montgomery Street, San Francisco, CA 94111	708

Title	Publisher	MMY–8 or T–2 (or date)
PERSONALITY TESTS: MISCELLANEOUS (Ch. 20)		
Adjective Check List (ACL)	Consulting Psychologists Press	495 (1980)
Barron-Welsh Art Scale	Consulting Psychologists Press	504
California Q-Sort Deck	Consulting Psychologists Press	(1979)
Chapin Social Insight Test	Consulting Psychologists Press	T–2:1125
Children's Embedded Figures Test	Consulting Psychologists Press	519
Embedded Figures Test	Consulting Psychologists Press	548
Famous Sayings	Psychological Test Specialists	T–2:1183
Group Embedded Figures Test	Consulting Psychologists Press	572
IPAT Humor Test of Personality	Institute for Personality and Ability Testing	T–2:1228
Objective-Analytic (O-A) Anxiety Battery	Institute for Personality and Ability Testing	T–2:1300
Objective-Analytic (O-A) Test Kit	Institute for Personality and Ability Testing	(1978)
Preschool Embedded Figures Test	Consulting Psychologists Press	T–2:1331
Welsh Figure Preference Test	Consulting Psychologists Press	T–2:1437 (1980)

MEASURES OF ENVIRONMENTAL QUALITIES AND ECOLOGICAL ATTITUDES (Ch. 20)

Title	Publisher	MMY–8 or T–2 (or date)
American Home Scale	Psychometric Affiliates	T–2:1039
Environmental Response Inventory	Consulting Psychologists Press	550
Home Index	Harrison G. Gough, 2240 Piedmont Avenue, University of California. Berkeley, CA 94720	468
The Inventory of College Leisure Activities Blank (Research Edition)	NCS Interpretive Scoring / Consulting Psychologists Press	T–2:1244 / 602
Social Climate Scales	Consulting Psychologists Press	681
Stern Activities Index	Psychological Research Center, 250 Machinery Hall, Syracuse University, Syracuse, NY 13210	T–2:1394
Stern Environment Indexes	Psychological Research Center, 250 Machinery Hall, Syracuse University, Syracuse, NY 13210	T–2:1395
Work Environment Preference Schedule	Psychological Corporation	712

References

ABRAHAMS, N. M., & ALF, E., JR. Pratfalls in moderator research. *Journal of Applied Psychology*, 1972, *56*, 245–251.

ADAMS, K. M. In search of Luria's battery: A false start. *Journal of Consulting and Clinical Psychology*, 1980, *48*, 511–516. (a)

ADAMS, K. M. An end of innocence for behavioral neurology? Adams replies. *Journal of Consulting and Clinical Psychology*, 1980, *48*, 522–524. (b)

ADCOCK, C. J. Thematic Apperception Test. *Sixth Mental Measurements Yearbook*, 1965, 533–535.

ADKINS, D. C. *Test construction: Development and interpretation of achievement tests* (2nd ed.). Columbus, Ohio: Merrill, 1974.

AHLSTRÖM, K. G. *Studies in spelling: I. Analysis of three different aspects of spelling ability*. Report No. 20, The Institute of Education, Uppsala University (Sweden), 1964.

ALBRIGHT, L. E., et al. Federal government in psychological testing: Is it here? A symposium. *Personnel Psychology*, 1976, *29*, 519–557.

ALLEN, M. J., & YEN, W. M. *Introduction to measurement theory*. Monterey, Calif.: Brooks/Cole, 1979.

ALLEN, R. M., & COLLINS, M. G. Suggestions for the adaptive administration of intelligence tests for those with cerebral palsy. *Cerebral Palsy Review*, 1955, *16*, 11–14.

ALLPORT, G. W. *Personality: A psychological interpretation*. New York: Holt, 1937.

ALLPORT, G. W., & ODBERT, H. S. Trait-names, a psycholexical study. *Psychological Monographs*, 1936, *47*(1, Whole No. 211).

AMERICAN ASSOCIATION ON MENTAL DEFICIENCY. *Adaptive Behavior Scale: Manual*. Washington, D.C.: Author, 1974.

AMERICAN PSYCHOLOGICAL ASSOCIATION. Minutes of the annual meeting of the Council of Representatives. *American Psychologist*, 1966, *21*, 1141. (Also reprinted in *Casebook on ethical standards of psychologists*. Washington, D.C.: American Psychological Association, 1974. Pp. 80–81).

AMERICAN PSYCHOLOGICAL ASSOCIATION, TASK FORCE ON EMPLOYMENT TESTING OF MINORITY GROUPS. Job testing and the disadvantaged. *American Psychologist*, 1969, *24*, 637–650.

AMERICAN PSYCHOLOGICAL ASSOCIATION. *Ethical principles in the conduct of research with human participants*. Washington, D.C.: Author, 1973.

AMERICAN PSYCHOLOGICAL ASSOCIATION, TASK FORCE ON HEALTH RESEARCH. Contributions of psychology to health research: Patterns, problems, and potential. *American Psychologist*, 1976, *31*, 263–274.

AMERICAN PSYCHOLOGICAL ASSOCIATION, DIVISION OF INDUSTRIAL-ORGANIZATIONAL PSYCHOLOGY. *Principles for the validation and use of personnel selection procedures* (2nd ed.). Berkeley, Calif.: Author, 1980.

AMERICAN PSYCHOLOGICAL ASSOCIATION. *Ethical principles of psychologists.* Washington, D.C.: Author, 1981.

AMES, L. B. The sequential patterning of prone progression in the human infant. *Genetic Psychology Monographs,* 1937, *19,* 409–460.

AMES, L. B., GILLESPIE, B. S., HAINES, J., & ILG, F. L. *The Gesell Institute's child from one to six: Evaluating the behavior of the preschool child.* New York: Harper & Row, 1979.

AMES, L. B., METRAUX, R. W., RODELL, J. L., & WALKER, R. N. Rorschach responses in old age. New York: Brunner/Mazel, 1973.

AMES, L. B., METRAUX, R. W., RODELL, J. L., & WALKER, R. N. *Child Rorschach responses: Developmental trends from two to ten years.* New York: Brunner/Mazel, 1974.

AMES, L. B., METRAUX, R. W., & WALKER, R. N. *Adolescent Rorschach responses: Developmental trends from ten to sixteen years.* New York: Brunner/Mazel, 1971.

ANASTASI, A. Practice and variability. *Psychological Monographs,* 1934, *45*(5, Whole No. 204).

ANASTASI, A. The nature of psychological "traits." *Psychological Review,* 1948, *55,* 127–138.

ANASTASI, A. The concept of validity in the interpretation of test scores. *Educational and Psychological Measurement,* 1950, *10,* 67–68.

ANASTASI, A. Age changes in adult test performance. *Psychological Reports,* 1956, *2,* 509.

ANASTASI, A. *Differential psychology* (3rd ed.). New York: Macmillan, 1958.

ANASTASI, A. Psychological tests: Uses and abuses. *Teachers College Record,* 1961, *62,* 389–393.

ANASTASI, A. (Ed.). *Individual differences.* New York: Wiley, 1965.

ANASTASI, A. Psychology, psychologists, and psychological testing. *American Psychologist,* 1967, *22,* 297–306.

ANASTASI, A. *Psychological testing* (3rd ed.). New York: Macmillan, 1968.

ANASTASI, A. On the formation of psychological traits. *American Psychologist,* 1970, *25,* 899–910.

ANASTASI, A. More on heritability: Addendum to the Hebb and Jensen interchange. *American Psychologist,* 1971, *26,* 1036–1037.

ANASTASI, A. Technical critique. In L. A. Crooks (Ed.), *Proceedings of Invitational Conference on "An investigation of sources of bias in the prediction of job performance: A six-year study."* Princeton, N.J.: Educational Testing Service, 1972. Pp. 79–88.

ANASTASI, A. Harassing a dead horse: Review of D. R. Green (Ed.), The aptitude–achievement distinction: Proceedings of the Second CTB/McGraw-Hill Conference on Issues in Educational Measurement. *Review of Education,* 1975, *1,* 356–362.

ANASTASI, A. *Fields of applied psychology* (2nd ed.). New York: McGraw-Hill, 1979.

ANASTASI, A. Abilities and the measurement of achievement. *New Directions for Testing and Measurement,* 1980, *5,* 1–10.

ANASTASI, A., & CORDOVA, F. A. Some effects of bilingualism upon the intelligence test performance of Puerto Rican children in New York City. *Journal of Educational Psychology,* 1953, *44,* 1–19.

ANASTASI, A., & DRAKE, J. An empirical comparison of certain techniques for estimating the reliability of speeded tests. *Educational and Psychological Measurement*, 1954, *14*, 529–540.

ANDERSON, J. E. The prediction of terminal intelligence from infant and preschool tests. *Thirty-ninth Yearbook, National Society for the Study of Education*, 1940, Part I, 385–403.

ANDERSON, S. B., & MESSICK, S. Social competency in young children. *Developmental Psychology*, 1974, *10*, 282–293.

ANDRISANI, P. J., & NESTEL, G. Internal-external control as contributor to and outcome of work experience. *Journal of Applied Psychology*, 1976, *61*, 156–165.

ANGOFF, W. H. Scales with nonmeaningful origins and units of measurement. *Educational and Psychological Measurement*, 1962, *22*, 27–34.

ANGOFF, W. H. Technical problems of obtaining equivalent scores on tests. *Journal of Educational Measurement*, 1964, *1*, 11–13.

ANGOFF, W. H. Can useful general-purpose equivalency tables be prepared for different college admissions tests? In A. Anastasi (Ed.), *Testing problems in perspective*. Washington, D.C.: American Council on Education, 1966. Pp. 251–264.

ANGOFF, W. H. (Ed.). *The College Board Admissions Testing Program: A technical report on research and development activities relating to the Scholastic Aptitude Test and achievement tests*. New York: College Entrance Examination Board, 1971. (a)

ANGOFF, W. H. Scales, norms, and equivalent scores. In R. L. Thorndike (Ed.), *Educational measurement* (2nd ed.). Washington, D.C.: American Council on Education, 1971. Ch. 15. (b)

ANGOFF, W. H. Criterion-referencing, norm-referencing, and the SAT. *College Board Review*, 1974, *92*, 3–5, 21.

ANGOFF, W. H., & MODU, C. C. *Equating the scales of the Prueba de Aptitud Academica and the Scholastic Aptitude Test*. College Entrance Examination Board, Research Report 3, 1973.

ANSBACHER, H. L. The Goodenough Draw-a-Man Test and primary mental abilities. *Journal of Consulting Psychology*, 1952, *16*, 176–180.

Army Air Forces aviation psychology program, research reports. Rep. Nos. 1–19. Washington, D.C.: Government Printing Office, 1947–1948.

ARNOLD, G. F. A technique for measuring the mental ability of the cerebral palsied. *Psychological Service Center Journal*, 1951, *3*, 171–180.

ARONOW, E., & REZNIKOFF, M. *Rorschach content interpretation*. New York: Grune & Stratton, 1976.

ARVEY, R. D. Unfair discrimination in the employment interview: Legal and psychological aspects. *Psychological Bulletin*, 1979, *86*, 736–765.

ASHER, S. R., SINGLETON, L. C., TINSLEY, B. R., & HYMEL, S. A reliable sociometric measure for preschool children. *Developmental Psychology*, 1979, *15*, 443–444.

ASTIN, A. W. *The college environment*. Washington, D.C.: American Council on Education, 1968. (a)

ASTIN, A. W. Undergraduate achievement and institutional "excellence." *Science*, 1968, *161*, 661–668. (b)

Astin, A. W., & Boruch, R. F. A "Link" system for assuring confidentiality of research data in longitudinal studies. *American Educational Research Journal,* 1970, *7,* 615–624.

Atkinson, J. W. (Ed.). *Motives in fantasy, action, and society.* New York: Van Nostrand, 1958.

Atkinson, J. W. Motivational determinants of intellective performance and cumulative achievement. In J. W. Atkinson & J. O. Raynor, *Motivation and achievement.* Washington, D.C.: Winston, 1974. Ch. 20.

Atkinson, J. W. Studying personality in the context of an advanced motivational psychology. *American Psychologist,* 1981, *36,* 117–128.

Atkinson, J. W., & Birch, D. *An introduction to motivation* (2nd ed.). New York: Van Nostrand, 1978.

Atkinson, J. W., & Feather, N. T. (Eds.). *A theory of achievement motivation.* New York: Wiley, 1966.

Atkinson, J. W., O'Malley, P. M. & Lens, W. Motivation and ability: Interactive psychological determinants of intellective performance, educational achievement, and each other. In W. H. Sewell, R. M. Hauser, & D. L. Featherman (Eds.), *Schooling and achievement in American society.* New York: Academic Press, 1976. Ch. 8.

Atkinson, J. W., & Raynor, J. O. (Eds.). *Motivation and achievement.* Washington, D.C.: Winston, 1974.

Atkinson, R. C. Teaching children to read using a computer. *American Psychologist,* 1974, *29,* 169–178.

Babad, E. Y., & Budoff, M. Sensitivity and validity of learning-potential measurement in three levels of ability. *Journal of Educational Psychology,* 1974, *66,* 439–447.

Bakan, D. Clinical psychology and logic. *American Psychologist,* 1956, *11,* 655–662.

Bakare, C. G. M. Social-class differences in the performance of Nigerian children on the Draw-a-Man test. In L. J. Cronbach & P. J. D. Drenth (Eds.), *Mental tests and cultural adaptation.* The Hague: Mouton, 1972. Pp. 355–363.

Baker, F. B. Automation of test scoring, reporting, and analysis. In R. L. Thorndike (Ed.), *Educational measurement* (2nd ed.). Washington, D.C.: American Council on Education, 1971. Ch. 8.

Baker, F. B. Advances in item analysis. *Review of Educational Research,* 1977, *47,* 151–178.

Baller, W. R., Charles, D. C., & Miller, E. L. Mid-life attainment of the mentally retarded: A longitudinal study. *Genetic Psychology Monographs,* 1967, *75,* 235–329.

Balma, M. J. The concept of synthetic validity. *Personnel Psychology,* 1959, *12,* 395–396.

Baltes, P. B. Longitudinal and cross-sectional sequences in the study of age and generation effects. *Human Development,* 1968, *11,* 145–171.

Baltes, P. B., Reese, H. W., & Lipsitt, L. P. Life-span developmental psychology. *Annual Review of Psychology,* 1980, *31,* 65–110.

Baltes, P. B., & Schaie, K. W. On the plasticity of intelligence in adulthood and old age. *American Psychologist,* 1976, *31,* 720–725.

BANDURA, A. *Principles of behavior modification*. New York: Holt, Rinehart & Winston, 1969.

BANDURA, A., & WALTERS, R. H. *Social learning and personality development*. New York: Holt, Rinehart & Winston, 1963.

BANNISTER, D., & MAIR, J. M. M. *The evaluation of personal constructs*. New York: Academic Press, 1968.

BARKER, R. G. *Ecological psychology*. Stanford, Calif.: Stanford University Press, 1968.

BARKER, R. G., and associates. *Habitats, environments, and human behavior*. San Francisco: Jossey-Bass, 1978.

BARRON, F. The psychology of creativity. In F. Barron et al., *New directions in psychology II*. New York: Holt, Rinehart & Winston, 1965. Pp. 3–134.

BARRON, F. *Creative person and creative process*. New York: Holt, Rinehart & Winston, 1969.

BART, W. M., & AIRASIAN, P. W. Determination of the ordering among seven Piagetian tasks by an ordering-theoretic method. *Journal of Educational Psychology*, 1974, *66*, 277–284.

BARTLETT, C. J., & EDGERTON, H. A. Stanine values for ranks for different numbers of things ranked. *Educational and Psychological Measurement*, 1966, *26*, 287–289.

BASS, A. R., & TURNER, J. N. Ethnic group differences in relationships among criteria of job performance. *Journal of Applied Psychology*, 1973, *57*, 101–109.

BASS, B. M. The leaderless group discussion. *Psychological Bulletin*, 1954, *51*, 465–492.

BASS, B. M. Validity studies of a proverbs personality test. *Journal of Applied Psychology*, 1957, *41*, 158–160.

BASS, B. M. Famous Sayings test: General manual. *Psychological Reports*, 1958, *4*, 479–497. (Monograph Supplement)

BAUGHMAN, E. E. Rorschach scores as a function of examiner difference. *Journal of Projective Techniques*, 1951, *15*, 243–249.

BAUGHMAN, E. E. The role of the stimulus in Rorschach responses. *Psychological Bulletin*, 1958, *55*, 121–147.

BAYLEY, N. On the growth of intelligence. *American Psychologist*, 1955, *10*, 805–818.

BAYLEY, N. Development of mental abilities. In P. H. Mussen (Ed.), *Carmichael's manual of child psychology*. New York: Wiley, 1970.

BAYLEY, N., & ODEN, M. H. The maintenance of intellectual ability in gifted adults. *Journal of Gerontology*, 1955, *10*, 91–107.

BAYLEY, N., & SCHAEFER, E. S. Correlations of maternal and child behaviors with the development of mental abilities. *Monographs of the Society for Research in Child Development*, 1964, *29*(6, Serial No. 97).

BAYROFF, A. G., & FUCHS, E. F. *Armed Services Vocational Aptitude Battery* (Tech. Res. Rep. 1161). Alexandria, Va.: U.S. Army Research Institute for the Behavioral and Social Sciences, February 1970.

BECKER, W. C. The matching of behavior rating and questionnaire personality factors. *Psychological Bulletin*, 1960, *57*, 201–212.

BEERE, C. A. *Women and women's issues: A handbook of tests and measures.* San Francisco: Jossey-Bass, 1979.

BEIER, J. J., & EKSTROM, R. B. Creating employment equity through the recognition of experiential learning. *Journal of Career Education,* 1979, *6,* 2–11.

BEJAR, I. I. Biased assessment of program impact due to psychometric artifacts. *Psychological Bulletin,* 1980, *87,* 513–524.

BELL, A., & ZUBEK, J. The effect of age on the intellectual performance of mental defectives. *Journal of Gerontology,* 1960, *15,* 285–295.

BELL, F. O., HOFF, A. L., & HOYT, K. B. Answer sheets do make a difference. *Personnel Psychology,* 1964, *17,* 65–71.

BELLAK, L. *The TAT, CAT, and SAT in clinical use* (3rd ed.). New York: Grune & Stratton, 1975.

BELLAK, L., & BELLAK, S. S. *Manual: Senior Apperception Technique.* Larchmont, N.Y.: C.P.S., 1973.

BELLAK, L., & HURVICH, M. S. A human modification of the Children's Apperception Test (CAT-H). *Journal of Projective Techniques and Personality Assessment,* 1966, *30,* 228–242.

BELMONT, J. M., & BUTTERFIELD, E. C. The instructional approach to developmental cognitive research. In R. V. Kail, Jr., & J. Hagen (Eds.), *Perspectives on the development of memory and cognition.* Hillsdale, N.J.: Erlbaum, 1977.

BEM, D. J., & ALLEN, A. On predicting some of the people some of the time: The search for cross-situational consistencies in behavior. *Psychological Review,* 1974, *81,* 506–520.

BEM, D. J., & FUNDER, D. C. Predicting more of the people more of the time: Assessing the personality of situations. *Psychological Review,* 1978, *85,* 485–501.

BEM, S. L. The measurement of psychological androgyny. *Journal of Consulting and Clinical Psychology,* 1974, *42,* 155–162.

BEM, S. L. On the utility of alternative procedures for assessing psychological androgyny. *Journal of Consulting and Clinical Psychology,* 1977, *45,* 196–205.

BEM, S. L. *Manual for the Bem Sex-Role Inventory.* Palo Alto, Calif.: Consulting Psychologists Press, 1981.

BEMIS, S. E. Occupational validity of the General Aptitude Test Battery. *Journal of Applied Psychology,* 1968, *52,* 240–244.

BENDER, L. A visual motor Gestalt test and its clinical use. *American Orthopsychiatric Association, Research Monographs,* 1938, No. 3.

BENNETT, G. K., & DOPPELT, J. E. *Test Orientation Procedure.* New York: Psychological Corporation, 1967.

BENNETT, G. K., SEASHORE, H. G., & WESMAN, A. G. *Fifth edition manual for the Differential Aptitude Tests, Forms S and T.* New York: Psychological Corporation, 1974.

BENTLER, P. M., JACKSON, D. N., & MESSICK, S. Identification of content and style: A two-dimensional interpretation of acquiescence. *Psychological Bulletin,* 1971, *76,* 186–204.

BENTLER, P. M., JACKSON, D. N., & MESSICK, S. A rose by any other name. *Psychological Bulletin,* 1972, *77,* 109–113.

BENTON, A. L. *Revised Visual Retention Test: Manual.* New York: Psychological Corporation, 1974.

BENTZ, V. J. (Chair). *Methodological implications of large scale validity studies of clerical occupations.* Symposium presented at the meeting of the American Psychological Association, Montreal, September 1980.

BERG, I. A. The deviation hypothesis: A broad statement of its assumptions and postulates. In I. A. Berg (Ed.), *Response set in personality assessment.* Chicago: Aldine, 1967. Pp. 146–190.

BERGNER, M., BOBBITT, R. A., et al. The Sickness Impact Profile: Development and final revision of a health status measure. *Medical Care,* 1981, *19*(8).

BERGNER, M., & GILSON, B. S. The Sickness Impact Profile: The relevance of social science to medicine. In L. Eisenberg & A. Kleinman (Eds.), *The relevance of social science to medicine.* Dordrecht, Holland: Reidel, 1981. Pp. 135–150.

BERK, R. A. (Ed.). *Criterion-referenced measurement: The state of the art.* Baltimore: Johns Hopkins University Press, 1980.

BERNARDIN, H. J., & PENCE, E. C. Effects of rater training: Creating new response sets and decreasing accuracy. *Journal of Applied Psychology,* 1980, *65*, 60–66.

BERNE, E. *Transactional analysis in psychotherapy.* New York: Grove Press, 1961.

BERNE, E. *Principles of group treatment.* New York: Oxford University Press, 1966.

BERNSTEIN, L. The examiner as an inhibiting factor in clinical testing. *Journal of Consulting Psychology,* 1956, *20*, 287–290.

BERNSTEIN, L., BERNSTEIN, R. S., & DANA, R. H. *Interviewing: A guide for health professionals* (2nd ed.). New York: Appleton-Century-Crofts, 1974.

BERRY, J. W. Radical cultural relativism and the concept of intelligence. In L. J. Cronbach & P. J. D. Drenth (Eds.), *Mental tests and cultural adaptations.* The Hague: Mouton, 1972. Pp. 77–88.

BERRY, J. W. *Human ecology and cognitive style: Comparative studies in cultural and psychological adaptation.* Beverly Hills, Calif.: Sage, 1976.

BIERI, J. Cognitive structures in personality. In H. M. Schroder & P. Suedfeld (Eds.), *Personality theory and information processing.* New York: Ronald, 1971.

BIERI, J., ATKINS, A. L., BRIAR, S., LEAMAN, R. L., MILLER, H., & TRIPODI, T. *Clinical and social judgment: The discrimination of behavioral information.* New York: Wiley, 1966.

BIESHEUVEL, S. (Ed.). *Methods for the measurement of psychological performance.* International Biological Program (IBP) Handbook No. 10. Oxford: Blackwell, 1969.

BIJOU, S. W., & PETERSON, R. F. Functional analysis in the assessment of children. In P. McReynolds (Ed.), *Advances in psychological assessment* (Vol. 2). Palo Alto, Calif.: Science and Behavior Books, 1971. Pp. 63–78.

BINET, A., & HENRI, V. La psychologie individuelle. *Année psychologique,* 1895, *2*, 411–463.

BINET, A., & SIMON, TH. Méthodes nouvelles pour le diagnostic du niveau intellectuel des anormaux. *Année psychologique,* 1905, *11*, 191–244.

BINGHAM, W. V., MOORE, B. V., & GUSTAD, J. *How to interview* (4th ed.). New York: Harper, 1959.

BIRREN, J. E. Increments and decrements in the intellectual status of the aged. *Psychiatric Research Reports,* 1968, *23*, 207–214.

BLAKE, R. H. Industrial application of tests developed for illiterate and semiliterate people. In L. J. Cronbach & P. J. D. Drenth (Eds.), *Mental tests and cultural adaptation*. The Hague: Mouton, 1972. Pp. 37–46.

BLANCHARD, W. H. The consensus Rorschach: Background and development. *Journal of Projective Techniques and Personality Assessment*, 1968, *32*, 327–330.

BLOCK, J. *The challenge of response sets: Unconfounding meaning, acquiescence, and social desirability in the MMPI*. New York: Irvington, 1965.

BLOCK, J. Remarks on Jackson's "review" of Block's challenge of response sets. *Educational and Psychological Measurement*, 1967, *27*, 499–502.

BLOCK, J. *Lives through time*. Berkeley, Calif.: Bancroft, 1971. (a)

BLOCK, J. On further conjectures regarding acquiescence. *Psychological Bulletin*, 1971, *76*, 205–210. (b)

BLOCK, J. The shifting definitions of acquiescence. *Psychological Bulletin*, 1972, *78*, 10–12.

BLOCK, J. *The Q sort method in personality assessment and psychiatric research*. Palo Alto, Calif.: Consulting Psychologists Press, 1978.

BLOOM, B. S. *Stability and change in human characteristics*. New York: Wiley, 1964.

BLOOM, B. S. Learning for mastery. *Evaluation Comment* (University of California at Los Angeles, Center for the Study of Evaluation of Instructional Programs), 1968, *1*, No. 2.

BLOOM, B. S. *Human characteristics and school learning*. New York: McGraw-Hill, 1976.

BLOOM, B. S., & BRODER, L. *Problem-solving processes of college students*. Chicago: University of Chicago Press, 1950.

BLOOM, B. S., DAVIS, A., & HESS, R. *Compensatory education for cultural deprivation*. New York: Holt, Rinehart & Winston, 1965.

BLOOMBERG, M. (Ed.). *Creativity: Theory and research*. New Haven, Conn.: College and University Press, 1973.

BOCK, R. D. Estimating item parameters and latent ability when responses are scored in two or more nominal categories. *Psychometrika*, 1972, *37*, 29–51.

BOLTON, T. L. The growth of memory in school children. *American Journal of Psychology*, 1891–1892, *4*, 362–380.

BOND, E. A. Tenth grade abilities and achievements. *Teachers College Contributions to Education*, 1940, No. 813.

BONJEAN, C. M., HILL, R. J., & McLEMORE, S. D. *Sociological measurement: An inventory of scales and indices*. San Francisco: Chandler, 1967.

BORING, E. G. *A history of experimental psychology* (Rev. ed.). New York: Appleton-Century-Crofts, 1950.

BORISLOW, B. The Edwards Personal Preference Schedule (EPPS) and fakability. *Journal of Applied Psychology*, 1958, *42*, 22–27.

BORMAN, W. C. Format and training effects on rating accuracy and rating errors. *Journal of Applied Psychology*, 1979, *64*, 410–421.

BORUCH, R. F., & CECIL, J. S. *Assuring confidentiality of social research data*. Philadelphia: University of Pennsylvania Press, 1979.

BOWER, E. M. *Early identification of emotionally handicapped children in school* (2nd ed.). Springfield, Ill.: Charles C Thomas, 1969.

BOWERS, K. Situationism in psychology: An analysis and a critique. *Psychological Review*, 1973, *80*, 307–336.

BRADWAY, K. P. An experimental study of factors associated with Stanford-Binet IQ changes from the preschool to the junior high school. *Journal of Genetic Psychology*, 1945, *66*, 107–128.

BRADWAY, K. P., & ROBINSON, N. M. Significant IQ changes in twenty-five years: A follow-up. *Journal of Educational Psychology*, 1961, *52*, 74–79.

BRADWAY, K. P., THOMPSON, C. W., & CRAVENS, R. B. Preschool IQ's after twenty-five years. *Journal of Educational Psychology*, 1958, *49*, 278–281. *Board Review*, 1977, No. 103, 2–6.

BRELAND, H. M. Can multiple-choice tests measure writing skills? *The College Monograph No. 8, The College Board*, 1979.

BRELAND, H. M. Population validity and college entrance measures. *Research*

BRIDGEMAN, B. Effects of test score feedback on immediately subsequent test performance. *Journal of Educational Psychology*, 1974, *66*, 62–66.

BRIEF, A. P. Peer assessment revisited: A brief comment on Kane and Lawler. *Psychological Bulletin*, 1980, *88*, 78–79.

BRISLIN, R. W., LONNER, W. J., & THORNDIKE, R. M. *Cross-cultural research methods*. New York: Wiley, 1974.

BROGDEN, H. E. An approach to the problem of differential prediction. *Psychometrika*, 1946, *11*, 139–154. (a)

BROGDEN, H. E. On the interpretation of the correlation coefficient as a measure of predictive efficiency. *Journal of Educational Psychology*, 1946, *37*, 65–76. (b)

BROGDEN, H. E. Increased efficiency of selection resulting from replacement of a single predictor with several differential predictors. *Educational and Psychological Measurement*, 1951, *11*, 173–196.

BROGDEN, H. E. A simple proof of a personnel classification theorem. *Psychometrika*, 1954, *19*, 205–208.

BROWN, A. L. The role of strategic behavior in retardate memory. In N. R. Ellis (Ed.), *International review of research in mental retardation* (Vol. 7). New York: Academic Press, 1974.

BROWN, B. (Ed.). *Found: Long-term gains from early intervention*. Boulder, Col.: Westview Press, 1978.

BROWN, C. W., & GHISELLI, E. E. Percent increase in proficiency resulting from use of selective devices. *Journal of Applied Psychology*, 1953, *37*, 341–345.

BROWN, S. R. Bibliography on Q technique and its methodology. *Perceptual and Motor Skills*, 1968, *26*, 587–613.

BUCHWALD, A. M. Values and the use of tests. *Journal of Consulting Psychology*, 1965, *29*, 49–54.

BUDOFF, M., & CORMAN, L. Demographic and psychometric factors related to improved performance on the Kohs learning potential procedure. *American Journal of Mental Deficiency*, 1974, *78*, 578–585.

BURNHAM, P. S. Prediction and performance. In *From high school to college: Readings for counselors*. New York: College Entrance Examination Board, 1965. Pp. 65–71.

BURNS, R. B. Age and mental ability: Retesting with thirty-three years' interval. *British Journal of Educational Psychology*, 1966, *36*, 116.

Burns, R. B. Relation of aptitudes to learning at different points in time during instruction. *Journal of Educational Psychology,* 1980, *72,* 785–795.

Buros, O. K. (Ed.). *Personality tests and reviews I.* Lincoln: University of Nebraska, Buros Institute of Mental Measurements, 1970.

Buros, O. K. (Ed.). *Tests in print II.* Lincoln: University of Nebraska, Buros Institute of Mental Measurements, 1974.

Buros, O. K. (Ed.). *Intelligence tests and reviews.* Lincoln: University of Nebraska, Buros Institute of Mental Measurements, 1975. (a)

Buros, O. K. (Ed.). *Personality tests and reviews II.* Lincoln: University of Nebraska, Buros Institute of Mental Measurements, 1975. (b)

Buros, O. K. (Ed.). *Vocational tests and reviews.* Lincoln: University of Nebraska, Buros Institute of Mental Measurements, 1975. (c)

Buros, O. K. (Ed.). *The eighth mental measurements yearbook.* Lincoln: University of Nebraska, Buros Institute of Mental Measurements, 1978.

Burt, C. *The factors of the mind: An introduction to factor-analysis in psychology.* New York: Macmillan, 1941.

Burt, C. Mental abilities and mental factors. *British Journal of Educational Psychology,* 1944, *14,* 85–89.

Burt, C. The structure of the mind; a review of the results of factor analysis. *British Journal of Educational Psychology,* 1949, *19,* 100–111; 176–199.

Burton, R. V. Generality of honesty reconsidered. *Psychological Review,* 1963, *70,* 481–499.

Burtt, H. E. *Legal psychology.* Englewood Cliffs, N.J.: Prentice-Hall, 1931.

Buss, A. R. An extension of developmental models that separate ontogenetic changes and cohort differences. *Psychological Bulletin,* 1973, *80,* 466–479.

Butcher, J. N., & Owen, P. L. Objective personality inventories: Recent research and some contemporary issues. In B. B. Wolman (Ed.), *Clinical diagnosis of mental disorders.* New York: Plenum, 1978. Ch. 15.

Butcher, J. N., & Pancheri, P. *A handbook of cross-national MMPI research.* Minneapolis: University of Minnesota Press, 1976.

Caldwell, M. B., & Smith, T. A. Intellectual structure of southern Negro children. *Psychological Reports,* 1968, *23,* 63–71.

Caldwell, O. W., & Courtis, S. A. *Then and now in education, 1845–1923.* Yonkers, N.Y.: World Book Co., 1923.

Campbell, D. P. A cross-sectional and longitudinal study of scholastic abilities over twenty-five years. *Journal of Counseling Psychology,* 1965, *12,* 55–61.

Campbell, D. P. *Handbook for the Strong Vocational Interest Blank.* Stanford, Calif.: Stanford University Press, 1971.

Campbell, D. P. *Manual for the Strong-Campbell Interest Inventory* (Rev. ed.). Stanford, Calif.: Stanford University Press, 1977.

Campbell, D. T. The indirect assessment of social attitudes. *Psychological Bulletin,* 1950, *47,* 15–38.

Campbell, D. T. Recommendations for APA test standards regarding construct, trait, and discriminant validity. *American Psychologist,* 1960, *15,* 546–553.

Campbell, D. T. Social attitudes and other acquired behavioral dispositions. In S. Koch (Ed.), *Psychology: A study of a science.* New York: McGraw-Hill, 1963. Vol. 6, pp. 94–172.

Campbell, D. T., & Fiske, D. W. Convergent and discriminant validation by the multitrait-multimethod matrix. *Psychological Bulletin,* 1959, *56,* 81–105.

CAMPBELL, J. T., CROOKS, L. A., MAHONEY, M. H., & ROCK, D. A. *An investigation of sources of bias in the prediction of job performance: A six-year study.* Princeton, N.J.: Educational Testing Service, 1973.

CAMPIONE, J. C., & BROWN, A. L. Toward a theory of intelligence: Contributions from research with retarded children. In R. J. Sternberg & D. K. Detterman (Eds.), *Human intelligence: Perspectives on its theory and measurement.* Norwood, N.J.: Ablex, 1979. Pp. 139–163.

CANFIELD, A. A. The "sten" scale—A modified C-scale. *Educational and Psychological Measurement,* 1951, *11,* 295–297.

Careers in Focus. New York: Gregg Division, McGraw-Hill Book Company, 1976.

CARLSON, A. B., & WERTS, C. E. *Relationship among law school predictors, law school performance, and bar examination results.* Law School Admission Council Report (LSAC-76-1), September 1976.

CARLSON, H. S. The AASPB story: The beginnings and first 16 years of the American Association of State Psychology Boards, 1961–1977. *American Psychologist,* 1978, *33,* 486–495.

CARROLL, H. A. What do the Meier-Seashore and the McAdory Tests measure? *Journal of Educational Research,* 1933, *26,* 661–665.

CARROLL, J. B. A model of school learning. *Teachers College Record,* 1963, *64,* 723–733.

CARROLL, J. B. Factors of verbal achievement. In A. Anastasi (Ed.), *Testing problems in perspective.* Washington, D.C.: American Council on Education, 1966. Pp. 406–413.

CARROLL, J. B. Problems of measurement related to the concept of learning for mastery. *Educational Horizons,* 1970, *48,* 71–80.

CARROLL, J. B. Stalking the wayward factors (Review of *The analysis of intelligence* by J. P. Guilford & R. Hoepfner). *Contemporary Psychology,* 1972, *17,* 321–324.

CARROLL, J. D. Multidimensional scaling. *Annual Review of Psychology,* 1980, *31,* 607–649.

CASHEN, V. M., & RAMSEYER, G. C. The use of separate answer sheets by primary age children. *Journal of Educational Measurement,* 1969, *6,* 155–158.

CATTELL, J. McK. Mental tests and measurements. *Mind,* 1890, *15,* 373–380.

CATTELL, R. B. *Personality and learning theory, Vol. I: The structure of personality and its environment.* New York: Springer, 1979.

CATTELL, R. B., EBER, H. W., & TATSUOKA, M. M. *Handbook for the Sixteen Personality Factor Questionnaire.* Champaign, Ill.: Institute for Personality and Ability Testing, 1970.

CATTELL, R. B., & LUBORSKY, L. B. Personality factors in response to humor. *Journal of Abnormal and Social Psychology,* 1947, *42,* 402–421.

CATTELL, R. B., & SCHUERGER, J. M. *Personality theory in action: Handbook for the Objective-Analytic (O-A) Test Kit.* Champaign, Ill.: Institute for Personality and Ability Testing, 1978.

CAUTELA, J. R. *Behavior analysis forms for clinical intervention.* Champaign, Ill.: Research Press, 1977.

CAUTELA, J. R., & KASTENBAUM, R. A reinforcement survey schedule for use in therapy, training, and research. *Psychological Reports,* 1967, *20,* 1115–1130.

CHAPMAN, L. J. Illustory correlation in observational report. *Journal of Verbal Learning and Verbal Behavior,* 1967, *6,* 151–155.

CHAPMAN, L. J., & CHAPMAN, J. P. Genesis of popular but erroneous psychodiagnostic observations. *Journal of Abnormal Psychology*, 1967, 72, 193–204.

CHAPMAN, L. J., & CHAPMAN, J. P. Illusory correlation as an obstacle to the use of valid psychodiagnostic signs. *Journal of Abnormal Psychology*, 1969, 74, 271–280.

CHARLES, D. C. Ability and accomplishment of persons earlier judged mentally deficient. *Genetic Psychology Monographs*, 1953, 47, 3–71.

CHARLES, D. C., & JAMES, S. T. Stability of average intelligence. *Journal of Genetic Psychology*, 1964, 105, 105–111.

CHRISTAL, R. E. Factor analytic study of visual memory. *Psychological Monographs*, 1958, 72(13, Whole No. 466).

CHRISTENSEN, A. L. *Luria's neuropsychological investigation*. New York: Spectrum, 1975.

CHRISTENSEN, A. L. *Luria's neuropsychological investigation* (2nd ed.). Copenhagen: Munksgaard, 1980.

CHUN, KI-TAEK, COBB, S., & FRENCH, J. R. P., JR. *Measures for psychological assessment*. Ann Arbor: Institute for Social Research, The University of Michigan, 1976.

CIMINERO, A. R., CALHOUN, K. S., & ADAMS, H. E. (Eds.). *Handbook of behavioral assessment*. New York: Wiley, 1977.

CIRCUS: *Comprehensive assessment in nursery school and kindergarten.* (Proceedings of a symposium presented at the meeting of the American Psychological Association, Montreal, August 1973). Princeton, N.J.: Educational Testing Service, 1973.

CLEARY, T. A. Test bias: Prediction of grades of Negro and white students in integrated colleges. *Journal of Educational Measurement*, 1968, 5, 115–124.

CLEARY, T. A., HUMPHREYS, L. G., KENDRICK, S. A., & WESMAN, A. Educational uses of tests with disadvantaged students. *American Psychologist*, 1975, 30, 15–41. (See also comments on pp. 88–96.)

CLEARY, T. A., LINN, R. L., & ROCK, D. A. An exploratory study of programmed tests. *Educational and Psychological Measurement*, 1968, 28, 347–349.

CLEMANS, W. V. An index of item-criterion relationship. *Educational and Psychological Measurement*, 1958, 18, 167–172.

CLEMANS, W. V. Test administration. In R. L. Thorndike (Ed.), *Educational measurement* (2nd ed.). Washington D.C.: American Council on Education, 1971. Ch. 7.

COHEN, E. Examiner differences with individual intelligence tests. *Perceptual and Motor Skills*, 1965, 20, 1324.

COHEN, J. The factorial structure of the WAIS between early adulthood and old age. *Journal of Consulting Psychology*, 1957, 21, 283–290. (a)

COHEN, J. A factor-analytically based rationale for the Wechsler Adult Intelligence Scale. *Journal of Consulting Psychology*, 1957, 21, 351–457. (b)

COHEN, J. Weighted kappa: Nominal scale agreement with provision for scale disagreement or partial credit. *Psychological Bulletin*, 1968, 70, 213–220.

COHEN, R. A. Conceptual styles, cultural conflict, and nonverbal tests. *American Anthropologist*, 1969, 71, 828–856.

COLE, M., & BRUNER, J. S. Cultural differences and inferences about psychological processes. *American Psychologist*, 1971, 26, 867–876.

COLE, S., & HUNTER, M. Pattern analysis of WISC scores achieved by culturally disadvantaged children. *Psychological Reports*, 1971, 29, 191–194.

COLEMAN, W., & CURETON, E. E. Intelligence and achievement: The "jangle fallacy" again. *Educational and Psychological Measurement*, 1954, 14, 347–351.

The College Board Review (Testing Supplement). A look at testing: Tensions and benefits. No. 117, Fall 1980.

COLLEGE ENTRANCE EXAMINATION BOARD. *The Admissions Testing Program guide for high schools and colleges, 1979–81*. New York: Author, 1979. (a)

COLLEGE ENTRANCE EXAMINATION BOARD. The effect of special preparation programs on score results of the Scholastic Aptitude Test. *Research and Development Update*, January 1979. (b) (Also reprinted in *The College Board News*, February 1979, p. 7.)

COLLEGE ENTRANCE EXAMINATION BOARD. *About the achievement tests*. New York: Author, 1981. (a)

COLLEGE ENTRANCE EXAMINATION BOARD. *Taking the SAT: A guide to the Scholastic Aptitude Test and the Test of Standard Written English*. New York: Author, 1981. (b)

COLLINS, B. E. Four components of the Rotter Internal-External Scale: Belief in a difficult world, a just world, a predictable world, and a politically responsive world. *Journal of Personality and Social Psychology*, 1974, 29, 381–391.

COMREY, A. L., BACKER, T. E., & GLASER, E. M. *A sourcebook for mental health measures*. Los Angeles: Human Interaction Research Institute, 1973.

CONGER, A. J., & JACKSON, D. N. Suppressor variables, prediction, and the interpretation of psychological relationships. *Educational and Psychological Measurement*, 1972, 32, 579–599.

CONRAD, L., TRISMEN, D., & MILLER, R. (Eds.). *Graduate Record Examinations technical manual*. Princeton, N.J.: Educational Testing Service, 1977.

CONSORTIUM FOR LONGITUDINAL STUDIES. *Lasting effects after preschool*. Washington, D.C.: U.S. Government Printing Office (017-090-00047-0), 1978.

CONSTANTINOPLE, A. Masculinity-femininity: An exception to a famous dictum? *Psychological Bulletin*, 1973, 80, 389–407.

COOLEY, W. W. Further relationships with the TALENT battery. *Personnel and Guidance Journal*, 1965, 44, 295–303.

COOLEY, W. W., & GLASER, R. The computer and individualized instruction. *Science*, 1969, 166, 574–582.

COOLEY, W. W., & MILLER, J. D. The Project TALENT tests as a national standard. *Personnel and Guidance Journal*, 1965, 43, 1038–1044.

CORAH, M. L., et al. Social desirability as a variable in the Edwards Personal Preference Schedule. *Journal of Consulting Psychology*, 1958, 22, 70–72.

COUCH, A., & KENISTON, K. Yeasayers and naysayers: Agreeing response set as a personality variable. *Journal of Abnormal and Social Psychology*, 1960, 60, 151–174.

Counseling from profiles: A casebook for the Differential Aptitude Tests (2nd ed.). New York: Psychological Corporation, 1977.

CRAIK, K. H. The assessment of places. In P. McReynolds (Ed.), *Advances in psychological assessment*. Palo Alto, Calif.: Science and Behavior Books, 1971. Vol. 2, Ch. 3.

CRAIK, K. H. Environmental psychology. *Annual Review of Psychology,* 1973, *24,* 403–421.

CRITES, J. O. Measurement of vocational maturity at adolescence: 1. Attitude test of the vocational development inventory. *Psychological Monographs,* 1965, 79(2, Whole No. 595). (a)

CRITES, J. O. Research frontier: The vocational development project at the University of Iowa. *Journal of Counseling Psychology,* 1965, *12,* 81–86. (b)

CRITES, J. O. *The maturity of vocational attitudes in adolescence.* Iowa City: University of Iowa, 1969.

CRONBACH, L. J. Statistical methods applied to Rorschach scores: A review. *Psychological Bulletin,* 1949, *46,* 393–429.

CRONBACH, L. J. Coefficient alpha and the internal structure of tests. *Psychometrika,* 1951, *16,* 297–334.

CRONBACH, L. J. Review of the BITCH Test. *Eighth Mental Measurements Yearbook,* 1978, Vol. I, p. 250.

CRONBACH, L. J., & DRENTH, P. J. D. (Eds.). *Mental tests and cultural adaptation.* The Hague: Mouton, 1972.

CRONBACH, L. J., & GLESER, G. C. *Psychological tests and personnel decisions* (2nd ed.). Urbana: University of Illinois Press, 1965.

CRONBACH, L. J., & MEEHL, P. E. Construct validity in psychological tests. *Psychological Bulletin,* 1955, *52,* 281–302.

CROWNE, D. P., & MARLOWE, D. *The approval motive: Studies in evaluative dependence.* New York: Wiley, 1964.

CULLER, R. E., & HOLAHAN, C. J. Test anxiety and academic performance: The effects of study-related behavior. *Journal of Educational Psychology,* 1980, *72,* 16–20.

CURETON, E. E. Validity, reliability, and baloney. *Educational and Psychological Measurement,* 1950, *10,* 94–96.

CURETON, E. E. Recipe for a cookbook. *Psychological Bulletin,* 1957, *54,* 494–497. (a)

CURETON, E. E. The upper and lower twenty-seven per cent rule. *Psychometrika,* 1957, *22,* 293–296. (b)

CURETON, E. E. Reliability and validity: Basic assumptions and experimental designs. *Educational and Psychological Measurement,* 1965, 25, 327–346.

CUTTER, F., & FARBEROW, N. L. The consensus Rorschach. In B. Klopfer, M. M. Meyer, F. B. Brawer, & W. G. Klopfer (Eds.), *Developments in the Rorschach technique* (Vol. 3). New York: Harcourt Brace Jovanovich, 1970.

DAHLSTROM, W. G., & DAHLSTROM, L. E. *Basic readings on the MMPI: A new selection on personality measurement.* Minneapolis: University of Minnesota Press, 1979.

DAHLSTROM, W. G., WELSH, G. S., & DAHLSTROM, L. E. *An MMPI handbook.* Vol. I, *Clinical interpretation.* Minneapolis: University of Minnesota Press, 1972.

DAHLSTROM, W. G., WELSH, G. S., & DAHLSTROM, L. E. *An MMPI handbook.* Vol. II, *Research developments and applications.* Minneapolis: University of Minnesota Press, 1975.

DAILEY, C. A. The life history as a criterion of assessment. *Journal of Counseling Psychology,* 1960, 7, 20–23.

DAILEY, J. T., SHAYCOFT, M. F., & ORR, D. B. *Calibration of Air Force selection tests to Project TALENT norms.* U.S. Air Force, Personnel Research Laboratory, PRL-TDR-62-6, May 1962.

D'ANDRADE, R. G. Trait psychology and componential analysis. *American Anthropologist,* 1965, *67,* 215–228.

DARLINGTON, R. B. Another look at cultural fairness. *Journal of Educational Measurement,* 1971, *8,* 71–82.

DARLINGTON, R. B. A defense of "rational" personnel selection, and two new methods. *Journal of Educational Measurement,* 1976, *13,* 43–52.

DARLINGTON, R. B., & STAUFFER, G. F. A method for choosing a cutting point on a test. *Journal of Applied Psychology,* 1966, *50,* 229–231.

DAS, R. S. Analysis of the components of reasoning in nonverbal tests and the structure of reasoning in a bilingual population. *Archiv für die gesamte Psychologie,* 1963, *115*(3), 217–229.

DASEN, P. K. (Ed.). *Piagetian psychology: Cross-cultural contributions.* New York: Halsted, 1977.

DAVIDS, A., & PILDNER, H., JR. Comparison of direct and projective methods of personality assessment under different conditions of motivation. *Psychological Monographs,* 1958, *72*(11, Whole No. 464).

DAVIS, P. C. A factor analysis of the Wechsler-Bellevue Scale. *Educational and Psychological Measurement,* 1956, *16,* 127–146.

DAVIS, W. E. Effect of prior failure on subjects' WAIS arithmetic subtest scores. *Journal of Clinical Psychology,* 1969, *25,* 72–73. (a)

DAVIS, W. E. Examiner differences, prior failure, and subjects' arithmetic scores. *Journal of Clinical Psychology,* 1969, *25,* 178–180. (b)

DAWES, R. M., & CORRIGAN, B. Linear models in decision making. *Psychological Bulletin,* 1974, *81,* 95–106.

DAY, M. C., & PARKER, R. K. (Eds.). *The preschool in action: Exploring early childhood programs.* Boston: Allyn & Bacon, 1977.

DEAN, R. S. Reliability of the WISC-R with Mexican-American children. *Journal of School Psychology,* 1977, *15,* 267–268.

DEAN, R. S. Predictive validity of the WISC-R with Mexican-American children. *Journal of School Psychology,* 1979, *17,* 55–58.

DEAN, R. S. Factor structure of the WISC-R with Anglos and Mexican-Americans. *Journal of School Psychology,* 1980, *18,* 234–239.

DELLAS, M. & GAIER, E. L. Identification of creativity: The individual. *Psychological Bulletin,* 1970, *73,* 55–73.

DEMMING, J. A., & PRESSEY, S. L. Tests "indigenous" to the adult and older years. *Journal of Counseling Psychology,* 1957, *4,* 144–148.

DENNIS, W. Goodenough scores, art experience, and modernization. *Journal of Social Psychology,* 1966, *68,* 211–228.

DENNY, J. P. Effects of anxiety and intelligence on concept formation. *Journal of Experimental Psychology,* 1966, *72,* 596–602.

DEUTSCH, M., FISHMAN, J. A., KOGAN, L., NORTH, R., & WHITEMAN, M. Guidelines for testing minority group children. *Journal of Social Issues,* 1964, *20,* 127–145.

DEWITT, L. J., & WEISS, D. J. *A computer software system for adaptive ability measurement* (Res. Rep. 74–1). Psychometric Methods Program, Department of Psychology, University of Minnesota, January 1974.

DICKEN, C. F. Simulated patterns on the Edwards Personal Preference Schedule. *Journal of Applied Psychology*, 1959, *43*, 372–378.

DICKINSON, T. L., & ZELLINGER, P. M. A comparison of the behaviorally anchored rating and mixed standard scale formats. *Journal of Applied Psychology*, ¹⁰⁸⁰, *65*, 147–154.

DIENER, E., & CRANDALL, R. *Ethics in social and behavioral research.* Chicago: University of Chicago Press, 1978.

DOLL, E. A. (Ed.). *The Oseretsky Tests of Motor Proficiency.* Minneapolis: American Guidance Service, 1946.

DOLL, E. A. *The measurement of social competence.* Minneapolis: American Guidance Service, 1953.

DOLL, E. A. *Vineland Social Maturity Scale: Manual of directions* (Rev. ed.). Minneapolis: American Guidance Service, 1965.

DONOFRIO, A. F. Clinical value of infant testing. *Perceptual and Motor Skills,* 1965, *21*, 571–574.

DOPPELT, J. E., & WALLACE, W. L. Standardization of the Wechsler Adult Intelligence Scale for older persons. *Journal of Abnormal and Social Psychology,* 1955, *51*, 312–330.

DORCUS, R. M., & JONES, M. H. *Handbook of employee selection.* New York: McGraw-Hill, 1950.

DRAKE, L. E., & OETTING, E. R. *An MMPI codebook for counselors.* Minneapolis: University of Minnesota Press, 1959.

DREGER, R. M. General temperament and personality factors related to intellectual performances. *Journal of Genetic Psychology,* 1968, *113*, 275–293.

DROEGE, R. C. Effects of practice on aptitude scores. *Journal of Applied Psychology,* 1966, *50*, 306–310.

DuBois, P. H. A test standardized on Pueblo Indian children. *Psychological Bulletin,* 1939, *36*, 523.

DuBois, P. H. A test-dominated society: China 1115 B.C.–1905 A.D. In A. Anastasi (Ed.), *Testing problems in perspective.* Washington, D.C.: American Council on Education, 1966. Pp. 29–36.

DuBois, P. H. *A history of psychological testing.* Boston: Allyn and Bacon, 1970.

DuBois, P. H. College Board Scholastic Aptitude Test. *Seventh Mental Measurements Yearbook,* 1972, p. 646.

DUNN, J. A. Inter- and intra-rater reliability of the new Harris-Goodenough Draw-A-Man Test. *Perceptual and Motor Skills,* 1967, *24*, 269–270.

DUNN, L(LOYD) M., & DUNN, L(EOTA) M. *Peabody Picture Vocabulary Test—Revised: Manual for Forms L and M.* Circle Pines, Minn.: American Guidance Service, 1981.

DUNNETTE, M. D. (Ed.). *Handbook of industrial and organizational psychology.* Chicago: Rand McNally, 1976.

DUNNETTE, M. D., & BORMAN, W. C. Personnel selection and classification systems. *Annual Review of Psychology,* 1979, *30*, 477–525.

DYER, H. S. Recycling the problems in testing. *Proceedings of the 1972 Invitational Conference on Testing Problems, Educational Testing Service,* 1973, 85–95.

EBBINGHAUS, H. Über eine neue Methode zur Prüfung geistiger Fähigkeiten und ihre Anwendung bei Schulkindern. *Zeitschrift für angewandte Psychologie,* 1897, *13*, 401–459.

EBEL, R. L. Content standard test scores. *Educational and Psychological Measurement,* 1962, *22,* 15–25.

EBEL, R. L. The social consequences of educational testing. *Proceedings of the 1963 Invitational Conference on Testing Problems, Educational Testing Service,* 1964, 130–143.

EBEL, R. L. *Measuring educational achievement.* Englewood Cliffs, N.J.: Prentice-Hall, 1965.

EBEL, R. L. The relation of item discrimination to test reliability. *Journal of Educational Measurement,* 1967, *4,* 125–128.

EBEL, R. L. Some limitations of criterion-referenced measurement. In G. H. Bracht, K. D. Hopkins, & J. C. Stanley (Eds.), *Perspectives in educational and psychological measurement.* Englewood Cliffs, N. J.: Prentice-Hall, 1972. Pp. 144–149.

EBEL, R. L. Evaluation and educational objectives. *Journal of Educational Measurement,* 1973, *10,* 273–279.

EBEL, R. L. *Essentials of educational measurement* (3rd ed.). Englewood Cliffs, N.J.: Prentice-Hall, 1979.

EBEL, R. L., & DAMRIN, D. E. Tests and examinations. *Encyclopedia of Educational Research* (3rd ed.), 1960, 1502–1517.

EDGERTON, H. A. A table for computing the phi coefficient. *Journal of Applied Psychology,* 1960, *44,* 141–145.

EDWARDS, A. J. Using vocabulary as a measure of general ability. *Personnel and Guidance Journal,* 1963, *42,* 153–154.

EDWARDS, A. L. *The social desirability variable in personality assessment and research.* New York: Dryden, 1957.

EDWARDS, A. L. Relationship between probability of endorsement and social desirability scale value for a set of 2,824 personality statements. *Journal of Applied Psychology,* 1966, *50,* 238–239.

EELLS, K., et al. *Intelligence and cultural differences.* Chicago: University of Chicago Press, 1951.

EISDORFER, C. The WAIS performance of the aged: A retest evaluation. *Journal of Gerontology,* 1963, *18,* 169–172.

EISENMAN, R., & PLATT, J. J. Authoritarianism, creativity, and other correlates of the Famous Sayings test. *Psychological Reports,* 1970, *26,* 267–271.

EKSTROM, R. B., FRENCH, J. W., & HARMAN, H. H. *Manual for kit of factor-referenced cognitive tests.* Princeton, N.J.: Educational Testing Service, 1976.

ENDLER, N. S., & HUNT, J. McV. Sources of behavioral variance as measured by the S-R Inventory of Anxiousness. *Psychological Bulletin,* 1966, *65,* 336–346.

ENDLER, N. S., & HUNT, J. McV. S-R inventories of hostility and comparisons of the proportions of variance from persons, responses, and situations for hostility and anxiousness. *Journal of Personality and Social Psychology,* 1968, *9,* 309–315.

ENDLER, N. S., & HUNT, J. McV. Generalizability of contributions from sources of variance in the S-R inventories of anxiousness. *Journal of Personality,* 1969, *37,* 1–24.

ENDLER, N. S., & MAGNUSSON, D. Toward an interactional psychology of personality. *Psychological Bulletin,* 1976, *83,* 956–974.

ENGELHART, M. D. A comparison of several item discrimination indices. *Journal of Educational Measurement,* 1965, *2,* 69–76.

ENTWISLE, D. R. To dispel fantasies about fantasy-based measures of achievement motivation. *Psychological Bulletin,* 1972, 77, 377–391.

EPSTEIN, S. Some theoretical considerations on the nature of ambiguity and the use of stimulus dimensions in projective techniques. *Journal of Consulting Psychology,* 1966, 30, 183–192.

EPSTEIN, S. The stability of behavior: I. On predicting most of the people much of the time. *Journal of Personality and Social Psychology,* 1979, 37, 1097–1121.

EPSTEIN, S. The stability of behavior: II. Implications for psychological research. *American Psychologist,* 1980, 35, 790–806.

EQUAL EMPLOYMENT OPPORTUNITY COMMISSION (EEOC). Guidelines on employee selection procedures. *Federal Register,* 1970, 35(149), 12333–12336.

ERIKSON, E. H. *Childhood and society.* New York: Norton, 1950.

ESCALONA, S. K. The use of infant tests for predictive purposes. *Bulletin of the Menninger Clinic,* 1950, 14, 117–128.

ESQUIROL, J. E. D. *Des maladies mentales considérées sous les rapports médical, hygiénique, et médico-légal* (2 vols.). Paris: Baillière, 1838.

ESTES, B. W. Influence of socioeconomic status on Wechsler Intelligence Scale for Children: An exploratory study. *Journal of Consulting Psychology,* 1953, 17, 58–62.

ESTES, B. W. Influence of socioeconomic status on Wechsler Intelligence Scale for Children: Addendum. *Journal of Consulting Psychology,* 1955, 19, 225–226.

ESTES, W. K. Learning theory and intelligence. *American Psychologist,* 1974, 29, 740–749.

ETS kit of factor-referenced cognitive tests. Princeton, N.J.: Educational Testing Service, 1976.

EXNER, J. E., JR. Variations in WISC performances as influenced by differences in pretest rapport. *Journal of General Psychology,* 1966, 74, 299–306.

EXNER, J. E., JR. *The Rorschach: A comprehensive system.* New York: Wiley, 1974.

EXNER, J. E., JR. *The Rorschach: A comprehensive system, Vol. 2: Current research and advanced interpretations.* New York: Wiley-Interscience, 1978.

EYDE, L. D., PRIMOFF, E. S., & HARDT, R. H. *A job element examination for State Troopers* (PRR-81-3). Washington, D.C.: Personnel Research and Development Center, U.S. Office of Personnel Management, February 1981 (National Technical Information Service, Springfield, Va. 22161).

FAN, C. T. *Item analysis table.* Princeton, N.J.: Educational Testing Service, 1952.

FAN, C. T. Note on construction of an item analysis table for the high-low-27-percent group method. *Psychometrika,* 1954, 19, 231–237.

FEAR, R. A. *The evaluation interview* (2nd ed.). New York: McGraw-Hill, 1973.

FELDHUSEN, J. F., & KLAUSMEIER, H. J. Anxiety, intelligence, and achievement in children of low, average, and high intelligence. *Child Development,* 1962, 33, 403–409.

FELDMAN, D. H., & BRATTON, J. C. Relativity and giftedness: Implications for equality of educational opportunity. *Exceptional Children,* 1972, 38, 491–492.

FELDT, L. S. Leisure Activities Blank. *Eighth Mental Measurements Yearbook,* 1978, pp. 887–888.

FERGUSON, G. A. On learning and human ability. *Canadian Journal of Psychology,* 1954, 8, 95–112.

FERGUSON, G. A. On transfer and the abilities of man. *Canadian Journal of Psychology,* 1956, *10,* 121–131.

FERGUSON, R. L., & NOVICK, M. R. Implementation of a Bayesian system for decision analysis in a program of individually prescribed instruction. *ACT Research Report* (American College Testing Program), No. 60, 1973.

FEUERSTEIN, R. *The dynamic assessment of retarded performers.* Baltimore: University Park Press, 1979.

FEUERSTEIN, R. *Instrumental enrichment: An intervention program for cognitive modifiability.* Baltimore: University Park Press, 1980.

FIELD, J. G. Two types of tables for use with Wechsler's Intelligence Scales. *Journal of Clinical Psychology,* 1960, *16,* 3–6.

FIGURELLI, J. C., & KELLER, H. R. The effects of training and socioeconomic class upon the acquisition of conservation concepts. *Child Development,* 1972, *43,* 293–298.

FINCHER, C. Personnel testing and public policy. *American Psychologist,* 1973, *28,* 489–497.

FINDLEY, W. G. Rationale for the evaluation of item discrimination statistics. *Educational and Psychological Measurement,* 1956, *16,* 175–180.

FINK, A. M., & BUTCHER, J. N. Reducing objections to personality inventories with special instructions. *Educational and Psychological Measurement,* 1972, *32,* 631–639.

FINKLE, R. B. Managerial assessment centers. In M. D. Dunnette (Ed.), *Handbook of industrial and organizational psychology.* Chicago: Rand McNally, 1976. Ch. 20.

FINLAYSON, D. S. The reliability of the marking of essays. *British Journal of Educational Psychology,* 1951, *21,* 126–134.

FISHBEIN, M. (Ed.). *Readings in attitude theory and measurement.* New York: Wiley, 1967.

FISKE, D. W. Can a personality construct be validated empirically? *Psychological Bulletin,* 1973, *80,* 89–92.

FISKE, D. W. Can a personality construct have a single validational pattern? Rejoinder to Huba and Hamilton. *Psychological Bulletin,* 1976, *83,* 877–879.

FISKE, D. W., & BAUGHMAN, E. E. Relationships between Rorschach scoring categories and the total number of responses. *Journal of Abnormal and Social Psychology,* 1953, *48,* 25–32.

FITZGIBBON, T. J. *The use of standardized instruments with urban and minority group pupils.* New York: Harcourt Brace Jovanovich, 1972. (ERIC No. ED 068-505.)

FJELD, S. P., & LANDFIELD, A. W. Personal construct consistency. *Psychological Reports,* 1961, *8,* 127–129.

FLANAGAN, J. C. Scientific development of the use of human resources: Progress in the Army Air Forces. *Science,* 1947, *105,* 57–60.

FLANAGAN, J. C. Critical requirements: A new approach to employee evaluation. *Personnel Psychology,* 1949, *2,* 419–425.

FLANAGAN, J. C. The critical incident technique. *Psychological Bulletin,* 1954, *51,* 327–358.

FLANAGAN, J. C. Symposium: Standard scores for aptitude and achievement tests: Discussion. *Educational and Psychological Measurement,* 1962, *22,* 35–39.

FLANAGAN, J. C. The first 15 years of project TALENT: Implications for career guidance. *Vocational Guidance Quarterly*, 1973, *22*, 8–14.

FLANAGAN, J. C., et al., *The American high school student*. Pittsburgh: Project TALENT Office, University of Pittsburgh, 1964.

FLANAGAN, J. C., SHAYCOFT, M. F., RICHARDS, J. M., JR., & CLAUDY, J. G. *Five years after high school*. Palo Alto, Calif.: American Institutes for Research, 1971.

FLAUGHER, R. L. Some points of confusion in discussing the testing of black students. In L. P. Miller (Ed.), *The testing of black students: A symposium*. Englewood Cliffs, N.J.: Prentice-Hall, 1974. Pp. 11–16.

FLAVELL, J. H. *The developmental psychology of Jean Piaget*. New York: Van Nostrand, 1963.

FLAVELL, J. H. Metacognition and cognitive monitoring: A new area of cognitive-developmental inquiry. *American Psychologist*, 1979, *34*, 906–911.

FLEISHMAN, E. A. Dimensional analysis of movement reactions. *Journal of Experimental Psychology*, 1958, *55*, 438–453.

FLEISHMAN, E. A. *The structure and measurement of physical fitness*. Englewood Cliffs, N.J.: Prentice-Hall, 1964.

FLEISHMAN, E. A. On the relation between abilities, learning, and human performance. *American Psychologist*, 1972, *27*, 1018–1032.

FLEISHMAN, E. A. Toward a taxonomy of human performance. *American Psychologist*, 1975, *30*, 1127–1149.

FORD, C., JR., & TYLER, L. E. A factor analysis of Terman and Miles' M-F test. *Journal of Applied Psychology*, 1952, *36*, 251–253.

FREDERIKSEN, C. H. Abilities, transfer, and information retrieval in verbal learning. *Multivariate Behavioral Research Monographs*, 1969, No. 69-2.

FREDERIKSEN, N. Factors in in-basket performance. *Psychological Monographs*, 1962, *76*(22, Whole No. 541).

FREDERIKSEN, N. Response set scores as predictors of performance. *Personnel Psychology*, 1965, *18*, 225–244.

FREDERIKSEN, N. In-basket tests and factors in administrative performance. In A. Anastasi (Ed.), *Testing problems in perspective*. Washington, D.C.: American Council on Education, 1966. Pp. 208–221. (a)

FREDERIKSEN, N. Validation of a simulation technique. *Organizational Behavior & Human Performance*, 1966, *1*, 87–109. (b)

FREDERIKSEN, N. Toward a taxonomy of situations. *American Psychologist*, 1972, *27*, 114–123.

FREDERIKSEN, N., & GILBERT, A. C. F. Replication of a study of differential predictability. *Educational and Psychological Measurement*, 1960, *20*, 759–767.

FREDERIKSEN, N., & MELVILLE, S. D. Differential predictability in the use of test scores. *Educational and Psychological Measurement*, 1954, *14*, 647–656.

FREEBERG, N. E. Relevance of rater–ratee acquaintance in the validity and reliability of ratings. *Journal of Applied Psychology*, 1969, *53*, 518–524.

FRENCH, J. W. The description of aptitude and achievement tests in terms of rotated factors. *Psychometric Monographs*, 1951, No. 5.

FRENCH, J. W. Effect of anxiety on verbal and mathematical examination scores. *Educational and Psychological Measurement*, 1962, *22*, 553–564.

FRENCH, J. W. The relationship of problem-solving styles to the factor composition of tests. *Educational and Psychological Measurement*, 1965, *25*, 9–28.

FRENCH, J. W. The logic of and assumptions underlying differential testing. In A. Anastasi (Ed.), *Testing problems in perspective.* Washington, D.C.: American Council on Education, 1966. Pp. 321–330.

FRIEDMAN, M., & ROSENMAN, R. H. The possible general causes of coronary artery disease. In M. Friedman (Ed.), *Pathogenesis of coronary artery disease.* New York: McGraw-Hill, 1969.

FRIEDMAN, R. B. A computer program for simulating the patient–physician encounter. *Journal of Medical Education,* 1973, *48,* 92–97.

FROMM, E., HARTMAN, L. D., & MARSCHAK, M. Children's intelligence tests as a measure of dynamic personality functioning. *American Journal of Orthopsychiatry,* 1957, *27,* 134–144.

FRYER, D. *Measurement of interests.* New York: Holt, 1931.

GAEL, S., GRANT, D. L., & RITCHIE, R. J. Employment test validation for minority and nonminority telephone operators. *Journal of Applied Psychology,* 1975, *60,* 411–419. (a)

GAEL, S., GRANT, D. L., & RITCHIE, R. J. Employment test validation for minority and nonminority clerks with work sample criteria. *Journal of Applied Psychology,* 1975, *60,* 420–426. (b)

GAGE, N. L., & CRONBACH, L. J. Conceptual and methodological problems in interpersonal perception. *Psychological Review,* 1955, *62,* 411–422.

GAGNÉ, R. *The conditions of learning.* New York: Holt, Rinehart & Winston, 1965.

GALASSI, J. P., DELO, J. S., GALASSI, M. D., & BASTIEN, S. The College Self-Expression Scale: A measure of assertiveness. *Behavior Therapy,* 1974, *5,* 165–171.

GALASSI, J. P., & GALASSI, M. D. *Instructions for administering and scoring the College Self-Expression Scale.* Chapel Hill: University of North Carolina, 1974.

GALTON, F. Psychometric experiments. *Brain,* 1879, *2,* 149–162.

GALTON, F. *Inquiries into human faculty and its development.* London: Macmillan, 1883.

GAMBLE, K. R. The Holtzman Inkblot Technique: A review. *Psychological Bulletin,* 1972, *77,* 172–194.

GARDNER, J. W. *Excellence.* New York: Harper, 1961.

GARZA, R. T., & WIDLAK, F. W. The validity of locus of control dimensions for Chicano populations. *Journal of Personality Assessment,* 1977, *41,* 635–643.

GAUDRY, E., & SPIELBERGER, C. D. *Anxiety and educational achievement.* New York: Wiley, 1974.

GERBERICH, J. R., GREENE, H. A., & JORGENSEN, A. N. *Measurement and evaluation in the modern school.* New York: McKay, 1962.

GESELL, A., et al. *The first five years of life.* New York: Harper, 1940.

GESELL, A., & AMATRUDA, C. S. *Developmental diagnosis* (2nd ed.). New York: Hoeber-Harper, 1947.

GESELL, A., ILG, F. L., & AMES, L. B. *Infant and child in the culture of today* (Rev. ed.). New York: Harper & Row, 1974.

GHISELLI, E. E. Differentiation of individuals in terms of their predictability. *Journal of Applied Psychology,* 1956, *40,* 374–377.

GHISELLI, E. E. The generalization of validity. *Personnel Psychology,* 1959, *12,* 397–402.

GHISELLI, E. E. The prediction of predictability. *Educational and Psychological Measurement,* 1960, *20,* 3–8.

GHISELLI, E. E. Moderating effects and differential reliability and validity. *Journal of Applied Psychology,* 1963, 47, 81–86.

GHISELLI, E. E. *The validity of occupational aptitude tests.* New York: Wiley, 1966.

GHISELLI, E. E. Interaction of traits and motivational factors in the determination of the success of managers. *Journal of Applied Psychology,* 1968, 52, 480–483.

GHISELLI, E. E. The validity of aptitude tests in personnel selection. *Personnel Psychology,* 1973, 26, 461–477.

GILBERT, H. B. On the IQ ban. *Teachers College Record,* 1966, 67, 282–285.

GILBERT, J. A. Researches on the mental and physical development of school children. *Studies from the Yale Psychological Laboratory,* 1894, 2, 40–100.

GINSBURG, H., & OPPER, S. *Piaget's theory of intellectual development: An introduction.* Englewood Cliffs, N.J.: Prentice-Hall, 1969.

GLASER, R. Instructional technology and the measurement of learning outcomes. *American Psychologist,* 1963, 18, 519–522.

GLASER, R., & NITKO, A. J. Measurement in learning and instruction. In R. L. Thorndike (Ed.), *Educational measurement* (2nd ed.). Washington, D.C.: American Council on Education, 1971. Ch. 17.

GLASSER, A. J., & ZIMMERMAN, I. L. *Clinical interpretation of the Wechsler Intelligence Scale for Children.* New York: Grune & Stratton, 1967.

GOFFENEY, B., HENDERSON, N. B., & BUTLER, B. V. Negro-white, male-female eight-month developmental scores compared with seven-year WISC and Bender Test scores. *Child Development,* 1971, 42, 595–604.

GOLDBERG, L. R. Diagnosticians versus diagnostic signs: The diagnosis of psychosis versus neurosis from the MMPI. *Psychological Monographs,* 1965, 79(9, Whole No. 602).

GOLDBERG, L. R. Seer over sign: The first "good" example? *Journal of Experimental Research in Personality,* 1968, 3, 168–171. (a)

GOLDBERG, L. R. Simple models or simple processes? Some research on clinical judgments. *American Psychologist,* 1968, 23, 483–496. (b)

GOLDBERG, L. R. Man versus model of man: A rationale, plus some evidence, for a method of improving on clinical inferences. *Psychological Bulletin,* 1970, 73, 422–432.

GOLDBERG, L. R. A historical survey of personality scales and inventories. In P. McReynolds (Ed.), *Advances in psychological assessment* (Vol. 2). Palo Alto, Calif.: Science and Behavior Books, 1971. Pp. 293–336.

GOLDBERG, L. R. Parameters of personality inventory construction and utilization: A comparison of prediction strategies and tactics. *Multivariate Behavioral Research Monographs,* 1972, No. 72–2.

GOLDEN, C. J. *Learning disabilities and brain dysfunction.* Springfield, Ill.: Charles C Thomas, 1978.

GOLDEN, C. J. *Clinical interpretation of objective psychological tests.* New York: Grune & Stratton, 1979.

GOLDEN, C. J. In reply to Adams's "In search of Luria's battery: A false start." *Journal of Consulting and Clinical Psychology,* 1980, 48, 517–521.

GOLDEN, C. J. The Luria-Nebraska Neuropsychological Battery: Theory and research. In P. McReynolds (Ed.), *Advances in psychological assessment* (Vol. 5). San Francisco: Jossey-Bass, 1981. Ch. 4. (a)

GOLDEN, C. J. A standardized version of Luria's neuropsychological tests: A quantitative and qualitative approach to neuropsychological evaluation. In S. B. Filskov & T. J. Boll (Eds.), *Handbook of clinical neuropsychology*. New York: Wiley-Interscience, 1981. Ch. 19. (b)

GOLDEN, C. J., HAMMEKE, T. A., & PURISCH, A. D. *The Luria-Nebraska Neuropsychological Battery: Manual*. Los Angeles: Western Psychological Services, 1980.

GOLDEN, M. Some effects of combining psychological tests on clinical inferences. *Journal of Consulting Psychology*, 1964, *28*, 440–446.

GOLDFRIED, M. R., & DAVISON, G. C. *Clinical behavior therapy*. New York: Holt, Rinehart & Winston, 1976.

GOLDFRIED, M. R., & D'ZURILLA, T. J. A behavioral-analytic model for assessing competence. In C. D. Spielberger (Ed.), *Current topics in clinical psychology*, Vol. 1. New York: Academic Press. 1969. Pp. 151–196.

GOLDFRIED, M. R., & KENT, R. N. Traditional versus behavioral personality assessment: A comparison of methodological and theoretical assumptions. *Psychological Bulletin*, 1972, *77*, 409–420.

GOLDFRIED, M. R., & LINEHAN, M. M. Basic issues in behavioral assessment. In A. R. Ciminero, K. S. Calhoun, & H. E. Adams (Eds.), *Handbook of behavioral assessment*. New York: Wiley, 1977. Ch. 2.

GOLDFRIED, M. R., STRICKER, G., & WEINER, I. R. *Rorschach handbook of clinical and research applications*. Englewood Cliffs, N.J.: Prentice-Hall, 1971.

GOLDING, S. L., & RORER, L. G. Illusory correlation and subjective judgment. *Journal of Abnormal Psychology*, 1972, *80*, 249–260.

GOLDMAN, B. A., & BUSCH, J. C. (Eds.). *Directory of unpublished experimental mental measures, Vol. II*. New York: Human Sciences Press, 1978.

GOLDMAN, B. A., & SAUNDERS, J. L. (Eds.). *Directory of unpublished experimental mental measures, Vol. I*. New York: Human Sciences Press, 1974.

GOLDMAN, L. *Using tests in counseling* (2nd ed.). Englewood Cliffs, N.J.: Prentice-Hall, 1971.

GOLDSCHMID, M. L. Role of experience in the acquisition of conservation. *Proceedings, 76th Annual Convention, American Psychological Association*, 1968, 361–362.

GOLDSCHMID, M. L., et al. A cross-cultural investigation of conservation. *Journal of Cross-Cultural Psychology*, 1973, *4*, 75–88.

GOLDSCHMID, M. L., & BENTLER, P. M. Dimensions and measurement of conservation. *Child Development*, 1968, *39*, 787–802. (a)

GOLDSCHMID, M. L. & BENTLER, P. M. *Manual: Concept Assessment Kit—Conservation*. San Diego, Calif.: Educational and Industrial Testing Service, 1968. (b)

GOLDSTEIN, K., & SCHEERER, M. Abstract and concrete behavior: An experimental study with special tests. *Psychological Monographs*, 1941, *53*(2, Whole No. 230).

GOLDSTEIN, K. M., & BLACKMAN, S. Assessment of cognitive style. In P. McReynolds (Ed.), *Advances in psychological assessment* (Vol. 4). San Francisco: Jossey-Bass, 1978. Ch. 11. (a)

GOLDSTEIN, K. M., & BLACKMAN, S. *Cognitive style: Five approaches and relevant research*. New York: Wiley-Interscience, 1978. (b)

GOODENOUGH, D. R. The role of individual differences in field dependence as a factor in learning and memory. *Psychological Bulletin,* 1976, *83,* 675–694.

GOODENOUGH, F. L. *Mental testing: Its history, principles, and applications.* New York: Rinehart, 1949.

GOODENOUGH, F. L., & HARRIS, D. B. Studies in the psychology of children's drawings: II. 1928–1949. *Psychological Bulletin,* 1950, *47,* 369–433.

GOODNOW, J. J. The nature of intelligent behavior: Questions raised by cross-cultural studies. In L. B. Resnick (Ed.), *The nature of intelligence.* Hillsdale, N.J.: Erlbaum, 1976. Ch. 9.

GORDON, E. The Music Aptitude Profile: A new and unique musical aptitude test battery. *Council for Research in Music Education,* 1965, No. 6, 12–16.

GORDON, E. *A three-year longitudinal predictive validity study of the Musical Aptitude Profile.* Iowa City: University of Iowa Press, 1967.

GORDON, E. W., & WILKERSON, D. A. *Compensatory education for the disadvantaged—programs and practices: Preschool through college.* New York: College Entrance Examination Board, 1966.

GORDON, L. V., & ALF, E. F. Acclimatization and aptitude test performance. *Educational and Psychological Measurement,* 1960, *20,* 333–337.

GORDON, M. A. *A study of the applicability of the same minimum qualifying scores for technical schools to white males, WAF, and Negro males* (Tech. Rep. No. 53–34). Lackland Air Force Base, Texas: Personnel Research Laboratory, 1953.

GORHAM, D. R. Validity and reliability studies of a computer-based scoring system for inkblot responses. *Journal of Consulting Psychology,* 1967, *31,* 65–70.

GORHAM, W. A. (Chair). *Computers and testing: Steps toward the inevitable conquest.* Symposium presented at the meeting of the American Psychological Association, Chicago, August 1975. (Also reprinted as PS-76-1, Personnel Research and Development Center, U.S. Office of Personnel Management, September, 1976.)

GORSUCH, R. L. *Factor analysis.* Philadelphia: Saunders, 1974.

GOTTFRIED, A. W., & BRODY, N. Interrelationships between and correlates of psychometric and Piagetian scales of sensorimotor intelligence. *Developmental Psychology,* 1975, *11,* 379–387.

GOUGH, H. G. A new dimension of status. I. Development of a personality scale. *American Sociological Review,* 1948, *13,* 401–409.

GOUGH, H. G. The Adjective Check List as a personality assessment research technique. *Psychological Reports,* 1960, *6,* 107–122.

GOUGH, H. G. A cluster analysis of Home Index status items. *Psychological Reports,* 1971, *28,* 923–929. (a)

GOUGH, H. G. Socioeconomic status as related to high school graduation and college attendance. *Psychology in the Schools,* 1971, *7,* 226–231. (b)

GOUGH, H. G., & HEILBRUN, A. B., JR. *The Adjective Check List bibliography (1980 edition).* Palo Alto, Calif.: Consulting Psychologists Press, 1980. (a)

GOUGH, H. G., & HEILBRUN, A. B., JR. *The Adjective Check List manual* (Rev. ed). Palo Alto, Calif.: Consulting Psychologists Press, 1980. (b)

GOULET, L. R., & BALTES, P. B. (Eds.). *Life-span developmental psychology: Research and theory.* New York: Academic Press, 1970.

GRAHAM, F. K., et al. Development three years after perinatal anoxia and other potentially damaging newborn experiences. *Psychological Monographs,* 1962, *76*(3, Whole No. 522).

GRAHAM, F. K., ERNHART, C. B., et al. Brain injury in the preschool child. *Psychological Monographs*, 1963, 77(10–11, Whole Nos. 573–574).

GRAHAM, J. R. *The MMPI: A practical guide*. New York: Oxford University Press, 1977.

GRANT, D. L., & BRAY, D. W. Contributions of the interview to assessment of management potential. *Journal of Applied Psychology*, 1969, 53, 24–34.

GRANT, D. L., & BRAY, D. W. Validation of employment tests for telephone company installation and repair occupations. *Journal of Applied Psychology*, 1970, 54, 7–14.

GREEN, B. F., JR. Comments on tailored testing. In W. H. Holtzman (Ed.), *Computer-assisted instruction, testing, and guidance*. New York: Harper & Row, 1970. Pp. 184–197.

GREEN, D. R. (Ed.). *The aptitude–achievement distinction: Proceedings of the Second CTB/McGraw-Hill Conference on Issues in Educational Measurement*. New York: McGraw-Hill, 1974.

GREEN, D. R., FORD, M. P., & FLAMER, G. B. (Eds.). *Measurement and Piaget: Proceedings of the CTB/McGraw-Hill Conference on Ordinal Scales of Cognitive Development*. New York: McGraw-Hill, 1971.

GREEN, R. F. Does a selection situation induce testees to bias their answers on interest and temperament tests? *Educational and Psychological Measurement*, 1951, 11, 503–515.

GREENWOOD, J. M., & McNAMARA, W. J. Interrater reliability in situational tests. *Journal of Applied Psychology*, 1967, 51, 101–106.

GRIBBONS, W. D., & LOHNES, P. R. *Emerging careers*. New York: Teachers College Press, 1968.

GRIBBONS, W. D., & LOHNES, P. R. *Career development from age 13 to age 25* (Final Report, Project No. 6-2151). Washington, D.C.: U.S. Office of Education, 1969.

GRONLUND, N. E. *Preparing criterion-referenced tests for classroom instruction*. New York: Macmillan, 1973.

GRONLUND, N. E. *Determining accountability for classroom instruction*. New York: Macmillan, 1974.

GRONLUND, N. E. *Constructing achievement tests* (2nd ed.). Englewood Cliffs, N.J.: Prentice-Hall, 1977.

GRONLUND, N. E. *Stating behavioral objectives for classroom instruction* (2nd ed.). New York: Macmillan, 1978.

GRONLUND, N. E. *Measurement and evaluation in teaching* (4th ed.). New York: Macmillan, 1981.

GROOMS, R. R., & ENDLER, N. S. The effect of anxiety on academic achievement. *Journal of Educational Psychology*, 1960, 51, 299–304.

GROSS, A. L., FAGGEN, J., & McCARTHY, K. The differential predictability of the college performance of males and females. *Educational and Psychological Measurement*, 1974, 34, 363–365.

GROSS, A. L., & SU, W. H. Defining a "fair" or "unbiased" selection model: A question of utilities. *Journal of Applied Psychology*, 1975, 60, 345–351.

GROSSMAN, H. (Ed.). *Manual on terminology and classification in mental retardation* (1973 revision). Washington, D.C.: American Association on Mental Deficiency, 1973.

GUERTIN, W. H., et al. Research with the Wechsler-Bellevue Intelligence Scale: 1950–1955. *Psychological Bulletin*, 1956, 53, 235–257.

GUERTIN, W. H., et al. Research with the Wechsler Intelligence Scales for Adults: 1955–60. *Psychological Bulletin,* 1962, *59,* 1–26.

GUERTIN, W. H., et al. Research with the Wechsler Intelligence Scales for Adults: 1960–1965. *Psychological Bulletin,* 1966, *66,* 385–409.

GUERTIN, W. H., et al. Research with the Wechsler Intelligence Scales for Adults: 1965–1970. *Psychological Record,* 1971, *21,* 289–339.

GUICCIARDI, G., & FERRARI, G. C. I testi mentali per l'esame degli alienati. *Rivista sperimentale di Freniatria,* 1896, *22,* 297–314.

Guide to the use of the Graduate Record Examinations, 1980–81. Princeton, N.J.: Educational Testing Service, 1980.

GUILFORD, J. P. Creative abilities in the arts. *Psychological Review,* 1957, *64,* 110–118.

GUILFORD, J. P. *Personality.* New York: McGraw-Hill, 1959.

GUILFORD, J. P. *The nature of human intelligence.* New York: McGraw-Hill, 1967.

GUILFORD, J. P., & FRUCHTER, B. *Fundamental statistics in psychology and education* (6th ed.). New York: McGraw-Hill, 1978.

GUILFORD, J. P., & HOEPFNER, R. *The analysis of intelligence.* New York: McGraw-Hill, 1971.

GUILFORD, J. P., & LACEY, J. I. (Eds.). *Printed classification tests* (AAF Aviation Psychology Program, Research Reports. Rep. No. 5). Washington, D.C.: U.S. Government Printing Office, 1947.

GUILFORD, J. P., & ZIMMERMAN, W. S. Fourteen dimensions of temperament. *Psychological Monographs,* 1956, *70*(10, Whole No. 417).

GUION, R. M. Recruiting, selection, and job placement. In M. D. Dunnette (Ed.), *Handbook of industrial and organizational psychology.* Chicago: Rand McNally, 1976, Ch. 8.

GUION, R. M. Content validity: Three years of talk—What's the action? *Public Personnel Management,* 1977, *6,* 407–414.

GULLIKSEN, H. *Theory of mental tests.* New York: Wiley, 1950.

GULLIKSEN, H. Looking back and ahead in psychometrics. *American Psychologist,* 1974, *29,* 251–261.

GULLIKSEN, H., & WILKS, S. S. Regression tests for several samples. *Psychometrika,* 1950, *15,* 91–114.

GUTKIN, T. B., & REYNOLDS, C. R. Factorial similarity of the WISC-R for white and black children from the standardization sample. *Journal of Educational Psychology,* 1981, *73,* 227–231.

GUTTMAN, I., & RAJU, N. S. A minimum loss function as determiner of optimal cutting scores. *Personnel Psychology,* 1965, *18,* 179–185.

GUTTMAN, L. A basis for scaling qualitative data. *American Sociological Review,* 1944, *9,* 139–150.

GUTTMAN, L. The Cornell technique for scale and intensity analysis. *Educational and Psychological Measurement,* 1947, *7,* 247–280.

HALL, J. A correlation of a modified form of Raven's Progressive Matrices (1938) with Wechsler Adult Intelligence Scale. *Journal of Consulting Psychology,* 1957, *21,* 23–26.

HALL, J. A., & HALBERSTADT, A. G. Masculinity and femininity in children: Development of the Children's Personal Attributes Questionnaire. *Developmental Psychology,* 1980, *16,* 270–280.

HALSTEAD, W. C. *Brain and intelligence: A quantitative study of the frontal lobes.* Chicago: University of Chicago Press, 1947.

HALVERSON, H. M. The acquisition of skill in infancy. *Journal of Genetic Psychology,* 1933, 43, 3–48.

HAMBLETON, R. K. Testing and decision-making procedures for selected individualized instructional programs. *Review of Educational Research,* 1974, 44, 371–400.

HAMBLETON, R. K. Latent trait models and their applications. In R. Traub (Ed.), *New directions for testing and measurement: Methodological developments* (No. 4). San Francisco: Jossey-Bass, 1979.

HAMBLETON, R. K. Test score validity and standard setting. In R. A. Berk (Ed.), *Criterion-referenced measurement: The state of the art.* Baltimore: Johns Hopkins University Press, 1980. Ch. 4.

HAMBLETON, R. K., & COOK, L. L. Latent trait models and their use in the analysis of educational test data. *Journal of Educational Measurement,* 1977, 14, 75–96.

HAMBLETON, R. K., & NOVICK, M. R. Toward an integration of theory and method for criterion-referenced tests. *Journal of Educational Measurement,* 1973, 10, 159–170.

HAMILTON, J. L., & BUDOFF, M. Learning potential among the moderately and severely mentally retarded. *Mental Retardation,* 1974, 12, 33–36.

HAMILTON, R. G., & ROBERTSON, M. H. Examiner influence on the Holtzman Inkblot Technique. *Journal of Projective Techniques and Personality Assessment,* 1966, 30, 553–558.

HAMMOND, K. R., HURSCH, C. J., & TODD, F. J. Analyzing the components of clinical inference. *Psychological Review,* 1964, 71, 438–456.

HARCOURT BRACE JOVANOVICH, TEST DEPARTMENT. The effect of separate answer document use on achievement test performance of Grade 3 and 4 pupils. *Special Report* No. 24, June 1973.

HARDT, R. H., EYDE, L. D., PRIMOFF, E. S., & TORDY, G. R. *The New York State Trooper job element examination: Final technical report.* Albany: New York State Police, January 1981. (National Technical Information Service, Springfield, Va. 22161.)

HARLOW, H. F. The formation of learning sets. *Psychological Review,* 1949, 56, 51–65.

HARLOW, H. F. Learning set and error factor theory. In S. Koch (Ed.), *Psychology: A study of a science* (Vol. 2). New York: McGraw-Hill, 1960. Pp. 492–537.

HARMAN, H. H. *Final report of research on assessing human abilities* (ONR Contract N00014-71-C-0117 Project NR 150 329). Princeton, N.J.: Educational Testing Service, July 1975.

HARMAN, H. H. *Modern factor analysis* (3rd. ed.). Chicago: University of Chicago Press, 1976.

HÄRNQVIST, K. Relative changes in intelligence from 13 to 18. *Scandinavian Journal of Psychology,* 1968, 9, 50–82.

HARRIS, C. W., & MCARTHUR, D. L. Another view of the relation of environment to mental abilities. *Journal of Educational Psychology,* 1974, 66, 457–459.

HARRIS, D. B. *Children's drawings as measures of intellectual maturity: A revision and extension of the Goodenough Draw-a-Man Test*. New York: Harcourt Brace Jovanovich, 1963.

HARRIS, J. A. The computer: Guidance tool of the future. In W. E. Coffman (Ed.), *Frontiers of educational measurement and information systems— 1973*. Boston: Houghton Mifflin, 1973. Ch. 7.

HARRISON, R. Thematic apperception methods. In B. B. Wolman (Ed.), *Handbook of clinical psychology*. New York: McGraw-Hill, 1965. Pp. 562–620.

HARTMANN, D. P., ROPER, B. L., & BRADFORD, D. C. Some relationships between behavioral and traditional assessment. *Journal of Behavioral Assessment*, 1979, *1*, 3–21.

HARTSHORNE, H., & MAY, M. A. *Studies in deceit*. New York: Macmillan, 1928.

HARTSHORNE, H., MAY, M. A., & MALLER, J. B. *Studies in service and self-control*. New York: Macmillan, 1929.

HARTSHORNE, H., MAY, M. A., & SHUTTLEWORTH, F. K. *Studies in the organization of character*. New York: Macmillan, 1930.

HARTSON, L. D. A five year study of objective tests for sectioning courses in English composition. *Journal of Applied Psychology*, 1930, *14*, 202–210.

HATHAWAY, S. R., & MEEHL, P. E. *An atlas for the clinical use of the MMPI*. Minneapolis: University of Minnesota Press, 1951.

HATHAWAY, S. R., & MONACHESI, E. D. *An atlas of juvenile MMPI Profiles*. Minneapolis: University of Minnesota Press, 1961.

HATHAWAY, S. R., & MONACHESI, E. D. *Adolescent personality and behavior*. Minneapolis: University of Minnesota Press, 1963.

HAVIGHURST, R. J. *Human development and education*. New York: Longmans Green, 1953.

HAWK, J. A. Linearity of criterion-GATB aptitude relationships. *Measurement and Evaluation in Guidance*, 1970, *2*, 249–251.

HAYES, S. P. Alternative scales for the mental measurement of the visually handicapped. *Outlook for the Blind*, 1942, *36*, 225–230.

HAYES, S. P. A second test scale for the mental measurement of the visually handicapped. *Outlook for the Blind*, 1943, *37*, 37–41.

HAYNES, R. B., TAYLOR, D. W., & SACKETT, D. L. (Eds.). *Compliance in health care*. Baltimore: Johns Hopkins University Press, 1979.

HEATON, R. K., BAADE, L. E., & JOHNSON, K. L. Neuropsychological test results associated with psychiatric disorders in adults. *Psychological Bulletin*, 1978, *85*, 141–162.

HEBB, D. O. A return to Jensen and his social science critics. *American Psychologist*, 1970, *25*, 568.

HEILBRUN, A. B. Social-learning theory, social desirability, and the MMPI. *Psychological Bulletin*, 1964, *61*, 377–387.

HENRY, W. E. *The analysis of fantasy: The thematic apperception technique in the study of personality*. New York: Wiley, 1956.

HENRY, W. E., & FARLEY, J. The validity of the Thematic Apperception Test in the study of adolescent personality. *Psychological Monographs*, 1959, *73*(17, Whole No. 487).

HENRYSSON, S. Gathering, analyzing, and using data on test items. In R. L. Thorndike (Ed.), *Educational Measurement* (2nd ed.). Washington, D.C.: American Council on Education, 1971. Ch. 5.

HERMAN, D. O. *The WISC-R, its development and usage: Some findings from sequential standardizations.* Paper presented at the meeting of the California Association of School Psychologists and Psychometrists and the National Association of School Psychologists, San Diego, March 1979.

HERRON, E. W. Psychometric characteristics of a thirty-item version of the group method of the Holtzman Inkblot Technique. *Journal of Clinical Psychology,* 1963, *19,* 450–453.

HERRON, E. W. Changes in inkblot perception with presentation of the Holtzman inkblot technique as an "intelligence test." *Journal of Projective Techniques and Personality Assessment,* 1964, *28,* 442–447.

HERZBERGER, S. D., LINNEY, J. A., SEIDMAN, E., & RAPPAPORT, J. Preschool and primary locus of control scale: Is it ready for use? *Developmental Psychology,* 1979, *15,* 320–324.

HEVERN, V. W. Recent validity studies of the Halstead-Reitan approach to clinical neuropsychological assessment: A critical review. *Clinical Neuropsychology,* 1980, *2,* 49–61.

HEWER, V. H. Are tests fair to college students from homes with low socioeconomic status? *Personnel and Guidance Journal,* 1965, *43,* 764–769.

HICKS, L. E. Some properties of ipsative, normative, and forced normative measures. *Psychological Bulletin,* 1970, *74,* 167–184.

HIGGINS, C., & SIVERS, C. H. A comparison of Stanford-Binet and Colored Raven Progressive Matrices IQs for children with low socioeconomic status. *Journal of Consulting Psychology,* 1958, *22,* 465–468.

HILL, E. F. *The Holtzman Inkblot Technique: A handbook for clinical application.* San Francisco: Jossey-Bass, 1972.

HILL, K. T., & SARASON, S. B. The relation of test anxiety and defensiveness to test and school performance over the elementary school years. *Monographs of the Society for Research in Child Development,* 1966, *31*(2, Serial No. 104).

HIMELSTEIN, P. Research with the Stanford-Binet, Form L-M: The first five years. *Psychological Bulletin,* 1966, *65,* 156–164.

HINKLE, L. E., JR., WHITNEY, L. H., & LEHMAN, E. W. Occupation, education, and coronary heart disease. *Science,* 1968, *161,* 238–246.

HOBBS, N. *The futures of children.* San Francisco: Jossey-Bass, 1975. (a)

HOBBS, N. (Ed.). *Issues in the classification of children* (Vols. 1 & 2). San Francisco: Jossey-Bass, 1975. (b)

HOFFMAN, B. *The tyranny of testing.* New York: Crowell-Collier, 1962.

HOGAN, R. Moral conduct and moral character: A psychological perspective. *Psychological Bulletin,* 1973, *79,* 217–232.

HOGAN, R., DeSOTO, C. B., & SOLANO. C. Traits, tests, and personality research. *American Psychologist,* 1977, *32,* 255–264.

HOLDEN, R. H. Improved methods in testing cerebral palsied children. *American Journal of Mental Deficiency,* 1951, *56,* 349–353.

HOLLAND, J. L. *The psychology of vocational choice.* Waltham, Mass.: Blaisdell, 1966.

HOLLAND, J. L. *Making vocational choices: A theory of careers.* Englewood Cliffs, N.J.: Prentice-Hall, 1973.

HOLLAND, J. L. *The Self-Directed Search: Professional manual, 1979 edition.* Palo Alto, Calif.: Consulting Psychologists Press, 1979.

HOLLAND, J. L., & GOTTFREDSON, G. D. Using a typology of persons and environments to explain careers: Some extensions and clarifications. *The Counseling Psychologist*, 1976, *6*, 20–29.

HOLLENBECK, G. P., & KAUFMAN, A. S. Factor analysis of the Wechsler Preschool and Primary Scale of Intelligence (WPPSI). *Journal of Clinical Psychology*, 1973, *29*, 41–45.

HOLLINGSHEAD, A. B. *Two-factor index of scoial position.* Unpublished manuscript, 1957. (Available from A. B. Hollingshead, Department of Sociology, Yale University, New Haven, Conn. 06510.)

HOLTZMAN, W. H. Holtzman Inkblot Technique. In A. I. Rabin (Ed.), *Projective techniques in personality assessment.* New York: Springer, 1968. Pp. 136–170.

HOLTZMAN, W. H. (Ed.). *Computer-assisted instruction, testing, and guidance.* New York: Harper & Row, 1970.

HOLTZMAN, W. H. The changing world of mental measurement and its social significance. *American Psychologist*, 1971, *26*, 546–553.

HOLTZMAN, W. H. (Chair). *Moral development* (Proceedings of the 1974 ETS Invitational Conference). Princeton, N.J.: Educational Testing Service, 1975. (a)

HOLTZMAN, W. H. New developments in Holtzman Inkblot Technique. In P. McReynolds (Ed.), *Advances in psychological assessment* (Vol. 3). San Francisco: Jossey-Bass, 1975. Ch. 6. (b)

HOLTZMAN, W. H., MOSELEY, E. C., REINEHR, R. C., & ABBOTT, E. Comparison of the group method and the standard individual version of the Holtzman Inkblot Technique. *Journal of Clinical Psychology*, 1963, *19*, 441–449.

HOLTZMAN, W. H., THORPE, J. S., SWARTZ, J. D., & HERRON, E. W. *Inkblot perception and personality—Holtzman Inkblot Technique.* Austin: University of Texas Press, 1961.

HONZIK, M. P. Environmental correlates of mental growth: Prediction from the family setting at 21 months. *Child Development*, 1967, *38*, 337–364.

HONZIK, M. P., MACFARLANE, J. W., & ALLEN, L. The stability of mental test performance between two and eighteen years. *Journal of Experimental Education*, 1948, *17*, 309–324.

HOOPER, F. H. Cognitive assessment across the life-span: Methodological implications of the organismic approach. In J. R. Nesselroade & H. W. Reese (Eds.), *Life-span developmental psychology: Methodological issues.* New York: Academic Press, 1973. Pp. 299–316.

HOPKINS, K. D., & STANLEY, J. C. *Educational and psychological measurement and evaluation* (6th ed.). Englewood Cliffs, N.J.: Prentice-Hall, 1981.

HORN, J. L. Human abilities: A review of research and theory in the early 1970s. *Annual Review of Psychology*, 1976, *27*, 437–485.

HORN, J. L., & DONALDSON, G. On the myth of intellectual decline in adulthood. *American Psychologist*, 1976, *31*, 701–719.

HORN, J. L., & KNAPP, J. R. On the subjective character of the empirical base of Guilford's structure-of-intellect model. *Psychological Bulletin*, 1973, *80*, 33–43.

HORST, P. *The prediction of personal adjustment.* New York: Social Science Research Council, 1941.

Horst, P. A technique for the development of a differential prediction battery. *Psychological Monographs,* 1954, *68*(9, Whole No. 380).

Howard, J. L., & Plant, W. T. Psychometric evaluation of an Operation Head Start program. *Journal of Genetic Psychology,* 1967, *111*, 281–288.

Huba, G. J., & Hamilton, D. L. On the generality of trait relations: Some analyses based on Fisk's paper. *Psychological Bulletin,* 1976, *83*, 868–876.

Huddleston, E. M. Measurement of writing ability at the college-entrance level: Objective vs. subjective testing techniques. *Journal of Experimental Education,* 1954, *22*, 165–213.

Hughes, R. B., & Lessler, K. A comparison of WISC and Peabody scores of Negro and white rural school children. *American Journal of Mental Deficiency,* 1965, *69*, 877–880.

Hull, C. L. *Aptitude testing.* Yonkers, N.Y.: World Book Co., 1928.

Hulten, C. E. The personal element in teachers' marks. *Journal of Educational Research,* 1925, *12*, 49–55.

Humphreys, L. G. Individual differences. *Annual Review of Psychology,* 1952, *3*, 131–150.

Humphreys, L. G. The organization of human abilities. *American Psychologist,* 1962, *17*, 475–483.

Humphreys, L. G. A skeptical look at the factor pure test. In C. Lunneborg (Ed.), *Current problems and techniques in multivariate psychology.* Seattle: University of Washington, 1970. Pp. 23–32.

Humphreys, L. G. Statistical definitions of test validity for minority groups. *Journal of Applied Psychology,* 1973, *58*, 1–4.

Humphreys, L. G. The construct of general intelligence. *Intelligence,* 1979, *3*, 105–120.

Hunt, E. Varieties of cognitive power. In L. B. Resnick (Ed.), *The nature of intelligence.* Hillsdale, N.J.: Erlbaum, 1976. Ch. 13.

Hunt, E., Frost, N., & Lunneborg, C. Individual differences in cognition. In G. Bower (Ed.), *The psychology of learning and motivation: Advances in research and theory* (Vol. 7). New York: Academic Press, 1973.

Hunt, J. McV. Reflections on a decade of early education. *Journal of Abnormal Child Psychology,* 1975, *3*, 275–330.

Hunt, J. McV. The utility of ordinal scales inspired by Piaget's observations. *Merrill-Palmer Quarterly,* 1976, *22*, 31–45.

Hunt, J. McV., & Kirk, G. E. Criterion-referenced tests of school readiness: A paradigm with illustrations. *Genetic Psychology Monographs,* 1974, *90*, 143–182.

Hunt, J. McV., Paraskevopoulos, J., Schickedanz, D., & Užgiris, I. Č. Variations in the mean ages of achieving object permanence under diverse conditions of rearing. In B. Z. Friedlander, G. M. Sterritt, & G. E. Kirk (Eds.), *The exceptional infant: Assessment and intervention* (Vol. 3). New York: Brunner/Mazel, 1975. Pp. 247–263.

Hunter, J. E. *A critical analysis of item means and item-test correlations to determine the presence or absence of content bias in achievement test items.* Paper presented at the National Institute of Education Conference on Test Bias, Annapolis, Md., December 1975.

HUNTER, J. E., & SCHMIDT, F. L. Critical analysis of the statistical and ethical implications of various definitions of *test bias. Psychological Bulletin,* 1976, *83,* 1053–1071.

HUNTER, J. E., & SCHMIDT, F. L. Differential and single-group validity of employment tests by race: A critical analysis of three recent studies. *Journal of Applied Psychology,* 1978, *63,* 1–11.

HUNTER, J. E., & SCHMIDT, F. L. Fitting people into jobs: The impact of personnel selection on national productivity. In M. D. Dunnette & E. A. Fleishman (Eds.), *Human performance and productivity, Vol. 1: Human capability assessment.* Hillsdale, N.J.: Erlbaum, 1981. Ch. 7.

HUNTER, J. E., SCHMIDT, F. L., & HUNTER, R. Differential validity of employment tests by race: A comprehensive review and analysis. *Psychological Bulletin,* 1979, *86,* 721–735.

HUNTER, J. E., SCHMIDT, F. L., & RAUSCHENBERGER, J. M. Fairness of psychological tests: Implications of four definitions for selection utility and minority hiring. *Journal of Applied Psychology,* 1977, *62,* 245–260.

HUSÉN, T. The influence of schooling upon IQ. *Theoria,* 1951, *17,* 61–88.

HUTT, M. L. *The Hutt Adaptation of the Bender-Gestalt Test* (3rd ed.). New York: Grune & Stratton, 1977.

IRETON, H., THWING, E., & GRAVEM, H. Infant mental development and neurological status, family socioeconomic status, and intelligence at age four. *Child Development,* 1970, *41,* 937–945.

IRONSON, G. H., & SUBKOVIAK, M. J. A comparison of several methods of assessing item bias. *Journal of Educational Measurement,* 1979, *16,* 209–225.

IRVINE, S. H. Factor analysis of African abilities and attainments: Constructs across cultures. *Psychological Bulletin,* 1969, *71,* 20–32. (a)

IRVINE, S. H. Figural tests of reasoning in Africa: Studies in the use of Raven's Matrices across cultures. *International Journal of Psychology,* 1969, *4,* 217–228. (b)

IVANCEVICH, J. M. Longitudinal study of the effects of rater training on psychometric error in ratings. *Journal of Applied Psychology,* 1979, *64,* 502–508.

JACKSON, D. N. Block's The challenge of response sets. *Educational and Psychological Measurement,* 1967, *27,* 207–219. (a)

JACKSON, D. N. Balanced scales, item overlap, and the stables of Augeas. *Educational and Psychological Measurement,* 1967, *27,* 502–507. (b)

JACKSON, D. N. *Personality Research Form manual.* Port Huron, Mich.: Research Psychologists Press, 1967. (c)

JACKSON, D. N. A sequential system for personality scale development. In C. D. Spielberger (Ed.), *Current topics in clinical and community psychology* (Vol. 2). New York: Academic Press, 1970. Pp. 61–96.

JACKSON, D. N. The dynamics of structured personality tests. *Psychological Review,* 1971, *78,* 229–248.

JACKSON, D. N. Structured personality assessment. In B. B. Wolman (Ed.), *Handbook of general psychology.* Englewood Cliffs, N.J.: Prentice-Hall, 1973. Pp. 775–792.

JACKSON, D. N. Reliability of the Jackson Personality Inventory. *Psychological Reports,* 1977, *40,* 613–614.

JACKSON, D. N. Interpreter's guide to the Jackson Personality Inventory. In P. McReynolds (Ed.), *Advances in psychological assessment* (Vol. 4). San Francisco: Jossey-Bass, 1978. Ch. 2.

JACKSON, D. N. *Jackson Vocational Interest Survey manual.* Port Huron, Mich.: Research Psychologists Press, 1977.

JACKSON, D. N., & MESSICK, S. Content and style in personality assessment. *Psychological Bulletin,* 1958, *55,* 243–252.

JACKSON, D. N., & MESSICK, S. Response styles and the assessment of psychopathology. In S. Messick & J. Ross (Eds.), *Measurement in personality and cognition.* New York: Wiley, 1962. Pp. 129–155.

JACKSON, D. N., NEILL, J. A., & BEVAN, A. R. An evaluation of forced-choice and true-false item formats in personality assessment. *Journal of Research in Personality,* 1973, *7,* 21–30.

JACKSON, D. N., & PAUNONEN, S. V. Personality structure and assessment. *Annual Review of Psychology,* 1980, *31,* 503–551.

JACKSON, D. N., & WILLIAMS, D. R. Occupational classification in terms of interest patterns. *Journal of Vocational Behavior,* 1975, *6,* 269–280.

JACOBS, A., & BARRON, R. Falsification of the Guilford-Zimmerman Temperament Survey: II. Making a poor impression. *Psychological Reports,* 1968, *23,* 1271–1277.

JACOBS, P. I., & VANDEVENTER, M. The learning and transfer of double-classification skills: A replication and extension. *Journal of Experimental Child Psychology,* 1971, *12,* 140–157.

JAEGER, R. M. The national test-equating study in reading (The Anchor Test Study). *NCME Measurement in Education,* 1973 *4*(4), 1–8.

JAEGER, R. M. (Ed.). Applications of latent trait models (Special Issue). *Journal of Educational Measurement,* 1977, *14*(2), 73–196.

JANKE, L. L., & HAVIGHURST, R. J. Relations between ability and social status in a midwestern community: II. Sixteen-year-old boys and girls. *Journal of Educational Psychology,* 1945, *36,* 499–509.

JENKINS, C. D., ZYZANSKI, S. J., & ROSENMAN, R. H. *Jenkins Activity Survey: Manual.* New York: Psychological Corporation, 1979.

JENKINS, J. J., & RUSSELL, W. A. Systematic changes in word association norms: 1910–1952. *Journal of Abnormal and Social Psychology,* 1960, *60,* 293–304.

JENSEN, A. R. Social class and verbal learning. In M. Deutsch, I. Katz, & A. R. Jensen (Eds.), *Social class, race, and psychological development.* New York: Holt, Rinehart & Winston, 1968. Ch. 4.

JENSEN, A. R. How much can we boost IQ and scholastic achievement? *Harvard Educational Review,* 1969, *39,* 1–123.

JENSEN, A. R. *Bias in mental testing.* New York: Free Press, 1980.

JENSEN, H. E., MASSEY, I. H., & VALENTINE, L. D., JR. *Armed Services Vocational Aptitude Battery development (ASVAB Forms 5, 6, and 7).* Brooks AFB, Texas: Air Force Human Resources Laboratory. MEPCOM Technical Research Note 77-3, December 1977.

JOHANSSON, C. B. *Manual for the Career Assessment Inventory.* Minneapolis: NCS Interpretive Scoring Systems, 1976.

JOHANSSON, C. B., & JOHANSSON, J. C. *Manual supplement for the Career Assessment Inventory.* Minneapolis: NCS Interpretive Scoring Systems, 1978.

JOHNSON, A. P. Notes on a suggested index of item validity: The U-L index. *Journal of Educational Psychology*, 1951, *42*, 499–504.

JOHNSON, O. G. *Tests and measurements in child development: Handbook II, Vols. 1 and 2.* San Francisco: Jossey-Bass, 1976.

JOHNSON, O. G., & BOMMARITO, J. W. *Tests and measurements in child development: Handbook I.* San Francisco: Jossey-Bass, 1971.

JONES, H. G. The evaluation of the significance of differences between scaled scores on the WAIS: Perpetuation of a fallacy. *Journal of Consulting Psychology*, 1956, *20*, 319–320.

JONES, L. V. A factor analysis of the Stanford-Binet at four age levels. *Psychometrika*, 1949, *14*, 299–331.

JONES, L. V. Primary abilities in the Stanford-Binet, age 13. *Journal of Genetic Psychology*, 1954, *84*, 125–147.

JONES, R. R., REID, J. B., & PATTERSON, G. R. Naturalistic observation in clinical assessment. In P. McReynolds (Ed.), *Advances in psychological assessment* (Vol. 3). San Francisco: Jossey-Bass, 1975. Ch. 2.

JORDAAN, J. P., & HEYDE, M. B. *Vocational maturity during the high school years.* New York: Teachers College Press, 1979.

JUNG, C. G. The association method. *American Journal of Psychology*, 1910, *21*, 219–269.

JURGENSEN, C. E. Table for determining phi coefficients. *Psychometrika*, 1947, *12*, 17–29.

KAGAN, J., & FREEMAN, M. Relation of childhood intelligence, maternal behaviors, and social class to behavior during adolescence. *Child Development*, 1963, *34*, 899–911.

KAGAN, J., SONTAG, L. W., BAKER, C. T., & NELSON, V. L. Personality and IQ change. *Journal of Abnormal and Social Psychology*, 1958, *56*, 261–266.

KAHN, R. L., & CANNELL, C. F. *The dynamics of interviewing: Theory, technique, and cases.* New York: Wiley, 1957.

KAHNEMAN, D., AND TVERSKY, A. On the psychology of prediction. *Psychological Review*, 1973, *80*, 237–251.

KAISER, H. F. A modified stanine scale. *Journal of Experimental Education*, 1958, *26*, 261.

KAISER, H. F., & MICHAEL, W. B. Domain validity and generalizability. *Educational and Psychological Measurement*, 1975, *35*, 31–35.

KANE, J. S., & LAWLER, E. E., III. Methods of peer assessment. *Psychological Bulletin*, 1978, *85*, 555–586.

KANE, J. S., & LAWLER, E. E., III. In defense of peer assessment: A rebuttal to Brief's critique. *Psychological Bulletin*, 1980, *88*, 80–81.

KANFER, F. H. Assessment for behavior modification. *Journal of Personality Assessment*, 1972, *36*, 418–423.

KANFER, F. H., & SASLOW, G. Behavioral diagnosis. In C. M. Franks (Ed.), *Behavior therapy: Appraisal and status.* New York: McGraw-Hill, 1969. Pp. 417–444.

KAPLAN, L. J. On the testing of nontestable children. *Bulletin of the Menninger Clinic*, 1975, *39*, 420–435.

KAPLAN, R. M. *Health status measurement for evaluation research and policy analysis.* Paper presented at the meeting of the American Psychological Association, Montreal, September 1980.

KAPLAN, R. M., BUSH, J. W., & BERRY, C. C. Health status: Types of validity and the index of well-being. *Health Services Research,* 1976, *11,* 478–507.

KARNES, F. A., & BROWN, K. E. Factor analysis of WISC-R for the gifted. *Journal of Educational Psychology,* 1980, *72,* 197–199.

KARSON, S., & O'DELL, J. W. *A guide to the clinical use of the 16 PF.* Champaign, Ill.: Institute for Personality and Ability Testing, 1976.

KATZ, E. The "Pointing Modification" of the Revised Stanford-Binet Intelligence Scales, Forms L and M, Years II through VI: A report of research in progress. *American Journal of Mental Deficiency,* 1958, *62,* 698–707.

KATZ, M. R. Can computers make guidance decisions for students? *College Board Review,* 1969, No. 72, 13–17.

KATZ, M. R. Career decision-making: A computer-based System of Interactive Guidance and Information (SIGI). *Proceedings of the 1973 Invitational Conference on Testing Problems.* Princeton, N.J.: Educational Testing Service, 1974. Pp. 43–69.

KAUFMAN, A. S. Piaget and Gesell: A psychometric analysis of tests built from their tasks. *Child Development,* 1971, *42,* 1341–1360.

KAUFMAN, A. S. A short form of the Wechsler Preschool and Primary Scale of Intelligence. *Journal of Consulting and Clinical Psychology,* 1972, *39,* 361–369.

KAUFMAN, A. S. Comparison of the WPPSI, Stanford-Binet, and McCarthy scales as predictors of first-grade achievement. *Perceptual and Motor Skills,* 1973, *36,* 67–73. (a)

KAUFMAN, A. S. The relationship of WPPSI IQs to SES and other background variables. *Journal of Clinical Psychology,* 1973, *29,* 354–357. (b)

KAUFMAN, A. S. Factor analysis of the WISC-R at eleven age levels between 6½ and 16½ years. *Journal of Counseling and Clinical Psychology,* 1975, *43,* 135–147. (a)

KAUFMAN, A. S. Factor structure of the McCarthy scales at five age levels between 2½ and 8½. *Educational and Psychological Measurement,* 1975, *35,* 641–656. (b)

KAUFMAN, A. S. *Intelligent testing with the WISC-R.* New York: Wiley, 1979.

KAUFMAN, A. S., & HOLLENBECK, G. P. Factor analysis of the standardization edition of the McCarthy scales. *Journal of Clinical Psychology,* 1973, *29,* 358–362.

KAUFMAN, A. S., & HOLLENBECK, G. P. Comparative structure of the WPPSI for blacks and whites. *Journal of Clinical Psychology,* 1974, *30,* 316–319.

KAUFMAN, A. S., & KAUFMAN, N. L. Tests built from Piaget's and Gesell's tasks as predictors of first-grade achievement. *Child Development,* 1972, *43,* 521–535.

KAUFMAN, A. S., & KAUFMAN, N. L. Black–white differences at ages 2½–8½ on the McCarthy Scales fo Children's Abilities. *Journal of School Psychology,* 1973, *11,* 196–206. (a)

KAUFMAN, A. S., & KAUFMAN, N. L. Sex differences on the McCarthy Scales of Children's Abilities. *Journal of Clinical Psychology,* 1973, *29,* 362–365. (b)

KAUFMAN, A. S., & KAUFMAN, N. L. Social class differences on the McCarthy scales for black and white children. *Perceptual and Motor Skills,* 1975, *41,* 205–206.

KAUFMAN, A. S., & KAUFMAN, N. L. *Clinical evaluation of young children with the McCarthy scales.* New York: Grune & Stratton, 1977.

KAUFMAN, A. S., & WATERSTREET, M. A. Determining a child's strong and weak areas of functioning on the Stanford-Binet: A simplification of Sattler's *SD* method. *Journal of School Psychology,* 1978, *16,* 72–78.

KAVRUCK, S. Thirty-three years of test research: A short history of test development in the U.S. Civil Service Commission. *American Psychologist,* 1956, *11,* 329–333.

KELLEY, T. L. *Interpretation of educational measurements.* Yonkers, N.Y.: World Book Co., 1927.

KELLEY, T. L. *Crossroads in the mind of man: A study of differentiable mental abilities.* Stanford, Calif.: Stanford University Press, 1928.

KELLEY, T. L. *Essential traits of mental life.* Cambridge, Mass.: Harvard University Press, 1935.

KELLEY, T. L. The selection of upper and lower groups for the validation of test items. *Journal of Educational Psychology,* 1939, *30,* 17–24.

KELLEY, T. L. Cumulative significance of a number of independent experiments: Reply to A. E. Traxler and R. N. Hilkert. *School and Society,* 1943, *57,* 482–484.

KELLY, G. A. *The psychology of personal constructs.* New York: Norton, 1955.

KELLY, G. A. *A theory of personality.* New York: Norton, 1963.

KELLY, G. A. A summary statement of a cognitively-oriented comprehensive theory of behavior. In J. C. Mancuso (Ed.), *Readings for a cognitive theory of personality.* New York: Holt, Rinehart & Winston, 1970. Pp. 27–58.

KELLY, J. A., & WORELL, J. New formulations of sex roles and androgyny: A critical review. *Journal of Consulting and Clinical Psychology,* 1977, *45,* 1101–1115.

KELZ, J. W. The development and evaluation of a measure of counselor effectiveness. *Personnel and Guidance Journal,* 1966, *44,* 511–516.

KENDALL, P. C., FINCH, A. J., LITTLE, V. L., CHIRICO, B. M., & OLLENDICK, T. H. Variations in a construct: Quantitative and qualitative differences in children's locus of control. *Journal of Consulting and Clinical Psychology,* 1978, *46,* 590–592.

KENNEDY, W. A., et al. The ceiling of the new Stanford-Binet. *Journal of Clinical Psychology,* 1960, *17,* 284–286.

KENNEDY, W. A., VAN DE REIT, V., & WHITE, J. C. A normative sample of intelligence and achievement of Negro elementary schoolchildren in the southeastern United States. *Monographs of the Society for Research in Child Development,* 1963, *28*(6, Serial No. 90).

KENT, G. H., & ROSANOFF, A. J. A study of association in insanity. *American Journal of Insanity,* 1910, *67,* 37–96; 317–390.

KENT, R. N., & FOSTER, S. L. Direct observational procedures: Methodological issues in naturalistic settings. In A. R. Ciminero, K. S. Calhoun, & H. E. Adams (Eds.), *Handbook of behavioral assessment.* New York: Wiley, 1977, Ch. 9.

KHAN, S. B. Development of mental abilities: An investigation of the "differentiation hypothesis." *Canadian Journal of Psychology,* 1970, *24,* 199–205.

KHAN, S. B. Learning and the development of verbal ability. *American Educational Research Journal,* 1972, *9,* 607–614.

KIM, J.-O., & MUELLER, C. W. *Introduction to factor analysis: What it is and how to do it (Quantitative applications in the social sciences,* No. 13). Beverly Hills, Calif.: Sage, 1978. (a)

KIM, J.-O., & MUELLER, C. W. *Factor analysis: Statistical methods and practical issues (Quantitative applications in the social sciences,* No. 14). Beverly Hills, Calif.: Sage, 1978. (b)

KING, L. M., HUNTER, J. E., & SCHMIDT, F. L. Halo in a multidimensional forced-choice performance evaluation scale. *Journal of Applied Psychology,* 1980, *65,* 507–516.

KING, W. L., & SEEGMILLER, B. Performance of 14- to 22-month-old black, first-born male infants on two tests of cognitive development. The Bayley Scales and the Infant Psychological Development Scale. *Developmental Psychology,* 1973, *8,* 317–326.

KINSLINGER, H. J. Application of projective techniques in personnel psychology since 1940. *Psychological Bulletin,* 1966, *66,* 134–149.

KIRCHNER, W. K. A note on the effect of privacy in taking typing tests. *Journal of Applied Psychology,* 1966, *50,* 373–374.

KIRK, S. A., & KIRK, W. D. *Psycholinguistic learning disabilities: Diagnosis and remediation.* Urbana, Ill.: University of Illinois Press, 1971.

KIRKPATRICK, J. J., EWEN, R. B., BARRETT, R. S., & KATZELL, R. A. *Testing and fair employment.* New York: New York University Press, 1968.

KJERULFF, K., & WIGGINS, N. H. Graduate student styles for coping with stressful situations. *Journal of Educational Psychology,* 1976, *68,* 247–254.

KLAUS, R. A., & GRAY, S. W. The early training project for disadvantaged children: A report after five years. *Monographs of the Society for Research in Child Development,* 1968, *33*(4, Serial No. 120).

KLEINMUNTZ, B. The computer as clinician. *American Psychologist,* 1975, *30,* 379–387.

KLINEBERG, O. An experimental study of speed and other factors in "racial" differences. *Archives of Psychology,* 1928, No. 93.

KLINGER, E. Fantasy need achievement as a motivational construct. *Psychological Bulletin,* 1966, *66,* 291–308.

KLOPFER, W. G. *The psychological report: Use and communication of psychological findings.* New York: Grune & Stratton, 1960.

KLOPFER, W. G., & TAULBEE, E. S. Projective tests. *Annual Review of Psychology,* 1976, *27,* 543–568.

KNAPP, R. R. The effects of time limits on the intelligence test performance of Mexican and American subjects. *Journal of Educational Psychology,* 1960, *51,* 14–20.

KNOBLOCH, H., & PASAMANICK, B. An evaluation of the consistency and predictive value of the 40-week Gesell Developmental Schedule. *Psychiatric Research Reports,* 1960, *13,* 10–41.

KNOBLOCH, H., & PASAMANICK, B. Predicting intellectual potential in infancy. *American Journal of Diseases of Children,* 1963, *106,* 43–51.

KNOBLOCH, H., & PASAMANICK, B. Prospective studies on the epidemiology of reproductive casualty: Methods, findings, and some implications. *Merrill-Palmer Quarterly,* 1966, *12,* 27–43.

KNOBLOCH, H., & PASAMANICK, B. Prediction from the assessment of neuromotor and intellectual status in infancy. In *Psychopathology of mental development.* New York: Grune & Stratton, 1967.

KNOBLOCH, H., & PASAMANICK, B. (Eds.). *Gesell and Amatruda's developmental diagnosis* (3rd ed.). Hagerstown, Md.: Harper & Row, 1974.

KNOELL, D. M., & HARRIS, C. W. A factor analysis of spelling ability. *Journal of Educational Research*, 1952, *46*, 95–111.

KOCH, H. L. *Twins and twin relations*. Chicago: University of Chicago Press, 1966.

KOGAN, N. *Cognitive styles in infancy and early childhood*. Hillsdale, N.J.: Erlbaum, 1976.

KOHLBERG, L. Stage and sequence: The cognitive-developmental approach to socialization. In D. Goslin (Ed.), *Handbook of socialization: Theory and research*. Chicago: Rand McNally, 1969.

KOHLBERG, L. The development of moral stages: Uses and abuses. *Proceedings, 1973 Invitational Conference on Testing Problems, Educational Testing Service*, 1974, 1–8.

KOPPITZ, E. M. *The Bender-Gestalt Test for young children*. New York: Grune & Stratton, 1964.

KOPPITZ, E. M. *The Bender Gestalt Test for young children: Research and application, 1963–1973*. New York: Grune & Stratton, 1975.

KOTSONIS, M. E., & PATTERSON, C. J. Comprehension-monitoring skills in learning-disabled children. *Developmental Psychology*, 1980, *16*, 541–542.

KRAEPELIN, E. Über die Beeinflüssung einfacher psychischer Vorgänge durch einige Arzneimittel. Jena: Fischer, 1892.

KRAEPELIN, E. Der psychologische Versuch in der Psychiatrie. *Psychologische Arbeiten*, 1895, *1*, 1–91.

KRAUSKOPF, C. J. Review of The BITCH test. *Eighth Mental Measurements Yearbook*, 1978, Vol. I, pp. 250–251.

KREITZBERG, C. B., & JONES, D. H. *An empirical study of the Broad-Range Test of Verbal Ability* (ETS Res. Rep. 80–5). Princeton, N.J.: Educational Testing Service, May 1980.

KRUG, S. E. *Clinical Analysis Questionnaire manual*. Champaign, Ill.: Institute for Personality and Ability Testing, 1980.

KUDER, G. F. The Occupational Interest Survey. *Personnel and Guidance Journal*, 1966, *45*, 72–77.

KUDER, G. F. Some principles of interest measurement. *Educational and Psychological Measurement*, 1970, *30*, 205–226.

KUDER, G. F. *Kuder Occupational Interest Survey, Revised: General manual*. Chicago: Science Research Associates, 1979.

KUDER, G. F., & RICHARDSON, M. W. The theory of estimation of test reliability. *Psychometrika*, 1937, *2*, 151–160.

KUHLMANN, F. A revision of the Binet-Simon system for measuring the intelligence of children. *Journal of Psycho-Asthenics, Monograph Supplement*, 1912, *1*, 1–41.

KURTINES, W., & GREIF, E. B. The development of moral thought: Review and evaluation of Kohlberg's approach. *Psychological Bulletin*, 1974, *81*, 453–470.

KURTZ, A. K. A research test of the Rorschach test. *Personnel Psychology*, 1948, *1*, 41–51.

LACHAR, D., & GDOWSKI, C. L. *Actuarial assessment of child and adolescent personality: An interpretive guide for the Personality Inventory for Children profile*. Los Angeles: Western Psychological Services, 1979.

LA FAVE, L. Essay vs. multiple-choice: Which test is preferable? *Psychology in the Schools*, 1966, *3*, 65–69.

La Fave, L., Haddad, J. & Marshall, N. Humor judgments as a function of identification classes. *Sociology and Social Research*, 1974, 58, 184–194.

Landy, F. J., & Farr, J. H. Performance rating. *Psychological Bulletin*, 1980, 87, 72–107.

Landy, F. J., Vance, R. J., Barnes-Farrell, J. L., & Steele, J. W. Statistical control of halo error in performance ratings. *Journal of Applied Psychology*, 1980, 65, 501–506.

Lanyon, R. I. A free-choice version of the EPPS. *Journal of Clinical Psychology*, 1966, 22, 202–205.

Lanyon, R. I. *A handbook of MMPI group profiles.* Minneapolis: University of Minnesota Press, 1968.

Lanyon, R. I., & Goodstein, L. D. *Personality assessment.* New York: Wiley, 1982.

Laosa, L. M., Swartz, J. D., & Diaz-Guerrero, R. Perceptual-cognitive and personality development of Mexican and Anglo-American children as measured by human figure drawings. *Developmental Psychology*, 1974, 10, 131–139.

Larkin, K. C., & Weiss, D. J. *An empirical investigation of computer-administered pyramidal ability testing.* Psychometrics Methods Program, Department of Psychology, University of Minnesota, Research Report 74-3, July 1974.

Laska, E. M., & Bank, R. (Eds.). *Safeguarding psychiatric privacy: Computer systems and their uses.* New York: Wiley, 1975.

Laumann, E. O., & House, J. S. Living room styles and social attributes: The patterning of material artifacts in a modern urban community. *Sociology and Social Research*, 1970, 54, 321–342.

Laurendeau, M., & Pinard, A. *Causal thinking in the child: A genetic and experimental approach.* New York: International Universities Press, 1962.

Laurendeau, M., & Pinard, A. *The development of the concept of space in the child.* New York: International Universities Press, 1970.

Lawrence, S. W., Jr. The effects of anxiety, achievement motivation, and task importance upon performance on an intelligence test. *Journal of Educational Psychology*, 1962, 53, 150–126.

Lawshe, C. H., & Balma, M. J. *Principles of personnel testing* (2nd ed.). New York: McGraw-Hill, 1966.

Lazarus, A. A. *Multimodal behavior therapy.* New York: Springer, 1976.

Leeds, C. H. Predictive validity of the *Minnesota Teacher Attitude Inventory*. *The Journal of Teacher Education* 1969, 20(1), 51–56.

Leeds, C. H. *The predictive validity of the Minnesota Teacher Attitude Inventory.* Final Report, Project No. 1-D-019, Grant No. OEG-4-71-0050. U.S. Office of Education, September 1972.

Lefcourt, H. M. *Locus of control: Current trends in theory and research.* Hillsdale, N.J.: Erlbaum, 1976.

Lehman, P. R. *Tests and measurements in music.* Englewood Cliffs, N.J.: Prentice-Hall, 1968.

Lennon, R. T. A comparison of results of three intelligence tests. In C. I. Chase & H. G. Ludlow (Eds.), *Readings in educational and psychological measurement.* Boston: Houghton Mifflin, 1966. Pp. 198–205. (a)

Lennon, R. T. Norms: 1963. In A. Anastasi (Ed.), *Testing problems in perspective.* Washington, D.C.: American Council on Education, 1966. Pp. 243–250. (b)

LERNER, B. Washington v. Davis: Quantity, quality, and equality in employment testing. In P. B. Kurland (Ed.), *1976 Supreme Court Review*. Chicago: University of Chicago Press, 1977. Pp. 263–316.

LERNER, B. Equal protection and external screening: Davis, De Funis, and Bakke. *Proceedings of the 1977 ETS Invitational Conference*, 1978, 3–27. (a)

LERNER, B. The Supreme Court and the APA, AERA, NCME test standards: Past references and future possibilities. *American Psychologist*, 1978, *33*, 915–919. (b)

LERNER, B. Tests and standards today: Attacks, counterattacks, and responses. *New Directions for Testing and Measurement*, 1979, *3*, 15–31.

LERNER, B. Employment discrimination: Adverse impact, validity, and equality. In P. B. Kurland & G. Casper (Eds.), *1979 Supreme Court Review*. Chicago: University of Chicago Press, 1980. Pp. 17–49. (a)

LERNER, B. The war on testing: Detroit Edison in perspective. *Personnel Psychology*, 1980, *33*, 11–16. (b)

LEVINE, H. G., & McGUIRE, C. Role-playing as an evaluative technique. *Journal of Educational Measurement*, 1968, *5*, 1–8.

LEVINSON, B. M. Traditional Jewish cultural values and performance on the Wechsler tests. *Journal of Educational Psychology*, 1959, *50*, 177–181.

LEVINSON, B. M. The WAIS quotient of subcultural deviation. *Journal of Genetic Psychology*, 1963, *103*, 123–131.

LEVITT, E. E., & TRUUMAA, A. *The Rorschach technique with children and adolescents: Application and norms*. New York: Grune & Stratton, 1972.

LEVONIAN, E. A statistical analysis of the 16 Personality Factor Questionnaire. *Educational and Psychological Measurement*, 1961, *21*, 589–596.

LEWINSOHN, P. M. The behavioral study and treatment of depression. In M. Hersen, R. M. Eisler, & P. M. Miller (Eds.), *Progress in behavior modification*. New York: Academic Press, 1975. Pp. 19–64.

LEWINSOHN, P. M., & GRAF, M. Pleasant activities and depression. *Journal of Consulting and Clinical Psychology*, 1973, *41*, 261–268.

LEWIS, J. F., & MERCER, J. R. The System of Multicultural Pluralistic Assessment: SOMPA. In W. A. Coulter & H. W. Morrow (Eds.), *Adaptive behavior: Concepts and measurements*. New York: Grune & Stratton, 1978. Pp. 185–212.

LEWIS, M. Infant intelligence tests: Their use and misuse. *Human Development*, 1973, *16*, 108–118.

LEWIS, M. (Ed). *Origins of intelligence: Infancy and early childhood*. New York: Plenum, 1976. (a)

LEWIS, M. What do we mean when we say "infant intelligence scores?" A sociopolitical question. In M. Lewis (Ed.), *Origins of intelligence: Infancy and childhood*. New York: Plenum, 1976, Ch. 1. (b)

LEWIS, M., & McGURK, H. Evaluation of infant intelligence: Infant intelligence scores—true or false? *Science*, 1972, *178*(4066), 1174–1177.

LEZAK, M. D. *Neuropsychological assessment*. New York: Oxford University Press, 1976.

LIDZ, C. S. *Improving assessment of schoolchidren*. San Francisco: Jossey-Bass, 1981.

LIKERT, R. A technique for the measurement of attitudes. *Archives of Psychology*, 1932, No. 140.

LINDGREN, B. W., & McELRATH, G. W. *Introduction to probability and statistics* (3rd ed.). New York: Macmillan, 1969.

LINDSLEY, D. B. The psychology of lie detection. In G. J. Dudycha et al., *Psychology for law enforcement officers.* Springfield, Ill.: Charles C Thomas, 1955. Ch. 4.

LINDZEY, G. On the classification of projective techniques. *Psychological Bulletin,* 1959, *56*, 158–168.

LINDZEY, G. *Projective techniques and cross-cultural research.* New York: Irvington, 1977.

LINDZEY, G., & HERMAN, P. S. Thematic Apperception Test: A note on reliability and situational validity. *Journal of Projective Techniques,* 1955, *19*, 36–42.

LINN, R. L. Test bias and the prediction of grades in law school. *Journal of Legal Education,* 1975, *27*, 293–323.

LINN, R. L. Single-group validity, differential validity, and differential prediction. *Journal of Applied Psychology,* 1978, *63*, 507–512.

LINN, R. L., & PITCHER, B. *Predictor score regions with significant differences in predicted law school grades from subgroup regression equations.* Law School Admission Council Reports (LSAC 76-2), February 1976.

LINN, R. L., ROCK, D. A., & CLEARY, T. A. The development and evaluation of several programmed testing methods. *Educational and Psychological Measurement,* 1969, *29*, 129–146.

LITTELL, W. M. The Wechsler Intelligence Scale for Children: Review of a decade of research. *Psychological Bulletin,* 1960, *57*, 132–156.

LITTLE, K. B., & SHNEIDMAN, E. S. Congruencies among interpretations of psychological test and anamnestic data. *Psychological Monographs,* 1959, *73*(6, Whole No. 476).

LOEHLIN, J., LINDZEY, G., & SPUHLER, J. N. *Race differences in intelligence.* San Francisco: Freeman, 1975.

LOEVINGER, J. The meaning and measurement of ego development. *American Psychologist,* 1966, *21*, 195–206. (a)

LOEVINGER, J. A theory of test response. In A. Anastasi (Ed.), *Testing problems in perspective.* Washington, D.C.: American Council on Education, 1966. Pp. 545–556. (b)

LOEVINGER, J., & OSSORIO, A. G. Evaluation of therapy by self-report: A paradox. *American Psychologist,* 1958, *13*, 366.

LOEVINGER, J., WESSLER, R., & REDMORE, C. *Measuring ego development.* Vol. 1: *Construction and use of a sentence completion test.* Vol. 2: *Scoring manual for women and girls.* San Francisco: Jossey-Bass, 1970.

LONDON, M., & BRAY, D. W. Ethical issues in testing and evaluation for personnel decisions. *American Psychologist,* 1980, *35*, 890–901.

LONNER, W. J., & ADAMS, H. L. Interest patterns of psychologists in nine Western nations. *Journal of Applied Psychology,* 1972, *56*, 141–151.

LORD, F. M. The relation of the reliability of multiple-choice tests to the distribution of item difficulties. *Psychometrika,* 1952, *17*, 181–194.

LORD, F. M. Item characteristic curves estimated without knowledge of their mathematical form—A confrontation of Birnbaum's logistic model. *Psychometrika,* 1970, *35*, 43–50. (a)

LORD, F. M. Some test theory for tailored testing. In W. H. Holtzman (Ed.), *Computer-assisted instruction, testing, and guidance.* New York: Harper & Row, 1970. Pp. 139–183. (b)

Lord, F. M. The self-scoring flexilevel test. *Journal of Educational Measurement,* 1971, 8, 147–151. (a)

Lord, F. M. A theoretical study of the measurement effectiveness of flexilevel tests. *Educational and Psychological Measurement* 1971, 31, 805–813, (b)

Lord, F. M. A theoretical study of two-stage testing. *Psychometrika,* 1971, 36, 227–241. (c)

Lord, F. M. Test theory and the public interest. *Proceedings of the 1976 ETS Invitational Conference,* 1976, 17–30.

Lord, F. M. *Applications of item response theory to practical testing problems.* Hillsdale, N.J.: Erlbaum, 1980.

Loret, P. G., Seder, A., Bianchini, J. C., & Vale, C. A. *Anchor Test Study: Equivalence and norms tables for selected reading achievement tests.* Washington, D.C.: U.S. Government Printing Office, 1974.

Loretan, J. O. Alternatives to intelligence testing. *Proceedings of the 1965 Invitational Conference on Testing Problems, Educational Testing Service,* 1966, 19–30.

Lorge, I. Schooling makes a difference. *Teachers College Record,* 1945, 46, 483–492.

Lotsof, E. J. Intelligence, verbal fluency, and the Rorschach test. *Journal of Consulting Psychology,* 1953, 17, 21–24.

Luborsky, L. B., & Cattell, R. B. The validation of personality factors in humor. *Journal of Personality,* 1947, 15, 283–291.

Luria, A. R. *The working brain.* New York: Basic, 1973.

Machover, K. *Personality projection in the drawing of the human figure: A method of personality investigation.* Springfield, Ill.: Charles C Thomas, 1949.

MacKinnon, D. W. The nature and nurture of creative talent. *American Psychologist,* 1962, 17, 484–495.

MacPhillamy, D. J., & Lewinsohn, P. M. Depression as a function of levels of desired and obtained pleasure. *Journal of Abnormal Psychology,* 1974, 83, 651–657.

MacPhillamy, D. J., & Lewinsohn, P. M. *Manual for the Pleasant Events Schedule.* Eugene, Ore.: Authors, 1976. (Available from P. M. Lewinsohn, Department of Psychology, University of Oregon, Eugene, Ore. 97403.)

Mahoney, M. J. *Cognition and behavior modification.* Cambridge, Mass.: Ballinger, 1974.

Mahoney, M. J. Reflections on the cognitive-learning trend in psychotherapy. *American Psychologist,* 1977, 32, 5–12.

Maier, M. H. *Effects of educational level on prediction of training success with the ACB.* U.S. Army Research Institute for the Behavioral and Social Sciences. Technical Research Note 225, June 1972.

Maier, M. H.. & Fuchs, E. F. *Development and evaluation of a new ACB and aptitude area system.* U.S. Army Research Institute for the Behavioral and Social Sciences, Technical Research Note 239, September 1972.

Maier, M. H., & Fuchs, E. F. *Effectiveness of selection and classification testing.* U.S. Army Research Institute for the Behavioral and Social Sciences. Research Report 1179, September 1973.

Maier, M. H., & Hirshfeld, S. F. *Criterion-referenced job proficiency testing: A large scale application.* U.S. Army Research Institute for the Behavioral and Social Sciences, Research Report 1193, February 1978.

MALONEY, M. P., & WARD, M. P. Ecology: Let's hear from the people: An objective scale for the measurement of ecological attitudes and knowledge. *American Psychologist,* 1973, *28,* 583–586.

MALONEY, M. P., WARD, M. P., & BRAUCHT, G. N. A revised scale for the measurement of ecological attitudes and knowledge. *American Psychologist,* 1975, *30,* 787–790.

MANDLER, G., & SARASON, S. B. A study of anxiety and learning. *Journal of Abnormal and Social Psychology,* 1952, *47,* 166–173.

MARJORIBANKS, K. Environment, social class, and mental abilities. *Journal of Educational Psychology,* 1972, *63,* 103–109.

MARJORIBANKS, K. Another view of the relation of environment to mental abilities. *Journal of Educational Psychology,* 1974, *66,* 460–463.

MARKS, P. A., SEEMAN, W., & HALLER, D. L. *The actuarial use of the MMPI with adolescents and adults.* Baltimore: Williams & Wilkins, 1974.

MASLING, J. The effects of warm and cold interaction on the administration and scoring of an intelligence test. *Journal of Consulting Psychology,* 1959, *23,* 336–341.

MASLING, J. The influence of situational and interpersonal variables in projective testing. *Psychological Bulletin,* 1960, *57,* 65–85.

MASLING, J. Differential indoctrination of examiners and Rorschach responses. *Journal of Consulting Psychology,* 1965, *29,* 198–201.

MASTERSON, S. The adjective checklist technique: A review and critique. In P. McReynolds (Ed.), *Advances in psychological assessment* (Vol. 4). San Francisco: Jossey-Bass, 1975. Ch. 7.

MATARAZZO, J. D. *Wechsler's measurement and appraisal of adult intelligence* (5th ed.). Baltimore: Williams & Wilkins, 1972.

MATARAZZO, J. D., & WIENS, A. N. *The interview: Research on its anatomy and structure.* Chicago: Aldine, 1972.

MAXFIELD, K. B., & BUCHHOLZ, S. *A social maturity scale for blind preschool children: A guide to its use.* New York: American Foundation for the Blind, 1957.

McBRIDE, J. R. *Adaptive mental testing: The state of the art* (Tech. Rep. 423). Alexandria, Va.: U.S. Army Research Institute for the Behavioral and Social Sciences, November 1979

McCALL, R. B. Toward an epigenetic conception of mental development in the first three years of life. In M. Lewis (Ed.), *Origins of intelligence: Infancy early childhood.* New York: Plenum, 1976. Ch. 4.

McCALL, R. B., APPELBAUM, M. I., & HOGARTY, P. S. Developmental changes in mental performance. *Monographs of the Society for Research in Child Development,* 1973, *38*(3, Serial No. 150).

McCALL, R. B., HOGARTY, P. S., & HURLBURT, N. Transitions in infant sensorimotor development and the prediction of childhood IQ. *American Psychologist,* 1972, *27,* 728–748.

McCALL, W. A. *How to measure in education.* New York: Macmillan, 1922.

McCARTHY, D. A study of the reliability of the Goodenough drawing test of intelligence. *Journal of Psychology,* 1944, *18,* 201–216.

McCLELLAND, D. C. Longitudinal trends in the relation of thought to action. *Journal of Consulting Psychology,* 1966, *30,* 479–483.

McCLELLAND, D. C. *The achieving society.* New York: Irvington, 1976.

McClelland, D. C., Atkinson, J. W., Clark, R. A., & Lowell, E. L. *The achievement motive*. New York: Irvington, 1976.

McCormick, E. J. Application of job analysis to indirect validity. *Personnel Psychology*, 1959, *12*, 395–420.

McCormick, E. J. Job and task analysis. In M. D. Dunnette (Ed.), *Handbook of industrial and organizational psychology*. Chicago: Rand McNally, 1976. Ch. 15.

McCormick, E. J. *Job analysis: Methods and applications*. New York: Amacom, 1979.

McCormick, E. J., & Ilgen, D. *Industrial psychology* (7th ed.). Englewood Cliffs, N.J.: Prentice-Hall, 1980.

McCormick, E. J., Jeanneret, P. R., & Meacham, R. C. A study of job characteristics and job dimensions as based on the Position Analysis Questionnaire (PAQ). *Journal of Applied Psychology*, 1972, 56, 347–368.

McFall, R. M., & Lillesand, D. B. Behavior rehearsal with modeling and coaching in assertion training. *Journal of Abnormal Psychology*, 1971, 77, 313–323.

McFall, R. M., & Twentyman, C. T. Four experiments on the relative contributions of rehearsal, modeling. and coaching to assertion training. *Journal of Abnormal Psychology*, 1973, *81*, 199–218.

McGee, M. G. Human spatial abilities: Psychometric studies and environmental, genetic, hormonal, and neurological influences. *Psychological Bulletin*, 1979, *86*, 889–918.

McKechnie, G. E. *ERI manual: Environmental Response Inventory*. Palo Alto, Calif.: Consulting Psychologists Press, 1974.

McKechnie, G. E. *Manual for the Leisure Activities Blank*. Palo Alto, Calif.: Consulting Psychologists Press, 1975.

McKechnie, G. E. Environmental dispositions: Concepts and measures. In P. McReynolds (Ed.), *Advances in psychological assessment*. San Francisco: Jossey-Bass, 1977. Ch. 4.

McKee, J. H. Subjective and (or versus) objective. *English Journal (College Edition)*, 1934, *23*, 127–133.

McKillip, R. H., & Wing, H. Application of a construct model in assessment for employment. In *Construct validity in psychological measurement: Proceedings of a colloquium on theory and application in education and employment*. Princeton, N.J.: Educational Testing Service, 1980.

McLeish, J. The validation of Seashore's measures of musical talent by factorial methods. *British Journal of Psychology, Statistical Section*, 1950, *3*, 129–140.

McNemar, Q. *The revision of the Stanford-Binet Scale: An analysis of the standardization data*. Boston: Houghton Mifflin, 1942.

McReynolds, P. (Ed.). *Advances in psychological assessment*. Palo Alto, Calif.: Science and Behavior Books. Vol. 1, 1968; Vol. 2, 1971.

McReynolds, P. (Ed.). *Advances in psychological assessment*. San Francisco: Jossey-Bass. Vol. 3, 1975; Vol. 4, 1978; Vol. 5, 1981.

McReynolds, P. The case for interactional assessment. *Behavioral Assessment*, 1979, *1*, 237–247.

McReynolds, P., & DeVoge, S. Use of improvisational techniques in assessment. In P. McReynolds (Ed.), *Advances in psychological assessment* (Vol. 4). San Francisco: Jossey-Bass, 1978. Ch. 6.

MEEHL, P. E. An investigation of a general normality or control factor in personality testing. *Psychological Monographs*, 1945, 59(4, Whole No. 274).

MEEHL, P. E. *Clinical versus statistical prediction: A theoretical analysis and a review of the evidence*. Minneapolis: University of Minnesota Press, 1954.

MEEHL, P. E. When shall we use our heads instead of the formula? *Journal of Counseling Psychology*, 1957, 4, 268–273.

MEEHL, P. E. Seer over sign: The first good example. *Journal of Experimental Research in Personality*, 1965, 1, 27–32.

MEEHL, P. E., & ROSEN, A. Antecedent probability and the efficiency of psychometric signs, patterns, or cutting scores. *Psychological Bulletin*, 1955, 52, 194–216.

MEEKER, M. N. *The structure of intellect: Its interpretation and uses*. Columbus: Charles E. Merrill, 1969.

MEGARGEE, E. I. The relation of response length to the Holtzman Inkblot Technique. *Journal of Consulting Psychology*, 1966, 30, 415–419.

MEGARGEE, E. I. *The California Psychological Inventory handbook*. San Francisco, Calif.: Jossey-Bass, 1972.

MEGARGEE, E. I., & PARKER, C. V. An exploration of the equivalence of Murrayan needs as assessed by the Adjective Check List, the TAT, and the Edwards Personal Preference Schedule. *Journal of Clinical Psychology*, 1968, 24, 47–51.

MEIER, N. C. *Art in human affairs*. New York: McGraw-Hill, 1942.

MELTON, A. W. (Ed.). *Apparatus tests*. (AAF Aviation Psychology Program, Research Reports. Rep. No. 4.) Washington, D.C.: U.S. Government Printing Office, 1947.

MENASCO, M. B., & CURRY, D. J. An assessment of the Role Construct Repertory Test. *Applied Psychological Measurement*, 1978, 2, 361–369.

MENNE, J. W., McCARTHY, W., & MENNE, J. A systems approach to the content validation of employee selection procedures. *Public Personnel Management*, 1976, 5, 387–396.

MERCER, J. R. *Labeling the mentally retarded*. Berkeley: University of California Press, 1973.

MERCER, J. R. Theoretical constructs of adaptive behavior: Movement from a medical to a social-ecological perspective. In W. A. Coulter & H. W. Morrow (Eds.), *Adaptive behavior: Concepts and measurements*. New York: Grune & Stratton, 1978. Pp. 59–82.

MERCER, J. R. *System of Multicultural Pluralistic Assessment (SOMPA): Technical manual*. New York: Psychological Corporation, 1979.

MERCER, J. R., & LEWIS, J. F. *System of Multicultural Pluralistic Assessment (SOMPA)*. New York: Psychological Corporation, 1978.

MESSER, S. B. Reflection-impulsivity: A review. *Psychological Bulletin*, 1976, 83, 1026–1052.

MESSICK, S. The criterion problem in the evaluation of instruction: Assessing possible, not just intended outcomes. In M. C. Wittrock & D. E. Wiley (Eds.), *The evaluation of instruction: Issues and problems*. New York: Holt, Rinehart & Winston, 1970. Pp. 183–202.

MESSICK, S. The context of assessment and the assessment of context. In *CIRCUS: Comprehensive assessment in nursery school and kindergarten*. (Proceedings of a symposium presented at the meeting of the American Psychological Association, Montreal, August 1973). Princeton, N.J.: Educational Testing Service, 1973. Pp. 33–38.

MESSICK, S. The standard problem: Meaning and values in measurement and evaluation. *American Psychologist*, 1975, *30*, 955–966.

MESSICK, S. *The effectiveness of coaching for the SAT: Review and reanalysis of research from the fifties to the FTC.* Princeton, N.J.: Educational Testing Service, 1980. (a)

MESSICK, S. Test validity and the ethics of assessment. *American Psychologist*, 1980, *35*, 1012–1027. (b).

MESSICK, S., and associates. *Individuality in learning.* San Francisco: Jossey-Bass, 1976.

MESSICK, S., & KOGAN, N. Personality consistencies in judgment: Dimensions of role construct. *Multivariate Behavioral Research*, 1966, *1*, 165–175.

MEYER, V., LIDDELL, A., & LYONS, M. Behavioral interviews. In A. R. Ciminero, K. S. Calhoun, & H. E. Adams (Eds.), *Handbook of behavioral assessment.* New York: Wiley, 1977. Ch. 5.

MIKLICH, D. R. Radio telemetry in clinical psychology and related areas. *American Psychologist*, 1975, *30*, 419–425.

MILGRAM, N. A. IQ constancy in disadvantaged Negro children. *Psychological Reports*, 1971, *29*, 319–326.

MILLER, H. G., WILLIAMS, R. G., & HALADYNA, T. M. *Beyond facts: Objective ways to measure thinking.* Englewood Cliffs, N.J.: Educational Technology, 1978.

MILLER, R. J. Cross-cultural research in the perception of pictorial materials. *Psychological Bulletin*, 1973, *80*, 135–150.

MILLMAN, J. *Determining test length* (Technical Paper No. 5). Los Angeles: Instructional Objectives Exchange. 1972.

MILLMAN, J. Passing scores and test lengths for domain-referenced measures. *Review of Educational Research*, 1973, *43*, 205–216.

MILLMAN, J. Criterion-referenced measurement. In M. W. Apple & M. J. Subkoviak, *Educational evaluation: Analysis and responsibility.* Berkeley, Calif.: McCutchan, 1974. Ch. 6.

MILLMAN, J., BISHOP, C. H., & EBEL, R. An analysis of test-wiseness. *Educational and Psychological Measurement*, 1965, *25*, 707–726.

MILLON, T. *Millon Clinical Multiaxial Inventory: Manual.* Minneapolis: NCS Interpretive Scoring Systems, 1977.

MILLON, T., GREEN, C. J., & MEAGHER, R. B., JR. The MBHI: A new inventory for the psychodiagnostician in medical settings. *Professional Psychology*, 1979, *10*, 529–539. (a)

MILLON, T., GREEN, C. J., & MEAGHER, R. B., JR. *Millon Behavioral Health Inventory: Manual.* Miami, Fla.: Clinical Assessment Systems, 1979. (b)

MILLS, R. B. Simulated stress in police recruit selection. *Journal of Police Science and Administration*, 1976, *4*, 179–186.

MISCHEL, W. *Personality and assessment.* New York: Wiley, 1968.

MISCHEL, W. Continuity and change in personality. *American Psychologist*, 1969, *24*, 1012–1018.

MISCHEL, W. Toward a cognitive social learning reconceptualization of personality. *Psychological Review*, 1973, *80*, 252–283.

MISCHEL, W. On the future of personality measurement. *American Psychologist*, 1977, *32*, 246–254.

MISCHEL, W. On the interface of cognition and personality: Beyond the person-situation debate. *American Psychologist*, 1979, *34*, 740–754.

MISCHEL, W., ZEISS, R., & ZEISS, A. Internal-external control and persistence: Validation and implications of the Stanford preschool internal-external scale. *Journal of Personality and Social Psychology,* 1974, *29,* 265–278.

MITCHELL, B. C. Predictive validity of the Metropolitan Readiness Tests and the Murphy-Durrell Reading Readiness Analysis for white and Negro pupils. *Educational and Psychological Measurement,* 1967, *27,* 1047–1054.

MOLLENKOPF, W. G. An experimental study of the effects on item-analysis data of changing item placement and test time limit. *Psychometrika,* 1950, *15,* 291–317. (a)

MOLLENKOPF, W. G. Predicted differences and differences between predictions. *Psychometrika,* 1950, *15,* 409–417. (b)

MOOS, R. H. Conceptualizations of human environments. *American Psychologist,* 1973, *28,* 652–663.

MOOS, R. H. *Evaluating treatment environments: A social ecological approach.* New York: Wiley, 1974. (a)

MOOS, R. H. *The Social Climate Scales: An overview.* Palo Alto, Calif.: Consulting Psychologists Press, 1974. (b)

MOOS, R. H. Assessment and impact of social climate. In P. McReynolds (Ed.), *Advances in psychological assessment* (Vol. 3). San Francisco: Jossey-Bass, 1975. Ch. 1. (a)

MOOS, R. H. *Evaluating correctional environments: With implications for community settings.* New York: Wiley, 1975. (b)

MOOS, R. H. *The human context: Environmental determinants of behavior.* New York: Wiley, 1976.

MORENO, J. L. *Who shall survive? Foundations of sociometry, group psychotherapy, and sociodrama* (2nd ed.). Beacon, N.Y.: Beacon House, 1953. (*Sociometry Monographs,* No. 29.)

MORIARTY, A. E. Children's ways of coping with the intelligence test. *Menninger Clinic Bulletin,* 1960, *24,* 115–127.

MORIARTY, A. E. Coping patterns of preschool children in response to intelligence test demands. *Genetic Psychology Monographs,* 1961, *64,* 3–127.

MORIARTY, A. E. *Constancy and IQ change: A clinical view of relationships between tested intelligence and personality.* Springfield, Ill.: Charles C Thomas, 1966.

MORROW, R. S. An analysis of the relations among tests of musical, artistic, and mechanical abilities. *Journal of Psychology,* 1938, *5,* 253–263.

MOWRER, O. H. "Q-technique"—Description, history, and critique. In O. H. Mowrer (Ed.), *Psychotherapy theory and research.* New York: Ronald, 1953. Pp. 316–375.

MURPHY, G., & KOVACH, J. K. *Historical introduction to modern psychology* (3rd ed.). New York: Harcourt Brace Jovanovich, 1972.

MURRAY, H. A., et al. *Explorations in personality.* New York: Oxford University Press, 1938.

MURRAY, H. A., & MACKINNON, D. W. Assessment of OSS personnel. *Journal of Consulting Psychology,* 1946, *10,* 76–80.

MURSTEIN, B. I. *Theory and research in projective techniques (emphasizing the TAT).* New York: Wiley, 1963.

MURSTEIN, B. I. Normative written TAT responses for a college sample. *Journal of Personality Assessment,* 1972, *36,* 213–217.

MUSSEN, P. H., & NAYLOR, H. K. The relationships between overt and fantasy aggression. *Journal of Abnormal and Social Psychology*, 1954, 49, 235–240.

NAY, W. R. *Multimethod clinical assessment*. New York: Gardner Press, 1979.

NAYLOR, J. C., & SHINE, L. C. A table for determining the increase in mean criterion score obtained by using a selection device. *Journal of Industrial Psychology*, 1965, 3, 33–42.

NEISSER, U. General, academic, and artificial intelligence. In L. B. Resnick (Ed.), *The nature of intelligence*. Hillsdale, N.J.: Erlbaum, 1976. Ch. 7.

NEISSER, U. The concept of intelligence. *Intelligence*, 1979, 3, 217–227.

NESSELROADE, J. R., & REESE, H. W. (Eds.). *Life-span developmental psychology: Methodological issues*. New York: Academic Press, 1973.

NICHOLS, J. G. Quality and equality in intellectual development: The role of motivation in education. *American Psychologist*, 1979, 34, 1071–1084.

NICHOLS, P. L., & BROMAN, S. H. Familial resemblance in infant mental development. *Developmental Psychology*, 1974. 10, 442–446.

NISBET, J. D. Symposium: Contributions to intelligence testing and the theory of intelligence: IV. Intelligence and age: Retesting with twenty-four years' interval. *British Journal of Educational Psychology*, 1957, 27, 190–198.

NORMAN, R. D. A revised deterioration formula for the Wechsler Adult Intelligence Scale. *Journal of Clinical Psychology*, 1966, 22, 287–294.

NOVACO, R. W. *Anger control*. Lexington, Mass.: Lexington Books, 1975.

NOVICK, M. R., & ELLIS, D. D., JR. Equal opportunity in educational and employment selection. *American Psychologist*, 1977, 32, 306–320.

NOVICK, M. R., & JACKSON, P. H. *Statistical methods for educational and psychological research*. New York: McGraw-Hill. 1974.

NOVICK, M. R., & LEWIS, C. Coefficient alpha and the reliability of composite measurements. *Psychometrika*, 1967, 32, 1–13.

NOWICKI, S., JR., & DUKE, M. P. A preschool and primary internal-external control scale. *Developmental Psychology*, 1974, 10, 874–880.

NOWICKI, S., JR., & DUKE, M. P. Preschool and primary locus of control scale: A reply. *Developmental Psychology*, 1979, 15, 325–328.

OEHRN, A. *Experimentelle Studien zur Individualpsychologie*. Dorpater disser., 1889. (Also in *Psychologische Arbeiten*, 1895, 1, 95–152.)

OLES, H. J., & DAVIS, G. D. Publishers violate APA standards on test distribution. *Psychological Reports*, 1977, 41, 713–714.

OLTON, R. M., & CRUTCHFIELD, R. S, Developing the skills of productive thinking. In P. H. Mussen, J. Langer, & M. Covington (Eds.), *Trends and issues in developmental psychology*. New York: Holt, Rinehart & Winston, 1969.

OOSTERHOF, A. C. Similarity of various item discrimination indices. *Journal of Educational Measurement*, 1976, 13, 145–150.

ORTAR, G. Is a verbal test cross-cultural? *Scripta Hierosolymitana* (Hebrew University, Jerusalem), 1963, 13, 219–235.

ORTAR, G. Some principles for adaptation of psychological tests. In L. J. Cronbach & P. J. D. Drenth (Eds.), *Mental tests and cultural adaptation*. The Hague: Mouton, 1972. Pp. 111–120.

OSGOOD, C. E., SUCI, G. J., & TANNENBAUM, P. H. *The measurement of meaning*. Urbana, Ill.: University of Illinois Press, 1957.

OSIPOV, S. H. *Theories of career development* (2nd ed.). New York: Appleton-Century-Crofts, 1973.

OSS Assessment Staff. *Assessment of men: Selection of personnel for the Office of Strategic Services.* New York: Rinehart, 1948.

Owens, W. A. Age and mental abilities: A longitudinal study. *Genetic Psychology Monographs,* 1953, *48,* 3–54.

Owens, W. A. Age and mental abilities: A second adult follow-up. *Journal of Educational Psychology,* 1966, 57, 311–325.

Owens, W. A. Toward one discipline of scientific psychology. *American Psychologist,* 1968, *23,* 782–785.

Owens, W. A. Background data. In M. D. Dunnette (Ed.), *Handbook of industrial and organizational psychology.* Chicago: Rand McNally, 1976. Ch. 14.

Owens, W. A., & Schoenfeldt, L. F. Toward a classification of persons. *Journal of Applied Psychology Monograph,* 1979, *65,* 569–607.

Owings, R. A., Petersen, G. A., Bransford, J. D., Morris, C. D., & Stein, B. S. Spontaneous monitoring and regulation of learning: A comparison of successful and less successful fifth graders. *Journal of Educational Psychology,* 1980, *72,* 250–256.

Palermo, D. S., & Jenkins, J. J. Frequency of superordinate responses to a word association test as a function of age. *Journal of Verbal Learning and Verbal Behavior,* 1963, *1,* 378–383.

Palmer, J. O. *The psychological assessment of children.* New York: Wiley, 1970.

Palmore, E. (Ed.). *Normal aging.* Durham, N.C.: Duke University Press, 1970.

Panell, R. C., & Laabs, G. J. Construction of a criterion-referenced, diagnostic test for an individualized instruction program. *Journal of Applied Psychology,* 1979, *64,* 255–261.

Paraskevopoulos, J., & Hunt, J. McV. Object construction and imitation under differing conditions of rearing. *Journal of Genetic Psychology,* 1971, *119,* 301–321.

Pasamanick, B., & Knobloch, H. Retrospective studies on the epidemiology of reproductive casualty: Old and new. *Merrill-Palmer Quarterly,* 1966, *12,* 7–26.

Pascal, G. R., & Suttell, B. J. *The Bender-Gestalt Test: Quantification and validity for adults.* New York: Grune & Stratton, 1951.

Passini, F. T., & Norman, W. T. A universal conception of personality structure. *Journal of Personality and Social Psychology,* 1966, *4,* 44–49.

Paul, G. L., & Eriksen, C. W. Effects of test anxiety on "real-life" examinations. *Journal of Personality,* 1964, *32,* 480–494.

Payne, J. E., Mercer, C. D., Payne, A., & Davison, R. G. *Head Start: A tragicomedy with epilogue.* New York: Behavioral Publications, 1973.

Pearlman, K. Job families: A review and discussion of their implications for personnel selection. *Psychological Bulletin,* 1980, *87,* 1–28.

Pearlman, K., Schmidt, F. L., & Hunter, J. E. Validity generalization results for tests used to predict job proficiency and training success in clerical occupations. *Journal of Applied Psychology,* 1980, *65,* 373–406.

Pearson, K. On lines and planes of closest fit to systems of points in space. *Philosophical Magazine, Series 6,* 1901, *2,* 559–572.

Peel, E. A. A note on practice effects in intelligence tests. *British Journal of Educational Psychology,* 1951, *21,* 122–125.

Peel, E. A. Practice effects between three consecutive tests of intelligence. *British Journal of Educational Psychology,* 1952, *22,* 196–199.

Peleg, R., & Adler, C. Compensatory education in Israel: Conceptions, attitudes, and trends. *American Psychologist,* 1977, *32,* 945–958.

Pellegrino, J. W., & Glaser, R. Cognitive correlates and components in the analysis of individual differences. *Intelligence,* 1979, *3,* 187–214.

Pemberton, C. L. The closure factors related to temperament. *Journal of Personality,* 1952, *21,* 159–175.

Petersen, N. S. *An expected utility model for "optimal" selection.* American College Testing Program, Technical Bulletin. No. 24, 1974.

Petersen, N. S., & Novick, M. R. An evaluation of some models for culture-fair selection. *Journal of Educational Measurement,* 1976, *13,* 3–29.

Peterson, D. *The clinical study of social behavior.* New York: Appleton-Century-Crofts, 1968.

Peterson, J. *Early conceptions and tests of intelligence.* Yonkers, N.Y.: World Book Co., 1926.

Phares, E. J. *Locus of control and personality.* Morristown, N.J.: General Learning Press, 1976.

Philippe, J. Jastrow—exposition d'anthropologie de Chicago—testes psychologiques. etc. *Année psychologique,* 1894, *1,* 522–526.

Pietrofesa, J. J. & Splete, H. *Career development: Theory and research.* New York: Grune & Stratton, 1975.

Pike, L. W., & Evans, F. R. Effects of special instruction for three kinds of mathematics aptitude items. *College Entrance Examination Board Research Report* 1, 1972.

Pinard, A., & Laurendeau, M. A scale of mental development based on the theory of Piaget: Description of a project. *Journal of Research in Science Teaching,* 1964, *2,* 253–260.

Pinder, C. C. Statistical accuracy and practical utility in the use of moderator variables. *Journal of Applied Psychology,* 1973, *57,* 214–221.

Pine, S. M. Applications of item characteristic curve theory to the problem of item bias. In D. J. Weiss (Ed.), *Applications of computerized adaptive testing* (Res. Rep. 77–1). Psychometric Methods Programs, Department of Psychology, University of Minnesota, March 1977.

Pinneau, S. R. *Changes in intelligence quotient from infancy to maturity.* Boston: Houghton Mifflin, 1961.

Pitcher, B. *The Law School Admission Test as a predictor of first-year law school grades, 1962–1963.* Statistical Report, Educational Testing Service, SR–65–32, 1965.

Pitcher, B. *A further study of predicting law school grades for female law students.* Law School Admission Council Reports (LSAC–75–3), October 1975.

Pitcher, B. *Subgroups validity study.* Law School Admission Council Reports (LSAC–76–6), October 1976.

Pittluck, P. *The relation between aggressive fantasy and overt behavior.* Unpublished doctoral dissertation. Yale University, 1950.

Plant, W. T., & Minium, E. W. Differential personality development in young adults of markedly different aptitude levels. *Journal of Educational Psychology,* 1967, *58,* 141–152.

POPHAM, W. J. Indices of adequacy for criterion-referenced test items. In W. J. Popham (Ed.), *Criterion-referenced measurement.* Englewood Cliffs, N.J.: Educational Technology Publications, 1971. Pp. 79–98.

POPHAM, W. J., & HUSEK, T. R. Implications of criterion-referenced measurement. *Journal of Educational Measurement,* 1969, 6, 1–9.

PORCH, B. E. *Porch Index of Communicative Ability in Children: Vol. 1.* Palo Alto, Calif.: Consulting Psychologists Press, 1979.

PORTEUS, S. D. *The psychology of a primitive people.* New York: Longmans, Green, 1931.

POSEY, C. Luck and examination grades. *Journal of Engineering Education,* 1932, 23, 292–296.

POSTMAN, L., & KEPPEL, G. *Norms of word association.* New York: Academic Press, 1970.

POWERS, D. E. *Comparing predictions of law school performance for black, Chicano, and white law students.* Law School Admission Council Report (LSAC–77–3), August 1977.

PREDIGER, D. J., & JOHNSON, R. W. *Alternatives to sex-restrictive vocational interest assessment.* (ACT Research Report No. 79). Iowa City: American College Testing Program, May 1979.

PRESCOTT, G. A., BALOW, I. H., HOGAN, T. P., & FARR, R. C. *Teacher's manual for administering and interpreting complete survey battery, Metropolitan Achievement Test: Elementary.* New York: Harcourt Brace Jovanovich, 1978.

PRIMOFF, E. S. Empirical validations of the J-coefficient. *Personnel Psychology,* 1959, 12, 413–418.

PRIMOFF, E. S. *How to prepare and conduct job element examinations* (Personnel Research and Development Center, Technical Study 75–1). Washington, D.C.: U.S. Government Printing Office, June 1975.

PRIMOFF, E. S. The use of self-assessments in examining. *Personnel Psychology,* 1980, 33, 283–290.

Privacy and behavioral research. Washington, D.C.: U.S. Government Printing Office, 1967.

Publication manual of the American Psychological Association. Washington, D.C.: American Psychological Association, 1974.

RABIN, A. I., & GUERTIN, W. H. Research with the Wechsler-Bellevue Test: 1945–1950. *Psychological Bulletin,* 1951, 48, 211–248.

RADCLIFFE, J. A. A note on questionnaire faking with 16PFQ and MPI. *Australian Journal of Psychology,* 1966, 18, 154–157.

RAMSAY, R. T. *Management guide to effective employment testing.* Chicago: Dartnell Corporation, 1981.

RAMSEY, P. H., & VANE, J. R. A factor analytic study of the Stanford-Binet with young children. *Journal of School Psychology,* 1970, 8, 278–284.

RAMSEYER, G. C., & CASHEN, V. M. The effect of practice sessions on the use of separate answer sheets by first and second graders. *Journal of Educational Measurement,* 1971, 8, 177–181.

RAND, Y., TANNENBAUM, A. J., & FEUERSTEIN, R. Effects of instrumental enrichment on the psychoeducational development of low-functioning adolescents. *Journal of Educational Psychology,* 1979, 71, 751–763.

RAPAPORT, D., et al. *Diagnostic psychological testing* (rev. ed. edited by R. R. Holt). New York: International Universities Press, 1968.

RASCH, G. An individualistic approach to item analysis. In P. F. Lazarsfeld & N. W. Henry (Eds.), *Readings in mathematical social sciences*. Cambridge, Mass.: MIT Press, 1966. Pp. 89–107.

REES, A. H., & PALMER, F. H. Factors related to change in mental test performance. *Developmental Psychology Monographs,* 1970, *3*(2, Part 2).

REICHENBERG-HACKETT, W. Changes in Goodenough drawings after a gratifying experience. *American Journal of Orthopsychiatry,* 1953, *23*, 501–517.

REILLY, R. R. A note on minority group test bias studies. *Psychological Bulletin,* 1973, *80*, 130–132.

REINERT, G. Comparative factor analytic studies of intelligence throughout the human life-span. In L. R. Goulet & P. B. Baltes (Eds.), *Life-span developmental psychology: Research and theory*. New York: Academic Press, 1970. Pp. 467–484.

REITAN, R. M. Certain differential effects of left and right cerebral lesions in human adults. *Journal of Comparative and Physiological Psychology,* 1955, *48*, 474–477.

REITAN, R. M. A research program on the psychological effects of brain lesions in human beings. In N. R. Ellis (Ed.), *International Review of Research in Mental Retardation* (Vol. 1). New York: Academic Press, 1966. Pp. 153–218.

REITAN, R. M., & DAVISON, L. A. (Eds.). *Clinical neuropsychology: Current status and applications*. New York: Halsted, 1974.

RENNINGER, C. R. (Ed.). *Approaches to privacy and security in computer systems*. Washington, D.C.: National Bureau of Standards, 1974. (U.S. Government Printing Office, No. C13, 10:404.)

RENTZ, R. R., & BASHAW, W. L. The National Reference Scale for reading: An application of the Rasch model. *Journal of Educational Measurement,* 1977, *14*, 161–179.

RESNICK, L. B. (Ed.). *The nature of intelligence*. Hillsdale, N.J.: Erlbaum, 1976.

RESNICK, L. B., & GLASER, R. Problem solving and intelligence. In L. B. Resnick (Ed.), *The nature of intelligence*. Hillsdale, N.J.: Erlbaum, 1976. Ch. 11.

The responsible use of tests: A position paper of AMEG, APGA, and NCME. *Measurement and Evaluation in Guidance,* 1972, *5*, 385–388.

REYNOLDS, H. H. Efficacy of sociometric ratings in predicting leadership success. *Psychological Reports,* 1966, *19*, 35–40.

REZMOVIC, E. L., & REZMOVIC, V. Empirical validation of psychological constructs: A secondary analysis. *Psychological Bulletin,* 1980, *87*, 66–71.

RICH, C. C., & ANDERSON, R. P. A tactual form of the Progressive Matrices for use with blind children. *Personnel and Guidance Journal,* 1965, *43*, 912–929.

RICHMAN, S. Research on the Examination for Professional Practice of Psychology. *Professional Practice of Psychology,* 1980, *1*, 45–50.

RIMOLDI, H. J. A note on Raven's Progressive Matrices Test. *Educational and Psychological Measurement,* 1948, *8*, 347–352.

ROBINSON, J. P., & SHAVER, P. R. *Measures of social psychological attitudes*. Ann Arbor, Mich.: Institute for Social Research, The University of Michigan, 1973.

ROBINSON, N. M., & ROBINSON, H. B. *The mentally retarded child* (2nd ed.). New York: McGraw-Hill, 1976.

RODGER, A. G. The application of six group intelligence tests to the same children, and the effects of practice. *British Journal of Educational Psychology,* 1936, *6,* 291–305.

ROGERS, C. R., & DYMOND, R. F. (Eds.). *Psychotherapy and personality change.* Chicago: University of Chicago Press, 1954.

RORER, L. G. The great response-style myth. *Psychological Bulletin,* 1965, *63,* 129–156.

RORER, L. G., HOFFMAN, P. J., LA FORGE, G. E., & HSIEH, KUO-CHENG. Optimum cutting scores to discriminate groups of unequal size and variance. *Journal of Applied Psychology,* 1966, *50,* 153–164.

RORSCHACH, H. (Transl. by P. Lemkau & B. Kronenburg.) *Psychodiagnostics: A diagnostic test based on perception.* Berne: Huber, 1942. (1st German ed., 1921; U.S. distributor, Grune & Stratton.)

ROSENMAN, R. H. The interview method of assessment of the coronary-prone behavior pattern. In T. M. Dembroski, S. M. Weiss, J. L. Shields, S. G. Haynes, & M. Feinleib (Eds.), *Coronary-prone behavior.* New York: Springer–Verlag, 1978.

ROSENMAN, R. H., FRIEDMAN, M., STRAUS, R., JENKINS, C. D., ZYZANSKI, S. J., & WURM, M. Coronary heart disease in the Western Collaborative Group Study. Final follow-up experience of 8½ years. *Journal of the American Medical Association,* 1975, *233,* 872–877.

ROSENTHAL, R. *Experimenter effects in behavioral research.* New York: Appleton-Century-Crofts, 1966.

ROSENTHAL, R., & ROSNOW, R. L. (Eds.). *Artifact in behavioral research.* New York: Academic Press, 1969.

ROSENZWEIG, S. *Revised scoring manual for the Rosenzweig Picture-Frustration Study, Form for Adults.* St. Louis: Author, 1950.

ROSENZWEIG, S. The Rosenzweig Picture-Frustration Study, Children's Form. In A. I. Rabin & M. Haworth (Eds.), *Projective techniques with children.* New York: Grune and Stratton, 1960. Pp. 149–176.

ROSENZWEIG, S. Sex differences in reaction to frustration among adolescents. In J. Zubin & A. Freedman (Eds.), *Psychopathology of adolescence.* New York: Grune and Stratton, 1970.

ROSENZWEIG, S. Aggressive behavior and the Rosenzweig Picture-Frustration (P-F) Study. *Journal of Clinical Psychology,* 1976, *32,* 885–891. (a)

ROSENZWEIG, S. *Manual for the Rosenzweig Picture-Frustration Study, Adolescent Form.* St. Louis: Author, 1976. (b)

ROSENZWEIG. S. *Manual for the Children's Form of the Rosenzweig Picture-Frustration (P-F) Study.* St. Louis: Rana House, 1977.

ROSENZWEIG, S. *Adult Form supplement to the basic manual of the Rosenzweig Picture-Frustration (P-F) Study.* St. Louis: Rana House, 1978. (a)

ROSENZWEIG, S. *Aggressive behavior and the Rosenzweig Picture-Frustration Study.* New York: Praeger. 1978. (b)

ROSENZWEIG, S. An investigation of the reliability of the Rosenzweig Picture-Frustration (P-F) Study, Children's Form. *Journal of Personality Assessment,* 1978, *42,* 483–488. (c)

ROSENZWEIG, S. *The Rosenzweig Picture-Frustration (P-F) Study: Basic manual.* St. Louis: Rana House, 1978. (d)

ROSENZWEIG, S., & ADELMAN, S. Construct validity of the Picture-Frustration Study. *Journal of Personality Assessment,* 1977, *41,* 578–588.

ROTTER, J. B. Generalized expectancies for internal versus external control of reinforcement. *Psychological Monographs,* 1966, *80* (1, Whole No. 609).

ROURKE, B. P. Brain-behavior relationships in children with learning disabilities: A research program. *American Psychologist,* 1975, *30,* 911–920.

RUCH, G. M. *The objective or new-type examination.* Glenville, Ill.: Scott Foresman, 1929.

RUCH, W. W. *A re-analysis of published differential validity studies.* Paper presented at the meeting of the American Psychological Association, Honolulu, September 1972.

RUEBHAUSEN, O. M., & BRIM. O. G.. JR. Privacy and behavioral research. *American Psychologist,* 1966, *21,* 423–437.

RULON, P. J. A simplified procedure for determining the reliability of a test of split-halves. *Harvard Educational Review,* 1939, *9,* 99–103.

RUSSELL SAGE FOUNDATION. *Guidelines for the collection, maintenance, and dissemination of pupil records.* New York: Author, 1970.

SAAL, F. E., DOWNEY, R. G., & LAHEY, M. A. Rating the ratings: Assessing the psychometric quality of rating data. *Psychological Bulletin,* 1980, *88,* 413–428.

SACHMAN, H. *An investigation of certain aspects of the validity of the formal Rorschach scoring system in relation to age, education, and vocabulary score.* Unpublished doctoral dissertation, Fordham University, 1952.

SACKS. E. L. Intelligence scores as a function of experimentally established social relationships between the child and examiner. *Journal of Abnormal and Social Psychology,* 1952, *47,* 354–358.

SAMEJIMA, F. Estimation of latent ability using a response pattern of graded scores. *Psychometric Monograph* No. 17, 1969.

SAMELSON, F. Response style. A psychologist's fallacy? *Psychological Bulletin,* 1972, *78,* 13–16.

SAMUDA, R. J. *Psychological testing of American minorities: Issues and consequencies.* New York: Dodd, Mead, 1975.

SANDERS, J. R. Complaints against psychologists adjudicated informally by APA's Committee on Scientific and Professional Ethics and Conduct. *American Psychologist,* 1979, *34,* 1139–1144.

SANDOVAL, J. H., & WHELAN, M. P. *Accuracy of judgments of WISC-R item difficulty for minority groups.* Paper presented at the meeting of the American Psychological Association, New York, September 1979.

SANFORD, N. (Ed.). Personality development during the college years. *Journal of Social Issues,* 1956, *12,* 3–70.

SARASON, I. G. Test anxiety and the intellectual performance of college students. *Journal of Educational Psychology,* 1961, *52,* 201–206.

SARASON, I. G. *Personality: An objective approach* (2nd ed.). New York: Wiley, 1972.

SARASON, I. G. (Ed.). *Test anxiety: Theory, research, and applications.* Hillsdale, N.J.: Erlbaum, 1980.

SARASON, S. B. *The clinical interaction, with special reference to the Rorschach.* New York: Harper, 1954.

SARASON, S. B., DAVIDSON, K. S., LIGHTHALL, F. F., WAITE, R. R., & RUEBUSH, B. K. *Anxiety in elementary school children.* New York: Wiley, 1960.

SARASON, S. B., & GLADWIN, T. *Psychological problems in mental deficiency* (3rd ed.). New York: Harper, 1959.

SARASON, S. B., HILL, K. T., & ZIMBARDO, P. A longitudinal study of the relation of test anxiety to performance on intelligence and achievement tests. *Monographs of the Society for Research in Child Development,* 1964, *29*(7, Serial No. 98).

SARBIN, T. R., TAFT, R., & BAILEY, D. E. *Clinical inference and cognitive theory.* New York: Holt, Rinehart & Winston, 1960.

SATTLER, J. M. Racial "experimenter effects" in experimentation, testing, interviewing, and psychotherapy. *Psychological Bulletin,* 1970, *73*, 137–160.

SATTLER, J. M. *Assessment of children's intelligence.* Philadelphia: Saunders, 1974.

SATTLER, J. M. Clinical and psychoeducational testing is alive. Review of A. S. Kaufman, Intelligent testing with the WISC-R. *Contemporary Psychology,* 1981, *26*, 30–31.

SATTLER, J. M. *Asssesment of children's intelligence and special abilities* (Rev. ed.). Boston: Allyn & Bacon, 1982.

SATTLER, J. M., & THEYE, F. Procedural, situational, and interpersonal variables in individual intelligence testing. *Psychological Bulletin,* 1967, *68*, 347–360.

SAUNDERS, D. R. Moderator variables in prediction. *Educational and Psychological Measurement,* 1956, *16*, 209–222.

SAWYER, J. Measurement *and* prediction, clinical *and* statistical. *Psychological Bulletin,* 1966, *66*, 178–200.

SCHAIE, J. P. Review of The Gerontological Apperception Test. *Eighth Mental Measurements Yearbook,* 1978, Vol. 1, pp. 829–830.

SCHAIE, K. W. A general model for the study of developmental problems. *Psychological Bulletin,* 1965, *64*, 92–107.

SCHAIE, K. W. Review of The Senior Apperception Technique. *Eighth Mental Measurements Yearbook,* 1978, Vol. 1, p. 1060.

SCHAIE, K. W., & GRIBBIN, K. Adult development and aging. *Annual Review of Psychology,* 1975, *26*, 65–96.

SCHAIE, K. W., LABOUVIE, G. V., & BUECH, B. U. Generational and cohort-specific differences in adult cognitive functioning: A fourteen-year study of independent samples. *Developmental Psychology,* 1973, *9*, 151–166.

SCHAIE, K. W., & LABOUVIE-VIEF, G. Generational versus ontogenetic components of change in cognitive behavior: A fourteen-year cross-sequential study. *Developmental Psychology,* 1974, *10*, 305–320.

SCHAIE, K. W., & STROTHER, C. R. A cross-sequential study of age changes in cognitive behavior. *Psychological Bulletin,* 1968, *70*, 671–680.

SCHERICH, H. H., & HANNA, G. S. Passage-dependence data in the selection of reading comprehension test items. *Educational and Psychological Measurement,* 1977, *37*, 991–997.

SCHMIDT, F. L., & BEMIS, S. E. *The behavioral consistency method of unassembled examining.* U.S. Office of Personnel Management, Technical Memorandum 79–21, November 1979.

SCHMIDT, F. L., BERNER, J. G., & HUNTER, J. E. Racial differences in validity of employment tests: Reality or illusion? *Journal of Applied Psychology,* 1973, *58*, 5–9.

SCHMIDT, F. L., GAST-ROSENBERG, I., & HUNTER, J. E. Validity generalization results for computer programmers. *Journal of Applied Psychology,* 1980, 65, 643–661.

SCHMIDT, F. L., & HUNTER, J. E. Development of a general solution to the problem of validity generalization. *Journal of Applied Psychology,* 1977, 62, 529–540.

SCHMIDT, F. L., HUNTER, J. E., McKENZIE, R. C., & MULDROW, T. W. Impact of valid selection procedures on work-force productivity. *Journal of Applied Psychology,* 1979, *64,* 609–626.

SCHMIDT, F. L., HUNTER, J. E., & PEARLMAN, K. Task differences as moderators of aptitude test validity in selection: A red herring. *Journal of Applied Psychology,* 1981, *66,* 166–185.

SCHMIDT, F. L., HUNTER, J. E., PEARLMAN, K., & SHANE, G. S. Further tests of the Schmidt-Hunter Bayesian validity generalization model. *Personnel Psychology,* 1979, *32,* 257–281.

SCHMIDT, F. L., HUNTER, J. E., & URRY, V. W. Statistical power in criterion-related validation studies. *Journal of Applied Psychology,* 1976, *61,* 473–485.

SCHMITT, N., MELLON, P. M., & BYLENGA, C. Sex differences in validity for academic and employment criteria, and different types of predictors. *Journal of Applied Psychology,* 1978, *63,* 145–150.

SCHOENFELDT, L. F., SCHOENFELDT, B. B., ACKER, S. R., & PERLSON, M. R. Content validity revisited: Test development of a content-oriented test of industrial reading. *Journal of Applied Psychology,* 1976, *61,* 581–588.

SCHRADER, W. B. *Summary of law school validity studies, 1948–1975* Law School Admission Council Report (LSAC 76–8), August 1977.

SCHUTZ, R. E. SRA Primary Mental Abilities, 1962 Edition. *Seventh Mental Measurements Yearbook,* 1972, Vol. II, pp. 1066–1068.

SCHWARZ, P. A. *Development and application of African ability tests: Summary Report.* American Institutes for Research, Contract ICAc–2155, AIR–C71–12/64–TR, 1964. (a)

SCHWARZ, P. A. *Development of manpower screening tests for the developing nations: Technical manual.* American Institutes for Research, Contract ICAc–2155, AIR–C71–6/64–TR, 1964. (b)

SCHWARZ, P. A., & KRUG, R. E. *Ability testing in developing countries: A handbook of principles and techniques.* New York: Praeger, 1972.

Scottish Council for Research in Education. *The trend of Scottish intelligence.* London: University of London Press, 1949.

SEASHORE, C. E. *Psychology of music.* New York: McGraw-Hill, 1938.

SEASHORE, H. G. Women are more predictable than men. *Journal of Counseling Psychology,* 1962, *9,* 261–270.

SEASHORE, H. G., WESMAN, A. G., & DOPPELT, J. E. The standardization of the Wechsler Intelligence Scale for Children. *Journal of Consulting Psychology,* 1950, *14,* 99–110.

SECHREST, L. Incremental validity: A recommendation. *Educational and Psychological Measurement,* 1963, *23,* 153–158.

SEGALL, M. H., CAMPBELL, D. T., & HERSKOVITS, M. J. *The influence of culture on visual perception.* Indianapolis: Bobbs-Merrill, 1966.

SEGUIN, E. *Idiocy: Its treatment by the physiological method.* (Reprinted from original ed. of 1866.) New York: Bureau of Publications, Teachers College, Columbia University, 1907.

SHAPIRA, Z., & DUNBAR, R. L. M. Testing Mintzberg's managerial roles classification using an in-basket simulation. *Journal of Applied Psychology,* 1980, *65,* 87–95.

SHARP, S. E. Individual psychology: A study in psychological method. *American Journal of Psychology,* 1898–1899, *10,* 329–391.

SHAW, M. E., & WRIGHT, J. M. *Scales for the measurement of attitudes.* New York: McGraw-Hill, 1967.

SHAYCOFT, M. F. *Handbook of criterion-referenced testing: Development, evaluation, and use.* New York: Garland STPM Press, 1979.

SHAYCOFT, M. F., NEYMAN, C. A., JR., & DAILEY, J. T. *Comparison of Navy recruits with male high school students on the basis of Project TALENT data.* Final Report, Nonr–3482(00), June 1962. (American Institutes for Research, Washington, D.C.)

SHORE, C. W., & MARION, R. *Suitability of using common selection test standards for Negro and white airmen* (AFHRL–TR–72–53). Lackland Air Force Base, Tex.: Personnel Research Division, Air Force Human Resources Laboratory, May 1972.

SHRADER, R. R. Validation studies on the Examinaton for Professional Practice in Psychology. *Professional Practice of Psychology,* 1980, *1,* 23–30.

SIGEL, I. E. How intelligence tests limit understanding of intelligence. *Merrill-Palmer Quarterly,* 1963, *9,* 39–56.

SIGEL, I. E. Where is preschool education going: Or are we en route without a map? *Proceedings 1972 Invitational Conference on Testing Problems, Educational Testing Service,* 1973, 99–116.

SIGI: A computer-based System of Interactive Guidance and Information. Princeton, N.J.: Educational Testing Service, 1974, 1975.

SILVERMAN, I., & SHULMAN, A. D. A conceptual model of artifact in attitude change studies. *Sociometry,* 1970, *33,* 97–107.

SILVERMAN, L. H. A Q-sort study of the validity of evaluations made from projective techniques. *Psychological Monographs,* 1959, *73*(7, Whole No. 477).

SILVERSTEIN, A. B. Validity of WPPSI short forms. *Journal of Consulting and Clinical Psychology,* 1968, *32,* 229–230. (a)

SILVERSTEIN, A. B. Validity of a new approach to the design of WAIS, WISC, and WPPSI short forms. *Journal of Consulting and Clinical Psychology,* 1968, *32,* 478–479. (b)

SILVERSTEIN, A. B. Reappraisal of the validity of WAIS, WISC, and WPPSI short forms. *Journal of Consulting and Clinical Psychology,* 1970, *34,* 12–14.

SILVERSTEIN, A. B. A corrected formula for assessing the validity of WAIS, WISC, and WPPSI short forms. *Journal of Clinical Psychology,* 1971, *27,* 212–213.

SILVERSTEIN, A. B. Factor structure of the Wechsler Intelligence Scale for Children for three ethnic groups. *Journal of Educational Psychology,* 1973, *65,* 408–410.

SIMON, H. A. Identifying basic abilities underlying intelligent performance of complex tasks. In L. B. Resnick (Ed.), *The nature of intelligence.* Hillsdale, N.J.: Erlbaum, 1976. Ch. 5.

SKOLNICK, A. Motivational imagery and behavior over twenty years. *Journal of Consulting Psychology,* 1966, *30,* 463–478.

SLOAN, W. The Lincoln-Oseretsky Motor Development Scale. *Genetic Psychology Monographs,* 1955, *51,* 183–252.

SMITH, A. Talkers and doers: Or education, intelligence, and WAIS verbal-performance ratios in psychiatric patients. *American Psychologist.* 1966, *21,* 687.

SMITH, P. C., &. KENDALL, L. M. Retranslation of expectations: An approach to the construction of unambiguous anchors for rating scales. *Journal of Applied Psychology,* 1963, *47,* 149–155.

SMITH, S. Language and non-verbal test performance of racial groups in Honolulu before and after a 14-year interval. *Journal of General Psychology,* 1942, *26,* 51–93.

SNIDER, J. G., & OSGOOD, C. E. (Eds.). *Semantic differential technique: A sourcebook.* Chicago: Aldine, 1969.

SNYDER, C. R., & LARSON, G. R. A further look at student acceptance of general personality interpretations. *Journal of Consulting and Clinical Psychology,* 1972, *38,* 384–388.

SNYGG, D., & COMBS, A. W. *Individual behavior: A perceptual approach to be-behavior* (Rev. ed.). New York: Harper, 1959.

SOMMER, R. *Diagnostik der Geisteskrankheiten für praktische Ärzte und Studierende. Wien und Leipzig: Urban und Schwarzenberg,* 1894.

SONTAG, L. W., BAKER. C. T., & NELSON, V. L. Mental growth and personality development: A longitudinal study. *Monographs of the Society for Research in Child Development,* 1958, *23*(2, Serial No. 68).

SPEARMAN, C. "General intelligence" objectively determined and measured. *American Journal of Psychology,* 1904, *15,* 201–293.

SPEARMAN, C. *The abilities of man.* New York: Macmillan, 1927.

SPENCE, J. T., & HELMREICH, R. L. *Masculinity and femininity: Their psychological dimensions, correlates, and antecedents.* Austin: University of Texas Press, 1978.

SPIELBERGER, C. D. (Ed.). *Anxiety: Current trends in theory and research* (Vol. 2). New York: Academic Press, 1972.

SPIELBERGER, C. D. *Test Anxiety Inventory: Preliminary professional manual.* Palo Alto, Calif.: Consulting Psychologists Press, 1980.

SPIELBERGER, C. D. and associates. *Preliminary manual for the State-Trait Anger Scale (STAS).* Center for Research in Community Psychology, University of South Florida, Tampa, Fla., August 1980.

SPIELBERGER, C. D.. ANTON, W. D., & BEDELL, J. The nature and treatment of test anxiety. In M. Zuckerman & C. D. Spielberger (Eds.), *Emotions and anxiety: New concepts, methods, and applications.* New York: LEA/Wiley, 1976. Ch. 10.

SPIELBERGER, C. D., CRANE, R. S., & ROSENMAN, R. H. The role of anger in Type-A behavior and heart disease. In C. D. Spielberger, I. G. Sarason, & P. B. Defares (Eds.), *Stress and anxiety* (Vol. 9). New York: McGraw-Hill/Hemisphere, 1982. Ch. 16.

SPIELBERGER, C. D., GONZALEZ, H. P., & FLETCHER, T. Test anxiety reduction, learning strategies, and academic performance. In H. F. O'Neil, Jr., and C. D. Spielberger (Eds.), *Cognitive and affective learning strategies.* New York: Academic Press, 1979. Ch. 5.

SPIELBERGER, C. D., GONZALEZ, H. P., TAYLOR, C. J., ALGAZE, B., & ANTON, W. D. Examination stress and test anxiety. In C. D. Spielberger & I. G. Sarason (Eds.), *Stress and anxiety* (Vol. 5). New York: Hemisphere, 1978. Pp. 167–191.

SPIELBERGER, C. D., GORSUCH, R. L., & LUSHENE, R. E. *STAI manual for the State-Trait Anxiety Inventory.* Palo Alto, Calif.: Consulting Psychologists Press, 1970.

SPIELBERGER, C. D., VAGG, P. R., BARKER, L. R., DONHAM, G. W., & WESTBERRY, L. G. The factor structure of the State-Trait Anxiety Inventory. In I. G. Sarason & C. D. Spielberger (Eds.), *Stress and anxiety* (Vol. 7). New York: Hemisphere, 1980. Pp. 95–109.

SPRANGER, E. (transl. by P. J. W. Pigors). *Types of men.* Halle: Niemeyer, 1928.

STAGNER, R. The gullibility of personnel managers. *Personnel Psychology,* 1958, *11,* 347–352.

STALNAKER, J. M. Essay and objective writing tests. *English Journal (College Edition),* 1933, *22,* 217–222.

Standards for educational and psychological tests. Washington, D.C.: American Psychological Association, 1974.

STANLEY, J. C. (Ed.). *Preschool programs for the disadvantaged: Five experimental approaches to early childhood education.* Baltimore: Johns Hopkins University Press, 1972.

STANLEY, J. C. (Ed.). *Compensatory education for children, ages two to eight.* Baltimore: Johns Hopkins University Press, 1973.

STARCH, D., & ELLIOTT, E. C. Reliability of grading high school work in English. *School Review,* 1912, *20,* 442–457.

STARCH, D., & ELLIOTT, E. C. Reliability of grading high school work in history. *School Review,* 1913, *21,* 676–681. (a)

STARCH, D., & ELLIOTT, E. C. Reliability of grading high school work in mathematics. *School Review,* 1913, *21,* 254–259. (b)

STARR, B. J., & KATKIN, E. S. The clinician as aberrant actuary: Illusory correlation and the Incomplete Sentences Blank. *Journal of Abnormal Psychology,* 1969, *74,* 670–675.

STECKLER, V. A review of the Nonreading Aptitude Test Battery. *Journal of Employment Counseling,* 1973, *10,* 17–20.

STEIN, M. I. *Stimulating creativity.* Vol. 1, *Individual procedures.* Vol. 2, *Group procedures.* New York: Academic Press, 1974, 1975.

STEP manual and technical report. Princeton, N.J.: Educational Testing Service, 1980.

STEPHENS, M. W., & DELYS, P. A locus of control measure for preschool children. *Developmental Psychology,* 1973, *9,* 55–65.

STEPHENSON, ·W. *The study of behavior: Q-technique and its methodology.* Chicago: University of Chicago Press, 1953.

STERN, G. G. *People in context: Measuring person–environment congruence in education and industry.* New York: Wiley, 1970.

STERNBERG, R. J. *Intelligence, information processing, and analogical reasoning: The componential analysis of human abilities.* Hillsdale, N.J.: Erlbaum, 1977.

STERNBERG, R. J. The nature of mental abilities. *American Psychologist,* 1979, *34,* 214–230.

STERNBERG, R. J., & DETTERMAN, D. K. (Eds.). *Human intelligence: Perspectives on its theory and measurement.* Norwood, N.J.: Ablex, 1979.

STERNBERG, R. J., & WEIL, E. M. An aptitude × strategy interaction in linear syllogistic reasoning. *Journal of Educational Psychology,* 1980, *72,* 226–239.

STICHT, T. G. (Ed.). *Reading for working: A functional literacy anthology* Alexandria, Va.: Human Resources Research Organization, 1975.

STONE, G. C., COHEN, F., ADLER, N. E., et al. *Health psychology—A handbook: Theories, applications, and challenges of a psychological approach to the health care system.* San Francisco: Jossey-Bass, 1979.

STOTT, L. H., & BALL, R. S. Infant and preschool mental tests: Review and evaluation. *Monographs of the Society for Research in Child Development,* 1965, *30*(3, Serial No. 101).

STRAUSS, A. A., & LEHTINEN, L. E. *Psychopathology and education of the brain-injured child.* New York: Grune & Stratton, 1947.

STRICKER, L. J. Compulsivity as a moderator variable: A replication and extension. *Journal of Applied Psychology,* 1966, *50,* 331–335.

STRICKER, L. J. "Test-wiseness" on personality scales. *Journal of Applied Psychology Monograph,* 1969, *53*(3, Part 2).

STRICKER, L. J. "SES" Indexes: What do they measure? *Basic and Applied Social Psychology,* 1980, *1*(1), 93–101.

STRONG, D. J., & FEDER, D. D. Measurement of the self-concept: A critique of the literature. *Journal of Counseling Psychology,* 1961, *8,* 170–178.

STRUNK, W., JR., & WHITE, E. B. *The elements of style* (3rd ed.). New York: Macmillan, 1979.

Summaries of court decisions on employment testing, 1968–1977. New York: Psychological Corporation, 1978.

SUMMERS, G. F. (Ed.). *Attitude measurement.* Chicago: Rand McNally, 1970.

SUNDBERG, N. D., SNOWDEN, L. R., & REYNOLDS, W. M. Toward assessment of personal competence and incompetence in life situations. *Annual Review of Psychology,* 1978, *29,* 179–221.

SUPER, D. E. A theory of vocational development. *American Psychologist,* 1953, *8,* 185–190.

SUPER, D. E. *The psychology of careers: An introduction to vocational development.* New York: Harper & Row, 1957.

SUPER, D. E. (Ed.). *The use of multifactor tests in guidance.* Washington, D.C.: American Personnel and Guidance Association, 1958. (Reprinted from *Personnel and Guidance Journal,* 1956, 1957.)

SUPER, D. E. *DAT Career Planning Program: Counselor's manual.* New York: Psychological Corporation, 1973.

SUPER, D. E. (Ed.). *Measuring vocational maturity for counseling and evaluation.* Washington, D.C.: Vocational Guidance Association, 1974.

SUPER, D. E. Vocational maturity in mid-career. *Vocational Guidance Quarterly,* 1977, *25,* 294–302.

SUPER, D. E. A life-span, life-space approach to career development. *Journal of Vocational Behavior,* 1980, *16,* 282–298.

SUPER, D. E., et al. *Computer-assisted counseling.* New York: Teachers College Press, 1970.

SUPER, D. E., & BOHN, M. J., Jr. *Occupational psychology.* Belmont, Calif.: Wadsworth, 1970.

SUPER, D. E., CRITES, J. O., HUMMEL, R. C., MOSER, H. P., OVERSTREET, P. L., & WARNATH, C. *Vocational development: A framework for research.* New York: Teachers College Press, 1957.

SUPER, D. E., & OVERSTREET, P. L. *The vocational maturity of ninth grade boys.* New York: Teachers College Press, 1960.

SWARTZ, J. D. Gamble's review of the Holtzman Inkblot Technique: Corrections and clarifications. *Psychological Bulletin,* 1973, 79, 378–379.

SWETS, J. A., & ELLIOTT, L. L. (Eds.). *Psychology and the handicapped child.* Washington, D.C.: U.S. Government Printing Office, 1974. (DHEW Publication No. OE–73–05000.)

SWEZEY, R. W., & PEARLSTEIN, R. B. *Guidebook for developing criterion-referenced tests.* Arlington, Va.: U.S. Army Research Institute for the Behavioral and Social Sciences, August 1975.

SYMONDS, P. M. *Diagnosing personality and conduct.* New York: Century, 1931.

TAFT, R. Multiple methods of personality assessment. *Psychological Bulletin,* 1959, 56, 333–352.

TALLENT, N. *Psychologicarl report writing.* Englewood Cliffs, N.J.: Prentice-Hall, 1977.

TALMAGE, H. (Ed.). *Systems of individualized education.* Berkeley, Calif.: McCutchan, 1975.

TASTO, D. L., HICKSON, R., & RUBIN, S. E. Scaled profile analysis of fear survey schedule factors. *Behavior Therapy,* 1971, 2, 543–549.

TAYLOR, C. W. (Ed.). *Climate for creativity: Report of the Seventh National Research Conference on Creativity.* New York: Pergamon, 1972.

TAYLOR, C. W., & BARRON, F. (Eds.). *Scientific creativity: Its recognition and development.* New York: Wiley, 1963.

TAYLOR, H. C., & RUSSELL, J. T. The relationship of validity coefficients to the practical effectiveness of tests in selection. Discussion and tables. *Journal of Applied Psychology,* 1939, 23, 565–578.

TEAHAN, J. E., & DREWS, E. M. A comparison of northern and southern Negro children on the WISC. *Journal of Consulting Psychology,* 1962, 26, 292.

TENOPYR, M. L. Content-construct confusion. *Personnel Psychology,* 1977, 30, 47–54.

TERMAN, L. M. *The measurement of intelligence.* Boston: Houghton Mifflin, 1916.

TERMAN, L. M., & MERRILL, M. A. *Measuring intelligence.* Boston: Houghton Mifflin, 1937.

TERMAN, L. M., & MERRILL, M. A. *Stanford-Binet Intelligence Scale: Manual for the third revision, Form L-M.* Boston: Houghton Mifflin, 1960.

TERMAN, L. M., & MERRILL, M. A. *Stanford-Binet Intelligence Scale: 1972 norms edition.* Boston: Houghton Mifflin, 1973.

TERMAN, L. M., & MILES, C. C. *Sex and personality: Studies in masculinity and femininity.* New York: McGraw-Hill, 1936.

TERMAN, L. M., & ODEN, M. H. *The gifted child grows up: Twenty-five years' follow-up of a superior group.* Stanford, Calif.: Stanford University Press, 1947.

TERMAN, L. M., & ODEN, M. H. *The gifted group at mid-life: Thirty-five years' follow-up of the superior child.* Stanford, Calif.: Stanford University Press, 1959.

TESINY. E. P., LEFKOWITZ, M. M., & GORDON, N. H. Childhood depression, locus of control, and school achievement. *Journal of Educational Psychology,* 1980, 72, 506–510.

Testing and public policy. (Special issue) *American Psychologist*, 1965, *20*, 857–992.

THARP, R. G., & WETZEL, R. J. *Behavior modification in the natural environment*. New York: Academic Press, 1969.

THOMAS, H. Psychological assessment instruments for use with human infants. *Merrill-Palmer Quarterly of Behavioral Development*, 1970, *16*, 179–223.

THOMSON, G. H. A hierarchy without a general factor. *British Journal of Psychology*, 1916, *8*, 271–281.

THOMSON, G. H. *The factorial analysis of human ability* (3rd ed.). Boston: Houghton Mifflin, 1948.

THORNDIKE, R. L. The effect of interval between test and retest on the constancy of the IQ. *Journal of Educational Psychology*, 1933, *24*, 543–549.

THORNDIKE, R. L. "Constancy" of the IQ. *Psychological Bulletin*, 1940, *37*, 167–186.

THORNDIKE, R. L. *Personnel selection: Test and measurement techniques*. New York: Wiley, 1949.

THORNDIKE, R. L. *The concepts of over- and under-achievement*. New York: Teachers College Press, 1963.

THORNDIKE, R. L. Causation of Binet IQ decrements. *Journal of Educational Measurement*, 1977, *14*, 197–202.

THORNDIKE, R. L., & HAGEN, E. *Measurement and evaluation in psychology and education* (4th ed.). New York: Wiley, 1977.

THORNTON, G. C., III, & ZORICH, S. Training to improve observer accuracy. *Journal of Applied Psychology*, 1980, *65*, 351–354.

THURSTONE, L. L. A method of scaling psychological and educational tests. *Journal of Educational Psychology*, 1925, *16*, 433–451.

THURSTONE, L. L. Primary mental abilities. *Psychometric Monographs*, 1938, No. 1.

THURSTONE, L. L. A factorial study of perception. *Psychometric Monographs*, 1944, No. 4.

THURSTONE, L. L. The calibration of test items. *American Psychologist*, 1947, *2*, 103–104. (a)

THURSTONE, L. L. *Multiple factor analysis*. Chicago: University of Chicago Press, 1947. (b)

THURSTONE, L. L. Some primary abilities in visual thinking. *Psychometric Laboratory, University of Chicago*, No. 59, August 1950.

THURSTONE, L. L. Creative talent. *Proceedings of the 1950 Invitational Conference on Testing Problems, Educational Testing Service*, 1951, 55–69. (Reprinted in A. Anastasi [Ed.], *Testing problems in perspective*. Washington, D.C.: American Council on Education, 1966. Pp. 414–428.)

THURSTONE, L. L. *The measurement of values*. Chicago: University of Chicago Press, 1959.

THURSTONE, L. L., & CHAVE, E. J. *The measurement of attitude*. Chicago: University of Chicago Press, 1929.

THURSTONE, L. L., & THURSTONE. T. G. Factorial studies of intelligence. *Psychometric Monographs*, 1941, No. 2.

TIEBOUT, C., & MEIER, N. C. Artistic ability and general intelligence. *Psychological Monographs*. 1936, *48*(1, Whole No. 213).

TITTLE, C. K., & ZYTOWSKI, D. G. (Eds.). *Sex-fair interest measurement: Research and implications*. Washington, D.C.: National Institute of Education, 1978.

TOLOR, A., & BRANNIGAN, G. G. *Research and clinical applications of the Bender-Gestalt Test.* Springfield, Ill.: Charles C Thomas, 1980.

TOLOR, A., & SCHULBERG, H. C. *An evaluation of the Bender-Gestalt Test.* Springfield, Ill.: Charles C Thomas, 1963.

TORDY. G. R., EYDE, L. D., PRIMOFF, E. S., & HARDT, R. H. *Job analysis of the position of New York State trooper: An application of the Job Element Method.* Albany: New York State Police, 1976.

TORRANCE, E. P. *Guiding creative talent.* Englewood Cliffs, N.J.: Prentice-Hall, 1962.

TORRANCE, E. P. *Education and the creative potential.* Minneapolis: University of Minnesota Press, 1963.

TORRANCE, E. P. *Rewarding creative behavior.* Englewood Cliffs, N.J.: Prentice-Hall, 1965.

TRACHT, V. S. Preliminary findings on testing the cerebral palsied with Raven's "Progressive Matrices." *Journal of Exceptional Children,* 1948, *15,* 77–79.

TRAXLER, A. E., & HILKERT, R. N. Effect of type of desk on results of machine-scored tests. *School and Society,* 1942, *56,* 277–296.

TRYON, G. S. The measurement and treatment of test anxiety. *Review of Educational Research,* 1980, *50,* 343–372.

TRYON, R. C. A theory of psychological components—An alternative to "mathematical factors." *Psychological Review,* 1935, *42,* 425–454.

TSUDZUKI, A., HATA, Y., & KUZE, T. (A study of rapport between examiner and subject.) *Japanese Journal of Psychology,* 1957, *27,* 22–28.

TUCKER, L. R. Experiments in multimode factor analysis. In A. Anastasi (Ed.), *Testing problems in perspective.* Washington, D.C.: American Council on Education, 1966. Pp. 369–379.

TUCKMAN, B. W. USES Nonreading Aptitude Test Battery, 1969 Edition. *Eighth Mental Measurements Yearbook,* 1978, Vol. I, p. 679.

TUDDENHAM, R. D. Soldier intelligence in World Wars I and II. *American Psychologist,* 1948, *3,* 54–56.

TUDDENHAM, R. D. Theoretical regularities and individual idiosyncracies. In D. R. Green, M. P. Ford, & G. B. Flamer (Eds.), *Measurement and Piaget.* New York: McGraw-Hill, 1971. Ch. 4.

TUDDENHAM, R. D., BLUMENKRANTZ, J., & WILKIN, W. R. Age changes on AGCT: A longitudinal study of average adults. *Journal of Consulting and Clinical Psychology,* 1968, *32,* 659–663.

TYLER, L. *The work of the counselor* (3rd ed.). Englewood Cliffs, N.J.: Prentice-Hall, 1969.

UCMAN, P. A normative study of the Goodenough-Harris Drawing Test on a Turkish sample. In L. J. Cronbach & P. J. D. Drenth (Eds.), *Mental tests and cultural adaptation.* The Hague: Mouton, 1972. Pp. 365–370.

ULRICH, L., & TRUMBO, D. The selection interview since 1949. *Psychological Bulletin,* 1965, *63,* 100–116.

Uniform guidelines on employee selection procedures (1978). *Federal Register,* 1978, *43*(166), 38296–38309.

URRY, V. W. Tailored testing: A successful application of latent trait theory. *Journal of Educational Measurement,* 1977, *14,* 181–196.

URRY, V. W. *Some variations on derivations by Primoff and their extensions.* (Personnel Research and Development Center, Technical Note 78–3). Washington, D.C.: U.S. Government Printing Office, August 1978.

Urry, V. W., & Dorans, N. J. *Tailored testing: Its theory and practice. Part 1. The basic model, the normal ogive submodels, and the tailoring algorithm.* San Diego, Calif.: Navy Personnel Research and Development Center, (in press).

U.S. Department of Labor, Employment and Training Administration. *Pretesting orientation exercise (Manual; Test booklet).* Washington, D.C.: U.S. Government Printing Office, 1968.

U.S. Department of Labor, Employment and Training Administration. *Manual for the USES General Aptitude Test Battery, Section III: Development.* Washington, D.C.: U.S. Government Printing Office, 1970. (a)

U.S. Department of Labor, Employment and Training Administration. *Pretesting orientation on the purposes of testing (Manual; Illustrations).* Washington, D.C.: U.S. Government Printing Office, 1970. (b)

U.S. Department of Labor, Employment and Training Administration. *Doing your best on aptitude tests.* Washington, D.C.: U.S. Government Printing Office, 1971.

U.S. Department of Labor, Employment and Training Administration. Development of USES aptitude test battery for teller (banking). *Technical Report S–259R75,* 1975.

U.S. Department of Labor, Employment and Training Administration. *Dictionary of occupational titles* (4th ed.). Washington, D.C.: U.S. Government Printing Office, 1977.

U.S. Department of Labor, Employment and Training Administration. *Guide for occupational exploration.* Washington, D.C.: U.S. Government Printing Office, 1979. (a) (Rev. ed. in press, 1981.)

U.S. Department of Labor, Employment and Training Administration. *Manual for the USES General Aptitude Test Battery. Section II: Occupational Aptitude Pattern Structure.* Washington, D.C.: U.S. Government Printing Office, 1979. (b)

U.S. Department of Labor, Employment and Training Administration. *Manual for the USES General Aptitude Test Battery. Section II-A: Development of the occupational aptitude pattern structure.* Washington, D.C.: U.S. Government Printing Office, 1980. (a)

U.S. Department of Labor, Employment and Training Administration. *Manual for the USES General Aptitude Test Battery. Section IV: Specific Aptitude Test Batteries.* Washington, D.C.: U.S. Government Printing Office, 1980. (b)

U.S. Department of Labor, Employment and Training Administration. *A new counselee assessment/occupational exploration system and its interest and aptitude dimensions* (USES Test Res. Rep. No. 35). Washington, D.C.: U.S. Government Printing Office, 1981.

U.S. Office of Personnel Management. *Equal employment opportunity court cases.* Washington. D.C.: U.S. Government Printing Office, 1979.

Užgiris, I. Č., & Hunt, J. McV. *Assessment in infancy: Ordinal Scales of Psychological Development.* Urbana: University of Illinois Press, 1975.

Vaidya, S., & Chansky, N. Cognitive development and cognitive style in mathematics achievement. *Journal of Educational Psychology,* 1980, 72, 326–330.

Van der Made-Van Bekkum, I. J. *Dutch word association norms.* Amsterdam: Swets & Zeitlinger N.V., 1971.

VARBLE, D. L. Current status of the Thematic Apperception Test. In P. Mc-Reynolds (Ed.), *Advances in psychological assessment* (Vol. 2). Palo Alto, Calif.: Science and Behavior Books, 1971. Pp. 216–235.

VERNON, P. E. The validation of civil service selection board procedures. *Occupational Psychology*, 1950, *24*, 75–95.

VERNON, P. E. *The structure of human abilities* (Rev. ed.). London: Methuen, 1961.

VERNON, P. E. *Intelligence and cultural environment.* London: Methuen, 1969.

VERNON, P. E., & MILLICAN, G. D. A further study of the reliability of English essays. *British Journal of Statistical Psychology*, 1954, *7*, 65–74.

VEROFF, J., ATKINSON, J. W., FELD, S. C., & GURIN, G. The use of thematic apperception to assess motivation in a nationwide interview study. In J. W. Atkinson, J. O. Raynor, et al. *Motivation and achievement.* Washington, D.C.: Winston, 1974. Ch. 3. (Distr. by Halsted Press Division, Wiley.)

VINITSKY, M. A forty-year follow-up on the vocational interests of psychologists and their relationship to career development. *American Psychologist*, 1973, *28*, 1000–1009.

WADE, T. C., & BAKER, T. B. Opinions and use of psychological tests: A survey of clinical psychologists. *American Psychologist*, 1977, *32*, 874–882.

WADE, T. C., BAKER, T. B., & HARTMANN, D. P. Behavior therapists' self-reported views and practices. *The Behavior Therapist*, 1979, *2*, 3–6.

WAHLSTROM, M., & BOERSMAN, F. J. The influence of test-wiseness upon achievement. *Educational and Psychological Measurement*, 1968, *28*, 413–420.

WAINWRIGHT, W. H. Cultural attitudes and clinical judgment. *International Journal of Social Psychiatry*, 1958, *4*, 105–107.

WAITE, R. R., SARASON, S. B., LIGHTHALL, F. F., & DAVIDSON, K. S. A study of anxiety and learning in children. *Journal of Abnormal and Social Psychology*, 1958, *57*, 267–270.

WALBERG, H. J., & MARJORIBANKS, K. Differential mental abilities and home environment: A canonical analysis. *Developmental Psychology*, 1973, *9*, 363–368.

WALD, A. *Sequential analysis.* New York: Wiley, 1947.

WALD, A. *Statistical decision function.* New York: Wiley, 1950.

WALLACE, W. L. College Board Scholastic Aptitude Test. *Seventh Mental Measurements Yearbook*, 1972, pp. 648–650.

WALLACH, M. A., & WING, C. W., JR. *The talented student: A validation of the creativity–intelligence distinction.* New York: Holt, Rinehart & Winston, 1969.

WALSH, T. M. Responses on the Famous Sayings Test of professional and non-professional personnel in a medical population. *Psychological Reports*, 1966, *18*, 151–157.

WALSH, W. B. Theories of person–environment interaction: Implications for the college student. *American College Testing Program, Monograph No. 10*, 1973.

WAND, B. Legislation to regulate psychologists and the practice of psychology in Canada: An overview *Professional Practice of Psychology*, 1980, *1*, 59–65.

WARD, J. The saga of Butch and Slim. *British Journal of Educational Psychology*, 1972, *42*, 267–289.

WARNER, W. L., MEEKER, M., & EELLS, K. *Social class in America: A manual of procedure for the measurement of social status.* Chicago: Science Research Associates, 1949.

WASIK, B. H., & WASIK, J. L. Performance of culturally deprived children on the Concept Assessment Kit—Conservation. *Child Development,* 1971, *42,* 1586–1590.

WEBB, E. J., CAMPBELL, D. T., SCHWARTZ, R. D., SECHREST, L., & GROVE, J. B. *Non-reactive measures in the social sciences, Second Edition.* Boston: Houghton Mifflin, 1981.

WECHSLER, D. *The measurement of adult intelligence.* Baltimore: Williams & Wilkins, 1939.

WECHSLER, D. *The measurement and appraisal of adult intelligence* (4th ed.). Baltimore: Williams & Wilkins, 1958.

WEISS, D. J. *The stratified adaptive computerized ability test* (Res. Rep. 73–3). Psychometric Methods Program, Department of Psychology, University of Minnesota, September 1973.

WEISS, D. J. *Strategies of adaptive ability measurement* (Res. Rep. 74–5). Psychometric Methods Program, Department of Psychology, University of Minnesota, December 1974.

WEISS, D. J. *Computerized ability testing, 1972–1975* (Final Report of Project NR 150–343). Psychometric Methods Program, Department of Psychology, University of Minnesota, April 1976.

WEISS, D. J., & BETZ, N. E. *Ability measurement: Conventional or adaptive?* (Res. Rep. 73–1). Psychometric Methods Program, Department of Psychology, University of Minnesota, February 1973.

WEISS, D. J., & Davison, M. L. Test theory and methods. *Annual Review of Psychology,* 1981, *32,* 629–658.

WEISSENBERG, P., & GRUENFELD, L. W. Relationships among leadership dimensions and cognitive style. *Journal of Applied Psychology,* 1966, *50,* 392–395.

WELSH, G. S. Adjective Check List description of Freud and Jung. *Journal of Personality Assessment,* 1975, *39,* 160–168. (a)

WELSH, G. S. *Creativity and intelligence: A personality approach.* Chapel Hill: Institute for Research in Social Science (University of North Carolina), 1975. (b)

WERNER, E. E., HONZIK, M. P., & SMITH, R. S. Prediction of intelligence and achievement at ten years from twenty months pediatric and psychologic examinations. *Child Development,* 1968, *39,* 1063–1075.

WERNER, H., & STRAUSS, A. A. Pathology of figure–background relation in the child. *Journal of Abnormal and Social Psychology,* 1941, *36,* 236–248.

WERNER, H., & STRAUSS, A. A. Impairment in thought process of brain-injured children. *American Journal of Mental Deficiency,* 1943, *47,* 291–295.

WESMAN, A. G. Effect of speed on item-test correlation coefficients. *Educational and Psychological Measurement,* 1949, *9,* 51–57.

WESMAN, A. G. Faking personality test scores in a simulated employment situation. *Journal of Applied Psychology.* 1952, *36,* 112–113.

WESMAN, A. G. Intelligent testing. *American Psychologist,* 1968, *23,* 267–274.

WHIMBEY, A. E. *Intelligence can be taught.* New York: Dutton, 1975.

WHIMBEY, A. E. Teaching sequential thought. The cognitive-skills approach. *Phi Delta Kappan,* 1977, *59,* 255–259.

WHIMBEY, A. E. Students can learn to be better problem solvers. *Educational Leadership,* 1980, *37,* 560–565.

WHIMBEY, A. E., & DENENBERG, V. H. Programming life histories: Creating individual differences by the experimental control of early experiences. *Multivariate Behavioral Research,* 1966, *1,* 279–286.

WHITEMAN, M. Intelligence and learning. *Merrill-Palmer Quarterly,* 1964, *10,* 297–309.

WICKER, A. W. Nature and assessment of behavior settings: Recent contributions from the ecological perspective. In P. McReynolds (Ed.), *Advances in psychological assessment* (Vol. 5). San Francisco: Jossey-Bass, 1981. Ch. 1.

WICKES, T. A., JR. Examiner influence in a testing situation. *Journal of Consulting Psychology,* 1956, *20,* 23–26.

WIENER, G., RIDER, R. V., & OPPEL, W. Some correlates of IQ change in children. *Child Development,* 1963, *34,* 61–67.

WIENER-LEVY, D., & EXNER, J. E., JR. The Rorschach comprehensive system: An overview. In P. McReynolds (Ed.), *Advances in psychological assessment* (Vol. 5). San Francisco: Jossey-Bass, 1981. Ch. 5.

WIENS, A. N. The Examination for Professional Practice in Psychology. *Professional Practice of Psychology,* 1980, *1,* 11–21.

WIGGINS, J. S. Strategic, method, and stylistic variance in the MMPI. *Psychological Bulletin,* 1962, *59,* 224–242.

WIGGINS, J. S. Social desirability estimation and "faking good" well. *Educational and Psychological Measurement,* 1966, *26,* 329–341. (a)

WIGGINS, J. S. Substantive dimensions of self-report in the MMPI item pool. *Psychological Monographs,* 1966, *80*(22, Whole No. 630). (b)

WIGGINS, J. S. *Personality and prediction: Principles of personality assessment.* Reading, Mass.: Addison-Wesley, 1973.

WIGGINS, J. S., & WINDER, C. L. The Peer Nomination Inventory: An empirically derived sociometric measure of adjustment in preadolescent boys. *Psychological Reports,* 1961, *9,* 643–677. (a)

WIGGINS, J. S., & WINDER, C. L. *Peer Nomination Inventory: Technical supplement.* Stanford, Calif.: Stanford University Press, 1961. (b)

WIGGINS, N. Individual viewpoints of social desirability. *Psychological Bulletin.* 1966, *66,* 68–77.

WIGGINS, N., & HOFFMAN, P. J. Three models of clinical judgment. *Journal of Abnormal Psychology,* 1968, *73,* 70–77.

WILD, C. L. *Summary of research on restructuring the Graduate Record Examinations Aptitude Test.* Princeton, N.J.: Educational Testing Service, 1979.

WILLARD, L. S. A comparison of Culture Fair Test scores with group and individual intelligence test scores of disadvantaged Negro children. *Journal of Learning Disabilities,* 1968, *1,* 584–589.

WILLIAMS, M. The effect of past experience on mental performance in the elderly. *British Journal of Medical Psychology,* 1960, *33,* 215–219.

WILLINGHAM, W. W. Predicting success in graduate education. *Science,* 1974, *183,* 273–278.

WILLIS, J. Group versus individual intelligence tests in one sample of emotionally disturbed children. *Psychological Reports,* 1970, *27,* 819–822.

WILLIS, S. L., BLIESZNER, R., & BALTES, P. B. Intellectual training research in aging: Modification of performance on the fluid ability of figural relations. *Journal of Educational Psychology,* 1981, *73,* 41–50.

WING, H. D. A factorial study of musical tests. *British Journal of Psychology*, 1941, *31*, 341–355.

WING, H. D. A revision of the Wing Musical Aptitude Test. *Journal of Research in Music Education*, 1962, *10*, 39–46.

WIRT, R. D., & LACHAR, D. The Personality Inventory for Children: Development and clinical applications. In P. McReynolds (Ed.), *Advances in psychological assessment* (Vol. 5). San Francisco. Jossey-Bass, 1981. Ch. 7.

WIRTZ, W. (Chair). *On further examination: Report of the Advisory Panel on the Scholastic Aptitude Test Score Decline*. New York: College Entrance Examination Board, 1977.

WISSLER, C. The correlation of mental and physical traits. *Psychological Monographs*, 1901, *3*(6, Whole No. 16).

WITKIN, H. A. *Cognitive styles in personal and cultural adaptation: Heinz Werner Lecture Series, Vol. 11, 1977*. Worcester. Mass.: Clark University Press, 1978.

WITKIN, H. A., et al. Social conformity and psychological differentiation. *International Journal of Psychology*, 1974, *9*, 11–29.

WITKIN, H. A., DYK, R. B., FATERSON, H. F., GOODENOUGH, D. R., & KARP, S. A. *Psychological differentiation: Studies in development*. New York: Wiley, 1962. (Reissued 1974.)

WITKIN, H. A., & GOODENOUGH, D. R. Field dependence and interpersonal behavior. *Psychological Bulletin*, 1977, *84*, 661–689.

WITKIN, H. A., LEWIS, H. B., HERTZMAN, M., MACHOVER. K., MEISSNER, P. B., & WAPNER, S. *Personality through perception: An experimental and clinical study*. New York: Harper, 1954. (Reprinted Westport, Conn.: Greenwood, 1972.)

WOHLWILL, J. F. Methodology and research strategy in the study of developmental change. In L. R. Goulet & P. B. Baltes (Eds.), *Life-span developmental psychology: Research and theory*. New York: Academic Press, 1970. Pp. 149–191.

WOLF, R. The measurement of environments. In A. Anastasi (Ed.), *Testing problems in perspective*. Washington, D.C.: American Council on Education, 1966. Pp. 491–503.

WOLF, T. H. *Alfred Binet*. Chicago: University of Chicago Press, 1973.

WOLK, R. L., & WOLK, R. B. *Manual: Gerontological Apperception Test*. New York: Human Sciences Press, 1971.

WOLPE, J. *The practice of behavior therapy* (2nd ed.). New York: Pergamon, 1973.

WOLPE, J., & LANG, P. J. A fear survey schedule for use in behavior therapy. *Behaviour Research and Therapy*, 1964, *2*, 27–30.

WOMER, F. B. *What is National Assessment?* Ann Arbor, Mich.: National Assessment of Educational Progress, 1970.

WORELL, J. Sex roles and psychological well-being: Perspectives on methodology. *Journal of Consulting and Clinical Psychology*, 1978. *46*, 777–791.

WRIGHT, B. D. Sample-free test calibration and person measurement. *Proceedings of the 1967 Invitational Conference on Testing Problems, Educational Testing Service*, 1968, 85–101.

WRIGHT, B. D. Solving measurement problems with the Rasch model. *Journal of Educational Measurement*, 1977, *14*, 97–116.

WRIGHT, B. D., & STONE, M. H. *Best test design: Rasch measurement.* Chicago: Mesa Press, 1979.

WRIGHTSTONE, J. W., HOGAN, T. P., & ABBOTT, M. M. Accountability in education and associated measurement problems. *Test Service Notebook 33.* New York: Harcourt Brace Jovanovich, 1972.

YAMAMOTO, K., & FRENGEL, B. A. An exploratory component analysis of the Minnesota tests of creative thinking. *California Journal of Educational Research,* 1966, *17,* 220–229.

YATES, A. J., et al. Symposium on the effects of coaching and practice in intelligence tests. *British Journal of Educational Psychology,* 1953, *23,* 147–162; 1954, *24,* 1–8, 57–63.

YERKES, R. M. (Ed.). Psychological examining in the United States Army. *Memoirs of the National Academy of Sciences,* 1921, *15.*

ZEDECK, S. Problems with the use of "moderator" variables. *Psychological Bulletin,* 1971, *76,* 295–310.

ZIGLER, E., & VALENTINE, J. (Eds.). *Project Head Start: A legacy of the war on poverty.* New York: Free Press, 1980.

ZIMBARDO, P., & EBBESEN, E. B. *Influencing attitudes and changing behavior.* Reading, Mass.: Addison-Wesley, 1970.

ZIMMERMAN, B. J., & ROSENTHAL, T. L. Conserving and retaining equalities and inequalities through observation and correction. *Developmental Psychology,* 1974, *10,* 260–268. (a)

ZIMMERMANN, B. J., & ROSENTHAL, T. L. Observational learning of rule-governed behavior by children. *Psychological Bulletin,* 1974, *81,* 29–42. (b)

ZIMMERMAN, I. L., & WOO-SAM, J. M. Research with the Wechsler Intelligence Scale for Children: 1960–1970. *Psychology in the Schools,* 1972, *9,* 232–271. (Special Monograph Supplement.)

ZIMMERMAN, I. L., WOO-SAM, J. M., & GLASSER, A. J. *The clinical interpretation of the Wechsler Adult Intelligence Scale.* New York: Grune & Stratton, 1973.

ZIMMERMAN, R., & BORNSTEIN, S. *Developmental Checklist.* Boston: Boston Center for Blind Children (undated).

ZUCKERMAN, M., & Gerbasi, K. C. Dimensions of the I-E scale and their relationship to other personality measures. *Educational and Psychological Measurement,* 1977, *37,* 159–175.

AUTHOR INDEX

Numbers in **boldface** type indicate bibliography pages.

SUBJECT INDEX